2nd Workshop on Representation Learning for NLP 2017

Held at ACL 2017

Vancouver, Canada
3 August 2017

ISBN: 978-1-5108-4576-3

ACL 2017

**The 55th Annual Meeting of the
Association for Computational Linguistics**

**Proceedings of the 2nd Workshop on Representation
Learning for NLP**

August 3, 2017
Vancouver, Canada

Introduction

Welcome to the 2nd Workshop on Representation Learning for NLP (RepL4NLP), held on August 3, 2017 and hosted by the 55th Annual Meeting of the Association for Computational Linguistics (ACL) in Vancouver, Canada. The workshop is sponsored by DeepMind, Facebook AI Research, and Microsoft Research.

The 2nd Workshop on Representation Learning for NLP aims to continue the spirit of previously successful workshops at ACL/NAACL/EACL, namely RepL4NLP at ACL'16, VSM at NAACL'15 and CVSC at ACL'13/EACL'14/ACL'15, which focused on vector space models of meaning, compositionality, and the application of deep neural networks and spectral methods to NLP. It provides a forum for discussing recent advances on these topics, as well as future research directions in linguistically motivated vector-based models in NLP.

Roi Reichart

Tim Rocktäschel

Hinrich Schütze

Holger Schwenk

Richard Socher

Mark Steedman

Karl Stratos

Sam Thomson

Yoshimasa Tsuruoka

Yulia Tsvetkov

Lyle Ungar

Oriol Vinyals

Andreas Vlachos

Dani Yogatama

Yi Yang

Table of Contents

Workshop Program

Thursday, August 3, 2017

09:30–09:45   **Welcome and Opening Remarks**

09:45–10:30   **Keynote Session**

09:45–10:30   *Learning Joint Embeddings of Vision and Language*
Sanja Fidler

A successful autonomous system needs to not only understand the visual world but also communicate its understanding with humans. To make this possible, language can serve as a natural link between high level semantic concepts and low level visual perception. In this talk, I'll discuss recent work in the domain of vision and language, covering topics such as image/video captioning and retrieval, and question-answering. I'll also talk about our recent work on task execution via language instructions.

10:30–11:00   **Coffee Break**

11:00–12:30   **Keynote Session**

11:00–11:45   *Learning Representations of Social Meaning*
Jacob Eisenstein

Language plays a critical role in structuring human relationships, while marking social properties of the speaker/writer, audience, and communicative situation. With the increasing availability of big social media datasets, computational linguists have begun to join with sociolinguists in working to elucidate language's social dimension. However, this promising synthesis is threatened by a theoretical mismatch between these two disciplines. Much of the research in the emerging field of computational sociolinguistics involves social-theoretical models that uncritically assign individuals to broad categories such as man/woman, black/white, northern/southern, and urban/rural. Meanwhile, sociolinguists have worked for decades to elaborate a more nuanced view of identity and social meaning, but it has proven difficult to reconcile these rich theoretical models with scalable quantitative research methods. In this talk, I will ask whether representation learning can help to bridge this gap. The key idea is to use learned representations to mediate between linguistic data and socially relevant metadata. I will describe applications of this basic approach in the context of clustering, latent variable models, and neural networks, with applications to gender, multi-community studies, and social network analysis.

Thursday, August 3, 2017 (continued)

11:45–12:30   *Representations in the Brain*
Alona Fyshe

What can the brain tell us about computationally-learned representations of words, phrases and beyond? And what can those computational representations tell us about the brain? In this talk I will describe several brain imaging experiments that explore the representation of language meaning in the brain, and relate those brain representations to computationally learned representations of language meaning.

12:30–14:00   Lunch

14:00–14:45   Keynote Session

14:00–14:45   *"A million ways to say I love you" or Learning to Paraphrase with Neural Machine Translation*
Mirella Lapata

Recognizing and generating paraphrases is an important component in many natural language processing applications. A well-established technique for automatically extracting paraphrases leverages bilingual corpora to find meaning-equivalent phrases in a single language by "pivoting" over a shared translation in another language. In the first part of the talk I will revisit bilingual pivoting in the context of neural machine translation and present a paraphrasing model based purely on neural networks. The proposed model represents paraphrases in a continuous space, estimates the degree of semantic relatedness between text segments of arbitrary length, and generates paraphrase candidates for any source input. In the second part of the talk I will illustrate how neural paraphrases can be seamlessly integrated in models of question answering and summarization, achieving competitive results across datasets and languages.

14:45–15:00   Best Paper Session

15:00–16:30   Poster Session, including Coffee Break

Sense Contextualization in a Dependency-Based Compositional Distributional Model
Pablo Gamallo

Context encoders as a simple but powerful extension of word2vec
Franziska Horn

Active Discriminative Text Representation Learning
Ye Zhang, Matthew Lease and Byron Wallace

Using millions of emoji occurrences to pretrain any-domain models for detecting emotion, sentiment and sarcasm
Bjarke Felbo, Alan Mislove, Anders Søgaard, Iyad Rahwan and Sune Lehmann

Evaluating Layers of Representation in Neural Machine Translation on Syntactic and Semantic Tagging
Yonatan Belinkov, Lluís Màrquez, Hassan Sajjad, Nadir Durrani, Fahim Dalvi and James Glass

Machine Comprehension by Text-to-Text Neural Question Generation
Xingdi Yuan, Tong Wang, Caglar Gulcehre, Alessandro Sordoni, Philip Bachman, Saizheng Zhang, Sandeep Subramanian and Adam Trischler

Emergent Predication Structure in Hidden State Vectors of Neural Readers
Hai Wang, Takeshi Onishi, Kevin Gimpel and David McAllester

Towards Harnessing Memory Networks for Coreference Resolution
Joe Cheri and Pushpak Bhattacharyya

Combining Word-Level and Character-Level Representations for Relation Classification of Informal Text
Dongyun Liang, Weiran Xu and Yinge Zhao

Regularized Topic Models for Sparse Interpretable Word Embeddings
Anna Potapenko and Artem Popov

Does the Geometry of Word Embeddings Help Document Classification? A Case Study on Persistent Homology-Based Representations
Paul Michel, Abhilasha Ravichander and Shruti Rijhwani

Adversarial Generation of Natural Language
Sandeep Subramanian, Sai Rajeswar, Francis Dutil, Chris Pal and Aaron Courville

Deep Active Learning for Named Entity Recognition
Yanyao Shen, Hyokun Yun, Zachary Lipton, Yakov Kronrod and Animashree Anandkumar

The Coadaptation Problem when Learning How and What to Compose
Andrew Drozdov and Samuel Bowman

Learning when to skim and when to read
Alexander Johansen and Richard Socher

Learning to Embed Words in Context for Syntactic Tasks
Lifu Tu, Kevin Gimpel and Karen Livescu

16:30–17:30   Panel Discussion

17:30–17:40   Closing Remarks

Sense Contextualization in a Dependency-Based Compositional Distributional Model

Pablo Gamallo
Centro Singular de Investigación en
Tecnoloxías da Información (CiTIUS)
Universidade de Santiago de Compostela, Galiza
`pablo.gamallo@usc.es`

Abstract

Little attention has been paid to distributional compositional methods which employ syntactically structured vector models. As word vectors belonging to different syntactic categories have incompatible syntactic distributions, no trivial compositional operation can be applied to combine them into a new compositional vector. In this article, we generalize the method described by Erk and Padó (2009) by proposing a dependency-base framework that contextualize not only lemmas but also selectional preferences. The main contribution of the article is to expand their model to a fully compositional framework in which syntactic dependencies are put at the core of semantic composition. We claim that semantic composition is mainly driven by syntactic dependencies. Each syntactic dependency generates two new compositional vectors representing the contextualized sense of the two related lemmas. The sequential application of the compositional operations associated to the dependencies results in as many contextualized vectors as lemmas the composite expression contains. At the end of the semantic process, we do not obtain a single compositional vector representing the semantic denotation of the whole composite expression, but one contextualized vector for each lemma of the whole expression. Our method avoids the troublesome high-order tensor representations by defining lemmas and selectional restrictions as first-order tensors (i.e. standard vectors). A corpus-based experiment is performed to both evaluate the quality of the compositional vectors built with our strategy, and to compare them to other approaches on distributional compositional semantics. The experiments show that our dependency-based compositional method performs as (or even better than) the state-of-the-art.

1 Introduction

Erk and Padó (2008) proposed a method in which the combination of two words, a and b, returns two vectors: a vector a' representing the sense of a given the selectional preferences imposed by b, and a vector b' standing for the sense of b given the (inverse) selectional preferences imposed by a. The main problem is that this approach does not propose any compositional model for sentences. Its objective is to simulate word sense disambiguation, but not to model semantic composition at any level of analysis. In Erk and Padó (2009), the authors briefly describe an extension of their model by proposing a recursive application of the compositional function. However, they only formalize the recursive application when the composite expression consits of two dependent words linked to the same head. So, they only explain how the head is contextualized by its dependents, but not the other way around. In addition, they do not model the influence of context on the selectional preferences. In other terms, their recursive model does not make use of contextualized selectional preferences.

In this article, we generalize the method described in Erk and Padó (2009) by proposing a dependency-base framework that contextualize both lemmas and selectional preferences. The main contribution of the article is to expand their model to a fully compositional framework in which syntactic dependencies are put at the core of semantic composition.

Proceedings of the 2nd Workshop on Representation Learning for NLP, pages 1–9,
Vancouver, Canada, August 3, 2017. ©2017 Association for Computational Linguistics

In our model, lemmas and selectional preferences are defined as unary-tensors (standard vectors), while syntactic dependencies are binary functions combining vectors in an iterative and incremental way.

For dealing with any sequence with N (lexical) words and $N-1$ dependencies linking them, the compositional process can be applied $N-1$ times dependency-by-dependency in two different ways: from left-to-right and from right-to-left. Figure 1 illustrates the incremental process of building the sense of words dependency-by-dependency from left-to-right. Given the composite expression "$a\ b\ c$" and its dependency analysis depicted in the first row of the figure, several compositional processes are driven by the two dependencies involved in the analysis (m and n). First, m is decomposed into two functions: the head function $m_\uparrow$, and the dependent one, $m_\downarrow$. The head function $m_\uparrow$ takes as input the sense of the head word b and the selectional preferences of a, noted here as a°, and returns a new denotation of the head word, $b_{m\uparrow}$, which represents the contextualized sense of b given a at the m relation. Similarly, the dependent function $m_\downarrow$ takes as input the sense of the dependent word a and the selectional preferences b°, and returns a new denotation of the dependent word: $a_{m\downarrow}$. The green box is used to highlight the result of each function. Next, the dependency n between b and c is also decomposed into the head and dependent functions: $n_\uparrow$ and $n_\downarrow$. Function $n_\uparrow$ combines the already contextualized head $b_{m\uparrow}$ with the selectional preferences c°, and returns a still more specific sense of the head: $b_{m\uparrow+n\uparrow}$. Finally, function $n_\downarrow$ takes as input the sense of the dependent word c and the already contextualized selectional preferences $b^\circ_{m\downarrow}$, and builds a contextualized sense of the dependent word: $c_{m\downarrow+n\downarrow}$. At the end of the process, we have not obtained one single sense for the whole expression "$a\ b\ c$", but one contextualized sense per word: $a_{m\downarrow}$, $b_{m\uparrow+n\uparrow}$, and $c_{m\downarrow+n\downarrow}$. Notice that the two words involved in the direct object dependency, b and c, have been contextualized twice since they inherit the restrictions of the subject dependency. The root word, b, is directly involved in the two dependencies and, then, is assigned an intermediate contextualized sense, $b_{m\uparrow}$, in the first combination with a.

In the second case, from right-to-left, the semantic process is applied in a similar way, but starting from the rightmost dependency, n, and ending by the leftmost one, m. At the end of the process, three contextualized word senses are also obtained which might be slightly different from those obtained by the left-to-right algorithm. The main difference is that a is now contextualized by both b and c, while c is just contextualized by b.

The iterative application of the syntactic dependencies found in a sentence is actually the process of building the contextualized sense of all the content words constituting that sentence. So, the whole sentence is not assigned only one meaning - which could be the contextualized sense of the *root* word-, but one sense per word, being the sense of the root just one of them, as in the work described in Weir et al. (Weir et al., 2016). This allows us to retrieve the contextualized sense of all constituent words within a sentence. The contextualized sense of any word might be required in further semantic processes, namely for dealing with co-reference resolution involving anaphoric pronouns. Such an elementary operation is prevented if the sense of the phrase is just one complex sense, as in most compositional approaches.

The rest of the article is organized as follows. In Section 2, several distributional compositional approaches are introduced and discussed. Next, in Section 3, our dependency-based compositional model is described. In Section 4, a corpus-based experiment is performed to build and evaluate the quality of compositional vectors. Finally, relevant conclusions are addressed in Section 5.

2   Related Work

To take into account "the mode of combination", some distributional approaches follow a strategy aligned with the formal semantics perspective in which functional words are represented as high-dimensional tensors (Coecke et al., 2010; Baroni and Zamparelli, 2010; Grefenstette et al., 2011; Krishnamurthy and Mitchell, 2013; Kartsaklis and Sadrzadeh, 2013; Baroni, 2013; Baroni et al., 2014). Using the abstract mathematical framework of category theory, they provide the distributional models of meaning with the elegant mechanism expressed by the principle of compositionality, where words interact with each other according to their type-logical identities (Kartsaklis, 2014). The categorial-based approaches define arguments as vectors while functions taking arguments (e.g., verbs or adjectives that combine with nouns) are n-order tensors, with the number

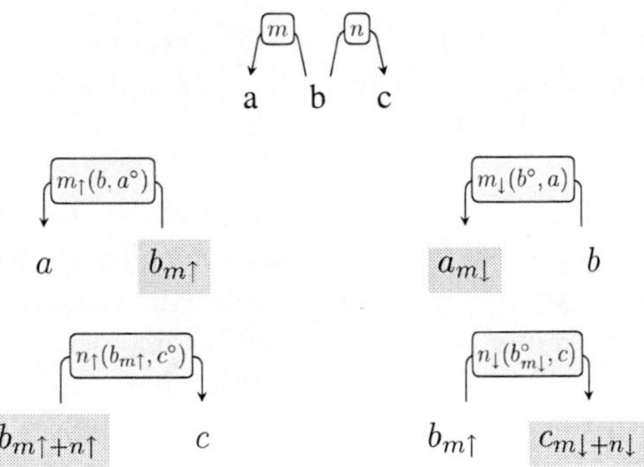

Figure 1: Syntactic analysis of the expression *"a b c"* and left-to-right construction of the contextualized word senses.

of arguments determining their order. Function application is the general composition operation. This is formalized as the tensor product, which is nothing more than a generalization of matrix multiplication in higher dimensions. However, this method results in an information scalability problem, since tensor representations grow exponentially (Kartsaklis et al., 2014).

In our approach, by contrast, we operate with only two types of semantic objects: first-order tensors (or standard vectors) for lemmas and preferences, and second-order functions for syntactic dependencies. This solves the scalability problem of high-order tensors. In addition, it also prevent us giving different categorical representations to verbs in different syntactic contexts. A verb is represented as a single vector which is contextualized as it is combined with its arguments.

Some of the approaches cited above induce the compositional meaning of the functional words from examples adopting regression techniques commonly used in machine learning (Baroni and Zamparelli, 2010; Krishnamurthy and Mitchell, 2013; Baroni, 2013; Baroni et al., 2014). In our approach, by contrast, functions associated with dependencies are just basic arithmetic operations on vectors, as in the case of the first arithmetic approaches to composition (Mitchell and Lapata, 2008, 2009, 2010; Guevara, 2010; Zanzotto et al., 2010). Arithmetic approaches are easy to implement and produce high-quality compositional vectors, which makes them a good choice for practical applications (Baroni et al., 2014).

However, given that our vector space is structured and enriched with syntactic information, the vectors built by composition cannot be a simple mixture of the input vectors as in the bag-of-words approaches (Mitchell and Lapata, 2008). Our syntax-based vector representation of two related words encodes incompatible information and there is no direct way of combining the information encoded in their respective vectors. Vectors of content words (nouns, verbs, adjectives, and adverbs) live into different and incompatible spaces because they are constituted by different types of syntactic contexts. So, they cannot be merged. To combine them, on the basis of previous work (Thater et al., 2010; Erk and Padó, 2008; Melamud et al., 2015), we distinguish between direct denotation and selectional preferences within a dependency relation. Our approach is an attempt to join the main ideas of these syntax-based and structured vector space models into an entirely compositional model. More precisely, we generalize the recursive model introduced by Erk and Pado (Erk and Padó, 2009) with the addition of contextualized selection preferences.

Finally, recent works make use of deep learning strategies to build compositional vectors, such as recursive neural network models (Socher et al., 2012; Hashimoto and Tsuruoka, 2015). Still in the deep learning paradigm, special attention deserves a syntax-based compositional version of C-BOW algorithm (Pham et al., 2015). Our method, however, requires transparent and structured vector spaces to model compositionality.

3   The Method

In our approach, composition is modeled in terms of recursive function application on word vectors driven by binary dependencies. Each dependency stands for two functions on vectors: the *head* function and the *dependent* one. Let us consider the *nominal subject* syntactic dependency, which denotes two functions represented by the following binary λ-expressions:

$$\lambda \mathbf{x}\, \lambda \mathbf{y}^{\circ}\; nsubj_{\uparrow}(\mathbf{x}, \mathbf{y}^{\circ}) \tag{1}$$
$$\lambda \mathbf{x}^{\circ}\, \lambda \mathbf{y}\; nsubj_{\downarrow}(\mathbf{x}^{\circ}, \mathbf{y}) \tag{2}$$

where $nsubj_{\uparrow}$ and $nsubj_{\downarrow}$ represent the head and dependent functions, respectively; $\mathbf{x}$, $\mathbf{x}^{\circ}$, $\mathbf{y}$, and $\mathbf{y}^{\circ}$ stand for vector variables. On the one hand, $\mathbf{x}$ and $\mathbf{y}$ represent the denotation of the head and dependent lemmas, respectively. They represent standard context distributions. On the other hand, $\mathbf{x}^{\circ}$ represents the selectional preferences imposed by the head, while $\mathbf{y}^{\circ}$ stands for the selectional preferences imposed by the dependent lemma. Selectional preferences are also vectors and the way we build them is described later.

Consider now the vectors of two specific lemmas, **cat** and **chase**, and their respective selectional preferences at the subject position. Each function application consists of multiplying the direct vector associated with a lemma and the selectional preferences imposed by the other lemma:

$$nsubj_{\uparrow}(\mathbf{chase}, \mathbf{cat}^{\circ}) = \mathbf{chase} \odot \mathbf{cat}^{\circ} = \mathbf{chase}_{nsubj\uparrow} \tag{3}$$
$$nsubj_{\downarrow}(\mathbf{chase}^{\circ}, \mathbf{cat}) = \mathbf{cat} \odot \mathbf{chase}^{\circ} = \mathbf{cat}_{nsubj\downarrow} \tag{4}$$

Each multiplicative operation results in a compositional vector which represents the contextualized sense of one of the two lemmas (either the head or the dependent). Component-wise multiplication has an intersective effect: the selectional preferences restricts the direct vector by assigning frequency 0 to those contexts that are not shared by both vectors. Here, $\mathbf{cat}^{\circ}$ and $\mathbf{chase}^{\circ}$ are selectional preferences resulting from the following vector addition:

$$\mathbf{cat}^{\circ} \;=\; \sum_{\mathbf{w}\in S_{\downarrow}(cat)} \mathbf{w} \tag{5}$$

$$\mathbf{chase}^{\circ} \;=\; \sum_{\mathbf{w}\in S_{\uparrow}(chase)} \mathbf{w} \tag{6}$$

where $S_{\downarrow}(cat)$ returns the vector set of those verbs having *cat* as subject (except the verb *chase*).

More precisely, given the nominal subject position, the new vector $\mathbf{cat}^{\circ}$ is obtained by adding the vectors $\{\mathbf{w}|\mathbf{w} \in S_{\downarrow}(cat)\}$ of those verbs (*eat, jump*, etc) that are combined with the noun *cat* in that syntactic context. Component-wise addition of vectors has an union effect. In more intuitive terms, $\mathbf{cat}^{\circ}$ stands for the inverse selectional preferences imposed by *cat* on any verb at the subject position. As this new vector consists of verbal contexts, it lives in the same vector space than verbs and, therefore, it can be combined with the direct vector of *chase*.

On the other hand, $S_{\uparrow}(chase)$ in equation 6 represents the vector set of nouns occurring as subjects of *chase* (except the noun *cat*). Given the subject position, the vector $\mathbf{chase}^{\circ}$ is obtained by adding the vectors $\{\mathbf{w}|\mathbf{w} \in S_{\uparrow}(chase)\}$ of those nouns (e.g. *dog, man, tiger*, etc) that might be at the subject position of the verb *chase*.

The incremental application of head and dependent functions contextualize the representation of each word in the phrase. Incrementality also model the influence of context on the selectional preferences. The incremental left-to-right interpretation of *"the cat chased a mouse"* is illustrated in Figure 2 (without considering the meaning of determiners nor verbal tense): First, the head and dependent functions associated with the subject dependency $nsubj$ build the compositional vectors $\mathbf{chase}_{nsubj\uparrow}$ and $\mathbf{cat}_{nsubj\downarrow}$. Then, the head function associated with $dobj$ produces a more elaborate chasing event, $\mathbf{chase}_{nsubj\uparrow+dobj\uparrow}$, which stands for the final contextualized sense of the root verb. In addition, the dependent function of $dobj$ yields a new nominal vector, $\mathbf{mouse}_{nsubj\downarrow+dobj\downarrow}$, whose internal information only can refer to a specific animal: *"the mouse chased by the cat"*. Notice that contextualization may disambiguate ambiguous words: in the context of a chasing event, *mouse* does not refer to a computer's device. In fact, to interpret *"the cat chased a mouse"*, it is required to interpret *"cat chased"* as a fragment that restricts the type of nouns that can appear at the direct object position: *mouse, rat, bird*, etc. In the same way *"police chases"* restricts the entities that can be chased by police officers: *thieves, robbers*, and so on.

In our approach, not only the lemmas are contextualized but also the selectional preferences. The contextualized selectional preferences,

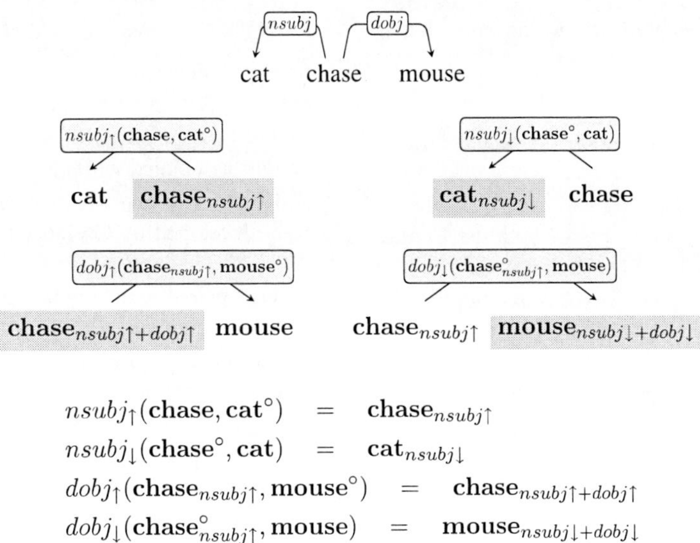

$$nsubj_\uparrow(\mathbf{chase},\mathbf{cat}^\circ) = \mathbf{chase}_{nsubj\uparrow}$$
$$nsubj_\downarrow(\mathbf{chase}^\circ,\mathbf{cat}) = \mathbf{cat}_{nsubj\downarrow}$$
$$dobj_\uparrow(\mathbf{chase}_{nsubj\uparrow},\mathbf{mouse}^\circ) = \mathbf{chase}_{nsubj\uparrow+dobj\uparrow}$$
$$dobj_\downarrow(\mathbf{chase}^\circ_{nsubj\uparrow},\mathbf{mouse}) = \mathbf{mouse}_{nsubj\downarrow+dobj\downarrow}$$

Figure 2: Syntactic analysis of the expression *"the cat chased a mouse"* and left-to-right construction of the contextualized word senses.

$\mathbf{chase}^\circ_{nsubj\uparrow}$, are obtained as follows:

$$\mathbf{chase}^\circ_{nsubj\uparrow} = \mathbf{cat}_{nsubj\downarrow} \odot \sum_{\mathbf{w}\in\, D_\uparrow(chase)} \mathbf{w} \tag{7}$$

where $D_\uparrow(chase)$ returns the vector set of those nouns that are in the direct object role of *chase* (except the noun *mouse*). The new vector resulting by this addition is combined by multiplication (intersection) with the contextualized dependent vector, $\mathbf{cat}_{nsubj\downarrow}$, to build the contextualized selectional preferences. In more intuitive terms, the selectional preferences built in equation 7 are constituted by selecting the contexts of the nouns appearing as direct object of *chase*, which are also part of *cat* after having been contextualized by the verb at the subject position. This is the major contribution with regard to the work described in Erk and Padó (2009).

The dependency-by-dependency functional application results in three contextualized word senses: $\mathbf{cat}_{nsubj\downarrow}$, $\mathbf{chase}_{nsubj\uparrow+dobj\uparrow}$ and $\mathbf{mouse}_{nsubj\downarrow+dobj\downarrow}$. They all together represent the meaning of the sentence in the left-to-right direction.

In the opposite direction, from right-to-left, the incremental process starts with the direct object dependency:

$$dobj_\uparrow(\mathbf{chase},\mathbf{mouse}^\circ) = \mathbf{chase}_{dobj\uparrow}$$
$$dobj_\downarrow(\mathbf{chase}^\circ,\mathbf{mouse}) = \mathbf{mouse}_{dobj\downarrow}$$
$$nsubj_\uparrow(\mathbf{chase}_{dobj\uparrow},\mathbf{cat}^\circ) = \mathbf{chase}_{dobj\uparrow+nsubj\uparrow}$$
$$nsubj_\downarrow(\mathbf{chase}^\circ_{dobj\uparrow},\mathbf{cat}) = \mathbf{cat}_{dobj\downarrow+nsubj\downarrow}$$
$$\tag{8}$$

In Equation 8, the verb *chase* is first restricted by *mouse* at the direct object position, and then by its subject *cat*. In addition, this noun is restricted by the vector $\mathbf{chase}^\circ_{dobj\downarrow}$, which represents the contextualized selectional preferences built by combining $\mathbf{mouse}_{dobj\downarrow}$ with the vectors of the nouns that are in the subject position of *chase* (except *cat*). This new compositional vector represents a very contextualized nominal concept: *"the cat that chased a mouse"*. The word *cat* and its specific sense can be related to anaphorical expressions by making use of co-referential relationships at the discourse level: e.g., pronoun *it*, other definite expressions (*"that cat"*, *"the cat"*), and so on.

4   Experiments

We carried out a corpus-based experiment based on compositional distributional similarity to check the quality of composite expressions, namely NOUN-VERB-NOUN constructions (NVN) incrementally composed with *nsubj* and *dobj* dependencies.

4.1 The Corpus and the Structured Vector Model

Our working corpus consists of both the English Wikipedia (dump file of November 2015[1]) and the British National Corpus (BNC)[2]. In total, the corpus contains about 2.5 billion word tokens. We used the rule-based dependency parser DepPattern (Gamallo and González, 2011; Gamallo, 2015) to perform syntactic analysis on the whole text.

Word vectors were built by computing their co-occurrences in syntactic contexts. Two different types of vectors were built from the corpus: nominal and verbal vectors. Then, for each word we filtered out non relevant contexts using simple count-based techniques inspired by those described in (Bordag, 2008; Padró et al., 2014; Gamallo, 2016), where matrices are stored in hash tables with only non-zero values. More precisely, the association between words and their contexts were weighted with the Dunning's likelihood ratio (Dunning, 1993) and then, for each word, only the N contexts with highest likelihood scores were stored in the hash table (where $N = 500$). So, the remaining contexts were removed from the hash (in standard vector/matrix representations, instead of removing contexts we should assign them zero values).

The process of matrix reduction resulted in the selection of $330,953$ nouns (most of them proper names) with $236,708$ different nominal contexts; and $6,618$ verbs with $140,695$ different verbal contexts. As the contexts of nouns and verbs are not compatible, we created two different vector spaces. Words and their contexts were stored in two hashes, one per vector space, which represent matrices containing only non-zero values. To build compositional vectors from these matrices, the strategy defined in the previous section was implemented in PERL giving rise to the software *Depfunc*[3]. Distributional similarity between pairs of composite expressions was performed using *Cosine*.

4.2 NVN Composite Expressions

This experiment consists of evaluating the quality of compositional vectors built by means of the consecutive application of head and dependency functions associated with nominal subject and direct object. The experiment is performed on the dataset developed by Grefenstette and Sadrzadeh (2011a). The dataset was built using transitive verbs paired with subjects and direct objects: NVN composites.

Given our compositional strategy, we are able to compositional build several vectors that somehow represent the meaning of the whole NVN composite expression. Take the expression *"the coach runs the team"*. If we follow the left-to-right strategy (noted *nv-n*), at the end of the compositional process, we obtain two fully contextualized senses:

nv-n_head The sense of the head *run*, as a result of being contextualized first by the preferences imposed by the subject and then by the preferences required by the direct object. We note *nv-n_head* the final sense of the head in a NVN composite expression following the left-to-right strategy.

nv-n_dep The sense of the object *team*, as a result of being contextualized by the preferences imposed by *run* previously combined with the subject *coach*. We note *nv-n_dep* the final sense of the direct object in a NVN composite expression following the left-to-right strategy.

If we follow the right-to-left strategy (noted *n-vn*), at the end of the compositional process, we obtain two fully contextualized senses:

n-nv_head The sense of the head *run* as a result of being contextualized first by the preferences imposed by the object and then by the subject.

n-nv_dep The sense of the subject *coach*, as a result of being contextualized by the preferences imposed by *run* previously combined with the object *team*.

Table 1 shows the Spearman's correlation values (ρ) between individual human similarity scores and the similarity values predicted by the different versions built from our *Depfunc* system. The best score was achieved by averaging the

---

Systems	ρ
non-compositional (V)	0.27
Depfunc (nv_head)	0.33
Depfunc (nv_dep)	0.19
Depfunc (vn_head)	0.36
Depfunc (vn_dep)	0.38
Depfunc (nv-n_head+dep)	0.35
Depfunc (nv-n_head)	0.33
Depfunc (nv-n_dep)	0.20
Depfunc (n-vn_head+dep)	**0.46**
Depfunc (n-vn_head)	0.36
Depfunc (n-vn_dep)	0.42
Depfunc (n-vn+nv-n)	0.44
Grefenstette and Sadrzadeh (2011)	0.28
Hashimoto and Tsuruoka (2014)	0.43
Polajnar et al. (2015)	0.35

Table 1: Spearman correlation for transitive expressions using the benchmark by Grefenstette and Sadrzadeh (2011)

head and dependent similarity values derived from the *n-vn* (right-to-left) strategy. Let us note that, for NVN composite expressions, the left-to-right strategy seems to build less reliable compositional vectors than the right-to-left counterpart. Besides, the combination of the two strategies (*n-vn+nv-n*) does not improve the results of the best one (*n-vn*).[4]

The score value obtained by our n-vn_head+dep right-to-left strategy outperforms other systems tested for this dataset: Grefenstette and Sadrzadeh (2011b); Polajnar et al. (2015), which are two works based on the categorical compositional distributional model of meaning of Coecke et al. (2010), and the neural network strategy described in Hashimoto and Tsuruoka (2015).

At the top of Table 1, we show the non-compositional baseline we have created for this dataset: similarity beteween single verbs. The table also shows four intermediate values resulting from comparing partial compositional constructions: the noun-verb (*nv_head* and *nv_dep*) and the verb-noun (*vn_head* and *vn_dep*) combinations. Two interesting remarks can be made from these values when they are compared with the full compositional constructions.

First, there is no clear improvement of performance if we compare the full compositional information of the two transitive constructions with the partial combinations. On the one hand, the full *nv-n* construction does not improve the scores obtained by the partial intransitive *nv*. On the other

hand, *n-vn* performs slightly better than *vn* but only in the case of the dependent function which makes use of contextualized selectional preferences: *n-vn_dep* = 0.42 / *vn_dep* = 0.38. The low performance at the second level of composition might call into question the use of contextualized vectors to build still more contextualized senses. The scarcity problem derived from the recursive combination of contextualized vectors is an important issue which could be faced with more corpus, and which we should analyze with more complex evaluation tests.

The second remark is about the difference between the two algorithms: left-to-righ and right-to-left. The scores achieved by the left-to-right algorithm (*nv*, *nv-n*) are clearly below those achieved by right-to-left (*vn*, *n-vn*) . This might be due to the weak semantic motivation of the selectional preferences involved in the subject dependency of transitive constructions in comparison to the direct object one. In fact, right-to-left and left-to-right function application produces quite different vectors because each algorithm corresponds to a particular hierarchy of constituents. Change of constituency implies different semantic entailments such as we can easily observe if we consider the different levels of constituency of noun modifiers (e.g. *"fastest American runner"* $\neq$ *"American fastest runner"*). Finally, the poor results of *nv* in this dataset might be explained because the subject role is less meaningful in transitive clauses than in intransitive ones. The subject of intransitive clauses is assigned a complex semantic role that tends to merge the notions of agent and patient. By contrast, the subject of transitive constructions tends to be just the agent of an action with an external patient.

5 Conclusions

In this paper, we described a distributional compositional model based on a transparent and syntactically structured vector space. The combination of two related lemmas gives rise to two vectors which represent the senses of the two contextualized lemmas. This process can be repeated until no syntactic dependency is found in the analyzed composite expression. The compositional interpretation of a composite expression builds the sense of each constituent lemma in an incremental way.

Substantial problems still remain unsolved. For instance there is no clear borderline between

---

[4]*n-vn+nv-n* is computed by averaging the similarities of both *n-vn_head+dep* and *nv-n_head+dep*

compositional and non-compositional expressions (collocations, compounds, or idioms). It seems to be obvious that vectors of full compositional units should be built by means of compositional operations and predictions based on their constituent vectors. It is also evident that vectors of entirely frozen expressions should be totally derived from corpus co-occurrences of the whole expressions without considering internal constituency. However, there are many expressions, in particular collocations (such as *"save time"*, *"go mad"*, *"heavy rain"*, ...) which can be considered as both compositional and non-compositional. In those cases, it is not clear which is the best method to build their distributional representation: predicted vectors by compositionality or corpus-observed vectors of the whole expression?

Another problem that has not been considered is how to represent the semantics of some grammatical words, namely determiners and auxiliary verbs (i.e., noun and verb specifiers). For this purpose, we think that it would be required a different functional approach, probably closer to the work described by Baroni (2014), who defines functions as linear transformations on vector spaces.

Finally, as we have outlined above, generated vectors tend to be too scarce when they are derived from the recursive combination of already contextualized vectors. Further experiments with more complex phrases and larger training corpora are required in order to deeply analyse this issue. For this purpose, we will explore the strategy defined in Kober et al. (2016) to improve sparse distributional representations.

In current work, we are defining richer semantic word models by combining WordNet features with semantic spaces based on distributional contexts (Gamallo and Pereira-Fariña, 2017). This hybrid method might also help overcome scarcity.

Acknowledgments

This work has received financial support from a 2016 BBVA Foundation Grant for Researchers and Cultural Creators, TelePares (MINECO, ref:FFI2014-51978-C2-1-R), the Consellería de Cultura, Educación e Ordenación Universitaria (accreditation 2016-2019, ED431G/08) and the European Regional Development Fund (ERDF).

References

Marco Baroni. 2013. Composition in distributional semantics. *Language and Linguistics Compass* 7:511–522.

Marco Baroni, Raffaella Bernardi, and Roberto Zamparelli. 2014. Frege in space: A program for compositional distributional semantics. *LiLT* 9:241–346.

Marco Baroni and Roberto Zamparelli. 2010. Nouns are vectors, adjectives are matrices: Representing adjective-noun constructions in semantic space. In *Proceedings of the 2010 Conference on Empirical Methods in Natural Language Processing*. Stroudsburg, PA, USA, EMNLP'10, pages 1183–1193.

Stefan Bordag. 2008. A Comparison of Co-occurrence and Similarity Measures as Simulations of Context. In *9th CICLing*. pages 52–63.

B. Coecke, M. Sadrzadeh, and S. Clark. 2010. Mathematical foundations for a compositional distributional model of meaning. *Linguistic Analysis* 36(1-4):345–384.

Ted Dunning. 1993. Accurate methods for the statistics of surprise and coincidence. *Computational Linguistics* 19(1):61–74.

Katrin Erk and Sebastian Padó. 2008. A structured vector space model for word meaning in context. In *Proceedings of EMNLP*. Honolulu, HI.

Katrin Erk and Sebastian Padó. 2009. Paraphrase assessment in structured vector space: Exploring parameters and datasets. In *Proceedings of the EACL Workshop on Geometrical Methods for Natural Language Semantics*. Athens, Greece.

Pablo Gamallo. 2015. Dependency parsing with compression rules. In *International Workshop on Parsing Technology (IWPT 2015)*. Bilbao, Spain.

Pablo Gamallo. 2016. Comparing explicit and predictive distributional semantic models endowed with syntactic contexts. *Language Resources and Evaluation* First online: 13 May 2016.

Pablo Gamallo and Isaac González. 2011. A grammatical formalism based on patterns of part-of-speech tags. *International Journal of Corpus Linguistics* 16(1):45–71.

Pablo Gamallo and Martín Pereira-Fariña. 2017. Compositional semantics using feature-based models from wordnet. In *1st Workshop on Sense, Concept and Entity Representations and their Applications, co-located at 15th Conference of the European Chapter of the Association for Computational Linguistics*. Association of Computational Linguistics (ACL), pages 1–10.

Edward Grefenstette and Mehrnoosh Sadrzadeh. 2011a. Experimental support for a categorical compositional distributional model of meaning. In *Conference on Empirical Methods in Natural Language Processing*.

Edward Grefenstette and Mehrnoosh Sadrzadeh. 2011b. Experimenting with transitive verbs in a discocat. In *Workshop on Geometrical Models of Natural Language Semantics (EMNLP-2011)*.

Edward Grefenstette, Mehrnoosh Sadrzadeh, Stephen Clark, Bob Coecke, and Stephen Pulman. 2011. Concrete sentence spaces for compositional distributional models of meaning. In *Proceedings of the Ninth International Conference on Computational Semantics*. IWCS '11, pages 125–134.

Emiliano Guevara. 2010. A regression model of adjective-noun compositionality in distributional semantics. In *Proceedings of the 2010 Workshop on GEometrical Models of Natural Language Semantics*. GEMS '10.

Kazuma Hashimoto and Yoshimasa Tsuruoka. 2015. Learning embeddings for transitive verb disambiguation by implicit tensor factorization. In *Proceedings of the 3rd Workshop on Continuous Vector Space Models and their Compositionality*. Association for Computational Linguistics, Beijing, China, pages 1–11. http://www.aclweb.org/anthology/W15-4001.

Dimitri Kartsaklis. 2014. Compositional operators in distributional semantics. *Springer Science Reviews* 2(1-2):161–177.

Dimitri Kartsaklis, Nal Kalchbrenner, and Mehrnoosh Sadrzadeh. 2014. Resolving lexical ambiguity in tensor regression models of meaning. In *Proceedings of the 52nd Annual Meeting of the Association for Computational Linguistics (Vol. 2: Short Papers)*. Association for Computational Linguistics, Baltimore, USA, pages 212–217.

Dimitri Kartsaklis and Mehrnoosh Sadrzadeh. 2013. Prior disambiguation of word tensors for constructing sentence vectors. In *Conference on Empirical Methods in Natural Language Processing (EMNLP 2013)*.

Thomas Kober, Julie Weeds, Jeremy Reffin, and David J. Weir. 2016. Improving sparse word representations with distributional inference for semantic composition. In *Proceedings of EMNLP 2016, Austin, Texas, USA*. pages 1691–1702. http://aclweb.org/anthology/D/D16/D16-1175.pdf.

Jayant Krishnamurthy and Tom Mitchell. 2013. *Proceedings of the Workshop on Continuous Vector Space Models and their Compositionality*, Association for Computational Linguistics, chapter Vector Space Semantic Parsing: A Framework for Compositional Vector Space Models, pages 1–10.

Oren Melamud, Ido Dagan, and Jacob Goldberger. 2015. Modeling word meaning in context with substitute vectors. In *NAACL HLT 2015, Denver, Colorado, USA*. pages 472–482. http://aclweb.org/anthology/N/N15/N15-1050.pdf.

Jeff Mitchell and Mirella Lapata. 2008. Vector-based models of semantic composition. In *Proceedings of ACL-08: HLT*. pages 236–244.

Jeff Mitchell and Mirella Lapata. 2009. Language models based on semantic composition. In *Proceedings of EMNLP*. pages 430–439.

Jeff Mitchell and Mirella Lapata. 2010. Composition in distributional models of semantics. *Cognitive Science* 34(8):1388–1439.

Muntsa Padró, Marco Idiart, Aline Villavicencio, and Carlos Ramisch. 2014. Nothing like good old frequency: Studying context filters for distributional thesauri. In *Proceedings of EMNLP 2014, Doha, Qatar*. pages 419–424.

Nghia The Pham, Germán Kruszewski, Angeliki Lazaridou, and Marco Baroni. 2015. Jointly optimizing word representations for lexical and sentential tasks with the C-PHRASE model. In *Proceedings of the 53rd Annual Meeting of the Association for Computational Linguistics and the 7th International Joint Conference on Natural Language Processing of the Asian Federation of Natural Language Processing, ACL 2015, July 26-31, 2015, Beijing, China, Volume 1: Long Papers*. pages 971–981. http://aclweb.org/anthology/P/P15/P15-1094.pdf.

Tamara Polajnar, Laura Rimell, and Stephen Clark. 2015. An exploration of discourse-based sentence spaces for compositional distributional semantics. In *Proceedings of the First Workshop on Linking Computational Models of Lexical, Sentential and Discourse-level Semantics*. Association for Computational Linguistics, Lisbon, Portugal, pages 1–11. http://aclweb.org/anthology/W15-2701.

Richard Socher, Brody Huval, Christopher D. Manning, and Andrew Y. Ng. 2012. Semantic compositionality through recursive matrix-vector spaces. In *Proceedings of the EMNLP-CoNLL'12*. Association for Computational Linguistics, Stroudsburg, PA, USA, pages 1201–1211. http://dl.acm.org/citation.cfm?id=2390948.2391084.

Stefan Thater, Hagen Fürstenau, and Manfred Pinkal. 2010. Contextualizing semantic representations using syntactically enriched vector models. In *Proceedings of the 48th Annual Meeting of the Association for Computational Linguistics*. Stroudsburg, PA, USA, pages 948–957.

David J. Weir, Julie Weeds, Jeremy Reffin, and Thomas Kober. 2016. Aligning packed dependency trees: A theory of composition for distributional semantics. *Computational Linguistics* 42(4):727–761.

Fabio Massimo Zanzotto, Ioannis Korkontzelos, Francesca Fallucchi, and Suresh Manandhar. 2010. Estimating linear models for compositional distributional semantics. In *Proceedings of the 23rd International Conference on Computational Linguistics*. COLING '10, pages 1263–1271.

Context encoders as a simple but powerful extension of word2vec

Franziska Horn
Machine Learning Group
Technische Universität Berlin, Germany
`franziska.horn@campus.tu-berlin.de`

Abstract

With a strikingly simple architecture and the ability to learn meaningful word embeddings efficiently from texts containing billions of words, word2vec remains one of the most popular neural language models used today. However, as only a single embedding is learned for every word in the vocabulary, the model fails to optimally represent words with multiple meanings and, additionally, it is not possible to create embeddings for new (out-of-vocabulary) words on the spot. Based on an intuitive interpretation of the continuous bag-of-words (CBOW) word2vec model's negative sampling training objective in terms of predicting context based similarities, we motivate an extension of the model we call context encoders (ConEc). By multiplying the matrix of trained word2vec embeddings with a word's average context vector, out-of-vocabulary (OOV) embeddings and representations for words with multiple meanings can be created based on the words' local contexts. The benefits of this approach are illustrated by using these word embeddings as features in the CoNLL 2003 named entity recognition (NER) task.

1 Introduction

Representation learning is very prominent in the field of natural language processing (NLP). For example, word embeddings learned by neural language models (NLM) were shown to improve the performance when used as features for supervised learning tasks such as named entity recognition (NER) (Collobert et al., 2011; Turian et al., 2010). The popular *word2vec* model (Mikolov et al., 2013a,b) learns meaningful word embed-

dings by considering only the words' local contexts and thanks to its shallow architecture it can be trained very efficiently on large corpora. The model, however, only learns a single representation for words from a fixed vocabulary. This means, if in a task we encounter a new word that was not present in the texts used for training, we cannot create an embedding for this word without repeating the time consuming training procedure of the model.[1] Additionally, a single embedding does not optimally represent words with multiple meanings. For example, "Washington" is both the name of a US state as well as a former president and only by taking into account the word's local context one can identify the proper sense.

Based on an intuitive interpretation of the continuous bag-of-words (CBOW) word2vec model's negative sampling training objective, we propose an extension of the model we call *context encoders* (ConEc). This allows for an easy creation of OOV embeddings as well as a better representation of words with multiple meanings simply by multiplying the trained word2vec embeddings with the words' average context vectors. As demonstrated on the CoNLL 2003 NER challenge, using the word embeddings created with ConEc instead of word2vec as features improves the classification performance significantly.

Related work In the past, NLM have addressed the issue of polysemy in various ways. For example, sense2vec is an extension of word2vec, where in a preprocessing step all words in the training corpus are annotated with their part-of-speech (POS)

---

[1] In practice the model is trained on such a large vocabulary that it is rare to encounter a word that does not have an embedding. Yet there are still scenarios where this is the case, for example, it is unlikely that the term "W10281545" is encountered in a regular training corpus, but we might still want its embedding to represent a search query like "whirlpool W10281545 ice maker part".

Proceedings of the 2nd Workshop on Representation Learning for NLP, pages 10–14,
Vancouver, Canada, August 3, 2017. ©2017 Association for Computational Linguistics

tag and then the embeddings are learned for tokens consisting of the words themselves and their POS tags, thereby generating different representations e.g. for words that are used both as a noun and verb (Trask et al., 2015). Other methods first cluster the contexts the words appear (Huang et al., 2012) or use additional resources such as wordnet to identify multiple meanings of words (Rothe and Schütze, 2015). One possibility to create OOV embeddings is to learn representations for all character n-grams in the texts and then compute the embedding of a word by combining the embeddings of the n-grams occurring in it (Bojanowski et al., 2016). However, none of these NLM are designed to solve both the OOV and polysemy problem at the same time and compared to word2vec they require more parameters, resources, or additional steps in the training procedure. ConEc on the other hand can generate OOV embeddings as well as better representations for words with multiple meanings simply by multiplying the matrix of trained word2vec embeddings with the words' average context vectors.

2 Background: CBOW word2vec trained with negative sampling

Word2vec learns d-dimensional vector representations, referred to as word embeddings, for all N words in the vocabulary. It is a shallow NLM with parameter matrices $W_0, W_1 \in \mathbb{R}^{N \times d}$, which are tuned iteratively by scanning huge amounts of texts sentence by sentence. Based on some context words the algorithm tries to predict the target word between them. Mathematically, this is realized by first computing the sum of the embeddings of the context words by selecting the appropriate rows from W_0. This vector is then multiplied by several rows selected from W_1: one of these rows corresponds to the target word, while the others correspond to k 'noise' words, selected at random (negative sampling). After applying a non-linear activation function, the backpropagation error is computed by comparing this output to a label vector $\mathbf{t} \in \mathbb{R}^{k+1}$, which is 1 at the position of the target word and 0 for all k noise words. After the training of the model is complete, the word embedding for a target word is the corresponding row of W_0.

3 Context Encoders

Similar words appear in similar contexts (Harris, 1954), for example, two words synonymous with each other could be exchanged for one another in almost all contexts without a reader noticing. Based on the context word co-occurrences, pairwise similarities between all N words of the vocabulary can be computed, resulting in a similarity matrix $S \in \mathbb{R}^{N \times N}$ (or for a single word w the vector $\mathbf{s}_w \in \mathbb{R}^N$) with similarity scores between 0 and 1. These similarities should be preserved in the word embeddings, e.g. the cosine similarity between the embedding vectors of two words used in similar contexts should be close to 1, or, more generally, the scalar product of the matrix with word embeddings $Y \in \mathbb{R}^{N \times d}$ should approximate S. Of course, the most straightforward way of obtaining word embeddings satisfying $YY^\top \approx S$ would be to compute the singular value decomposition (SVD) of the similarity matrix S and use the eigenvectors corresponding to the d largest eigenvalues (Levy et al., 2014, 2015). As our vocabulary typically comprises several $10,000$ words, however, performing an SVD of the corresponding similarity matrix is computationally far too expensive. Yet, while the similarity matrix would be huge, it would also be quite sparse, as many words are of course not synonymous with each other. If we picked a small number k of random words, chances are their similarities to a target word would be close to 0. So, while the product of a single word's embedding $\mathbf{y}_w \in \mathbb{R}^d$ and the matrix of all embeddings Y should result in a vector $\hat{\mathbf{s}}_w \in \mathbb{R}^N$ close to the true similarities $\mathbf{s}_w$ of this word, if we only consider a small subset of $\hat{\mathbf{s}}_w$ corresponding to the word itself and k random words, it is sufficient if this approximates the binary vector $\mathbf{t}_w \in \mathbb{R}^{k+1}$, which is 1 for the word itself and 0 elsewhere.

The CBOW word2vec model trained with negative sampling can therefore be interpreted as a neural network (NN) that predicts a word's similarities to other words (Fig. 1). During training, for each occurrence i of a word w in the texts, a binary vector $\mathbf{x}_{w_i} \in \mathbb{R}^N$, which is 1 at the positions of the context words of w and 0 elsewhere, is used as input to the network and multiplied by a set of weights W_0 to arrive at an embedding $\mathbf{y}_{w_i} \in \mathbb{R}^d$ (the summed rows of W_0 corresponding to the context words). This embedding is then multiplied by another set of weights W_1, which corresponds to the full matrix of word embeddings Y, to produce the output of the network, a vector $\hat{\mathbf{s}}_{w_i} \in \mathbb{R}^N$ containing the approximated similarities of the word w to all other words. The training error is then computed by comparing a subset of the output to a binary target vector $\mathbf{t}_{w_i} \in \mathbb{R}^{k+1}$, which serves as an approximation of the true similarities $\mathbf{s}_w$ when considering only a small number of random words. We refer to this interpretation of the model as *context encoders* (ConEc), as it is closely related to similarity encoders (SimEc), a dimensionality reduction method used for learning similarity preserving representations of data points (Horn and Müller, 2017).

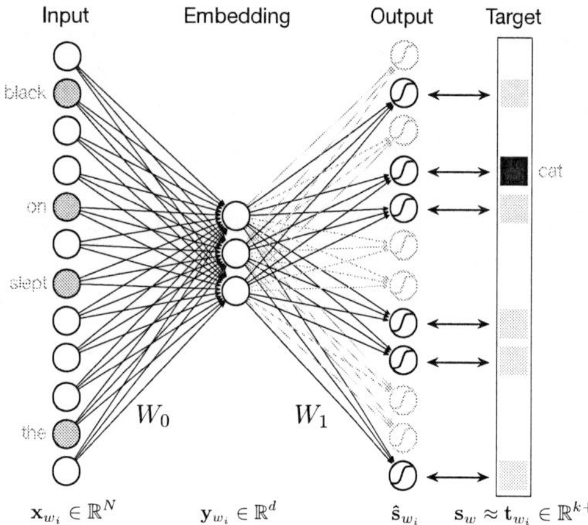

Figure 1: Context encoder (ConEc) NN architecture corresponding to the CBOW word2vec model trained with negative sampling.

While the training procedure of ConEc is identical to that of word2vec, there is a difference in the computation of a word's embedding after the training is complete. In the case of word2vec, the word embedding is simply the row of the tuned W_0 matrix. When considering the idea behind the optimization procedure, however, we instead propose to create the representation of a target word w by multiplying W_0 with the word's average context vector $\mathbf{x}_w$, as this better resembles how the word embeddings are computed during training.

We distinguish between a word's 'global' and 'local' average context vector (CV): The global CV is computed as the average of all binary CVs $\mathbf{x}_{w_i}$ corresponding to the M_w occurrences of w in the whole training corpus:

$$\mathbf{x}_{w_{\text{global}}} = \frac{1}{M_w} \sum_{i=1}^{M_w} \mathbf{x}_{w_i},$$

while the local CV $\mathbf{x}_{w_{\text{local}}}$ is computed likewise but considering only the m_w occurrences of w in a single document. We can now compute the embedding of a word w by multiplying W_0 with the

weighted average between both CVs:

$$\mathbf{y}_w = \left(a \cdot \mathbf{x}_{w_{\text{global}}} + (1 - a)\, \mathbf{x}_{w_{\text{local}}}\right)^\top W_0 \qquad (1)$$

with $a \in [0, 1]$. The choice of a determines how much emphasis is placed on the word's local context, which helps to distinguish between multiple meanings of the word (Melamud et al., 2015).[2] As an out-of-vocabulary word does not have a global CV (as it never occurred in the training corpus), its embedding is computed solely based on the local context, i.e. setting $a = 0$.

With this new perspective on the model and optimization procedure, another advancement is feasible. Since the context words are merely a sparse feature vector used as input to a NN, there is no reason why this input vector should not contain other features about the target word as well. For example, the feature vector $\mathbf{x}_w$ could be extended to contain information about the word's case, part-of-speech (POS) tag, or other relevant details. While this would increase the dimensionality of the first weight matrix W_0 to include the additional features when mapping the input to the word's embedding, the training objective and therefore also W_1 would remain unchanged. These additional features could be especially helpful if details about the words would otherwise get lost in preprocessing (e.g. by lowercasing) or to retain information about a word's position in the sentence, which is ignored in a BOW approach. These extended ConEcs are expected to create embeddings that distinguish even better between the words' different senses by taking into account, for example, if the word is used as a noun or verb in the current context, similar to the sense2vec algorithm (Trask et al., 2015). But instead of learning multiple embeddings per term explicitly, like sense2vec, only the dimensionality of the input vector is increased to include the POS tag of the current word as a feature, which is expected to improve generalization if few training examples are available.

4 Experiments

The word embeddings learned by word2vec and context encoders are evaluated on the CoNLL 2003 NER benchmark task (Tjong et al., 2003). We use a CBOW word2vec model trained with negative sampling as described above where $k = 13$, the embedding dimensionality d is 200 and we use a context window of 5 words. The word embeddings

---

[2]This implicitly assumes a word is only used in a single sense in one document.

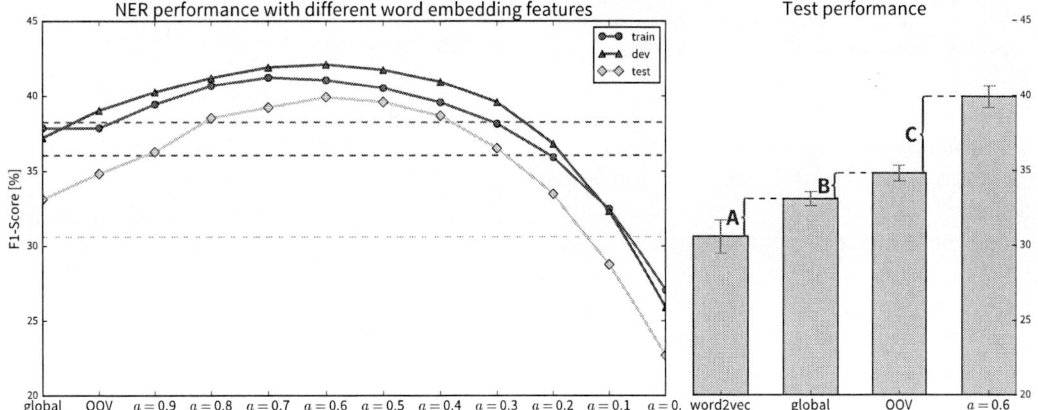

Figure 2: Results of the NER task based on three random initializations of the word2vec model. *Left panel:* Overall results, where the mean performance using word2vec embeddings (*dashed lines*) is considered as our baseline, all other embeddings are computed with ConEcs using various combinations of the words' global and local CVs. *Right panel:* Increased performance (mean and standard deviation) on the test fold when using ConEc: Multiplying the word2vec embeddings with global CVs yields a performance gain of 2.5 percentage points (*A*). By additionally using local CVs to create OOV word embeddings we gain another 1.7 points (*B*). When using a combination of global and local CVs (with $a = 0.6$) to distinguish between the different meanings of words, the F1-score increases by another 5.1 points (*C*), yielding a F1-score of 39.92%, which marks a significant improvement compared to the 30.59% reached with word2vec features.

created by ConEc are built directly on top of the word2vec model by multiplying the original embeddings (W_0) with the respective context vectors. Code to replicate the experiments is available online.[3]

Named Entity Recognition The main advantage of context encoders is that they can use local context to create OOV embeddings and distinguish between the different senses of words. The effects of this are most prominent in a task such as NER, where the local context of a word can make all the difference, e.g. to distinguish between the "Chicago Bears" (an organization) and the city of Chicago (a location). We tested this on the CoNLL 2003 NER task by using the word embeddings as features together with a logistic regression classifier. The reported F1-scores were computed using the official evaluation script. The results achieved with various word embeddings on the training, development and test part of the CoNLL task are reported in Fig. 2. Please note that we are using this task as an extrinsic evaluation to illustrate the advantages of ConEc embeddings over the regular word2vec embeddings. To isolate the effects on the performance, we are only using these word embeddings

as features, while of course the performance on this NER challenge is typically much higher when other features such as a word's case or POS tag are included as well.

The word2vec embeddings were trained on the documents used in the training part of the task and OOV words in the development and test parts are represented as zero vectors.[4] With three parameter settings we illustrate the advantages of ConEc:

A) Multiplying the word2vec embeddings by the words' average context vectors generally improves the embeddings. To show this, ConEc word embeddings were computed using only global CVs (Eq. 1 with $a = 1$), which means OOV words again have a zero representation. With these embeddings (labeled 'global' in Fig. 2) the performance improves on the dev and test folds of the task.

B) Useful OOV embeddings can be created from the local context of a new word. To show this, the ConEc embeddings for words from the training vocabulary ($w \in N$) were computed as in A), but now the embeddings for OOV words ($w' \notin N$) were computed using local CVs (Eq. 1 with $a = 1 \ \forall w \in N$ and $a = 0 \ \forall w' \notin N$; referred to as 'OOV' in the figure). The training performance

---

[3] https://github.com/cod3licious/conec

[4] Since this is a very small corpus, we trained word2vec for 25 iterations on these documents.

stays the same, of course, as here all words have an embedding based on their global contexts, but there is a jump in the ConEc performance on the dev and test folds, where OOV words now have a representation based on their local contexts.

C) Better embeddings for a word with multiple meanings can be created by using a combination of the word's average global and local CVs as input to the ConEc. To show this, the OOV embeddings were computed as in B), but now for the words occurring in the training vocabulary, the local context was taken into account as well by setting $a < 1$ (Eq. 1 with $a \in [0, 1)\ \forall w \in N$ and $a = 0\ \forall w' \notin N$). The best performances on all folds are achieved when averaging the global and local CVs with around $a = 0.6$ before multiplying them with the word2vec embeddings, which clearly shows that ConEc embeddings created by incorporating local context can help distinguish between multiple meanings of words.

5   Conclusion

Context encoders are a simple but powerful extension of the CBOW word2vec model trained with negative sampling. By multiplying the matrix of trained word2vec embeddings with the words' average context vectors, ConEcs are able to easily create OOV embeddings on the spot as well as distinguish between multiple meanings of words based on their local contexts. The benefits of this were demonstrated on the CoNLL NER challenge.

Acknowledgments

I would like to thank Antje Relitz, Ivana Balažević, Christoph Hartmann, Klaus-Robert Müller, and other anonymous reviewers for their helpful comments on earlier versions of this manuscript. Franziska Horn acknowledges funding from the Elsa-Neumann scholarship from the TU Berlin.

References

Piotr Bojanowski, Edouard Grave, Armand Joulin, and Tomas Mikolov. 2016. Enriching word vectors with subword information. *arXiv preprint arXiv:1607.04606* .

Ronan Collobert, Jason Weston, Léon Bottou, Michael Karlen, Koray Kavukcuoglu, and Pavel Kuksa. 2011. Natural language processing (almost) from scratch. *The Journal of Machine Learning Research* 12:2493–2537.

Zellig S Harris. 1954. Distributional structure. *Word* 10(2-3):146–162.

Franziska Horn and Klaus-Robert Müller. 2017. Learning similarity preserving representations with neural similarity encoders. *arXiv preprint arXiv:1702.01824* .

Eric H Huang, Richard Socher, Christopher D Manning, and Andrew Y Ng. 2012. Improving word representations via global context and multiple word prototypes. In *Proceedings of the 50th Annual Meeting of the Association for Computational Linguistics: Long Papers-Volume 1*. ACL, pages 873–882.

Omer Levy, Yoav Goldberg, and Ido Dagan. 2015. Improving distributional similarity with lessons learned from word embeddings. *Transactions of the Association for Computational Linguistics* 3:211–225.

Omer Levy, Yoav Goldberg, and Israel Ramat-Gan. 2014. Linguistic regularities in sparse and explicit word representations. In *CoNLL*. pages 171–180.

Oren Melamud, Ido Dagan, and Jacob Goldberger. 2015. Modeling word meaning in context with substitute vectors. In *Human Language Technologies: The 2015 Annual Conference of the North American Chapter of the ACL.*

Tomas Mikolov, Kai Chen, Greg Corrado, and Jeffrey Dean. 2013a. Efficient estimation of word representations in vector space. *arXiv preprint arXiv:1301.3781* .

Tomas Mikolov, Ilya Sutskever, Kai Chen, Greg S Corrado, and Jeff Dean. 2013b. Distributed representations of words and phrases and their compositionality. In *Advances in neural information processing systems*. pages 3111–3119.

Sascha Rothe and Hinrich Schütze. 2015. Autoextend: Extending word embeddings to embeddings for synsets and lexemes. *arXiv preprint arXiv:1507.01127* .

EF Tjong, Kim Sang, and F De Meulder. 2003. Introduction to the CoNLL-2003 Shared Task: Language-Independent Named Entity Recognition. In Walter Daelemans and Miles Osborne, editors, *Proceedings of CoNLL-2003*. Edmonton, Canada, pages 142–147.

Andrew Trask, Phil Michalak, and John Liu. 2015. sense2vec-a fast and accurate method for word sense disambiguation in neural word embeddings. *arXiv preprint arXiv:1511.06388* .

Joseph Turian, Lev Ratinov, and Yoshua Bengio. 2010. Word representations: a simple and general method for semi-supervised learning. In *Proceedings of the 48th annual meeting of the association for computational linguistics*. Association for Computational Linguistics, pages 384–394.

Machine Comprehension by Text-to-Text Neural Question Generation

Xingdi Yuan[1,*]   Tong Wang[1,*]   Caglar Gulcehre[2,*†]   Alessandro Sordoni[1,*]

Philip Bachman[1]   Sandeep Subramanian[2,†]   Saizheng Zhang[2,†]   Adam Trischler[1]

[1]Microsoft Maluuba, [2]Montreal Institute for Learning Algorithms, Université de Montréal

{eric.yuan,tong.wang,alsordon,phbachma,adam.trischler}@microsoft.com

gulcehrc@iro.umontreal.ca, sandeep.subramanian@gmail.com, saizheng.zhang@umontreal.ca

Abstract

We propose a recurrent neural model that generates natural-language questions from documents, conditioned on answers. We show how to train the model using a combination of supervised and reinforcement learning. After teacher forcing for standard maximum likelihood training, we fine-tune the model using policy gradient techniques to maximize several rewards that measure question quality. Most notably, one of these rewards is the performance of a question-answering system. We motivate question generation as a means to improve the performance of question answering systems. Our model is trained and evaluated on the recent question-answering dataset *SQuAD*.

1 Introduction

People ask questions to improve their knowledge and understanding of the world. Questions can be used to access the knowledge of others or to direct one's own information-seeking behavior. Here we study the generation of natural-language questions by machines, based on text passages. This task is synergistic with *machine comprehension* (MC), which pursues the understanding of written language by machines at a near-human level. Because most human knowledge is recorded in text, this would enable transformative applications.

Many machine comprehension datasets have been released recently. These generally comprise (document, question, answer) triples (Hermann et al., 2015; Hill et al., 2015; Rajpurkar et al., 2016; Trischler et al., 2016a; Nguyen et al., 2016), where the goal is to predict an answer, conditioned on a document and question. The availability of large

---

*Equal contribution.

† Supported by funding from Maluuba.

Text Passage

in 1066[1,2], duke william ii[3] of normandy conquered england killing king harold ii at the battle of hastings. **the invading normans and their descendants**[4] replaced the anglo-saxons as the ruling class of england.

Questions Generated by our System

1) when did the battle of hastings take place?
2) in what year was the battle of hastings fought?
3) who conquered king harold ii at the battle of hastings?
4) who became the ruling class of england?

Table 1: Examples of conditional question generation given a context and an answer from the *SQuAD* dataset, using the scheme referred to as $R_{\text{PPL} + \text{QA}}$ below. Bold text in the passage indicates the answers used to generate the numbered questions.

labeled datasets has spurred development of increasingly advanced models for question answering (QA) from text (Kadlec et al., 2016; Trischler et al., 2016b; Seo et al., 2016; Wang et al., 2016; Shen et al., 2016).

In this paper we reframe the standard MC task: rather than *answering* questions about a document, we teach machines to *ask* questions. Our work has several motivations. First, we believe that posing appropriate questions is an important aspect of information acquisition in intelligent systems. Second, learning to ask questions may improve the ability to answer them. Singer and Donlan (1982) demonstrated that having students devise questions before reading can increase scores on subsequent comprehension tests. Third, answering the questions in most existing QA datasets is an *extractive* task – it requires selecting some span of text within the document – while question asking is comparatively *abstractive* – it requires generation of text that may not appear in the document. Fourth, asking good questions involves skills beyond those used to answer them. For instance, in existing QA

Proceedings of the 2nd Workshop on Representation Learning for NLP, pages 15–25,
Vancouver, Canada, August 3, 2017. ©2017 Association for Computational Linguistics

datasets, a typical (document, question) pair specifies a unique answer. Conversely, a typical (document, answer) pair may be associated with multiple questions, since a valid question can be formed from any information or relations which uniquely specify the given answer. Finally, a mechanism to ask informative questions about documents (and eventually answer them) has many practical applications, e.g.: generating training data for question answering (Serban et al., 2016; Yang et al., 2017), synthesising frequently asked question (FAQ) documentation, and automatic tutoring systems (Lindberg et al., 2013).

We adapt the sequence-to-sequence approach of Cho et al. (2014) for generating questions, conditioned on a document and answer: first we encode the document and answer, then output question words sequentially with a decoder that conditions on the document and answer encodings. We augment the standard encoder-decoder approach with several modifications geared towards the question generation task. During training, in addition to maximum likelihood for predicting questions from (document, answer) tuples, we use policy gradient optimization to maximize several auxiliary rewards. These include a language-model-based score for fluency and the performance of a pretrained question-answering model on generated questions. We show quantitatively that policy gradient increases the rewards earned by generated questions at test time, and provide examples to illustrate the qualitative effects of different training schemes. To our knowledge, we present the first end-to-end, text-to-text model for question generation.

2 Related Work

Recently, automatic question generation has received increased attention from the research community. It has been harnessed, for example, as a means to build automatic tutoring systems (Heilman and Smith, 2010; Ali et al., 2010; Lindberg et al., 2013; Labutov et al., 2015; Mazidi and Nielsen, 2015), to reroute queries to community question-answering systems (Zhao et al., 2011), and to enrich training data for question-answering systems (Serban et al., 2016; Yang et al., 2017).

Several earlier works process documents as individual sentences using syntactic (Heilman and Smith, 2010; Ali et al., 2010; Kumar et al., 2015) or semantic-based parsing (Mannem et al., 2010;

Lindberg et al., 2013), then reformulate questions using hand-crafted rules acting on parse trees. These traditional approaches generate questions with a high word overlap with the original text that pertain specifically to the given sentence by re-arranging the sentence parse tree. An alternative approach is to use generic question templates whose slots can be filled with entities from the document (Lindberg et al., 2013; Chali and Golestanirad, 2016). Labutov et al. (2015), for example, use ontology-derived templates to generate high-level questions related to larger portions of the document. These approaches comprise pipelines of independent components that are difficult to tune for final performance measures.

More recently, neural networks have enabled end-to-end training of question generation systems. Serban et al. (2016) train a neural system to convert knowledge base (KB) triples into natural-language questions. The head and the relation form a context for the question and the tail serves as the answer. Similarly, we assume that the answer is known *a priori*, but we extend the context to encompass a span of unstructured text. Mostafazadeh et al. (2016) use a neural architecture to generate questions from images rather than text. Contemporaneously with this work, Yang et al. (2017) developed generative domain-adaptive networks, which perform question generation as an auxiliary task in training a QA system. The main goal of their question generation is data augmentation, thus questions themselves are not evaluated. In contrast, our work focuses primarily on developing a neural model for question generation that could be applied to a variety of downstream tasks that includes question answering.

Our model shares similarities with recent end-to-end neural QA systems, e.g. Seo et al. (2016); Wang et al. (2016). I.e., we use an encoder-decoder structure, where the encoder processes answer and document (instead of question and document) and our decoder generates a question (instead of an answer). While existing question answering systems typically extract the answer from the document, our decoder is a fully generative model.

Finally, we relate the recent body of works that apply reinforcement learning to natural language generation, such as Li et al. (2016); Ranzato et al. (2016); Kandasamy and Bachrach (2017); Zhang and Lapata (2017). We similarly apply a REINFORCE-style (Williams, 1992) algorithm to maximize various rewards earned by generated questions.

3 Encoder-Decoder Model for Question Generation

We adapt the simple encoder-decoder architecture first outlined by Cho et al. (2014) to the question generation problem. Particularly, we base our model on the attention mechanism of Bahdanau et al. (2015) and the *pointer-softmax* copying mechanism of Gulcehre et al. (2016). In question generation, we can condition our encoder on two different sources of information (compared to the single source in neural machine translation (NMT)): a document that the question should be about and an answer that should fit the generated question. Next, we describe how we adapt the encoder and decoder architectures in detail.

3.1 Encoder

Our encoder is a neural model acting on two input sequences: the document, $D = (d_1, \ldots, d_n)$ and the answer, $A = (a_1, \ldots, a_m)$. Sequence elements d_i, $a_j \in \mathbb{R}^{D_e}$ are given by embedding vectors (Bengio et al., 2001).

In the first stage of encoding, similar to current question answering systems, e.g. (Seo et al., 2016), we augment each document word embedding with a binary feature that indicates if the document word belongs to the answer. Then, we run a bidirectional long short-term memory (Hochreiter and Schmidhuber, 1997) (LSTM) network on the augmented document sequence, producing *annotation* vectors $\mathbf{h}^d = (\mathbf{h}^d_1, \ldots, \mathbf{h}^d_n)$. Here, $\mathbf{h}^d_i \in \mathbb{R}^{D_h}$ is the concatenation of the network's forward ($\vec{\mathbf{h}}^d_i$) and backward hidden states ($\overleftarrow{\mathbf{h}}^d_i$) for input token i, i.e., $\mathbf{h}^d_i = [\vec{\mathbf{h}}^d_i; \overleftarrow{\mathbf{h}}^d_i]$.[1]

Our model operates on QA datasets where the answer is extractive; thus, we encode the answer A using the annotation vectors corresponding to the answer word positions in the document. We assume that, without loss of generality, A consists of the sequence of words $(d_s, \ldots, d_e)$ in the document, s.t. $1 \leq s \leq e \leq n$. We concatenate the annotation sequence $(\mathbf{h}^d_s, \ldots, \mathbf{h}^d_e)$ with the corresponding answer word embeddings $(a_s, \ldots, a_e)$, i.e., $[\mathbf{h}^d_j; a_j], s \leq j \leq e$, then apply a second bidirectional LSTM (biLSTM) over the resulting sequence of vectors to obtain the extractive condition

encoding $\mathbf{h}^a \in \mathbb{R}^{D_h}$. We form $\mathbf{h}^a$ by concatenating the final hidden states from each direction of the biLSTM.

We also compute an initial state $\mathbf{s}_0 \in \mathbb{R}^{D_s}$ for the decoder using the annotation vectors and the extractive condition encoding:

$$\mathbf{r} = \mathbf{L}\mathbf{h}^a + \frac{1}{n} \sum_i^{|D|} \mathbf{h}^d_i, \quad \mathbf{s}_0 = \tanh\left(\mathbf{W}_0 \mathbf{r} + \mathbf{b}_0\right),$$

where $\mathbf{L} \in \mathbb{R}^{D_h \times D_h}$, $\mathbf{W}_0 \in \mathbb{R}^{D_s \times D_h}$, and $\mathbf{b}_0 \in \mathbb{R}^{D_s}$ are model parameters.[2]

3.2 Decoder

Our decoder is a neural model that generates outputs y_t sequentially to yield the question sequence $Q = \{y_t\}$. At each time-step t, the decoder models a conditional distribution parametrized by θ,

$$p_\theta(y_t | y_{<t}, D, A), \tag{1}$$

where $y_{<t}$ represents the outputs at earlier timesteps. In question generation, output y_t is a word sampled according to (1).

When formulating questions based on documents, it is common to refer to phrases and entities that appear directly in the text. We therefore incorporate into our decoder a mechanism for copying relevant words from D. We use the pointer-softmax formulation (Gulcehre et al., 2016), which has two output layers: the *shortlist* softmax and the *location* softmax. The shortlist softmax places a distribution over words in a predefined output vocabulary. The location softmax is a pointer network (Vinyals et al., 2015) that places a distribution over document tokens to be copied. A source switching network enables the model to interpolate between these distributions.

In more detail, the decoder is a recurrent neural network. Its internal state, $\mathbf{s}_t \in \mathbb{R}^{D_s}$, evolves according to the long short-term memory update (Hochreiter and Schmidhuber, 1997), i.e.,

$$\mathbf{s}_t = \text{LSTM}(\mathbf{s}_{t-1}, y_{t-1}, \mathbf{v}_t), \tag{2}$$

where $\mathbf{v}_t$ is a the context vector computed from the document and answer encodings.

At every time-step t, the model computes a soft-alignment score over the document to decide which words are more relevant to the question being generated. As in a traditional NMT architecture, the decoder computes a relevance weight α_{tj} for the jth

---

[1] We use the notation $[\cdot; \cdot]$ to denote concatenation of two vectors throughout the paper.

[2] Let $|X|$ denote the length of sequence X.

word in the document when generating the tth word in the question. Alignment score vector $\boldsymbol{\alpha}_t \in \mathbb{R}^{|D|}$ is computed with a single layer feedforward neural network $f(\cdot)$ using the $\tanh(\cdot)$ activation function. The scores $\boldsymbol{\alpha}_t$ are also used as the location softmax distribution. The network defined by $f(\cdot)$ computes energies according to (3) for the alignments, and the normalized alignments α_{tj} are computed as in (4):

$$e_{tj} = \exp(f(\mathbf{h}_j^d, \mathbf{h}^a, y_t, \mathbf{s}_{t-1})), \qquad (3)$$

$$\alpha_{tj} = \frac{\exp(e_{tj})}{\sum_{i=1}^{T} \exp(e_{ij})}. \qquad (4)$$

To compute the context vector $\mathbf{v}_t$ used in (2), we first construct context vector $\mathbf{c}_t$ for the document and then concatenate it with $\mathbf{h}^a$:

$$\mathbf{c}_t = \sum_{i=1}^{|D|} \alpha_{ti} \mathbf{h}_i^d, \qquad (5)$$

$$\mathbf{v}_t = [\mathbf{c}_t; \mathbf{h}^a]. \qquad (6)$$

We use a deep output layer (Pascanu et al., 2013) at each time-step for the shortlist softmax vector $\mathbf{o}_t$. This layer fuses the information coming from $\mathbf{s}_t$, $\mathbf{v}_t$ and y_{t-1} through a simple MLP to predict the word logits for the softmax as in (7). Parameters of the softmax layer are denoted as $\mathbf{W}_o \in \mathbb{R}^{|V| \times D_h}$ and $\mathbf{b}_o \in \mathbb{R}^{|V|}$, where $|V|$ is the size of the shortlist vocabulary (we used 2000 words).

$$\begin{aligned} \mathbf{e}_t &= g(\mathbf{s}_t, \mathbf{v}_t, y_{t-1}) \\ \mathbf{o}_t &= \mathrm{softmax}(\mathbf{W}_o \mathbf{e}_t + \mathbf{b}_o) \end{aligned} \qquad (7)$$

A source switching variable z_t enables the model to interpolate between document copying and generation from shortlist. It is computed by an MLP with two hidden layers using tanh units (Gulcehre et al., 2016). Similarly to the computation of the shortlist softmax, the switching network takes $\mathbf{s}_t$, $\mathbf{v}_t$ and y_{t-1} as inputs. Its output layer generates the scalar z_t through the logistic sigmoid activation function.

Finally, $p_\theta(y_t|y_{<t}, D, A)$ is approximated by the full pointer-softmax $\mathbf{p}_t \in \mathbb{R}^{|V|+|D|}$ by concatenating $\mathbf{o}_t$ and $\boldsymbol{\alpha}_t$ after both are weighted by z_t:

$$\mathbf{p}_t = [z_t \mathbf{o}_t; \; (1 - z_t)\boldsymbol{\alpha}_t]. \qquad (8)$$

As is standard in NMT, during decoding we use a beam search (Graves, 2012) to maximize (approximately) the conditional probability of an output sequence. We discuss this in more detail in the following section.

3.3 Training

The model is trained initially to minimize the negative log-likelihood of the training data under the model distribution,

$$\mathcal{L} = -\sum_t \log p_\theta(y_t|y_{<t}, D, A), \qquad (9)$$

where, in the decoder as defined in (2), the previous token y_{t-1} comes from the source sequence rather than the model output (this is called *teacher forcing*).

Based on our knowledge of the task, we introduce additional training signals to aid the model's learning. First, we encourage the model not to generate answer words in the question. We use the soft answer-suppression constraint given in (10) with the penalty hyperparameter λ_s; $\bar{A}$ denotes the set of words that appear in the answer but not in the ground-truth question:

$$\mathcal{L}_s = \lambda_s \sum_t \sum_{\bar{a} \in \bar{A}} p_\theta(y_t = \bar{a}|y_{<t}, D, A). \qquad (10)$$

We also encourage variety in the output words to counteract the degeneracy often observed in NLG systems towards common outputs (Sordoni et al., 2015). This is achieved with a loss term that maximizes entropy in the output softmax (8), i.e.,

$$\mathcal{L}_e = \lambda_e \sum_t \mathbf{p}_t^T \log \mathbf{p}_t. \qquad (11)$$

4 Policy Gradient Optimization

As described above, we use teacher forcing to train our model to generate text by maximizing ground-truth likelihood. Teacher forcing introduces critical differences between the training phase (in which the model is driven by ground-truth sequences) and the testing phase (in which the model is driven by its own outputs) (Bahdanau et al., 2016). Significantly, teacher forcing prevents the model from making and learning from mistakes during training. This is related to the observation that maximizing ground-truth likelihood does not teach the model how to distribute probability mass among examples other than the ground-truth, some of which may be valid questions and some of which may be completely incoherent. This is especially problematic in language, where there are often many ways to say the same thing. A reinforcement learning (RL) approach, by which a model is rewarded or penalized for its own actions, could mitigate these issues – though likely at the expense of reduced stability during training. A properly designed reward, maximized via RL, could provide a model with more information about how to distribute probability mass among sequences that do not occur in the training set (Norouzi et al., 2016).

We investigate the use of RL to fine-tune our question generation model. Specifically, we perform policy gradient optimization following a period of "pretraining" on maximum likelihood, using a combination of scalar rewards correlated to question quality. We detail this process below. To make clear that the model is acting freely without teacher forcing, we indicate model-generated tokens with $\hat{y}_t$ and sequences with $\hat{Y}$.

4.1 Rewards

Question answering (QA) One obvious measure of a question's quality is whether it can be answered correctly given the context document D. We therefore feed model-generated questions into a pretrained question-answering system and use that system's accuracy as a reward. We use the recently proposed Multi-Perspective Context Matching (MPCM) (Wang et al., 2016) model as our reference QA system, *sans* character-level encoding. Broadly, that model takes in a generated question $\hat{Y}$ and a document D, processes them through bidirectional recurrent neural networks, applies an attention mechanism, and points to the start and end tokens of the answer in D. After training a MPCM model on the *SQuAD* dataset, the reward $R_{\mathrm{QA}}(\hat{Y})$ is given by MPCM's answer accuracy on $\hat{Y}$ in terms of the F1 score, a token-based measure proposed by Rajpurkar et al. (2016) that accounts for partial word matches:

$$R_{\mathrm{QA}}(\hat{Y}) = \mathrm{F1}(\hat{A}, A), \qquad (12)$$

where $\hat{A} = \mathrm{MPCM}(\hat{Y})$ is the answer to the generated question by the MPCM model. Optimizing the QA reward could lead to 'friendly' questions that are either overly simplistic or that somehow cheat by exploiting quirks in the MPCM model. One obvious way to cheat would be to inject answer words into the question. We prevented this by masking these out in the location softmax, a hard version of the answer suppression loss (10).

Fluency (PPL) Another measure of quality is a question's fluency – i.e., is it stated in proper, grammatical English? As simultaneously proposed in Zhang and Lapata (2017), we use a language model to measure and reward the fluency of generated questions. In particular, we use the perplexity assigned to $\hat{Y}$ by an LSTM language model:

$$R_{\mathrm{PPL}}(\hat{Y}) = -2^{-\frac{1}{T}\sum_{t=1}^{T}\log_2 p_{\mathrm{LM}}(\hat{y}_t|\hat{y}_{<t})}, \qquad (13)$$

where the negation is to reward the model for minimizing perplexity. The language model is trained through maximum likelihood estimation on over $80,000$ human-generated questions from *SQuAD* (the training set).

Combination For the total scalar reward earned by the word sequence $\hat{Y}$, we also test a weighted combination of the individual rewards:

$$R_{\mathrm{PPL+QA}}(\hat{Y}) = \lambda_{\mathrm{QA}} R_{\mathrm{QA}}(\hat{Y}) + \lambda_{\mathrm{PPL}} R_{\mathrm{PPL}}(\hat{Y}),$$

where λ_{QA} and λ_{PPL} are hyperparameters. The individual reward functions use neural models to tune the neural question generator. This is reminiscent of recent work on GANs (Goodfellow et al., 2014) and actor-critic methods (Bahdanau et al., 2016). We treat the reward models as black boxes, rather than attempting to optimize them jointly or backpropagate error signals through them. We leave these directions for future work.

We also experimented with several other rewards, most notably the BLEU score (Papineni et al., 2002) between $\hat{Y}$ and the ground-truth question for the given document and answer, and a softer measure of similarity between output and ground-truth based on skip-thought vectors (Kiros et al., 2015). Empirically, we were unable to obtain consistent improvements on these rewards through training, though this may be an issue with hyperparameter settings.

4.2 REINFORCE

We use the REINFORCE algorithm (Williams, 1992) to maximize the model's expected reward. For each generated question $\hat{Y}$, we define the loss

$$\mathcal{L}_{\mathrm{RL}} = -\mathbb{E}_{\hat{Y}\sim\pi(\hat{Y}|D,A)}[R(\hat{Y})], \qquad (14)$$

where π is the policy to be trained. The policy is a distribution over discrete actions, i.e. words $\hat{y}_t$ that make up the sequence $\hat{Y}$. It is the distribution induced at the output layer of the encoder-decoder model (8), initialized with the parameters determined through likelihood optimization.[3]

---

[3]The policy also depends on the switch values but we omit these for brevity.

REINFORCE approximates the expectation in (14) with independent samples from the policy distribution, yielding the policy gradient

$$\nabla \mathcal{L}_{\text{RL}} \approx \sum_{t=1} \nabla \log \pi(\hat{y}_t | \hat{y}_{<t}, D, A) \frac{R(\hat{Y}) - \mu_R}{\sigma_R}. \tag{15}$$

The optional μ_R and σ_R are the running mean and standard deviation of the reward, which push $R(\hat{Y})$ toward zero mean and unit variance. This "whitening" of rewards is a simple version of PopArt (van Hasselt et al., 2016), and we found empirically that it stabilized learning.

It is straightforward to combine policy gradient with maximum likelihood, as both gradients can be computed by backpropagating through a properly reweighted sequence-level log-likelihood. The sequences for policy gradient are sampled from the model and weighted by a whitened reward, and the likelihood sequences are sampled from the training set and weighted by 1.

4.3 Training Scheme

Instead of sampling from the model's output distribution, we use beam-search to generate questions from the model and approximate the expectation in Eq. 14. Empirically we found that rewards could not be improved through training without this approach. Randomly sampling from the model's distribution may not be as effective for estimating the modes of the generation policy and it may introduce more variance into the policy gradient.

Beam search keeps a running set of candidates that expands and contracts adaptively. At each time-step t, k output words that maximize the probabilities of their respective paths are selected and added to the candidate sequences, where k is the beam size. The probabilities of these candidates are given by their accumulated log-likelihood up to t.[4]

Given a complete sample from the beam search and its accumulated log-likelihood, the gradient in (15) can be estimated as follows. After calculating the reward with a sequence generated by beam search, we use the sample to teacher-force the decoder so as to recreate exactly the model states from which the sequence was generated. The model can then be accurately updated by cou-

pling the parameter-independent reward with the log-likelihood of the generated sequence. This approach adds a computational overhead but it significantly increases the initial reward values earned by the model and stabilizes policy gradient training.

We also further tune the likelihood during policy gradient optimization to prevent the model from overwriting its earlier training. We combine the policy gradient update to the model parameters, $\nabla \mathcal{L}_{\text{RL}}$, with an update from $\nabla \mathcal{L}$ based on teacher forcing on the ground-truth signal.

5 Experiments

5.1 Dataset

We conducted our experiments on the *SQuAD* dataset for machine comprehension (Rajpurkar et al., 2016), a large-scale, human-generated corpus of (document, question, answer) triples. Documents are paragraphs from 536 high-PageRank Wikipedia articles covering a variety of subjects. Questions are posed by crowdworkers in natural language and answers are spans of text in the related paragraph highlighted by the same crowdworkers. There are 107,785 question-answer pairs in total, including 87,599 training instances and 10,570 development instances.

5.2 Baseline Seq2Seq System

Our baseline system, denoted "Seq2Seq," is based on the encoder-decoder architecture with attention and pointer-softmax outlined in Bahdanau et al. (2015) and Gulcehre et al. (2016). This is essentially the model outlined in Section 3, with a few key differences: (i) since the baseline was originally designed for translation, its encoder and decoder vocabularies are separate; (ii) the baseline conditions question generation on the answer simply by setting $\mathbf{h}^a$ as the average of the document encodings corresponding to the answer positions in D; (iii) the baseline has no constraint on generating answer words in the question (Equation (10)); and (iv) the baseline does not include the entropy-based loss defined in (11).

5.3 Quantitative Evaluation

We use several automatic evaluation metrics to judge the quality of generated questions with respect to the ground-truth questions from the dataset. We are undertaking a large-scale human evaluation to determine how these metrics align with human judgments. The first metric is BLEU (Papineni

---

[4]We also experimented with a stochastic version of beam search by randomly sampling k words from top-$2k$ predictions sorted by candidate sequence probability at each time step. No performance improvement was observed.

	NLL	BLEU	F1	QA	PPL
Seq2Seq	45.8	4.9	31.2	45.6	153.2
Our System	**35.3**	10.2	39.5	65.3	175.7
+ PG (R_{PPL})	35.7	9.2	38.2	61.1	**155.6**
+ PG (R_{QA})	39.8	**10.5**	**40.1**	**74.2**	300.9
+ PG ($R_{\text{PPL+QA}}$)	39.0	9.2	37.8	70.2	183.1
Question LM	-	-	-	-	87.7
MPCM	-	-	-	70.5	-

Table 2: Automatic metrics on *SQuAD*'s dev set. NLL is the negative log-likelihood. BLEU and F1 are computed with respect to the ground-truth questions. QA is the F1 obtained by the MPCM model answers to generated questions and PPL is the perplexity computed with the question language model (LM) (lower is better). PG denotes policy gradient training. The bottom two lines report performance on ground-truth questions.

Text Passage

...the court of justice accepted that a requirement to speak **gaelic** to teach in a dublin design college could be justified as part of the public policy of promoting the irish language.

Generated Questions

1) what did the court of justice not claim to do?

2) what language did the court of justice say should be justified as part of the public language?

3) what language did the court of justice decide to speak?

4) what language did the court of justice adopt a requirement to speak?

5) what language did the court of justice say should be justified as part of?

Table 3: Examples of generated questions given a context and an answer. Questions are generated by the five systems in Table 2, in order.

et al., 2002), a standard in machine translation, which computes $\{1,2,3,4\}$-gram matches between generated and ground-truth questions. Next we use F1, which focuses on unigram matches (Rajpurkar et al., 2016). We also report fluency and QA performance metrics used in our reward computation. Fluency is measured by the perplexity (PPL) of the generated question computed by the pretrained question language model. The PPL score is proportional to the marginal probability $p(\hat{Y})$ estimated from the corpus. The QA performance is measured by running the pretrained MPCM model on the generated questions and measuring F1 between the predicted answer and the conditioning answer.

5.4 Results and qualitative analysis

Our results for automatic evaluation on *SQuAD*'s development set are presented in Table 2. Implementation details for all models are given in the supplementary material. One striking feature is that BLEU scores are quite low for all systems tested, which relates to our earlier argument that a typical (document, answer) pair may be associated with multiple semantically-distinct questions. This seems to be born out by the result since most generated samples look reasonable despite low BLEU scores (see Tables 1, 3).

Our system vs. Seq2Seq   Comparing our model to the Seq2Seq baseline, we see that all metrics improve notably with the exception of PPL. Interestingly, our system performs worse in terms of PPL despite achieving lower negative log-likelihood. This, along with the improvements in BLEU, F1 and QA, suggests that our system learns a more powerful conditional model at the expense of accurately modelling the marginal distribution over questions. It is likely challenging for the model to allocate probability mass to rarer keywords that are helpful to recover the desired answer while also minimizing perplexity. We illustrate with samples from both models, specifically the first two samples in Table 3. The Seq2Seq baseline generated a well-formed English question, which is also quite vague – it is only weakly conditioned on the answer. On the other hand, our system's generated question is more specific, but still not correct given the context and perhaps less fluent given the repetition of the word *language*. We found that our proposed entropy regularization helped to avoid over-fitting and worked nicely in tandem with dropout: the training loss for our regularized model was 26.6 compared to 22.0 for the Seq2Seq baseline that used only dropout regularization.

Policy gradient (R_{PPL}: $\lambda_{\text{PPL}} = 0.1$)   Policy gradient training with the negative perplexity of the pretrained language model improves the generator's PPL score as desired, which approaches that of the baseline Seq2Seq model. However, QA, F1, and BLEU scores decrease. This aligns with the above observation that fluency and answerability (as measured by the automatic scores) may be in competition. As an example, the third sample in Table 3 is more fluent than the previous examples but does not refer to the desired answer.

Training	Generated Questions	QA	PPL
R_{PPL}	what was the name of the library that was listed on the grainger market?	0	73.2
R_{QA}	the grainger market architecture was listed in 1954 by what?	100	775
R_{QA+PPL}	what language did the grainger market architecture belong to?	0	257
R_{PPL}	what are the main areas of southern california?	0	114
R_{QA}	southern california is famous for what?	16.6	269
R_{QA+PPL}	what is southern california known for?	16.6	179
R_{PPL}	what was the goal of the imperial academy of medicine?	19.1	44.3
R_{QA}	why were confucian scholars attracted to the medical profession?	73.7	405
R_{QA+PPL}	what did the confucian scholars believe were attracted to the medical schools?	90.9	135
R_{PPL}	what is an example of a theory that can be solved in theory?	0	38
R_{QA}	in complexity theory, it is known as what?	100	194
R_{QA+PPL}	what is an example of a theory that can cause polynomial-time solutions to be useful?	100	37

Table 4: Comparison of questions from different reward combinations on the same text and answer.

Policy gradient (R_{QA}: $\lambda_{QA} = 1.0$) Policy gradient is very effective at maximizing the QA reward, gaining 8.9% in accuracy over the improved Seq2Seq model and improving most other metrics as well. The fact that QA score is 3.7% higher than that obtained on the ground-truth questions suggests that the question generator may have learned to exploit MPCM's answering mechanism, and the higher reported perplexity suggests questions under this scheme may be less fluent. We explore this in more detail below. The fourth sample in Table 3, in contrast to the others, is clearly answered by the context word *gaelic* as desired.

Policy gradient (R_{PPL+QA}: $\lambda_{PPL} = 0.25$, $\lambda_{QA} = 0.5$) We attempted to improve fluency and answerability in tandem by combining QA and PPL rewards. The PPL reward adds a prior towards questions that look natural. According to Table 2, this optimization scheme yields a good balance of performance, improving over the maximum-likelihood model by a large margin in terms of QA performance and gaining back some PPL. In the sample shown in Table 3, however, the question is specific to the answer but ends prematurely.

In Table 4 we provide additional generated samples from the different PG rewards. This table reveals one of the 'tricks' encouraged by the QA reward for improving MPCM performance: questions are often phrased with the interrogative 'wh' word at the end. This gives the language high perplexity, since such questions are rarer in the training data, but brings the question form closer to the form of the source text for answer matching.

5.5 Discussion

Looking through examples revealed certain difficulties in the task and some pathologies in the model that should be rectified through future work.

Entities and Verbs Similar entities and related verbs are often swapped, e.g., *miami* for *jacksonville* in a question about population. This issue could be mitigated by biasing the pointer softmax towards the document for certain word types.

Abstraction We desire a system that generates *interesting* questions, which are not limited to re-ordering words from the context but exhibit some abstraction. Rewards from existing QA systems do not seem beneficial for this purpose. Questions generated through NLL training show more abstraction at the expense of decreased specificity.

Commonsense and Reasoning Commonsense understanding appears critical for generating questions that are well-posed and show abstraction from the original text. Likewise, the ability to reason about and compose relations between entities could lead to more abstract and interesting questions. The existing model has no such capacities.

Evaluation Due to the large number of possible questions given a predefined answer, it is challenging to evaluate the outputs using standard overlap-based metrics such as BLEU. In this sense, question generation from text is similar to other tasks with large output spaces (Galley et al., 2015) and may benefit from corpora with multiple ground-truth questions associated to a quality rating (Mostafazadeh et al., 2016).

6   Conclusion and Future Work

We proposed a recurrent neural model that generates natural-language questions conditioned on text passages and predefined answers. We showed how to train this model using a combination of maximum likelihood and policy gradient optimization, and demonstrated both quantitatively and qualitatively how several reward combinations affect the generated outputs. We are now undertaking a human evaluation to determine the correlation between rewards and human judgments, improving our model, and testing on additional datasets.

One of our interests is to build models that seek information autonomously through question asking, as people do. This would entail, among other things, the direct sampling of interesting, informative questions from documents, i.e., modelling distribution $p(Q|D)$ rather than the distribution conditioned on the answer, $p(Q|D, A)$, as in this work. The present work may serve as a useful first step toward this goal, since the larger problem can be tackled by factorizing $p(Q|D) = \sum_A p(Q|D, A)p(A|D)$ and first sampling a document's likely answers according to modelled distribution $p(A|D)$.

References

Husam Ali, Yllias Chali, and Sadid A Hasan. 2010. Automation of question generation from sentences. *Proc. of QG2010: The Third Workshop on Question Generation* .

Dzmitry Bahdanau, Philemon Brakel, Kelvin Xu, Anirudh Goyal, Ryan Lowe, Joelle Pineau, Aaron Courville, and Yoshua Bengio. 2016. An actor-critic algorithm for sequence prediction. *arXiv preprint arXiv:1607.07086* .

Dzmitry Bahdanau, Kyunghyun Cho, and Yoshua Bengio. 2015. Neural machine translation by jointly learning to align and translate. *International Conference on Learning Representations (ICLR)* .

Yoshua Bengio, Réjean Ducharme, and Pascal Vincent. 2001. A neural probabilistic language model. In Todd K. Leen, Thomas G. Dietterich, and Volker Tresp, editors, *NIPS'2000*. MIT Press, pages 932–938.

Yllias Chali and Sina Golestanirad. 2016. Ranking automatically generated questions using common human queries. *Proc. of INLG* .

Kyunghyun Cho, Bart Van Merriënboer, Caglar Gulcehre, Dzmitry Bahdanau, Fethi Bougares, Holger Schwenk, and Yoshua Bengio. 2014. Learning phrase representations using rnn encoder-decoder for statistical machine translation. *arXiv preprint arXiv:1406.1078* .

François Chollet. 2015. keras. `https://github.com/fchollet/keras`.

Michel Galley, Chris Brockett, Alessandro Sordoni, Yangfeng Ji, Michael Auli, Chris Quirk, Margaret Mitchell, Jianfeng Gao, and Bill Dolan. 2015. deltableu: A discriminative metric for generation tasks with intrinsically diverse targets. *arXiv preprint arXiv:1506.06863* .

Ian Goodfellow, Jean Pouget-Abadie, Mehdi Mirza, Bing Xu, David Warde-Farley, Sherjil Ozair, Aaron Courville, and Yoshua Bengio. 2014. Generative adversarial nets. In *Advances in neural information processing systems*. pages 2672–2680.

Alex Graves. 2012. Sequence transduction with recurrent neural networks. *arXiv preprint arXiv:1211.3711* .

Caglar Gulcehre, Sungjin Ahn, Ramesh Nallapati, Bowen Zhou, and Yoshua Bengio. 2016. Pointing the unknown words. *arXiv preprint arXiv:1603.08148* .

Michael Heilman and Noah A Smith. 2010. Good question! statistical ranking for question generation. In *Human Language Technologies: The 2010 Annual Conference of the North American Chapter of the Association for Computational Linguistics*. Association for Computational Linguistics, pages 609–617.

Karl Moritz Hermann, Tomas Kocisky, Edward Grefenstette, Lasse Espeholt, Will Kay, Mustafa Suleyman, and Phil Blunsom. 2015. Teaching machines to read and comprehend. In *Advances in Neural Information Processing Systems*. pages 1693–1701.

Felix Hill, Antoine Bordes, Sumit Chopra, and Jason Weston. 2015. The goldilocks principle: Reading children's books with explicit memory representations. *arXiv preprint arXiv:1511.02301* .

Sepp Hochreiter and Jürgen Schmidhuber. 1997. Long short-term memory. *Neural Computation* 9.8:1735–1780.

Rudolf Kadlec, Martin Schmid, Ondrej Bajgar, and Jan Kleindienst. 2016. Text understanding with the attention sum reader network. *arXiv preprint arXiv:1603.01547* .

Kirthevasan Kandasamy and Yoram Bachrach. 2017. Batch policy gradient methods for improving neural conversation models. *Proc. of ICLR* .

Diederik P Kingma and Jimmy Ba. 2014. Adam: A method for stochastic optimization. In *International Conference on Learning Representations (ICLR)*.

Ryan Kiros, Yukun Zhu, Ruslan R Salakhutdinov, Richard Zemel, Raquel Urtasun, Antonio Torralba, and Sanja Fidler. 2015. Skip-thought vectors. In *Advances in neural information processing systems*. pages 3294–3302.

Girish Kumar, Rafael E Banchs, and Luis Fernando D'Haro Enriquez. 2015. Revup: Automatic gap-fill question generation from educational texts. *Proc. of ACL* .

Igor Labutov, Sumit Basu, and Lucy Vanderwende. 2015. Deep questions without deep understanding. *Proc. of ACL* .

Jiwei Li, Will Monroe, Alan Ritter, Michel Galley, Jianfeng Gao, and Dan Jurafsky. 2016. Deep reinforcement learning for dialogue generation. *Proc. of EMNLP* .

David Lindberg, Fred Popowich, and John Nesbit Phil Winne. 2013. Generating natural language questions to support learning on-line. *Proc. of ENLG* .

Prashanth Mannem, Rashmi Prasad, and Aravind Joshi. 2010. Question generation from paragraphs at upenn: Qgstec system description. In *Proceedings of QG2010: The Third Workshop on Question Generation*. pages 84–91.

Karen Mazidi and Rodney D Nielsen. 2015. Leveraging multiple views of text for automatic question generation. In *International Conference on Artificial Intelligence in Education*. Springer, pages 257–266.

Nasrin Mostafazadeh, Ishan Misra, Jacob Devlin, Margaret Mitchell, Xiaodong He, and Lucy Vanderwende. 2016. Generating natural questions about an image. *arXiv preprint arXiv:1603.06059* .

Tri Nguyen, Mir Rosenberg, Xia Song, Jianfeng Gao, Saurabh Tiwary, Rangan Majumder, and Li Deng. 2016. Ms marco: A human generated machine reading comprehension dataset. *arXiv preprint arXiv:1611.09268* .

Mohammad Norouzi, Samy Bengio, Zhifeng Chen, Navdeep Jaitly, Mike Schuster, Yonghui Wu, and Dale Schuurmans. 2016. Reward augmented maximum likelihood for neural structured prediction. In *Advances In Neural Information Processing Systems*.

Kishore Papineni, Salim Roukos, Todd Ward, and Wei-Jing Zhu. 2002. Bleu: a method for automatic evaluation of machine translation. In *Proceedings of the 40th annual meeting on association for computational linguistics*. Association for Computational Linguistics, pages 311–318.

Razvan Pascanu, Caglar Gulcehre, Kyunghyun Cho, and Yoshua Bengio. 2013. How to construct deep recurrent neural networks. *arXiv preprint arXiv:1312.6026* .

Jeffrey Pennington, Richard Socher, and Christopher D. Manning. 2014. Glove: Global vectors for word representation. In *Empirical Methods in Natural Language Processing (EMNLP)*. pages 1532–1543. http://www.aclweb.org/anthology/D14-1162.

Pranav Rajpurkar, Jian Zhang, Konstantin Lopyrev, and Percy Liang. 2016. Squad: 100,000+ questions for machine comprehension of text. *arXiv preprint arXiv:1606.05250* .

Marc'Aurelio Ranzato, Sumit Chopra, Michael Auli, and Wojciech Zaremba. 2016. Sequence level training with recurrent neural networks. *Proc. of ICLR* .

Minjoon Seo, Aniruddha Kembhavi, Ali Farhadi, and Hannaneh Hajishirzi. 2016. Bidirectional attention flow for machine comprehension. *arXiv preprint arXiv:1611.01603* .

Iulian Vlad Serban, Alberto García-Durán, Caglar Gulcehre, Sungjin Ahn, Sarath Chandar, Aaron Courville, and Yoshua Bengio. 2016. Generating factoid questions with recurrent neural networks: The 30m factoid question-answer corpus. *Proc. of ACL* .

Yelong Shen, Po-Sen Huang, Jianfeng Gao, and Weizhu Chen. 2016. Reasonet: Learning to stop reading in machine comprehension. *arXiv preprint arXiv:1609.05284* .

Harry Singer and Dan Donlan. 1982. Active comprehension: Problem-solving schema with question generation for comprehension of complex short stories. *Reading Research Quarterly* pages 166–186.

Alessandro Sordoni, Michel Galley, Michael Auli, Chris Brockett, Yangfeng Ji, Margaret Mitchell, Jian-Yun Nie, Jianfeng Gao, and Bill Dolan. 2015. A neural network approach to context-sensitive generation of conversational responses. *arXiv preprint arXiv:1506.06714* .

Nitish Srivastava, Geoffrey Hinton, Alex Krizhevsky, Ilya Sutskever, and Ruslan Salakhutdinov. 2014. Dropout: A simple way to prevent neural networks from overfitting. *J. Mach. Learn. Res.* 15(1):1929–1958. http://dl.acm.org/citation.cfm?id=2627435.2670313.

Theano Development Team. 2016. Theano: A Python framework for fast computation of mathematical expressions. *arXiv e-prints* abs/1605.02688. http://arxiv.org/abs/1605.02688.

Adam Trischler, Tong Wang, Xingdi Yuan, Justin Harris, Alessandro Sordoni, Philip Bachman, and Kaheer Suleman. 2016a. Newsqa: A machine comprehension dataset. *arXiv preprint arXiv:1611.09830* .

Adam Trischler, Zheng Ye, Xingdi Yuan, Phil Bachman, Alessandro Sordoni, and Kaheer Suleman. 2016b. Natural language comprehension with the epireader. In *Empirical Methods on Natural Language Processing (EMNLP)*.

Hado P van Hasselt, Arthur Guez, Matteo Hessel, Volodymyr Mnih, and David Silver. 2016. Learning values across many orders of magnitude. In *Advances in Neural Information Processing Systems.* pages 4287–4295.

Oriol Vinyals, Meire Fortunato, and Navdeep Jaitly. 2015. Pointer networks. In *Advances in Neural Information Processing Systems.* pages 2692–2700.

Zhiguo Wang, Haitao Mi, Wael Hamza, and Radu Florian. 2016. Multi-perspective context matching for machine comprehension. *arXiv preprint arXiv:1612.04211* .

Ronald J Williams. 1992. Simple statistical gradient-following algorithms for connectionist reinforcement learning. *Machine learning* 8(3-4):229–256.

Zhilin Yang, Junjie Hu, Ruslan Salakhutdinov, and William W Cohen. 2017. Semi-supervised qa with generative domain-adaptive nets. *arXiv preprint arXiv:1702.02206* .

Xingxing Zhang and Mirella Lapata. 2017. Sentence simplification with deep reinforcement learning. *arXiv preprint arXiv:1703.10931* .

Shiqi Zhao, Haifeng Wang, Chao Li, Ting Liu, and Yi Guan. 2011. Automatically generating questions from queries for community-based question answering. *Proc. of IJCNLP* .

Supplementary Material

A Implementation details

All models are implemented using Keras (Chollet, 2015) with Theano (Theano Development Team, 2016) backend. We used Adam (Kingma and Ba, 2014) with an initial learning rate 2e-4 for both maximum likelihood and policy gradient updates. Word embeddings were initialized with the GloVe vectors (Pennington et al., 2014) and updated during training. The hidden size for all RNNs is 768.

Dropout (Srivastava et al., 2014) is applied with a rate of 0.3 to the embedding layers as well as all the RNNs (between both input-hidden and hidden-hidden connections).

Both λ_s for answer-suppression and λ_e for entropy maximization are set to 0.01. We used beam search with a beam size of 32 in all experiments. The reward weights used in policy gradient training are listed in Table 5. These parameters are selected using grid search based on validation QA reward.

	QA_{MPCM}	$\text{PPL}_{\text{Quest. LM}}$
λ_{QA}	1.0	-
λ_{PPL}	-	0.1
$\lambda_{\text{PPL+QA}}$	0.5	0.25

Table 5: Hyperparameter settings for policy gradient training.

Emergent Predication Structure
in Hidden State Vectors of Neural Readers

Hai Wang[*] **Takeshi Onishi**[*] **Kevin Gimpel** **David McAllester**
Toyota Technological Institute at Chicago
6045 S. Kenwood Ave., Chicago, Illinois 60637, USA
`{haiwang,tonishi,kgimpel,mcallester}@ttic.edu`

Abstract

A significant number of neural architectures for reading comprehension have recently been developed and evaluated on large cloze-style datasets. We present experiments supporting the emergence of "predication structure" in the hidden state vectors of these readers. More specifically, we provide evidence that the hidden state vectors represent atomic formulas $\Phi[c]$ where Φ is a semantic property (predicate) and c is a constant symbol entity identifier.

1 Introduction

Reading comprehension is a type of question answering task where the answer is to be found in a passage about particular entities and events. In particular, the entities and events should not be mentioned in structured databases of general knowledge. Reading comprehension problems are intended to measure a system's ability to extract semantic information about entities and relations directly from unstructured text.

Several large scale reading comprehension datasets have been introduced recently, including the CNN & Daily Mail datasets (Hermann et al., 2015), the Children's Book Test (CBT) (Hill et al., 2016), and the Who-did-What dataset (Onishi et al., 2016). The large sizes of these datasets enable the application of deep learning. These are all cloze-style datasets where a question is constructed by deleting a word or phrase from an article summary (in CNN/Daily Mail), from a sentence in a children's story (in CBT), or by deleting a person from the first sentence of a different news article on the same entities and events (in Who-did-What).

---

[*] Authors contributed equally.

In this paper we present empirical evidence for the emergence of predication structure in a certain class of neural readers. To understand predication structure, it is helpful to review the anonymization performed in the CNN/Daily Mail dataset. In this dataset named entities are replaced by anonymous entity identifiers such as "entity37". The passage might contain "entity52 gave entity24 a rousing applause" and the question might be "X received a rounding applause from entity52". The task is to fill in X from a given multiple choice list of candidate entity identifiers. A fixed relatively small set of the same entity identifiers are used over all the problems and the same problem is presented many times with different entity identifiers shuffled. This prevents a given entity identifier from having any semantically meaningful vector embedding. The embeddings of the entity identifiers are presumably just pointers to semantics-free tokens. We will write entity identifiers as logical constant symbols such as c rather than strings such as "entity37".

"Aggregation" readers, including Memory Networks (Weston et al., 2015; Sukhbaatar et al., 2015), the Attentive Reader (Hermann et al., 2015), and the Stanford Reader (Chen et al., 2016), use bidirectional LSTMs or GRUs to construct a contextual embedding h_t of each position t in the passage and also an embedding h_q of the question q. They then select an answer c using a criterion similar to

$$\operatorname*{argmax}_{c} \sum_{t} <h_t, h_q> \ <h_t, e(c)> \quad (1)$$

where $e(c)$ is the vector embedding of the constant symbol (entity identifier) c. In practice the inner-product $<h_t, h_q>$ is normalized over t using a softmax to yield attention weights α_t over t and

Proceedings of the 2nd Workshop on Representation Learning for NLP, pages 26–36,
Vancouver, Canada, August 3, 2017. ©2017 Association for Computational Linguistics

(1) becomes

$$\underset{c}{\operatorname{argmax}} \; < e(c), \sum_t \alpha_t h_t > . \qquad (2)$$

Here $\sum_t \alpha_t h_t$ can be viewed as a vector representation of the passage.

We argue that for aggregation readers, roughly defined by (2), the hidden state h_t of the passage at position (or word) t can be viewed as a vector concatenation $h_t = [s(\Phi_t), s(c_t)]$ where Φ_t is a property (or statement or predicate) being stated of a particular constant symbol c_t. Here $s(\Phi_t)$ and $s(c_t)$ are unknown emergent embeddings of Φ_t and c_t respectively. A logician might write this as $h_t = \Phi_t[c_t]$. Furthermore, the question can be interpreted as having the form $\Psi[x]$ where the problem is to find a constant symbol c such that the passage implies $\Psi[c]$. Assuming $h_t = [s(\Phi_t), s(c_t)]$, $h_q = [s(\Psi), 0]$, and $e(c) = [0, s(c)]$, we can rewrite (1) as

$$\underset{c}{\operatorname{argmax}} \sum_t \; < s(\Phi_t), s(\Psi) > \; < s(c_t), s(c) > .$$
$$(3)$$

The first inner product in (3) is interpreted as measuring the extent to which $\Phi_t[x]$ implies $\Psi[x]$ for any x. The second inner product is interpreted as restricting t to positions talking about the constant symbol c.

Note that the posited decomposition of h_t is not explicit in (2) but instead must emerge during training. We present empirical evidence that this structure does emerge. The empirical evidence is somewhat tricky as the direct sum structure that divides h_t into its two parts need not be axis aligned and therefore need not literally correspond to vector concatenation.

We also consider a second class of neural readers that we call "explicit reference" readers. Explicit reference readers avoid (2) and instead use

$$\underset{c}{\operatorname{argmax}} \sum_{t \in R(c)} \alpha_t \qquad (4)$$

where $R(c)$ is the subset of the positions where the constant symbol (entity identifier) c occurs. Note that if we identify α_t with $< s(\Phi_t), s(\Psi) >$ and assume that $< s(c), s(c_t) >$ is either 0 or 1 depending on whether $c = c_t$, then (3) and (4) agree. In explicit reference readers the hidden state h_t need not carry a pointer to c_t as the restriction on t is independent of learned representations. Explicit reference readers include the Attention Sum Reader (Kadlec et al., 2016), the Gated Attention Reader (Dhingra et al., 2017), and the Attention-over-Attention Reader (Cui et al., 2017).

So far we have only considered anonymized datasets that require the handling of semantics-free constant symbols. However, even for non-anonymized datasets such as Who-did-What, it is helpful to add features which indicate which positions in the passage are referring to which candidate answers. This indicates, not surprisingly, that reference is important in question answering. The fact that explicit reference features are needed in aggregation readers on non-anonymized data indicates that reference is not being solved by the aggregation readers. However, as reference seems to be important for cloze-style question answering, these problems may ultimately provide training data from which reference resolution can be learned.

Sections 2 and 3 review various existing datasets and models respectively. In the CNN dataset the vector embeddings of entity identifiers such as "entity32" are clearly interpretable as vector representations of semantics-free constant symbols. However, to the best of our knowledge the emergent decomposition of the hidden state vectors into a concatenation of a property vector and an entity vector has not been previously described or empirically investigated in the literature. Section 4 presents the logical structure interpretation of aggregation readers in more detail and the empirical evidence supporting it. Section 5 proposes new models that enforce the direct sum structure of the hidden state vectors. It is shown that these new models perform well on the Who-did-What dataset provided that reference annotations are added as input features. Section 5 also describes additional linguistic features that can be added to the input embeddings and show that these improve the performance of existing models resulting in the best single-model performance to date on the Who-did-What dataset.

2 A Brief Survey of Datasets

Before presenting various models for machine comprehension we give a general formulation of the machine comprehension task. We take an instance of the task to be a four tuple $(q, p, a, \mathcal{A})$, where q is a question given as a sequence of words containing a special token for a "blank" to be filled in, p is a document consisting of a sequence of words, $\mathcal{A}$ is a set of possible answers and $a \in \mathcal{A}$ is the ground truth answer. All words are drawn from a vocabulary $\mathcal{V}$. We assume that all possible answers are words from the vocabulary, that is $\mathcal{A} \subseteq \mathcal{V}$, and that the ground truth answer appears in the document, that is $a \in p$. The problem can be described as that of selecting the answer $a \in \mathcal{A}$ that answers question q based on information from p. We now briefly summarize important features of the related datasets in reading comprehension.

CNN & Daily Mail: Hermann et al. (2015) constructed these datasets from a large number of news articles from the CNN and Daily Mail news websites. The main article is used as the context, while the cloze style question is formed from one short article summary sentence appearing in conjunction with the published article. To avoid the model using external world knowledge when answering the question, the named entities in the entire dataset were replaced by anonymous entity IDs which were then further shuffled for each example. This forces models to rely on the context document to answer each question. In this anonymized corpus the entity identifiers are taken to be a part of the vocabulary and the answer set $\mathcal{A}$ consists of the entity identifiers occurring in the passage.

Who-did-What (WDW): The Who-did-What dataset (Onishi et al., 2016) contains 127,000 multiple choice cloze questions constructed from the LDC English Gigaword newswire corpus (David and Cieri, 2003). In contrast with CNN and Daily Mail, WDW avoids using article summaries for question formation. Instead, each problem is formed from two independent articles: one is given as the passage to be read and a different article on the same entities and events is used to form the question. Further, WDW avoids anonymization — each choice is a person named entity. In this dataset the answer set $\mathcal{A}$ consists of the person named entities occurring in the passage. Finally, the problems have been filtered to remove a fraction that are easily solved by simple baselines. It has two training sets. The larger training set ("relaxed") is created using less baseline filtering, while the smaller training set ("strict") uses the same filtering as the validation and test sets.

Other Related Datasets. It is also worth mentioning several related datasets. The MCTest dataset (Richardson et al., 2013) consists of children's stories and questions written by crowd-sourced workers. The dataset only contains 660 documents and is too small to train deep models. The bAbI dataset (Weston et al., 2016) is constructed automatically using synthetic text generation and can be perfectly answered by hand-written algorithms (Lee et al., 2016). The SQuAD dataset (Rajpurkar et al., 2016) consists of passage-question pairs where the passage is a Wikipedia article and the questions are written via crowdsourcing. The dataset contains over 100,000 problems, but the answer is often a word sequence which is difficult to handle with the reader models considered here. The Children's Book Test (CBT) (Hill et al., 2016) takes any sequence of 21 consecutive sentences from a children's book: the first 20 sentences are used as the passage, and the goal is to infer a missing word in the 21st sentence. The task complexity varies with the type of the omitted word (verb, preposition, named entity, or common noun). The LAMBADA dataset (Paperno et al., 2016) is a word prediction dataset which requires a broad discourse context, though the correct answer might not actually be contained in the context. Nevertheless, when the correct answer is in the context, neural readers can be applied effectively (Chu et al., 2017).

3 Aggregation Readers and Explicit Reference Readers

As outlined in the introduction, here we classify readers into aggregation readers and explicit reference readers. Aggregation readers appeared first in the literature and include Memory Networks (Weston et al., 2015; Sukhbaatar et al., 2015), the Attentive Reader (Hermann et al., 2015), and the Stanford Reader (Chen et al., 2016). In this section we define aggregation readers more specifically by equations (7) and (9) below. Explicit reference readers include the Attention-Sum Reader (Kadlec et al., 2016), the Gated-Attention Reader (Dhingra et al., 2017), and the Attention-over-Attention Reader (Cui et al., 2017). In this section we define explicit reference readers more specifically by equation (13) below. We first present the Stanford Reader as a paradigmatic aggregation reader and the Attention-Sum Reader as a paradigmatic explicit reference reader.

3.1 Aggregation Readers

Stanford Reader. The Stanford Reader (Chen et al., 2016) computes a bidirectional LSTM representation of both the passage and the question.

$$h \;=\; \text{biLSTM}(e(p)) \tag{5}$$
$$h_q \;=\; [\text{fLSTM}(e(q))_{|q|}, \text{bLSTM}(e(q))_1] \tag{6}$$

In equations (5) and (6) we have that $e(p)$ is the sequence of word embeddings $e(w_i)$ for $w_i \in p$ and similarly for $e(q)$. The expression $\text{biLSTM}(s)$ denotes the sequence of hidden state vectors resulting from running a bidirectional LSTM on the vector sequence s. We write $\text{biLSTM}(s)_i$ for the ith vector in this sequence. Similarly $\text{fLSTM}(s)$ and $\text{bLSTM}(s)$ denote the sequence of vectors resulting from running a forward LSTM and a backward LSTM respectively and $[\cdot, \cdot]$ denotes vector concatenation. The Stanford Reader, and various other readers, then compute a bilinear attention over the passage which is used to construct a single weighted vector representation of the passage.

$$\alpha_t = \underset{t}{\text{softmax}}\; h_t^\top W_\alpha\, h_q \quad o = \sum_t \alpha_t h_t \tag{7}$$

Finally, they compute a probability distribution P over the answers:

$$P(\cdot|d, q, \mathcal{A}) \;=\; \underset{a \in \mathcal{A}}{\text{softmax}}\; e_o(a)^\top o \tag{8}$$
$$\hat{a} \;=\; \underset{a \in \mathcal{A}}{\text{argmax}}\; e_o(a)^\top o \tag{9}$$

Here $e_o(a)$ is the "output embedding" of the answer a. On the CNN dataset the Stanford Reader trains an output embedding for each of the roughly 550 entity identifiers used in the dataset. For datasets in which the answer might be any word in $\mathcal{V}$, output embeddings must be trained for the entire vocabulary.

The reader is trained with log-loss $-\log P(a|p, q, \mathcal{A})$ where a is the correct answer. At test time the reader is scored on the percentage of problems where $\hat{a} = a$.

Memory Networks. Memory Networks (Weston et al., 2015; Sukhbaatar et al., 2015) use (7) and (9) but have more elaborate methods of constructing "memory vectors" h_t not involving LSTMs. Memory networks use (7) and (9) but replace (8) with

$$P(\cdot|p, q, \mathcal{A}) = P(\cdot|p, q) = \underset{w \in \mathcal{V}}{\text{softmax}}\; e_o(w)^\top o. \tag{10}$$

It should be noted that (10) trains output vectors over the whole vocabulary rather than just those items occurring in the choice set $\mathcal{A}$. This is empirically significant in non-anonymized datasets such as CBT and Who-did-What where choices at test time may never have occurred as choices in the training data.

Attentive Reader. The Stanford Reader was derived from the Attentive Reader (Hermann et al., 2015). The Attentive Reader uses $\alpha_t = \text{softmax}_t\, \text{MLP}([h_t, h_q])$ instead of (7). Here $\text{MLP}(x)$ is the output of a multi layer perceptron given input x. Also, the answer distribution in the Attentive Reader is defined over the full vocabulary rather than just the candidate answer set $\mathcal{A}$:

$$P(\cdot|p, q, \mathcal{A}) = \underset{w \in \mathcal{V}}{\text{softmax}}\; e_o(w)^\top \text{MLP}([o, h_q]) \tag{11}$$

Equation (11) is similar to (10) in that it leads to the training of output vectors for the full vocabulary rather than just those items appearing in choice sets in the training data. As in memory networks, this leads to improved performance on non-anonymized datasets.

3.2 Explicit Reference Readers

Attention-Sum Reader. In the Attention-Sum Reader (Kadlec et al., 2016), h and q are computed with equations (5) and (6) as in the Stanford Reader but using GRUs rather than LSTMs. The attention α_t is computed similarly to (7) but using a simple inner product $\alpha_t = \text{softmax}_t\; h_t^\top h_q$ rather than a trained bilinear form. Most significantly, however, equations (8) and (9) are replaced by the following where $t \in R(a, p)$ indicates that a reference to candidate answer a occurs at position t in p.

$$P(a|p, q, \mathcal{A}) \;=\; \sum_{t \in R(a,p)} \alpha_t \tag{12}$$
$$\hat{a} \;=\; \underset{a}{\text{argmax}} \sum_{t \in R(a,p)} \alpha_t \tag{13}$$

Here we think of $R(a, p)$ as the set of references to a in the passage p. It is important to note that (12) is an equality and that $P(a|p, q, \mathcal{A})$ is not normalized to the members of $R(a, p)$. When training with the log-loss objective this drives the attention α_t to be normalized — to have support only on the positions t with $t \in R(a, p)$ for some a. See the heat maps in the supplementary material.

Gated-Attention Reader. The Gated-Attention Reader (Dhingra et al., 2017) involves a K-layer biGRU architecture defined by the following equations.

$$h_q^\ell = [\text{fGRU}(e(q))_{|q|}, \text{bGRU}(e(q))_1] \; 1 \le \ell \le K$$
$$h^1 = \text{biGRU}(e(p))$$
$$h^\ell = \text{biGRU}(h^{\ell-1} \odot h_q^{\ell-1}) \; 2 \le \ell \le K$$

Here the question embeddings h_q^ℓ for different values of ℓ are computed with different GRU model parameters. Here $h \odot h_q$ abbreviates the sequence $h_1 \odot h_q, h_2 \odot h_q, \ldots h_{|p|} \odot h_q$. Note that for $K = 1$ we have only h_q^1 and h^1 as in the attention-sum reader. An attention is then computed over the final layer h^K with $\alpha_t = \text{softmax}_t \, (h_t^K)^\top \, h_q^K$ in the Attention-Sum Reader. This reader uses (12) and (13).

Attention-over-Attention Reader. The Attention-over-Attention Reader (Cui et al., 2017) uses a more elaborate method to compute the attention α_t. We will use t to range over positions in the passage and j to range over positions in the question. The model is then defined by the following equations.

$$h = \text{biGRU}(e(p)) \qquad h_q = \text{biGRU}(e(q))$$

$$\alpha_{t,j} = \text{softmax}_t \, h_t^\top h_{q,j} \quad \beta_{t,j} = \text{softmax}_j \, h_t^\top h_{q,j}$$

$$\beta_j = \tfrac{1}{|p|} \sum_t \beta_{t,j} \qquad \alpha_t = \sum_j \beta_j \alpha_{t,j}$$

Note that the final equation defining α_t can be interpreted as applying the attention β_j to the attentions $\alpha_{t,j}$. This reader uses (12) and (13).

4 Emergent Predication Structure

As discussed in the introduction the entity identifiers such as "entity37" introduced in the CNN/Daily Mail datasets cannot be assigned any semantics other than their identity. We should think of them as pointers or semantics-free constant symbols. Despite this undermining of semantics, aggregation readers using (7) and (9) are able to perform well. Here we posit that this is due to an emergent predication structure in the hidden vectors h_t. Intuitively we want to think of the hidden state vector h_t as a concatenation $[s(\Phi_t), s(a_t)]$ where Φ_t is a property being asserted of entity a_t at the positon t in the passage. Here $s(\Phi_t)$ and $s(a_t)$ are emergent embeddings of the property and entity respectively, We also think

of the vector representation q of the question as having the form $[s(\Psi), 0]$ and the vector embedding $e_o(a)$ as having the form $[0, s(a)]$.

Unfortunately, the decomposition of h_t into this predication structure need not be axis aligned. Rather than posit an axis-aligned concatenation we posit that the hidden vector space H is a possibly non-aligned direct sum

$$H = S \oplus E \tag{14}$$

where S is a subspace of "statement vectors" and E is an orthogonal subspace of "entity pointers". Each hidden state vector $h \in H$ then has a unique decomposition as $h = \Psi + e$ for $\Psi \in S$ and $e \in E$. This is equivalent to saying that the hidden vector space H is some rotation of a concatenation of the vector spaces S and E. In this non-axis aligned model we also assume emergent embeddings $s(\Phi)$ and $s(a)$ with $s(\Phi) \in S$ and $s(a) \in E$. We will also assume that the latent spaces are learned in such a way that explicit entity output embeddings satisfy $e_o(a) \in E$.

We now present empirical evidence for this decomposition structure. This structure implies $e_o(a)^\top h_t$ equals $e_o(a)^\top s(a_t)$. This suggests the following for some fixed positive constant c.

$$e_o(a)^\top h_t = \begin{cases} c & \text{if } t \in R(a,p) \\ 0 & \text{otherwise} \end{cases} \tag{15}$$

We note that if $e_o(a)^\top s(a)$ was different for different constant a then answers would be biased toward constant symbols where this product was larger. But we need to have that all constant symbols are equivalent. We note that (15) gives

$$\operatorname*{argmax}_a e_o(a)^\top o = \operatorname*{argmax}_a e_o(a)^\top \sum_t \alpha_t h_t$$
$$= \operatorname*{argmax}_a \sum_t \alpha_t \, e_o(a)^\top h_t = \operatorname*{argmax}_a \sum_{t \in R(a,p)} \alpha_t$$

and hence (9) and (13) agree — the aggregation readers and the explicit reference readers are using essentially the same answer selection criterion.

Empirical evidence for (15) is given in the first three rows of Table 1. The first row empirically measures the constant c in (15) by measuring $e_0(a)^\top h_t$ for those cases where $t \in R(a,p)$. The second row measures "0" in (15) by measuring $e_o(a)^\top h_t$ in those cases where $t \notin R(a,p)$. The third row shows that this inner product falls off significantly just one word before or after the

	CNN Dev			CNN Test		
	samples	mean	variance	samples	mean	variance
$e_o(a)^\top h_t, \quad t \in R(a,p)$	222,001	10.66	2.26	164,746	10.70	2.45
$e_o(a)^\top h_t, \quad t \notin R(a,p)$	93,072,682	-0.57	1.59	68,451,660	-0.58	1.65
$e_o(a)^\top h_{t\pm1}, \quad t \in R(a,p)$	443,878	2.32	1.79	329,366	2.25	1.84
$\mathrm{Cosine}(h_q, h_t), \quad \exists a\, t \in R(a,p)$	222,001	0.22	0.11	164,746	0.22	0.12
$\mathrm{Cosine}(h_q, e_o(a)), \quad \forall a$	103,909	-0.03	0.04	78,411	-0.03	0.04

Table 1: Statistics to support (15) and (16). These statistics are computed for the Stanford Reader.

position of the answer word. Additional evidence for (15) is given in Figure 1 showing that the output vectors $e_o(a)$ for different entity identifiers a are nearly orthogonal. Orthogonality of the output vectors is required by (15) provided that each output vector $e_o(a)$ is in the span of the hidden state vectors $h_{t,p}$ for which $t \in R(a,p)$. Intuitively, the mean of all vectors $h_{t,p}$ with $t \in R(a,p)$ should be approximately equal to $e_o(a)$. Empirically this will only be approximately true.

Equation (15) would suggest that the vector embedding of the constant symbols should have dimension at least as large as the number of distinct constants. However, in practice it is sufficient that $e_o(a)^\top s(a')$ is small for $a \neq a'$. This allows the vector embeddings of the constants to have dimension much smaller than the number of constants. We have experimented with two-sparse constant symbol embeddings where the number of embedding vectors in dimension d is $2d(d-1)$ (d choose 2 times the four ways of setting the signs of the non-zero coordinates). Although we do not report results here, these designed and untrained constant embeddings worked reasonably well.

As further support for (15) we give heat maps for $e_o(a)^\top h_t$ for different identifiers a and heat maps for α_t for different readers in the supplementary material.

As another testable predication we note that the posited decomposition of the hidden state vectors implies

$$h_q^\top (h_i + e_o(a)) = h_q^\top h_i. \tag{16}$$

This equation is equivalent to $h_q^\top e_o(a) = 0$. Experimentally, however, we cannot expect $h_q^\top e_o(a)$ to be exactly zero and (16) seems to provides a more experimentally meaningful test. Empirical evidence for (16) is given in the fourth and fifth rows of Table 1. The fourth row measures the

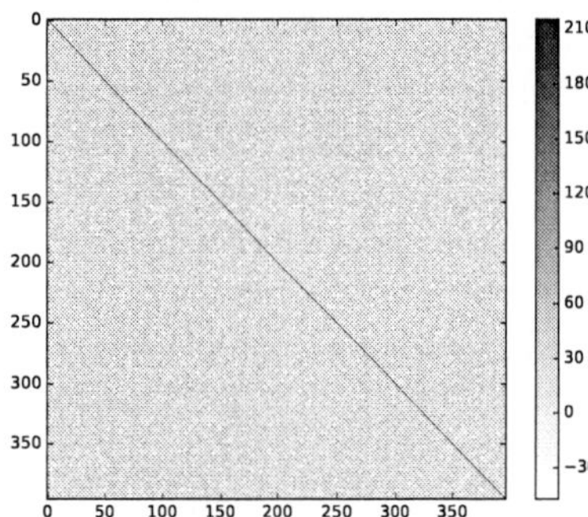

Figure 1: Plot of $e_o(a_i)^\top e_o(a_j)$ from Stanford Reader trained on CNN dataset, where rows range over i values and columns range over j values. Off-diagonal values have mean 25.6 and variance 17.2 while diagonal values have mean 169 and variance 17.3.

cosine of the angle between the question vector h_q and the hidden state h_t averaged over passage positions t at which some entity identifier occurs. The fifth row measures the cosine of the angle between h_q and $e_o(a)$ averaged over the entity identifiers a.

A question asks for a value of x such that a statement $\Psi[x]$ is implied by the passage. For a question Ψ we might even suggest the following vectorial interpretation of entailment.

$$\Phi[x] \text{ implies } \Psi[x] \quad \text{iff} \quad \Phi^\top \Psi \geq ||\Psi||_1.$$

This interpretation is exactly correct if some of the dimensions of the vector space correspond to predicates, Ψ is a 0-1 vector representing a conjunction predicates, and Φ is also 0-1 on these dimensions indicating whether a predicate is implied by the context. Of course in practice one expects the dimension to be smaller than the number of possible predicates.

5 Pointer Annotation Readers

It is of course important to note that anonymization provides reference information—anonymization assumes that one can determine coreference so as to replace coreferent phrases with the same entity identifier. Anonymization allows the reference set $R(a, p)$ to be directly read off of the passage. Still, an aggregation reader must learn to recover this explicit reference structure.

Aggregation readers can have difficulty when anonymization is not done. The Stanford Reader achieves just better than 45% on the Who-did-What dataset while the Attention-Sum Reader can get near 60% (see Table 2). But if we anonymize the Who-did-What dataset and then re-train the Stanford Reader, the accuracy jumps to near 65%. Anonymization greatly reduces the number of output word embeddings $e_o(a)$ to be learned. We need to learn only output embeddings for the relatively small number of entity identifiers needed for the question. Anonymization suppresses the semantics of the reference phrases and leaves only a semantics-free entity identifier. This suppression of semantics may facilitate the separation of the hidden state vector space H into a direct sum $S \oplus E$ with $s(\Phi) \in S$ and $e_o(a), s(a) \in E$.

A third, and perhaps more important effect of anonymization is to provide reference information. Anonymization explicitly marks positions of candidate answers and establishes coreference. A natural question is whether this information can be provided without anonymization by simply adding additional coreference features to the input. Here we evaluate two architectures inspired by this question. This evaluation is done on the Who-did-What dataset which is not anonymized. In each architecture we add features to the input to mark the occurrences of candidate answers. These models are simpler than the Stanford Reader but perform comparably. This comparable performance in Table 2 further supports our analysis of logical structure in aggregation readers.

One-Hot Pointer Reader: The Stanford Reader uses input embeddings of words and output embeddings of entity identifiers. In the Who-did-What dataset each problem has at most five choices in the multiple choice answer list. This means that we need only five entity identifiers and we can use a five dimensional one-hot vector rep-

resentation for answer identifiers.

If an answer choice exists at position t in the passage let i_t be the index of that choice on the answer choice list. If no answer choice occurs at position t we let i_t be zero. We define $e'(i)$ to be the zero vector if $i = 0$ and otherwise to be the one-hot vector for i (i.e., the five-dimensional vector with zeroes at all positions except with a one at position i). We define "pointer annotation" to be the result of concatenating $e'(i_t)$ as additional features to the word embedding $e(w_t)$ for token w_t in the passage:

$$\bar{e}(w_t) = [e(w_t), e'(i_t)] \qquad (17)$$

We feed the new $\bar{e}(w_t)$ to the readers for each token w_t. We define a "one-hot pointer reader" by designating the last five dimensions of the hidden state as indicators of the answer and take the probability of choice i to be defined as

$$p(i|d, q) = \operatorname*{softmax}_{i \in \mathcal{A}} o_i \qquad (18)$$

where o is computed by (7) and o_i is the ith-to-last dimension of vector o. Table 2 shows results using this reader, showing performance comparable to the Stanford Reader with anonymization.

General Pointer Reader: In the CNN dataset there are roughly 550 entity identifiers and a one-hot representation may not be desirable because it would enlarge the embedding space too much. Instead we can let $e'(i)$ be a fixed set of "pointer vectors"—vectors distributed widely on the unit sphere so that for $i \neq j$ we have that $e'(i)^\top e'(j)$ is small. We again use (17) but replace (18) with

$$p(i|d, q) = \operatorname*{softmax}_{i} [0, e'(i)]^\top o \qquad (19)$$

where "0" stands for a sufficient number of zeroes in order to make the dimensions match. We refer to this as a "general pointer reader". In this reader, the pointer embeddings $e'(i)$ are held fixed and not trained. Even though not shown here, in preliminary experiments, this reader yield similar performance to the one hot pointer reader while permitting smaller embedding dimensionality.

Linguistic Features: Each model can be modified to include additional input features for each input token in the question and passage. More specifically we can add the following features to the word embeddings: whether the current token occurs in the question; the frequency of the current token in the passage; the position of the token's first occurrence in the passage as a percentage of the passage length; and whether the text surrounding the token matches the text surrounding the placeholder in the question. More details of the experimental setup are provided in the appendix.

Table 2 shows results when adding these features to the Gated-Attention Reader, Stanford Reader, and One-Hot Pointer Reader, showing large improvements to all readers and leading to the best single-model performance reported to-date on the Who-did-What dataset.

6 Discussion

Explicit reference architectures rely on reference resolution—a specification of which phrases in the given passage refer to candidate answers. Our experiments indicate that all existing readers benefit greatly from this externally provided information. Aggregation readers seem to demonstrate a stronger learning ability in that they essentially learn to mimic explicit reference readers by identifying reference annotation and using it appropriately. This is done most clearly in the pointer reader architectures. Furthermore, we have argued for, and given experimental evidence for, an interpretation of aggregation readers as learning emergent predication structure—a factoring of neural representations into a direct sum of a statement (predicate) representation and an entity (argument) representation.

At a very high level our analysis and experiments support a central role for reference resolution in reading comprehension. Automating reference resolution in neural models, and demonstrating its value on appropriate datasets, would seem to be an important area for future research.

There is great interest in learning representations for natural language understanding. The current state of the art in reading comprehension is such that systems still benefit from externally provided linguistic features including externally annotated reference resolution. It would be interesting to develop fully automated neural readers that perform as well as readers using externally provided annotations.

Acknowledgments

We thank NVIDIA Corporation for donating GPUs used in this research.

References

Frederic Bastien, Pascal Lamblin, Razvan Pascanu, James Bergstra, Ian J. Goodfellow, Arnaud Bergeron, Nicolas Bouchard, and Yoshua Bengio. 2012. Theano: new features and speed improvements. In *NIPS Workshop on Deep Learning and Unsupervised Feature Learning*.

Danqi Chen, Jason Bolton, and Christopher D. Manning. 2016. A thorough examination of the CNN/Daily Mail reading comprehension task. In *Proceedings of the 54th Annual Meeting of the Association for Computational Linguistics (Volume 1: Long Papers)*.

Zewei Chu, Hai Wang, Kevin Gimpel, and David McAllester. 2017. Broad context language modeling as reading comprehension. In *Proceedings of the 15th Conference of the European Chapter of the ACL (EACL)*.

Yiming Cui, Zhipeng Chen, Si Wei, Shijin Wang, Ting Liu, and Guoping Hu. 2017. Attention-over-attention neural networks for reading comprehension. In *Proceedings of the 55th Annual Meeting of the Association for Computational Linguistics (Volume 1: Long Papers)*.

Graff David and Christopher Cieri. 2003. English Gigaword LDC2003T05. Linguistic Data Consortium.

Bhuwan Dhingra, Hanxiao Liu, Zhilin Yang, William W. Cohen, and Ruslan Salakhutdinov. 2017. Gated-attention readers for text comprehension. In *Proceedings of the 55th Annual Meeting of the Association for Computational Linguistics (Volume 1: Long Papers)*.

Karl Moritz Hermann, Tomas Kocisky, Edward Grefenstette, Lasse Espeholt, Will Kay, Mustafa Suleyman, and Phil Blunsom. 2015. Teaching machines to read and comprehend. In *Advances in Neural Information Processing Systems*.

Felix Hill, Antoine Bordes, Sumit Chopra, and Jason Weston. 2016. The Goldilocks principle: Reading children's books with explicit memory representations. In *Proceedings of the 4th International Conference on Learning Representations*.

Pennington Jeffrey, Richard Socher, and Christopher D. Manning. 2014. GloVe: Global vectors for word representation. In *Proceedings of the Conference on Empirical Methods on Natural Language Processing (EMNLP)*.

Rudolf Kadlec, Martin Schmid, Ondřej Bajgar, and Jan Kleindienst. 2016. Text understanding with the attention sum reader network. In *Proceedings of the 54th Annual Meeting of the Association for Computational Linguistics (Volume 1: Long Papers)*.

Diederik P. Kingma and Jimmy Ba. 2015. Adam: A method for stochastic optimization. In *Proceedings of the 3rd International Conference on Learning Representations*.

Who did What	Validation	Test
Attention Sum Reader (Onishi et al., 2016)	59.8	58.8
Gated Attention Reader (Onishi et al., 2016)	60.3	59.6
NSE (Munkhdalai and Yu, 2016)	66.5	66.2
Gated Attention + Linguistic Features[+]	72.2	**72.8**
Stanford Reader	46.1	45.8
Attentive Reader with Anonymization	55.7	55.5
Stanford Reader with Anonymization	64.8	64.5
One-Hot Pointer Reader	65.1	64.4
One-Hot Pointer Reader + Linguistic Features[+]	69.3	68.7
Stanford with Anonymization + Linguistic Features[+]	69.7	**69.2**
Human Performance	-	84

Table 2: Accuracy on Who-did-What dataset. Each result is based on a single model. Results for neural readers other than NSE are based on replications of those systems. All models were trained on the relaxed training set which uniformly yields better performance than the restricted training set. The first group of models are explicit reference models and the second group are aggregation models. + indicates anonymization with better reference identifier.

Moontae Lee, Xiaodong He, Scott Wen tau Yih, Jianfeng Gao, Li Deng, and Paul Smolensky. 2016. Reasoning in vector space: An exploratory study of question answering. In *Proceedings of the 4th International Conference on Learning Representations*.

Tsendsuren Munkhdalai and Hong Yu. 2016. Reasoning with memory augmented neural networks for language comprehension. *arXiv* .

Takeshi Onishi, Hai Wang, Mohit Bansal, Kevin Gimpel, and David McAllester. 2016. Who did What: A large-scale person-centered cloze dataset. In *Proceedings of the 2016 Conference on Empirical Methods in Natural Language Processing*.

Denis Paperno, Germán Kruszewski, Angeliki Lazaridou, Ngoc Quan Pham, Raffaella Bernardi, Sandro Pezzelle, Marco Baroni, Gemma Boleda, and Raquel Fernandez. 2016. The LAMBADA dataset: Word prediction requiring a broad discourse context. In *Proceedings of the 54th Annual Meeting of the Association for Computational Linguistics (Volume 1: Long Papers)*.

Pranav Rajpurkar, Jian Zhang, Konstantin Lopyrev, and Percy Liang. 2016. SQuAD: 100,000+ questions for machine comprehension of text. In *Proceedings of the 2016 Conference on Empirical Methods in Natural Language Processing*.

Pascanu Razvan, Tomas Mikolov, and Yoshua Bengio. 2013. On the difficulty of training recurrent neural networks. In *Proceedings of International Conference on Machine Learning (ICML)*.

Matthew Richardson, Christopher JC Burges, and Erin Renshaw. 2013. MCTest: A challenge dataset for the open-domain machine comprehension of text. In *Proceedings of the Conference on Empirical Methods on Natural Language Processing (EMNLP)*.

Andrew M. Saxe, James L. McClelland, and Surya Ganguli. 2013. Exact solutions to the nonlinear dynamics of learning in deep linear neural networks. *arXiv* .

Sainbayar Sukhbaatar, Arthur Szlam, Jason Weston, and Rob Fergus. 2015. End-to-end memory networks. In *Advances in Neural Information Processing Systems*.

Bart van Merrienboer, Dzmitry Bahdanau, Vincent Dumoulin, Dmitriy Serdyuk, David Warde-farley, Jan Chorowski, and Yoshua Bengio. 2015. Blocks and fuel: Frameworks for deep learning. *arXiv* .

Jason Weston, Antoine Bordes, Sumit Chopra, Alexander M. Rush, Bart van Merrienboer, Armand Joulin, and Tomas Mikolov. 2016. Towards AI complete question answering: A set of prerequisite toy tasks. In *Proceedings of the 4th International Conference on Learning Representations*.

Jason Weston, Sumit Chopra, and Antoine Bordes. 2015. Memory networks. In *Proceedings of the 3rd International Conference on Learning Representations*.

A Supplemental Material

A.1 Experiment Details

We implemented the neural readers using Theano (Bastien et al., 2012) and Blocks (van Merrienboer et al., 2015) and train them on a single NVIDIA Tesla K40 GPU. Negative log-likelihood is employed as training criterion. We used stochastic gradient descent (SGD) with the Adam update rule (Kingma and Ba, 2015) and set the learning rate to 0.0005.

For the Stanford Reader and One-Hot Pointer Reader, we use the Stanford Reader's default settings. For the Gated-Attention reader, the lookup table was initialized using pre-trained GloVe (Jeffrey et al., 2014) vectors.[1] Input to hidden state weights were initialized by random orthogonal matrices (Saxe et al., 2013) and biases were initialized to zero. Hidden to hidden state weights were initialized by identity matrices to force the model to remember longer information. To compute the attention weight, we use $\alpha_t = h_t^\top W_\alpha h_q$ and initialize W_α with random uniform distribution. We also use gradient clipping (Razvan et al., 2013) with a threshold of 10 and mini-batches of size 32.

During training we randomly shuffle all examples within each epoch. To speed up training, we always pre-fetch 10 batches worth of examples and sort them according to document length as done by Kadlec et al. (2016). When using anonymization, we randomly reshuffle the entity identifier to match the procedure proposed by Hermann et al. (2015).

During training we evaluate the accuracy after each epoch and stop training when the accuracy on the validation set starts decreasing. We tried limiting the vocabulary to the most frequent tokens but did not observe any performance improvement compared with using all distinct tokens as the vocabulary. Since part of our experiments need to check word embedding assignment issues, we finally use all the distinct tokens as vocabulary. To find the optimal embedding and hidden state dimension, we tried several groups of different combinations, and the optimal values were 200 and 384, respectively.

When anonymizing the Who-did-What dataset, we can either use simple string matching to replace answers in the question and passage with entity identifiers, or we can use the Stanford named entity recognizer (NER)[2] to detect named entities and replace the answer named entities in the question and passage with entity identifiers. We found the latter to bring 2% improvement compared with simple string matching.

A.2 Heat Maps for Stanford Reader for Different Answer Candidates

We randomly choose one article from the CNN dataset and show $\mathrm{softmax}(e_o(a)^\top h_t)$ for $t \in [0, |p|]$ for each answer candidate a in Figures 2-6. Red color indicates larger probability and orange indicates smaller probability and the remaining indicates very low probability that can be ignored. From these figures, we can see that our assumption that $e_o(a)$ is used to pick up its occurrence is reasonable.

@entity0 (@entity1) six survivors of the @entity0 kosher supermarket siege in january are suing a @entity5 media outlet for what they call dangerous live broadcasting during the hostage - taking . according to @entity0 prosecutor 's spokeswoman @entity10 , the lawsuit was filed march 27 and a preliminary investigation was opened by the prosecutor 's office wednesday . the media outlet , @entity1 affiliate @entity16 , is accused of endangering the lives of the hostages , who were hiding in a cold room during the attack , by broadcasting their location live during the siege . @entity23 in a statement friday said one of its journalists " mentioned only once the presence of a woman hidden inside the @entity27 , on the basis of police sources on the ground . " " immediately , the chief editor felt that this information should not be released . it therefore has subsequently never been repeated on air or posted on - screen . @entity16 regrets that the mention of this information could cause concern to the hostages , as well as their relatives , that their lives were in danger , " the statement said . gunman @entity47 , also suspected in the slaying of a police officer , stormed the @entity27 @entity51 supermarket on january 9 , killing four people and taking others hostage . he was killed in the police operation to end the siege . a 24 - year - old supermarket employee , @entity57 - born @entity56 , was hailed as a hero afterward when it emerged that he had risked his life to hide 15 customers from @entity47 in the cold room . the hostage - taking was the culmination of three days of terror in @entity0 that began with the january 7 shooting of 12 people at the offices of @entity5 satirical magazine @entity69 . the two brothers blamed for that attack , @entity72 and @entity73 , were killed on january 9 after a violent standoff at an industrial site . the terror attacks claimed the lives of 17 people and put @entity5 on a heightened state of alert . @entity1 's @entity80 reported from @entity0 , and @entity81 wrote from @entity82 . @entity1 's @entity83 contributed to this report .
query: they hid in a cold room during the attack in @entity0 by gunman @placeholder

Figure 2: Heat map when $a = $ entity0.

@entity0 (@entity1) six survivors of the @entity0 kosher supermarket siege in january are suing a @entity5 media outlet for what they call dangerous live broadcasting during the hostage - taking . according to @entity0 prosecutor 's spokeswoman @entity10 , the lawsuit was filed march 27 and a preliminary investigation was opened by the prosecutor 's office wednesday . the media outlet , @entity1 affiliate @entity16 , is accused of endangering the lives of the hostages , who were hiding in a cold room during the attack , by broadcasting their location live during the siege . @entity23 in a statement friday said one of its journalists " mentioned only once the presence of a woman hidden inside the @entity27 , on the basis of police sources on the ground . " " immediately , the chief editor felt that this information should not be released . it therefore has subsequently never been repeated on air or posted on - screen . @entity16 regrets that the mention of this information could cause concern to the hostages , as well as their relatives , that their lives were in danger , " the statement said . gunman @entity47 , also suspected in the slaying of a police officer , stormed the @entity27 @entity51 supermarket on january 9 , killing four people and taking others hostage . he was killed in the police operation to end the siege . a 24 - year - old supermarket employee , @entity57 - born @entity56 , was hailed as a hero afterward when it emerged that he had risked his life to hide 15 customers from @entity47 in the cold room . the hostage - taking was the culmination of three days of terror in @entity0 that began with the january 7 shooting of 12 people at the offices of @entity5 satirical magazine @entity69 . the two brothers blamed for that attack , @entity72 and @entity73 , were killed on january 9 after a violent standoff at an industrial site . the terror attacks claimed the lives of 17 people and put @entity5 on a heightened state of alert . @entity1 's @entity80 reported from @entity0 , and @entity81 wrote from @entity82 . @entity1 's @entity83 contributed to this report .
query: they hid in a cold room during the attack in @entity0 by gunman @placeholder

Figure 3: Heat map when $a = $ entity1.

A.3 Heat Maps for Other Readers

We randomly choose one article from the CNN dataset and show the attention map $\alpha_t = $

[1] http://nlp.stanford.edu/data/glove. 6B.zip

[2] http://nlp.stanford.edu/software/ CRF-NER.shtml

Figure 4: Heat map when $a = $ entity16.

Figure 5: Heat map when $a = $ entity27.

Figure 6: Heat map when $a = $ entity47.

softmax($h_q^\top W_a h_t$) for different readers (in Attention Sum and Gated Attention Reader, W_α is identity matrix). In Figures 7-9, we can see that all readers put essentially all weight on the entity identifiers.

Figure 7: Heat map α_t for Stanford Reader.

Figure 8: Heat map α_t for Gated Attention Reader.

Figure 9: Heat map α_t for Attention Sum Reader.

Towards Harnessing Memory Networks for Coreference Resolution

Joe Cheri Ross and **Pushpak Bhattacharyya**
Department of Computer Science & Engineering,
Indian Institute of Technology Bombay, India
`{joe,pb}@cse.iitb.ac.in`

Abstract

Coreference resolution task demands comprehending a discourse, especially for anaphoric mentions which require semantic information for resolving antecedents. We investigate into how *memory networks* can be helpful for coreference resolution when posed as question answering problem. The comprehension capability of memory networks assists coreference resolution, particularly for the mentions those require semantic and context information. We experiment memory networks for coreference resolution, with 4 synthetic datasets generated for coreference resolution with varying difficulty levels. Our system's performance is compared with a traditional coreference resolution system to show why memory networks can be promising for coreference resolution.

1 Introduction

Coreference resolution resolves anaphoric mentions against the co-referring entities by integrating syntactic, semantic and pragmatic knowledge (Carbonell and Brown, 1988). Even when syntactic knowledge has a crucial role in resolving many coreferential mentions, semantic knowledge is a much more challenging aspect of coreference (Durrett and Klein, 2013). This makes the attempts to bring significant improvement to the state-of-the-art results difficult.

There has been quite a few research in coreference resolution to bring in semantic knowledge through identification of semantic class of the entities (Ng, 2007a,b) and incorporating world knowledge with the help of sources like Wikipedia (Ponzetto and Strube, 2006; Rahman and Ng, 2011). The semantic analysis approach for coreference resolution discussed by Hobbs (1978) takes semantics into consideration. Vincent Ng

(2007b) discusses a pattern-based feature to identify corefering expressions through extracted patterns. Kehler *et. al.* (2004) make use of predicate-argument statistics based on co-occurrence to resolve coreference. Despite these significant contributions, the achieved results show the incapability to emulate the human process of coreference resolution. The potential of memory networks (Weston et al., 2014) towards comprehending the context of a discourse motivates this initiative.

A few psycholinguistic studies on memory based processing of anaphora, investigate the processing of antecedent information from a memory representation of the discourse (Dell et al., 1983; Gernsbacher, 1989; Gerrig and McKoon, 1998; Sanford and Garrod, 1989, 2005). Experiments by Nieuwland and Martin (2016) verify the interaction between the recognition memory network and the canonical frontal-temporal language network in the human process of coreference resolution. These insights confirm the applicability of memory networks for the task.

Memory networks integrate a memory component and inference capability which are jointly used to comprehend a discourse and perform reasoning based on that (Weston et al., 2014; Sukhbaatar et al., 2015; Kumar et al., 2015). Variants of memory networks, specially designed for question answering tasks, read from the external memory multiple times before delivering the answer. Internally, they compute a representation for the input story and the question. The question representation initiates a search through the memory representation of the input and extracts relevant facts. In the subsequent step, the answer module generates the answer based on the information got from the memory module (Sukhbaatar et al., 2015; Kumar et al., 2015). We utilize memory networks for coreference resolution, modeling it as a question answering task. The context of the mentions and its relative salience in a discourse are beneficial to resolve coreference. In practice, there are 2 ways in which coreference resolution can be as-

Proceedings of the 2nd Workshop on Representation Learning for NLP, pages 37–42,
Vancouver, Canada, August 3, 2017. ©2017 Association for Computational Linguistics

sisted by memory networks, *viz.* (i) for end-to-end coreference resolution, identifying the antecedents for the anaphoric mentions (ii) for identifying the relevant sentences for resolving anaphoric mentions using attention mechanism.

End-to-end memory networks proposed by Sukhbaatar *et al.*(2015) for question answering is taken for our experiments. They performed question answering experiments with Facebook's synthetic dataset bAbI (Weston et al., 2015). For our experiments we create another set of synthetic data with varying difficulty levels, targeting coreference resolution. Here, each instance is a discourse and the question is on an anaphoric mention in the discourse, with answer as its antecedent. Experiment results with memory networks on bAbI dataset is reported in terms of the accuracy of the answers whereas, our experiments also evaluate attention mechanism accuracy. We compare the prediction accuracy of memory networks with an existing state-of-the-art coreference resolution system on the same synthetic dataset. We also report results on a few modifications on memory networks.

2   Memory Networks

The end-to-end memory networks described in Sukhbaatar *et al.*(2015) takes input as sentences in a story $(x_1, x_2, ...x_n)$, query (q) and outputs the answer (a). The sentences in the input story $(\{x_i\})$ forms the memory vectors $(\{m_i\})$, getting the word embeddings of the words within. The initial internal state u is formed from the word embeddings of the input query. The input story and the query are embedded in a continous space through different embedding matrices (A and B), each of size $d \times V$, where V is the size of vocabulary and d is the embedding dimension.

Figure 1 shows the memory networks architecture with an example. The memory module has an attention mechanism responsible for identifying attention weights for each memory vector. Softmax over the dot product between the query representation (u_1) and each memory vector gives the probability (attention weights) associated with each memory vector w.r.t to its relevance to the given query. Attention weights are utilized to compute the weighted sum (o_1) of the memory vectors. The input query representation (u_1) is added to o_1 to obtain u_2. The above steps in the memory module are iterated depending on

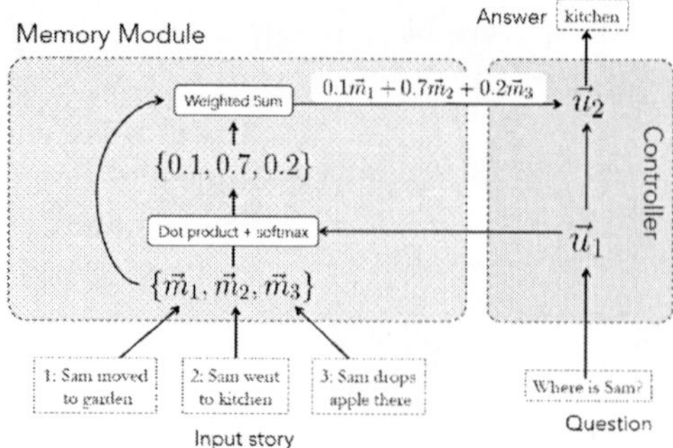

Figure 1: End-to-end memory networks (Weston, 2016)

the number of *hops*. In each subsequent iteration, u_{k+1} is computed taking u_k from the previous iteration as the input representation.

$$u_{k+1} = u_k.H + o_k \tag{1}$$

A linear mapping H updates u between the hops. The answer module computes $Softmax(W(o_k + u_k)$, predicting the output answer after defined number of hops.

3   Coreference Resolution as Question Answering

For our experiments with memory networks, coreference resolution is posed as a question answering problem, where the input story is the discourse containing entities and an anaphoric mention. The question is on an anaphoric mention and the answer is the antecedent entity. The following is one of the simple cases from the synthetic data.

```
Sandra went to the garden.
Mary moved to the hallway.
She is in the garden.
Who is She?        Ans:  Sandra
```

3.1   Modifications to the Network

Restricting Vocabulary: The above described memory networks architecture is designed for question answering tasks which include tasks having answers with words outside of the input story. On the other hand, the answers in our task for coreference resolution are restricted to words within the discourse. We have introduced a modification to the answer module to switch off words outside the discourse. Our proposed modification takes a one-hot representation of the words present in a discourse. A masking layer is introduced at the output layer of the answer module. The mask vector (X_{mask}) with dimension V, has bits set for the words present in the discourse. The added layer performs element-wise multiplication between X_{mask} and the preceding output as shown in Equation 2 before the softmax is applied.

$$Softmax((o_k + u_k).X_{mask}) \qquad (2)$$

Initialization of H: In the available implementation, the hidden layer matrix H in equation 1 is initialized with random values sampled from a normal distribution. To give uniform importance to the components in question representation initially, this modification uniformly initialize H with ones.

tanh **activation:** As mentioned in Section 2, the probability associated with a memory vector is computed by softmax over the dot product between query representation and each memory vector. This modification applies *tanh* activation before the softmax is computed. The clipping of higher values by the *tanh* activation helps to avoid getting skewed attention weights.

While the first modification is specific to coreference resolution, the latter 2 are task independent.

4 Experiments

Our experiments are designed to see how memory networks can help the task of coreference resolution. All the experiments are carried out with the synthetic data.

4.1 Synthetic Dataset

Most existing memory networks based question answering research depend on synthetic dataset inorder to reduce the adverse effect of noise in real-world data (Weston et al., 2015) . On similar lines, we generate 4 sets of data with different difficulty levels, keeping the vocabulary size minimal and maintaining an uniform syntactic structure. It is difficult to make valid observations with a dataset like Ontonotes (Pradhan et al., 2007) considering the diversity in sentence structure and the vocabulary size. Since the task is posed as a question answering problem each data instance has one pronominal reference to the one of the entities in the discourse. The ques tion here is on

the anaphoric mention and the answer is the antecedent mention. The 4 datasets are generated from 4 different templates randomizing the names and verbs. This synthetic data is constructed in a way such that, resolution of anaphoric mentions requires semantic knowledge to be available from the context. Each generated discourse has different names, actions and locations randomly picked from a pre-defined set of names, actions and locations. From the generated instances, 20% are taken for testing resulting in 11520 training instances and 2880 test instances in each dataset [1].

4.2 Experiment Setup

All the results are reported on the test data from 4 synthetic datasets. One of the state-of-the-art coreference resolution systems, Cort (Martschat et al., 2015) is chosen to compare with end-to-end memory networks (MemN2N). All the results reported with MemN2N are averaged across 10 different executions with different seeds used for training data shuffling. This is done to make the results independent of data-shuffling during training. The hyper-parameters are fixed as *embedding size=20, hops=3* under the training configuration as *optimizer=Adam, #epochs=100, batch size=32, learning rate=0.01*. To make the results of Cort comparable with the answer prediction accuracy of memory networks, accuracy of Cort is computed based on the number of correctly identified coreferent mentions, instead of CoNLL score (Pradhan et al., 2012). This evaluation is valid since there is only one coreferent chain comprising 2 mentions in each synthetic dataset instance. We experiment Cort with the available pre-trained coreference model and with the model trained on training data from the corresponding synthetic dataset.

We also check for the effectiveness of attention mechanism in memory networks to aid coreference resolution, through attention mechanism accuracy. Attention mechanism accuracy indicates, given an anaphoric mention, how capable the memory networks approach approach is in identifying the probable sentences to find the antecedent. The synthetic dataset has information about sentences those are relevant to the answer for each discourse instance. Attention weights obtained from memory networks are analyzed to get

---

[1]Dataset is available for download at `http://www.cfilt.iitb.ac.in/~coreference/memnet`

the sentences from the input discourse with higher attention, which in turn is used to compute attention accuracy.

5   Results

Table 2 compares the antecedent prediction accuracy between Cort and MemN2N. The results shows the superiority of memory networks over Cort (on both pre-trained and synthetic data trained models) in considering the context while resolving coreference. The existing feature based approaches have an inclination towards syntactical clues. Table 1 discusses prediction accuracy and attention accuracy with MemN2N and the modifications described in Section 3.1. We observe that most of the mis-predictions stem from attention errors, *i.e.* a wrong answer usually comes from a wrongly high-weighted sentence. This shows the strong dependence of the answer module on the attention mechanism.

Masking of the absent words in the discourse (MASK) has helped to improve the prediction accuracy of datasets 3 and 4. *Masking helps to filter out the irrelevant words reducing the false predictions.* This improvement is very intuitive since restriction of prediction to document words is relevant to the task of coreference resolution.

The initialization of H with ones helps to reach an accuracy of 100% for datasets 1 and 2 and brings significant improvement to attention accuracy. While there is no noticeable accuracy improvement for dataset 3 and there is a reduction in accuracy for dataset 4, the improvement in attention accuracy is quite significant.

$tanh$ activation helps the system to improve the prediction accuracy significantly on datasets 3 and 4, but not for datasets 1 and 2 which have already achieved highest prediction accuracy. For datasets 1 and 2 the attention accuracy has improved compared to MEMN2N and MASK, but not compared to H-INIT. There is a considerable improvement in prediction accuracy and attention accuracy with datasets 3 and 4. $tanh$ activation enables clipping of values before softmax is applied, thereby preventing attention weights from getting skewed towards 0 or 1. We observed with many test instances that, when $tanh$ is not applied the memory vector with the largest attention weight in the first hop tends to remain the largest in the subsequent hops as well. $tanh$ activation resolves this by reducing the skewness. *Errors pertaining to*

location related pronouns with datasets 3 and 4 in the other experiments are getting reduced considerably here, resulting in improvement in accuracy.

5.1   Analysis of Cort Results

Here we explain why an existing coreference resolution approach fails to consider context based clues through analysis of distance (in terms of sentence) between the anaphoric mention and the identified antecedent in the synthetic test data. Figure 2 shows the distance distribution of coreferent mentions in the gold annotation for all the datasets. Sentence distances in the range 1-4 are denoted using different colors. The random sentences in DS2 and DS4 make the distance distribution broader. Figures 3 and 4 show the distance distribution of Cort output. Cort could not detect the pronominal mention 'there' making the number of coreferent distances in DS3 and DS4 less than the number of test data instances shown in the ground truth figure.

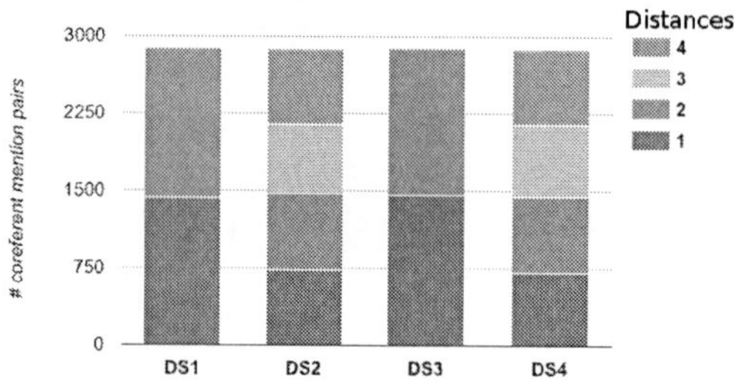

Figure 2: Distribution of distance between coreferent mentions identified by Cort (pre-trained model)

In a coreference resolution approach like Cort, syntactic features play a major role. Figure 3 shows distance distribution of coreferent mentions identified by Cort with pre-trained model trained on Ontonotes dataset. The preceding entity which forms subject in a sentence is likely to be the antecedent of an anaphoric mention in a dataset like ontonotes. When executed with pre-trained model, this leads to picking the recent subject mention as the antecedent making the distribution biased to 1. These features are designed considering the general behaviour of datasets like ontonotes, but does not work for cases where semantic/context knowledge is important.

When trained with synthetic training set, the

Experiment	Dataset 1		Dataset 2		Dataset 3		Dataset 4	
	pred. acc.	att. acc.	pred. acc.	att. acc.	pred. acc.	att. acc.	pred. acc.	att. acc.
MemN2N	99.05	85.06	99.23	78.56	89.99	76.53	88.51	73.37
MASK	99.06	85.06	99.23	78.56	92.28	76.53	89.02	73.37
H-INIT	**100**	**99.83**	**100**	**99.53**	92.94	87.87	86.98	75.61
TANH	99.99	87.05	98.34	93.02	**99.75**	**92.4**	**99.55**	**89.32**

Table 1: Antecedent prediction accuracy (pred. acc.) and attention accuracy (att. acc.) with MemN2N and its modifications. (Accuracy in %. Best results shown in bold.)

Experiment	DS 1	DS 2	DS 3	DS 4
Cort-pre	63.02	35.17	32.5	17.40
Cort-synth	80.42	79.90	40.66	41.04
MemN2N	99.05	99.23	89.99	88.51

Table 2: Comparison of antecedent prediction accuracy (%) of MemN2N with Cort. (DS: Dataset Cort-pre: results with Cort on available pre-trained model Cort-synth: results with Cort on model trained with synthetic training data)

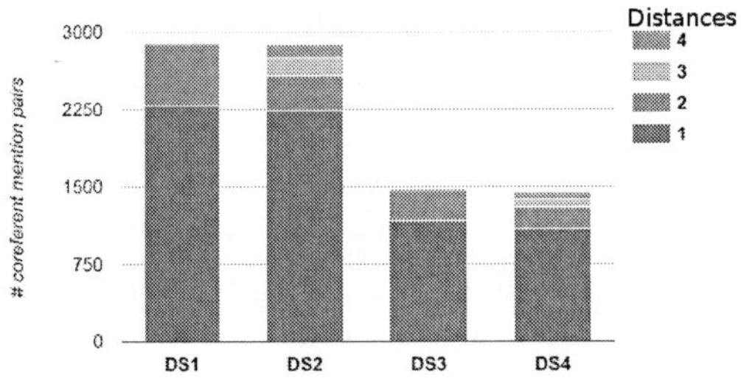

Figure 3: Distribution of distance between coreferent mentions identified by Cort (pre-trained model)

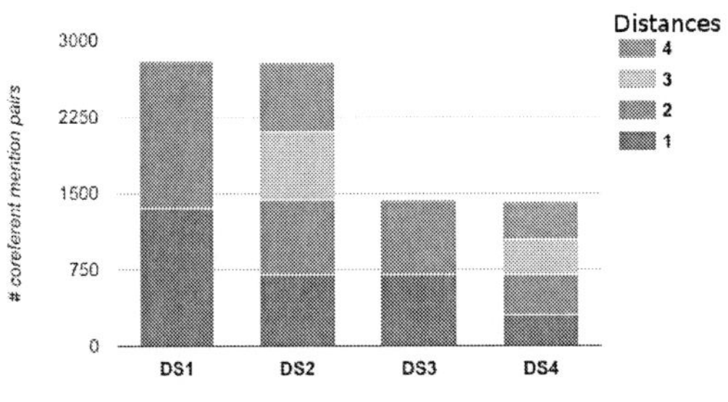

Figure 4: Distribution of distance between coreferent mentions identified by Cort (synthetic-trained model)

antecedents are not always the subject mentions in the preceding sentence based on the evidence learned from the training data. This makes the distribution of distances spread to higher distances. Even though the accuracy has improved over the experiment with pre-trained model, it is behind memory networks. From our observations, we could infer that certain other features (most likely *next_token* and *preceding_token* features) in Cort take the lead role here. This makes the system to take coreference decision based on some not so relevant patterns (based on afore-mentioned features) seen in the training data, leading to inferior performance compared to memory networks.

These observations conclude that even when syntactical clues can help coreference resolution to much extent, that is not sufficient to deal with all the cases where semantic understanding is required.

6 Conclusion

In this paper, we investigated into the suitability of posing coreference resolution as a question answering problem based on memory networks, taking motivation from psycholinguistics studies establishing the role of working memory during resolving coreferences. The experimental results comparing Cort with memory networks demonstrate the potential of memory networks. We also found that the task-driven modifications when applied, help to achieve better prediction and attention accuracy. While this work is a step towards identifying the potential of memory networks for coreference resolution, experiments are restricted to synthetic data. In the future, we propose to investigate on an architecture on real-world data, either through attention mechanism to assist existing approaches or through an end-to-end framework for coreference resolution.

References

Jaime G Carbonell and Ralf D Brown. 1988. Anaphora resolution: a multi-strategy approach. In *Proceedings of the 12th conference on Computational linguistics-Volume 1*. Association for Computational Linguistics, pages 96–101.

Gary S Dell, Gail McKoon, and Roger Ratcliff. 1983. The activation of antecedent information during the processing of anaphoric reference in reading. *Journal of Verbal Learning and Verbal Behavior* 22(1):121–132.

Greg Durrett and Dan Klein. 2013. Easy victories and uphill battles in coreference resolution. In *EMNLP*. pages 1971–1982.

Morton Ann Gernsbacher. 1989. Mechanisms that improve referential access. *Cognition* 32(2):99–156.

Richard J Gerrig and Gail McKoon. 1998. The readiness is all: The functionality of memory-based text processing. *Discourse Processes* 26(2-3):67–86.

Jerry R Hobbs. 1978. Resolving pronoun references. *Lingua* 44(4):311–338.

Andrew Kehler, Douglas E Appelt, Lara Taylor, and Aleksandr Simma. 2004. The (non) utility of predicate-argument frequencies for pronoun interpretation. In *HLT-NAACL*. volume 4, pages 289–296.

Ankit Kumar, Ozan Irsoy, Jonathan Su, James Bradbury, Robert English, Brian Pierce, Peter Ondruska, Ishaan Gulrajani, and Richard Socher. 2015. Ask me anything: Dynamic memory networks for natural language processing. *arXiv preprint arXiv:1506.07285* .

Sebastian Martschat, Patrick Claus, and Michael Strube. 2015. Plug latent structures and play coreference resolution. *ACL-IJCNLP 2015* page 61.

Vincent Ng. 2007a. Semantic class induction and coreference resolution. In *Proc. of the ACL*. pages 536–543.

Vincent Ng. 2007b. Shallow semantics for coreference resolution. In *Proceedings of the 20th International Joint Conference on Artifical Intelligence*. IJCAI'07, pages 1689–1694.

Mante Nieuwland and Andrea E Martin. 2016. A neural oscillatory signature of reference. *bioRxiv* page 072322.

Simone Paolo Ponzetto and Michael Strube. 2006. Exploiting semantic role labeling, wordnet and wikipedia for coreference resolution. In *Proceedings of the main conference on HLT-NAACL*. Association for Computational Linguistics, pages 192–199.

Sameer Pradhan, Alessandro Moschitti, Nianwen Xue, Olga Uryupina, and Yuchen Zhang. 2012. Conll-2012 shared task: Modeling multilingual unrestricted coreference in ontonotes. In *Joint Conference on EMNLP and CoNLL-Shared Task*. Association for Computational Linguistics, pages 1–40.

Sameer S Pradhan, Eduard Hovy, Mitch Marcus, Martha Palmer, Lance Ramshaw, and Ralph Weischedel. 2007. Ontonotes: A unified relational semantic representation. *International Journal of Semantic Computing* 1(04):405–419.

Altaf Rahman and Vincent Ng. 2011. Coreference resolution with world knowledge. In *Proc. of the 49th Annual Meeting of the Association for Computational Linguistics: Human Language Technologies-Volume 1*. Association for Computational Linguistics, pages 814–824.

AJ Sanford and SC Garrod. 1989. What, when, and how?: Questions of immediacy in anaphoric reference resolution. *Language and Cognitive Processes* 4(3-4):SI235–SI262.

Anthony J Sanford and Simon C Garrod. 2005. Memory-based approaches and beyond. *Discourse Processes* 39(2-3):205–224.

Sainbayar Sukhbaatar, Jason Weston, Rob Fergus, et al. 2015. End-to-end memory networks. In *Advances in neural information processing systems*. pages 2440–2448.

Jason Weston. 2016. *ICML 2016 Tutorial on Memory Networks for Language Understanding*. http://www.thespermwhale.com/jaseweston/icml2016/icml2016-memnn-tutorial.pdf.

Jason Weston, Antoine Bordes, Sumit Chopra, Alexander M Rush, Bart van Merriënboer, Armand Joulin, and Tomas Mikolov. 2015. Towards ai-complete question answering: A set of prerequisite toy tasks. *arXiv preprint arXiv:1502.05698* .

Jason Weston, Sumit Chopra, and Antoine Bordes. 2014. Memory networks. *arXiv preprint arXiv:1410.3916* .

Combining Word-Level and Character-Level Representations for Relation Classification of Informal Text

Dongyun Liang, Weiran Xu, Yinge Zhao,
PRIS, Beijing University of Posts and Telecommunications, China
{dongyunliang, xuweiran}@bupt.edu.cn yingezhao@outlook.com

Abstract

Word representation models have achieved great success in natural language processing tasks, such as relation classification. However, it does not always work on informal text, and the morphemes of some misspelling words may carry important short-distance semantic information. We propose a hybrid model, combining the merits of word-level and character-level representations to learn better representations on informal text. Experiments on two dataset of relation classification, SemEval-2010 Task8 and a large-scale one we compile from informal text, show that our model achieves a competitive result in the former and state-of-the-art with the other.

1 Introduction

Deep learning has made significant progress in natural language processing, and most of approaches treat word representations as the cornerstone. Though it is effective, word-level representation is inherently problematic: it assumes that each word type has its own vector that can vary independently; most words only occur once in training data and out-of-vocabulary(OOV) words cannot be addressed. A word may typically include a root and one or more affixes (*rock-s, red-ness, quick-ly, run-ning, un-expect-ed*), or more than one root in a compound (*black-board, rat-race*). It is reasonable to assume that words which share common components(root, prefix, suffix)may be potentially related, while word-level representation considers each word separately. On the other hand, new words enter English from every area of life, e.g. *Chillaxing* - Blend of *chilling* and *relaxing*, represent taking a break from stressful activities to rest or relax. Whereas the vocabulary size

of word-level model is fixed beforehand, the lack of these word representations may lose important semantic information.

Especially on informal text, the problems of word-level representation will be amplified and hard to ignore. Recently, character-level representation, which takes characters as atomic units to derive the embeddings, demonstrates that it can memorize the arbitrary aspects of word orthography. Parameters of these simple model are less, and it will be not ideal when processing long sentence. Combining word-level and character-level representations attempts to overcome the weaknesses of the two representations.

We utilize a Bidirectional Gated Recurrent Unit (Bi-GRU) (Chung et al., 2014) and Convolutional Neural Networks(CNN) to capture two-level semantic representations respectively. While character-level information is likely to be drowned out by word-level information if simply connected, we adopt Highway Networks (Srivastava et al., 2015) to balance both. To evaluate our model, we evaluate on a public benchmark: SemEval-2010 Task8. This dataset is small and restricted in their relation types and their syntactic and lexical variations, and it is still unknown whether learning on the range of the specific relation transfers well to informal text. As such, we introduce a large-scale dataset based on the corpus and queries of TAC-KBP Slot Filling Track (Surdeanu and Ji, 2014) between 2009 to 2014, which contains 48k relation sentences, called KBP-SF48[1].

TAC-KBP corpus comes from newswire, Web, post and discussion forum documents actually comprised of informal content, including language mismatch and spelling errors. We extract sentences from slots and fillers of Slot Filling Evalua-

---

[1]https://github.com/waterblas/KBP-SF48

43

Proceedings of the 2nd Workshop on Representation Learning for NLP, pages 43–47,
Vancouver, Canada, August 3, 2017. ©2017 Association for Computational Linguistics

tion with position indicators to keep the same format as SemEval-2010 Task8. For instance, the following sentence with two nominals surrounded by position indicators belong to *org:founded_by* relation:

Bharara's office brought insider trading charges against <e1>Raj Rajaratnam <e1/>, the co-founder of hedge fund <e2>Galleon Group<e2/>.

2 Related Work

Some works (Mikolov et al., 2013; Pennington et al., 2014) started to learn semantic representations of word by unsupervised approaches. Recently, relation classification has focused on neural networks. Zeng et al. (2014) utilized CNN to learn patterns of relations from raw text data to make representative progress, but a potential problem is that CNN is not suitable for learning long-distance semantic information. Santos et al. (2015) proposed a similar model named CR-CNN, and replaced the cost function with a ranking-based function. Some models (Xu et al., 2015; Cai et al., 2016) leveraged the shortest dependency path(SDP) between two nominals. Others (Zhou et al., 2016; Wang et al., 2016) employed attention mechanism to capture more important semantic information.

Working to a new dataset KBP37, Zhang and Wang (2015) proposed a framework based on a bidirectional Recurrent Neural Network(RNN). However, all these methods depend on learning word-level distributed representation without utilizing morphological feature.

Recent work captures word orthography using character-based neural networks. dos Santos and Zadrozny (2014) proposed a deep neural network to learn character-level representation of words for POS Tagging. Zhang et al. (2015) demonstrated the effectiveness of character-level CNN in text classification. Kim et al. (2015) employed CNN and a highway network to learn rich semantic and orthographic features from encoding characters. There were some models (Ling et al., 2015; Dhingra et al., 2016) based on RNN structures, which can memorize arbitrary aspects of word orthography over characters.

Our model uses multi-channel GRU units and CNN architecture to learn the representations of word-level and character-level, and project it to a softmax output layer for relation classification.

3 Model

As shown in Figure 1, the model learns word-level and character-level representations respectively, and combines them with interaction to get the final representation.

3.1 Word-level

Given a relation sentence consisting of words $w_1, w_2, ..., w_m$, each w_i is defined as a one hot vector 1_{w_i}, with value 1 at index w_i and 0 in all other dimensionality. We multiply a matrix $P_W \in \mathbb{R}^{d_w \times |V|}$ by 1_{w_i} to project the word w_i into its word embedding x_i, as with a lookup table:

$$x_i = P_W w_i \tag{1}$$

where d_w is the size of word embedding and V is the vocabulary of training set.

Then input the $x_1, x_2, ..., x_m$ sequence to a Bi-GRU network iteratively. Each GRU unit apply the following transformations:

$$
\begin{aligned}
r_t &= \sigma(W_r x_t + U_r h_{t-1} + b_r) \\
z_t &= \sigma(W_z x_t + U_z h_{t-1} + b_z) \\
h_t &= (1 - z_t) \odot h_{t-1} + z_t \odot \widetilde{h}_t \\
\widetilde{h}_t &= \tanh(W_h x_t + U_h(r_t \odot h_{t-1}) + b_h)
\end{aligned}
\tag{2}
$$

where z_t is a set of update gates, r_t is a set of reset gates and $\odot$ is an element-wise multiplication. W_r, W_z, W_h and U_r, U_z, U_h are weight matrices to be learned, and $\widetilde{h}_t$ is the candidate activation. We use element-wise sum to combine the forward and backward pass final states as word-level representation: $h_m^w = [\overrightarrow{h_m} + \overleftarrow{h_0}]$.

3.2 Character-level

To capture morphological features, we use convolutions to learn local n-gram features at the lower network layer. As character-level input, original sentence is decomposed into a sequence of characters, including special characters, such as white-space. We first project each character into a character embedding x_i by a lookup table whose mechanism is exactly as Eq.1.

Given the $x_1, x_2, , x_n$ embedding sequence, we compose the matrix $D^k \in \mathbb{R}^{kd_c \times n}$ to execute convolutions with same padding:

$$C^k = \tanh(W_{con}^k D^k) \tag{3}$$

where d_c is the size of word embedding and each column i in D^k consists of the concatenation of

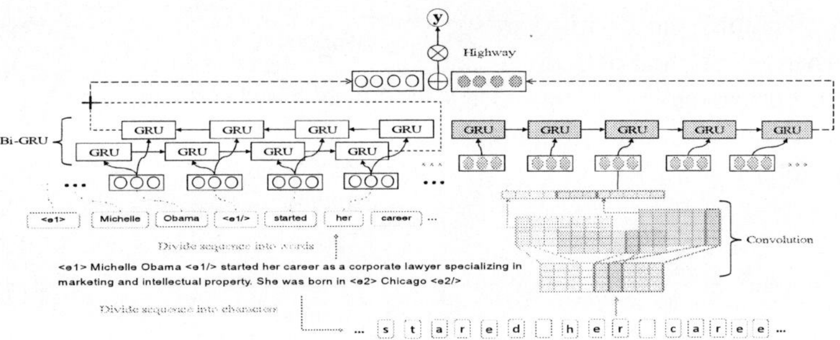

Figure 1: Hybrid model combining word-level and character-level representation.

vectors (i.e. k embeddings centered at the i-th character), W_{con}^{k} is a weight matrix of convolution layer, and $C^{k} \in \mathbb{R}^{c \times n}$ is the output of the convolution with c filters. We use p groups of filters with varying widths to obtain n-gram feature, and concatenate them by column:

$$C = C^{k_1} \oplus C^{k_2} \oplus ... \oplus C^{k_p} \quad (4)$$

The next step, $c_i, ..., c_n$ denoted by the column vector of C are fed as input sequence to a forward-GRU network(Eq.2), and we pick up final states activation h_n^c as character-level representation.

3.3 Combination

Instead of fully connected network layer, we utilize Highway Networks to emphasize impact of character level. Highway can be used to adaptively copy or transform representations, even when large depths are not required. We apply this idea to retain some independence of word and character when merging with interaction. Let h^* be the concatenation of h_m^w and h_n^c, The combination z is obtained by the Highway Network:

$$\begin{aligned} z = t \odot g(W_H h^* + b_H) + (1 - t) \odot h^* \\ t = \sigma(W_T h^* + b_T) \end{aligned} \quad (5)$$

where g is a nonlinear function $(\tanh)$, t is referred to as the transform gate, and $(1 - t)$ as the carry gate. W_T and W_H are square weight matrices, and b_T and b_H are bias vectors.

3.4 Training

Training our model for classifying sentence relation is a processes to optimizing the whole parameters θ of network layers. Given a input sentence X and the candidate set of relation Y, the classifier returns output $\hat{y}$ as follows:

$$\hat{y} = \arg \max_{y \in Y} p(y|X, \theta) \quad (6)$$

We let the combination vector z through a softmax layer to give the distribution $y = softmax(W_f z + b_f)$.

The training objective is the penalized cross-entropy loss between predicted and true relation:

$$J(\theta) = -\frac{1}{N} \sum_{i=1}^{N} \sum_{j=1}^{m} t_{i,j} \log(y_{i,j}) + \lambda \|\theta\|_F^2 \quad (7)$$

where N is the mini-batch size, m is the size of relation set, $t \in \mathbb{R}^m$ denotes the one-hot represented ground truth, $y_{i,j}$ is the predicted probability that the $i-$th sentence belongs to class j, and λ is a coefficient of L2 regularization.

4 Experiments

4.1 Dataset

We evaluate our model on two dataset. SemEval-2010 Task8 dataset contains 9 directional relations and an Other class.

There exist dataset derived from TAC-KBP for relation classification, such as KBP37(20k example for evaluation) collected by (Zhang and Wang, 2015). Based on this and more public corpus of resent years, we introduce a new larger scale dataset, called KBP-SF48. There are 48,340 annotated examples distributed among 40 relations(excluding *no_relation* and *org:website*), including 33,838 sentences for training that consists of 102 unique characters, 9,668 for testing and 4,834 for validation.

Compared to SemEval-2010 Task8, the relation type of KBP-SF48 is designed to build a Knowledge Base from unstructured text, including quite a few informal documents, and the specific nominals that belongs to these relations can be filled in specific slots. There exists non-directional and the directional corresponding relations (e.g. per:children & per:parents and org:members & org:member_of).

4.2 Results

Model	F1
SVM (Rink and Harabagiu, 2010)	82.2
CNN (Zeng et al., 2014)	82.7
SDP-LSTM (Xu et al., 2015)	83.7
Att-BLSTM (Zhou et al., 2016)	84.0
BRCNN (Cai et al., 2016)	86.3
Ours	84.1

Table 1: Comparison on SemEval-2010 Task8.

Table 1 compares our model with other previous state-of-the-art methods on SemEval-2010 Task8 dataset. Rink and Harabagiu (2010) built a SVM classifier on a variety of handcrafted features, and achieved an F1-score of 82.2%. Xu et al. (2015) achieved an F1-score of 83.7% via heterogeneous information along the SDP. BRCNN (Cai et al., 2016) combined CNN and two-channel LSTM units to learns features along SDP, and made use of POS tags, NER and WordNet hypernyms. Att-BLSTM (Zhou et al., 2016) only operated attention mechanism on Bidirectional Long Short-Term Memory(BLSTM) units with word vector.

Our model yields an F1-score of 84.1%, and outperforms most of the existing competing approaches without using any human-designed features and lexical resources.

On KBP-SF48 benchmark, we evaluate our model by top 1 precision, and mean rank of correct relation because of the existence of non-directional relations,

We reproduce the results on our own to show the performances of the other systems with the same train/dev/test splits, and ablate different aspects of the proposed model to show the impact of every component of our architecture. As is seen from Table 2, our model achieves a state-of-the-art result on KBP-SF48 dataset. Our model has already outperformed the RNN-based (Zhang and Wang, 2015) model of the KBP37 dataset,

Model	Precision @1	Mean Rank
RNN-based (Zhang and Wang, 2015)	68.9%	2.01
CNN (Zeng et al., 2014)	79.1%	1.55
BLSTM and Att-BLSTM (Zhou et al., 2016)	78.9% 80.2%	1.59 1.51
Character-level Only (Dhingra et al., 2016)	74.9%	1.85
Word-level Only	78.4%	1.60
Full connected network	80.9%	1.51
Ours	81.7%	1.45

Table 2: Comparison on KBP-SF48

a small scale dataset based on TAC-KBP Slot Filling Track. We compare our results against some state-of-the-art methods (Zeng et al., 2014; Zhou et al., 2016) of SemEval-2010 Task8, and our model achieves a better result by combining character feature into word-level representation. Then, we illustrate Bi-GRU architecture of Tweet2Vec (Dhingra et al., 2016), a pure character-level composition model, to show the effectiveness of character-level representation. Next, we get rid of the impact of characters to do word-level only experiment, and replace the highway with a fully connected layer. These clean comparisons demonstrate that the character-level and Highway network help to learn a better representation for classification.

5 Conclusion

In this paper, we propose a hybrid model that combines word-level and character-level representations. This model encodes characters by a cascade of CNN and GRU units, encodes words by Bi-GRU units, and uses Highway Network to combine. We demonstrate that our model achieves competitive results on the popular benchmark SemEval-2010 Task8 and achieves a better performance at learning character features on the KBP-SF48 dataset without relying on any lexical resources. In future, we plan to add interactions for each word with the corresponding positional characters.

References

Rui Cai, Xiaodong Zhang, and Houfeng Wang. 2016. Bidirectional recurrent convolutional neural network for relation classification. In *Proceedings of the 54th Annual Meeting of the Association for Computational Linguistics*. pages 756–765.

Junyoung Chung, Caglar Gulcehre, KyungHyun Cho, and Yoshua Bengio. 2014. Empirical evaluation of gated recurrent neural networks on sequence modeling. *arXiv preprint arXiv:1412.3555* .

Bhuwan Dhingra, Zhong Zhou, Dylan Fitzpatrick, Michael Muehl, and William W Cohen. 2016. Tweet2vec: Character-based distributed representations for social media. *arXiv preprint arXiv:1605.03481* .

Cícero Nogueira dos Santos and Bianca Zadrozny. 2014. Learning character-level representations for part-of-speech tagging. In *ICML*. pages 1818–1826.

Yoon Kim, Yacine Jernite, David Sontag, and Alexander M Rush. 2015. Character-aware neural language models. *arXiv preprint arXiv:1508.06615* .

Wang Ling, Tiago Luís, Luís Marujo, Ramón Fernandez Astudillo, Silvio Amir, Chris Dyer, Alan W Black, and Isabel Trancoso. 2015. Finding function in form: Compositional character models for open vocabulary word representation. *arXiv preprint arXiv:1508.02096* .

Tomas Mikolov, Kai Chen, Greg Corrado, and Jeffrey Dean. 2013. Efficient estimation of word representations in vector space. *arXiv preprint arXiv:1301.3781* .

Jeffrey Pennington, Richard Socher, and Christopher D Manning. 2014. Glove: Global vectors for word representation. In *EMNLP*. volume 14, pages 1532–43.

Bryan Rink and Sanda Harabagiu. 2010. Utd: Classifying semantic relations by combining lexical and semantic resources. *ACL 2010* page 256.

Cicero Nogueira dos Santos, Bing Xiang, and Bowen Zhou. 2015. Classifying relations by ranking with convolutional neural networks. *arXiv preprint arXiv:1504.06580* .

Rupesh K Srivastava, Klaus Greff, and Jürgen Schmidhuber. 2015. Training very deep networks. In *Advances in neural information processing systems*. pages 2377–2385.

Mihai Surdeanu and Heng Ji. 2014. Overview of the english slot filling track at the tac2014 knowledge base population evaluation. In *Proc. Text Analysis Conference (TAC2014)*.

Linlin Wang, Zhu Cao, Gerard de Melo, and Zhiyuan Liu. 2016. Relation classification via multi-level attention cnns. In *Proceedings of the 54th Annual Meeting of the Association for Computational Linguistics*. pages 1298–1307.

Yan Xu, Lili Mou, Ge Li, Yunchuan Chen, Hao Peng, and Zhi Jin. 2015. Classifying relations via long short term memory networks along shortest dependency paths. In *Proceedings of Conference on Empirical Methods in Natural Language Processing*.

Daojian Zeng, Kang Liu, Siwei Lai, Guangyou Zhou, Jun Zhao, et al. 2014. Relation classification via convolutional deep neural network. In *COLING*. pages 2335–2344.

Dongxu Zhang and Dong Wang. 2015. Relation classification via recurrent neural network. *arXiv preprint arXiv:1508.01006* .

Xiang Zhang, Junbo Zhao, and Yann LeCun. 2015. Character-level convolutional networks for text classification. In *Advances in Neural Information Processing Systems*. pages 649–657.

Peng Zhou, Wei Shi, Jun Tian, Zhenyu Qi, Bingchen Li, Hongwei Hao, and Bo Xu. 2016. Attention-based bidirectional long short-term memory networks for relation classification. In *The 54th Annual Meeting of the Association for Computational Linguistics*. page 207.

Transfer Learning for Neural Semantic Parsing

Xing Fan, Emilio Monti, Lambert Mathias, and Markus Dreyer
Amazon.com
{fanxing, mathias, mddreyer}@amazon.com, monti@amazon.co.uk

Abstract

The goal of semantic parsing is to map natural language to a machine interpretable meaning representation language (MRL). One of the constraints that limits full exploration of deep learning technologies for semantic parsing is the lack of sufficient annotation training data. In this paper, we propose using sequence-to-sequence in a multi-task setup for semantic parsing with a focus on transfer learning. We explore three multi-task architectures for sequence-to-sequence modeling and compare their performance with an independently trained model. Our experiments show that the multi-task setup aids transfer learning from an auxiliary task with large labeled data to a target task with smaller labeled data. We see absolute accuracy gains ranging from 1.0% to 4.4% in our in-house data set, and we also see good gains ranging from 2.5% to 7.0% on the ATIS semantic parsing tasks with syntactic and semantic auxiliary tasks.

1 Introduction

Conversational agents, such as Alexa, Siri and Cortana, solve complex tasks by interacting and mediating between the end-user and multiple backend software applications and services. Natural language is a simple interface used for communication between these agents. However, to make natural language machine-readable we need to map it to a representation that describes the semantics of the task expressed in the language. Semantic parsing is the process of mapping a natural-language sentence into a formal machine-readable representation of its meaning. This poses a challenge in a multi-tenant system that has to interact with multiple backend knowledge sources each with their own semantic formalisms and custom schemas for accessing information, where each formalism has various amount of annotation training data.

Recent works have proven sequence-to-sequence to be an effective model architecture (Jia and Liang, 2016; Dong and Lapata, 2016) for semantic parsing. However, because of the limit amount of annotated data, the advantage of neural networks to capture complex data representation using deep structure (Johnson et al., 2016) has not been fully explored. Acquiring data is expensive and sometimes infeasible for task-oriented systems, the main reasons being multiple formalisms (e.g., SPARQL for WikiData (Vrandečić and Krötzsch, 2014), MQL for Freebase (Flanagan, 2008)), and multiple tasks (question answering, navigation interactions, transactional interactions). We propose to exploit these multiple representations in a multi-task framework so we can minimize the need for a large labeled corpora across these formalisms. By suitably modifying the learning process, we capture the common structures that are implicit across these formalisms and the tasks they are targeted for.

In this work, we focus on a sequence-to-sequence based transfer learning for semantic parsing. In order to tackle the challenge of multiple formalisms, we apply three multi-task frameworks with different levels of parameter sharing. Our hypothesis is that the encoder-decoder paradigm learns a canonicalized representation across all tasks. Over a strong single-task sequence-to-sequence baseline, our proposed approach shows accuracy improvements across the target formalism. In addition, we show that even when the auxiliary task is syntactic parsing we can achieve good gains in semantic parsing that are comparable to the published state-of-the-art.

Proceedings of the 2nd Workshop on Representation Learning for NLP, pages 48–56,
Vancouver, Canada, August 3, 2017. ©2017 Association for Computational Linguistics

2 Related Work

There is a large body of work for semantic parsing. These approaches fall into three broad categories – completely supervised learning based on fully annotated logical forms associated with each sentence (Zelle and Mooney, 1996; Zettlemoyer and Collins, 2012) using question-answer pairs and conversation logs as supervision (Artzi and Zettlemoyer, 2011; Liang et al., 2011; Berant et al., 2013) and distant supervision (Cai and Yates, 2013; Reddy et al., 2014). All these approaches make assumptions about the task, features and the target semantic formalism.

On the other hand, neural network based approaches, in particular the use of recurrent neural networks (RNNs) and encoder-decoder paradigms (Sutskever et al., 2014), have made fast progress on achieving state-of-the art performance on various NLP tasks (Vinyals et al., 2015; Dyer et al., 2015; Bahdanau et al., 2014). A key advantage of RNNs in the encoder-decoder paradigm is that very few assumptions are made about the domain, language and the semantic formalism. This implies they can generalize faster with little feature engineering.

Full semantic graphs can be expensive to annotate, and efforts to date have been fragmented across different formalisms, leading to a limited amount of annotated data in any single formalism. Using neural networks to train semantic parsers on limited data is quite challenging. Multi-task learning aims at improving the generalization performance of a task using related tasks (Caruana, 1998; Ando and Zhang, 2005; Smith and Smith, 2004). This opens the opportunity to utilize large amounts of data for a related task to improve the performance across all tasks. There has been recent work in NLP demonstrating improved performance for machine translation (Dong et al., 2015) and syntactic parsing (Luong et al., 2015).

In this work, we attempt to merge various strands of research using sequence-to-sequence modeling for semantic parsing with focusing on improving semantic formalisms with small amount of training data using a multi-task model architecture. The closest work is Herzig and Berant (2017). Similar to this work, the authors use a neural semantic parsing model in a multi-task framework to jointly learn over multiple knowledge bases. Our work differs from their work in that we focus our attention on transfer learning, where we have access to a large labeled resource in one task and want another semantic formalism with access to limited training data to benefit from a multi-task learning setup. Furthermore, we also demonstrate that we can improve semantic parsing tasks by using large data sources from an auxiliary task such as syntactic parsing, thereby opening up the opportunity for leveraging much larger datasets. Finally, we carefully compare multiple multi-task architectures in our setup and show that increased sharing of both the encoder and decoder along with shared attention results in the best performance.

3 Problem Formulation

3.1 Sequence-to-Sequence Formulation

Our semantic parser extends the basic encoder-decoder approach in Jia and Liang (2016). Given a sequence of inputs $x = x_1, \ldots, x_m$, the sequence-to-sequence model will generate an output sequence of $y = y_1, \ldots, y_n$. We encode the input tokens $x = x_1, \ldots, x_m$ into a sequence of embeddings $h = h_1, \ldots, h_m$

$$h_i = f_{\text{encoder}}(E_x(x_i), h_{i-1}) \qquad (1)$$

First, an input embedding layer E_x maps each word x_i to a fixed-dimensional vector which is then fed as input to the network f to obtain the hidden state representation h_i. The embedding layer E_x could contain one single word embedding lookup table or a combination of word and gazetteer embeddings, where we concatenate the output from each table. For the encoder and decoder, we use a stacked Gated Recurrent Units (GRU) (Cho et al., 2014).[1] The hidden states are then converted to one fixed-length context vector per output index, $c_j = \phi_j(h_1, \ldots, h_m)$, where ϕ_j summarizes all input hidden states to form the context for a given output index j.[2]

The decoder then uses these fixed-length vectors c_j to create the target sequence through the following model. At each time step j in the output sequence, a state s_j is calculated as

$$s_j = f_{\text{decoder}}(E_y(y_{j-1}), s_{j-1}, c_j) \qquad (2)$$

---

[1] In order to speedup training, we use a right-to-left GRU instead of a bidirectional GRU.

[2] In a vanilla decoder, each $\phi_j(h_1, \ldots, h_m) \stackrel{\text{def}}{=} h_m$, i.e, the hidden representation from the last state of the encoder is used as context for every output time step j.

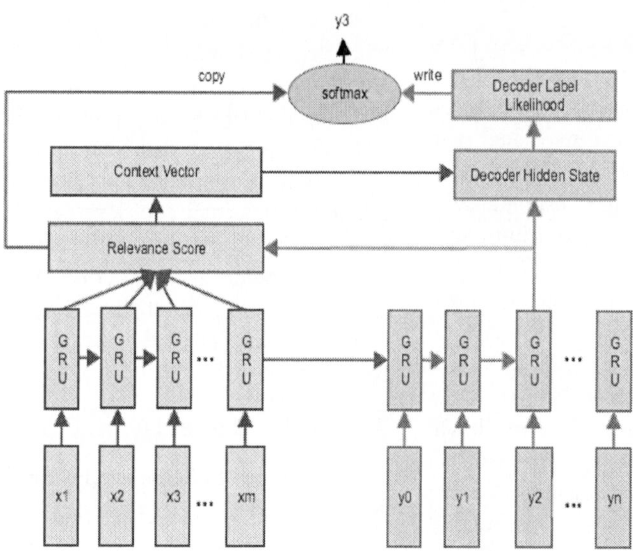

Figure 1: An example of how the decoder output y_3 is generated.

Here, E_y maps any output symbol to a fixed-dimensional vector. Finally, we compute the probability of the output symbol y_j given the history $y_{<j}$ using Equation 3.

$$p(y_j \mid y_{<j}, \boldsymbol{x}) \propto \exp(\boldsymbol{O}[\boldsymbol{s}_j; \boldsymbol{c}_j]) \qquad (3)$$

where the matrix $\boldsymbol{O}$ projects the concatenation of $\boldsymbol{s}_j$ and $\boldsymbol{c}_j$, denoted as $[\boldsymbol{s}_j; \boldsymbol{c}_j]$, to the final output space. The matrix $\boldsymbol{O}$ are part of the trainable model parameters. We use an attention mechanism (Bahdanau et al., 2014) to summarize the context vector $\boldsymbol{c}_j$,

$$c_j = \phi_j(h_1, \ldots, h_m) = \sum_{i=1}^{m} \alpha_{ji}\, h_i \qquad (4)$$

where $j \in [1, \ldots, n]$ is the step index for the decoder output and α_{ji} is the attention weight, calculated using a softmax:

$$\alpha_{ji} = \frac{\exp(e_{ji})}{\sum_{i'=1}^{m} \exp(e_{ji'})} \qquad (5)$$

where e_{ji} is the relevance score of each context vector $\boldsymbol{c}_j$, modeled as:

$$e_{ji} = g(\boldsymbol{h}_i, \boldsymbol{s}_j) \qquad (6)$$

In this paper, the function g is defined as follows:

$$g(\boldsymbol{h}_i, \boldsymbol{s}_j) = \boldsymbol{v}^\mathsf{T} \tanh(\boldsymbol{W}_1 \boldsymbol{h}_i + \boldsymbol{W}_2 \boldsymbol{s}_j) \qquad (7)$$

where $\boldsymbol{v}$, $\boldsymbol{W}_1$ and $\boldsymbol{W}_2$ are trainable parameters.

In order to deal with the large vocabularies in the output layer introduced by the long tail of entities in typical semantic parsing tasks, we use a copy mechanism (Jia and Liang, 2016). At each time step j, the decoder chooses to either copy a token from the encoder's input stream or to write a token from the the decoder's fixed output vocabulary. We define two actions:

1. WRITE[y] for some $y \in \mathcal{V}_{\text{decoder}}$, where $\mathcal{V}_{\text{decoder}}$ is the output vocabulary of the decoder.

2. COPY[i] for some $i \in 1, \ldots, m$, which copies one symbol from the m input tokens.

We formulate a single softmax to select the action to take, rewriting Equation 3 as follows:

$$p(a_j = \text{WRITE}[y_j] \mid y_{<j}, \boldsymbol{x}) \propto \exp(\boldsymbol{O}[\boldsymbol{s}_j; \boldsymbol{c}_j]) \qquad (8)$$

$$p(a_j = \text{COPY}[i] \mid y_{<j}, \boldsymbol{x}) \propto \exp(e_{ji}) \qquad (9)$$

The decoder is now a softmax over the actions a_j; Figure 1 shows how the decoder's output $\boldsymbol{y}$ at the third time step y_3 is generated. At each time step, the decoder will make a decision to copy a particular token from input stream or to write a token from the fixed output label pool.

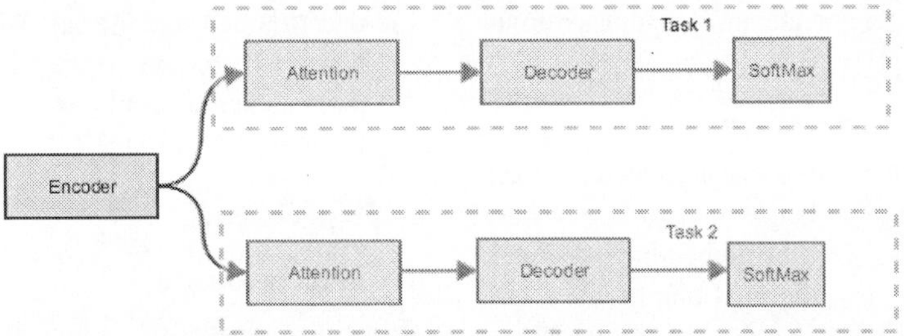

(a) *one-to-many*: A multi-task architecture where only the encoder is shared across the two tasks.

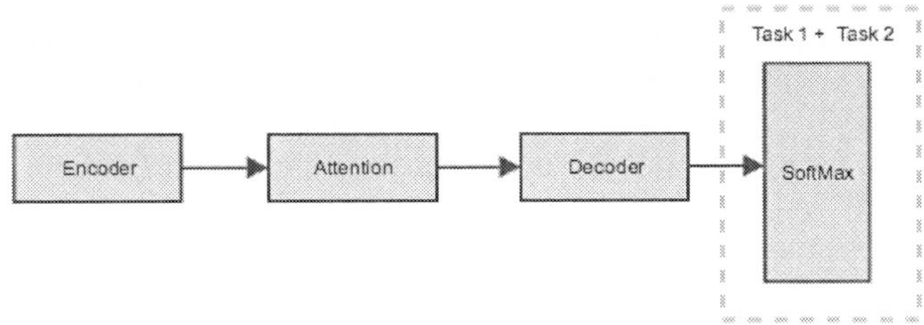

(b) *one-to-one*: A multi-task architecture where both the encoder and decoder along with the attention layer are shared across the two tasks.

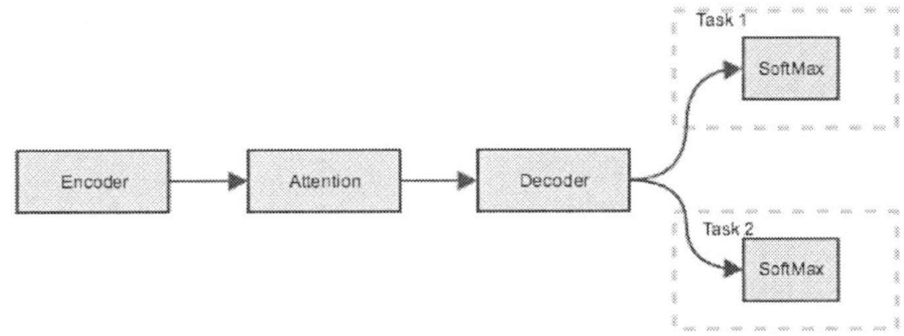

(c) *one-to-shareMany*: A multi-task architecture where both the encoder and decoder along with the attention layer are shared across the two tasks, but the final softmax output layer is trained differently, one for each task.

Figure 2: Three multi-task architectures.

3.2 Multi-task Setup

We focus on training scenarios where multiple training sources K are available. Each source K can be considered a domain or a task, which consists of pairs of utterance x and annotated logical form y. There are no constraints on the logical forms having the same formalism across the K domains. Also, the tasks K can be different, e.g., we can mix semantic parsing and syntactic parsing tasks. We also assume that given an utterance, we already know its associated source K in both training and testing.

In this work, we explore and compare three multi-task sequence-to-sequence model architectures: one-to-many, one-to-one and one-to-shareMany.

3.2.1 One-to-Many Architecture

This is the simplest extension of sequence-to-sequence models to the multi-task case. The encoder is shared across all the K tasks, but the decoder and attention parameters are not shared. The shared encoder captures the English language sequence, whereas each decoder is trained to predict its own formalism. This architecture is shown in Figure 2a. For each minibatch, we uniformly sample among all training sources, choosing one source to select data exclusively from. Therefore, at each model parameter update, we only update the encoder, attention module and the decoder for the selected source, while the parameters for the other $K-1$ decoder and attention modules remain the same.

3.2.2 One-to-One Architecture

Figure 2b shows the one-to-one architecture. Here we have a single sequence-to-sequence model across all the tasks, i.e., the embedding, encoder, attention, decoder and the final output layers are shared across all the K tasks. In this architecture, the number of parameters is independent of the number of tasks K. Since there is no explicit representation of the domain/task that is being decoded, the input is augmented with an artificial token at the start to identify the task the same way as in Johnson et al. (2016).

3.2.3 One-to-ShareMany Architecture

We show the model architecture for one-to-shareMany in Figure 2c. The model modifies the one-to-many model by encouraging further sharing of the decoder weights. Compared with the one-to-one model, the one-to-shareMany differs in the following aspects:

- Each task has its own output layer. Our hypothesis is that by separating the tasks in the final layer we can still get the benefit of sharing the parameters, while fine-tuning for specific tasks in the output, resulting in better accuracy on each individual task.

- The one-to-one requires a concatenation of all output labels from training sources. During training, every minibatch needs to be forwarded and projected to this large softmax layer. While for one-to-ShareMany, each minibatch just needs to be fed to the softmax associated with the chosen source. Therefore, the one-to-shareMany is faster to train especially in cases where the output label size is large.

- The one-to-one architecture is susceptible to data imbalance across the multiple tasks, and typically requires data upsampling or downsampling. While for one-to-shareMany we can alternate the minibatches amongst the K sources using uniform selection.

From the perspective of neural network optimization, mixing the small training data with a large data set from the auxiliary task can be also seen as adding noise to the training process and hence be helpful for generalization and to avoid overfitting. With the auxiliary tasks, we are able to train large size modesl that can handle complex task without worrying about overfitting.

4 Experiments

4.1 Data Setup

We mainly consider two Alexa dependency-based semantic formalisms in use – an Alexa meaning representation language (AlexaMRL), which is a lightweight formalism used for providing built-in functionality for developers to develop their own skills.[3] The other formalism we consider is the one used by Evi,[4] a question-answering system used in Alexa. Evi uses a proprietary formalism for semantic understanding; we will call this the Evi meaning representation language (EviMRL). Both these formalisms aim to represent natural language. While the EviMRL is aligned with an internal schema specific to the knowledge base (KB), the AlexaMRL is aligned with an RDF-based open-source ontology (Guha et al., 2016). Figure 3 shows two example utterances and their parses in both EviMRL and AlexaMRL formalisms.

Our training set consists of $200K$ utterances – a fraction of our production data, annotated using AlexaMRL – as our main task. For the EviMRL task, we have $> 1M$ utterances data set for training. We use a test set of $30K$ utterances for AlexaMRL testing, and $366K$ utterances for EviMRL testing. To show the effectiveness of our proposed method, we also use the ATIS corpora as the small task for our transfer learning framework, which has 4480 training and 448 test utterances (Zettlemoyer and Collins, 2007). We also include an auxiliary task such as syntactic parsing in order to demonstrate the flexibility of the multi-task paradigm. We use $34K$ WSJ training data for syntactic constituency parsing as the large task, similar to the corpus in Vinyals et al. (2015).

We use Tensorflow (Abadi et al., 2016) in all our experiments, with extensions for the copy mechanism. Unless stated otherwise, we train all models for 10 epochs, with a fixed learning rate of 0.5 for the first 6 epochs and halve it subsequently for every epoch. The mini-batch size used is 128. The encoder and decoder use a 3-layer GRU with 512

---

[3]For details see `https://tinyurl.com/lnfh9py`.

[4]`https://www.evi.com`

```
AlexaMRL
"play madonna from the playlist"
PlaybackAction( object( MusicCreativeWork ) ) object( byArtist( name( Person( "mandonna" ) ) ) ) object(
type( MusicCreativeWork( "playlist" ) ) )

EviMRL
"what is the elevation of the san francisco"
Is_the_elevation_of@now( obj_1( "san  francisco" ) )

ATIS
"flight from dallas to san francisco"
lambda $0 e ( and ( flight $0 ) ( from $0 "dallas" ) ( to $0 "san francisco" ) )

WSJ
"the next province ?"
Top( FRAG( NP( DT JJ NN ) . ) )
```

Figure 3: Example utterances for the multiple semantic formalisms

hidden units. We apply dropout with probability of 0.2 during training. All models are initialized with pre-trained 300-dimension GloVe embeddings (Pennington et al., 2014). We also apply label embeddings with 300 dimension for the output labels that are randomly initialized and learned during training. The input sequence is reversed before sending it to the encoder (Vinyals et al., 2015). We use greedy search during decoding. The output label size for EviMRL is $2K$ and for Alexa is < 100. For the multi-task setup, we use a vocabulary size of about $50K$, and for AlexaMRL independent task, we use a vocabulary size of about $20K$. We post-process the output of the decoder by balancing the brackets and determinizing the units of production to avoid duplicates.

4.2 AlexaMRL Transfer Learning Experiments

We first study the effectiveness of the multi-task architecture in a transfer learning setup. Here we consider EviMRL as the large source auxiliary task and the AlexaMRL as the target task we want to transfer learn. We consider various data sizes for the target task – $10K$, $50K$ and $100K$ and $200K$ by downsampling. For each target data size, we compare a single-task setup, trained on the target task only, with the the various multi-task setups from Section 3.2 – independent, one-to-one, one-to-many, and one-to-manyShare. Figure 4 summarizes the results. The x-axis lists the four model architecture, and y-axis is the accuracy. The positive number above the mark of one-to-one, one-to-many and one-to-manyShare represents the absolute accuracy gain compared with the independent model. For the $10k$ independent

model, we reduce the hidden layer size from 512 to 256 to optimize the performance.

In all cases, the multi-task architectures provide accuracy improvements over the independent architecture. By jointly training across the two tasks, the model is able to leverage the richer syntactic/semantic structure of the larger task (EviMRL), resulting in an improved encoding of the input utterance that is then fed to the decoder resulting in improved accuracy over the smaller task (Alexa-MRL).

We take this sharing further in the one-to-one and one-to-shareMany architecture by introducing shared decoder parameters, which forces the model to learn a common canonical representation for solving the semantic parsing task. Doing so, we see further gains across all data sizes in 4. For instance, in the 200k case, the absolute gain improves from $+2.0$ to $+2.7$. As the training data size for the target task increases, we tend to see relatively less gain from model sharing. For instance, in 10k training cases, the absolute gain from the one-to-one and one-to-manyshared is 1.6, this gain reduces to 0.7 when we have 200k training data.

When we have a small amount of training data, the one-to-shareMany provides better accuracy compared with one-to-one. For instance, we see 1.0 and 0.6 absolute gain from one-to-one to one-to-shareMany for 10k and 50k cases respectively. However, no gain is observed for 100k and 200k training cases. This confirms the hypothesis that for small amounts of data, having a dedicated output layer is helpful to guide the training.

Transfer learning works best when the source data is large, thereby allowing the smaller task to leverage the rich representation of the larger task.

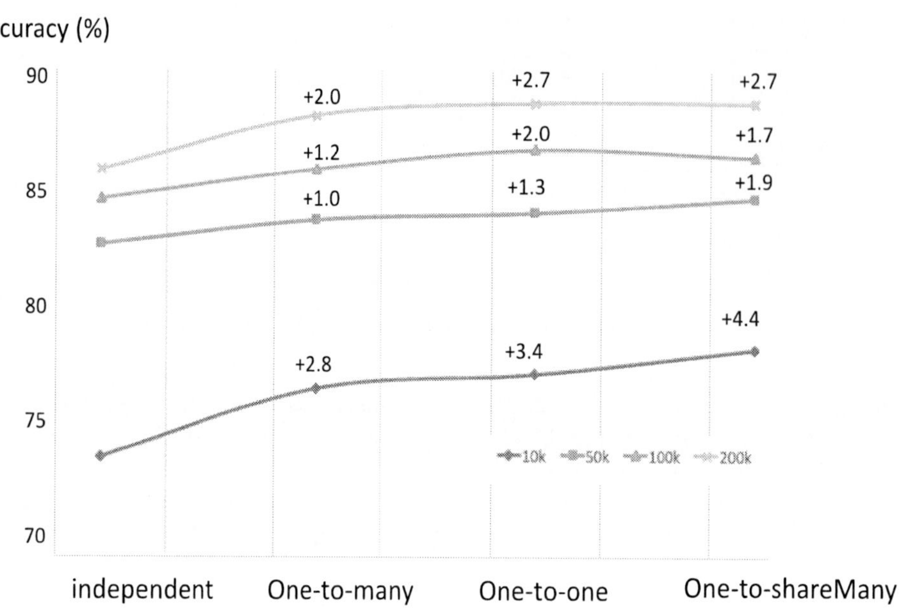

Figure 4: *Accuracy for AlexaMRL.*

However, as the training data size increases, the accuracy gains from the shared architectures become smaller – the largest gain of 4.4% absolute is observed in the $10K$ setting, but as the data increases to $200K$ the improvements are almost halved to about 2.7%.

In Table 1, we summarize the numbers of parameters in each of the four model architectures and their step time.[5] As expected, we see comparable training time for one-to-many and one-to-shareMany, but 10% step time increase for one-to-one. We also see that one-to-one and one-to-shareMany have similar number of parameter, which is about 15% smaller than one-to-many due to the sharing of weights. The one-to-shareMany architecture is able to get the increased sharing while still maintaining reasonable training speed per step-size.

We also test the accuracy of EviMRL with the transfer learning framework. To our surprise, the EviMRL task also benefits from the AlexMRL task. We observe an absolute increase of accu-

Model architecture	param. size	step time
independent	15 million	0.51
one-to-many	33 million	0.66
one-to-one	28 million	0.71
one-to-shareMany	28 million	0.65

Table 1: parameter size and training time comparision for independent and multi-task models

racy of 1.3% over the EviMRL baseline.[6] This observation reinforces the hypothesis that combining data from different semantic formalisms helps the generalization of the model by capturing common sub-structures involved in solving semantic parsing tasks across multiple formalisms.

4.3 Transfer Learning Experiments on ATIS

Here, we apply the described transfer learning setups to the ATIS semantic parsing task (Zettlemoyer and Collins, 2007). We use a single GRU layer of 128 hidden states to train the independent model. During transfer learning, we increase the model size to two hidden layers each with 512 hid-

---

[5]In our experiment, it is the training time for a 128 size minibatches update on Nvidia Tesla K80 GPU

[6]The baseline is at 90.9% accuracy for the single task sequence-to-sequence model

den states. We adjust the minibatch size to 20 and dropout rate to 0.2 for independent model and 0.7 for multi-task model. We post-process the model output, balancing the braces and removing duplicates in the output. The initial learning rate has been adjusted to 0.8 using the dev set. Here, we only report accuracy numbers for the independent and one-to-shareMany frameworks. Correctness is based on denotation match at utterance level. We summarize all the results in Table 2.

System	Test accuracy
Previous work	
Zettlemoyer and Collins (2007)	**84.6**
Kwiatkowski et al. (2011)	82.8
Poon (2013)	83.5
Zhao and Huang (2014)	84.2
Jia and Liang (2016)	83.3
Dong and Lapata (2016)	84.2
Our work	
Independent model	77.2
+ WSJ constituency parsing	79.7
+ EviMRL semantic parsing	84.2

Table 2: Accuracy on ATIS

Our independent model has an accuracy of 77.2%, which is comparable to the published baseline of 76.3% reported in Jia and Liang (2016) before their data recombination. To start with, we first consider using a related but complementary task – syntactic constituency parsing, to help improve the semantic parsing task. By adding WSJ constituency parsing as an auxiliary task for ATIS, we see a 3% relative improvement in accuracy over the independent task baseline. This demonstrates that the multi-task architecture is quite general and is not constrained to using semantic parsing as the auxiliary task. This is important as it opens up the possibility of using significantly larger training data on tasks where acquiring labels is relatively easy.

We then add the EviMRL data of $> 1M$ instances to the multi-task setup as a third task, and we see further relative improvement of 5%, which is comparable to the published state of the art (Zettlemoyer and Collins, 2007) and matches the neural network setup in Dong and Lapata (2016).

5 Conclusion

We presented sequence-to-sequence architectures for transfer learning applied to semantic parsing. We explored multiple architectures for multi-task decoding and found that increased parameter sharing results in improved performance especially when the target task data has limited amounts of training data. We observed a 1.0-4.4% absolute accuracy improvement on our internal test set with 10k-200k training data. On ATIS, we observed a $> 6\%$ accuracy gain.

The results demonstrate the capabilities of sequence-to-sequence modeling to capture a canonicalized representation between tasks, particularly when the architecture uses shared parameters across all its components. Furthermore, by utilizing an auxiliary task like syntactic parsing, we can improve the performance on the target semantic parsing task, showing that the sequence-to-sequence architecture effectively leverages the common structures of syntax and semantics. In future work, we want to use this architecture to build models in an incremental manner where the number of sub-tasks K continually grows. We also want to explore auxiliary tasks across multiple languages so we can train multilingual semantic parsers simultaneously, and use transfer learning to combat labeled data sparsity.

References

Martín Abadi, Ashish Agarwal, Paul Barham, Eugene Brevdo, Zhifeng Chen, Craig Citro, Greg S Corrado, Andy Davis, Jeffrey Dean, Matthieu Devin, et al. 2016. Tensorflow: Large-scale machine learning on heterogeneous distributed systems. *arXiv preprint arXiv:1603.04467* .

Rie Kubota Ando and Tong Zhang. 2005. A framework for learning predictive structures from multiple tasks and unlabeled data. *Journal of Machine Learning Research* 6(Nov):1817–1853.

Yoav Artzi and Luke Zettlemoyer. 2011. Bootstrapping semantic parsers from conversations. In *Proceedings of the conference on empirical methods in natural language processing*. Association for Computational Linguistics, pages 421–432.

Dzmitry Bahdanau, Kyunghyun Cho, and Yoshua Bengio. 2014. Neural machine translation by jointly learning to align and translate. *arXiv preprint arXiv:1409.0473* .

Jonathan Berant, Andrew Chou, Roy Frostig, and Percy Liang. 2013. Semantic parsing on Freebase from question-answer pairs. In *EMNLP*. volume 2, page 6.

Qingqing Cai and Alexander Yates. 2013. Semantic parsing Freebase: Towards open-domain semantic parsing. In *Second Joint Conference on Lexical and Computational Semantics (* SEM)*. volume 1, pages 328–338.

Rich Caruana. 1998. Multitask learning. In *Learning to learn*, Springer, pages 95–133.

Kyunghyun Cho, Bart Van Merriënboer, Caglar Gulcehre, Dzmitry Bahdanau, Fethi Bougares, Holger Schwenk, and Yoshua Bengio. 2014. Learning phrase representations using rnn encoder-decoder for statistical machine translation. *arXiv preprint arXiv:1406.1078* .

Daxiang Dong, Hua Wu, Wei He, Dianhai Yu, and Haifeng Wang. 2015. Multi-task learning for multiple language translation. In *ACL (1)*. pages 1723–1732.

Li Dong and Mirella Lapata. 2016. Language to logical form with neural attention. *arXiv preprint arXiv:1601.01280* .

Chris Dyer, Miguel Ballesteros, Wang Ling, Austin Matthews, and Noah A. Smith. 2015. Transition-based dependency parsing with stack long short-term memory. *arXiv preprint arXiv:1505.08075* .

David Flanagan. 2008. Mql reference guide. *Metaweb Technologies, Inc* page 2.

Ramanathan V Guha, Dan Brickley, and Steve Macbeth. 2016. Schema. org: Evolution of structured data on the web. *Communications of the ACM* 59(2):44–51.

Jonathan Herzig and Jonathan Berant. 2017. Neural semantic parsing over multiple knowledge-bases. *https://arxiv.org/abs/1702.01569* .

Robin Jia and Percy Liang. 2016. Data recombination for neural semantic parsing. *arXiv preprint arXiv:1606.03622* .

Melvin Johnson, Mike Schuster, Quoc V Le, Maxim Krikun, Yonghui Wu, Zhifeng Chen, Nikhil Thorat, Fernanda Viégas, Martin Wattenberg, Greg Corrado, et al. 2016. Google's multilingual neural machine translation system: Enabling zero-shot translation. *arXiv preprint arXiv:1611.04558* .

Tom Kwiatkowski, Luke Zettlemoyer, Sharon Goldwater, and Mark Steedman. 2011. Lexical generalization in ccg grammar induction for semantic parsing. In *Proceedings of the Conference on Empirical Methods in Natural Language Processing*. Association for Computational Linguistics, pages 1512–1523.

Percy Liang, Michael I Jordan, and Dan Klein. 2011. Learning dependency-based compositional semantics. In *Proceedings of the 49th Annual Meeting of the Association for Computational Linguistics: Human Language Technologies-Volume 1*. Association for Computational Linguistics, pages 590–599.

Minh-Thang Luong, Quoc V Le, Ilya Sutskever, Oriol Vinyals, and Lukasz Kaiser. 2015. Multi-task sequence to sequence learning. *arXiv preprint arXiv:1511.06114* .

Jeffrey Pennington, Richard Socher, and Christopher D Manning. 2014. Glove: Global vectors for word representation. In *EMNLP*. volume 14, pages 1532–1543.

Hoifung Poon. 2013. Grounded unsupervised semantic parsing. In *ACL (1)*. Citeseer, pages 933–943.

Siva Reddy, Mirella Lapata, and Mark Steedman. 2014. Large-scale semantic parsing without question-answer pairs. *Transactions of the Association for Computational Linguistics* 2:377–392.

David A. Smith and Noah A. Smith. 2004. Bilingual parsing with factored estimation: Using english to parse korean. In *EMNLP*.

Ilya Sutskever, Oriol Vinyals, and Quoc V Le. 2014. Sequence to sequence learning with neural networks. In *Advances in neural information processing systems*. pages 3104–3112.

Oriol Vinyals, Łukasz Kaiser, Terry Koo, Slav Petrov, Ilya Sutskever, and Geoffrey Hinton. 2015. Grammar as a foreign language. In *Advances in Neural Information Processing Systems*. pages 2773–2781.

Denny Vrandečić and Markus Krötzsch. 2014. Wikidata: a free collaborative knowledgebase. *Communications of the ACM* 57(10):78–85.

John M Zelle and Raymond J Mooney. 1996. Learning to parse database queries using inductive logic programming. In *Proceedings of the national conference on artificial intelligence*. pages 1050–1055.

Luke S. Zettlemoyer and Michael Collins. 2007. Online learning of relaxed CCG grammars for parsing to logical form. In *EMNLP*. pages 678–687.

Luke S. Zettlemoyer and Michael Collins. 2012. Learning to map sentences to logical form: Structured classification with probabilistic categorial grammars. *arXiv preprint arXiv:1207.1420* .

Kai Zhao and Liang Huang. 2014. Type-driven incremental semantic parsing with polymorphism. *arXiv preprint arXiv:1411.5379* .

Modeling Large-Scale Structured Relationships with Shared Memory for Knowledge Base Completion

Yelong Shen[*] and **Po-Sen Huang**[*] and **Ming-Wei Chang** and **Jianfeng Gao**

Microsoft Research, Redmond, WA, USA

{yeshen,pshuang,minchang,jfgao}@microsoft.com

Abstract

Recent studies on knowledge base completion, the task of recovering missing relationships based on recorded relations, demonstrate the importance of learning embeddings from multi-step relations. However, due to the size of knowledge bases, learning multi-step relations directly on top of observed triplets could be costly. Hence, a manually designed procedure is often used when training the models. In this paper, we propose Implicit ReasoNets (IRNs), which is designed to perform multi-step inference *implicitly* through a controller and shared memory. Without a human-designed inference procedure, IRNs use training data to *learn* to perform multi-step inference in an embedding neural space through the shared memory and controller. While the inference procedure does not explicitly operate on top of observed triplets, our proposed model outperforms all previous approaches on the popular FB15k benchmark by more than 5.7%.

1 Introduction

Knowledge bases such as WordNet (Fellbaum, 1998), Freebase (Bollacker et al., 2008), or Yago (Suchanek et al., 2007) contain many real-world facts expressed as triples, e.g., (Bill Gates, FOUNDEROF, Microsoft). These knowledge bases are useful for many downstream applications such as question answering (Berant et al., 2013; Yih et al., 2015) and information extraction (Mintz et al., 2009). However, despite the formidable size of knowledge bases, many important facts are still missing. For example, West et al. (2014) showed that 21% of the 100K most frequent

PERSON entities have no recorded nationality in a recent version of Freebase. We seek to infer unknown entities based on the observed entities and relations. Thus, the knowledge base completion (KBC) task has emerged an important open research problem (Nickel et al., 2011).

Neural-network based methods have been very popular for solving the KBC task. Following Bordes et al. (2013), one of the most popular approaches for KBC is to learn vector-space representations of entities and relations during training, and then apply linear or bi-linear operations to infer the missing relations at test time. However, several recent papers demonstrate limitations of prior approaches relying upon vector-space models alone (Guu et al., 2015; Toutanova et al., 2016; Lin et al., 2015a). By themselves, there is no straightforward way to capture the structured relationships between multiple triples adequately. For example, assume that we want to fill in the missing relation for the triple (Obama, NATIONALITY, ?), a multi-step search procedure might be needed to discover the evidence in the observed triples such as (Obama, BORNIN, Hawaii) and (Hawaii, PARTOF, U.S.A). To address this issue, Guu et al. (2015); Toutanova et al. (2016); Neelakantan et al. (2015); Das et al. (2016); Lin et al. (2015a) propose different approaches of injecting structured information based on the human-designed inference procedure (e.g., random walk) that directly operates on the observed triplets. Unfortunately, due to the size of knowledge bases, these newly proposed approaches suffer from some limitations, as most paths are not informative for inferring missing relations, and it is prohibitive to consider all possible paths during the training time.

In this paper, we propose Implicit ReasoNets (IRNs) that take a different approach from prior work on KBC by addressing the challenges of performing multi-step inference through the design of

---

[*]These authors contributed equally.

57

Proceedings of the 2nd Workshop on Representation Learning for NLP, pages 57–68,
Vancouver, Canada, August 3, 2017. ©2017 Association for Computational Linguistics

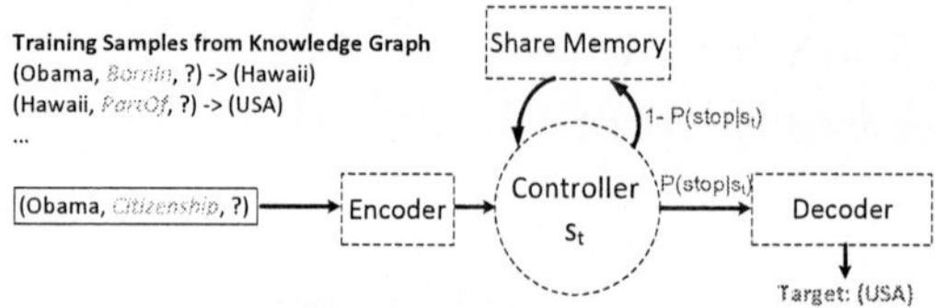

Figure 1: An overview of the IRN for KBC tasks.

controller and *shared memory*. We design a shared memory component to store KB information implicitly. That is, the model needs to determine what information it should store. Moreover, instead of explicitly manipulating the observed triples based on the human-designed inference procedure, the proposed model learns the multi-step inference procedure implicitly, i.e., without human intervention. Specifically, our model makes the prediction several times while forming different intermediate representations along the way. The controller determines how many steps the model should proceed given an input. At each step, a new representation is formed by taking the current representation and a context vector generated by accessing the shared memory. The detailed process is introduced in Section 3.3 and an overview of the model is shown in Figure 1.

The main contributions of our paper are as follows:

- We propose Implicit ReasoNets (IRNs), which use a shared memory guided by a controller to model multi-step structured relationships implicitly.

- We evaluate IRNs and demonstrate that our proposed model achieves the state-of-the-art results on the popular FB15k benchmark, surpassing prior approaches by more than 5.7%.

- Our analysis shows that the multi-step inference is crucial to the performance of our model.

2 Knowledge Base Completion Task

The goal of Knowledge Base Completion (KBC) tasks is to predict a head or a tail entity given the relation type and the other entity, i.e. predicting the head entity h given a triplet $(?, R, t)$ with relation R and tail entity t, or predicting the tail entity t given a triplet $(h, R, ?)$ with head entity h and relation R, where ? denotes the missing entity.

Early work on KBC focuses on learning symbolic rules. Schoenmackers et al. (2010) learns inference rules from a sequence of triplets, e.g., (X, COUNTRYOFHEADQUARTERS, Y) is implied by (X, ISBASEDIN, A) and (A, STATELOCATEDIN, B) and (B, COUNTRYLOCATEDIN, Y). However, enumerating all possible relations is intractable when the knowledge base is large, since the number of distinct sequences of triplets increases rapidly with the number of relation types. Also, the rules-based methods cannot be generalized to paraphrase alternations.

Recent approaches (Bordes et al., 2013; Socher et al., 2013) achieve better generalization by operating on embedding representations, where the vector similarity can be regarded as semantic similarity.

In the evaluation, models compute the similarity between the output prediction and all entities. Mean rank and precision of the target entity are used as metrics for evaluation.

3 Proposed Model

Our proposed model uses the same setup as in the embedding type of approaches (Bordes et al., 2013; Socher et al., 2013), i.e., the model first takes a triplet with a missing entity, $(h, R, ?)$, as input, then maps the input into the neural space through embeddings, and finally outputs a prediction vector of the missing entity. Given that our model is a neural model, we use the *encoder* module to transform the input triplet $(h, R, ?)$ to a continuous representation. For generating the prediction results, the *decoder* module takes the generated continuous representation and outputs a predicted vector, which can be used to find the nearest entity embedding. Basically, we use encoder and decoder modules to convert the tasks between symbolic space and neural space.

The main differences between our model and previous proposed models is that we make the prediction several times while forming *multiple* intermediate continuous representations along the way. Given an intermediate representation, the *controller* judges if the representation encodes enough information for us to produce the output prediction or not. If the controller agrees, we produce the current prediction as our final output. Otherwise, the controller generates a new continuous representation by taking current representation and a context vector generated by accessing the *shared memory*. Then the new presentation will be fed into

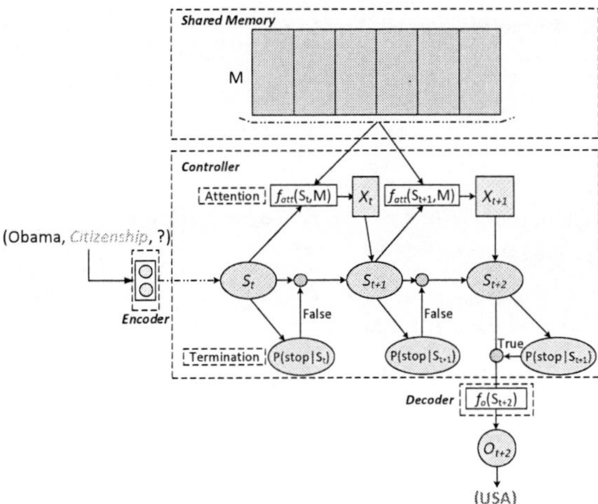

Figure 2: A running example of the IRN architecture. Given the input (Obama, CITIZENSHIP, ?), the model iteratively reformulates the input vector via the current input vector and the attention vector over the shared memory, and determines to stop when an answer is found.

the controller, and the whole process is performed repeatedly until the controller stops the process. Note that the number of steps varies according to the complexity of each example.

3.1 Inference

Encoder/Decoder Given an input $(h, R, ?)$, the encoder module retrieves the entity h and relation R embeddings from an embedding matrix, and then concatenates the two vectors as the intermediate representation s_1.

The decoder module outputs a prediction vector $f_o(s_t) = \tanh(W_o s_t + b_o)$ based on the intermediate representation s_t, which is a nonlinear projection from the controller hidden state and W_o and b_o are the weight matrix and bias vector, respectively. W_o is a k-by-n matrix, where k is the number of the possible entities, and n is the dimension of the hidden vector s_t.

Shared Memory The shared memory is denoted as $M = \{m_i\}_{i=1}^{|M|}$, which consists of a list of vectors. During training, the shared memory, which is shared across all training instances, is first randomly initialized and then is jointed learned with the controller on training data.

Controller The controller has two roles in our model. First, it needs to judge if the process should be stopped. If yes, the output will be generated. Otherwise, it needs to generate a new represen-

tation based on previous representation and the context vector generated from shared memory. The controller is a recurrent neural network and controls the process by keeping internal state sequences to track the current search process and history. The controller uses an attention mechanism to fetch information from relevant memory vectors in M, and decides if the model should output the prediction or continue to update the input vector in the next step.

To judge the process should be continued or not, the model estimates $P(\texttt{stop}|s_t)$ by a logistical regression module: $\texttt{sigmoid}(W_c s_t + b_c)$, where the weight matrix W_c and bias vector b_c are learned during training. With probability $P(\texttt{stop}|s_t)$, the process will be stopped, and the decoder will be called to generate the output.

With probability $1 - P(\texttt{stop}|s_t)$, the controller needs to generate the next representation $s_{t+1} = \text{RNN}(s_t, x_t)$. The attention vector x_t at t-th step is generated based on the current internal state s_t and the shared memory M. Specifically, the attention score $a_{t,i}$ on a memory vector m_i given a state s_t is computed as

$$a_{t,i} \propto \lambda \cos(W_1 m_i, W_2 s_t),$$

where λ is set to 10 in our experiments and the weight matrices W_1 and W_2 are learned during training. The attention vector x_t can be written as $x_t = f_{\texttt{att}}(s_t, M) = \sum_i^{|M|} a_{t,i} m_i$.

Overall Process The inference process is formally described in Algorithm 1. Given input (Obama, NATIONALITY, ?), the encoder module converts it to a vector s_1 by concatenating entity/relation embedding lookup. Second, at step t, with probability $P(\texttt{stop}|s_t)$, model outputs the prediction vector o_i. With probability $1 - P(\texttt{stop}|s_t)$, the state s_{i+1} is updated based on the previous state s_i and the vector x_t generated by performing attention over the shared memory.

We iterate the process till a predefined maximum step $T_{\max}$. At test time, the model outputs a prediction o_j where the step j has the maximum termination probability. Note that the overall framework is generic to different applications by tailoring the encoder/decoder to a target application. An example of shortest path synthesis task is shown in Appendix B.

Algorithm 1 Inference Process of IRNs
```
Lookup entity and relation embeddings, h and r.
Set s₁ = [h, r]                        ▷ Encoder
while True do
    u ~ [0, 1]
    if u > P(stop|sₜ) then
        xₜ = f_att(sₜ, M)              ▷ Access Memory
        s_{t+1} = RNN(sₜ, xₜ), t ← t + 1
    else
        Generate output oₜ = f_o(sₜ)   ▷ Decoder
        break                          ▷ Stop
    end if
end while
```

3.2 Training Objectives

In this section, we introduce the training objectives to train our model. While our process is stochastic, the model mainly needs to decide the number of steps for generating the intermediate representations for each example. Since the number of steps the model should take for each example is unknown in the training data, we optimize the expected reward directly, motivated by the REINFORCE algorithm (Williams, 1992).

The expected reward at step t can be obtained as follows. At t-step, given the representation vector s_t, the model generates the output score o_t as $f_o(s_t)$. We convert the output score to a probability by the following steps. The probability of selecting a prediction $\hat{y} \in D$ is approximated as $p(\hat{y}|o_t) = \frac{\exp(-\gamma d(o_t, \hat{y}))}{\sum_{y_k \in D} \exp(-\gamma d(o_t, y_k))}$, where $d(o, y) = \|o - y\|_1$ is the L_1 distance between output o and the target entity y, and D is the set of all possible entities. In our experiments, we set γ to 5 and sample 20 negative examples in D to speed up training. Assume that ground truth target entity embedding is y^*, the expected reward at time t is:

$$J(s_t|\theta) = \sum_{\hat{y}} R(\hat{y}) \frac{\exp(-\gamma d(o_t, \hat{y}))}{\sum_{\bar{y} \in D} \exp(-\gamma d(o, \bar{y}))}$$

$$= \frac{\exp(-\gamma d(o_t, y^*))}{\sum_{\bar{y} \in D} \exp(-\gamma d(o, \bar{y}))},$$

where R is the reward function, and we assign the reward to be 1 when we make a correct prediction on the target entity, and 0 otherwise.

Next, we can calculate the reward by summing them over each step. The overall probability of model terminated at time t is $\Pi_{i=1}^{t-1}(1-v_i)v_t$, where $v_i = P(\text{stop}|s_i, \theta)$. Therefore, the overall objec-

tive function can be written as

$$J(\theta) = \sum_{t=1}^{T_{\max}} \Pi_{i=1}^{t-1}(1 - v_i)v_t J(s_t|\theta). \quad (1)$$

Then, the parameters can be updated through back-propagation.

3.3 Motivating Examples

We now describe the motivating examples to explain the design of shared memory that implicitly stores KB information and the design of the controller that implicitly learns the inference procedure.

Shared Memory Suppose, in a KBC task, the input is (Obama, NATIONALITY, ?) and the model is required to answer the missing entity (answer: U.S.A). Our model can learn to utilize and store information in the shared memory through the controller. When a new information from a new instance is received (e.g., (Obama, BORNIN, Hawaii)), the model first uses its controller to find relevant information (e.g., (Hawaii, PARTOF, U.S.A)). If the relevant information is not found, the model learns to store the information to memory vectors by gradient update in order to answer the missing entity correctly. Due to the limited size of the shared memory, the model cannot store all new information explicitly. Thus, the model needs to learn to utilize the shared memory efficiently to lower the training loss. If a related information from a new instance is received, the model learns to do inference by utilizing the controller to go over existing memory vectors iteratively. In this way, the model could learn to do inference and correlate training instances via memory cells without explicitly storing new information.

Controller The design of the controller allows the model to iteratively reformulate its representation through incorporating context information retrieved from the shared memory. Without explicitly providing human-designed inference procedure, during the iterative progress, the controller needs to explore the multi-step inference procedure on its own. Suppose a given input triplet is not able to be resolved in one step. The controller needs to utilize its reformulation capability to explore different representations and make a prediction correctly in order to lower the training loss.

Table 1: The knowledge base completion (link prediction) results on WN18 and FB15k.

Model	Additional Information	WN18		FB15k	
		Hits@10 (%)	MR	Hits@10 (%)	MR
SE (Bordes et al., 2011)	NO	80.5	985	39.8	162
Unstructured (Bordes et al., 2014)	NO	38.2	304	6.3	979
TransE (Bordes et al., 2013)	NO	89.2	251	47.1	125
TransH (Wang et al., 2014)	NO	86.7	303	64.4	87
TransR (Lin et al., 2015b)	NO	92.0	225	68.7	77
CTransR (Lin et al., 2015b)	NO	92.3	218	70.2	75
KG2E (He et al., 2015)	NO	93.2	348	74.0	59
TransD (Ji et al., 2015)	NO	92.2	212	77.3	91
TATEC (García-Durán et al., 2015)	NO	-	-	76.7	58
NTN (Socher et al., 2013)	NO	66.1	-	41.4	-
DISTMULT (Yang et al., 2014)	NO	94.2	-	57.7	-
STransE (Nguyen et al., 2016)	NO	94.7 (93)	244 (**206**)	79.7	69
RTransE (García-Durán et al., 2015)	Path	-	-	76.2	50
PTransE (Lin et al., 2015a)	Path	-	-	84.6	58
NLFeat (Toutanova et al., 2015)	Node + Link Features	94.3	-	87.0	-
Random Walk (Wei et al., 2016)	Path	94.8	-	74.7	-
IRN	NO	**95.3**	249	**92.7**	**38**

Table 2: The performance of IRNs with different memory sizes and inference steps on FB15k, where $|M|$ and T_{max} represent the number of memory vectors and the maximum inference step, respectively.

$|M|$	T_{max}	FB15k	
		Hits@10 (%)	MR
64	1	80.7	55.7
64	2	87.4	49.2
64	5	**92.7**	38.0
64	8	88.8	**32.9**
32	5	90.1	38.7
64	5	**92.7**	38.0
128	5	92.2	36.1
512	5	90.0	35.3
4096	5	88.7	**34.7**

4 Experimental Results

In this section, we evaluate the performance of our model on the benchmark FB15k and WN18 datasets for KBC (Bordes et al., 2013). These datasets contain multi-relations between head and tail entities. Given a head entity and a relation, the model produces a ranked list of the entities according to the score of the entity being the tail entity of this triple. To evaluate the ranking, we report **mean rank (MR)**, the mean of rank of the correct entity across the test examples, and **hits@10**, the proportion of correct entities ranked in the top-10 predictions. Lower MR or higher hits@10 indicates a better prediction performance. We follow the evaluation protocol in Bordes et al. (2013) to report filtered results, where negative examples N are removed from the dataset. In this case, we avoid some negative examples being valid and ranked above the target triplet.

We use the same hyper-parameters of our model for both FB15k and WN18 datasets. Entity embeddings (which are not shared between input and output modules) and relation embedding are both 100-dimensions. We use the encoder module and decoder module to encode input entities and relations, and output entities, respectively. There are 64 memory vectors with 200 dimensions each, initialized by random vectors with unit L_2-norm. We use single-layer GRU with 200 cells as the search controller. We set the maximum inference step T_{max} of the IRN to 5. We randomly initialize all model parameters, and use SGD as the training algorithm with mini-batch size of 64. We set the learning rate to a constant number, 0.01. To prevent the model from learning a trivial solution by increasing entity embeddings norms, we follow Bordes et al. (2013) to enforce the L_2-norm of the entity embeddings as 1. We use hits@10 as the validation metric for the IRN. Following the work (Lin et al., 2015a), we add reverse relations into the training triplet set to increase the training data.

Following Nguyen et al. (2016), we divide the results of previous work into two groups. The first group contains the models that directly optimize a scoring function for the triples in a knowledge base without using extra information. The second group of models make uses of additional information from multi-step relations. For example, RTransE (García-Durán et al., 2015) and PTransE

Table 3: Hits@10 (%) in the relation category on FB15k. (M stands for Many)

Model	Predicting head h				Predicting tail t			
	1-1	1-M	M-1	M-M	1-1	1-M	M-1	M-M
SE (Bordes et al., 2011)	35.6	62.6	17.2	37.5	34.9	14.6	68.3	41.3
Unstructured (Bordes et al., 2014)	34.5	2.5	6.1	6.6	34.3	4.2	1.9	6.6
TransE (Bordes et al., 2013)	43.7	65.7	18.2	47.2	43.7	19.7	66.7	50.0
TransH (Wang et al., 2014)	66.8	87.6	28.7	64.5	65.5	39.8	83.3	67.2
TransR (Lin et al., 2015b)	78.8	89.2	34.1	69.2	79.2	37.4	90.4	72.1
CTransR (Lin et al., 2015b)	81.5	89.0	34.7	71.2	80.8	38.6	90.1	73.8
KG2E (He et al., 2015)	**92.3**	94.6	66.0	69.6	**92.6**	67.9	94.4	73.4
TransD (Ji et al., 2015)	86.1	95.5	39.8	78.5	85.4	50.6	94.4	81.2
TATEC (García-Durán et al., 2015)	79.3	93.2	42.3	77.2	78.5	51.5	92.7	80.7
STransE (Nguyen et al., 2016)	82.8	94.2	50.4	80.1	82.4	56.9	93.4	83.1
PTransE (Lin et al., 2015a)	91.0	92.8	60.9	83.8	91.2	74.0	88.9	86.4
IRN	87.2	**96.1**	**84.8**	**92.9**	86.9	**90.5**	**95.3**	**94.1**

(Lin et al., 2015a) models are extensions of the TransE (Bordes et al., 2013) model by explicitly exploring multi-step relations in the knowledge base to regularize the trained embeddings. The NLFeat model (Toutanova et al., 2015) is a log-linear model that makes use of simple node and link features.

Table 1 presents the experimental results. According to the table, our model significantly outperforms previous baselines, regardless of whether previous approaches use additional information or not. Specifically, on FB15k, the MR of our model surpasses all previous results by 12, and our hit@10 outperforms others by 5.7%. On WN18, the IRN obtains the highest hit@10 while maintaining similar MR results compared to previous work.[*]

To better understand the behavior of IRNs, we report the results of IRNs with different memory sizes and different T_{max} on FB15k in Table 2. We find the performance of IRNs increases significantly if the number of inference step increases. Note that an IRN with $T_{max} = 1$ is the case that an IRN without the shared memory. Interestingly, given $T_{max} = 5$, IRNs are not sensitive to memory sizes. In particular, larger memory always improves the MR score, but the best hit@10 is obtained by $|M| = 64$ memory vectors. A possible reason is that the best memory size is determined by the complexity of the tasks.

We evaluate hits@10 results on FB15k with respect to the relation categories. Following the evaluation in Bordes et al. (2013), we categorize the relations according to the cardinalities of their associated head and tail entities in four types: 1-1,

1-Many, Many-1, and Many-Many. A given relation is 1-1 if a head entity can appear with at most one tail entity, 1-Many if a head entity can appear with many tail entities, Many-1 if multiple heads can appear with the same tail entity, and Many-Many if multiple head entities can appear with multiple tail entities. The detailed results are shown in Table 3. The IRN significantly improves the hits@10 results in the Many-1 category on predicting the head entity (18.8%), the 1-Many category on predicting the tail entity (16.5%), and the Many-Many category (over 8% in average).

In order to show the inference procedure determined by IRNs, we map the representation s_t back to human-interpretable entity and relation names in the KB. In Table 4, we show a randomly sampled example with its top-3 closest triplets (h, R, ?) in terms of L_2-distance, and top-3 answer predictions along with the termination probability at each step. Throughout our observation, the inference procedure is quite different from the traditional inference chain that people designed in the symbolic space (Schoenmackers et al., 2010). The potential reason is that IRNs operate in the neural space. Instead of connecting triplets that share exactly the same entity as in the symbolic space, IRNs update the representations and connects other triplets in the semantic space instead. As we can observe in the examples of Table 4, the model reformulates the representation s_t at each step and gradually increases the ranking score of the correct tail entity with higher termination probability during the inference process. In the last step of Table 4, the closest tuple (Phoenix Suns, /BASKETBALL_ROSTER_POSITION/POSITION) is actually within the training set with a tail entity Forward-center, which is the same as the tar-

[*]Nguyen et al. (2016) reported two results on WN18, where the first one is obtained by choosing to optimize hits@10 on the validation set, and second one is obtained by choosing to optimize MR on the validation set. We list both of them in Table 1.

Table 4: Interpret the state s_t in each step via finding the closest (entity, relation) tuple, and the corresponding the top-3 predictions and termination probability. "Rank" stands for the rank of the target entity and "Term. Prob." stands for termination probability.

Input: (Milwaukee Bucks, /BASKETBALL_ROSTER_POSITION/POSITION)
Target: Forward-center

Step	Term. Prob.	Rank		Top 3 Entity, Relation/Prediction
1	6.85e-6	5	(Entity, Relation)	1. (Milwaukee Bucks, /BASKETBALL_ROSTER_POSITION/POSITION) 2. (Milwaukee Bucks, /SPORTS_TEAM_ROSTER/POSITION) 3. (Arizona Wildcats men's basketball, /BASKETBALL_ROSTER_POSITION/POSITION)
			Prediction	1. Swingman 2. Punt returner 3. Return specialist
2	0.012	4	(Entity, Relation)	1. (Phoenix Suns, /BASKETBALL_ROSTER_POSITION/POSITION) 2. (Minnesota Golden Gophers men's basketball, /BASKETBALL_ROSTER_POSITION/POSITION) 3. (Sacramento Kings, /BASKETBALL_ROSTER_POSITION/POSITION)
			Prediction	1. Swingman 2. Sports commentator 3. Wide receiver
3	0.987	1	(Entity, Relation)	1. (Phoenix Suns, /BASKETBALL_ROSTER_POSITION/POSITION) 2. (Minnesota Golden Gophers men's basketball, /BASKETBALL_ROSTER_POSITION/POSITION) 3. (Sacramento Kings, /BASKETBALL_ROSTER_POSITION/POSITION)
			Prediction	1. **Forward-center** 2. Swingman 3. Cabinet of the United States

get entity. Hence, the whole inference process can be thought as the model iteratively reformulates the representations in order to minimize its distance to the target entity in neural space.

To understand what the model has learned in the shared memory in the KBC tasks, in Table 5, we visualize the shared memory in an IRN trained from FB15k. We compute the average attention scores of each relation type on each memory cell. In the table, we show the top 8 relations, ranked by the average attention scores, of some memory cells. These memory cells are activated by certain semantic patterns within the knowledge graph. It suggests that the shared memory can efficiently capture the relationships implicitly. We can still see a few noisy relations in each clustered memory cell, e.g., "bridge-player-teammates/teammate" relation in the "film" memory cell, and "olympic-medal-honor/medalist" in the "disease" memory cell.

We provide some more IRN prediction examples at each step from FB15k as shown in Appendix A. In addition to the KBC tasks, we construct a synthetic task, shortest path synthesis, to evaluate the inference capability over a shared memory as shown in the Appendix B.

5 Related Work

Link Prediction and Knowledge Base Completion Given that R is a relation, h is the head entity, and t is the tail entity, most of the embedding models for link prediction focus on finding the scoring function $f_r(h, t)$ that represents the implausibility of a triple. (Bordes et al., 2011, 2014, 2013; Wang et al., 2014; Ji et al., 2015; Nguyen et al., 2016). In many studies, the scoring function $f_r(h, t)$ is linear or bi-linear. For example, in TransE (Bordes et al., 2013), the function is implemented as $f_r(h, t) = \|h + r - t\|$, where $\mathbf{h}$, $\mathbf{r}$ and $\mathbf{t}$ are the corresponding vector representations.

Recently, different studies (Guu et al., 2015; Lin et al., 2015a; Neelakantan et al., 2015; Das et al., 2016; Toutanova et al., 2016) demonstrate the importance for models to also learn from multi-step relations. Learning from multi-step relations injects the structured relationships between triples into the model. However, this also poses a technical challenge of considering exponential numbers of multi-step relationships. Prior approaches address this issue by designing path-mining algorithms (Lin et al., 2015a) or considering all possible paths using a dynamic programming algorithm with the restriction of using linear or bi-linear models only (Toutanova et al., 2016). Neelakantan et al.

Table 5: Shared memory visualization in an IRN trained on FB15k, where we show the top 8 relations, ranked by the average attention scores, of some memory cells. The first row in each column represents the interpreted relation.

"family"	"person"	"film", "award"
lived-with/participant	person/gender	film-genre/films-in-this-genre
breakup/participant	person/nationality	film/cinematography
marriage/spouse	military-service/military-person	cinematographer/film
vacation-choice/vacationer	government-position-held/office-holder	award-honor/honored-for
support/supported-organization	leadership/role	netflix-title/netflix-genres
marriage/location-of-ceremony	person/ethnicity	director/film
canoodled/participant	person/parents	award-honor/honored-for
dated/participant	person/place-of-birth	bridge-player-teammates/teammate

"disease"	"sports"	"tv program"
disease-cause/diseases	sports-team-roster/team	tv-producer-term/program
crime-victim/crime-type	basketball-roster-position/player	tv-producer-term/producer-type
notable-person-with-medical-condition/condition	basketball-roster-position/player	tv-guest-role/episodes-appeared-in
cause-of-death/parent-cause-of-death	baseball-player/position-s	tv-program/languages
disease/notable-people-with-this-condition	appointment/appointed-by	tv-guest-role/actor
olympic-medal-honor/medalist	batting-statistics/team	tv-program/spin-offs
disease/includes-diseases	basketball-player-stats/team	award-honor/honored-for
disease/symptoms	person/profession	tv-program/country-of-origin

(2015) and Das et al. (2016) use an RNN to model the multi-step relationships over a set of random walk paths on the observed triplets. Toutanova and Chen (2015) shows the effectiveness of using simple node and link features that encode structured information on FB15k and WN18. In our work, the IRN outperforms prior results and shows that similar information can be captured by the model without explicitly designing inference procedures on the observed triplets. Our model can be regarded as a recursive function that iteratively update the representation in such a way that its distance to the target entity in the neural space is minimized, i.e., $\|f_{\text{IRN}}(\mathbf{h}, \mathbf{r}) - \mathbf{t}\|$.

Studies such as (Riedel et al., 2013) show that incorporating textual information can further improve the KBC tasks. It would be interesting to incorporate the information outside the knowledge bases in our model in the future.

Neural Frameworks Sequence-to-sequence models (Sutskever et al., 2014; Cho et al., 2014) have shown to be successful in many applications such as machine translation and conversation modeling (Sordoni et al., 2015). While sequence-to-sequence models are powerful, recent work has shown the necessity of incorporating an external memory to perform inference in simple algorithmic tasks (Graves et al., 2014, 2016).

Compared IRNs to Memory Networks (MemNN) (Weston et al., 2014; Sukhbaatar et al., 2015; Miller et al., 2016) and Neural Turing Machines (NTM) (Graves et al., 2014, 2016), the biggest difference between our model and the existing frameworks is the controller and the use of the shared memory. We follow Shen et al. (2017) for using a controller module to dynamically perform a multi-step inference depending on the complexity of the instance. MemNN and NTM explicitly store inputs (such as graph definition, supporting facts) in the memory. In contrast, in IRNs, we do not explicitly store all the observed inputs in the shared memory. Instead, we directly operate on the shared memory, which modeling the structured relationships implicitly. During training, we randomly initialize the memory and update the memory jointly with the controller with respect to task-specific objectives via back-propagation, instead of explicitly defining memory write operations as in NTM.

6 Conclusion

In this paper, we propose Implicit ReasoNets (IRNs), which perform inference over a shared memory that stores large-scale structured relationships implicitly. The inference process is guided by a controller to access the memory that is shared across instances. We demonstrate and analyze the multi-step inference capability of IRNs in the knowledge base completion tasks. Our model, without using any explicit knowledge base information in the inference procedure, outperforms all prior approaches on the popular FB15k benchmark by more than 5.7%.

For future work, we aim to further extend IRNs

in two ways. First, inspired from Ribeiro et al. (2016), we would like to develop techniques to exploit ways to generate human understandable reasoning interpretation from the shared memory. Second, we plan to apply IRNs to infer the relationships in unstructured data such as natural language. For example, given a natural language query such as "are rabbits animals?", the model can infer a natural language answer implicitly in the shared memory without performing inference directly on top of huge amounts of observed sentences such as "all mammals are animals" and "rabbits are animals". We believe that the ability to perform inference implicitly is crucial for modeling large-scale structured relationships.

References

Jonathan Berant, Andrew Chou, Roy Frostig, and Percy Liang. 2013. Semantic parsing on Freebase from question-answer pairs. In *Proceedings of EMNLP*.

Kurt Bollacker, Colin Evans, Praveen Paritosh, Tim Sturge, and Jamie Taylor. 2008. Freebase: A collaboratively created graph database for structuring human knowledge. In *Proceedings of SIGMOD-08*. pages 1247–1250.

Antoine Bordes, Xavier Glorot, Jason Weston, and Yoshua Bengio. 2014. A semantic matching energy function for learning with multi-relational data. *Machine Learning* 94(2):233–259.

Antoine Bordes, Nicolas Usunier, Alberto Garcia-Duran, Jason Weston, and Oksana Yakhnenko. 2013. Translating embeddings for modeling multi-relational data. In *Advances in Neural Information Processing Systems*. pages 2787–2795.

Antoine Bordes, Jason Weston, Ronan Collobert, and Yoshua Bengio. 2011. Learning structured embeddings of knowledge bases. In *Proceedings of the Twenty-Fifth AAAI Conference on Artificial Intelligence*. pages 301–306.

Kyunghyun Cho, Bart Van Merriënboer, Caglar Gulcehre, Dzmitry Bahdanau, Fethi Bougares, Holger Schwenk, and Yoshua Bengio. 2014. Learning phrase representations using rnn encoder-decoder for statistical machine translation. *arXiv preprint arXiv:1406.1078* .

Rajarshi Das, Arvind Neelakantan, David Belanger, and Andrew McCallum. 2016. Chains of reasoning over entities, relations, and text using recurrent neural networks. *arXiv preprint arXiv:1607.01426* .

C. Fellbaum. 1998. *WordNet: An Electronic Lexical Database*. MIT Press.

Alberto García-Durán, Antoine Bordes, and Nicolas Usunier. 2015. Composing relationships with translations. In *EMNLP*. pages 286–290.

Alberto García-Durán, Antoine Bordes, Nicolas Usunier, and Yves Grandvalet. 2015. Combining two and three-way embeddings models for link prediction in knowledge bases. *CoRR* abs/1506.00999.

Alex Graves, Greg Wayne, and Ivo Danihelka. 2014. Neural turing machines. *arXiv preprint arXiv:1410.5401* .

Alex Graves, Greg Wayne, Malcolm Reynolds, Tim Harley, Ivo Danihelka, Agnieszka Grabska-Barwińska, Sergio Gómez Colmenarejo, Edward Grefenstette, Tiago Ramalho, John Agapiou, et al. 2016. Hybrid computing using a neural network with dynamic external memory. *Nature* .

Kelvin Guu, John Miller, and Percy Liang. 2015. Traversing knowledge graphs in vector space. *arXiv preprint arXiv:1506.01094* .

Shizhu He, Kang Liu, Guoliang Ji, and Jun Zhao. 2015. Learning to represent knowledge graphs with gaussian embedding. In *Proceedings of the 24th ACM International on Conference on Information and Knowledge Management*. pages 623–632.

Guoliang Ji, Shizhu He, Liheng Xu, Kang Liu, and Jun Zhao. 2015. Knowledge graph embedding via dynamic mapping matrix. In *ACL*. pages 687–696.

Yankai Lin, Zhiyuan Liu, Huanbo Luan, Maosong Sun, Siwei Rao, and Song Liu. 2015a. Modeling relation paths for representation learning of knowledge bases. In *Proceedings of the Conference on Empirical Methods for Natural Language Processing (EMNLP)*.

Yankai Lin, Zhiyuan Liu, Maosong Sun, Yang Liu, and Xuan Zhu. 2015b. Learning entity and relation embeddings for knowledge graph completion. In *Proceedings of the Twenty-Ninth AAAI Conference on Artificial Intelligence*. AAAI'15, pages 2181–2187.

Alexander Miller, Adam Fisch, Jesse Dodge, Amir-Hossein Karimi, Antoine Bordes, and Jason Weston. 2016. Key-value memory networks for directly reading documents. In *EMNLP*.

Mike Mintz, Steven Bills, Rion Snow, and Daniel Jurafsky. 2009. Distant supervision for relation extraction without labeled data. In *Proceedings of ACL-IJCNLP-09*. pages 1003–1011.

Arvind Neelakantan, Benjamin Roth, and Andrew McCallum. 2015. Compositional vector space models for knowledge base completion. *arXiv preprint arXiv:1504.06662* .

Dat Quoc Nguyen, Kairit Sirts, Lizhen Qu, and Mark Johnson. 2016. STransE: a novel embedding model of entities and relationships in knowledge bases. In *NAACL*. pages 460–466.

Maximilian Nickel, Volker Tresp, and Hans-Peter Kriegel. 2011. A three-way model for collective learning on multi-relational data. In *Proceedings of the 28th International Conference on Machine Learning*. pages 809–816.

Marco Tulio Ribeiro, Sameer Singh, and Carlos Guestrin. 2016. "Why Should I Trust You?": Explaining the Predictions of Any Classifier. In *KDD*.

Sebastian Riedel, Limin Yao, Andrew McCallum, and Benjamin M. Marlin. 2013. Relation extraction with matrix factorization and universal schemas. In *HLT-NAACL*. pages 74–84.

Stefan Schoenmackers, Oren Etzioni, Daniel S Weld, and Jesse Davis. 2010. Learning first-order horn clauses from web text. In *Proceedings of the 2010 Conference on Empirical Methods in Natural Language Processing*. Association for Computational Linguistics, pages 1088–1098.

Yelong Shen, Po-Sen Huang, Jianfeng Gao, and Weizhu Chen. 2017. ReasoNet: Learning to stop reading in machine comprehension. In *KDD*.

Richard Socher, Danqi Chen, Christopher D. Manning, and Andrew Y. Ng. 2013. Reasoning With Neural Tensor Networks For Knowledge Base Completion. In *Advances in Neural Information Processing Systems*.

Alessandro Sordoni, Michel Galley, Michael Auli, Chris Brockett, Yangfeng Ji, Margaret Mitchell, Jian-Yun Nie, Jianfeng Gao, and Bill Dolan. 2015. A neural network approach to context-sensitive generation of conversational responses. *arXiv preprint arXiv:1506.06714* .

F. M. Suchanek, G. Kasneci, and G. Weikum. 2007. Yago: A Core of Semantic Knowledge. In *WWW*.

Sainbayar Sukhbaatar, Jason Weston, Rob Fergus, et al. 2015. End-to-end memory networks. In *Advances in Neural Information Processing Systems*. pages 2440–2448.

Ilya Sutskever, Oriol Vinyals, and Quoc V Le. 2014. Sequence to sequence learning with neural networks. In *Advances in Neural Information Processing Systems*. pages 3104–3112.

Kristina Toutanova and Danqi Chen. 2015. Observed versus latent features for knowledge base and text inference. In *Proceedings of the 3rd Workshop on Continuous Vector Space Models and their Compositionality*. pages 57–66.

Kristina Toutanova, Danqi Chen, Patrick Pantel, Hoifung Poon, Pallavi Choudhury, and Michael Gamon. 2015. Representing text for joint embedding of text and knowledge bases. In *EMNLP*.

Kristina Toutanova, Xi Victoria Lin, Scott Wen tau Yih, Hoifung Poon, and Chris Quirk. 2016. Compositional learning of embeddings for relation paths in knowledge bases and text. In *ACL*.

Zhen Wang, Jianwen Zhang, Jianlin Feng, and Zheng Chen. 2014. Knowledge graph embedding by translating on hyperplanes. In *Proceedings of the Twenty-Eighth AAAI Conference on Artificial Intelligence*. pages 1112–1119.

Zhuoyu Wei, Jun Zhao, and Kang Liu. 2016. Mining inference formulas by goal-directed random walks. In *EMNLP*.

Robert West, Evgeniy Gabrilovich, Kevin Murphy, Shaohua Sun, Rahul Gupta, and Dekang Lin. 2014. Knowledge base completion via search-based question answering. In *Proceedings of the 23rd International Conference on World Wide Web*. ACM, pages 515–526.

Jason Weston, Sumit Chopra, and Antoine Bordes. 2014. Memory networks. *arXiv preprint arXiv:1410.3916* .

Ronald J. Williams. 1992. Simple statistical gradient-following algorithms for connectionist reinforcement learning. *Machine Learning* 8:229–256.

Bishan Yang, Wen-tau Yih, Xiaodong He, Jianfeng Gao, and Li Deng. 2014. Embedding entities and relations for learning and inference in knowledge bases. *CoRR* abs/1412.6575.

Wen-tau Yih, Ming-Wei Chang, Xiaodong He, and Jianfeng Gao. 2015. Semantic parsing via staged query graph generation: Question answering with knowledge base. In *Proc. of ACL*.

A Inference Steps in KBC

To analyze the behavior of IRNs in each inference step, we further pick some examples for the tail entity prediction in Table 6. Interestingly, we observed that the model can gradually increase the ranking score of the correct tail entity during the inference process.

B Analysis: Applying IRNs to a Shortest Path Synthesis Task

To further understand the inference procedure of IRNs, we construct a synthetic task, shortest path synthesis, to evaluate the inference capability over a shared memory. The motivations of applying our model to this task are as follows. First, we want to evaluate IRNs on another task requiring multi-step inference. Second, we select the *sequence generation* task so that we are able to analyze the inference capability of IRNs in details.

In the shortest path synthesis task, as illustrated in Figure 3, a training instance consists of a start node and an end node (e.g., $215 \rightsquigarrow 493$) of an underlying weighted directed graph that is unknown to models. The output of each instance is the shortest path between the given start and end nodes of the underlying graph (e.g., $215 \rightarrow 101 \rightarrow 493$). Specifically, models can only observe the start-end node pairs as input and their shortest path as output. The whole graph is unknown to the models and the edge weights are not revealed in the training data. At test time, a path sequence is considered correct if it connects the start node and the end node of the underlying graph, and the cost of the predicted path is the same as the optimal path.

We construct the underlying graph as follows: on a three-dimensional unit-sphere, we randomly generate a set of nodes. For each node, we connect its K-nearest neighbors and use the euclidean distance between two nodes to construct a graph. We randomly sample two nodes and compute its shortest path if it is connected between these two nodes. Given the fact that all the sub-paths within a shortest path are shortest paths, we incrementally create the dataset and remove the instances which are a sub-path of previously selected paths or are super-set of previous selected paths. In this case, all the shortest paths can not be answered through directly copying from another instance. In addition, all the weights in the graph are hidden and not shown in the training data, which increases the difficulty of the tasks. We set $k = 50$ as a default value.

Note that the task is very difficult and *cannot* be solved by dynamic programming algorithms since the weights on the edges are not revealed to the algorithms or the models. To recover some of the shortest paths at the test time, the model needs to infer the correct path from the observed instances. For example, assume that we observe two instances in the training data, "$A \rightsquigarrow D$: $A \rightarrow B \rightarrow G \rightarrow D$" and "$B \rightsquigarrow E$: $B \rightarrow C \rightarrow E$". In order to answer the shortest path between A and E, the model needs to infer that "$A \rightarrow B \rightarrow C \rightarrow E$" is a possible path between A and E. If there are multiple possible paths, the model has to decide which one is the shortest one using statistical information.

In the experiments, we construct a graph with 500 nodes and we randomly assign two nodes to form an edge. We split 20,000 instances for training, 10,000 instances for validation, and 10,000 instances for testing. We create the training and testing instances carefully so that the model needs to perform inference to recover the correct path. We describe the details of the graph and data construction parts in the appendix section. A sub-graph of the data is shown in Figure 3.

For the settings of the IRN, we switch the output module to a GRU decoder for a sequence generation task. We assign reward $r_T = 1$ if all the prediction symbols are correct and 0 otherwise. We use a 64-dimensional embedding vector for input symbols, a GRU controller with 128 cells, and a GRU decoder with 128 cells. We set the maximum inference step $T_{\max}$ to 5.

We compare the IRN with two baseline approaches: dynamic programming without edge-weight information and a standard sequence-to-sequence model (Sutskever et al., 2014) using a similar parameter size to our model. Without knowing the edge weights, dynamic programming only recovers 589 correct paths at test time. The sequence-to-sequence model recovers 904 correct paths. The IRN outperforms both baselines, recovering 1,319 paths. Furthermore, 76.9% of the predicted paths from IRN are *valid* paths, where a path is valid if the path connects the start and end node nodes of the underlying graph. In contrast, only 69.1% of the predicted paths from the sequence-to-sequence model are valid.

To further understand the inference process of the IRN, Figure 3 shows the inference process of a test instance. Interestingly, to make the correct pre-

Table 6: An inference example of FB15k dataset. Given a head entity and a relation, the predictions of IRN in different steps associated with the corresponding termination probabilities.

Input: (Dean Koontz, /PEOPLE/PERSON/PROFESSION)
Target: Film Producer

Step	Termination Prob.	Answer Rank	Predict top-3 entities		
1	0.018	9	Author	TV. Director	Songwriter
2	0.052	7	Actor	Singer	Songwriter
3	0.095	4	Actor	Singer	Songwriter
4	0.132	4	Actor	Singer	Songwriter
5	0.702	3	Actor	Singer	**Film Producer**

Input: (War and Peace, /FILM/FILM/PRODUCED_BY)
Target: Carlo Ponti

Step	Termination Prob.	Answer Rank	Predict top-3 entities		
1	0.001	13	Scott Rudin	Stephen Woolley	Hal B. Wallis
2	5.8E-13	7	Billy Wilder	William Wyler	Elia Kazan
3	0.997	1	**Carlo Ponti**	King Vidor	Hal B. Wallis

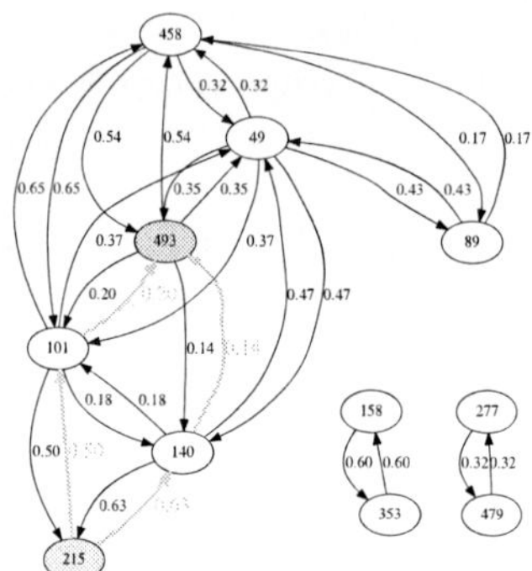

Step	Termination Probability	Distance	Predictions
1	0.001	N/A	$215 \rightarrow 158 \rightarrow 89 \rightarrow 458 \rightarrow 493$
2	~ 0	N/A	$215 \rightarrow 479 \rightarrow 277 \rightarrow 353 \rightarrow 493$
3	~ 0	N/A	$215 \rightarrow 49 \rightarrow 493$
4	~ 0	0.77	$215 \rightarrow 140 \rightarrow 493$
5	0.999	0.70	$215 \rightarrow 101 \rightarrow 493$

Figure 3: An example of the shortest path synthesis dataset, given an input "$215 \rightsquigarrow 493$" (Answer: $215 \rightarrow 101 \rightarrow 493$). Note that we only show the nodes that are related to this example here. The corresponding termination probability and prediction results are shown in the table. The model terminates at step 5.

diction on this instance, the model has to perform a fairly complicated inference.[†] We observe that the model cannot find a connected path in the first three steps. Finally, the model finds a valid path at the forth step and predict the correct shortest path sequence at the fifth step.

[†] In the example, to find the right path, the model needs to search over observed instances "$215 \rightsquigarrow 448: 215 \rightarrow 101 \rightarrow 448$" and "$76 \rightsquigarrow 493: 76 \rightarrow 308 \rightarrow 101 \rightarrow 493$", and to figure out the distance of "$140 \rightarrow 493$" is longer than "$101 \rightarrow 493$" (there are four shortest paths between $101 \rightarrow 493$ and three shortest paths between $140 \rightarrow 493$ in the training set).

Knowledge Base Completion: Baselines Strike Back

Rudolf Kadlec and **Ondrej Bajgar** and **Jan Kleindienst**
IBM Watson
V Parku 4, 140 00 Prague, Czech Republic
{rudolf_kadlec, obajgar, jankle}@cz.ibm.com

Abstract

Many papers have been published on the knowledge base completion task in the past few years. Most of these introduce novel architectures for relation learning that are evaluated on standard datasets such as FB15k and WN18. This paper shows that the accuracy of almost all models published on the FB15k can be outperformed by an appropriately tuned baseline — our reimplementation of the Dist-Mult model. Our findings cast doubt on the claim that the performance improvements of recent models are due to architectural changes as opposed to hyperparameter tuning or different training objectives. This should prompt future research to re-consider how the performance of models is evaluated and reported.

1 Introduction

Projects such as Wikidata[1] or earlier Freebase (Bollacker et al., 2008) have successfully accumulated a formidable amount of knowledge in the form of $\langle$entity1 - relation - entity2$\rangle$ triplets. Given this vast body of knowledge, it would be extremely useful to teach machines to reason over such knowledge bases. One possible way to test such reasoning is knowledge base completion (KBC).

The goal of the KBC task is to fill in the missing piece of information into an incomplete triple. For instance, given a query $\langle$Donald Trump, president of, ?$\rangle$ one should predict that the target entity is USA.

More formally, given a set of entities $\mathcal{E}$ and a set of binary relations $\mathcal{R}$ over these entities, a *knowledge base* (sometimes also referred to as a knowl-

edge *graph*) can be specified by a set of triplets $\langle h, r, t \rangle$ where $h, t \in \mathcal{E}$ are head and tail entities respectively and $r \in \mathcal{R}$ is a relation between them. In *entity* KBC the task is to predict either the tail entity given a query $\langle h, r, ? \rangle$, or to predict the head entity given $\langle ?, r, t \rangle$.

Not only can this task be useful to test the generic ability of a system to reason over a knowledge base, but it can also find use in expanding existing incomplete knowledge bases by deducing new entries from existing ones.

An extensive amount of work has been published on this task (for a review see (Nickel et al., 2015; Nguyen, 2017), for a plain list of citations see Table 2). Among those DistMult (Yang et al., 2015) is one of the simplest.[2] Still this paper shows that even a simple model with proper hyperparameters and training objective evaluated using the standard metric of Hits@10 can outperform 27 out of 29 models which were evaluated on two standard KBC datasets, WN18 and FB15k (Bordes et al., 2013).

This suggests that there may be a huge space for improvement in hyper-parameter tuning even for the more complex models, which may be in many ways better suited for relational learning, e.g. can capture directed relations.

2 The Model

Inspired by the success of word embeddings in natural language processing, distributional models for KBC have recently been extensively studied. Distributional models represent the entities and sometimes even the relations as N-dimensional real vectors[3], we will denote these vectors by bold font, $\mathbf{h}, \mathbf{r}, \mathbf{t} \in \mathbb{R}^N$.

---

[1]https://www.wikidata.org/

[2]We could even say too simple given that it assumes symmetry of all relations which is clearly unrealistic.

[3]Some models represent relations as matrices instead.

Proceedings of the 2nd Workshop on Representation Learning for NLP, pages 69–74,
Vancouver, Canada, August 3, 2017. ©2017 Association for Computational Linguistics

The DistMult model was introduced by Yang et al. (2015). Subsequently Toutanova and Chen (2015) achieved better empirical results with the same model by changing hyper-parameters of the training procedure and by using negative-log likelihood of softmax instead of L1-based max-margin ranking loss. Trouillon et al. (2016) obtained even better empirical result on the FB15k dataset just by changing DistMult's hyper-parameters.

DistMult model computes a score for each triplet $\langle \mathbf{h}, \mathbf{r}, \mathbf{t} \rangle$ as

$$s(\mathbf{h}, \mathbf{r}, \mathbf{t}) = \mathbf{h}^T \cdot W_{\mathbf{r}} \cdot \mathbf{t} = \sum_{i=1}^{N} h_i r_i t_i$$

where $W_{\mathbf{r}}$ is a diagonal matrix with elements of vector $\mathbf{r}$ on its diagonal. Therefore the model can be alternatively rewritten as shown in the second equality.

In the end our implementation normalizes the scores by a softmax function. That is

$$P(t|h, r) = \frac{exp(s(h, r, t))}{\sum_{\bar{t} \in \mathcal{E}_{h,r}} exp(s(h, r, \bar{t}))}$$

where $\mathcal{E}_{h,r}$ is a set of candidate answer entities for the $\langle h, r, ? \rangle$ query.

3 Experiments

Datasets. In our experiments we use two standard datasets WN18 derived from WordNet (Fellbaum, 1998) and FB15k derived from the Freebase knowledge graph (Bollacker et al., 2008).

Method. For evaluation, we use the *filtered* evaluation protocol proposed by Bordes et al. (2013). During training and validation we transform each triplet $\langle h, r, t \rangle$ into two examples: tail query $\langle h, r, ? \rangle$ and head query $\langle ?, r, t \rangle$. We train the model by minimizing negative log-likelihood (NLL) of the ground truth triplet $\langle h, r, t \rangle$ against randomly sampled pool of M negative triplets $\langle h, r, t' \rangle, t' \in \mathcal{E} \setminus \{t\}$ (this applies for tail queries, head queries are handled analogically).

In the filtered protocol we rank the validation or test set triplet against all corrupted (supposedly untrue) triplets – those that do not appear in the train, valid and test dataset (excluding the test set triplet in question itself). Formally, for a query $\langle h, r, ? \rangle$ where the correct answer is t, we compute the rank of $\langle h, r, t \rangle$ in a candidate set $C_{h,r} = \{\langle h, r, t' \rangle : \forall t' \in \mathcal{E}\} \setminus (Train \cup Valid \cup Test) \cup \{\langle h, r, t \rangle\}$, where $Train$, $Valid$ and $Test$ are sets of true triplets. Head queries $\langle ?, r, t \rangle$ are handled analogically. Note that softmax normalization is suitable under the filtered protocol since exactly one correct triplet is guaranteed to be among the candidates.

In our preliminary experiments on FB15k, we varied the batch size b, embedding dimensionality N, number of negative samples in training M, L2 regularization parameter and learning rate lr. Based on these experiments we fixed lr=0.001, L2=0.0 and we decided to focus on influence of batch size, embedding dimension and number of negative samples. For final experiments we trained several models from hyperparameter range: $N \in \{128, 256, 512, 1024\}$, $b \in \{16, 32, 64, 128, 256, 512, 1024, 2048\}$ and $M \in \{20, 50, 200, 500, 1000, 2000\}$.

We train the final models using Adam (Kingma and Ba, 2015) optimizer ($lr = 0.001, \beta_1 = 0.9, \beta_2 = 0.999, \epsilon = 10^{-8}, decay = 0.0$). We also performed limited experiments with Adagrad, Adadelta and plain SGD. Adagrad usually required substantially more iterations than ADAM to achieve the same performance. We failed to obtain competitive performance with Adadelta and plain SGD. On FB15k and WN18 validation datasets the best hyper-parameter combinations were $N = 512, b = 2048, M = 2000$ and $N = 256, b = 1024, M = 1000$, respectively. Note that we tried substantially more hyperparameter combinations on FB15k than on WN18. Unlike most previous works we do not normalize neither entity nor relation embeddings.

To prevent over-fitting, we stop training once Hits@10 stop improving on the validation set. On the FB15k dataset our Keras (Chollet, 2015) based implementation with TensorFlow (Abadi et al., 2015) backend needed about 4 hours to converge when run on a single GeForce GTX 1080 GPU.

Results. Besides single models, we also evaluated performance of a simple ensemble that averages predictions of multiple models. This technique consistently improves performance of machine learning models in many domains and it slightly improved results also in this case.

The results of our experiments together with previous results from the literature are shown in Table 2. DistMult with proper hyperparameters twice achieves the second best score and once the third best score in three out of four commonly reported benchmarks (mean rank (MR) and

Hits@10 on WN18 and FB15k). On FB15k only the IRN model (Shen et al., 2016) shows better Hits@10 and the ProjE (Shi and Weniger, 2017) has better MR.

Our implementation has the best reported mean reciprocal rank (MRR) on FB15k, however this metric is not reported that often. MRR is a metric of ranking quality that is less sensitive to outliers than MR.

On WN18 dataset again the IRN model together with R-GCN+ shows better Hits@10. However, in MR and MRR DistMult performs poorly. Even though DistMult's inability to model asymmetric relations still allows it to achieve competitive results in Hits@10 the other metrics clearly show its limitations. These results highlight qualitative differences between FB15k and WN18 datasets.

Interestingly on FB15k recently published models (including our baseline) that use only **r** and **h** or **t** as their input outperform models that utilize richer features such as text or knowledge base path information. This shows a possible gap for future improvement.

Table 1 shows accuracy (Hits@1) of several models that reported this metric. On WN18 our implementation performs worse than HolE and ComplEx models (that are equivalent as shown by Hayashi and Shimbo (2017)). On FB15k our implementation outperforms all other models.

3.1 Hyper-parameter influence on FB15k

In our experiments on FB15k we found that increasing the number of negative examples M had a positive effect on performance.

Another interesting observation is that batch size has a strong influence on final performance. Larger batch size always lead to better results, for instance Hits@10 improved by 14.2% absolute when the batch size was increased from 16 to 2048. See Figure 1 for details.

Compared to previous works that trained DistMult on these datasets (for results see bottom of Table 2) we use different training objective than Yang et al. (2015) and Trouillon et al. (2017) that optimized max margin objective and NLL of softplus activation function ($softplus(x) = ln(1 + e^x)$), respectively. Similarly to Toutanova and Chen (2015) we use NLL of softmax function, however we use ADAM optimizer instead of RProp (Riedmiller and Braun, 1993).

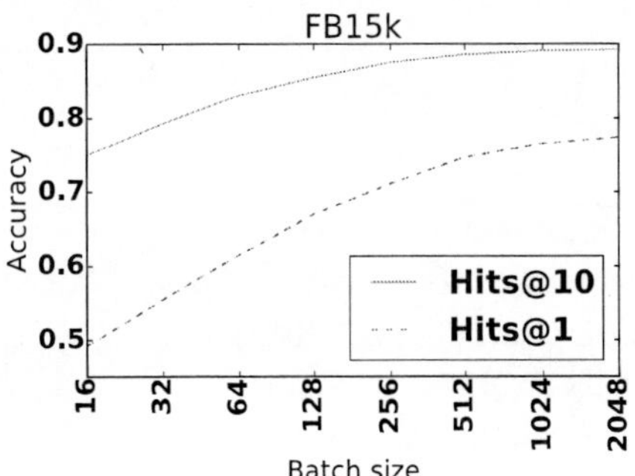

Figure 1: Influence of batch size on Hits@10 and Hits@1 metrics for a single model with $N = 512$ and $M = 2000$.

Method	Accuracy(Hits@1)	
	WN18	FB15k
HolE [†]	93.0	40.2
DistMult [‡]	72.8	54.6
ComplEx [‡]	**93.6**	59.9
R-GCN+ [♯]	67.9	60.1
DistMult ensemble	78.4	**79.7**

Table 1: Accuracy (Hits@1) results sorted by performance on FB15k. Results marked by [†], [‡] and [♯] are from (Nickel et al., 2016), (Trouillon et al., 2017) and (Schlichtkrull et al., 2017), respectively. Our implementation is listed in the last row.

4 Conclusion

Simple conclusions from our work are: 1) Increasing batch size dramatically improves performance of DistMult, which raises a question whether other models would also significantly benefit from similar hyper-parameter tuning or different training objectives; 2) In the future it might be better to focus more on metrics less frequently used in this domain, like Hits@1 (accuracy) and MRR since for instance on WN18 many models achieve similar, very high Hits@10, however even models that are competitive in Hits@10 underperform in Hits@1, which is the case of our DistMult implementation.

A lot of research focus has recently been centred on the filtered scenario which is why we decided to use it in this study. An advantage is that it is easy to evaluate. However the scenario trains the model to expect that there is only a single correct answer among the candidates which is unrealistic in the context of knowledge bases. Hence

Method	Filtered						Extra features
	WN18			**FB15k**			
	MR	H10	MRR	MR	H10	MRR	
SE (Bordes et al., 2011)	985	80.5	-	162	39.8	-	None
Unstructured (Bordes et al., 2014)	304	38.2	-	979	6.3	-	
TransE (Bordes et al., 2013)	251	89.2	-	125	47.1	-	
TransH (Wang et al., 2014)	303	86.7	-	87	64.4	-	
TransR (Lin et al., 2015b)	225	92.0	-	77	68.7	-	
CTransR (Lin et al., 2015b)	218	92.3	-	75	70.2	-	
KG2E (He et al., 2015)	331	92.8	-	59	74.0	-	
TransD (Ji et al., 2015)	212	92.2	-	91	77.3	-	
lppTransD (Yoon et al., 2016)	270	94.3	-	78	78.7	-	
TranSparse (Ji et al., 2016)	211	93.2	-	82	79.5	-	
TATEC (Garcia-Duran et al., 2016)	-	-	-	58	76.7	-	
NTN (Socher et al., 2013)	-	66.1	0.53	-	41.4	0.25	
HolE (Nickel et al., 2016)	-	94.9	**0.938**	-	73.9	0.524	
STransE (Nguyen et al., 2016)	**206**	93.4	0.657	69	79.7	0.543	
ComplEx (Trouillon et al., 2017)	-	94.7	<u>**0.941**</u>	-	84.0	0.692	
ProjE wlistwise (Shi and Weniger, 2017)	-	-	-	<u>**34**</u>	88.4	-	
IRN (Shen et al., 2016)	249	**95.3**	-	**38**	<u>**92.7**</u>	-	
RTransE (García-Durán et al., 2015)	-	-	-	50	76.2	-	Path
PTransE (Lin et al., 2015a)	-	-	-	58	84.6	-	
GAKE (Jun Feng and Zhu, 2015)	-	-	-	119	64.8	-	
Gaifman (Niepert, 2016)	352	93.9	-	75	84.2	-	
Hiri (Liu et al., 2016)	-	90.8	0.691	-	70.3	0.603	
R-GCN+ (Schlichtkrull et al., 2017)	-	**96.4**	0.819	-	84.2	0.696	
NLFeat (Toutanova and Chen, 2015)	-	94.3	**0.940**	-	87.0	**0.822**	Text
TEKE_H (Wang and Li, 2016)	<u>**114**</u>	92.9	-	108	73.0	-	
SSP (Xiao et al., 2017)	**156**	93.2	-	82	79.0	-	
DistMult (orig) (Yang et al., 2015)	-	94.2	0.83	-	57.7	0.35	None
DistMult (Toutanova and Chen, 2015)	-	-	-	-	79.7	0.555	
DistMult (Trouillon et al., 2017)	-	93.6	0.822	-	82.4	0.654	
Single DistMult (this work)	655	94.6	0.797	42.2	**89.3**	0.798	
Ensemble DistMult (this work)	457	**95.0**	0.790	**35.9**	90.4	<u>**0.837**</u>	

Table 2: Entity prediction results. MR, H10 and MRR denote evaluation metrics of mean rank, Hits@10 (in %) and mean reciprocal rank, respectively. The three best results for each metric are in bold. Additionally the best result is underlined. The first group (above the first double line) lists models that were trained only on the knowledge base and they do not use any additional input besides the source entity and the relation. The second group shows models that use path information, e.g. they consider paths between source and target entities as additional features. The models from the third group were trained with additional textual data. In the last group we list various implementations of the DistMult model including our implementation on the last two lines. Since DistMult does not use any additional features these results should be compared to the models from the first group. "NLFeat" abbreviates Node+LinkFeat model from (Toutanova and Chen, 2015). The results for NTN (Socher et al., 2013) listed in this table are taken from Yang et al. (2015). This table was adapted from (Nguyen, 2017).

future research could focus more on the *raw* scenario which however requires using other information retrieval metrics such as *mean average precision* (MAP), previously used in KBC for instance by Das et al. (2017).

We see this preliminary work as a small contribution to the ongoing discussion in the machine learning community about the current strong focus on state-of-the-art empirical results when it might be sometimes questionable whether they were achieved due to a better model/algorithm or just by more extensive hyper-parameter search. For broader discussion see (Church, 2017).

In light of these results we think that the field would benefit from a large-scale empirical comparative study of different KBC algorithms, similar to a recent study of word embedding models (Levy et al., 2015).

References

Martin Abadi, Ashish Agarwal, Paul Barham, Eugene Brevdo, Zhifeng Chen, Craig Citro, Greg Corrado, Andy Davis, Jeffrey Dean, Matthieu Devin, Sanjay Ghemawat, Ian Goodfellow, Andrew Harp, Geoffrey Irving, Michael Isard, Yangqing Jia, Lukasz Kaiser, Manjunath Kudlur, Josh Levenberg, Dan Man, Rajat Monga, Sherry Moore, Derek Murray, Jon Shlens, Benoit Steiner, Ilya Sutskever, Paul Tucker, Vincent Vanhoucke, Vijay Vasudevan, Oriol Vinyals, Pete Warden, Martin Wicke, Yuan Yu, and Xiaoqiang Zheng. 2015. TensorFlow : Large-Scale Machine Learning on Heterogeneous Distributed Systems .

Kurt Bollacker, Colin Evans, Praveen Paritosh, Tim Sturge, and Jamie Taylor. 2008. Freebase: A collaboratively created graph database for structuring human knowledge. In *Proceedings of the 2008 ACM SIGMOD International Conference on Management of Data*. ACM, New York, NY, USA, SIGMOD '08, pages 1247–1250. https://doi.org/10.1145/1376616.1376746.

Antoine Bordes, Xavier Glorot, Jason Weston, and Yoshua Bengio. 2014. A semantic matching energy function for learning with multi-relational data. *Machine Learning* 94(2):233–259.

Antoine Bordes, Nicolas Usunier, Jason Weston, and Oksana Yakhnenko. 2013. Translating Embeddings for Modeling Multi-Relational Data. *NIPS* 26:2787–2795. https://doi.org/10.1007/s13398-014-0173-7.2.

Antoine Bordes, Jason Weston, Ronan Collobert, and Yoshua Bengio. 2011. Learning structured embeddings of knowledge bases. In *Conference on artificial intelligence*. EPFL-CONF-192344.

Francois Chollet. 2015. Keras https://github.com/fchollet/keras/.

Kenneth Ward Church. 2017. Emerging trends: I did it, I did it, I did it, but... *Natural Language Engineering* 23(03):473–480. https://doi.org/10.1017/S1351324917000067.

Rajarshi Das, Arvind Neelakantan, David Belanger, and Andrew Mccallum. 2017. Chains of Reasoning over Entities, Relations, and Text using Recurrent Neural Networks. *EACL* .

Christiane Fellbaum. 1998. *WordNet*. Wiley Online Library.

Alberto García-Durán, Antoine Bordes, and Nicolas Usunier. 2015. Composing Relationships with Translations. In *Conference on Empirical Methods in Natural Language Processing (EMNLP 2015)*. Lisbonne, Portugal, pages 286–290. https://doi.org/10.18653/v1/D15-1034.

Alberto Garcia-Duran, Antoine Bordes, Nicolas Usunier, and Yves Grandvalet. 2016. Combining Two And Three-Way Embeddings Models for Link Prediction in Knowledge Bases. *Journal of Artificial Intelligence Research* 55:715—-742. https://doi.org/10.1613/jair.5013.

Katsuhiko Hayashi and Masashi Shimbo. 2017. On the Equivalence of Holographic and Complex Embeddings for Link Prediction pages 1–8. http://arxiv.org/abs/1702.05563.

Shizhu He, Kang Liu, Guoliang Ji, and Jun Zhao. 2015. Learning to Represent Knowledge Graphs with Gaussian Embedding. *CIKM '15 Proceedings of the 24th ACM International on Conference on Information and Knowledge Management* pages 623–632. https://doi.org/10.1145/2806416.2806502.

Guoliang Ji, Shizhu He, Liheng Xu, Kang Liu, and Jun Zhao. 2015. Knowledge Graph Embedding via Dynamic Mapping Matrix. *Proceedings of the 53rd Annual Meeting of the Association for Computational Linguistics and the 7th International Joint Conference on Natural Language Processing (Volume 1: Long Papers)* pages 687–696. http://www.aclweb.org/anthology/P15-1067.

Guoliang Ji, Kang Liu, Shizhu He, and Jun Zhao. 2016. Knowledge Graph Completion with Adaptive Sparse Transfer Matrix. *Proceedings of the 30th Conference on Artificial Intelligence (AAAI 2016)* pages 985–991.

Minlie Huang Yang Yang Jun Feng and Xiaoyan Zhu. 2015. GAKE: Graph Aware Knowledge Emebdding. In *Proceedings of the 27th International Conference on Computational Linguistics (COLING'16)*. pages 641–651.

Diederik P. Kingma and Jimmy Lei Ba. 2015. Adam: a Method for Stochastic Optimization. *International Conference on Learning Representations* pages 1–13.

Omer Levy, Yoav Goldberg, and Ido Dagan. 2015. Improving Distributional Similarity with Lessons Learned from Word Embeddings. *Transactions of the Association for Computational Linguistics* 3:211–225. https://doi.org/10.1186/1472-6947-15-S2-S2.

Yankai Lin, Zhiyuan Liu, and Maosong Sun. 2015a. Modeling relation paths for representation learning of knowledge bases. *CoRR* abs/1506.00379. http://arxiv.org/abs/1506.00379.

Yankai Lin, Zhiyuan Liu, Maosong Sun, Yang Liu, and Xuan Zhu. 2015b. Learning Entity and Relation Embeddings for Knowledge Graph Completion. *Proceedings of the Twenty-Ninth AAAI Conference on Artificial Intelligence Learning* pages 2181–2187.

Qiao Liu, Liuyi Jiang, Minghao Han, Yao Liu, and Zhiguang Qin. 2016. Hierarchical random walk inference in knowledge graphs. In *Proceedings of the 39th International ACM SIGIR conference on Research and Development in Information Retrieval.* ACM, pages 445–454.

Dat Quoc Nguyen. 2017. An overview of embedding models of entities and relationships for knowledge base completion https://arxiv.org/pdf/1703.08098.pdf.

Dat Quoc Nguyen, Kairit Sirts, Lizhen Qu, and Mark Johnson. 2016. STransE: a novel embedding model of entities and relationships in knowledge bases. *Proceedings of the 2016 Conference of the North American Chapter of the Association for Computational Linguistics: Human Language Technologies* pages 460–466. https://doi.org/10.18653/v1/N16-1054.

Maximilian Nickel, Kevin Murphy, Volker Tresp, and Evgeniy Gabrilovich. 2015. A Review of Relational Machine Learning for Knowledge Graph. *Proceedings of the IEEE* (28):1–23. https://doi.org/10.1109/JPROC.2015.2483592.

Maximilian Nickel, Lorenzo Rosasco, and Tomaso Poggio. 2016. Holographic Embeddings of Knowledge Graphs. *AAAI* pages 1955–1961. http://arxiv.org/abs/1510.04935.

Mathias Niepert. 2016. Discriminative gaifman models. In *Advances in Neural Information Processing Systems.* pages 3405–3413.

Martin Riedmiller and Heinrich Braun. 1993. A direct adaptive method for faster backpropagation learning: The rprop algorithm. In *Neural Networks, 1993., IEEE International Conference on.* IEEE, pages 586–591.

Michael Schlichtkrull, Thomas N. Kipf, Peter Bloem, Rianne van den Berg, Ivan Titov, and Max Welling. 2017. Modeling Relational Data with Graph Convolutional Networks http://arxiv.org/abs/1703.06103.

Yelong Shen, Po-Sen Huang, Ming-Wei Chang, and Jianfeng Gao. 2016. Implicit reasonet: Modeling large-scale structured relationships with shared memory. *arXiv preprint arXiv:1611.04642* .

Baoxu Shi and Tim Weniger. 2017. ProjE : Embedding Projection for Knowledge Graph Completion. *AAAI* .

Richard Socher, Danqi Chen, Christopher D. Manning, and Andrew Y. Ng. 2013. Reasoning With Neural Tensor Networks for Knowledge Base Completion. *Proceedings of the Advances in Neural Information Processing Systems 26 (NIPS 2013)* .

Kristina Toutanova and Danqi Chen. 2015. Observed versus latent features for knowledge base and text inference. *Proceedings of the 3rd Workshop on Continuous Vector Space Models and their Compositionality* pages 57–66.

Théo Trouillon, Christopher R. Dance, Johannes Welbl, Sebastian Riedel, Éric Gaussier, and Guillaume Bouchard. 2017. Knowledge Graph Completion via Complex Tensor Factorization http://arxiv.org/abs/1702.06879.

Théo Trouillon, Johannes Welbl, Sebastian Riedel, Eric Gaussier, and Guillaume Bouchard. 2016. Complex Embeddings for Simple Link Prediction. *Proceedings of ICML* 48:2071–2080. http://arxiv.org/pdf/1606.06357v1.pdf.

Zhen Wang, Jianwen Zhang, Jianlin Feng, and Zheng Chen. 2014. Knowledge Graph Embedding by Translating on Hyperplanes. *AAAI Conference on Artificial Intelligence* pages 1112–1119.

Zhigang Wang and Juanzi Li. 2016. Text-enhanced representation learning for knowledge graph. In *Proceedings of the Twenty-Fifth International Joint Conference on Artificial Intelligence.* AAAI Press, pages 1293–1299.

Han Xiao, Minlie Huang, and Xiaoyan Zhu. 2017. Ssp: Semantic space projection for knowledge graph embedding with text descriptions. In *Pro- ceedings of the 31st AAAI Conference on Artificial In- telligence.*

Bishan Yang, Wen-tau Yih, Xiaodong He, Jianfeng Gao, and Li Deng. 2015. Embedding Entities and Relations for Learning and Inference in Knowledge Bases. *ICLR* page 12. http://arxiv.org/abs/1412.6575.

Hee-geun Yoon, Hyun-je Song, Seong-bae Park, and Se-young Park. 2016. A Translation-Based Knowledge Graph Embedding Preserving Logical Property of Relations. *Naacl* pages 1–9.

Sequential Attention:
A Context-Aware Alignment Function for Machine Reading

Sebastian Brarda[*]
Center for Data Science
New York University
sb5518@nyu.edu

Philip Yeres[*]
Center for Data Science
New York University
yeres@nyu.edu

Samuel R. Bowman
Center for Data Science
and Department of Linguistics
New York University
bowman@nyu.edu

Abstract

In this paper we propose a neural network model with a novel *Sequential Attention* layer that extends soft attention by assigning weights to words in an input sequence in a way that takes into account not just how well that word matches a query, but how well surrounding words match. We evaluate this approach on the task of reading comprehension (on the *Who did What* and *CNN* datasets) and show that it dramatically improves a strong baseline—the *Stanford Reader*—and is competitive with the state of the art.

1 Introduction

Soft attention (Bahdanau et al., 2014), a differentiable method for selecting the inputs for a component of a model from a set of possibilities, has been crucial to the success of artificial neural network models for natural language understanding tasks like reading comprehension that take short passages as inputs. However, standard approaches to attention in NLP select words with only very indirect consideration of their context, limiting their effectiveness. This paper presents a method to address this by adding explicit context sensitivity into the soft attention scoring function.

We demonstrate the effectiveness of this approach on the task of *cloze*-style reading comprehension. A problem in the cloze style consists of a passage p, a question q and an answer a drawn from among the entities mentioned in the passage. In particular, we use the *CNN* dataset (Hermann et al., 2015), which introduced the task into widespread use in evaluating neural networks for language understanding, and the newer and more

---

[*] These authors contributed equally to this work.

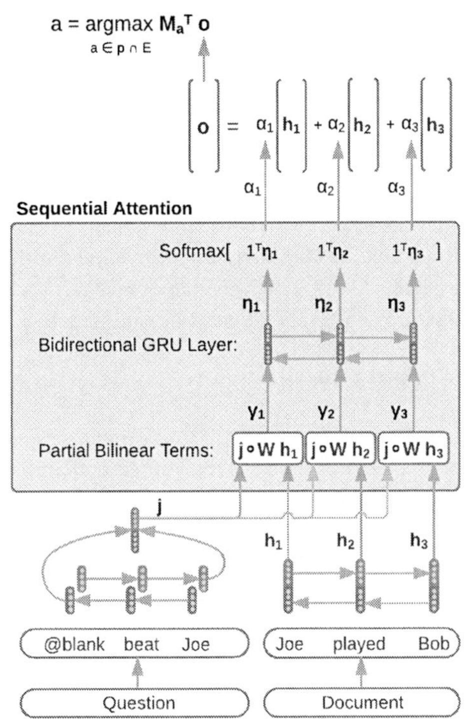

Figure 1: The Sequential Attention Model. RNNs first encode the question into a vector j and the document into a sequence of vectors H. For each word index i in the document, a scoring vector γ_i is then computed from j and h_i using a function like the partial bilinear function shown here. These vectors are then used as inputs to another RNN layer, the outputs of which (η_i) are summed elementwise and used as attention scores (α_i) in answer selection.

carefully quality-controlled *Who did What* dataset (Onishi et al., 2016).

In standard approaches to soft attention over passages, a *scoring function* is first applied to every word in the source text to evaluate how closely

75

Proceedings of the 2nd Workshop on Representation Learning for NLP, pages 75–80,
Vancouver, Canada, August 3, 2017. ©2017 Association for Computational Linguistics

that word matches a *query vector* (here, a function of the question). The resulting scores are then normalized and used as the weights in a weighted sum which produces an *output* or *context* vector summarizing the most salient words of the input, which is then used in a downstream model (here, to select an answer).

In this work we propose a novel scoring function for soft attention that we call *Sequential Attention* (SA), shown in Figure 1. In an SA model, a mutiplicative interaction scoring function is used to produce a scoring *vector* for each word in the source text. A newly-added bidirectional RNN then consumes those vectors and uses them to produce a context-aware scalar score for each word. We evaluate this scoring function within the context of the *Stanford Reader* (Chen et al., 2016), and show that it yields dramatic improvements in performance. On both datasets, it is outperformed only by the *Gated Attention Reader* (Dhingra et al., 2016), which in some cases has access to features not explicitly seen by our model.

2   Related Work

In addition to Chen et al. (2016)'s *Stanford Reader* model, there have been several other modeling approaches developed to address these reading comprehension tasks.

Seo et al. (2016) introduced the *Bi-Directional Attention Flow* which consists of a multi-stage hierarchical process to represent context at different levels of granularity; it use the concatenation of passage word representation, question word representation, and the element-wise product of these vectors in their attention flow layer. This is a more complex variant of the classic bi-linear term that multiplies this concatenated vector with a vector of weights, producing attention scalars. Dhingra et al. (2016)'s *Gated-Attention Reader* integrates a multi-hop structure with a novel attention mechanism, essentially building query specific representations of the tokens in the document to improve prediction. This model conducts a classic dot-product soft attention to weight the query representations which are then multiplied element-wise with the context representations, and fed into the next layer of RNN. After several hidden layers that repeat the same process, the dot product between the context representation and the query is used to compute a classic soft-attention.

Outside the task of reading comprehension there has been other work on soft attention over text, largely focusing on the problem of attending over single sentences. Luong et al. (2015) study several issues in the design of soft attention models in the context of translation, and introduce the bilinear scoring function. They also propose the idea of attention input-feeding where the original attention vectors are concatenated with the hidden representations of the words and fed into the next RNN step. The goal is to make the model fully aware of the previous alignment choices.

In work largely concurrent to our own, Kim et al. (2017) explore the use of conditional random fields (CRFs) to impose a variety of constraints on attention distributions achieving strong results on several sentence level tasks.

3   Modeling

Given the tuple (passage, question, answer), our goal is to predict $\Pr(a|d, q)$ where a refers to answer, d to passage, and q to question. We define the words of each passage and question as $d = d_1, .., d_m$ and $q = q_1, ..., q_l$, respectively, where exactly one q_i contains the token @*blank*, representing a blank that can be correctly filled in by the answer. With calibrated probabilities $\Pr(a|d, q)$, we take the $\operatorname{argmax}_a \Pr(a|d, q)$ where possible a's are restricted to the subset of anonymized entity symbols present in d. In this section, we present two models for this reading comprehension task: Chen et al. (2016)'s *Stanford Reader*, and our version with a novel attention mechanism which we call the *Sequential Attention* model.

3.1   Stanford Reader

Encoding Each word or entity symbol is mapped to a d-dimensional vector via embedding matrix $E \in \mathbb{R}^{d \times |V|}$. For simplicity, we denote the vectors of the passage and question as $d = d_1, .., d_m$ and $q = q_1, ..., q_l$, respectively. The *Stanford Reader* (Chen et al., 2016) uses bidirectional GRUs (Cho et al., 2014) to encode the passage and questions. For the passage, the hidden state is defined: $h_i = \operatorname{concat}(\overrightarrow{h_i}, \overleftarrow{h_i})$. Where contextual embeddings d_i of each word in the passage are encoded in both directions.

$$\overleftarrow{h_i} = \operatorname{GRU}(\overleftarrow{h_{i+1}}, d_i) \tag{1}$$

$$\overrightarrow{h_i} = \operatorname{GRU}(\overrightarrow{h_{i-1}}, d_i) \tag{2}$$

And for the question, the last hidden representation of each direction is concatenated:

$$j = \text{concat}(\overrightarrow{j_l}, \overleftarrow{j_1}) \tag{3}$$

Attention and answer selection The Stanford Reader uses bilinear attention (Luong et al., 2015):

$$\alpha_i = \text{softmax}_i(j \mathbf{W} h_i) \tag{4}$$

Where $\mathbf{W}$ is a learned parameters matrix of the bilinear term that computes the similarity between j and h_i with greater flexibility than a dot product. The output vector is then computed as a linear combination of the hidden representations of the passage, weighted by the attention coefficients:

$$o = \sum \alpha_i h_i \tag{5}$$

The prediction is the answer, a, with highest probability from among the anonymized entities:

$$a = \underset{a \in p \cap entities}{\text{argmax}} \; M_a^T o \tag{6}$$

Here, $\mathbf{M}$ is the weight matrix that maps the output to the entities, and M_a represents the column of a certain entity. Finally a softmax layer is added on top of $M_a^T o$ with a negative log-likelihood objective for training.

3.2   Sequential Attention

In the *Sequential Attention* model instead of producing a single scalar value α_i for each word in the passage by using a bilinear term, we define the vectors γ_i with a partial-bilinear term[1]. Instead of doing the dot product as in the bilinear term, we conduct an element wise multiplication to produce a vector instead of a scalar:

$$\gamma_i = j \circ \mathbf{W} h_i \tag{7}$$

Where $\mathbf{W}$ is a matrix of learned parameters. It is also possible to use an element-wise multiplication, thus prescinding the parameters $\mathbf{W}$:

$$\gamma_i = j \circ h_i \tag{8}$$

We then feed the γ_i vectors into a new bidirectional GRU layer to get the hidden attention η_i vector representation.

$$\overleftarrow{\eta_i} = \text{GRU}(\overleftarrow{\eta_{i+1}}, \gamma_i) \tag{9}$$

---

[1] Note that doing softmax over the sum of the terms of the γ_i vectors would lead to the same α_i of the Stanford Reader.

$$\overrightarrow{\eta_i} = \text{GRU}(\overrightarrow{\eta_{i-1}}, \gamma_i) \tag{10}$$

We concatenate the directional η vectors to be consistent with the structure of previous layers.

$$\eta_i = \text{concat}(\overrightarrow{\eta_i}, \overleftarrow{\eta_i}) \tag{11}$$

Finally, we compute the α weights as below, and proceed as before.

$$\alpha_i = \text{softmax}_i(1^\top \eta_i]) \tag{12}$$

$$o = \sum \alpha_i h_i \tag{13}$$

$$a = \underset{a \in p \cap entities}{\text{argmax}} \; M_a^T o \tag{14}$$

4   Experiments and Results

We evaluate our model on two tasks, *CNN* and Who did What (*WDW*). For CNN, we used the anonymized version of the dataset released by Hermann et al. (2015), containing 380,298 training, 3,924 dev, and 3,198 test examples. For *WDW* we used Onishi et al. (2016)'s data generation script to reproduce their *WDW* data, yielding 127,786 training, 10,000 dev, and 10,000 test examples.[2] We used the strict version of *WDW*.

Training We implemented all our models in Theano (Theano Development Team, 2016) and Lasagne (Dieleman et al., 2015) and used the Stanford Reader (Chen et al., 2016) open source implementation as a reference. We largely used the same hyperparameters as Chen et al. (2016) in the Stanford Reader: $|V| = 50K$, embedding size $d = 100$, *GloVe* (Pennington et al., 2014) word embeddings[3] for initialization, hidden size $h = 128$. The size of the hidden layer of the bidirectional RNN used to encode the attention vectors is double the size of the one that encodes the words, since it receives vectors that result from the concatenation of GRUs that go in both directions, $\eta \in \mathbb{R}^{256}$. Attention and output parameters were

---

[2] In the WDW data we found 340 examples in the strict training set, 545 examples in the relaxed training set, 20 examples in the test set, and 30 examples in the validation set that were not answerable because the anonymized answer entity did not exist in the passage. We removed these examples, reducing the size of the WDW test set by 0.2%, to 9,980. We believe this difference is not significant and did not bias the comparison between models.

[3] The GloVe word vectors used were pretrained with 6 billion tokens with an uncased vocab of 400K words, and were obtained from Wikipedia 2014 and Gigaword 5.

Model	WDW Strict	CNN
Attentive Reader	53%	63%
Stanford Reader	65.6%	73.4%
+ SA partial-bilinear	67.2%	77.1%
Gated Att. Reader	**71.2%**	**77.9%**

Table 1: Accuracy on *WDW* and CNN test sets

initialized from a $U \sim (-0.01, 0.01)$ while GRU weights were initialized from a $N \sim (0, 0.1)$. Learning was carried out with SGD with a learning rate of 0.1, batch size of 32, gradient clipping of norm 10 and dropout of 0.2 in all the vertical layers[4] (including the *Sequential Attention* layer). Also, all the anonymized entities were relabeled according to the order of occurrence, as in the *Stanford Reader*. We trained all models for 30 epochs.

4.1 Results

Who did What In our experiments the *Stanford Reader* (SR) achieved an accuracy of 65.6% on the strict *WDW* dataset compared to the 64% that Onishi et al. (2016) reported. The *Sequential Attention* model (SA) with partial-bilinear scoring function got 67.21%, which is the second best performance on the *WDW* leaderboard, only surpassed by the 71.2% from the *Gated Attention Reader* (GA) with *qe-comm* (Li et al., 2016) features and fixed GloVe embeddings. However, the GA model without *qe-comm* features and fixed embeddings performs significantly worse at 67%. We did not use these features in our SA models, and it is likely that adding these features could further improve SA model performance. We also experimented with fixed embeddings in SA models, but fixed embeddings reduced SA performance.

Another experiment we conducted was to add 100K training samples from *CNN* to the *WDW* data. This increase in the training data size boosted accuracy by 1.4% with the SR and 1.8% with the *Sequential Attention* model reaching a 69% accuracy. This improvement strongly suggests that the gap in performance/difficulty between the CNN and the *WDW* datasets is partially related to the difference in the training set sizes

---

[4]We also tried increasing the hidden size to 200, using 200d GloVe word representations and increasing the dropout rate to 0.3. Finally we increased the number of hidden encoding layers to two. None of these changes resulted in significant performance improvements in accordance with Chen et al. (2016).

which results in overfitting.

CNN For a final sanity check and a fair comparison against a well known benchmark, we ran our *Sequential Attention* model on exactly the same *CNN* data used by Chen et al. (2016).

The *Sequential Attention* model with partial-bilinear attention scoring function took an average of 2X more time per epoch to train vs. the *Stanford Reader*. However, our model converged in only 17 epochs vs. 30 for the *SR*. The results of training the *SR* on *CNN* were slightly lower than the 73.6% reported by Chen et al. (2016). The *Sequential Attention* model achieved 77.1% accuracy, a 3.7% gain with respect to *SR*.

4.1.1 Model comparison on CNN

After achieving good performance with *SA* we wanted to understand what was driving the increase in accuracy. It is clear that *SA* has more trainable parameters compared to *SR*. However, it was not clear if the additional computation required to learn those parameters should be allocated in the attention mechanism, or used to compute richer hidden representations of the passage and questions. Additionally, the bilinear parameters increase the computational requirements, but their impact on performance was not clear. To answer these questions we compared the following models: i) *SR* with dot-product attention; ii) *SR* with bilinear attention; iii) *SR* with two layers (to compute the hidden question and passage representations) and dot-product attention; iv) *SR* with two layers and bilinear attention; v) *SA* with elementwise multiplication scoring function; vi) *SA* with partial-bilinear scoring function.

Surprisingly, the element-wise version of *SA* performed better than the partial-bilinear version, with an accuracy of 77.3% which, to our knowledge, has only been surpassed by Dhingra et al. (2016) with their *Gated-Attention Reader* model.

Additionally, 1-layer *SR* with dot-product attention got 0.3% lower accuracy than the 1-layer *SR* with bilinear attention. These results suggest that the bilinear parameters do not significantly improve performance over dot-product attention.

Adding an additional GRU layer to encode the passage and question in the *SR* model increased performance over the original 1-layer model. With dot-product attention the increase was 1.1% whereas with bilinear attention, the increase was 1.3%. However, these performance in-

Question: Women 's 1,500 m world champion @entity4 headlines the track action at the Asian Games Tuesday as India 's @entity5 stunned top seed @placeholder to win the men 's tennis title . (**Correct Answer: @entity5**)	
Stanford Reader Context Attention (Prediction: @entity4): china 's @entity0 defeated uzbekistan 's @entity1 to win the asian games women 's singles gold on tuesday for her second title in guangzhou . @entity0 , who had linked up with compatriot @entity2 to win the women 's team event , claimed a 7-5 , 6-2 victory in front of a packed house at the tennis centre . india 's @entity3 had earlier won the men 's title with a straight sets triumph over another @entity4 , top seed @entity5 .	**Sequential Attention Context Attention: (Prediction @entity5)** china 's @entity0 defeated uzbekistan 's @entity1 to win the asian games women 's singles gold on tuesday for her second title in guangzhou . @entity0 , who had linked up with compatriot @entity2 to win the women 's team event , claimed a 7-5 , 6-2 victory in front of a packed house at the tennis centre . india 's @entity3 had earlier won the men 's title with a straight sets triumph over another @entity4 , top seed @entity5 .

Figure 2: Representative sample output for the Stanford Reader and our model.

Model	CNN	Params
SR, dot prod. att.	73.1%	5.44×10^6
SR, bilinear att.	73.4%	5.50×10^6
SR, 2-layer, dot prod. att.	74.2%	5.83×10^6
SR, 2-layer, bilinear att.	74.7%	5.90×10^6
SA, element-wise att.	77.3%	5.73×10^6
SA, partial-bilinear att.	77.1%	5.80×10^6

Table 2: Accuracy on CNN test sets and number of trainable parameters for various Stanford Reader (SR) and Sequential Attention (SA) models.

creases were considerably less than the lift from using an *SA* model (and SA has fewer parameters).

4.2 Discussion

The difference between our *Sequential Attention* and standard approaches to attention is that we conserve the distributed representation of similarity for each token and use that contextual information when computing attention over other words. In other words, when the bilinear attention layer computes $\alpha_i = \text{softmax}_i(\boldsymbol{j}\mathbf{W}\boldsymbol{h_i})$, it only cares about the magnitude of the resulting α_i (the amount of attention that it gives to that word). Whereas if we keep the vector $\boldsymbol{\gamma_i}$ we can also know which were the dimensions of the distributed representation of the attention that weighted in that decision. Furthermore, if we use that information to feed a new GRU, it helps the model to learn how to assign attention to surrounding words.

Compared to *Sequential Attention*, *Bidirectional attention flow* uses a considerably more complex architecture with a query representations for each word in the question. Unlike the *Gated Attention Reader*, SA does not require intermediate soft attention and it uses only one additional RNN layer. Furthermore, in SA no dot product is required to compute attention, only the sum of the

elements of the η vector. SA's simpler architecture performs close to the state-of-the-art.

Figure 2 shows some sample model behavior. In this example and elsewhere, *SA* results in less sparse attention vectors compared to *SR*, and this helps the model assign attention not only to potential target strings (anonymized entities) but also to relevant contextual words that are related to those entities. This ultimately leads to richer semantic representations $o = \sum \alpha_i \boldsymbol{h_i}$ of the passage.

Finally, we found: i) bilinear attention does not yield dramatically higher performance compared to dot-product attention; ii) bilinear parameters do not improve SA performance; iii) Increasing the number of layers in the attention mechanism yields considerably greater performance gains with fewer parameters compared to increasing the number of layers used to compute the hidden representations of the question and passage.

5 Conclusion and Discussion

In this this paper we created a novel and simple model with a *Sequential Attention* mechanism that performs near the state of the art on the *CNN* and *WDW* datasets by improving the bilinear and dot-product attention mechanisms with an additional bi-directional RNN layer. This additional layer allows local alignment information to be used when computing the attentional score for each token. Furthermore, it provides higher performance gains with fewer parameters compared to adding an additional layer to compute the question and passage hidden representations. For future work we would like to try other machine reading datasets such as *SQuAD* and *MS MARCO*. Also, we think that some elements of the *SA* model could be mixed with ideas applied in recent research from Dhingra et al. (2016) and Seo et al. (2016). We believe that the *SA* mechanism may benefit other tasks as well, such as machine translation.

Acknowledgements

This paper was the result of a term project for the NYU Course DS-GA 3001, Natural Language Understanding with Distributed Representations. Bowman acknowledges support from a Google Faculty Research Award and gifts from Tencent Holdings and the NVIDIA Corporation.

References

Dzmitry Bahdanau, Kyunghyun Cho, and Yoshua Bengio. 2014. Neural machine translation by jointly learning to align and translate. *CoRR* abs/1409.0473. http://arxiv.org/abs/1409.0473.

Danqi Chen, Jason Bolton, and Christopher D. Manning. 2016. A thorough examination of the cnn/daily mail reading comprehension task. *CoRR* abs/1606.02858. http://arxiv.org/abs/1606.02858.

Kyunghyun Cho, Bart van Merrienboer, Çaglar Gülçehre, Fethi Bougares, Holger Schwenk, and Yoshua Bengio. 2014. Learning phrase representations using RNN encoder-decoder for statistical machine translation. *CoRR* abs/1406.1078. http://arxiv.org/abs/1406.1078.

Bhuwan Dhingra, Hanxiao Liu, William W. Cohen, and Ruslan Salakhutdinov. 2016. Gated-attention readers for text comprehension. *CoRR* abs/1606.01549. http://arxiv.org/abs/1606.01549.

Sander Dieleman, Jan Schlter, Colin Raffel, Eben Olson, Sren Kaae Snderby, Daniel Nouri, Daniel Maturana, Martin Thoma, Eric Battenberg, Jack Kelly, Jeffrey De Fauw, Michael Heilman, Diogo Moitinho de Almeida, Brian McFee, Hendrik Weideman, Gbor Takcs, Peter de Rivaz, Jon Crall, Gregory Sanders, Kashif Rasul, Cong Liu, Geoffrey French, and Jonas Degrave. 2015. Lasagne: First release. https://doi.org/10.5281/zenodo.27878.

Karl Moritz Hermann, Tomás Kociský, Edward Grefenstette, Lasse Espeholt, Will Kay, Mustafa Suleyman, and Phil Blunsom. 2015. Teaching machines to read and comprehend. *CoRR* abs/1506.03340. http://arxiv.org/abs/1506.03340.

Yoon Kim, Carl Denton, Luong Hoang, and Alexander M. Rush. 2017. Structured attention networks. *CoRR* abs/1702.00887. http://arxiv.org/abs/1702.00887.

Peng Li, Wei Li, Zhengyan He, Xuguang Wang, Ying Cao, Jie Zhou, and Wei Xu. 2016. Dataset and neural recurrent sequence labeling model for open-domain factoid question answering. *CoRR* abs/1607.06275. http://arxiv.org/abs/1607.06275.

Minh-Thang Luong, Hieu Pham, and Christopher D. Manning. 2015. Effective approaches to attention-based neural machine translation. *CoRR* abs/1508.04025. http://arxiv.org/abs/1508.04025.

Takeshi Onishi, Hai Wang, Mohit Bansal, Kevin Gimpel, and David A. McAllester. 2016. Who did what: A large-scale person-centered cloze dataset. *CoRR* abs/1608.05457. http://arxiv.org/abs/1608.05457.

Jeffrey Pennington, Richard Socher, and Christopher D. Manning. 2014. Glove: Global vectors for word representation. In *Empirical Methods in Natural Language Processing (EMNLP)*. pages 1532–1543. http://www.aclweb.org/anthology/D14-1162.

Min Joon Seo, Aniruddha Kembhavi, Ali Farhadi, and Hannaneh Hajishirzi. 2016. Bidirectional attention flow for machine comprehension. *CoRR* abs/1611.01603. http://arxiv.org/abs/1611.01603.

Theano Development Team. 2016. Theano: A python framework for fast computation of mathematical expressions. *CoRR* abs/1605.02688. http://arxiv.org/abs/1605.02688.

Semantic Vector Encoding and Similarity Search
Using Fulltext Search Engines

Jan Rygl and **Jan Pomikálek** and
Radim Řehůřek
RaRe Technologies
jimmy@rare-technologies.com
honza@rare-technologies.com
radim@rare-technologies.com

Michal Růžička and **Vít Novotný** and
Petr Sojka
Faculty of Informatics, Masaryk University
Botanická 68a, 602 00 Brno, Czechia
mruzicka@mail.muni.cz,
witiko@mail.muni.cz,
sojka@fi.muni.cz
ORCID: 0000-0001-5547-8720,
0000-0002-3303-4130, 0000-0002-5768-4007

Abstract

Vector representations and vector space modeling (VSM) play a central role in modern machine learning. We propose a novel approach to 'vector similarity searching' over dense semantic representations of words and documents that can be deployed on top of traditional inverted-index-based fulltext engines, taking advantage of their robustness, stability, scalability and ubiquity. We show that this approach allows the indexing and querying of dense vectors in text domains. This opens up exciting avenues for major efficiency gains, along with simpler deployment, scaling and monitoring. The end result is a fast and scalable vector database with a tunable trade-off between vector search performance and quality, backed by a standard fulltext engine such as Elasticsearch. We empirically demonstrate its querying performance and quality by applying this solution to the task of semantic searching over a dense vector representation of the entire English Wikipedia.

1 Introduction

The vector space model (Salton et al., 1975) of representing documents in high-dimensional vector spaces has been validated by decades of research and development. Extensive deployment of inverted-index-based information retrieval (IR) systems has led to the availability of robust open source IR systems such as Sphinx, Lucene or its popular, horizontally scalable extensions of Elasticsearch and Solr.

Representations of document semantics based solely on first order document-term statistics, such as TF-IDF or Okapi BM25, are limited in their expressiveness and search recall. Today, approaches based on distributional semantics and deep learning allow the construction of semantic vector space models representing words, sentences, paragraphs or even whole documents as vectors in high-dimensional spaces (Deerwester et al., 1990; Blei et al., 2003; Mikolov et al., 2013).

The ubiquity of semantic vector space modeling raises the challenge of efficient searching in these dense, high-dimensional vector spaces. We would naturally want to take advantage of the design and optimizations behind modern fulltext engines like Elasticsearch so as to meet the scalability and robustness demands of modern IR applications. This is the research challenge addressed in this paper.

The rest of the paper describes novel ways of encoding dense vectors into text documents, allowing the use of traditional inverted index engines, and explores the trade-offs between IR accuracy and speed. Being motivated by pragmatic needs, we describe the results of experiments carried out on real datasets measured on concrete, practical software implementations.

2 Semantic Vector Encoding
for Inverted-Index Search Engines

2.1 Related Work

The standard representation of documents in the Vector Space Model (VSM) (Salton and Buckley, 1988) uses term feature vectors of very high dimensionality. To map the feature space onto a smaller and denser latent semantic subspace, we may use a body of techniques, including Latent Semantic Analysis (LSA) (Deerwester et al., 1990), Latent Dirichlet Allocation (LDA) (Blei et al., 2003) or the many variants of Locality-sensitive hashing (LSH) (Gionis et al., 1999).

Throughout the long history of VSM developments, many other methods for improving search

Proceedings of the 2nd Workshop on Representation Learning for NLP, pages 81–90,
Vancouver, Canada, August 3, 2017. ©2017 Association for Computational Linguistics

efficiency have been explored. Weber et al. ran one of the first rigorous studies that dealt with the ineffectiveness of the VSM and the so-called curse of dimensionality. They evaluated several data partitioning and vector approximation schemes, achieving significant nearest-neighbour search speedup in (Weber and Böhm, 2000). The scalability of similarity searching through a new index data structures design is described in (Zezula et al., 2006). Dimensionality reduction techniques proposed in (Digout et al., 2004) allow a robust speedup while showing that not all features are equally discriminative and have a different impact on efficiency, due to their density distribution. Boytsov shows that the k-NN search can be a replacement for term-based retrieval when the term-document similarity matrix is dense.

Recently, deep learning approaches and tools like doc2vec (Le and Mikolov, 2014) construct *semantic* representations of documents D as $d = |D|$ (dense) vectors in an n-dimensional vector space.

To take advantage of ready-to-use and optimized systems for term indexing and searching, we have developed a method for representing points in a semantic vector space encoded as plain text strings. In our experiments, we will be using Elasticsearch (Gormley and Tong, 2015) in its 'vanilla' setup. We do not utilize any advanced features of Elasticsearch, such as custom scoring, tokenization or a n-gram analyzers. Thus, our method does not depend on any functionality that is specific to Elasticsearch, and it is possible (and sometimes even desirable) to substitute Elasticsearch with other fulltext engine implementations.

2.2 Our Vector to String Encoding Method

Let our query be a document, represented by its vector $\vec{q}$, for which we aim to find the top k most similar documents in D. We want to search efficiently, indexing and deleting documents from the index in near-real-time, and in a manner that could scale by eventual parallelization, re-using the significant research and engineering effort that went into designing and implementing systems like Elasticsearch.

Conceptually, our method consists of encoding vector features into string tokens (feature tokens), creating a text document from each dense vector. These encoded documents are consequently indexed in traditional inverted-index-based search engines. At query time, we encode the query vector and retrieve the subset of similar vectors E, $|E| \ll |D|$, using the engine's fulltext search functionality. Finally, the small set of candidate vectors E is re-ranked by calculating the exact similarity metric (such as cosine similarity) to the query vector. This makes the search effectively a *two-phase process*, with our encoded fulltext search as the first phase and candidate re-ranking as the second.

2.2.1 Encoding Vectors

The core of our method of encoding vectors into strings lies in encoding the vector feature values at a *selected precision* as character strings – feature tokens.[1] This is best demonstrated on a small example: Let us take a semantic vector of three dimensions, $\vec{w} = [0.12, -0.13, 0.065]$. Each feature token starts with its feature identification (e.g. a feature number such as 0, 1 etc.) followed by a precision encoding schema identifier (such as P2, I10 etc.) and the encoded feature value (such as i0d12, ineg0d2 etc.) depending on the particular encoding method. We propose and evaluate three encoding methods:

rounding Feature values are rounded to a fixed number of decimal positions and stored as a string that encodes both the feature identification and its value. Rounding to two decimal places produces representation of $\vec{w}$ as ['0P2i0d12', '1P2ineg0d13', '2P2i0d07'].

interval quantizes $\vec{w}$ into intervals of fixed length. For example, with an interval width of 0.1, feature values fall into intervals starting at 0.1, −0.2 and 0.0, which we encode as d1, d2 and d0, respectively. Combined with the interval length denotation of I10, the full vector is encoded into the tokens $\vec{w}$ = ['0I10i0d1', '1I10ineg0d2', '2I10i0d0'].

combined Rounding and interval encoding used together. Rounding $\vec{w}$ to three decimal places and using intervals of length 0.2, we get the representation of $\vec{w}$ as feature tokens ['0P3i0d120', '1P3ineg0d130', '2P3i0d065', '0I5i0d0', '1I5ineg0d2', '2I5i0d0'].

---

[1] We avoid the use of any special characters such as plus (+) or minus (−) signs, white spaces etc. inside the tokens. This is used as a safeguard against any unintended tokenization within the fulltext search system, so as to avoid having to define custom tokenizers.

The intuition behind all these encoding schemes is a trade-off between *increasing feature sparsity* and *retaining search quality*: we show that some types of sparsification actually lead to little loss of quality, allowing an efficient use of inverted-index IR engines.

2.2.2 High-Pass Filtering Techniques

The rationale behind the next two techniques is to filter out semantic vector features of low importance, further increasing feature sparsity. This improves performance at the expense of quality.

Trim: In the trimming phase, a fixed threshold – such as 0.1 – is used. Feature tokens in the query with an absolute value of the feature below the threshold are simply discarded from the query. In the case of our example vector $\vec{w} = [0.12, -0.13, 0.065]$, the tokens representing the third feature value 0.065 are removed since $|0.065| < 0.1$.

Best: Features of each vector are ordered according to their absolute value and only a fixed number of the highest-valued features are added to the index, discarding the rest. As an example, with $best = 1$, only the second feature of -0.13 (the highest absolute value) would be considered from $\vec{w}$.

Note that in both cases, this type of filtering is only meaningful when the feature ranges are comparable. In our experiments all vectors are normalized to unit length, ranging absolute values of features from zero (no feature importance) to one (maximal feature importance).

2.3 Space and Time Requirements

In this section we summarize and compare the theoretical space and time requirements of our proposed vector-to-string encoding and filtering methods with a baseline of a naive, linear brute force search. The inverted-index-based analysis is based on the documentation of the Lucene search engine implementation[2].

While the running time of the naive search is stable and predictable, the efficiency of the other optimization methods depends on the data set, such as its vocabulary size and the expected postings list sparsity, after the feature token encoding and filtering. On the other hand, performance can be influenced by how the method is configured – for

example, the expected number of distinct feature values depends on the precision of the rounding of the feature values that was used.

The efficiency trade-offs are summarized in Table 1. Each document is represented as a vector $\vec{d}$ of n features computed by LSA over TF-IDF.

Baseline – naive brute force search: The naive baseline method avoids using a fulltext search altogether, and instead stores all d 'indexed' vectors in their original dense vector representation in RAM, as an $n \times d$ matrix. At query time, it computes a similarity between the query vector $\vec{q}$ and each of the indexed document vectors $\vec{d}$, in a single linear scan through the matrix, and returns the top k vectors with the best score.

Efficiency of a naive brute force search: The index is a matrix of floats of size nd resulting in $O(nd)$ space complexity. We have chosen the cosine similarity as our similarity metric. To calculate cossim between the query and all d documents, vector $\vec{q}$ of length n has to be multiplied with a length-normalized matrix of dimensionality $n \times d$, e.g. $O(nd)$. Using the resulting vector of d scores, we then pick the k nearest documents as the final query result, in $O(d)$.

Efficiency of encoding: We investigate the efficiency of our vector-to-string encoding when a general inverted-index-based search engine is used to index and search through them.

At worst, we store one token per dimension for each vector. We need $O(nd)$ space to store all indexed documents, as is the case with the naive search. In practice, there are several different constants as naive search saves one float per feature (four bytes), while our feature tokens are compressed string-encoded feature values and indices of the sparse feature positions in the inverted index.

Each dimension of the query vector $\vec{q}$ contains a string-encoded feature q_j. For each q_j we fetch a list of documents c_i together with term frequency t_n in that document: $\mathrm{tf}(t_n, c_i)$.

For each of these $(c_i, \mathrm{tf}(t_n, c_i))$ pairs we add the corresponding score value to the score of document c_i in a list of result-candidate documents. The score computation contains a vector dot-product operation in the dimension of the size v of feature vocabulary V that can be computed in $O(v)$. Document c_i is added to the set C of all result-candidate documents, which we sort in $O(c \log c)$ time and return the top k results. The whole search is per-

---

[2]https://lucene.apache.org/core/6_5_1/index.html

formed in $O(n \cdot p \cdot v + c \log c)$ steps, where p is the expected postings list size and $c = |C|$.

Efficiency of high-pass filtering: We approximate the full feature vector by storing only the most significant features, e.g. only the top m dimensions. When compared with a naive search, we save on space: only $O(md)$, $m \ll n$ values are needed.

For each feature value q_j we have to find all documents with the same feature value. We are able to find the feature set in $O(\log j)$ steps, where j is the number of distinct indexed values of the feature. Consequently, we retrieve the matched documents in $O(l)$ time, where l is the number of documents in the index with the appropriate feature value.

Each of the found documents is added to set C and its score is incremented for this hit. If represented with an appropriate data structure, such as a hash table, we are able to add and increment scores of the items in $O(1)$ time. Having all $c = |C|$ candidate documents over all the separate feature-searches, we pick and return the top k items in $O(c)$ time.

Combined, $O(n \cdot (\log j + l) + c)$ steps are needed for the search, where j is the expected number of distinct indexed values per feature and l is the number of documents in the index per feature value.

3 Experimental Setup

To evaluate our method, we used ScaleText (Rygl et al., 2016) based on Elasticsearch (Gormley and Tong, 2015) as our fulltext IR system. The evaluation dataset was the whole of the English Wikipedia consisting of 4,181,352 articles.

3.1 Quality Evaluation

The aim of the quality evaluation was to investigate how well the approximate 'encoded vector' search performs in comparison with the exact naive brute-force search, using cosine similarity as the similarity metric. Cosine similarity is definitely not the only possible metric – we selected cosine similarity as we needed a fully automatic evaluation, without any need of human judgement, and because cosine similarity suits our upstream application logic perfectly.

We converted all Wikipedia documents into vectors using LSA with 400 features. We then randomly selected 1,000 documents from our Wikipedia dataset to act as our query vectors. By doing a naive brute force scan over all the vectors (the whole dataset), we identified the 10 most similar ones for each query vector. This became our 'gold standard'.

We encoded the dataset vectors into various string representations, as described in Section 2.2.1 and stored them in Elasticsearch.

For evaluating the search, we pruned the values in the query vectors (see Section 2.2.2) and encoded them into a string representation. Using these strings, we performed 1,000 Elasticsearch searches. For each query, we measured the overlap between the retrieved documents and the gold standard using Precision@k or the Normalized Discounted Cumulative Gain ($nDCG_k$). The mean cumulative loss between the ideal and the actual cosine similarities of the top k results (avg. diff.) is also reported.

Note that since we re-rank $|E|$ results obtained from Elasticsearch (see Section 2.2), the positions on which the gold standard vectors were originally returned by the fulltext engine are irrelevant.

Apart from the vector dimensionality n (the number of LSA **features**), we monitored the **trim** threshold and the number of **best** features as described in Section 2.2.2. We also experimented with the number of vectors E retrieved for each Elasticsearch query as the **page** parameter.

To provide a comparison with an established search approach, and to serve as a baseline, we also evaluated indexing and searching using the native fulltext indexing and searching capabilities of Elasticsearch. In this case, the plain fulltext of every article was sent directly to the fulltext search engine as a string, without any vector conversions or preprocessing. For querying, we use the *More Like This (MLT) Query* API of Elasticsearch.[3] Any data processing during indexing and querying was done by Elasticsearch in its default settings with a single exception: we evaluated multiple values of the `max_query_terms` parameter of the MLT API. We tested the default value (25) plus values corresponding to the values of the **best** parameter used for the evaluation of our method.

We report mainly on the *avg. diff.*, i.e. the mean difference between the ideal and the actual cosine similarities of the first ten retrieved documents to a query, averaged over all 1,000 queries. We also report *Precision@10*, i.e. the ratio of the gold stan-

---

[3]`https://www.elastic.co/guide/en/elasticsearch/reference/5.2/query-dsl-mlt-query.html`

Table 1: Comparison of encoding methods in terms of space and time. n is the number of semantic vector features, d is the number of semantic vectors, m is the number of semantic vector features after high-pass filtering, p is the expected postings list size (inverted index sparsity), v is the expected vocabulary size per a feature, c is the number of result-candidate semantic vectors, j the expected number of distinct indexed values of the feature, and l the expected number of documents in the index per a feature value. For details see Section 2.3.

	naive search	token encoding	high-pass filtering
space	$O(nd)$	$O(nd)$	$O(md)$
time	$O(nd)$	$O(n \cdot p \cdot v + c \log c)$	$O(n \cdot (\log j + l) + c)$

dard documents in the first ten results averaged over all 1,000 queries, and on *Normalized Discounted Cumulative Gain (nDCG$_{10}$)* (Manning et al., 2008, Section 8.4), where the relevance value of a retrieved document is taken to be its cosine similarity to the query.

3.2 Speed Evaluation

In this section, we evaluate the performance of feature token strings searches in Elasticsearch, using various Elasticsearch configurations as well as various vector filtering parameters.

Our Elasticsearch cluster consisted of 6 nodes, with 32 GiB RAM and 8 CPUs each, for a total of 192 GiB and 48 cores.

We experimented with several Elasticsearch parameters: the number of Elasticsearch index shards (6, 12, 24, 48, 96; always using one replica), the number of LSA features (100, 200, 400), a trim threshold of LSA vector values (none, 0.05, 0.10, 0.20), the number of Elasticsearch results used (Elasticsearch page size; 20, 80, 320, 640), parallel querying (1 [serial], 4, 16) and the cluster querying strategy (querying single-node or round-robin querying of 5 different Elasticsearch nodes). Each evaluation batch consisted of 128 queries (randomly selected for each batch) that were used to ask Elasticsearch one-by-one or in parallel in multiple queues depending on the evaluation setup.

We report *ES avg./std. [s]* – the average number of seconds per request Elasticsearch took (the 'took' time from the Elasticsearch response, i.e. the search time inside Elasticsearch) and its standard deviation, *Request avg./std. [s]* – the average number of seconds and its standard deviation per request including communication overhead with Elasticsearch to get the results (i.e. the time of the client to get the answer), *Total time [s]* – total number of seconds for processing all requests in the batch. This can differ from the sum of average request times when executing queries in parallel. The number of features in query vectors that passed through threshold trimming is reported as *Vec. size avg./std.*

4   Results

4.1   Quality Evaluation

Results of the quality evaluation are summarized in Table 2. The results of our method in different settings are put side by side with the results of the brute-force naive search and with Elasticsearch's native More Like This (MLT) search. For the MLT results, the `max_query_terms` Elasticsearch parameter is reported in the **best** column since both the semantics and the impact on the search speed are similar.

Figure 1 illustrates the impact of feature value filtering and the number of retrieved search candidates from Elasticsearch (page size) on its accuracy. It can be seen that avg. diff. decreases logarithmically with the page size. The results improve all the way up to 640 search results (the maximum value we have tried), which is expected as this increases the size of the subset E that is consequently ordered (re-ranked) in phase 2 with the precise but more costly exact algorithm. Increasing the size of E increases the chance of the inclusion of relevant results.

The shape of the curve suggests that there would only be a slight improvement in accuracy, and this would be at the cost of a substantial drop in performance. The impact of including only a limited number of features with the highest absolute value (see Section 2.2.2), is rather low. This is an excellent result with regard to performance as it means we may effectively sparsify the query vector with very little impact on search quality. We observe little difference between no filtering (searching by

Table 2: Results of quality evaluation. 400 LSA features were used. See Section 3.1 for more details. Only the subset of results with the top $nDCG_{10}$ scores are shown. Results with Precision@$10 \geq 0.9$ are shown in bold, with avg. diff. ≤ 0.002 in italics.

Trim	Best	Page	Min. P@10	Avg. P@10	Max. P@10	$nDCG_{10}$	Avg. diff.
naive search		***10***	***1.0***	***1.0000***	***1.0***	***1.0000***	***0.0000***
MLT	17	10	0.0	0.1967	1.0	0.9206	0.1799
MLT	25	10	0.0	0.2029	1.0	0.9221	0.1698
MLT	40	10	0.0	0.2077	1.0	0.9224	0.1619
MLT	90	10	0.0	0.2120	1.0	0.9210	0.1580
MLT	400	10	0.0	0.2114	1.0	0.9211	0.1568
0.00	160	17	0.0	0.4275	1.0	0.9840	0.0220
0.00	320	17	0.0	0.5281	1.0	0.9949	0.0149
0.00	640	17	0.0	0.6340	1.0	0.9989	0.0101
0.00	40	40	0.0	0.5090	1.0	0.9870	0.0142
0.00	80	40	0.0	0.6215	1.0	0.9940	0.0085
0.00	160	40	0.0	0.7254	1.0	0.9980	0.0051
0.00	320	40	0.1	0.8181	1.0	0.9998	0.0030
0.00	*640*	*40*	*0.0*	*0.8883*	*1.0*	*0.9989*	*0.0016*
0.00	10	90	0.0	0.3927	1.0	0.9940	0.0323
0.00	20	90	0.0	0.5167	1.0	0.9950	0.0147
0.00	40	90	0.0	0.6314	1.0	0.9970	0.0084
0.00	80	90	0.1	0.7306	1.0	0.9994	0.0051
0.00	160	90	0.1	0.8185	1.0	0.9994	0.0029
0.00	*320*	*90*	*0.0*	*0.8818*	*1.0*	*0.9988*	*0.0017*
0.00	***640***	***90***	***0.0***	***0.9282***	***1.0***	***0.9989***	***0.0010***
0.00	20	all	0.1	0.5730	1.0	1.0000	0.0124
0.00	80	all	0.3	0.7870	1.0	1.0000	0.0044
0.00	***320***	***all***	***0.4***	***0.9050***	***1.0***	***1.0000***	***0.0016***
0.00	***640***	***all***	***0.4***	***0.9460***	***1.0***	***1.0000***	***0.0010***
0.05	160	17	0.0	0.4276	1.0	0.9837	0.0220
0.05	320	17	0.0	0.5280	1.0	0.9948	0.0149
0.05	640	17	0.0	0.6341	1.0	0.9989	0.0101
0.05	40	40	0.0	0.5088	1.0	0.9870	0.0142
0.05	80	40	0.0	0.6216	1.0	0.9940	0.0085
0.05	160	40	0.0	0.7255	1.0	0.9980	0.0051
0.05	320	40	0.1	0.8177	1.0	0.9992	0.0030
0.05	*640*	*40*	*0.0*	*0.8880*	*1.0*	*0.9988*	*0.0016*
0.05	10	90	0.0	0.3927	1.0	0.9940	0.0323
0.05	20	90	0.0	0.5168	1.0	0.9950	0.0147
0.05	40	90	0.0	0.6313	1.0	0.9970	0.0084
0.05	80	90	0.0	0.7305	1.0	0.9990	0.0051
0.05	160	90	0.1	0.8187	1.0	0.9997	0.0029
0.05	*320*	*90*	*0.0*	*0.8815*	*1.0*	*0.9988*	*0.0017*
0.05	***640***	***90***	***0.0***	***0.9281***	***1.0***	***0.9988***	***0.0010***
0.05	10	all	0.0	0.3923	1.0	0.9960	0.0321
0.05	20	all	0.0	0.5154	1.0	0.9976	0.0149
0.05	40	all	0.0	0.6320	1.0	0.9985	0.0085
0.05	80	all	0.0	0.7321	1.0	0.9990	0.0051
0.05	160	all	0.0	0.8179	1.0	0.9990	0.0030
0.05	*320*	*all*	*0.1*	*0.8810*	*1.0*	*0.9992*	*0.0018*
0.05	***640***	***all***	***0.1***	***0.9302***	***1.0***	***0.9991***	***0.0009***
0.10	320	17	0.0	0.4981	1.0	0.9888	0.0171
0.10	640	17	0.0	0.6008	1.0	0.9969	0.0117
0.10	160	40	0.0	0.4409	1.0	0.9771	0.0216
0.10	320	40	0.0	0.5432	1.0	0.9891	0.0148
0.10	640	40	0.0	0.6435	1.0	0.9968	0.0099
0.10	320	90	0.0	0.5434	1.0	0.9893	0.0148
0.10	640	90	0.0	0.6436	1.0	0.9968	0.0099
0.10	160	all	0.0	0.4410	1.0	0.9770	0.0216
0.10	320	all	0.0	0.5431	1.0	0.9889	0.0148
0.10	640	all	0.0	0.6438	1.0	0.9972	0.0099

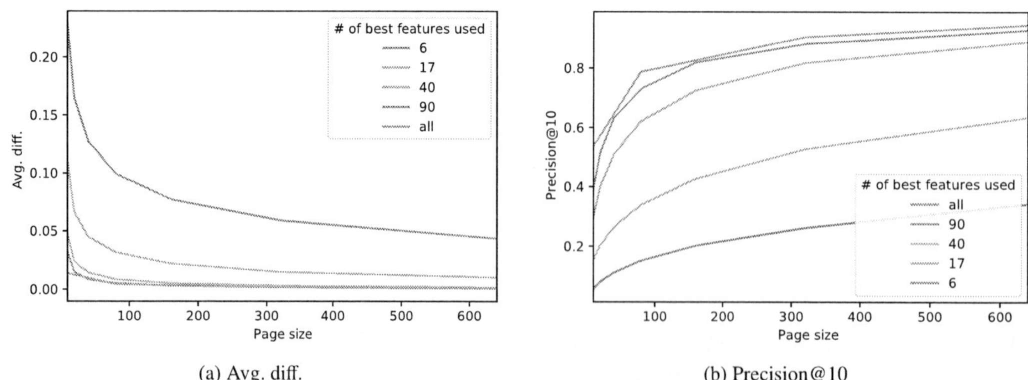

(a) Avg. diff.

(b) Precision@10

Figure 1: The impact of the number of best features selected (with no trimming) and the page size (the number of search results retrieved from Elasticsearch) on Avg. diff. and Precision@10.

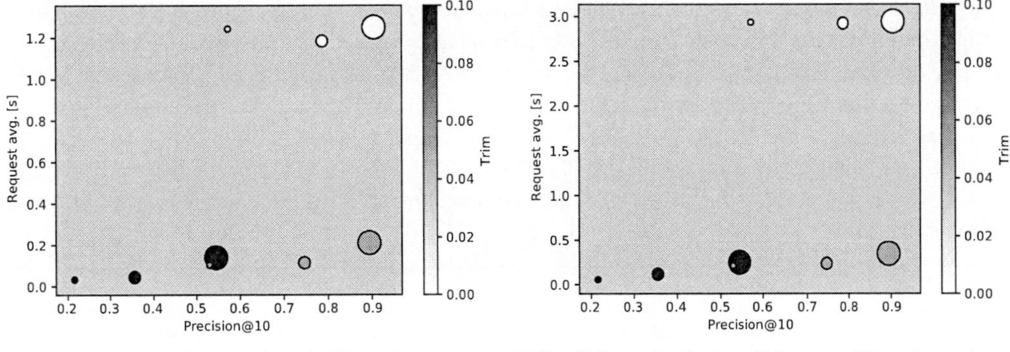

(a) Consecutive querying of 128 queries   (b) Parallel querying in 4 parallel queues, 32 queries each (128 queries in total)

Figure 2: The impact of value filtering and the number of retrieved search results on the average request time. The *x-axis* shows the *average precision*, the *y-axis* the *average request time*. The *size* of the points indicates the *number of retrieved results*: large = Elasticsearch page size 320, medium = page size 80, small = 20. The *color* of the points indicates the *trim thresholds*: white = 0.00 (no filtering), gray = 0.05, black = 0.10.

all 400 encoded features) and trimming to only the 90 best query vector values. However, trimming to as low as 6 values results in a significant increase in avg. diff. See Figure 1a.

Our methods scores above the MLT baseline in all of the followed metrics, even with aggressive high-pass filtering and with a small page size.

We expect that similar setup parameters will work similarly, at least for general multi-topic text datasets. Its behaviour for a dramatically different dataset, such as images instead of texts, or without normalized feature ranges, cannot be directly inferred and remains to be investigated in our future work. However, we expect our speed optimization methods to be applicable in some form, with the concrete parameters to be validated on the particular dataset and algorithmic setup.

4.2 Speed Evaluation

Selected results of our speed evaluation are summarized in Table 3. For clarity, we selected only the configurations using 400 LSA features and 48 Elasticsearch shards, as this setup turned out to provide the optimal performance on the Elasticsearch cluster and dataset we used according to the quality evaluation (see Section 4.1), where the same parameters were used.

The speed of the native Elasticsearch MLT search is summarized in Table 4. The speed is comparable to our method when high-pass filtering is involved.

Figure 2 displays the impact of value filtering and the number of retrieved search results on the average request time. Comparing consecutive queries (Figure 2a) with four parallel queries on the same Elasticsearch cluster configuration (Figure 2b) shows that at the expense of doubling the response time, we are able to answer four requests in parallel.

The best results in Figure 2 are located in the bottom right corner where the precision is high and the response time is low. For our dataset and algorithm (LSA with 400 features), the best overall results are represented by the largest gray dots, i.e. retrieving 320 vectors from Elasticsearch while filtering the query vector to roughly 90 values via trimming with a threshold of 0.05.

To achieve the optimal results, we suggest retrieving as large a set of candidates (Elasticsearch page size, E) as the response-time constraints allow, as the page size seems to have significantly lower influence on the response time compared to trimming, while having a significant positive effect on accuracy.

Our experiments were done on the Wikipedia dataset. Wikipedia is a multi-topic dataset – articles are on a wide variety of different topics using different keywords (names of people, places and things, etc) and notation (text only articles, articles on mathematics using formulae, articles on chemistry using different formulae, etc) are included. This provides enough room for the machine learning algorithms to build features that reflect these

Table 3: Results of speed evaluation using 400 LSA features, batches of 128 queries and 48 Elasticsearch shards. Column *Parallel q.* shows the number of parallel queries used together, *Trim* is the threshold for high-pass filtering of the features, *Page* is the number of vectors retrieved from Elasticsearch for each query (see Section 2.2.2), *ES avg./std.* is the average and standard deviation of the number of seconds per request Elasticsearch took, *Request avg./std.* is the average and deviation of the number of seconds per request including processing overheads, *Total time* is the total number of seconds for processing all requests, *Vec. size avg./std.* is the average/deviation of the number of values in query vectors that passed high-pass filtering.

Parallel q.	Trim	Page	ES avg. [s]	ES std. [s]	Request avg. [s]	Request std. [s]	Total time [s]	Vec. size avg.	Vec. size std.
1	0.00	20	1.1949	0.0737	1.2418	0.2864	160.760	400.0000	0.0000
1	0.00	80	1.1656	0.0710	1.1829	0.0713	153.246	400.0000	0.0000
1	0.00	320	1.2066	0.0893	1.2494	0.0894	161.783	400.0000	0.0000
1	0.05	20	0.0935	0.0202	0.1013	0.0204	14.521	93.5781	20.9268
1	0.05	80	0.0935	0.0214	0.1119	0.0228	15.898	91.5781	22.9822
1	0.05	320	0.1635	0.1014	0.2085	0.1032	28.360	87.2500	20.6908
1	0.10	20	0.0241	0.0057	0.0320	0.0057	5.574	19.3516	4.4222
1	0.10	80	0.0259	0.0059	0.0435	0.0061	7.107	19.0469	4.3027
1	0.10	320	0.0940	0.0966	0.1383	0.0971	19.357	18.0703	4.7863
4	0.00	20	2.9093	0.3943	2.9325	0.3989	94.750	400.0000	0.0000
4	0.00	80	2.8842	0.2968	2.9211	0.3004	94.548	400.0000	0.0000
4	0.00	320	2.8621	0.2897	2.9439	0.2938	95.290	400.0000	0.0000
4	0.05	20	0.1919	0.0491	0.2094	0.0531	7.212	89.3516	21.9351
4	0.05	80	0.2027	0.0525	0.2327	0.0563	7.948	93.2422	20.6166
4	0.05	320	0.2583	0.0983	0.3442	0.1025	11.538	86.3203	24.1855
4	0.10	20	0.0422	0.0080	0.0550	0.0078	2.253	18.8047	4.4547
4	0.10	80	0.0703	0.0708	0.1151	0.0884	4.174	19.5547	4.2625
4	0.10	320	0.1547	0.1093	0.2468	0.1161	8.411	17.8750	4.4459
16	0.00	20	11.5664	3.2998	11.6019	3.3018	94.480	400.0000	0.0000
16	0.00	80	11.5408	2.6209	11.6033	2.6262	94.535	400.0000	0.0000
16	0.00	320	11.5144	3.7843	11.7623	3.7645	95.112	400.0000	0.0000
16	0.05	20	0.7870	0.1988	0.8116	0.2020	6.896	88.4141	21.6681
16	0.05	80	0.7253	0.2309	0.8802	0.3051	7.463	87.9063	23.1528
16	0.05	320	0.8511	0.2350	1.0453	0.2491	9.332	89.9141	23.0604
16	0.10	20	0.1354	0.0182	0.1660	0.0169	1.625	18.4375	3.9484
16	0.10	80	0.1845	0.0859	0.2613	0.0891	2.400	18.7656	4.8404
16	0.10	320	0.4181	0.1442	0.6213	0.2065	5.416	18.0703	4.3807

unique markers of particular topics and makes particular features significantly irrelevant for particular documents in the dataset.

For general multi-topic text datasets, we recommend trimming features values by their absolute value below 5% of the maximum (i.e. between −0.05 and 0.05 in our experiments). Trimming more feature tokens decreases the precision with almost no influence on the response times, while keeping more feature tokens in the index has almost no positive effect on the precision but slows down the search significantly.

5 Conclusions

In this paper we have demonstrated a novel method for the conversion of semantic vectors into a set of string 'feature tokens' that can be subsequently indexed in a standard inverted-index-based fulltext search engine, such as Elasticsearch.

Two techniques of feature tokens filtering were demonstrated to further significantly speed up the search process, with an acceptably low impact on the quality of the results.

Using Elasticsearch MLT on document texts as a baseline, our method performs better than the baseline on all the followed metrics. With sufficient query vector feature reduction, our method is faster

Table 4: Results of speed evaluation using the native Elasticsearch More Like This (MLT) search (no parallel queries) using 48 shards. `max_query_terms` is the maximum number of query terms per query that were selected by Elasticsearch. *ES avg./std.* is the average and standard deviation of the number of seconds per request Elasticsearch took.

System	max_query_terms	ES avg. [s]	ES std. [s]
MLT	17	0.0468	0.0233
MLT	25	0.0595	0.0270
MLT	40	0.0745	0.0322
MLT	90	0.1090	0.0490
MLT	400	0.1458	0.0978

than MLT. With moderate query vector feature reduction, we can achieve excellent approximation of the gold standard while being only marginally slower than the MLT.

An important conclusion from our experiments is that the search speed can be improved even with filtering the query vectors alone and without the need to trim index vectors. A pleasant practical consequence of this finding is that a vector search engine based on our proposed scheme could allow the users to define the filtering parameters dynamically, at search time rather than at indexing time. In this way, we let the users choose the approximation trade-off between the search speed and accuracy, i.e. use weaker filtering parameters for searches where accuracy is critical, and more aggressive filtering where speed is critical.

In our future work we will focus on the validation of our techniques on different types of data (such as images or audio data) and different text representations (such as doc2vec) in specific domains (such as question answering).

Acknowledgments

Funding by TA ČR Omega grant TD03000295 is gratefully acknowledged.

References

David M. Blei, Andrew Y. Ng, Michael I. Jordan, and John Lafferty. 2003. Latent Dirichlet Allocation. *Journal of Machine Learning Research* 3:993–1022. http://dl.acm.org/citation.cfm?id=944919.944937.

Leonid Boytsov. 2017. Efficient and Accurate Non-Metric *k*-NN Search with Applications to Text Matching. Thesis proposal, School of Computer Science, Carnegie Mellon University. http://boytsov.info/pubs/proposal_boytsov.pdf.

Scott Deerwester, Susan T. Dumais, George W. Furnas, Thomas K. Landauer, and Richard Harshman. 1990. Indexing by Latent Semantic Analysis. *Journal of the American Society for Information Science* 41(6):391–407.

Christian Digout, Mario A. Nascimento, and Alexandru Coman. 2004. Similarity search and dimensionality reduction: Not all dimensions are equally useful. In YoonJoon Lee, Jianzhong Li, Kyu-Young Whang, and Doheon Lee, editors, *Proc. of Database Systems for Advanced Applications: 9th Int. Conf., DASFAA 2004, Jeju Island, Korea, March 17–19, 2003*. Springer, pages 831–842. https://doi.org/10.1007/978-3-540-24571-1_73.

Aristides Gionis, Piotr Indyk, and Rajeev Motwani. 1999. Similarity search in high dimensions via hashing. In *VLDB '99, Proceedings of 25th International Conference on Very Large Data Bases, September 7–10, 1999, Edinburgh, Scotland, UK*. pages 518–529. http://www.vldb.org/conf/1999/P49.pdf.

Clinton Gormley and Zachary Tong. 2015. *Elasticsearch: The Definitive Guide*. O'Reilly Media, Inc., 1st edition.

Quoc V. Le and Tomas Mikolov. 2014. Distributed representations of sentences and documents. *CoRR* abs/1405.4053. http://arxiv.org/abs/1405.4053.

Christopher D. Manning, Prabhakar Raghavan, and Hinrich Schütze. 2008. *Introduction to Information Retrieval*. Cambridge University Press, New York, NY, USA.

Tomas Mikolov, Ilya Sutskever, Kai Chen, Greg S Corrado, and Jeff Dean. 2013. Distributed representations of words and phrases and their compositionality. In *Advances in Neural Information Processing Systems*. pages 3111–3119.

Jan Rygl, Petr Sojka, Michal Růžička, and Radim Řehůřek. 2016. ScaleText: The Design of a Scalable, Adaptable and User-Friendly Document System for Similarity Searches: Digging for Nuggets of Wisdom in Text. In Aleš Horák, Pavel Rychlý, and Adam Rambousek, editors, *Proceedings of the Tenth Workshop on Recent Advances in Slavonic Natural Language Processing, RASLAN 2016*. Tribun EU, Brno, pages 79–87. https://nlp.fi.muni.cz/raslan/2016/paper08-Rygl_Sojka_etal.pdf.

Gerard Salton and Chris Buckley. 1988. Term-weighting approaches in automatic text retrieval. *Information Processing and Management* 24:513–523.

Gerard Salton, Anita Wong, and Chung-Shu Yang. 1975. A vector space model for automatic indexing. *Communications of the ACM* 18(11):613–620. https://doi.org/10.1145/361219.361220.

Roger Weber and Klemens Böhm. 2000. Trading quality for time with nearest-neighbor search. In Carlo Zaniolo, Peter C. Lockemann, Marc H. Scholl, and Torsten Grust, editors, *Proc. of Advances in Database Technology — EDBT 2000: 7th Int. Conf. on Extending Database Technology Konstanz, Germany, March 27–31, 2000*. Springer, pages 21–35. https://doi.org/10.1007/3-540-46439-5_2.

Roger Weber, Hans-Jörg Schek, and Stephen Blott. 1998. A quantitative analysis and performance study for similarity-search methods in high-dimensional spaces. In *Proc. of the 24rd International Conference on Very Large Data Bases*. Morgan Kaufmann Publishers Inc., San Francisco, CA, USA, VLDB '98, pages 194–205. http://dl.acm.org/citation.cfm?id=645924.671192.

Pavel Zezula, Giuseppe Amato, Vlastislav Dohnal, and Michal Batko. 2006. *Similarity Search: The Metric Space Approach*, volume 32 of *Advances in Database Systems*. Springer.

Multi-task Domain Adaptation for Sequence Tagging

Nanyun Peng and **Mark Dredze**
Human Language Technology Center of Excellence
Center for Language and Speech Processing
Johns Hopkins University, Baltimore, MD, 21218
`npeng1@jhu.edu, mdredze@cs.jhu.edu`

Abstract

Many domain adaptation approaches rely on learning cross domain shared representations to transfer the knowledge learned in one domain to other domains. Traditional domain adaptation only considers adapting for one task. In this paper, we explore multi-task representation learning under the domain adaptation scenario. We propose a neural network framework that supports domain adaptation for multiple tasks simultaneously, and learns shared representations that better generalize for domain adaptation. We apply the proposed framework to domain adaptation for sequence tagging problems considering two tasks: Chinese word segmentation and named entity recognition. Experiments show that multi-task domain adaptation works better than disjoint domain adaptation for each task, and achieves the state-of-the-art results for both tasks in the social media domain.

1 Introduction

Many natural language processing tasks have abundant annotations in formal domain (news articles) but suffer a significant performance drop when applied to a new domain, where only a small number of annotated examples are available. The idea behind domain adaptation is to leverage annotations from high-resource (source) domains to improve predictions in low-resource (target) domains by training a predictor for a single task across different domains.

Domain adaptation work tends to focus on changes in data distributions, e.g. different words are used in each domain. Domain adaptation methods include unsupervised (Blitzer et al.,

2006) and supervised (Daumé III, 2007) variants, depending on whether there exists no or some training data in the target domain. This paper considers the case of supervised domain adaptation, where we have a limited amount of target domain training data, but much more training data in a source domain.

Work on domain adaptation mostly follows two approaches: parameter tying (i.e. linking similar features during learning) (Dredze and Crammer, 2008; Daumé III, 2007, 2009; Finkel and Manning, 2009; Kumar et al., 2010; Dredze et al., 2010), and learning cross domain representations (Blitzer et al., 2006, 2007; Glorot et al., 2011; Chen et al., 2012; Yang and Eisenstein, 2015). Often times, domain adaptation is formulated as learning a single model for the same task across domains, although with a focus on maximizing target domain performance. This is similar in spirit to multi-task learning (MTL) (Caruana, 1997) which jointly learns models for several tasks, for example. learning a single data representation common to each task (Ando and Zhang, 2005; Collobert et al., 2011; Liu et al., 2016c; Peng and Dredze, 2016; Yang et al., 2016; Liu et al., 2016a). Given the similarity between domain adaptation and MTL, it is natural to ask: can domain adaptation benefit from jointly learning across several tasks?

This paper investigates how MTL can induce better representations for domain adaptation. There are several benefits. First, learning multiple tasks provides more training data for learning. Second, MTL provides a better inductive learning bias so that the learned representations better generalize. Third, considering several tasks in domain adaptation opens up the opportunities to adapt from a different domain *and* a different task, a mismatch setting which has not previously been explored. We present a representation learning

Proceedings of the 2nd Workshop on Representation Learning for NLP, pages 91–100,
Vancouver, Canada, August 3, 2017. ©2017 Association for Computational Linguistics

framework based on MTL that incorporates parameter tying strategies common in domain adaptation. Our framework is based on a bidirectional long short-term memory network with a conditional random fields (BiLSTM-CRFs) (Lample et al., 2016) for sequence tagging. We consider sequence tagging problem since they are common in NLP applications and have been demonstrated to benefit from learning representations (Lample et al., 2016; Yang et al., 2016; Peng and Dredze, 2016; Ma and Hovy, 2016).

This paper makes the following contributions:

- A neural MTL domain adaptation framework that considers several tasks *simultaneously* when doing domain adaptation.

- A new domain/task mismatch setting: where you have two datasets from two different, but related domains and tasks.

- State-of-the-art results on Chinese word segmentation and named entity recognition in social media data.

2 Model

We begin with a brief overview of our model, and then instantiate each layer with specific neural architectures to conduct multi-task domain adaptation for sequence tagging. Figure 1 summarizes the entire model presented in this section.

A representation learner that is shared across all domains and tasks, and learns robust data representations for features. This feeds a domain projection layer, with one projection for each domain that transforms the learned representations for different domains into the same shared space. As a result, the final layer of task specific models, which learns feature weights for different tasks, can be shared across domains since the learned representations (features) for different domains are now in the same space. The framework is flexible in both the number of tasks and domains. Increasing the number of domains linearly increases domain projection parameters, with the number of other model parameters unchanged. Similarly, increasing the number of tasks only linearly increases the number of task specific model parameters. If there is only one domain, then the framework reduces to a multi-task learning framework, and similarly, the framework reduces to a standard domain adaptation framework if there is only one task.

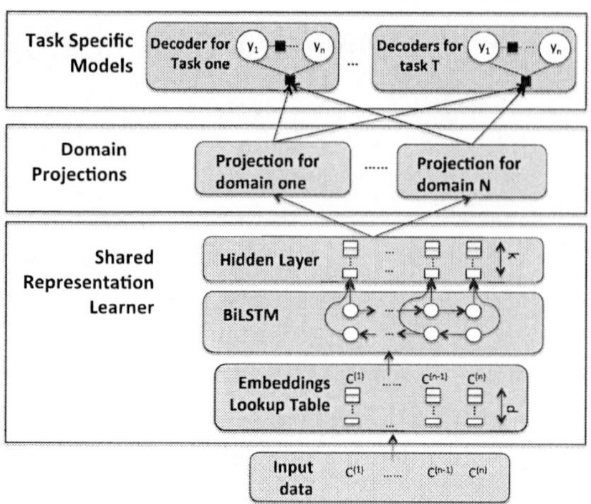

Figure 1: An overview of our proposed model framework. The bottom layer is shared by all tasks and domains. The domain projections contain one projection per domain and the task specific models (top layer) contain one model per task.

The shared representation learner, domain projections and task specific models can be instantiated based on the application. In this paper, we focus on sequence tagging problems. We now introduce our instantiated neural architecture for multi-task domain adaptation for sequence tagging.

2.1 BiLSTM for representation learning

Long short-term memory (LSTM) (Hochreiter and Schmidhuber, 1997) is a type of recurrent neural network (RNN) that models interdependencies in sequential data. It addresses the vanishing or exploding gradients (Bengio et al., 1994; Pascanu et al., 2013) problems of vanilla RNNs by using a series of gates (input, forget and output gates) to control how memory is propagated in the hidden states of the model, and thus effectively captures long-distance dependencies between the inputs.

Many NLP applications use bi-directional LSTMs (BiLSTM) (Dyer et al., 2015) to scan both left-to-right and right-to-left, which capture left and right context. The hidden vectors produced by both LSTMs are concatenated to form the final output vector $h_t = \overrightarrow{h_t} \oplus \overleftarrow{h_t}$. BiLSTMs have become a common building block for learning representations in NLP and have achieved impressive performance in problems such as sequence tagging (Lample et al., 2016; Yang et al., 2016; Ma and Hovy, 2016), relation classification (Xu et al., 2015; Zhang et al., 2015), and syntactic parsing (Kiperwasser and Goldberg, 2016; Cross and Huang, 2016). We use a BiLSTM as our representation learner. It produces a hidden vector for each token in the sentence, which we denote as:

$$h_t = \text{BiLSTM}(x_{1:n}, t) \tag{1}$$

where $x_{1:n}$ denotes the whole input sequence of length n, and t denotes the t-th position. The representation for the whole sequence is thus denoted as $\boldsymbol{h} = h_{1:n}$.

2.2 Domain Projections

Domain adaptation requires learning a shared representation that generalizes across domains. Ideally, parameter estimation of the BiLSTM should learn to produce such robust features. However, this may place a heavy burden on the BiLSTM; it does not know the identity of each domain yet must still learns how to map two heterogeneous input types to the same representation. To reduce this burden, we introduce a domain projection layer, which relies on explicit domain specific transformation functions to produce shared representations. We place this transformation between the representation learner and the task specific predictor to alleviates pressure on the representation learner to learn cross domain representations. Note that the domain projection layer works *jointly* with the representation learner to produce shared representations. We experiment with two simple strategies for domain projections which are based on previous lines of work in domain adaptation.

2.2.1 Domain Masks

The first strategy is inspired by Daumé III (2007) and Yang and Hospedales (2015), which split the representations into several regions, with one region shared among domains, and others specific for each domain. As a result, the BiLSTM representation learner will learn to put the features that are suitable to be shared across domains into the shared region, and domain specific features to the corresponding region for the domain.

We implement this strategy by defining domain masks $\boldsymbol{m}_d$, which is a vector for the dth domain. The mask $\boldsymbol{m}_d$ has value 1 for the effective dimensions of domain d and domain shared region, and 0 for all other dimensions. For example, assume we have two domains and a k dimensional hidden vector for features, the first $k/3$-dimensions is shared between the two domains, while the $k/3+1$ to $2k/3$ dimensions are used only for domain 1,

and the remaining dimensions for domain 2. The mask for domain 1 and domain 2 would be:

$$\boldsymbol{m}_1 = [\vec{1}, \vec{1}, \vec{0}], \quad \boldsymbol{m}_2 = [\vec{1}, \vec{0}, \vec{1}]. \tag{2}$$

We can then apply these masks directly to the hidden vectors $\boldsymbol{h}$ learned by the BiLSTM to produce a projected hidden state $\hat{\boldsymbol{h}}$:

$$\hat{\boldsymbol{h}} = \boldsymbol{m}_d \odot \boldsymbol{h}, \tag{3}$$

where $\odot$ denotes element-wise multiplication. Since only a subset of the dimensions are used as features in each domain, the BiLSTM will be encouraged to learn to partition the dimensions of the output hidden vectors into domains.

Note that in Daumé III (2007), the domain masks operate on hand engineered features, thus only affect feature weights. However, here the domain masks will change the parameters learned in BiLSTMs as well, changing the learned features. Therefore, training data from one domain will also change the other domains' representation. When we jointly train with data from all domains, the model has to balance the training objectives for all domains simultaneously.

2.2.2 Linear Projection

The second domain adaptation strategy we explore is a linear transformation to each domain, denoted as T_d. Given a k-dimensional vector representation $\boldsymbol{h}$, T_d is a $k \times k$ matrix that projects the learned BiLSTM hidden vector to a common space that can be used by a shared task specific model. We use the transformation:

$$\hat{\boldsymbol{h}} = T_d \boldsymbol{h}. \tag{4}$$

We learn T_d for each domain jointly with other model parameters. While this model has greater freedom in learning representations across domains, it relies on the training data to learn a good transformation, and does not explicitly partition the representations into domain regions.

2.3 Task Specific Neural-CRF Models

Multi-task domain adaptation *simultaneously* considers several tasks adapting domains since the related tasks would help induce more robust data representations for domain adaptation. Additionally, it enables leveraging more data to learn better domain projections. The goal of a task specific model is to learn parameters to project the shared representations to the desired outputs for the corresponding task. Different tasks that define different output spaces need separate task specific models.

For our applications to sequence tagging problems, we choose Conditional Random Fields (CRFs) (Lafferty et al., 2001) as task specific models, since it is widely used in previous work and is shown to benefit from learning representations (Peng and Dredze, 2015; Lample et al., 2016; Ma and Hovy, 2016). These "Neural-CRFs" define the conditional probability of a sequence of labels given the input as:

$$p(\boldsymbol{y}^k|\boldsymbol{x}^k;W) = \frac{\prod_{i=1}^{n} \exp\left(W^T F(y_{i-1}^k, y_i^k, \psi(\boldsymbol{x}^k))\right)}{Z^k},$$

where i indexes the position in the sequence, F is the feature function, and $\psi(\boldsymbol{x}^k)$ defines a transformation of the original input, in our case $\psi(\boldsymbol{x}^k) = BiLSTM(\boldsymbol{x}^k)$. Z^k is the partition function defined as:

$$Z^k = \sum_{\boldsymbol{y} \in \mathcal{Y}} \prod_{i=1}^{n} \exp\left(W^T F(y_{i-1}^k, y_i^k, \psi(\boldsymbol{x}^k))\right).$$

2.3.1 Sharing Task Specific Models

We could create a CRF decoder for each task and domain. This is the practice of some (Yang and Hospedales, 2015) who consider domain adaptation, or multi-domain learning, a special case of MTL, and learn separate models for the same task from different domains.

Instead, we argue that learning a single model for a task regardless of the number of domains draws strong connections to the traditional domain adaptation literature. It enjoys the benefit of increasing the amount of training data for each task by considering different domains, and better handles the problem of shifts in data distributions by explicitly considering different domains. Therefore, we use a single CRF per *task*, shared across all domains.

3 Parameter Estimation

The proposed neural architecture for multi-task domain adaptation can be trained end-to-end by maximizing data log-likelihood. As there are $D \times T$ [1] datasets, the final loss function is a linear combination of the log-likelihood of each dataset. For simplicity, we give each dataset equal weight when forming the linear combination.

---

[1] D denotes the number of domains and T the number of tasks

Training Model training is a straightforward application of gradient based back-propagation. We use alternating optimization among each dataset with stochastic gradient descent (SGD). To prevent training from skewing the model to a specific dataset due to the optimization order, we subsample the number of instances used in each epoch with a fraction λ w.r.t. the smallest dataset size, which is tuned as a hyper-parameter on development data. A separate learning rate is tuned for each dataset, and we decay the learning rate when results on development data do not improve after 5 consecutive epochs. We train for up to 30 epochs and use early stopping (Caruana et al., 2001; Graves et al., 2013) as measured on development data. We select the best model for each dataset based on hyper-parameter tuning. We use dropout on the embeddings and the BiLSTM output vectors as in Ma and Hovy (2016).

Initialization We use pre-trained Chinese embeddings provided by Peng and Dredze (2015) with dimension 100. All other model parameters are initialized uniformly at random in the range of $[-1, 1]$.

Inference For training the CRFs, we use marginal inference and maximize the marginal probabilities of the labels in the training data. At test time, the label sequence with highest conditional probability $y^* = \arg\max p(y|x; \Omega)$ is obtained by MAP inference.

Hyper-parameters Our hyper-parameters include the initial learning rate (per dataset, in the range of [0.005, 0.01, 0.02]), the dropout rate for the input embedding and the hidden vectors (in the range of [0, 0.1, 0.2]), and the subsample coefficient for each setting (in the range of [5, 10, 15]). We tune these hyper-parameter using beam search on development data. For convenience, the embedding and the LSTM hidden vector dimensions are set to 100 and 150 respectively.

4 Experimental Setup

We test the effectiveness of the multi-task domain adaptation framework on two sequence tagging problems: Chinese word segmentation (CWS) and named entity recognition (NER). We consider two domains: news and social media, with news the source domain and social media the target domain.

Dataset	#Train	#Dev	#Test
SighanCWS	39,567	4,396	4,278
SighanNER	16,814	1,868	4,636
WeiboCWS	1,600	200	200
WeiboNER	1,350	270	270

Table 1: Datasets statistics.

4.1 Datasets

We consider two domains: news and social media for the two tasks: CWS and NER. This results in four datasets: news CWS data comes from the SIGHAN 2005 shared task (*SighanCWS*) (Emerson, 2005), news NER data comes from the SIGHAN 2006 shared task (*SighanNER*) (Levow, 2006), social CWS data (*WeiboSeg*) created by Zhang et al. (2013), and social NER data (*WeiboNER*) created by Peng and Dredze (2015).

Both *SighanCWS* and *SighanNER* contain several portions[2]; we use those for simplified Chinese (PKU and MSR respectively). The datasets do not have development data, so we hold out the last 10% of training data for development. *SighanNER* contains three entity types (person, organization and location), while *WeiboNER* is annotated with four entity types (person, organization, location and geo-political entity), including named and nominal mentions. To match the two tag sets, we only use named mentions in *WeiboNER* and merge geo-political entities and locations. The 2000 annotated instances in *WeiboSeg* were meant only for evaluation, so we split the data ourselves using an 8:1:1 split for training, development, and test. Hyper-parameters are tuned on the development data and we report the precision, recall, and F1 score on the test portion. Detailed data statistics is shown in Table 1.

4.2 Baselines

We consider two baselines common in domain adaptation experiments. The first baseline only considers a single dataset at a time (*separate*) by training *separate* models just on in-domain training data. The second baseline (*mix*) uses out-of-domain training data for the same task by mixing it with the in-domain data. For both the baselines, we use the BiLSTM-CRFs neural architec-

---

[2]The portions are annotated by different institutes, and cover both traditional and simplified Chinese

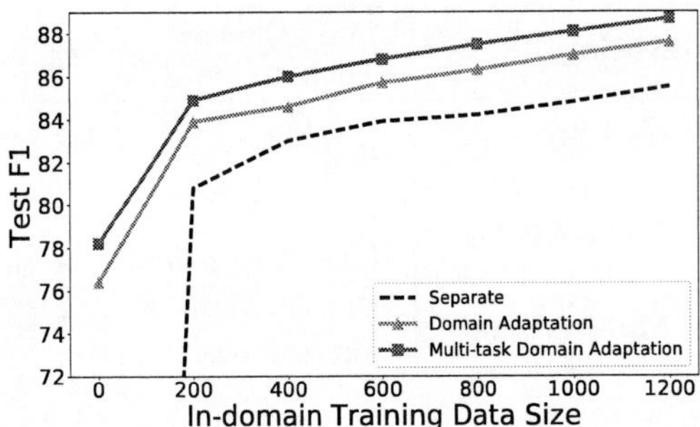

(a)

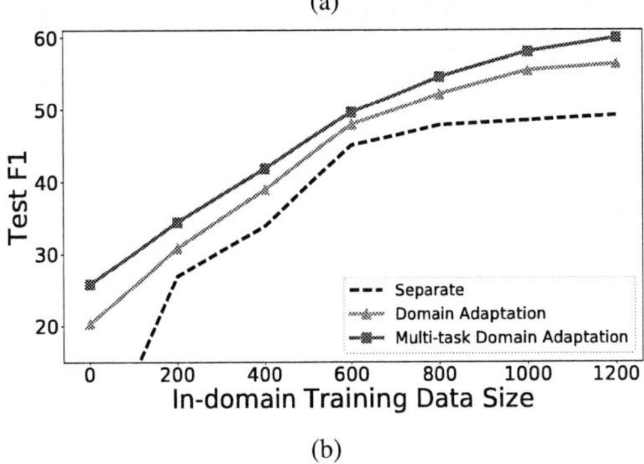

(b)

Figure 2: The effect of training data size on social media CWS (top) and NER (bottom) tasks. With more in-domain training data we see diminishing returns from domain adaptation. Our proposed multi-task domain adaptation framework is also applicable for unsupervised domain adaptation (with no in-domain training data).

ture (Lample et al., 2016), which achieved state-of-the-art results on NER and other sequence tagging tasks (Peng and Dredze, 2016; Ma and Hovy, 2016; Yang et al., 2016).

5 Experimental Results

5.1 Main Results

Table 2 presents the results for domain adaptation to the target domain (social media) test data . The baseline method *Mix* improves over *Separate* as it benefits from the increased training data. The single task domain adaptation models are a special case of the proposed multi-task domain adaptation framework: with only one task specific model in the top layer (CWS or NER). Both of our approaches (domain mask and linear projection) improve over the baseline methods. Knowing the domain of the training data helps the model better learn effective representations. Finally, we see further improvements in the multi-task domain adaptation setting. By considering additional tasks in

Settings	Datasets / Methods	CWS			NER		
		Prec	Recall	F1	Prec	Recall	F1
Baseline	Separate	86.2	85.7	86.0	57.2	42.1	48.5
	Mix	87.0	86.1	86.5	60.9	44.0	51.1
Domain Adapt	Domain Mask	88.7	87.1	87.9	68.2	48.6	56.8
	Linear Projection	88.0	87.5	87.7	73.3	45.8	56.4
Multi-task DA	Domain Mask	**89.7**	88.3	**89.0**	60.2	**52.3**	**59.9**
	Linear Projection	89.1	**88.6**	88.9	**68.6**	49.5	57.5

Table 2: Test results for CWS and Chinese NER on the target social media domain. The first two rows are baselines (Section 4.2,) followed by two domain adaptation models that only considers one task a time. The last two rows are the proposed multi-task domain adaptation framework building upon the two domain adaptation models, respectively. Domain adaptation models leverage out-of-domain training data and *significantly* improve over the *Separate* baseline, as well as the *Mix* baseline which trains with the out-of-domain data without considering domain shift. Multi-task domain adaptation further *significantly* improves over traditional domain adaptation on both domain adaptation models and achieved the new state-of-the-art results on the two tasks.

addition to domains, we achieve new state-of-the-art results on the two tasks. We compare to the best published results from Zhang et al. (2013) and Peng and Dredze (2016) with F1 scores of 87.5% (CWS) and 55.3% (NER), respectively.

Statistical Significance We measures statistical significance using McNemars chi-square test (McNemar, 1947) for paired significant test. We treated the predicted spans (not tokens) that agreed with the ground truth as positive, otherwise negative. For the NER task, we only count the spans that corresponds to named entities. We compare the best baseline (*mix*) and the two domain adaptation models, as well as between the domain adaptation models and their multi-task domain adaptation counterpart. Both the domain adaptation models *significantly* improved over the *mix* baseline ($p < 0.01$), and the multi-task domain adaptation methods *significantly* improved over their single task domain adaptation counterpart ($p < 0.01$). We cannot conduct paired significance tests with the best published results since we do not have access to their outputs.

5.2   In-domain Training Data

We also conducted several experiments to show the flexibility of our multi-task domain adaptation framework and analyze the behavior of the models by varying the training data.

We first consider the effect of in-domain training data size. Figure 2 shows the test F1 for the *Separate* baseline which only considers in-domain training data compared with both a single-task domain adaptation model and a multi-task domain adaptation model. For simplicity, we only show the curve for the *Domain Mask* variant. As expected, we observe diminishing returns with additional in-domain training data on both tasks, but domain adaptation and multi-task domain adaptation methods suffer less from the diminishing return, especially on the NER task (Figure 2a). The curves for domain adaptation and multi-task domain adaptation also appear to be smoother, as they leverage more data to learn input representations, and thus are more robust.

When we have no in-domain training data, the problem reduces to unsupervised domain adaptation. Our framework applies here as well, and multi-task domain adaptation achieves performance close to the *Separate* baseline with only 200 in-domain training examples.

5.3   Model Variations

The multi-task domain adaptation framework is flexible regarding the number of domains and tasks, thus the number of datasets. Table 3 shows the results for several model variations, grouped by the number of training datasets. With one dataset, it is just the standard supervised learning setting, which reduces to our *Separate* baseline.

With two datasets, the framework can do multi-task learning (with two datasets from the same domain but different tasks), single task domain adaptation (with two datasets for the same task but from different domains), and a novel mismatch setting (with two datasets from *both* different domains *and* different tasks). As shown in the second

Dataset Numbers	Datasets / Methods	CWS			NER		
		Prec	Recall	F1	Prec	Recall	F1
One Dataset	Separate	86.2	85.7	86.0	57.2	42.1	48.5
Two Datasets	Multi-task	87.7	86.2	86.9	59.1	44.9	51.1
	Domain Adaptation	88.7	87.1	87.9	68.2	48.6	56.8
	Mismatch	87.8	86.3	87.1	60.8	45.0	51.7
Four Datasets	All Multi-task	88.7	87.7	88.2	67.2	48.5	56.4
	Multi-task DA	89.7	88.3	89.0	60.2	52.3	59.9

Table 3: Model variations grouped by number of training datesets.

section of Table 3, including additional training data – no matter from another task, domain or both – always improves the performance. A hidden factor not shown in the table is the additional dataset's size. For multi-task learning, since we are look at the social media domain, the additional dataset size is small. This is probably the reason why the *Mismatch* setting leveraging data from a different task *and* domain surprisingly outperformed multi-task learning. *Domain adaptation* enjoys both the benefits of a large amount of additional training data and an aligned task, thus achieving the best results among the two dataset settings.

When conducting multi-task domain adaptation, we are leveraging four datasets. One concern is that the performance gains only come from additional training data, instead of the deliberately designed framework (Joshi et al., 2012). We thus also compare with a strategy which treats the same task for a different domain as a different task. The corresponding neural architecture is a shared BiLSTM with four separate task-specific models: we call it the *All Multi-task* setting. The results show that explicitly modeling data domains gives extra benefit than blindly throwing in more training data. We found the same benefits when experimenting with three datasets (instead of 2 or 4).

6 Related Work

The previous work on domain adaptation exclusively focused on building a unified model for *a* task across domain. However, we argue that a flexible framework for domain adaptation on several tasks simultaneously would be beneficial. To the best of our knowledge, the work that is closest to ours is Yang and Hospedales (2015), which provided a unified perspective for multi-task learning and multi-domain learning (a more general case of domain adaptation) under the same perspective of representation learning. However, they only focused on exploring the common ground of multi-task learning and multi-domain learning, and did not explore the possibility of having multi-task learning to help domain adaptation. We briefly review previous work on domain adaptation and multi-task learning below.

6.1 Domain Adaptation

In domain adaptation, or more general multi-domain learning, the goal is to learn a single model that can produce accurate predictions for multiple domains. An important characteristic of learning across domains is that each domain represents data drawn from a different distribution, yet share many commonalities. The larger the difference between these distributions, the larger the generalization error when learning across domains (Ben-David et al., 2010; Mansour et al., 2009).

As a result, a long line of work in multi-domain learning concerns learning shared representations, such as through identifying alignments between features (Blitzer et al., 2007, 2006), learning with deep networks (Glorot et al., 2011), using transfer component analysis (Pan et al., 2011), learning feature embeddings (Yang and Eisenstein, 2015) and kernel methods for learning low dimensional domain structures (Gong et al., 2012), among others. Another line sought for feature weight tying (Dredze and Crammer, 2008; Daumé III, 2007, 2009; Finkel and Manning, 2009; Kumar et al., 2010; Dredze et al., 2010) to transfer the learned feature weights across domains.

We combined the two lines and explored joint learning with multiple tasks.

6.2 Multi-task Learning

The goal of MTL (Caruana, 1997; Ando and Zhang, 2005) is to improve performance on different tasks by learning them jointly.

With recent progress in deep representation learning, new work considers MTL with neural networks in a general framework: learn a shared representations for all the tasks, and then a task specific predictor. The representations shared by tasks go from lower level word representations (Collobert and Weston, 2008; Collobert et al., 2011), to higher level contextual representations learned by Recurrent Neural Networks (RNNs) (Liu et al., 2016b; Yang et al., 2016; Peng et al., 2017) or other neural architectures (Liu et al., 2016a; Søgaard and Goldberg, 2016; Benton et al., 2017). MTL has helped in many NLP tasks, such as sequence tagging (Collobert et al., 2011; Peng and Dredze, 2016; Søgaard and Goldberg, 2016; Yang et al., 2016), text classification (Liu et al., 2016b,a), and discourse analysis (Liu et al., 2016c).

We expand the spectrum by exploring how multi-task learning can help domain adaptation.

7 Conclusion

We have presented a framework for multi-task domain adaptation, and instantiated a neural architecture for sequence tagging problems. The framework is composed of a shared representation learner for all datasets, a domain projection layer that learns one projection per domain, and a task-specific model layer that learns one set of feature weights per task. The proposed neural architecture can be trained end-to-end, and achieved the state-of-the-art results for Chinese word segmentation and NER on social media domain.

With this framework in mind, there are several interesting future directions to explore. First, we considered common domain adaptation schemas with our domain mask and linear projection. However, there are many more sophisticated methods that we can consider integrating into our model (Blitzer et al., 2007; Yang and Eisenstein, 2015). Second, we only experimented with sequence tagging problems. However, the proposed framework is generally applicable to other problems such as text classification, parsing, and machine translation. We plan to explore these applications in the future. Finally, our work draws on two traditions in multi-domain learning: parameter sharing (on the task specific models) and representation learning (the shared representation learner). We plan to explore how other domain adaptation methods can be realized in a deep architecture.

References

Rie Kubota Ando and Tong Zhang. 2005. A framework for learning predictive structures from multiple tasks and unlabeled data. *The Journal of Machine Learning Research* .

Shai Ben-David, John Blitzer, Koby Crammer, Alex Kulesza, Fernando Pereira, and Jennifer Wortman Vaughan. 2010. A theory of learning from different domains. *Machine learning* .

Yoshua Bengio, Patrice Simard, and Paolo Frasconi. 1994. Learning long-term dependencies with gradient descent is difficult. *IEEE Transactions on Neural Networks* .

Adrian Benton, Margaret Mitchell, and Dirk Hovy. 2017. Multi-task learning for mental health using social media text. In *Proceedings of EACL.*

John Blitzer, Mark Dredze, Fernando Pereira, et al. 2007. Biographies, bollywood, boom-boxes and blenders: Domain adaptation for sentiment classification. In *Proceedings of ACL.*

John Blitzer, Ryan McDonald, and Fernando Pereira. 2006. Domain adaptation with structural correspondence learning. In *Proceedings of EMNLP.*

Rich Caruana. 1997. Multitask learning. *Machine learning* .

Rich Caruana, vSteve Lawrence, and Lee Giles. 2001. Overfitting in neural nets: Backpropagation, conjugate gradient, and early stopping. In *Proceedings of NIPS.*

Minmin Chen, Zhixiang Xu, Fei Sha, and Kilian Q Weinberger. 2012. Marginalized denoising autoencoders for domain adaptation. In *Proceedings of ICML.*

Ronan Collobert and Jason Weston. 2008. A unified architecture for natural language processing: Deep neural networks with multitask learning. In *Proceedings of ICML.*

Ronan Collobert, Jason Weston, Léon Bottou, Michael Karlen, Koray Kavukcuoglu, and Pavel Kuksa. 2011. Natural language processing (almost) from scratch. *The Journal of Machine Learning Research* .

James Cross and Liang Huang. 2016. Span-based constituency parsing with a structure-label system and provably optimal dynamic oracles. In *Proceedings of EMNLP.*

Hal Daumé III. 2007. Frustratingly easy domain adaptation. In *Proceedings of ACL.*

Hal Daumé III. 2009. Bayesian multitask learning with latent hierarchies. In *Proceedings of UAI.*

Mark Dredze and Koby Crammer. 2008. Online methods for multi-domain learning and adaptation. In *Proceedings of EMNLP.*

Mark Dredze, Alex Kulesza, and Koby Crammer. 2010. Multi-domain learning by confidence-weighted parameter combination. *Machine Learning* .

Chris Dyer, Miguel Ballesteros, Wang Ling, Austin Matthews, and Noah A Smith. 2015. Transition-based dependency parsing with stack long short-term memory. In *Proceedings of ACL*.

Thomas Emerson. 2005. The second international chinese word segmentation bakeoff. In *Proceedings of the fourth SIGHAN workshop on Chinese language Processing*.

Jenny Rose Finkel and Christopher D Manning. 2009. Hierarchical bayesian domain adaptation. In *Proceedings of NAACL*.

Xavier Glorot, Antoine Bordes, and Yoshua Bengio. 2011. Domain adaptation for large-scale sentiment classification: A deep learning approach. In *Proceedings of ICML*.

Boqing Gong, Yuan Shi, Fei Sha, and Kristen Grauman. 2012. Geodesic flow kernel for unsupervised domain adaptation. In *Proceedings of CVPR*.

Alan Graves, Abdel-rahman Mohamed, and Geoffrey Hinton. 2013. Speech recognition with deep recurrent neural networks. In *Proceedings of ICASSP*.

Sepp Hochreiter and Jürgen Schmidhuber. 1997. Long short-term memory. *Neural computation* .

Mahesh Joshi, William W Cohen, Mark Dredze, and Carolyn P Rosé. 2012. Multi-domain learning: when do domains matter? In *Proceedings of EMNLP*.

Eliyahu Kiperwasser and Yoav Goldberg. 2016. Simple and accurate dependency parsing using bidirectional LSTM feature representations. *Transactions of the Association for Computational Linguistics* .

Abhishek Kumar, Avishek Saha, and Hal Daume. 2010. Co-regularization based semi-supervised domain adaptation. In *Proceedings of NIPS*.

John Lafferty, Andrew McCallum, and Fernando CN Pereira. 2001. Conditional random fields: Probabilistic models for segmenting and labeling sequence data. In *Proceedings of ICML*.

Guillaume Lample, Miguel Ballesteros, Sandeep Subramanian, Kazuya Kawakami, and Chris Dyer. 2016. Neural architectures for named entity recognition. In *Proceedings of NAACL*.

Gina-Anne Levow. 2006. The third international chinese language processing bakeoff: Word segmentation and named entity recognition. In *Proceedings of the Fifth SIGHAN Workshop on Chinese Language Processing*.

Pengfei Liu, Xipeng Qiu, and Xuanjing Huang. 2016a. Deep multi-task learning with shared memory. In *Proceedings of EMNLP*.

Pengfei Liu, Xipeng Qiu, and Xuanjing Huang. 2016b. Recurrent neural network for text classification with multi-task learning. In *Proceedings of IJCAI*.

Yang Liu, Sujian Li, Xiaodong Zhang, and Zhifang Sui. 2016c. Implicit discourse relation classification via multi-task neural networks. In *Proceedings of AAAI*.

Xuezhe Ma and Eduard Hovy. 2016. End-to-end sequence labeling via bi-directional lstm-cnns-crf. In *Proceedings of ACL*.

Yishay Mansour, Mehryar Mohri, and Afshin Rostamizadeh. 2009. Domain adaptation: Learning bounds and algorithms. In *Proceedings of COLT*.

Quinn McNemar. 1947. Note on the sampling error of the difference between correlated proportions or percentages. *Psychometrika* 12(2):153–157.

Sinno Jialin Pan, Ivor W Tsang, James T Kwok, and Qiang Yang. 2011. Domain adaptation via transfer component analysis. *IEEE Transactions on Neural Networks* .

Razvan Pascanu, Tomas Mikolov, and Yoshua Bengio. 2013. On the difficulty of training recurrent neural networks. In *Proceedings of ICML*.

Nanyun Peng and Mark Dredze. 2015. Named entity recognition for chinese social media with jointly trained embeddings. In *Proceedings of EMNLP*. Lisboa, Portugal.

Nanyun Peng and Mark Dredze. 2016. Improving named entity recognition for chinese social media with word segmentation representation learning. In *Proceedings of ACL*.

Nanyun Peng, Hoifung Poon, Chris Quirk, Kristina Toutanova, and Wen-tau Yih. 2017. Cross-sentence n-ary relation extraction with graph lstms. *Transactions of the Association for Computational Linguistics* 5:101–115.

Anders Søgaard and Yoav Goldberg. 2016. Deep multi-task learning with low level tasks supervised at lower layers. In *Proceedings of the 54th Annual Meeting of the Association for Computational Linguistics*. Association for Computational Linguistics, volume 2, pages 231–235.

Yan Xu, Lili Mou, Ge Li, Yunchuan Chen, Hao Peng, and Zhi Jin. 2015. Classifying relations via long short term memory networks along shortest dependency paths. In *Proceedings of EMNLP*.

Yi Yang and Jacob Eisenstein. 2015. Unsupervised multi-domain adaptation with feature embeddings. In *Proceedings of NAACL*.

Yongxin Yang and Timothy M Hospedales. 2015. A unified perspective on multi-domain and multi-task learning. *Proceedings of ICLR* .

Zhilin Yang, Ruslan Salakhutdinov, and William Cohen. 2016. Multi-task cross-lingual sequence tagging from scratch. *arXiv preprint arXiv:1603.06270*
.

Longkai Zhang, Li Li, Zhengyan He, Houfeng Wang, and Ni Sun. 2013. Improving chinese word segmentation on micro-blog using rich punctuations. In *Proceedings of ACL*.

Shu Zhang, Dequan Zheng, Xinchen Hu, and Ming Yang. 2015. Bidirectional long short-term memory networks for relation classification. In *Proceedings of 29th Pacific Asia Conference on Language, Information and Computation*.

Beyond Bilingual: Multi-sense Word Embeddings using Multilingual Context

Shyam Upadhyay[1]   Kai-Wei Chang[2]   Matt Taddy[3]   Adam Kalai[3]   James Zou[4]

[1]University of Illinois at Urbana-Champaign, Urbana, IL, USA
[2]University of Virginia, Charlottesville, VA, USA
[3]Microsoft Research, Cambridge, MA, USA
[4]Stanford University, Stanford, CA, USA
upadhya3@illinois.edu, kw@kwchang.net
{taddy,adum}@microsoft.com, jamesyzou@gmail.com

Abstract

Word embeddings, which represent a word as a point in a vector space, have become ubiquitous to several NLP tasks. A recent line of work uses bilingual (two languages) corpora to learn a different vector for each sense of a word, by exploiting crosslingual signals to aid sense identification. We present a multi-view Bayesian non-parametric algorithm which improves multi-sense word embeddings by (a) using multilingual (i.e., more than two languages) corpora to significantly improve sense embeddings beyond what one achieves with bilingual information, and (b) uses a principled approach to learn a variable number of senses per word, in a data-driven manner. Ours is the first approach with the ability to leverage multilingual corpora efficiently for multi-sense representation learning. Experiments show that multilingual training significantly improves performance over monolingual and bilingual training, by allowing us to combine different parallel corpora to leverage multilingual context. Multilingual training yields comparable performance to a state of the art monolingual model trained on five times more training data.

1   Introduction

Word embeddings (Turian et al., 2010; Mikolov et al., 2013, *inter alia*) represent a word as a point in a vector space. This space is able to capture semantic relationships: vectors of words with similar meanings have high cosine similarity (Turney, 2006; Turian et al., 2010). Use of embeddings as features has been shown to benefit several NLP tasks and serve as good initializations for deep architectures ranging from dependency parsing (Bansal et al., 2014) to named entity recognition (Guo et al., 2014b).

Although these representations are now ubiquitous in NLP, most algorithms for learning word-embeddings do not allow a word to have different meanings in different contexts, a phenomenon known as polysemy. For example, the word *bank* assumes different meanings in financial (eg. "bank pays interest") and geographical contexts (eg. "river bank") and which cannot be represented adequately with a single embedding vector. Unfortunately, there are no large sense-tagged corpora available and such polysemy must be inferred from the data during the embedding process.

| I got high **interest** on my savings from the bank. | Je suis un grand **[intérêt]** sur mes économies de la banque. | 我得到了我的储蓄从银行高**[利息]**。 |
| My **interest** lies in History. | Mon **[intérêt]** réside dans l'Histoire. | 我的**[兴趣]**在于历史。 |

Figure 1: **Benefit of Multilingual Information (beyond bilingual)**: Two different senses of the word "interest" and their translations to French and Chinese (word translation shown in **[bold]**). While the surface form of both senses are same in French, they are different in Chinese.

Several attempts (Reisinger and Mooney, 2010; Neelakantan et al., 2014; Li and Jurafsky, 2015) have been made to infer multi-sense word representations by modeling the sense as a latent variable in a Bayesian non-parametric framework. These approaches rely on the "one-sense per collocation" heuristic (Yarowsky, 1995), which assumes that presence of nearby words correlate with the sense of the word of interest. This heuristic provides only a weak signal for sense identification, and such algorithms require large amount of training data to achieve competitive perfor-

101

Proceedings of the 2nd Workshop on Representation Learning for NLP, pages 101–110,
Vancouver, Canada, August 3, 2017. ©2017 Association for Computational Linguistics

mance.

Recently, several approaches (Guo et al., 2014a; Šuster et al., 2016) propose to learn multi-sense embeddings by exploiting the fact that different senses of the same word may be translated into different words in a foreign language (Dagan and Itai, 1994; Resnik and Yarowsky, 1999; Diab and Resnik, 2002; Ng et al., 2003). For example, *bank* in English may be translated to *banc* or *banque* in French, depending on whether the sense is financial or geographical. Such bilingual distributional information allows the model to identify which sense of a word is being used during training.

However, bilingual distributional signals often do not suffice. It is common that polysemy for a word survives translation. Fig. 1 shows an illustrative example – both senses of *interest* get translated to *intérêt* in French. However, this becomes much less likely as the number of languages under consideration grows. By looking at Chinese translation in Fig. 1, we can observe that the senses translate to different surface forms. Note that the opposite can also happen (i.e. same surface forms in Chinese, but different in French). Existing crosslingual approaches are inherently bilingual and cannot naturally extend to include additional languages due to several limitations (details in Section 4). Furthermore, works like (Šuster et al., 2016) sets a fixed number of senses for each word, leading to inefficient use of parameters, and unnecessary model complexity.[1]

This paper addresses these limitations by proposing a multi-view Bayesian non-parametric word representation learning algorithm which leverages multilingual distributional information. Our representation learning framework is the first multilingual (not bilingual) approach, allowing us to utilize arbitrarily many languages to disambiguate words in English. To move to multilingual system, it is necessary to ensure that the embeddings of each foreign language are relatable to each other (i.e., they live in the same space). We solve this by proposing an algorithm in which word representations are learned *jointly* across languages, using English as a bridge. While large parallel corpora between two languages are scarce, using our approach we can concatenate multiple parallel corpora to obtain a large multilingual corpus. The parameters are estimated in

a Bayesian nonparametric framework that allows our algorithm to only associate a word with a new sense vector when evidence (from either same or foreign language context) requires it. As a result, the model infers different number of senses for each word in a data-driven manner, avoiding wasting parameters.

Together, these two ideas – multilingual distributional information and nonparametric sense modeling – allow us to disambiguate multiple senses using far less data than is necessary for previous methods. We experimentally demonstrate that our algorithm can achieve competitive performance after training on a small multilingual corpus, comparable to a model trained monolingually on a much larger corpus. We present an analysis discussing the effect of various parameters – choice of language family for deriving the multilingual signal, crosslingual window size etc. and also show qualitative improvement in the embedding space.

2   Related Work

Work on inducing multi-sense embeddings can be divided in two broad categories – two-staged approaches and joint learning approaches. Two-staged approaches (Reisinger and Mooney, 2010; Huang et al., 2012) induce multi-sense embeddings by first clustering the contexts and then using the clustering to obtain the sense vectors. The contexts can be topics induced using latent topic models(Liu et al., 2015a,b), or Wikipedia (Wu and Giles, 2015) or coarse part-of-speech tags (Qiu et al., 2014). A more recent line of work in the two-staged category is that of retrofitting (Faruqui et al., 2015; Jauhar et al., 2015), which aims to infuse semantic ontologies from resources like WordNet (Miller, 1995) and Framenet (Baker et al., 1998) into embeddings during a post-processing step. Such resources list (albeit not exhaustively) the senses of a word, and by retro-fitting it is possible to tease apart the different senses of a word. While some resources like WordNet (Miller, 1995) are available for many languages, they are not exhaustive in listing all possible senses. Indeed, the number senses of a word is highly dependent on the task and cannot be pre-determined using a lexicon (Kilgarriff, 1997). Ideally, the senses should be inferred in a data-driven manner, so that new senses not listed in such lexicons can be discovered. While re-

---

[1]Most words in conventional English are monosemous, i.e. single sense (eg. the word *monosemous*)

cent work has attempted to remedy this by using parallel text for retrofitting sense-specific embeddings (Ettinger et al., 2016), their procedure requires creation of *sense graphs*, which introduces additional tuning parameters. On the other hand, our approach only requires two tuning parameters (prior α and maximum number of senses T).

In contrast, joint learning approaches (Neelakantan et al., 2014; Li and Jurafsky, 2015) jointly learn the sense clusters and embeddings by using non-parametrics. Our approach belongs to this category. The closest non-parametric approach to ours is that of (Bartunov et al., 2016), who proposed a multi-sense variant of the skip-gram model which learns the different number of sense vectors for all words from a large monolingual corpus (eg. English Wikipedia). Our work can be viewed as the multi-view extension of their model which leverages both monolingual and crosslingual distributional signals for learning the embeddings. In our experiments, we compare our model to monolingually trained version of their model.

Incorporating crosslingual distributional information is a popular technique for learning word embeddings, and improves performance on several downstream tasks (Faruqui and Dyer, 2014; Guo et al., 2016; Upadhyay et al., 2016). However, there has been little work on learning multi-sense embeddings using crosslingual signals (Bansal et al., 2012; Guo et al., 2014a; Šuster et al., 2016) with only (Šuster et al., 2016) being a joint approach. (Kawakami and Dyer, 2015) also used bilingual distributional signals in a deep neural architecture to learn context dependent representations for words, though they do not learn separate sense vectors.

3 Model Description

Let $E = \{x^e_1, .., x^e_i, .., x^e_{N_e}\}$ denote the words of the English side and $F = \{x^f_1, .., x^f_i, .., x^f_{N_f}\}$ denote the words of the foreign side of the parallel corpus. We assume that we have access to word alignments $A_{e \to f}$ and $A_{f \to e}$ mapping words in English sentence to their translation in foreign sentence (and vice-versa), so that x^e and x^f are aligned if $A_{e \to f}(x^e) = x^f$.

We define $\text{Nbr}(x, L, d)$ as the neighborhood in language L of size d (on either side) around word x in its sentence. The English and foreign neighboring words are denoted by y^e and y^f, respec-

tively. Note that y^e and y^f need not be translations of each other. Each word x^f in the foreign vocabulary is associated with a dense vector $\boldsymbol{x}^f$ in $\mathbb{R}^m$, and each word x^e in English vocabulary admits at most T sense vectors, with the kth sense vector denoted as $\boldsymbol{x}^e_k$.[2] As our main goal is to model multiple senses for words in English, we do not model polysemy in the foreign language and use a single vector to represent each word in the foreign vocabulary.

We model the joint conditional distribution of the context words y^e, y^f given an English word x^e and its corresponding translation x^f on the parallel corpus:

$$P(y^e, y^f \mid x^e, x^f; \alpha, \theta), \qquad (1)$$

where θ are model parameters (i.e. all embeddings) and α governs the hyper-prior on latent senses.

Assume x^e has multiple senses, which are indexed by the random variable z, Eq. (1) can be rewritten,

$$\int_\beta \sum_z P(y^e, y^f z, \beta \mid x^e, x^f, \alpha; \theta) d\beta$$

where β are the parameters determining the model probability on each sense for x^e (i.e., the weight on each possible value for z). We place a Dirichlet process (Ferguson, 1973) prior on sense assignment for each word. Thus, adding the word-x subscript to emphasize that these are word-specific senses,

$$P(z_x = k \mid \beta_x) = \beta_{xk} \prod_{r=1}^{k-1} (1 - \beta_{xr}) \quad (2)$$

$$\beta_{xk} \mid \alpha \overset{ind}{\sim} Beta(\beta_{xk} \mid 1, \alpha), \quad k = 1, \dots . \quad (3)$$

That is, the potentially infinite number of senses for each word x have probability determined by the sequence of independent *stick-breaking weights*, β_{xk}, in the constructive definition of the DP (Sethuraman, 1994). The hyper-prior concentration α provides information on the number of senses we expect to observe in our corpus.

After conditioning upon word sense, we decompose the context probability,

$$P(y^e, y^f \mid z, x^e, x^f; \theta) =$$
$$P(y^e \mid x^e, x^f, z; \theta) P(y^f \mid x^e, x^f, z; \theta).$$

---

[2] We also maintain a context vector for each word in the English and Foreign vocabularies. The context vector is used as the representation of the word when it appears as the context for another word.

Both the first and the second terms are sense-dependent, and each factors as,

$$P(y \mid x^e, x^f, z = k; \theta) \propto \Psi(x^e, z = k, y)\Psi(x^f, y)$$
$$= \exp(\boldsymbol{y}^T \boldsymbol{x}_k^e)\exp(\boldsymbol{y}^T \boldsymbol{x}^f) = \exp(\boldsymbol{y}^T(\boldsymbol{x}_k^e + \boldsymbol{x}^f)),$$

where x_k^e is the embedding corresponding to the kth sense of the word x^e, and y is either y^e or y^f. The factor $\Psi(x^e, z = k, y)$ use the corresponding sense vector in a skip-gram-like formulation. This results in total of 4 factors,

$$P(y^e, y^f \mid z, x^e, x^f; \theta) \propto \Psi(x^e, z, y^e)\Psi(x^f, y^f)$$
$$\Psi(x^e, z, y^f)\Psi(x^f, y^e)$$
$$(4)$$

See Figure 2 for illustration of each factor. This modeling approach is reminiscent of (Luong et al., 2015), who jointly learned embeddings for two languages l_1 and l_2 by optimizing a joint objective containing 4 skip-gram terms using the aligned pair (x^e, x^f)– two predicting monolingual contexts $l_1 \to l_1, l_2 \to l_2$, and two predicting crosslingual contexts $l_1 \to l_2, l_2 \to l_1$.

Learning. Learning involves maximizing the log-likelihood,

$$P(y^e, y^f \mid x^e, x^f; \alpha, \theta) =$$
$$\int_\beta \sum_z P(y^e, y^f, z, \beta \mid x^e, x^f, \alpha; \theta)d\beta$$

for which we use variational approximation. Let $q(z, \beta) = q(z)q(\beta)$ where

$$q(z) = \prod_i q(z_i) \quad q(\beta) = \prod_{w=1}^{V}\prod_{k=1}^{T}\beta_{wk}$$
$$(5)$$

are the fully factorized variational approximation of the true posterior $P(z, \beta \mid y^e, y^f, x^e, x^f, \alpha)$, where V is the size of english vocabulary, and T is the maximum number of senses for any word. The optimization problem solves for $\theta, q(z)$ and $q(\beta)$ using the stochastic variational inference technique (Hoffman et al., 2013) similar to (Bartunov et al., 2016) (refer for details).

The resulting learning algorithm is shown as Algorithm 1. The first for-loop (line 1) updates the English sense vectors using the crosslingual and monolingual contexts. First, the expected sense distribution for the current English word w is computed using the current estimate of $q(\beta)$ (line 4). The sense distribution is updated (line 7) using the combined monolingual and crosslingual contexts

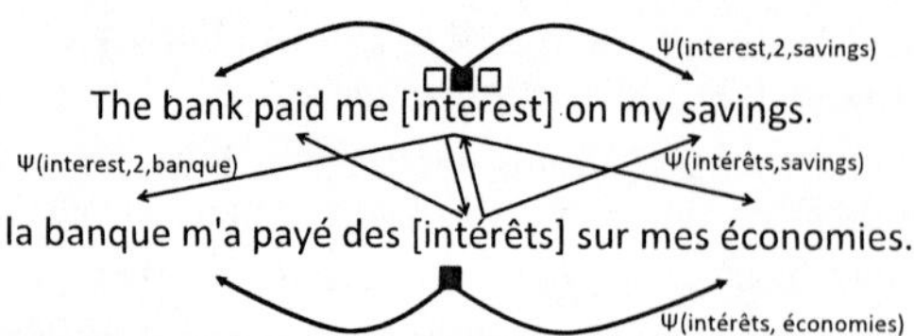

Figure 2: The aligned pair (*interest,intérêt*) is used to predict monolingual and crosslingual context in both languages (see factors in eqn. (4)). We pick each sense (here 2nd) vector for *interest*, to perform weighted update. We only model polysemy in English.

(line 5) and re-normalized (line 8). Using the updated sense distribution $q(\beta)$'s sufficient statistics is re-computed (line 9) and the global parameter θ is updated (line 10) as follows,

$$\theta \leftarrow \theta + \rho_t \nabla_\theta \sum_{k \mid z_{ik} > \epsilon} \sum_{y \in y_c} z_{ik} \log p(y \mid x_i, k, \theta)$$
$$(6)$$

Note that in the above sum, a sense participates in a update only if its probability exceeds a threshold ϵ (= 0.001). The final model retains sense vectors whose sense probability exceeds the same threshold. The last for-loop (line 11) jointly optimizes the foreign embeddings using English context with the standard skip-gram updates.

Disambiguation. Similar to (Bartunov et al., 2016), we can disambiguate the sense for the word x^e given a monolingual context y^e as follows,

$$P(z \mid x^e, y^e) \propto$$
$$P(y^e \mid x^e, z; \theta) \sum_\beta P(z \mid x^e, \beta)q(\beta)$$
$$(7)$$

Although the model trains embeddings using both monolingual and crosslingual context, we only use monolingual context at test time. We found that so long as the model has been trained with multilingual context, it performs well in sense disambiguation on new data even if it contains only monolingual context. A similar observation was made by (Šuster et al., 2016).

4 Multilingual Extension

Bilingual distributional signal alone may not be sufficient as polysemy may survive translation in the second language. Unlike existing approaches, we can easily incorporate multilingual distributional signals in our model. For using languages l_1 and l_2 to learn multi-sense embeddings for English, we train on a concatenation of En-l_1 parallel corpus with an En-l_2 parallel corpus. This technique can easily be generalized to more than

---

Algorithm 1 Psuedocode of Learning Algorithm

Input: parallel corpus $E = \{x_1^e, .., x_i^e, .., x_{N_e}^e\}$ and $F = \{x_1^f, .., x_i^f, .., x_{N_f}^f\}$ and alignments $A_{e \to f}$ and $A_{f \to e}$, Hyper-parameters α and T, window sizes d, d'.

Output: $\theta, q(\beta), q(\mathbf{z})$

1: **for** $i = 1$ to N_e **do** $\triangleright$ update english vectors
2:    $w \leftarrow x_i^e$
3:    **for** $k = 1$ to T **do**
4:       $z_{ik} \leftarrow \mathbb{E}_{q(\beta_w)}[\log p(z_i = k|, x_i^e)]$
5:       $y_c \leftarrow \text{Nbr}(x_i^e, E, d) \cup \text{Nbr}(x_i^f, F, d') \cup \{x_i^f\}$
       where $x_i^f = A_{e \to f}(x_i^e)$
6:       **for** y in y_c **do**
7:          SENSE-UPDATE(x_i^e, y, z_i)
8:       Renormalize z_i using softmax
9:       Update suff. stats. for $q(\beta)$ like (Bartunov et al., 2016)
10:       Update θ using eq. (6)
11: **for** $i = 1$ to N_f **do** $\triangleright$ jointly update foreign vectors
12:    $y_c \leftarrow \text{Nbr}(x_i^f, F, d) \cup \text{Nbr}(x_i^e, E, d') \cup \{x_i^e\}$
       where $x_i^e = A_{f \to e}(x_i^f)$
13:    **for** y in y_c **do**
14:       SKIP-GRAM-UPDATE(x_i^f, y)
15: **procedure** SENSE-UPDATE(x_i, y, z_i)
16:    $z_{ik} \leftarrow z_{ik} + \log p(y|x_i, k, \theta)$

---

two foreign languages to obtain a large multilingual corpus.

Value of $\Psi(y^e, x^f)$**.** The factor modeling the dependence of the English context word y^e on foreign word x^f is crucial to performance when using multiple languages. Consider the case of using French and Spanish contexts to disambiguate the financial sense of the English word *bank*. In this case, the (financial) sense vector of *bank* will be used to predict vector of *banco* (Spanish context) and *banque* (French context). If vectors for *banco* and *banque* do not reside in the same space or are not close, the model will incorrectly assume they are different contexts to introduce a new sense for *bank*. This is precisely why the bilingual models, like that of (Šuster et al., 2016), cannot be extended to multilingual setting, as they pre-train the embeddings of second language before running the multi-sense embedding process. As a result of naive pre-training, the French and Spanish vectors of semantically similar pairs like (*banco,banque*) will lie in different spaces and need not be close. A similar reason holds for (Guo et al., 2014a), as

Corpus	Source	Lines (M)	EN-Words (M)
En-Fr	EU proc.	≈ 10	250
En-Zh	FBIS news	≈ 9.5	286
En-Es	UN proc.	≈ 10	270
En-Fr	UN proc.	≈ 10	260
En-Zh	UN proc.	≈ 8	230
En-Ru	UN proc.	≈ 10	270

Table 1: Corpus Statistics (in millions). Horizontal lines demarcate corpora from the same domain.

they use a two step approach instead of joint learning.

To avoid this, the vector for pairs like *banco* and *banque* should lie in the same space and close to each other and the sense vector for *bank*. The $\Psi(y^e, x^f)$ term attempts to ensure this by using the vector for *banco* and *banque* to predict the vector of *bank*. This way, the model brings the embedding space for Spanish and French closer by using English as a bridge language during joint training. A similar idea of using English as a bridging language was used in the models proposed in (Hermann and Blunsom, 2014) and (Coulmance et al., 2015). Beside the benefit in the multilingual case, the $\Psi(y^e, x^f)$ term improves performance in the bilingual case as well, as it forces the English and second language embeddings to remain close in space.

To show the value of $\Psi(y^e, x^f)$ factor in our experiments, we ran a variant of Algorithm 1 without the $\Psi(y^e, x^f)$ factor, by only using monolingual neighborhood $Nbr(x_i^f, F)$ in line 12 of Algorithm 1. We call this variant ONE-SIDED model and the model in Algorithm 1 the FULL model.

5   Experimental Setup

We first describe the datasets and the preprocessing methods used to prepare them. We also describe the Word Sense Induction task that we used to compare and evaluate our method.

Parallel Corpora. We use parallel corpora in English (En), French (Fr), Spanish (Es), Russian (Ru) and Chinese (Zh) in our experiments. Corpus statistics for all datasets used in our experiments are shown in Table 1. For En-Zh, we use the FBIS parallel corpus (LDC2003E14). For En-Fr, we use the first 10M lines from the Giga-EnFr corpus released as part of the WMT shared task (Callison-Burch et al., 2011). Note that the domain from which parallel corpus has been derived can affect the final result. To understand what choice of languages provide suitable disambiguation signal, it is necessary to control for domain in all parallel corpora. To this end, we also used the En-Fr, En-Es, En-Zh and En-Ru sections of the MultiUN parallel corpus (Eisele and Chen, 2010). Word alignments were generated using `fast_align` tool (Dyer et al., 2013) in the symmetric intersection mode. Tokenization and other preprocessing were performed using `cdec` [3] toolkit. Stanford Segmenter (Tseng et al., 2005) was used to preprocess the Chinese corpora.

Word Sense Induction (WSI). We evaluate our approach on word sense induction task. In this task, we are given several sentences showing usages of the same word, and are required to cluster all sentences which use the same sense (Nasiruddin, 2013). The predicted clustering is then compared against a provided gold clustering. Note that WSI is a harder task than Word Sense Disambiguation (WSD)(Navigli, 2009), as unlike WSD, this task does not involve any supervision or explicit human knowledge about senses of words. We use the disambiguation approach in eq. (7) to predict the sense given the target word and four context words.

To allow for fair comparison with earlier work, we use the same benchmark datasets as (Bartunov et al., 2016) – Semeval-2007, 2010 and Wikipedia Word Sense Induction (WWSI). We report Adjusted Rand Index (ARI) (Hubert and Arabie, 1985) in the experiments, as ARI is a more strict and precise metric than F-score and V-measure.

Parameter Tuning. For fairness, we used five context words on either side to update each English word-vectors in all the experiments. In the monolingual setting, all five words are English; in the multilingual settings, we used four neighboring English words plus the one foreign word aligned to the word being updated ($d = 4$, $d' = 0$ in Algorithm 1). We also analyze effect of varying d', the context window size in the foreign sentence on the model performance.

We tune the parameters α and T by maximizing the log-likelihood of a held out English text.[4] The parameters were chosen from the following values $\alpha = \{0.05, 0.1, .., 0.25\}$, $T = \{5, 10, .., 30\}$. All models were trained for 10 iteration with a decay-

---

[3] `github.com/redpony/cdec`
[4] first 100k lines from the En-Fr Europarl (Koehn, 2005)

ing learning rate of 0.025, decayed to 0. Unless otherwise stated, all embeddings are 100 dimensional.

Under various choice of α and T, we identify only about 10-20% polysemous words in the vocabulary using monolingual training and 20-25% polysemous using multilingual training. It is evident using the non-parametric prior has led to substantially more efficient representation compared to previous methods with fixed number of senses per word.

6 Experimental Results

Setting	S-2007	S-2010	WWSI	avg. ARI	SCWS
En-Fr					
Mono	.044	.064	.112	.073	41.1
One-Sided	.054	.074	**.116**	.081	**41.9**
Full	**.055**	**.086**	.105	**.082**	41.8
En-Zh					
Mono	.054	.074	.073	.067	42.6
One-Sided	**.059**	.084	.078	.074	**45.0**
Full	.055	**.090**	**.079**	**.075**	41.7
En-FrZh					
Mono	.056	.086	.103	.082	**47.3**
One-Sided	**.067**	.085	.113	.088	44.6
Full	.065	**.094**	**.120**	**.093**	41.9

Table 2: Results on word sense induction (left four columns) in ARI and contextual word similarity (last column) in percent correlation. Language pairs are separated by horizontal lines. Best results shown in **bold**.

We performed extensive experiments to evaluate the benefit of leveraging bilingual and multilingual information during training. We also analyze how the different choices of language family (i.e. using more distant vs more similar languages) affect performance of the embeddings.

6.1 Word Sense Induction Results.

The results for WSI are shown in Table 2. Recall that the One-Sided model is the variant of Algorithm 1 without the $\Psi(y^e, x^f)$ factor. Mono refers to the AdaGram model of (Bartunov et al., 2016) trained on the English side of the parallel corpus. In all cases, the Mono model is outperformed by One-Sided and Full models, showing the benefit of using crosslingual signal in training. Best performance is attained by the multilingual model (En-FrZh), showing value of multilingual signal. The value of $\Psi(y^e, x^f)$ term is also verified by the fact that the One-Sided model performs worse than the Full model.

Train Setting	S-2007		S-2010		WWSI		Avg. ARI	
	En-FrEs	En-RuZh	En-FrEs	En-FrEs	En-FrEs	En-RuZh	En-FrEs	En-RuZh
(1) MONO	.035	.033	.046	.049	.054	.049	.045	.044
(2) ONE-SIDED	.044	**.044**	.055	.063	.062	.057	.054	.055
(3) FULL	**.046**	.040	**.056**	**.070**	**.068**	**.069**	**.057**	**.059**
(3) - (1)	.011	.007	.010	.021	.014	.020	.012	.015

Table 3: Effect (in ARI) of language family distance on WSI task. Best results for each column is shown in **bold**. The improvement from MONO to FULL is also shown as (3) - (1). Note that this is not comparable to results in Table 2, as we use a different training corpus to control for the domain.

We can also compare (unfairly to our FULL model) to the best results described in (Bartunov et al., 2016), which achieved ARI scores of 0.069, 0.097 and 0.286 on the three datasets respectively after training 300 dimensional embeddings on English Wikipedia ($\approx$ 100M lines). Note that, as WWSI was derived from Wikipedia, training on Wikipedia gives AdaGram model an undue advantage, resulting in high ARI score on WWSI. In comparison, our model did not train on English Wikipedia, and uses 100 dimensional embeddings. Nevertheless, even in the unfair comparison, it noteworthy that on S-2007 and S-2010, we can achieve comparable performance (0.067 and 0.094) with multilingual training to a model trained on almost 5 times more data using higher (300) dimensional embeddings.

6.2 Contextual Word Similarity Results.

For completeness, we report correlation scores on Stanford contextual word similarity dataset (SCWS) (Huang et al., 2012) in Table 2. The task requires computing similarity between two words given their contexts. While the bilingually trained model outperforms the monolingually trained model, surprisingly the multilingually trained model does not perform well on SCWS. We believe this may be due to our parameter tuning strategy.[5]

6.3 Effect of Language Family Distance.

Intuitively, choice of language can affect the result from crosslingual training as some languages may provide better disambiguation signals than others. We performed a systematic set of experiment to evaluate whether we should choose languages from a closer family (Indo-European languages) or farther family (Non-Indo European Languages)

as training data alongside English.[6] To control for domain here we use the MultiUN corpus. We use En paired with Fr and Es as Indo-European languages, and English paired with Ru and Zh for representing Non-Indo-European languages.

From Table 3, we see that using Non-Indo European languages yield a slightly higher improvement on an average than using Indo-European languages. This suggests that using languages from a distance family aids better disambiguation. Our findings echo those of (Resnik and Yarowsky, 1999), who found that the tendency to lexicalize senses of an English word differently in a second language, correlated with language distance.

6.4 Effect of Window Size.

Figure 3d shows the effect of increasing the crosslingual window (d') on the average ARI on the WSI task for the En-Fr and En-Zh models. While increasing the window size improves the average score for En-Zh model, the score for the En-Fr model goes down. This suggests that it might be beneficial to have a separate window parameter per language. This also aligns with the observation earlier that different language families have different suitability (bigger crosslingual context from a distant family helped) and requirements for optimal performance.

7 Qualitative Illustration

As an illustration for the effects of multilingual training, Figure 3 shows PCA plots for 11 sense vectors for 9 words using monolingual, bilingual and multilingual models. From Fig 3a, we note that with monolingual training the senses are poorly separated. Although the model infers two senses for *bank*, the two senses of *bank* are close to financial terms, suggesting their distinction was not recognized. The same observation can be

---

[5]Most works tune directly on the test dataset for Word Similarity tasks (Faruqui et al., 2016)

[6] (Šuster et al., 2016) compared different languages but did not control for domain.

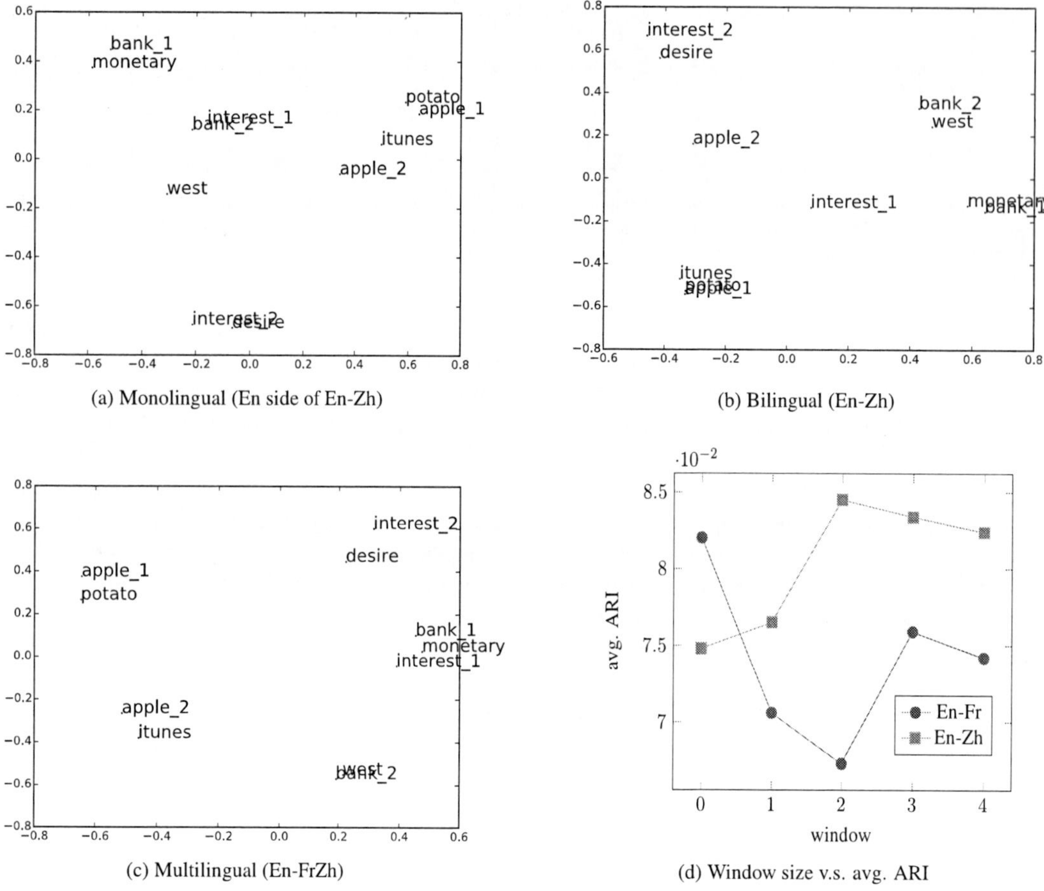

(a) Monolingual (En side of En-Zh)

(b) Bilingual (En-Zh)

(c) Multilingual (En-FrZh)

(d) Window size v.s. avg. ARI

Figure 3: **Qualitative:** PCA plots for the vectors for {*apple, bank, interest, itunes, potato, west, monetary, desire*} with multiple sense vectors for *apple*,*interest* and *bank* obtained using monolingual (3a), bilingual (3b) and multilingual (3c) training. **Window Tuning:** Figure 3d shows tuning window size for En-Zh and En-Fr.

made for the senses of *apple*. In Fig 3b, with bilingual training, the model infers two senses of *bank* correctly, and two sense of *apple* become more distant. The model can still improve eg. pulling *interest* towards the financial sense of *bank*, and pulling *itunes* towards *apple_2*. Finally, in Fig 3c, all senses of the words are more clearly clustered, improving over the clustering of Fig 3b. The senses of *apple*, *interest*, and *bank* are well separated, and are close to sense-specific words, showing the benefit of multilingual training.

8 Conclusion

We presented a multi-view, non-parametric word representation learning algorithm which can leverage multilingual distributional information. Our approach effectively combines the benefits of crosslingual training and Bayesian non-parametrics. Ours is the first multi-sense representation learning algorithm capable of using multilingual distributional information efficiently, by combining several parallel corpora to obtained a large multilingual corpus. Our experiments show how this multi-view approach learns high-quality embeddings using substantially less data and parameters than prior state-of-the-art. We also analyzed the effect of various parameters such as choice of language family and cross-lingual window size on the performance. While we focused on improving the embedding of English words in this work, the same algorithm could learn better multi-sense embedding for other languages. Exciting avenues for future research include extending our approach to model polysemy in foreign language. The sense vectors can then be aligned across languages, to generate a multilingual Wordnet like resource, in a completely unsupervised manner thanks to our joint training paradigm.

References

Collin F Baker, Charles J Fillmore, and John B Lowe. 1998. The berkeley framenet project. In *ACL*.

Mohit Bansal, John DeNero, and Dekang Lin. 2012. Unsupervised translation sense clustering. In *NAACL*.

Mohit Bansal, Kevin Gimpel, and Karen Livescu. 2014. Tailoring continuous word representations for dependency parsing. In *ACL*.

Sergey Bartunov, Dmitry Kondrashkin, Anton Osokin, and Dmitry Vetrov. 2016. Breaking sticks and ambiguities with adaptive skip-gram. *AISTATS* .

Chris Callison-Burch, Philipp Koehn, Christof Monz, and Omar F Zaidan. 2011. Findings of the 2011 workshop on statistical machine translation. In *WMT Shared Task*.

Jocelyn Coulmance, Jean-Marc Marty, Guillaume Wenzek, and Amine Benhalloum. 2015. Transgram, fast cross-lingual word-embeddings. In *EMNLP*.

Ido Dagan and Alon Itai. 1994. Word sense disambiguation using a second language monolingual corpus. *Computational linguistics* .

Mona Diab and Philip Resnik. 2002. An unsupervised method for word sense tagging using parallel corpora. In *ACL*.

Chris Dyer, Victor Chahuneau, and Noah A Smith. 2013. A simple, fast, and effective reparameterization of ibm model 2. In *NAACL*.

Andreas Eisele and Yu Chen. 2010. MultiUN: A multilingual corpus from united nation documents. In *LREC*.

Allyson Ettinger, Philip Resnik, and Marine Carpuat. 2016. Retrofitting sense-specific word vectors using parallel text. In *NAACL*.

Manaal Faruqui, Jesse Dodge, Sujay K. Jauhar, Chris Dyer, Eduard Hovy, and Noah A. Smith. 2015. Retrofitting word vectors to semantic lexicons. In *NAACL*.

Manaal Faruqui and Chris Dyer. 2014. Improving vector space word representations using multilingual correlation. In *EACL*.

Manaal Faruqui, Yulia Tsvetkov, Pushpendre Rastogi, and Chris Dyer. 2016. Problems with evaluation of word embeddings using word similarity tasks. In *1st RepEval Workshop*.

Thomas S Ferguson. 1973. A bayesian analysis of some nonparametric problems. *The annals of statistics* .

Jiang Guo, Wanxiang Che, Haifeng Wang, and Ting Liu. 2014a. Learning sense-specific word embeddings by exploiting bilingual resources. In *COLING*.

Jiang Guo, Wanxiang Che, Haifeng Wang, and Ting Liu. 2014b. Revisiting embedding features for simple semi-supervised learning. In *EMNLP*.

Jiang Guo, Wanxiang Che, David Yarowsky, Haifeng Wang, and Ting Liu. 2016. A representation learning framework for multi-source transfer parsing. In *AAAI*.

Karl Moritz Hermann and Phil Blunsom. 2014. Multilingual Distributed Representations without Word Alignment. In *ICLR*.

Matthew D Hoffman, David M Blei, Chong Wang, and John William Paisley. 2013. Stochastic variational inference. *JMLR* .

Eric H Huang, Richard Socher, Christopher D Manning, and Andrew Y Ng. 2012. Improving word representations via global context and multiple word prototypes. In *ACL*.

Lawrence Hubert and Phipps Arabie. 1985. Comparing partitions. *Journal of classification* .

Sujay Kumar Jauhar, Chris Dyer, and Eduard Hovy. 2015. Ontologically grounded multi-sense representation learning for semantic vector space models. In *NAACL*.

Kazuya Kawakami and Chris Dyer. 2015. Learning to represent words in context with multilingual supervision. *ICLR Workshop* .

Adam Kilgarriff. 1997. I don't believe in word senses. *Computers and the Humanities* .

Philipp Koehn. 2005. Europarl: A parallel corpus for statistical machine translation. In *MT summit*. volume 5, pages 79–86.

Jiwei Li and Dan Jurafsky. 2015. Do multi-sense embeddings improve natural language understanding? *EMNLP* .

Pengfei Liu, Xipeng Qiu, and Xuanjing Huang. 2015a. Learning context-sensitive word embeddings with neural tensor skip-gram model. In *IJCAI*.

Yang Liu, Zhiyuan Liu, Tat-Seng Chua, and Maosong Sun. 2015b. Topical word embeddings. In *AAAI*.

Thang Luong, Hieu Pham, and Christopher D. Manning. 2015. Bilingual word representations with monolingual quality in mind. In *Workshop on Vector Space Modeling for NLP*.

Tomas Mikolov, Wen-tau Yih, and Geoffrey Zweig. 2013. Linguistic regularities in continuous space word representations. In *NAACL*.

George A Miller. 1995. Wordnet: a lexical database for english. *Communications of the ACM* .

Mohammad Nasiruddin. 2013. A state of the art of word sense induction: A way towards word sense disambiguation for under-resourced languages. *arXiv preprint arXiv:1310.1425* .

Roberto Navigli. 2009. Word sense disambiguation: A survey. *ACM Computing Surveys (CSUR)* .

Arvind Neelakantan, Jeevan Shankar, Alexandre Passos, and Andrew McCallum. 2014. Efficient non-parametric estimation of multiple embeddings per word in vector space. In *EMNLP*.

Hwee Tou Ng, Bin Wang, and Yee Seng Chan. 2003. Exploiting parallel texts for word sense disambiguation: An empirical study. In *ACL*.

Lin Qiu, Yong Cao, Zaiqing Nie, Yong Yu, and Yong Rui. 2014. Learning word representation considering proximity and ambiguity. In *AAAI*.

Joseph Reisinger and Raymond J. Mooney. 2010. Multi-prototype vector-space models of word meaning. In *NAACL*.

Philip Resnik and David Yarowsky. 1999. Distinguishing systems and distinguishing senses: New evaluation methods for word sense disambiguation. *NLE* .

Jayaram Sethuraman. 1994. A constructive definition of dirichlet priors. *Statistica sinica* .

Huihsin Tseng, Pichuan Chang, Galen Andrew, Daniel Jurafsky, and Christopher Manning. 2005. A conditional random field word segmenter for sighan bake-off 2005. In *Proc. of SIGHAN*.

Joseph Turian, Lev Ratinov, and Yoshua Bengio. 2010. Word representations: a simple and general method for semi-supervised learning. In *ACL*.

Peter D. Turney. 2006. Similarity of semantic relations. *Computational Linguistics* .

Shyam Upadhyay, Manaal Faruqui, Chris Dyer, and Dan Roth. 2016. Cross-lingual models of word embeddings: An empirical comparison. In *ACL*.

Simon Šuster, Ivan Titov, and Gertjan van Noord. 2016. Bilingual learning of multi-sense embeddings with discrete autoencoders. In *NAACL*.

Zhaohui Wu and C Lee Giles. 2015. Sense-aaware semantic analysis: A multi-prototype word representation model using wikipedia. In *AAAI*.

David Yarowsky. 1995. Unsupervised word sense disambiguation rivaling supervised methods. In *ACL*.

DocTag2Vec: An Embedding Based Multi-label Learning Approach for Document Tagging

Sheng Chen[♯]*, Akshay Soni[†], Aasish Pappu[‡], Yashar Mehdad[§]

[♯]University of Minnesota-Twin Cities, Minneapolis, MN 55455, USA
[†]Yahoo Research, Sunnyvale, CA 94089, USA and [‡]New York, NY 10036, USA
[§]Airbnb, San Francisco, CA 94103, USA
`chen2832@umn.edu {akshaysoni,aasishkp}@yahoo-inc.com`
`yashar.mehdad@airbnb.com`

Abstract

Tagging news articles or blog posts with relevant tags from a collection of predefined ones is coined as document tagging in this work. Accurate tagging of articles can benefit several downstream applications such as recommendation and search. In this work, we propose a novel yet simple approach called DocTag2Vec to accomplish this task. We substantially extend Word2Vec and Doc2Vec – two popular models for learning distributed representation of words and documents. In DocTag2Vec, we simultaneously learn the representation of words, documents, and tags in a joint vector space during training, and employ the simple k-nearest neighbor search to predict tags for unseen documents. In contrast to previous multi-label learning methods, DocTag2Vec directly deals with raw text instead of provided feature vector, and in addition, enjoys advantages like the learning of tag representation, and the ability of handling newly created tags. To demonstrate the effectiveness of our approach, we conduct experiments on several datasets and show promising results against state-of-the-art methods.

1 Introduction

Every hour, several thousand blog posts are actively shared on social media; for example, blogging sites such as Tumblr[1] had more than 70 billion posts by January 2014 across different communities (Chang et al., 2014). In order to reach

---

*This work was done when the author was an intern at Yahoo.

[1]tumblr.com

right audience or community, authors often assign keywords or "#tags" (hashtags) to these blog posts. Besides being topic-markers, it was shown that hashtags also serve as group identities (Bruns and Burgess, 2011), and as brand labels (Page, 2012). On Tumblr, authors are allowed to create their own tags or choose existing tags to label their blog. Creating or choosing tags for maximum outreach can be a tricky task and authors may not be able to assign all the relevant tags. To alleviate this problem, algorithm-driven document tagging has emerged as a potential solution in recent times. Automatically tagging these blogs has several downstream applications, e.g., blog search, cluster similar blogs, show topics associated with trending tags, and personalization of blog posts. For better user engagement, the personalization algorithm could match user interests with the tags associated with a blog post.

From machine learning perspective, document tagging is by nature a *multi-label learning* (MLL) problem, where the input space is certain feature space $\mathcal{X}$ of document and the output space is the power set $2^{\mathcal{Y}}$ of a finite set of tags $\mathcal{Y}$. Given training data $\mathcal{Z} \subset \mathcal{X} \times 2^{\mathcal{Y}}$, we want to learn a function $f : \mathcal{X} \mapsto 2^{\mathcal{Y}}$ that predicts tags for unseen documents. As shown in Figure 1a, during training a standard MLL algorithm (big blue box) one typically attempts to fit the prediction function (small blue box) into feature vectors of documents and the corresponding tags. Note that feature vectors are generated *separately* before training, and tags for each document are encoded as a $|\mathcal{Y}|$-dimensional binary vector with one representing the presence and zero otherwise. In prediction phase, the learned prediction function will output relevant tags for the input feature vector of an unseen document. Following such a paradigm, many generic algorithms have been developed for MLL (Weston et al., 2011; Prabhu and Varma,

111

Proceedings of the 2nd Workshop on Representation Learning for NLP, pages 111–120,
Vancouver, Canada, August 3, 2017. ©2017 Association for Computational Linguistics

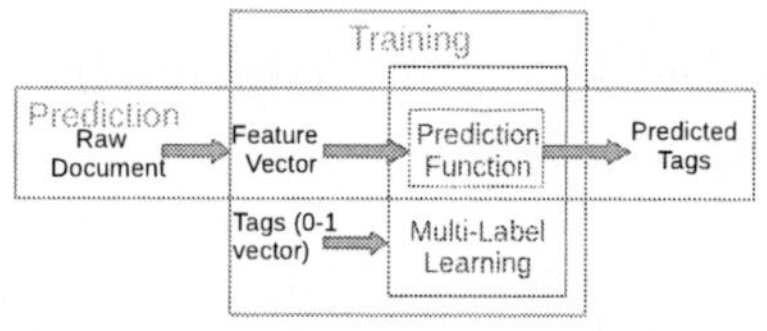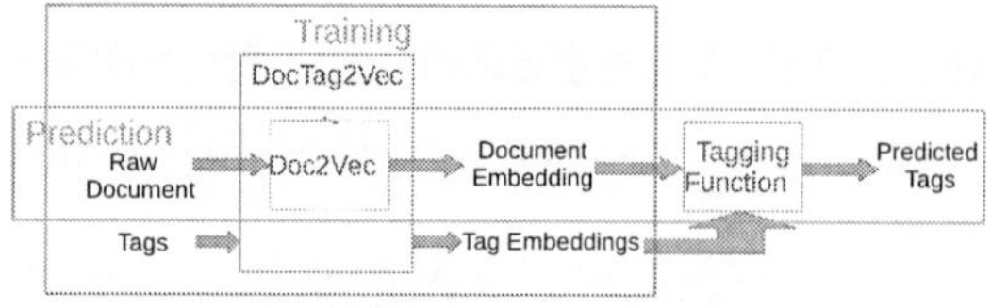

(a) standard multi-label learning   (b) proposed method (DocTag2Vec)

Figure 1: Comparison of standard multi-label learning framework and the proposed method

2014; Bhatia et al., 2015). With a surge of text content created by users online, such as blog posts, Wikipedia entries, etc., the algorithms for document tagging has many challenges. Firstly, time sensitive news articles are generated on a daily basis, and it is important for an algorithm to assign tags before they loose freshness. Secondly, new tagged documents could be fed into the training system, thus incrementally adapting the system to new training data without re-training from scratch is also critical. Thirdly, we might face a very large set of candidate tags that can change dynamically, as new things are being invented.

In view of the aforementioned challenges, in this paper we propose a new and simple approach for document tagging: DocTag2Vec. Our approach is motivated by the line of works on learning distributed representation of words and documents, e.g., Word2Vec (Mikolov et al., 2013) and Doc2Vec (a.k.a. Paragraph Vector) (Le and Mikolov, 2014). Word2Vec and Doc2Vec aim at learning low-dimensional feature vectors (i.e., embeddings) for words and documents from large corpus in an *unsupervised* manner, such that similarity between words (or documents) can be reflected by some distance metric on their embeddings. The general assumption behind Word2Vec and Doc2Vec is that more frequent co-occurrence of two words inside a small neighborhood of document should imply higher semantic similarity between them (see Section 2.2 for details). The DocTag2Vec extends this idea to document and tag by positing that document and its associated tags should share high semantic similarity, which allows us to learn the embeddings of tags along with documents (see Section 2.3 for details). Our method has two striking differences compared with standard MLL frameworks: firstly, our method directly works with raw text and *does not* need feature vectors extracted in advance. Secondly, our DocTag2Vec produces tag embeddings, which carry semantic information that are generally not available from standard MLL frame-

work. During training, DocTag2Vec directly takes the raw documents and tags as input and learns their embeddings using *stochastic gradient descent* (SGD). In terms of prediction, a new document will be first embedded using a Doc2Vec component inside the DocTag2Vec, and tags are then assigned by searching for the nearest tags embedded around the document. Overall the proposed approach has the following merits.

- The SGD training supports the incremental adjustment of DocTag2Vec to new data.

- The prediction uses the simple k-nearest neighbor search among tags instead of documents, whose running time does not scale up as training data increase.

- Since our method represent each individual tag using its own embedding vector, it it easy to dynamically incorporate new tags.

- The output tag embeddings can be used in other applications.

Related Work: Multi-label learning has found several applications in social media and web, like sentiment and topic analysis (Huang et al., 2013a), social text stream analysis (Ren et al., 2014), and online advertising (Agrawal et al., 2013). MLL has also been applied to diverse Natural Language Processing (NLP) tasks. However to the best of our knowledge we are the first to propose embedding based MLL approach to a NLP task. MLL has been applied to Word Sense Disambiguation (WSD) problem for polysemic adjectives (Boleda et al., 2007). (Huang et al., 2013b) proposed a joint model to predict sentiment and topic for tweets and (Surdeanu et al., 2012) proposed a multi-instance MLL based approach for relation extraction with distant supervision.

Recently learning embeddings of words and sentences from large unannotated corpus has gained immense popularity in many NLP tasks, such as Named Entity Recognition (Passos et al., 2014; Lample et al., 2016; Ma and Hovy, 2016), sentiment classification (Socher et al., 2011; Tang

112

et al., 2014; dos Santos and Gatti, 2014) and summarization (Kaageback et al., 2014; Rush et al., 2015; Li et al., 2015). Also, vector space modeling has been applied to search re-targeting (Grbovic et al., 2015a) and query rewriting (Grbovic et al., 2015b).

Given many potential applications, document tagging has been a very active research area. In information retrieval, it is often coined as content-based *tag recommendation* problem (Chirita et al., 2007), for which numbers of approaches were proposed, such as (Heymann et al., 2008), (Song et al., 2008b), (Song et al., 2008a) and (Song et al., 2011). Personalized tag recommendation is also studied in the literature (Symeonidis et al., 2008; Rendle et al., 2009). In machine learning community, a lot of general MLL algorithms have been developed, with application to document tagging, including compressed-sensing based approach (Hsu et al., 2009), WSABIE (Weston et al., 2011), ML-CSSP (Bi and Kwok, 2013), LEML (Yu et al., 2014), FastXML (Prabhu and Varma, 2014), SLEEC (Bhatia et al., 2015) to name a few.

Paper Organization: The rest of the paper is organized as follows. In Section 2, we first give a brief review of Word2Vec and Doc2Vec models, and then present training and prediction step respectively for our proposed extension, Doc-Tag2Vec. In Section 3, we demonstrate the effectiveness of our DocTag2Vec approach through experiments on several datasets. In the end, Section 4 is dedicated to conclusions and future works.

2 Proposed Approach

In this section, we present details of DocTag2Vec. For the ease of exposition, we first introduce some mathematical notations followed by a brief review for two widely-used embedding models: Word2Vec and Doc2Vec.

2.1 Notation

We let V be the size of vocabulary (i.e., set of unique words), N be the number of documents in the training set, M be the size of tag set, and K be the dimension of the vector space of embedding. We denote the vocabulary as $\mathcal{W} = \{w_1, \ldots, w_V\}$, set of documents as $\mathcal{D} = \{d_1, \ldots, d_N\}$, and the set of tags as $\mathcal{T} = \{t_1, \ldots, t_M\}$. Each document $d \in \mathcal{D}$ is basically a sequence of n_d words represented by $(w_1^d, w_2^d, \ldots, w_{n_d}^d)$, and is associated with M_d tags $\mathcal{T}_d = \{t_1^d, \ldots, t_{M_d}^d\}$. Here the sub-script d of n and M suggests that the number of word and tag is different from document to document. For convenience, we use the shorthand $w_i^d :$ w_j^d, $i \leq j$, to denote the subsequence of words $w_i^d, w_{i+1}^d, \ldots, w_{j-1}^d, w_j^d$ in document d. Correspondingly, we denote $\mathbf{W} = [\mathbf{w}_1, \ldots, \mathbf{w}_V] \in \mathbb{R}^{K \times V}$ as the matrix for word embeddings, $\mathbf{D} = [\mathbf{d}_1, \ldots, \mathbf{d}_N] \in \mathbb{R}^{K \times N}$ as the matrix for document embeddings, and $\mathbf{T} = [\mathbf{t}_1, \ldots, \mathbf{t}_M] \in \mathbb{R}^{K \times M}$ as the matrix for tag embeddings. Sometimes we may use the symbol d_i interchangeably with the embedding vector $\mathbf{d}_i$ to refer to the i-th document, and use $\mathbf{d}_d$ to denote the vector representation of document d. Similar conventions apply to word and tag embeddings. Besides we let $\sigma(\cdot)$ be the sigmoid function, i.e., $\sigma(a) = 1/(1 + \exp(-a))$.

2.2 Word2Vec and Doc2Vec

The proposed approach is inspired by the work of Word2Vec, an unsupervised model for learning embedding of words. Essentially, Word2Vec embeds all words in the training corpus into a low-dimensional vector space, so that the semantic similarities between words can be reflected by some distance metric (e.g., cosine distance) defined on their vector representations. The way to train Word2Vec model is to minimize the loss function associated with certain classifier with respect to both *feature vectors* (i.e., word embeddings) and *classifier parameters*, such that the nearby words are able to predict each other. For example, in *continuous bag-of-word* (CBOW) framework, Word2Vec specifically minimizes the following average negative log probability

$$\sum_{d \in \mathcal{D}} \sum_{i=1}^{n_d} - \log p(w_i^d \mid w_{i-c}^d : w_{i-1}^d, w_{i+1}^d : w_{i+c}^d) \, ,$$

where c is the size of context window inside which words are defined as "nearby". To ensure the conditional probability above is legitimate, one usually needs to evaluate a partition function, which may lead to a computationally prohibitive model when the vocabulary is large. A popular choice to bypass such issue is to use hierarchical softmax (HS) (Morin and Bengio, 2005), which factorizes the conditional probability into products of some simple terms. The hierarchical softmax relies on the construction of a binary tree $\mathcal{B}$ with V leaf nodes, each of which corresponds to a particular word in the vocabulary $\mathcal{W}$. HS is parameterized by a matrix $\mathbf{H} \in \mathbb{R}^{K \times (V-1)}$, whose columns are respectively mapped to a unique non-leaf node of $\mathcal{B}$. Additionally, we define $\text{Path}(w) = \{(i,j) \in \mathcal{B} \mid \text{edge } (i,j) \text{ is on the path from root to word } w\}$. Then the negative log probability is given as

$$-\log p(w_i^d \mid w_{i-c}^d : w_{i-1}^d, w_{i+1}^d : w_{i+c}^d)$$

$$= -\log \prod_{(u,v) \in \text{Path}(w_i^d)} \sigma\left(\text{child}(v) \cdot \langle \mathbf{g}_i^d, \mathbf{h}_v \rangle\right)$$

$$= -\sum_{(u,v) \in \text{Path}(w_i^d)} \log \sigma\left(\text{child}(v) \cdot \langle \mathbf{g}_i^d, \mathbf{h}_v \rangle\right) ,$$

$$\mathbf{g}_i^d = \sum_{\substack{-c \le j \le c \\ j \ne 0}} \mathbf{w}_{i+j}^d ,$$

where $\text{child}(u,v)$ is equal to 1 if v is the left child of u and 0 otherwise. Figure 2a shows the model architecture of CBOW Word2Vec. Basically $\mathbf{g}_i^d$ is the input feature for HS classifier corresponding to projection layer in Figure 2a , which essentially summarizes the feature vectors of context words surrounding w_i^d, and other options like averaging of $\mathbf{w}_{i+j}^d$ can also be applied. This Word2Vec model can be directly extended to Distributed memory (DM) Doc2Vec model by conditioning the probability of w_i^d on d as well as $w_{i-c}^d, \ldots, w_{i+c}^d$, which yields

$$-\log p(w_i^d \mid w_{i-c}^d : w_{i-1}^d, w_{i+1}^d : w_{i+c}^d, d)$$

$$= -\sum_{(u,v) \in \text{Path}(w_i^d)} \log \sigma\left(\text{child}(v) \cdot \langle \tilde{\mathbf{g}}_i^d, \mathbf{h}_v \rangle\right) ,$$

$$(1)$$

$$\tilde{\mathbf{g}}_i^d = \mathbf{d}_d + \sum_{\substack{-c \le j \le c \\ j \ne 0}} \mathbf{w}_{i+j}^d . \qquad (2)$$

The architecture of DM Doc2Vec model is illustrated in Figure 2b. Instead of optimizing some rigorously defined probability function, both Word2Vec and Doc2Vec can be trained using other objectives, e.g., negative sampling (NEG) (Mikolov et al., 2013).

2.3   Training for DocTag2Vec

Our approach, DocTag2Vec, extends the DM Doc2Vec model by adding another component for learning tag embeddings. In addition to predicting target word w_i^d using context $w_{i-c}^d, \ldots, w_{i+c}^d$, as shown in Figure 2c, DocTag2Vec also uses the document embedding to predict each associated tag, with hope that they could be closely embedded. The joint objective is given by

$$\sum_{d \in \mathcal{D}} \sum_{i=1}^{n_d} \left(-\log p(w_i^d \mid w_{i-c}^d : w_{i-1}^d, w_{i+1}^d : w_{i+c}^d, d) \right.$$

$$\left. - \alpha \sum_{t \in \mathcal{T}_d} \log p(t \mid d) \right) ,$$

where α is a tuning parameter. As discussed for Word2Vec, the problem of evaluating costly partition function is also faced by the newly introduced probability $p(t \mid d)$. Different from the conditional probability of w_i^d, the probability $p(t \mid d)$ cannot be modeled using hierarchical softmax, as the columns of parameter matrix do not have one-to-one correspondence to tags (remember that we need to obtain a vector representation for each tag). Motivated by the idea of negative sampling used in Word2Vec, we come up with the following objective for learning tag embedding rather than stick to a proper probability function,

$$-\sum_{t \in \mathcal{T}_d} \log \sigma\left(\langle \mathbf{d}_t, \mathbf{t}_t \rangle\right) + r \cdot \mathbb{E}_{\mathbf{t} \sim p}\left[\log \sigma\left(-\langle \mathbf{d}_t, \mathbf{t} \rangle\right)\right] ,$$

$$(3)$$

where p is a discrete distribution over all tag embeddings $\{\mathbf{t}_1, \ldots, \mathbf{t}_M\}$ and r is a integer-valued hyperparameter. The goal of such objective is to differentiate the tag t from the draws according to p, which is chosen as *uniform distribution* for simplicity in our practice. Now the final loss function for DocTag2Vec is the combination of (1) and (3),

$$\ell(\mathbf{W}, \mathbf{D}, \mathbf{T}, \mathbf{H}) = \sum_{d \in \mathcal{D}} \sum_{i=1}^{n_d}$$

$$\left(\underbrace{- \sum_{(u,v) \in \text{Path}(w_i^d)} \log \sigma\left(\text{child}(v) \cdot \langle \tilde{\mathbf{g}}_i^d, \mathbf{h}_v \rangle\right)}_{\text{DM Doc2Vec with hierarchical softmax}} - \right.$$

$$\left. \underbrace{\alpha \sum_{t \in \mathcal{T}_d} \log \sigma\left(\langle \mathbf{d}_t, \mathbf{t}_t \rangle\right) + r \cdot \mathbb{E}\left[\log \sigma\left(-\langle \mathbf{d}_t, \mathbf{t} \rangle\right)\right]}_{\text{tag embedding with negative sampling}} \right)$$

$$(4)$$

We minimize $\ell(\mathbf{W}, \mathbf{D}, \mathbf{T}, \mathbf{H})$ using stochastic gradient descent (SGD). To avoid exact calculation of the expectation in negative sampling, at each iteration we sample r i.i.d. instances of $\mathbf{t}$ from distribution p, denoted by $\{\mathbf{t}_p^1, \mathbf{t}_p^2, \ldots, \mathbf{t}_p^r\}$, to stochastically approximate the expectation, i.e., $\sum_{j=1}^r \log \sigma(-\langle \mathbf{d}_t, \mathbf{t}_p^j \rangle) \approx r \cdot \mathbb{E}\left[\log \sigma\left(-\langle \mathbf{d}_t, \mathbf{t} \rangle\right)\right]$.

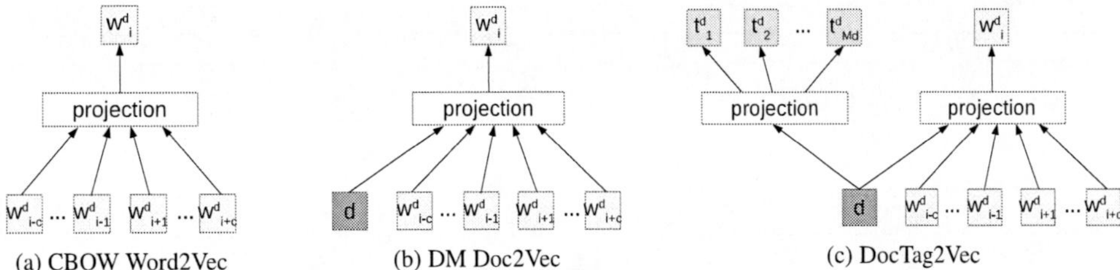

Figure 2: Model architectures of different embedding approaches

2.4 Prediction for DocTag2Vec

Unlike Word2Vec and Doc2Vec, which only target on learning high-quality embeddings of words and documents, DocTag2Vec needs to make predictions of relevant tags for new documents. To this end, we first embed the new document via the Doc2Vec component within DocTag2Vec and then perform k-nearest neighbor (k-NN) search among tags. To be specific, given a new document d, we first optimize the objective (1) with respect to $\mathbf{d}_d$ by fixing $\mathbf{W}$ and $\mathbf{H}$. Note that this is the standard inference step for new document embedding in Doc2Vec. Once $\mathbf{d}_d$ is obtained, we search for the k-nearest tags to it based on cosine similarity. Hence the prediction function is given as

$$f_k(\mathbf{d}_d) = \left\{ i \,|\, u_i \text{ is in the largest } k \text{ entries} \right.$$
$$\left. \text{of } \mathbf{u} = \overline{\mathbf{T}}^T \mathbf{d}_d \right\}, \tag{5}$$

where $\overline{\mathbf{T}}$ is column-normalized version of $\mathbf{T}$. To boost the prediction performance of DocTag2Vec, we apply the *bootstrap aggregation* (a.k.a. bagging) technique to DocTag2Vec. Essentially we train b DocTag2Vec learners using different randomly sampled subset of training data, resulting in b different tag predictors $f^1_{k'}(\cdot), \ldots, f^b_{k'}(\cdot)$ along with their tag embedding matrices $\mathbf{T}^1, \ldots, \mathbf{T}^b$. In general, the number of nearest neighbors k' for individual learner can be different from k. In the end, we combine the predictions from different models by selecting from $\bigcup_{j=1}^{b} f^j_{k'}(\mathbf{d}_d)$ the k tags with the largest aggregated similarities with $\mathbf{d}_d$,

$$f^{bag}_k(\mathbf{d}_d) = \left\{ i \,|\, u_i \text{ is in the largest } k \text{ entries of } \mathbf{u}, \right.$$
$$\left. \text{where } u_i = \sum_{j=1}^{b} \mathbb{I}\{i \in f^j_{k'}(\mathbf{d}_d)\} \cdot \langle \overline{\mathbf{t}}^j_i, \overline{\mathbf{d}}_d \rangle \right\}.$$

3 Experiments

3.1 Datasets

In this subsection, we briefly describe the datasets included in our experiments. It is worth noting that DocTag2Vec method needs raw texts as input instead of extracted features. Therefore many benchmark datasets for evaluating multi-label learning algorithms are not suitable for our setting. For the experiment, we primarily focus on the diversity of the source of tags, which capture different aspects of documents. The statistics of all datasets are provided in Table 1.

Public datasets:

- **Wiki10**: The wiki10 dataset contains a subset of English Wikipedia documents, which are tagged collaboratively by users from the social bookmarking site *Delicious*[1]. We remove the two uninformative tags, "wikipedia" and "wiki", from the collected data.

- **WikiNER**: WikiNER has a larger set of English Wikipedia documents. The tags for each document are the named entities inside it, which is detected automatically by some named entity recognition (NER) algorithm.

Proprietary datasets

- **Relevance Modeling (RM)**: The RM dataset consists of two sets of financial news article in Chinese and Korean respectively. Each article is tagged with related ticker symbols of companies given by editorial judgement.

- **News Content Taxonomy (NCT)**: NCT dataset is a collection of news articles annotated by editors with topical tags from a taxonomy tree. The closer the tag is to the root, the more general the topic is. For such tags with hierarchical structure, we also evaluate our method separately for tags of general topics (depth=2) and specific topics (depth=3).

3.2 Baselines and Hyperparameter Setting

The baselines include one of the state-of-the-art multi-label learning algorithms called SLEEC

Dataset	#training point	#testing point	#unique tags	Avg #tags per document
Wiki10	14095	6600	31177	17.27
WikiNER	89521	10000	67179	22.96
Relevance Modeling (Chinese)	4505	500	391	1.02
Relevance Modeling (Korean)	1292	500	261	1.07
NCT (all)	40305	9546	883	1.88
NCT (general)	39401	9389	294	1.76
NCT (specific)	17278	4509	412	1.41

Table 1: Statistics of datasets

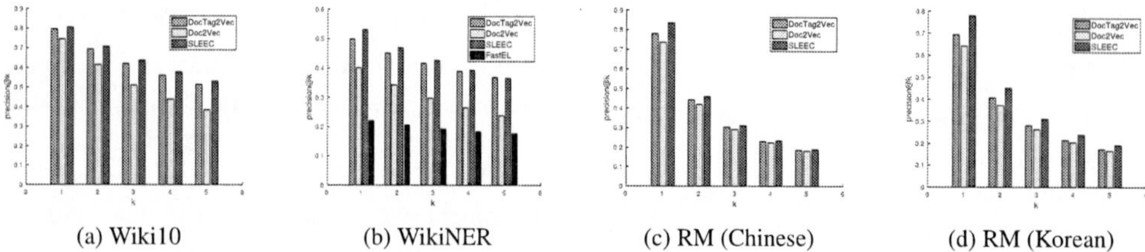

(a) Wiki10 (b) WikiNER (c) RM (Chinese) (d) RM (Korean)

Figure 3: Precision on Wiki10, WikiNER and Relevance Modeling dataset

(Bhatia et al., 2015), a variant of DM Doc2Vec, and an unsupervised entity linking system, FastEL (Blanco et al., 2015), which is specific to WikiNER dataset. SLEEC is based on non-linear dimensionality reduction of binary tag vectors, and use a sophisticated objective function to learn the prediction function. For comparison, we use the TF-IDF representation of document as the input feature vector for SLEEC, as it yields better result than embedding based features like Doc2Vec feature. To extend DM Doc2Vec for tagging purpose, basically we replace the document d shown in Figure 2b with tags $t_1^d, \ldots, t_{M_d}^d$, and train the Doc2Vec to obtain the tag embeddings. During testing, we perform the same steps as DocTag2Vec to predict the tags, i.e., inferring the embedding of test document followed by k-NN search. FastEL is unsupervised appproach for entity linking of web-search queries that walks over a sequence of words in query and aims to maximize the likelihood of linking the text span to an entity in Wikipedia. FastEL model calculates the conditional probabilities of an entity given every substring of the input document, however avoid computing entit to entity joint dependencies, thus making the process efficient. We built FastEL model using query logs that spanned 12 months and Wikipedia anchor text extracted from Wikipedia dumps dated November 2015. We choose an entity linker baseline because it is a simple way of detecting topics/entities that are semantically associated with a document.

Regarding hyperparameter setting, both SLEEC and DocTag2Vec aggregate multiple learners to enhance the prediction accuracy, and we set the number of learners to be 15. For SLEEC, we tune the rest of hyperparameters using grid search. For SLEEC and DocTag2Vec, we set the number of epochs for SGD to be 20 and the window size c to be 8. To train each individual learner, we randomly sample 50% training data. In terms of the nearest neighbor search, we set $k' = 10$ for Wiki10 and WikiNER while keeping $k' = 5$ for others. For the rest of hyperparameters, we also apply grid search to find the best ones. For DocTag2Vec, we additionally need to set the number of negative tags r and the weight α in (4). Typically r ranges from 1 to 5, and $r = 1$ gives the best performance on RM and NCT datasets. Empirically good choice for α is between 0.5 and 5. For FastEL, we consider a sliding window of size 5 over the raw-text (no punctuations) of document to generate entity candidates. We limit the number of candidates per document to 50.

3.3 Results

We use $precision@k$ as the evaluation metric for the performance. Figure 3 shows the precision plot of different approaches against choices of k on Wiki10, WikiNER and RM dataset. On Wiki10, we see that the precision of our DocTag2Vec is close to the one delivered by SLEEC, while Doc2Vec performs much worse. We observe similar result on WikiNER except for the precision@1, but our precision catches up as k increases. For RM dataset, SLEEC outperforms our approach, and we conjecture that such gap is due to the small size of training data, from which DocTag2Vec is not able to learn good embeddings. It

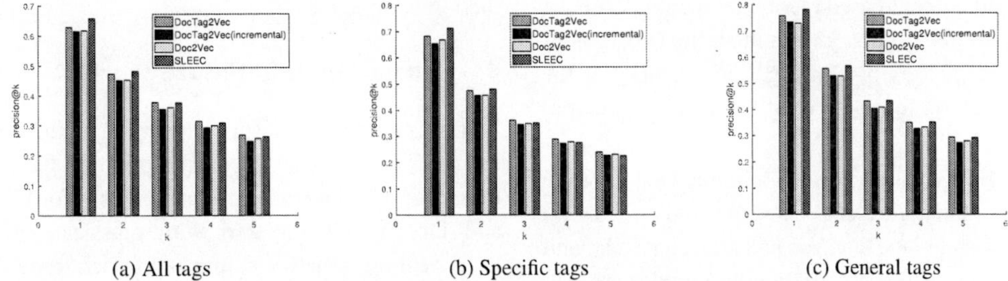

(a) All tags   (b) Specific tags   (c) General tags

Figure 4: Precision on News Content Taxonomy dataset

	DocTag2Vec	DocTag2Vec (incremental)	Doc2Vec	SLEEC
NCT (all tags)	0.6702	0.6173	0.6389	0.6524
NCT (specific tags)	0.8111	0.7678	0.7810	0.7624
NCT (general tags)	0.7911	0.7328	0.7521	0.7810

Table 2: Overall Recall on News Content Taxonomy dataset

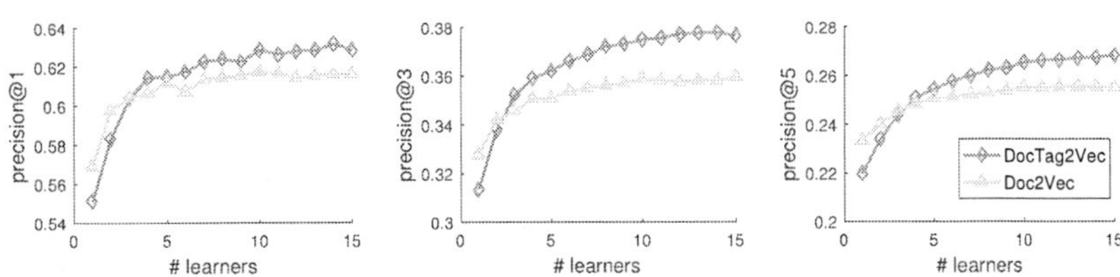

Figure 5: Precision vs. number of learners on NCT dataset

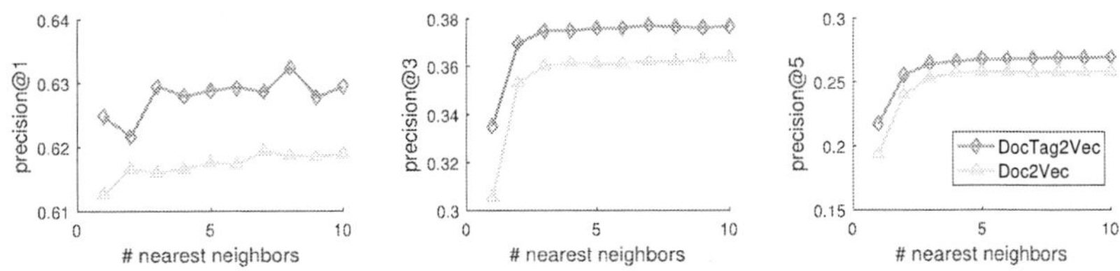

Figure 6: Precision vs. number of nearest neighbors on NCT dataset

News excerpt	Editorial tags	Prediction (top 3)	
		Predicted tags	similarity
The world is definitely getting warmer, according to the U.S. National Atmospheric and Oceanic Administration. For its annual "State of the Climate" report, NOAA for the first time gathered data on 37 climate indicators, such as air and sea temperatures, sea level, humidity, and snow cover in one place, and found that, taken together, the measurements show an "unmistakable upward trend" in temperature. Three hundred scientists analyzed the information and concluded it's "undeniable" that the planet has warmed since 1980, with the last decade taking the record for hottest ever recorded.	/Nature & Environment/ Natural Phenomena	/Nature & Environment/ Environment/Climate Change	1.99
		/Science/ Meteorology	0.64
		/Nature & Environment/Natural Phenomena/Weather	0.57
Business software maker Epicor Software Corp. said Thursday that its second-quarter loss narrowed as revenue climbed. For the April-June quarter, Epicor's loss totaled $1 million, or 2 cents per share, compared with a loss of $6.7 million, or 11 cents per share, in the year-ago quarter. When excluding one-time items, Epicor earned 13 cents per share, which is what analysts polled by Thomson Reuters expected. Revenue rose 9 percent to $109.2 million, beating analyst estimates for $105.2 million.	/Business/Sectors & Industries/ Information Technology/Internet Software & Services /Finance/Investment & Company Information	/Finance/Investment & Company Information/ Company Earnings	2.25
		/Finance/Investment & Company Information	1.23
		/Finance/Investment & Company Information/ Stocks & Offerings	0.32
TicketLiquidator, the leading provider of the world's most extensive ticket inventory for hard-to-find, low priced tickets, today announced that tickets are available for the Orlando Magic vs. Cleveland Cavaliers game on Wednesday, November 11th at Orlando's Amway Arena. The much-anticipated matchup features LeBron James, who is now in the final year of his contract with the Cavaliers.	/Sports & Recreation/ Baseball	/Sports & Recreation/Basketball	4.07
		/Arts & Entertainment/Events/Tickets	3.42
		/Sports & Recreation/Baseball	0.96

Table 3: Examples of Better Prediction over Editorial Judgement

is to be noted that SLEEC requires proper features as input and does not work directly with raw documents; while DocTag2Vec learns vector representation of documents that are not only useful for multilabel learning but also as features for other tasks like sentiment analysis, hate speech detection, and content based recommendation. We have demonstrated improvements in all the above mentioned use-cases of DocTag2Vec vectors but the discussion on those is out of the scope of this paper.

For NCT dataset, we also train the DocTag2Vec incrementally, i.e., each time we only feed 100 documents to DocTag2Vec and let it run SGD, and we keep doing so until all training samples are presented. As shown in Figure 4, our DocTag2Vec outperform Doc2Vec baseline, and delivers competitive or even better precision in comparision with SLEEC. Also, the incremental training does not sacrifice too much precision, which makes DocTag2Vec even appealing. The overall recall of DocTag2Vec is also slightly better than SLEEC, as shown in Table 2. Figure 5 and 6 include the precision plot against the number of learners b and the number of nearest neighbors k' for individual learner, respectively. It is not difficult to see that after $b = 10$, adding more learners does not give significant improvement on precision. For nearest neighbor search, $k' = 5$ would suffice.

3.4 Case Study for NCT dataset

For NCT dataset, when we examine the prediction for individual articles, it turns out surprisingly that there are a significant number of cases where DocTag2Vec outputs better tags than those by editorial judgement. Among all these cases, we include a few in Table 3 showing the superiority of the tags given by DocTag2Vec sometimes. For the first article, we can see that the three predicted tags are all related to the topic, especially the one with highest similarity, */Nature & Environment/ Environment/Climate Change*, seems more pertinent compared with the editor's. Similarly, we predict */Finance/Investment & Company Information/Company Earnings* as the most relevant topic for the second article, which is more precise than its parent */Finance/Investment & Company Information*. Besides our approach can even find the wrong tags assigned by the editor. The last piece of news is apparently about NBA, which should have the tag */Sports & Recreation/Basketball* as predicted, while the editor annotates them with the incorrect one, */Sports & Recreation/Baseball*. On the other hand, by looking at the similarity scores associated with the predicted tags, we can see that higher score in general implies higher aboutness, which can also be used as a quantification of prediction confidence.

4   Conclusions and Future Work

In this paper, we present a simple method for document tagging based on the popular distributional representation learning models, Word2Vec and Doc2Vec. Compared with classical multi-label learning methods, our approach provides several benefits, such as allowing incremental update of model, handling the dynamical change of tag set, as well as producing feature representation for tags. The document tagging can benefit a number of applications on social media. If the text content over web is correctly tagged, articles or blog posts can be pushed to the right users who are likely to be interested. And such good personalization will potentially improve the users engagement. In future, we consider extending our approach in a few directions. Given that tagged documents are often costly to obtain, it would be interesting to extend our approach to a semi-supervised setting, where we can incorporate large amounts of unannotated documents to enhance our model. On the other hand, with the recent progress in graph embedding for social network (Yang et al., 2016; Grover and Leskovec, 2016), we may be able to improve the tag embedding by exploiting the representation of users and interactions between tags and users on social networks.

Acknowledgements

The authors would like to thank the anonymous reviewers for their encouraging and thoughtful comments.

References

R. Agrawal, A. Gupta, Y. Prabhu, and M. Varma. 2013. Multi-label learning with millions of labels: Recommending advertiser bid phrases for web pages. In *Proceedings of the 22Nd International Conference on World Wide Web*. WWW '13.

K. Bhatia, H. Jain, P. Kar, M. Varma, and P. Jain. 2015. Sparse local embeddings for extreme multi-label classification. In *Proceedings of the 28th International Conference on Neural Information Processing Systems*. pages 730–738.

W. Bi and J. Kwok. 2013. Efficient multi-label classification with many labels. In *Proceedings of the 30th International Conference on Machine Learning (ICML-13)*. pages 405–413.

Roi Blanco, Giuseppe Ottaviano, and Edgar Meij. 2015. Fast and space-efficient entity linking for queries. In *Proceedings of the Eighth ACM International Conference on Web Search and Data Mining*. ACM, pages 179–188.

Gemma Boleda, Sabine Schulte im Walde, and Toni Badia. 2007. Modelling polysemy in adjective classes by multi-label classification. In *EMNLP-CoNLL*. pages 171–180.

Axel Bruns and Jean E Burgess. 2011. The use of twitter hashtags in the formation of ad hoc publics. In *Proceedings of the 6th European Consortium for Political Research (ECPR) General Conference 2011*.

Yi Chang, Lei Tang, Yoshiyuki Inagaki, and Yan Liu. 2014. What is tumblr: A statistical overview and comparison. *ACM SIGKDD Explorations Newsletter* 16(1):21–29.

P.-A. Chirita, S. Costache, W. Nejdl, and S. Handschuh. 2007. P-tag: Large scale automatic generation of personalized annotation tags for the web. In *Proceedings of the 16th International Conference on World Wide Web*. pages 845–854.

Cícero Nogueira dos Santos and Maira Gatti. 2014. Deep convolutional neural networks for sentiment analysis of short texts. In *COLING*. pages 69–78.

M. Grbovic, N. Djuric, V. Radosavljevic, and N. Bhamidipati. 2015a. Search retargeting using directed query embeddings. In *Proceedings of the 24th International Conference on World Wide Web*. pages 37–38.

M. Grbovic, N. Djuric, V. Radosavljevic, F. Silvestri, and N. Bhamidipati. 2015b. Context- and content-aware embeddings for query rewriting in sponsored search. In *Proceedings of the 38th International ACM SIGIR Conference on Research and Development in Information Retrieval*. pages 383–392.

A. Grover and J. Leskovec. 2016. Node2vec: Scalable feature learning for networks. In *Proceedings of the 22Nd ACM SIGKDD International Conference on Knowledge Discovery and Data Mining*. KDD '16.

P. Heymann, D. Ramage, and H. Garcia-Molina. 2008. Social tag prediction. In *Proceedings of the 31st Annual International ACM SIGIR Conference on Research and Development in Information Retrieval*. pages 531–538.

D. J Hsu, S. M Kakade, J. Langford, and T. Zhang. 2009. Multi-label prediction via compressed sensing. In *Advances in Neural Information Processing Systems 22*, pages 772–780.

S. Huang, W. Peng, J. Li, and D. Lee. 2013a. Sentiment and topic analysis on social media: A multi-task multi-label classification approach. In *Proceedings of the 5th Annual ACM Web Science Conference*. WebSci '13.

Shu Huang, Wei Peng, Jingxuan Li, and Dongwon Lee. 2013b. Sentiment and topic analysis on social media: a multi-task multi-label classification approach. In *Proceedings of the 5th annual acm web science conference*. ACM, pages 172–181.

Mikael Kaageback, Olof Mogren, Nina Tahmasebi, and Devdatt Dubhashi. 2014. Extractive summarization using continuous vector space models. In *Proceedings of the 2nd Workshop on Continuous Vector Space Models and their Compositionality (CVSC) EACL*. pages 31–39.

Guillaume Lample et al. 2016. Neural architectures for named entity recognition. *arXiv preprint arXiv:1603.01360*.

Q. V. Le and T. Mikolov. 2014. Distributed representations of sentences and documents. In *ICML*. volume 14, pages 1188–1196.

Jiwei Li, Minh-Thang Luong, and Dan Jurafsky. 2015. A hierarchical neural autoencoder for paragraphs and documents. *arXiv preprint arXiv:1506.01057*.

Xuezhe Ma and Eduard Hovy. 2016. End-to-end sequence labeling via bi-directional LSTM-CNNs-CRF. *arXiv preprint arXiv:1603.01354*.

T. Mikolov, I. Sutskever, K. Chen, G. S. Corrado, and J. Dean. 2013. Distributed representations of words and phrases and their compositionality. In *Advances in Neural Information Processing Systems 26*, pages 3111–3119.

Frederic Morin and Yoshua Bengio. 2005. Hierarchical probabilistic neural network language model. In *AISTATS05*. pages 246–252.

Ruth Page. 2012. The linguistics of self-branding and micro-celebrity in twitter: The role of hashtags. *Discourse & Communication* 6(2):181–201.

Alexandre Passos, Vineet Kumar, and Andrew McCallum. 2014. Lexicon infused phrase embeddings for named entity resolution. *arXiv preprint arXiv:1404.5367*.

Y. Prabhu and M. Varma. 2014. Fastxml: A fast, accurate and stable tree-classifier for extreme multi-label learning. In *Proceedings of the 20th ACM SIGKDD International Conference on Knowledge Discovery and Data Mining*. pages 263–272.

Z. Ren, M.-H. Peetz, S. Liang, W. van Dolen, and M. de Rijke. 2014. Hierarchical multi-label classification of social text streams. In *Proceedings of the 37th International ACM SIGIR Conference on Research & Development in Information Retrieval*. SIGIR '14.

S. Rendle, L. Balby Marinho, A. Nanopoulos, and L. Schmidt-Thieme. 2009. Learning optimal ranking with tensor factorization for tag recommendation. In *Proceedings of the 15th ACM SIGKDD International Conference on Knowledge Discovery and Data Mining*. pages 727–736.

Alexander M Rush, Sumit Chopra, and Jason Weston. 2015. A neural attention model for abstractive sentence summarization. *arXiv preprint arXiv:1509.00685* .

Richard Socher, Jeffrey Pennington, Eric H Huang, Andrew Y Ng, and Christopher D Manning. 2011. Semi-supervised recursive autoencoders for predicting sentiment distributions. In *Proceedings of the Conference on Empirical Methods in Natural Language Processing*. Association for Computational Linguistics, pages 151–161.

Y. Song, L. Zhang, and C. L. Giles. 2008a. A sparse gaussian processes classification framework for fast tag suggestions. In *Proceedings of the 17th ACM Conference on Information and Knowledge Management*. pages 93–102.

Y. Song, L. Zhang, and C. L. Giles. 2011. Automatic tag recommendation algorithms for social recommender systems. *ACM Trans. Web* 5(1):4:1–4:31.

Y. Song, Z. Zhuang, H. Li, Q. Zhao, J. Li, W.-C. Lee, and C. L. Giles. 2008b. Real-time automatic tag recommendation. In *Proceedings of the 31st Annual International ACM SIGIR Conference on Research and Development in Information Retrieval*. pages 515–522.

Mihai Surdeanu, Julie Tibshirani, Ramesh Nallapati, and Christopher D Manning. 2012. Multi-instance multi-label learning for relation extraction. In *Proceedings of the 2012 Joint Conference on Empirical Methods in Natural Language Processing and Computational Natural Language Learning*. Association for Computational Linguistics, pages 455–465.

P. Symeonidis, A. Nanopoulos, and Y. Manolopoulos. 2008. Tag recommendations based on tensor dimensionality reduction. In *Proceedings of the 2008 ACM Conference on Recommender Systems*. pages 43–50.

Duyu Tang, Furu Wei, Nan Yang, Ming Zhou, Ting Liu, and Bing Qin. 2014. Learning sentiment-specific word embedding for twitter sentiment classification. In *ACL (1)*. pages 1555–1565.

J. Weston, S. Bengio, and N. Usunier. 2011. Wsabie: Scaling up to large vocabulary image annotation. In *Proceedings of the Twenty-Second International Joint Conference on Artificial Intelligence - Volume Volume Three*. pages 2764–2770.

Z. Yang, W. W. Cohen, and R. Salakhutdinov. 2016. Revisiting semi-supervised learning with graph embeddings. In *Proceedings of the 33nd International Conference on Machine Learning, ICML 2016, New York City, NY, USA, June 19-24, 2016*.

H.-F. Yu, P. Jain, P. Kar, and I. S. Dhillon. 2014. Large-scale multi-label learning with missing labels. In *International Conference on Machine Learning (ICML)*. volume 32.

Binary Paragraph Vectors

Karol Grzegorczyk and **Marcin Kurdziel**
AGH University of Science and Technology
Department of Computer Science
Krakow, Poland
{kgr,kurdziel}@agh.edu.pl

Abstract

Recently Le & Mikolov described two log-linear models, called Paragraph Vector, that can be used to learn state-of-the-art distributed representations of documents. Inspired by this work, we present *Binary Paragraph Vector* models: simple neural networks that learn short binary codes for fast information retrieval. We show that binary paragraph vectors outperform autoencoder-based binary codes, despite using fewer bits. We also evaluate their precision in transfer learning settings, where binary codes are inferred for documents unrelated to the training corpus. Results from these experiments indicate that binary paragraph vectors can capture semantics relevant for various domain-specific documents. Finally, we present a model that simultaneously learns short binary codes and longer, real-valued representations. This model can be used to rapidly retrieve a short list of highly relevant documents from a large document collection.

1 Introduction

One of the significant challenges in contemporary information processing is the sheer volume of available data. Gantz and Reinsel (2012), for example, claim that the amount of digital data in the world doubles every two years. This trend underpins efforts to develop algorithms that can efficiently search for relevant information in huge datasets. One class of such algorithms, represented by, e.g., Locality Sensitive Hashing (Indyk and Motwani, 1998), relies on hashing data into short, locality-preserving binary codes (Wang et al., 2014). The codes can then be used to group the data into buckets, thereby enabling sublinear search for relevant information, or for fast comparison of data items. Most of the algorithms from this family are data-oblivious, i.e. can generate hashes for any type of data. Nevertheless, some methods target specific kind of input data, like text or image.

In this work we focus on learning binary codes for text documents. An important work in this direction has been presented by Salakhutdinov and Hinton (2009). Their *semantic hashing* leverages autoencoders with sigmoid bottleneck layer to learn binary codes from a word-count bag-of-words (BOW) representation. Salakhutdinov & Hinton report that binary codes allow for up to 20-fold improvement in document ranking speed, compared to real-valued representation of the same dimensionality. Moreover, they demonstrate that semantic hashing codes used as an initial document filter can improve precision of TF-IDF-based retrieval. Learning binary representation from BOW, however, has its disadvantages. First, word-count representation, and in turn the learned codes, are not in itself stronger than TF-IDF. Second, BOW is an inefficient representation: even for moderate-size vocabularies BOW vectors can have thousands of dimensions. Learning fully-connected autoencoders for such high-dimensional vectors is impractical. Salakhutdinov & Hinton restricted the BOW vocabulary in their experiments to 2000 most frequent words.

Binary codes have also been applied to cross-modal retrieval where text is one of the modalities. Specifically, Wang et al. (2013) incorporated tag information that often accompany text documents, while Masci et al. (2014) employed siamese neural networks to learn single binary representation for text and image data.

Recently several works explored simple neural models for unsupervised learning of distributed

Proceedings of the 2nd Workshop on Representation Learning for NLP, pages 121–130,
Vancouver, Canada, August 3, 2017. ©2017 Association for Computational Linguistics

representations of words, sentences and documents. Mikolov et al. (2013) proposed log-linear models that learn distributed representations of words by predicting a central word from its context (CBOW model) or by predicting context words given the central word (Skip-gram model). The CBOW model was then extended by Le and Mikolov (2014) to learn distributed representations of documents. Specifically, they proposed Paragraph Vector Distributed Memory (PV-DM) model, in which the central word is predicted given the context words and the document vector. During training, PV-DM learns the word embeddings and the parameters of the softmax that models the conditional probability distribution for the central words. During inference, word embeddings and softmax weights are fixed, but the gradients are backpropagated to the inferred document vector. In addition to PV-DM, Le & Mikolov studied also a simpler model, namely Paragraph Vector Distributed Bag of Words (PV-DBOW). This model predicts words in the document given only the document vector. It therefore disregards context surrounding the predicted word and does not learn word embeddings. Le & Mikolov demonstrated that paragraph vectors outperform BOW and bag-of-bigrams in information retrieval task, while using only few hundreds of dimensions. These models are also amendable to learning and inference over large vocabularies. Original CBOW network used hierarchical softmax to model the probability distribution for the central word. One can also use noise-contrastive estimation (Gutmann and Hyvärinen, 2010) or importance sampling (Cho et al., 2015) to approximate the gradients with respect to the softmax logits.

An alternative approach to learning representation of pieces of text has been recently described by Kiros et al. (2015). Networks proposed therein, inspired by the Skip-gram model, learn to predict surrounding sentences given the center sentence. To this end, the center sentence is encoded by an encoder network and the surrounding sentences are predicted by a decoder network conditioned on the center sentence code. Once trained, these models can encode sentences without resorting to backpropagation inference. However, they learn representations at the sentence level but not at the document level.

In this work we present Binary Paragraph Vector models, an extensions to PV-DBOW and PV-DM that learn short binary codes for text documents. One inspiration for binary paragraph vectors comes from a recent work by Lin et al. (2015) on learning binary codes for images. Specifically, we introduce a sigmoid layer to the paragraph vector models, and train it in a way that encourages binary activations. We demonstrate that the resultant binary paragraph vectors significantly outperform semantic hashing codes. We also evaluate binary paragraph vectors in transfer learning settings, where training and inference are carried out on unrelated text corpora. Finally, we study models that simultaneously learn short binary codes for document filtering and longer, real-valued representations for ranking. While Lin et al. (2015) employed a supervised criterion to learn image codes, binary paragraph vectors remain unsupervised models: they learn to predict words in documents.

2   Binary paragraph vector models

The basic idea in binary paragraph vector models is to introduce a sigmoid nonlinearity before the softmax that models the conditional probability of words given the context. If we then enforce binary or near-binary activations in this nonlinearity, the probability distribution over words will be conditioned on a bit vector context, rather than real-valued representation. The inference in the model proceeds like in Paragraph Vector, except the document code is constructed from the sigmoid activations. After rounding, this code can be seen as a distributed binary representation of the document.

In the simplest Binary PV-DBOW model (Figure 1) the dimensionality of the real-valued document embeddings is equal to the length of the binary codes. Despite this low dimensional representation – a useful binary hash will typically have 128 or fewer bits – this model performed surprisingly well in our experiments. Note that we cannot simply increase the embedding dimension-

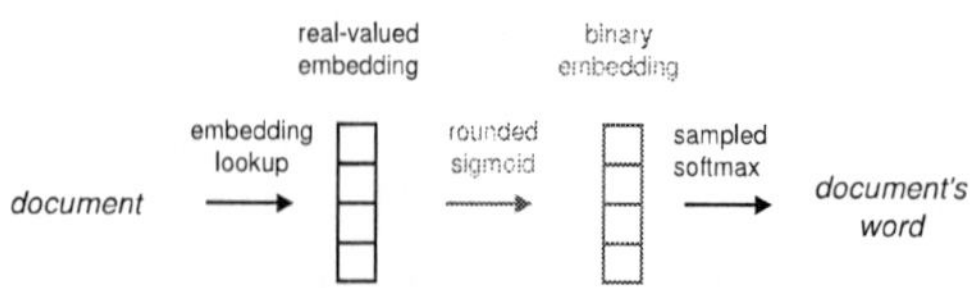

Figure 1: The Binary PV-DBOW model. Modifications to the original PV-DBOW model are highlighted.

ality in Binary PV-DBOW in order to learn better codes: binary vectors learned in this way would be too long to be useful in document hashing. The retrieval performance can, however, be improved by using binary codes for initial filtering of documents, and then using a representation with higher capacity to rank the remaining documents by their similarity to the query. Salakhutdinov and Hinton (2009), for example, used semantic hashing codes for initial filtering and TF-IDF for ranking. A similar document retrieval strategy can be realized with binary paragraph vectors. Furthermore, we can extend the Binary PV-DBOW model to simultaneously learn short binary codes and higher-dimensional real-valued representations. Specifically, in the Real-Binary PV-DBOW model (Figure 2) we introduce a linear projection between the document embedding matrix and the sigmoid nonlinearity. During training, we learn the softmax parameters and the projection matrix. During inference, softmax weights and the projection matrix are fixed. This way, we simultaneously obtain a high-capacity representation of a document in the embedding matrix, e.g. 300-dimensional real-valued vector, and a short binary representation from the sigmoid activations. One advantage of

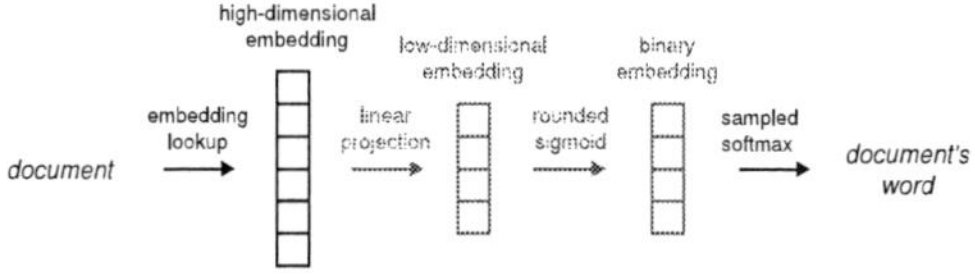

Figure 2: The Real-Binary PV-DBOW model. Modifications to the original PV-DBOW model are highlighted.

using the Real-Binary PV-DBOW model over two separate networks is that we need to store only one set of softmax parameters (and a small projection matrix) in the memory, instead of two large weight matrices. Additionally, only one model needs to be trained, rather than two distinct networks.

Binary document codes can also be learned by extending distributed memory models. Le and Mikolov (2014) suggest that in PV-DM, a context of the central word can be constructed by either concatenating or averaging the document vector and the embeddings of the surrounding words. However, in Binary PV-DM (Figure 3) we always construct the context by concatenating the relevant vectors before applying the sigmoid nonlinearity. This way, the length of binary codes is not tied to

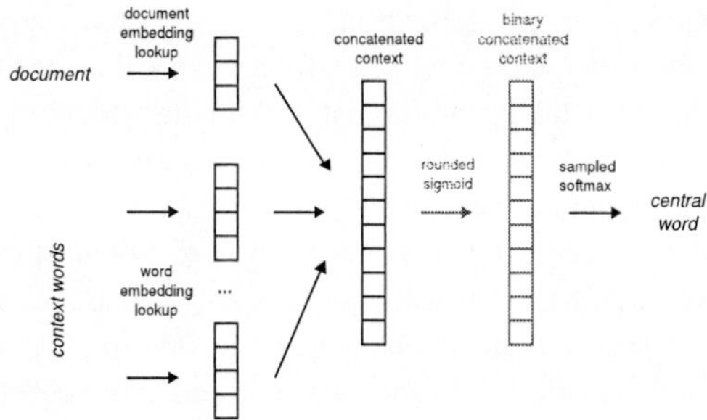

Figure 3: The Binary PV-DM model. Modifications to the original PV-DM model are highlighted.

the dimensionality of word embeddings.

Softmax layers in the models described above should be trained to predict words in documents given binary context vectors. Training should therefore encourage binary activations in the preceding sigmoid layers. This can be done in several ways. In semantic hashing autoencoders Salakhutdinov and Hinton (2009) added noise to the sigmoid coding layer. Error backpropagation then countered the noise, by forcing the activations to be close to 0 or 1. Another approach was used by Krizhevsky and Hinton (2011) in autoencoders that learned binary codes for small images. During the forward pass, activations in the coding layer were rounded to 0 or 1. Original (i.e. not rounded) activations were used when backpropagating errors. Alternatively, one could model the document codes with stochastic binary neurons. Learning in this case can still proceed with error backpropagation, provided that a suitable gradient estimator is used alongside stochastic activations. We experimented with the methods used in semantic hashing and Krizhevsky's autoencoders, as well as with the two biased gradient estimators for stochastic binary neurons discussed by Bengio et al. (2013). We also investigated the slope annealing trick (Chung et al., 2016) when training networks with stochastic binary activations. From our experience, binary paragraph vector models with rounded activations are easy to train and learn better codes than models with noise-based binarization or stochastic neurons. We therefore use Krizhevsky's binarization in our models.

3 Experiments

To assess the performance of binary paragraph vectors, we carried out experiments on three datasets: 20 Newsgroups[1], a cleansed version (also called v2) of Reuters Corpus Volume 1[2] (RCV1) and English Wikipedia[3]. As paragraph vectors can be trained with relatively large vocabularies, we did not perform any stemming of the source text. However, we removed stop words as well as words shorter than two characters and longer than 15 characters. Results reported by (Li et al., 2015) indicate that performance of PV-DBOW can be improved by including *n-grams* in the model. We therefore evaluated two variants of Binary PV-DBOW: one predicting words in documents and one predicting words and bigrams. Since 20 Newsgroups is a relatively small dataset, we used all words and bigrams from its documents. This amounts to a vocabulary with slightly over one million elements. For the RCV1 dataset we used words and bigrams with at least 10 occurrences in the text, which gives a vocabulary with approximately 800 thousands elements. In case of English Wikipedia we used words and bigrams with at least 100 occurrences, which gives a vocabulary with approximately 1.5 million elements.

The 20 Newsgroups dataset comes with reference train/test sets. In case of RCV1 we used half of the documents for training and the other half for evaluation. In case of English Wikipedia we held out for testing randomly selected 10% of the documents. We perform document retrieval by selecting queries from the test set and ordering other test documents according to the similarity of the inferred codes. We use Hamming distance for binary codes and cosine similarity for real-valued representations. Results are averaged over queries. We assess the performance of our models with precision-recall curves and two popular information retrieval metrics, namely mean average precision (MAP) and the normalized discounted cumulative gain at the 10th result (NDCG@10) (Järvelin and Kekäläinen, 2002). The results depend, of course, on the chosen document relevancy measure. Relevancy measure for the 20 Newsgroups dataset is straightforward: a retrieved document is relevant to the query if they both belong to the same newsgroup. In RCV1 each document belongs to a hierarchy of topics,

making the definition of relevancy less obvious. In this case we adopted the relevancy measure used by Salakhutdinov and Hinton (2009). That is, the relevancy is calculated as the fraction of overlapping labels in a retrieved document and the query document. Overall, our selection of test datasets and relevancy measures for 20 Newsgroups and RCV1 follows Salakhutdinov and Hinton (2009), enabling comparison with semantic hashing codes. To assess the relevancy of articles in English Wikipedia we can employ categories assigned to them. However, unlike in RCV1, Wikipedia categories can have multiple parent categories and cyclic dependencies. Therefore, for this dataset we adopted a simplified relevancy measure: two articles are relevant if they share at least one category. We also removed from the test set categories with less than 20 documents as well as documents that were left with no categories. Overall, the relevancy is measured over more than $11,800$ categories, making English Wikipedia harder than the other two benchmarks.

We use AdaGrad (Duchi et al., 2011) for training and inference in all experiments reported in this work. During training we employ dropout (Srivastava et al., 2014) in the embedding layer. To facilitate models with large vocabularies, we approximate the gradients with respect to the softmax logits using the method described by Cho et al. (2015). Binary PV-DM networks use the same number of dimensions for document codes and word embeddings.

Performance of 128- and 32-bit binary paragraph vector codes is reported in Table 1 and in Figure 4. For comparison we also report performance of real-valued paragraph vectors. Note that the binary codes perform very well, despite their far lower capacity: on 20 Newsgroups and RCV1 the 128-bit Binary PV-DBOW trained with bigrams approaches the performance of the real-valued paragraph vectors, while on English Wikipedia its performance is slightly lower. Furthermore, Binary PV-DBOW with bigrams outperforms semantic hashing codes: comparison of precision-recall curves from Figures 4a and 4b with Salakhutdinov and Hinton (2009, Figures 6 & 7) shows that 128-bit codes learned with this model outperform 128-bit semantic hashing codes on 20 Newsgroups and RCV1. Moreover, the 32-bit codes from this model outperform 128-bit semantic hashing codes on the RCV1 dataset, and

---

[1]Available at `http://qwone.com/~jason/20Newsgroups`

[2]Available at `http://trec.nist.gov/data/reuters/reuters.html`

[3]A snapshot from April 5th, 2016

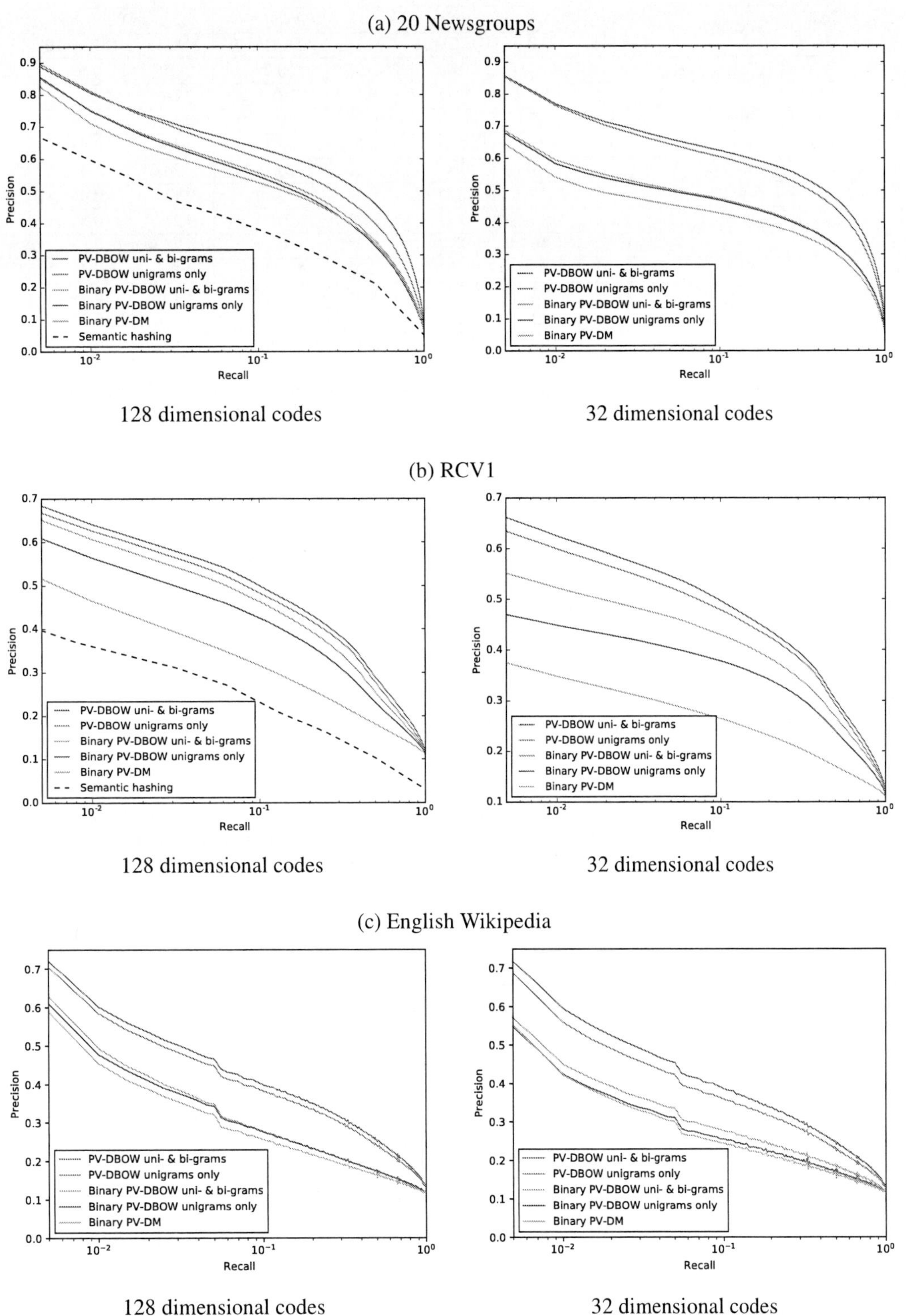

Figure 4: Precision-recall curves for the 20 Newsgroups, RCV1 and the English Wikipedia. Cosine similarity was used with real-valued representations and the Hamming distance with binary codes. For comparison we also included semantic hashing results reported by Salakhutdinov and Hinton (2009, Figures 6 & 7).

Code size	Model	With bigrams	20 Newsgroups		RCV1		English Wikipedia	
			MAP	NDCG@10	MAP	NDCG@10	MAP	NDCG@10
128	PV-DBOW	no	0.4	0.75	0.25	0.79	0.25	0.59
		yes	0.45	0.75	0.27	0.8	0.26	0.6
	Binary PV-DBOW	no	0.34	0.69	0.22	0.74	0.18	0.48
		yes	**0.35**	**0.69**	**0.24**	**0.77**	**0.18**	**0.49**
	PV-DM	N/A	0.41	0.73	0.23	0.78	0.24	0.59
	Binary PV-DM		0.34	0.65	0.18	0.69	0.16	0.46
32	PV-DBOW	no	0.43	0.71	0.26	0.75	0.23	0.55
		yes	0.46	0.72	0.27	0.77	0.25	0.58
	Binary PV-DBOW	no	0.32	0.53	0.22	0.6	0.16	0.41
		yes	**0.32**	**0.54**	**0.25**	**0.66**	**0.17**	**0.44**
	PV-DM	N/A	0.43	0.7	0.23	0.77	0.23	0.55
	Binary PV-DM		0.29	0.49	0.17	0.53	0.15	0.41

Table 1: Information retrieval results. The best results with binary models are highlighted.

on the 20 Newsgroups dataset give similar precision up to approximately 3% recall and better precision for higher recall levels. Note that the difference in this case lies not only in retrieval precision: the short 32-bit Binary PV-DBOW codes are more efficient for indexing than long 128-bit semantic hashing codes.

We also compared binary paragraph vectors against codes constructed by first inferring short, real-valued paragraph vectors and then using a separate hashing algorithm for binarization. When the dimensionality of the paragraph vectors is equal to the size of binary codes, the number of network parameters in this approach is similar to that of Binary PV models. We experimented with two standard hashing algorithms, namely random hyperplane projection (Charikar, 2002) and iterative quantization (Gong and Lazebnik, 2011). Paragraph vectors in these experiments were inferred using PV-DBOW with bigrams. Results reported in Table 2 show no benefit from using a separate algorithm for binarization. On the 20 Newsgroups and RCV1 datasets Binary PV-DBOW yielded higher MAP than the two baseline approaches. On English Wikipedia iterative quantization achieved MAP equal to Binary PV-DBOW, while random hyperplane projection yielded lower MAP. Some gain in precision of top hits can be observed for iterative quantization, as indicated by NDCG@10. However, precision of top hits can also be improved by querying with Real-Binary PV-DBOW model (Section 3.2). It is also worth noting that end-to-end inference in Binary PV models is more convenient than inferring real-valued vectors and then using another algorithm for hashing.

Li et al. (2015) argue that PV-DBOW outperforms PV-DM on a sentiment classification task, and demonstrate that the performance of PV-DBOW can be improved by including bigrams in the vocabulary. We observed similar results with Binary PV models. That is, including bigrams in the vocabulary usually improved retrieval precision. Also, codes learned with Binary PV-DBOW provided higher retrieval precision than Binary PV-DM codes. Furthermore, to choose the context size for the Binary PV-DM models, we evaluated several networks on validation sets taken out of the training data. The best results were obtained with a minimal one-word, one-sided context window. This is the distributed memory architecture most similar to the Binary PV-DBOW model.

Hashing algorithm	20 Newsgroups		RCV1		English Wikipedia	
	MAP	NDCG@10	MAP	NDCG@10	MAP	NDCG@10
Random hyperplane projection	0.27	0.53	0.21	0.66	0.16	0.44
Iterative quantization	0.31	0.58	0.23	0.68	0.17	0.46

Table 2: Information retrieval results for 32-bit binary codes constructed by first inferring 32d real-valued paragraph vectors and then employing a separate hashing algorithm for binarization. Paragraph vectors were inferred using PV-DBOW with bigrams.

3.1 Transfer learning

In the experiments presented thus far we had at our disposal training sets with documents similar to the documents for which we inferred binary codes. One could ask a question, if it is possible to use binary paragraph vectors without collecting a domain-specific training set? For example, what if we needed to hash documents that are not associated with any available domain-specific corpus? One solution could be to train the model with a big generic text corpus, that covers a wide variety of domains. Lau and Baldwin (2016) evaluated this approach for real-valued paragraph vectors, with promising results. It is not obvious, however, whether short binary codes would also perform well in similar settings. To shed light on this question we trained Binary PV-DBOW with

bigrams on the English Wikipedia, and then inferred binary codes for the test parts of the 20 Newsgroups and RCV1 datasets. The results are presented in Table 3 and in Figure 5. The model trained on an unrelated text corpus gives lower retrieval precision than models with domain-specific training sets, which is not surprising. However, it still performs remarkably well, indicating that the semantics it captured can be useful for different text collections. Importantly, these results were obtained without domain-specific finetuning.

	MAP	NDCG@10
20 Newsgroups	0.24	0.51
RCV1	0.18	0.66

Table 3: Information retrieval results for the Binary PV-DBOW model trained on an unrelated text corpus. Results are reported for 128-bit codes.

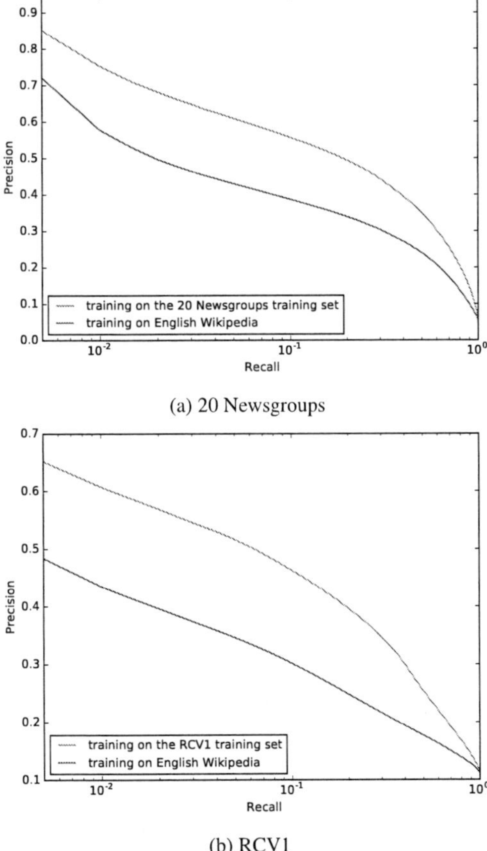

(a) 20 Newsgroups

(b) RCV1

Figure 5: Precision-recall curves for the baseline Binary PV-DBOW models and a Binary PV-DBOW model trained on an unrelated text corpus. Results are reported for 128-bit codes.

3.2 Retrieval with Real-Binary models

As pointed out by Salakhutdinov and Hinton (2009), when working with large text collections one can use short binary codes for indexing and a representation with more capacity for ranking. Following this idea, we proposed Real-Binary PV-DBOW model (Section 2) that can simultaneously learn short binary codes and high-dimensional real-valued representations. We begin evaluation of this model by comparing retrieval precision of real-valued and binary representations learned by it. To this end, we trained a Real-Binary PV-DBOW model with 28-bit binary codes and 300-dimensional real-valued representations on the 20 Newsgroups and RCV1 datasets. Results are reported in Figure 6. The real-valued representations learned with this model give lower precision than PV-DBOW vectors but, importantly, improve precision over binary codes for top ranked documents. This justifies their use alongside binary codes.

Using short binary codes for initial filtering of documents comes with a tradeoff between the retrieval performance and the recall level. For example, one can select a small subset of similar documents by using 28–32 bit codes and retrieving documents within small Hamming distance to the query. This will improve retrieval performance, and possibly also precision, at the cost of recall. Conversely, short codes provide a less fine-grained hashing and can be used to index documents within larger Hamming distance to the

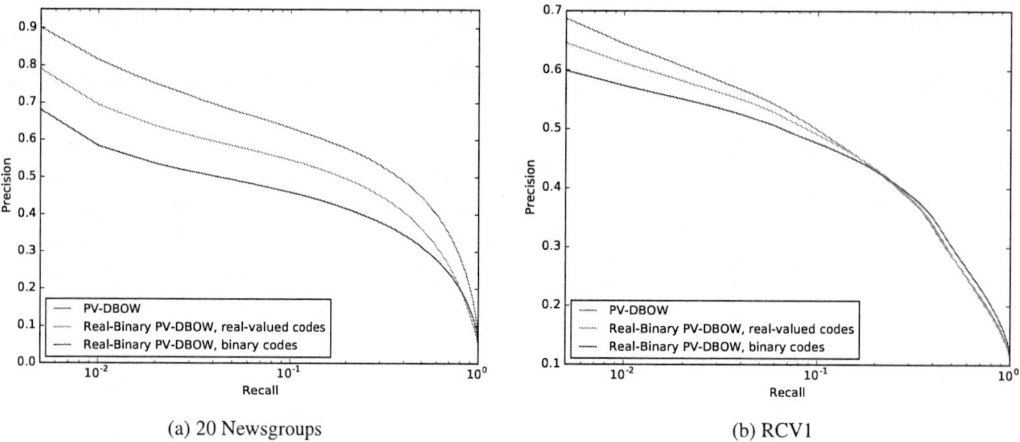

(a) 20 Newsgroups   (b) RCV1

Figure 6: Information retrieval results for binary and real-valued codes learned by the Real-Binary PV-DBOW model with bigrams. Results are reported for 28-bit binary codes and 300d real-valued codes. A 300d PV-DBOW model is included for reference.

query. They can therefore be used to improve recall at the cost of retrieval performance, and possibly also precision. For these reasons, we evaluated Real-Binary PV-DBOW models with different code sizes and under different limits on the Hamming distance to the query. In general, we cannot expect these models to achieve 100% recall under the test settings. Furthermore, recall will vary on query-by-query basis. We therefore decided to focus on the NDCG@10 metric in this evaluation, as it is suited for measuring model performance when a short list of relevant documents is sought, and the recall level is not known. MAP and precision-recall curves are not applicable in these settings.

Information retrieval results for Real-Binary PV-DBOW are summarized in Table 4. The model gives higher NDCG@10 than 32-bit Binary PV-DBOW codes (Table 1). The difference is large when the initial filtering is restrictive, e.g. when using 28-bit codes and 1-2 bit Hamming distance limit. Real-Binary PV-DBOW can therefore be useful when one needs to quickly find a short list of relevant documents in a large text collection, and the recall level is not of primary importance. If needed, precision can be further improved by using plain Binary PV-DBOW codes for filtering and standard DBOW representation for raking (Table 4, column B). Note, however, that PV-DBOW model would then use approximately 10 times more parameters than Real-Binary PV-DBOW.

4 Conclusion

In this article we presented simple neural networks that learn short binary codes for text documents. Our networks extend Paragraph Vector by introducing a sigmoid nonlinearity before the softmax that predicts words in documents. Binary codes inferred with the proposed networks achieve higher retrieval precision than semantic hashing codes on two popular information retrieval benchmarks. They also retain a lot of their precision when trained on an unrelated text corpus. Finally, we presented a network that simultaneously learns short binary codes and longer, real-valued representations.

Code size	Radius	NDCG@10					
		20 NG		RCV1		Wikipedia	
		A	B	A	B	A	B
28	1	0.79	0.85	0.77	0.85	0.66	0.7
	2	0.72	0.8	0.73	0.81	0.62	0.65
24		0.65	0.79	0.7	0.76	0.56	0.59
	3	0.63	0.76	0.69	0.74	0.5	0.55

Table 4: Information retrieval results for the Real-Binary PV-DBOW model. Real-valued representations have 300 dimensions. (A) Binary codes are used for selecting documents within a given Hamming distance to the query and real-valued representations are used for ranking. (B) For comparison, variant A was repeated with binary codes inferred using plain Binary PV-DBOW and real-valued representation inferred using original PV-DBOW model.

The best codes in our experiments were inferred with Binary PV-DBOW networks. The Binary PV-DM model did not perform so well. Li et al. (2015) made similar observations for Paragraph Vector models, and argue that in distributed memory model the word context takes a lot of the burden of predicting the central word from the document code. An interesting line of future research could, therefore, focus on models that account for word order, while learning good binary codes. It is also worth noting that Le and Mikolov (2014) constructed paragraph vectors by combining DM and DBOW representations. This strategy may proof useful also with binary codes, when employed with hashing algorithms designed for longer codes, e.g. with multi-index hashing (Norouzi et al., 2012).

Acknowledgments

This research is supported by National Science Centre, Poland grant no. 2013/09/B/ST6/01549 "Interactive Visual Text Analytics (IVTA): Development of novel, user-driven text mining and visualization methods for large text corpora exploration." This research was carried out with the support of the "HPC Infrastructure for Grand Challenges of Science and Engineering" project, cofinanced by the European Regional Development Fund under the Innovative Economy Operational Programme. This research was supported in part by PL-Grid Infrastructure.

A Visualization of Binary PV codes

For an additional comparison with semantic hashing, we used t-distributed Stochastic Neighbor Embedding (van der Maaten and Hinton, 2008) to construct two-dimensional visualizations of codes learned by Binary PV-DBOW with bigrams. We used the same subsets of newsgroups and RCV1 topics that were used by Salakhutdinov and Hinton (2009, Figure 5). Codes learned by Binary PV-DBOW (Figure 7) appear slightly more clustered.

References

Yoshua Bengio, Nicholas Léonard, and Aaron Courville. 2013. Estimating or propagating gradients through stochastic neurons for conditional computation. *arXiv preprint arXiv:1308.3432* .

(a) A subset of the 20 Newsgroups dataset: green - soc.religion.christian, red - talk.politics.guns, blue - rec.sport.hockey, brown - talk.politics.mideast, magenta - comp.graphics, black - sci.crypt.

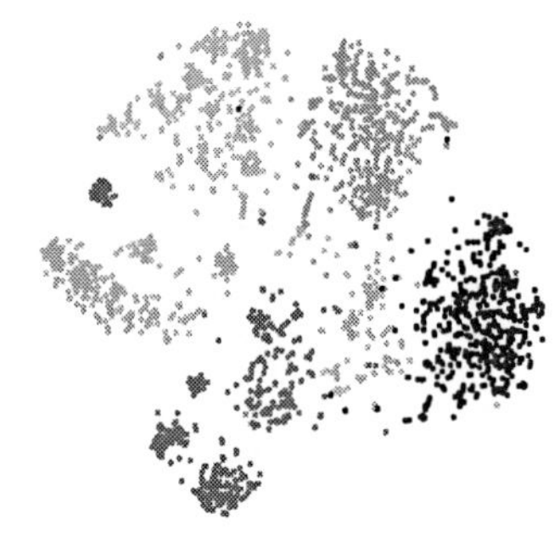

(b) A subset of the RCV1 dataset: green - disasters and accidents, red - government borrowing, blue - accounts/earnings, magenta - energy markets, black - EC monetary/economic.

Figure 7: t-SNE visualizations of 128 dimensional binary paragraph vector codes; the Hamming distance was used to calculate code similarity.

Moses S Charikar. 2002. Similarity estimation techniques from rounding algorithms. In *Proceedings of the thiry-fourth annual ACM symposium on Theory of computing*. ACM, pages 380–388.

Sébastien Jean Kyunghyun Cho, Roland Memisevic, and Yoshua Bengio. 2015. On using very large target vocabulary for neural machine translation. In *Proceedings of the 53rd Annual Meeting of the Association for Computational Linguistics and the 7th International Joint Conference on Natural Language Processing*. ACL, volume 1, pages 1–10.

Junyoung Chung, Sungjin Ahn, and Yoshua Bengio. 2016. Hierarchical multiscale recurrent neural networks. *arXiv preprint arXiv:1609.01704* .

John Duchi, Elad Hazan, and Yoram Singer. 2011. Adaptive subgradient methods for online learning and stochastic optimization. *Journal of Machine Learning Research* 12(Jul):2121–2159.

John Gantz and David Reinsel. 2012. The digital universe in 2020: Big data, bigger digital shadows, and biggest growth in the far east. Technical report, IDC.

Yunchao Gong and Svetlana Lazebnik. 2011. Iterative quantization: A procrustean approach to learning binary codes. In *Computer Vision and Pattern Recognition (CVPR), 2011 IEEE Conference on*. IEEE, pages 817–824.

Michael Gutmann and Aapo Hyvärinen. 2010. Noise-contrastive estimation: A new estimation principle for unnormalized statistical models. In *International Conference on Artificial Intelligence and Statistics*. pages 297–304.

Piotr Indyk and Rajeev Motwani. 1998. Approximate nearest neighbors: towards removing the curse of dimensionality. In *Proceedings of the thirtieth annual ACM symposium on Theory of computing*. ACM, pages 604–613.

Kalervo Järvelin and Jaana Kekäläinen. 2002. Cumulated gain-based evaluation of ir techniques. *ACM Transactions on Information Systems (TOIS)* 20(4):422–446.

Ryan Kiros, Yukun Zhu, Ruslan R Salakhutdinov, Richard Zemel, Raquel Urtasun, Antonio Torralba, and Sanja Fidler. 2015. Skip-thought vectors. In *Advances in neural information processing systems*. pages 3294–3302.

Alex Krizhevsky and Geoffrey E Hinton. 2011. Using very deep autoencoders for content-based image retrieval. In *Proceedings of the 19th European Symposium on Artificial Neural Networks*. pages 489–494.

Jey Han Lau and Timothy Baldwin. 2016. An empirical evaluation of doc2vec with practical insights into document embedding generation. In *Proceedings of the 1st Workshop on Representation Learning for NLP*. Association for Computational Linguistics, pages 78–86.

Quoc Le and Tomas Mikolov. 2014. Distributed representations of sentences and documents. In *Proceedings of The 31st International Conference on Machine Learning*. pages 1188–1196.

Bofang Li, Tao Liu, Xiaoyong Du, Deyuan Zhang, and Zhe Zhao. 2015. Learning document embeddings by predicting n-grams for sentiment classification of long movie reviews. *arXiv preprint arXiv:1512.08183* .

Kevin Lin, Huei Fang Yang, Jen Hao Hsiao, and Chu Song Chen. 2015. Deep learning of binary hash codes for fast image retrieval. In *Proceedings of the IEEE Conference on Computer Vision and Pattern Recognition Workshops*. pages 27–35.

Jonathan Masci, Michael M Bronstein, Alexander M Bronstein, and Jürgen Schmidhuber. 2014. Multimodal similarity-preserving hashing. *IEEE transactions on pattern analysis and machine intelligence* 36(4):824–830.

Tomas Mikolov, Kai Chen, Greg Corrado, and Jeffrey Dean. 2013. Efficient estimation of word representations in vector space. *arXiv preprint arXiv:1301.3781* .

Mohammad Norouzi, Ali Punjani, and David J Fleet. 2012. Fast search in hamming space with multi-index hashing. In *Computer Vision and Pattern Recognition (CVPR), 2012 IEEE Conference on*. IEEE, pages 3108–3115.

Ruslan Salakhutdinov and Geoffrey E Hinton. 2009. Semantic hashing. *International Journal of Approximate Reasoning* 50(7):969–978.

Nitish Srivastava, Geoffrey E Hinton, Alex Krizhevsky, Ilya Sutskever, and Ruslan Salakhutdinov. 2014. Dropout: A simple way to prevent neural networks from overfitting. *The Journal of Machine Learning Research* 15(1):1929–1958.

Laurens van der Maaten and Geoffrey Hinton. 2008. Visualizing data using t-SNE. *Journal of Machine Learning Research* 9(Nov):2579–2605.

Jingdong Wang, Heng Tao Shen, Jingkuan Song, and Jianqiu Ji. 2014. Hashing for similarity search: A survey. *arXiv preprint arXiv:1408.2927* .

Qifan Wang, Dan Zhang, and Luo Si. 2013. Semantic hashing using tags and topic modeling. In *Proceedings of the 36th international ACM SIGIR conference on Research and development in information retrieval*. ACM, pages 213–222.

Representing Compositionality based on Multiple Timescales Gated Recurrent Neural Networks with Adaptive Temporal Hierarchy for Character-Level Language Models

Moirangthem Dennis Singh, Jegyung Son, Minho Lee
School of Electronics Engineering
Kyungpook National University
Daegu, South Korea
{mdennissingh,wprud4,mholee}@gmail.com

Abstract

A novel character-level neural language model is proposed in this paper. The proposed model incorporates a biologically inspired temporal hierarchy in the architecture for representing multiple compositions of language in order to handle longer sequences for the character-level language model. The temporal hierarchy is introduced in the language model by utilizing a Gated Recurrent Neural Network with multiple timescales. The proposed model incorporates a timescale adaptation mechanism for enhancing the performance of the language model. We evaluate our proposed model using the popular Penn Treebank and Text8 corpora. The experiments show that the use of multiple timescales in a Neural Language Model (NLM) enables improved performance despite having fewer parameters and with no additional computation requirements. Our experiments also demonstrate the ability of the adaptive temporal hierarchies to represent multiple compositonality without the help of complex hierarchical architectures and shows that better representation of the longer sequences lead to enhanced performance of the probabilistic language model.

1 Introduction

Language Modeling is a fundamental task central to Natural Language Processing (NLP) and language understanding. A character-level language model (CLM) can be interpreted as a probability estimation method for the next character given a sequence of characters as input. From the perspective of sequence generation, predicting one character at a time has higher importance since it allows the network to invent novel words and strings. CLMs are commonly used for modeling new words and there have been successful techniques that use generative language models (LMs) based on characters or phonemes (Sutskever et al., 2011).

Recurrent neural networks have been applied to CLMs (Sutskever et al., 2011; Graves, 2013). Recently Kim et al. (2016b) introduced a LM with explicit hierarchical architecture to work at character levels and word levels. Cooijmans et al. (2017) introduced recurrent batch normalization into CLMs which significantly improved the performance. However, since the population statistics are estimated separately for each time step, the model is computationally intensive particularly for a CLM where the number of steps are more than conventional word level LMs. Similarly, Krueger and Memisevic (2016) introduced regularization in CLMs using a norm-stabilizer and reported an increased training time for higher levels of regularization.

In spite of the recent successes, CLMs still have inferior performance compared to its equivalent word-level models (Mikolov et al., 2012) since these LMs need to consider longer history of tokens to properly predict the next one. In order to improve the performance of the CLMs, there is a need for better representation of the additional levels of compositionality and the richer discourse structure found in CLMs.

Heinrich et al. (2012) used multiple timescale RNNs to learn the linguistic hierarchy for speech related tasks and Ding et al. (2016) demonstrated that, during listening to connected speech, cortical activity of different timescales concurrently tracked the time course of abstract linguistic compositionality at different hierarchical levels, such as words, phrases and sentences. In this work,

131

Proceedings of the 2nd Workshop on Representation Learning for NLP, pages 131–138,
Vancouver, Canada, August 3, 2017. ©2017 Association for Computational Linguistics

we propose a character-level recurrent neural network (RNN) LM that employs an adaptive multiple timescales approach to incorporate temporal hierarchies in the architecture to enhance the representation of multiple compositionalities. Our proposed model includes a novel timescale update mechanism which enhances the adaptation of the temporal hierarchy during the learning process. We build the temporal hierarchical structure using fast and slow context units to imitate different timescales. This temporal hierarchy concept is implemented based on the multiple timescales gated recurrent unit (MTGRU) (Kim et al., 2016a) that incorporates multiple timescales at different layers of the RNN.

Our model, inspired by the concept of temporal hierarchy found in the human brain (Botvinick, 2007; Meunier et al., 2010), demonstrates the ability to capture multiple compositionalities similar to the findings of Ding et al. (2016). This better representation learning capability enhances the ability of our model to handle longer sequences for the CLM. The resulting LM is a much simpler model that does not incorporate explicit hierarchical structures or normalization techniques. We show that our CLM with the biologically inspired temporal hierarchy is able to achieve performance comparable to the existing state-of-the-art CLMs evaluated over the Penn Treebank (PTB) and Text8 corpora.

2 Related Works

Recent advances in distributed representation learning have demonstrated promising results in language modeling. Distributed representation learning approaches are a group of methods in which real-valued vectors are trained to capture the underlying meaning in the input. Bengio et al. (2003) demonstrated that the probabilistic language models can achieve much better generalization.

Out-of-vocabulary words have always been a problem in language tasks. To address the rare word problem in language generation, Alexandrescu and Kirchhoff (2006) represented a word as a set of shared factor embeddings. In another approach, Sutskever et al. (2011) introduced NLMs that incorporated a character-level model with both input and output as characters. CLMs are also capable of generating novel words and are suitable for addressing the rare word problem.

Training a CLM has been a difficult task and its performance has been lower than the word-level LMs. Handling longer sequences is critical to improve the performance of CLMs and it remains a challenge. Mikolov et al. (2012) proposed an alternative approach, where subword-level models are trained to benefit from the word-level LMs. Pachitariu and Sahani (2013) proposed impulse-response LMs for improving RNN LMs. Recently, several studies on RNN based CLMs have been proposed, mostly using the Long short-term memory (LSTM) (Graves, 2013; Cooijmans et al., 2017; Zhang et al., 2016), where numerous regularization and normalization techniques have been applied to enhance the performance of CLMs. Additionally, weight generation networks (Ha et al., 2017), hierarchical architectures (Chung et al., 2017) in conjunction with the normalization techniques have been proposed to achieve state-of-the-art performance.

We propose a different approach for our CLM by using a simpler biologically inspired temporal hierarchy model. Recently, Ding et al. (2016) demonstrated strong evidence for a neural tracking of hierarchical linguistic structures in the brain. The study performed experiments to determine whether neural representation of language (speech) tracks hierarchical linguistic structures, rather than prosodic and statistical transitional probability cues. In simpler terms, the brain tracks and represents linguistic structures hierarchically. Similar findings have been shown in Meunier et al. (2010) and Botvinick (2007), but Ding et al. (2016) was the first to confirm the same in the domain of language. The authors hypothesized that concurrent neural tracking of hierarchical linguistic structures provides a mechanism for temporally integrating smaller linguistic units into larger structures. Therefore, our knowledge of the hierarchical nature of linguistic structures and the theory of linguistic compositionality have been shown to be biologically plausible. Previous works have applied this hierarchical structure to RNNs in movement tracking (Paine and Tani, 2004), sensorimotor control systems (Yamashita and Tani, 2008) and speech recognition (Heinrich et al., 2012). Based on the above conclusions, we adopt the multiple timescales concept to implement the temporal hierarchy architecture for representing multiple compositionalities which will help in handling longer sequences for our CLM.

Moreover, Yamashita and Tani (2008) had tested their model performance over different values of the timescale τ to investigate the impact of multiple timescales in RNNs. They showed that different setting of the timescales significantly affects the performance and a higher τ-ratio(τ-slow/τ-fast) improved the performance. In this spirit, we implement an adaptive timescale update method for better performance compared to a model with static timescales.

3 Proposed Character-Level Neural Language Model

A character-level language model (CLM) estimates a probability distribution over w_{t+1} given a sequence $w_{1:t} = [w_1, \ldots, w_t]$. We propose a recurrent neural network based CLM with temporal hierarchies using a multilayer gated recurrent neural network. Gated RNNs such as LSTM (Hochreiter and Schmidhuber, 1997) and Gated Recurrent Unit (GRU) (Cho et al., 2014) address the problem of learning long range dependencies. GRU and LSTM have been shown to yield comparable performance (Chung et al., 2014). These gated recurrent architectures are known to address the vanishing gradient problem efficiently and multilayer architectures are known to be able to learn expressive and complex features. However, the phenomenon responsible for these algorithms to approach human performance on speech and language tasks cannot be ascertained owing to our lack of understanding or insight into the actual representations that are being learned. However, due to our lack of understanding or insight into the actual representations being learned, it is difficult to ascertain the phenomenon responsible for these algorithms to approach human performance on speech and language tasks. Therefore, concurrent to the studies of temporal hierarchy in neuroscience (Ding et al., 2016), we formulated a hypothesis that multilayer gated recurrent neural networks can represent compositional hierarchies in the learning process that involves a monotonically increasing timescale hierarchy. We argue that hierarchical temporal representations capture the linguistic hierarchy of the input and are primarily responsible for better performance of multilayer gated recurrent architectures.

We propose a Multiple Timescales Gated Recurrent Unit (MTGRU) with adaptive timescales for our language model. The MTGRU, which

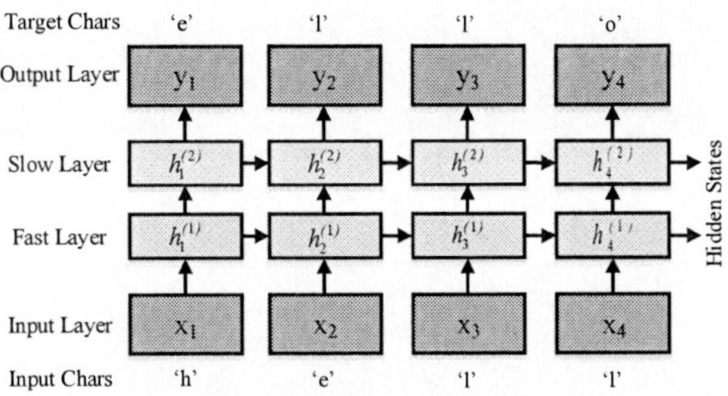

Figure 1: Proposed character-level neural language model.

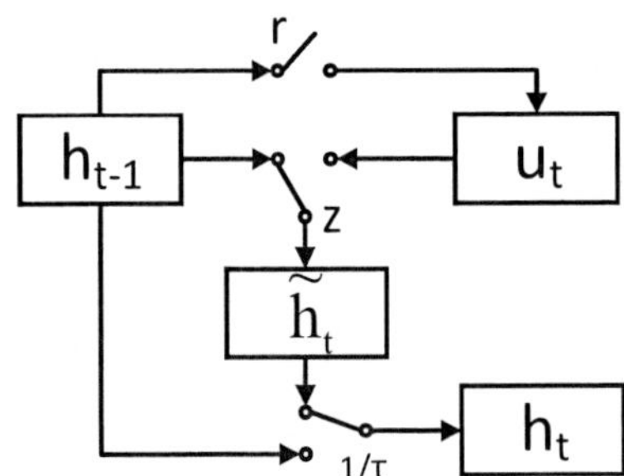

Figure 2: A Multiple Timescales Gated Recurrent Unit.

has a temporal hierarchical architecture, is implemented in the framework of a language model as shown in Figure 1. We find that the multiple timescales model is primarily responsible for explicitly guiding each layer of the neural network to facilitate in learning of features operating over increasingly slower timescales, corresponding to subsequent levels in the compositional hierarchy. The temporal hierarchy in the network is implemented by applying a timescale constant at the end of a conventional GRU unit, essentially adding another constant gating unit that modulates the mixture of past and current hidden states. In an MT-GRU, each step takes as input $\mathbf{x}_t, \mathbf{h}_{t-1}$ and produces the hidden $\mathbf{h_t}$. The time constant τ added to the activation $\mathbf{h}_t$ of the MTGRU is shown in Eq. (1). τ is used to control the timescale of each GRU cell. Larger τ results in slower cell outputs but it makes the cell focus on the slow features of a dynamic sequence input. The MTGRU model is illustrated in Figure 2.

133

$$r_t = \sigma(W_{xr}x_t + W_{hr}h_{t-1})$$
$$z_t = \sigma(W_{xz}x_t + W_{hz}h_{t-1})$$
$$u_t = \tanh(W_{xu}x_t + W_{hu}(r_t \odot h_{t-1})) \quad (1)$$
$$\tilde{h}_t = z_t h_{t-1} + (1 - z_t)u_t$$
$$h_t = \tilde{h}_t \frac{1}{\tau} + (1 - \frac{1}{\tau})h_{t-1}$$

where $\sigma(\cdot)$ and $\tanh(\cdot)$ are the sigmoid and tangent hyperbolic activation functions, $\odot$ denotes the element-wise multiplication operator, and $\mathbf{r}_t$, $\mathbf{z}_t$ are referred to as *reset*, *update* gates respectively. $\mathbf{u}_t$ and $\tilde{\mathbf{h}}_t$ are the candidate activation and candidate hidden state of the MTGRU.

We build the multilayer MTGRU-CLM with a different timescale τ for each layer. Based on our hypothesis that later layers should learn features that operate over slower timescales, we set larger τ as we go up the layers. We use the bits-per-character (BPC) as the evaluation metric. The timescale τ is initialized for each layers at the start of the training.

We implement the proposed timescale update mechanism by adaptively increasing the τ during the training process as it is known that just higher τ-ratio, without timescale adaptation, leads to improved performance (Yamashita and Tani, 2008). As we proceed with the training epochs, whenever the validation negative log-likelihood (NLL) (shown in Eq.(2)) stopped decreasing, the timescale τ is updated. A $growth\_factor$ is used to determine the growth rate of the timescales. We update the timescales only after training has completed for a particular number of epochs (max_epoch). The timescale update mechanism is presented in Algorithm 1. In order to prevent deteriorated performance over large increases in the timescales, smaller growth factors are set for the experiments.

$$-\frac{1}{N}\sum_{n=1}^{N}\sum_{t=1}^{T}\log P\left(w_t^n \mid w_1^n \ldots w_{t-1}^n; \theta\right) \quad (2)$$

where N is the number of training sequences, T is the length of the nth sequence, θ is the model parameter, and w_t^n is the token at time t of sequence n and so on.

4   Experiments and Results

We evaluate our CLM on the Penn Treebank (PTB) corpus (Marcus et al., 1993) and on the much larger Text8 corpus (Mahoney, 2009). We use orthogonal initialization for all the weight matrices and use stochastic gradient descent with gradient clipping at 1.0 and step rule determined by Adam (Kingma and Ba, 2014). We report the hyperparameter values that were explored in our experiments in Table 1. The timescale for the fast layer is initialized to 1 in all the experiments as $\tau = 1$ defines the default or the input timescale.

We also conduct an additional experiment for the comparison of computational efficiency of our model with normalization based techniques. The details of all the experiments are described in the sections below.

4.1   Penn Treebank (PTB) Corpus

The PTB corpus is divided to train, valid, and test sets following Mikolov and Zweig (2012). For this experiment we use 600 units in each layer of the 2 layer MTGRU network. We train on non-overlapping sequences of length 100 with a mini-batch size of 64 and a learning rate of 0.002. We initialize the timescales τ as $\{1, 1.3\}$ for the fast and the slow layers respectively. We set the $growth\_factor$ to 1.05 with a max_epoch of 25. The size of our model is 3.7M parameters.

We also implemented the batch normalized gated recurrent unit (BN-GRU) following Cooijmans et al. (2017) as a baseline to compare with

---

Input: Current Timescale τ
Output: Updated Timescale τ
if *current_epoch > max_epoch* **then**
    read $growth\_factor$;
    if *the validation NLL did not decrease*
    then
        $\tau = \tau * growth\_factor$;
        return τ;
    else
        return τ;
    end
end

Algorithm 1: Timescale adaptation in MTGRU

τ	$\{1.2, 1.3, 1.35, 1.4\}$
$growth\_factor$	$\{1.01, 1.05, 1.1, 1.15\}$
learning rate	$\{$1e-2, 1e-3, 1e-4, 2e-3$\}$
minibatch size	$\{32, 64, 128\}$

Table 1: Grid of hyperparameters explored in the experiments.

Model	BPC	Size
Zhang et al. (2016)	1.49	-
Mikolov et al. (2012)	1.41	-
Krueger and Memisevic (2016)	1.39	4.25M*
BN-GRU	1.39	4.1M
Mikolov et al. (2012)	1.37	-
Cooijmans et al. (2017)	1.32	4.25M*
Ha et al. (2017)	1.31	4.25M
MTGRU-CLM	1.27	3.7M
Ha et al. (2017)	1.27	4.91M
Chung et al. (2017)	1.24	5.35M*
MTGRU-CLM-Adaptive	1.24	3.7M
Ha et al. (2017)	1.22	14.41M

Table 2: Bits-Per-Character on PTB test and size of the models. **MTGRU-CLM** and **MTGRU-CLM-Adaptive** correspond to our CLMs with a constant timescale and an adaptive timescales respectively. *These are estimated model sizes as the actual number of parameters is not available in the literature.

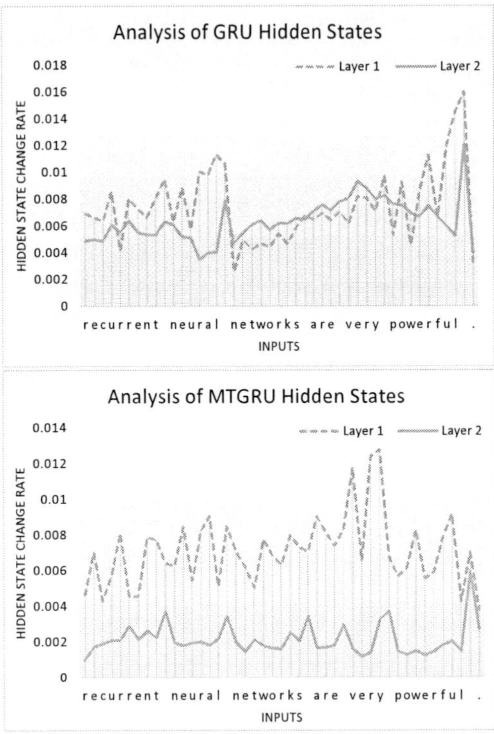

Figure 3: Hidden state representation of GRU-CLM and MTGRU-CLM-Adaptive.

our model. We use early-stopping on validation-set performance and the resulting model is evaluated over the test set and the results are summarized in Table 2. Our model performed comparable to the current state-of-the-art models with a test BPC of 1.24. We also illustrate the performance of our model in Table 4 under the different settings of τ and $growth\_factor$ given in Table 1.

For further analysis, we graph the hidden state change rate of each layer by measuring the $L2$ distance between the past and current hidden states of the MTGRU-CLM-Adaptive and the GRU CLM, over the input time steps as shown in Figure 3. The models are trained on the PTB set with the same set of parameters. In this graph, "spikes" can be interpreted as events where the input representation at each layer is varying significantly. The first(fast) layer, where the layer of the recurrent unit is exposed directly to the input (as illustrated in Fig. 1), the spiking corresponds to each character of the input. Looking at the second(slow) layer graph of MTGRU, we can observe the larger spikes correspond to the end of each word, while the same is not true in the case of GRU. It is evident that MTGRU learns better representation of each word by utilizing the temporal hierarchy without any explicit architectural hierarchy. These findings are consistent with the previous studies on speech where in speech sounds, syllable-level

information on short time scale is integrated into word-level information over a longer time scale (Yamashita and Tani, 2008; Ding et al., 2016).

4.2 Text8 Corpus

The Text8 corpus consists of 100M characters extracted from the Wikipedia corpus. We follow Mikolov and Zweig (2012) and divide the train, valid, and test sets accordingly in order to compare with previous works. Since Text8 contains only alphabets and spaces, the total number of symbols is just 27. We use 1200 units in each layer of the 2 layer MTGRU network and it is trained over non-overlapping sequences of length 180. The mini-batch size is set to 128 and the learning rate is 0.001. The timescales τ is initialized as $\{1, 1.3\}$ for the fast and the slow layers respectively with a $growth\_factor$ of 1.05. The max_epoch parameter is set to be 25. The size of this model is 14.5M parameters. The performance of the resulting model with early-stopping on validation-set is shown in Table 3. We also report the performance of the BN-GRU baseline model on the Text8 corpus. The MTGRU-CLM-Adaptive model obtains a test BPC of 1.29 which is comparable to the

Model	BPC	Size
Mikolov et al. (2012)	1.54	-
Zhang et al. (2016)	1.49	-
Pachitariu and Sahani (2013)	1.48	-
BN-GRU	1.39	16.1M
Cooijmans et al. (2017)	1.36	16.22M*
MTGRU-CLM	1.34	14.5M
Chung et al. (2017)	1.32	21M*
Chung et al. (2017)	1.29	21M*
MTGRU-CLM-Adaptive	1.29	14.5M

Table 3: Bits-Per-Character on Text8 test and size of the Models. **MTGRU-CLM** and **MTGRU-CLM-Adaptive** correspond to our CLMs with a constant timescale and an adaptive timescales respectively. *These are estimated parameter sizes as the actual value is not available in the literature.

Corpus	BPC
PTB Corpus	1.26±0.0158
Text8 Corpus	1.31±0.0187

Table 4: Performance of the proposed model under different timescale updates. These are the performance of the model under different settings of τ and $growth\_factors$ as shown in Table 1.

current state-of-the-art. The performance of this model under different τ and $growth\_factor$ settings given in Table 1 is shown in Table 4.

4.3 Comparison of Computing Efficiency

In order to compare the computation efficiency of MTGRU with the baselines, we replicated the Sequential MNIST experiment from Cooijmans et al. (2017) using our implementation of LSTM, GRU, Batch Normalized (BN)-LSTM, BN-GRU, MTGRU, and MTGRU-Adaptive following the same experimental conditions. Despite the faster convergence of BN-LSTM, BN-GRU, MTGRU, and MTGRU-Adaptive as illus-

Model	Accuracy	Train Time
LSTM	98.89%	14 hours
GRU	98.56%	15 hours
BN-LSTM	99.01%	41 hours
BN-GRU	98.97%	43 hours
MTGRU	99.26%	17 hours
MTGRU-Adaptive	99.37%	17 hours

Table 5: Sequential MNIST classification results with training duration of 100K steps.

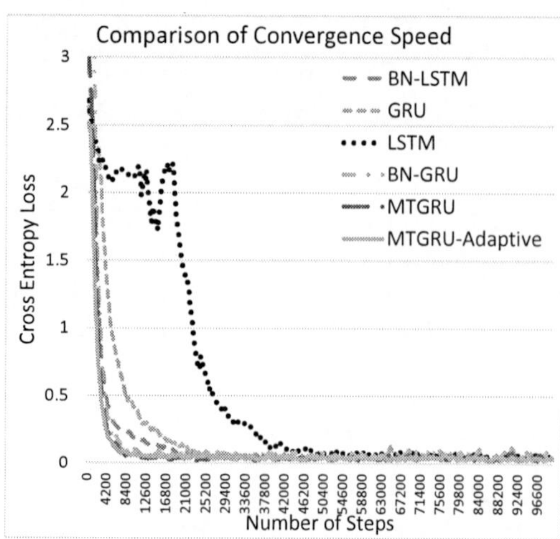

Figure 4: Comparison of convergence speed of the various models for Sequential MNIST classification task.

trated in Figure 4, the total time taken to train 100K steps of BN-LSTM, BN-GRU significantly increased compared to LSTM and GRU while the training time of MTGRU and MTGRU-Adaptive remained comparable to GRU as shown in Table 5. The experiments were performed on one machine with an Nvidia Titan-X GPU. Moreover, Kim et al. (2016a) already demonstrated much faster convergence in the case of MTGRU when compared to GRU in sequence-to-sequence tasks.

5 Discussion

The proposed method based on a biologically inspired hierarchical structure can represent multiple compositions of language by virtue of the adaptive multiple timescales in each layer. Sensitivity of the human brain to the compositional structure of language was recently confirmed by Ding et al. (2016). By recording the activity of listeners brains using magnetoencephalography (MEG), it was found that the brain activates or spikes when it is presented with individual words, phrases, or a whole sentence. We successfully replicated this property in our model and it achieves significant performance gains despite having a simpler structure and lesser number of parameters. Our model's ability to represent compositions of language at the word level is illustrated in Figure 3. This illustration validates our hypothesis that multilayer gated recurrent neural networks can represent compositional hierarchies similar to the human brain.

The enhanced performance of the proposed CLM illustrates that our approach can give better generalization performance without the help of complex hierarchical architectures. The results indicate that the temporal hierarchies with the adaptive timescale approach can represent the compositonality better and increases the capability of the model to handle longer sequences for the CLM. The results also demonstrate that our multilayer MTGRU model with adaptive timescale performs comparable to the current state-of-the-art models despite having fewer parameters and a simpler architecture. The temporal hierarchy approach eliminates the need for complex structures and normalization techniques (Cooijmans et al., 2017; Krueger and Memisevic, 2016; Chung et al., 2017; Ha et al., 2017) for the LM task, thereby increasing the computational efficiency of our model.

6 Conclusion

Our approach incorporates temporal hierarchies in a character-level NLM to improve the performance of the language model without introducing additional parameters. The proposed approach takes into account the need for a biologically plausible structure and a model to implement simpler hierarchies for handling different level of language compositions in order to tackle the longer sequences problem in CLMs. Our approach with adaptive timescales enables a simpler model with a better representation of language to achieve significant performance gains over existing models with larger complexities and also alleviates the need of additional computations.

Acknowledgment

This research was supported by ICT R&D program of MSIP/IITP [R7124-16-0004, Development of Intelligent Interaction Technology Based on Context Awareness and Human Intention Understanding] (70%) and by the National Research Foundation of Korea (NRF) grant funded by the Korea government (MSIP) (No. NRF-2016M3C1B6929647) (30%).

References

Andrei Alexandrescu and Katrin Kirchhoff. 2006. Factored neural language models. In *Proceedings of the Human Language Technology Conference of the NAACL, Companion Volume: Short Papers*. Association for Computational Linguistics, pages 1–4.

Yoshua Bengio, Réjean Ducharme, Pascal Vincent, and Christian Jauvin. 2003. A neural probabilistic language model. *journal of machine learning research* 3(Feb):1137–1155.

Matthew M Botvinick. 2007. Multilevel structure in behaviour and in the brain: a model of fuster's hierarchy. *Philosophical Transactions of the Royal Society B: Biological Sciences* 362(1485):1615–26. https://doi.org/10.1098/rstb.2007.2056.

Kyunghyun Cho, Bart van Merrienboer, Çaglar Gülçehre, Fethi Bougares, Holger Schwenk, and Yoshua Bengio. 2014. Learning phrase representations using RNN encoder-decoder for statistical machine translation. *CoRR* abs/1406.1078. http://arxiv.org/abs/1406.1078.

Junyoung Chung, Sungjin Ahn, and Yoshua Bengio. 2017. Hierarchical multiscale recurrent neural networks. In *Proceeding of the International Conference on Learning Representations*.

Junyoung Chung, Çaglar Gülçehre, KyungHyun Cho, and Yoshua Bengio. 2014. Empirical evaluation of gated recurrent neural networks on sequence modeling. *CoRR* abs/1412.3555. http://arxiv.org/abs/1412.3555.

Tim Cooijmans, Nicolas Ballas, César Laurent, Çağlar Gülçehre, and Aaron Courville. 2017. Recurrent batch normalization. In *Proceeding of the International Conference on Learning Representations*.

Nai Ding, Lucia Melloni, Hang Zhang, Xing Tian, and David Poeppel. 2016. Cortical tracking of hierarchical linguistic structures in connected speech. *Nature neuroscience* 19(1):158–164.

Alex Graves. 2013. Generating sequences with recurrent neural networks. *arXiv preprint arXiv:1308.0850* .

David Ha, Andrew Dai, and Quoc V Le. 2017. Hypernetworks. In *Proceeding of the International Conference on Learning Representations*.

Stefan Heinrich, Cornelius Weber, and Stefan Wermter. 2012. Adaptive learning of linguistic hierarchy in a multiple timescale recurrent neural network. In *International Conference on Artificial Neural Networks*. Springer, pages 555–562.

Sepp Hochreiter and Jürgen Schmidhuber. 1997. Long short-term memory. *Neural computation* 9(8):1735–1780.

Minsoo Kim, Moirangthem Dennis Singh, and Minho Lee. 2016a. Towards abstraction from extraction: Multiple timescale gated recurrent unit for summarization. *ACL 2016* pages 70–77.

Yoon Kim, Yacine Jernite, David Sontag, and Alexander M Rush. 2016b. Character-aware neural language models. In *Proceedings of the Thirtieth AAAI Conference on Artificial Intelligence*. AAAI Press, pages 2741–2749.

Diederik Kingma and Jimmy Ba. 2014. Adam: A method for stochastic optimization. *arXiv preprint arXiv:1412.6980* .

David Krueger and Roland Memisevic. 2016. Regularizing rnns by stabilizing activations. In *Proceeding of the International Conference on Learning Representations*.

Matt Mahoney. 2009. Large text compression benchmark. *URL: http://www. mattmahoney. net/text/text. html* .

Mitchell P Marcus, Mary Ann Marcinkiewicz, and Beatrice Santorini. 1993. Building a large annotated corpus of english: The penn treebank. *Computational linguistics* 19(2):313–330.

D. Meunier, R. Lambiotte, A. Fornito, K. D. Ersche, and E. T. Bullmore. 2010. Hierarchical modularity in human brain functional networks. *ArXiv e-prints* .

Tomáš Mikolov, Ilya Sutskever, Anoop Deoras, Hai-Son Le, Stefan Kombrink, and Jan Cernocky. 2012. Subword language modeling with neural networks. *preprint (http://www. fit. vutbr. cz/imikolov/rnnlm/char. pdf)* .

Tomas Mikolov and Geoffrey Zweig. 2012. Context dependent recurrent neural network language model. In *SLT*. pages 234–239.

Marius Pachitariu and Maneesh Sahani. 2013. Regularization and nonlinearities for neural language models: when are they needed? *arXiv preprint arXiv:1301.5650* .

Rainer W. Paine and Jun Tani. 2004. Motor primitive and sequence self-organization in a hierarchical recurrent neural network. *Neural Networks* 17(89):1291 – 1309. New Developments in Self-Organizing Systems.

Ilya Sutskever, James Martens, and Geoffrey E Hinton. 2011. Generating text with recurrent neural networks. In *Proceedings of the 28th International Conference on Machine Learning (ICML-11)*. pages 1017–1024.

Yuichi Yamashita and Jun Tani. 2008. Emergence of functional hierarchy in a multiple timescale neural network model: A humanoid robot experiment. *PLoS Comput Biol* 4(11):1–18. https://doi.org/10.1371/journal.pcbi.1000220.

Saizheng Zhang, Yuhuai Wu, Tong Che, Zhouhan Lin, Roland Memisevic, Ruslan R Salakhutdinov, and Yoshua Bengio. 2016. Architectural complexity measures of recurrent neural networks. In *Advances in Neural Information Processing Systems*. pages 1822–1830.

Learning Bilingual Projections of Embeddings
for Vocabulary Expansion in Machine Translation

Pranava Swaroop Madhyastha[*]
Department of Computer Science
University of Sheffield
Sheffield, S1 4DP, UK
p.madhyastha@sheffield.ac.uk

Cristina España-Bonet[*]
University of Saarland
DFKI, German Research Center
for Artificial Intelligence
Saarbrücken, Germany
cristinae@dfki.de

Abstract

We propose a simple log-bilinear softmax-based model to deal with vocabulary expansion in machine translation. Our model uses word embeddings trained on significantly large unlabelled monolingual corpora and learns over a fairly small, word-to-word bilingual dictionary. Given an out-of-vocabulary source word, the model generates a probabilistic list of possible translations in the target language using the trained bilingual embeddings. We integrate these translation options into a standard phrase-based statistical machine translation system and obtain consistent improvements in translation quality on the English–Spanish language pair. When tested over an out-of-domain testset, we get a significant improvement of 3.9 BLEU points.

1 Introduction

Data-driven machine translation systems are able to translate words that have been seen in the training parallel corpora, however translating unseen words is still a major challenge for even the best performing systems. The amount of parallel data is finite (and sometimes scarce) and, therefore, word types like named entities, domain specific content words, or infrequent terms are rare. This lack of information can potentially result in incomplete or erroneous translations.

This problem has been actively studied in the field of machine translation (MT) (Habash, 2008; Daumé III and Jagarlamudi, 2011; Marton et al., 2009; Rapp, 1999; Dou and Knight,

2012; Irvine and Callison-Burch, 2013). Lexicon-based resources have been used for resolving unseen content words by exploiting a combination of monolingual and bilingual resources (Rapp, 1999; Callison-Burch et al., 2006; Zhao et al., 2015). In this context, distributed word representations, or word embeddings (WE), have been recently applied to resolve unseen word related problems (Mikolov et al., 2013b; Zou et al., 2013). In general, word representations capture rich linguistic relationships and several works (Gouws et al., 2015; Wu et al., 2014) try to use them to improve MT systems. However, very few approaches use them directly to resolve the out-of-vocabulary (OOV) problem in MT systems.

Previous research in MT systems suggests that a significant number of named entities (NE) can be handled by using simple pre or post-processing methods, e.g., transliteration techniques (Hermjakob et al., 2008; Al-Onaizan and Knight, 2002). However, a change in domain results in a significant increase in the number of unseen content words for which simple pre or post-processing methods are sub-optimal (Zhang et al., 2012).

Our work is inspired by the recent advances (Zou et al., 2013; Zhang et al., 2014) in applications of word embeddings to the task of vocabulary expansion in the context of statistical machine translation (SMT). Our focus in this paper is to resolve unseen content words by using continuous word embeddings on both the languages and learn a model over a small seed lexicon to map the embedding spaces. To this extent, our work is similar to Ishiwatari et al. (2016) where the authors map distributional representations using a linear regression method similar to Mikolov et al. (2013b) and insert a new feature based on cosine similarity metric into the MT system. On the other hand, there is a rich body of recent literature that focuses on obtaining bilingual word

---

[*] This work was done while the authors were in TALP Research Center, Universitat Politècnica de Catalunya, Barcelona.

Proceedings of the 2nd Workshop on Representation Learning for NLP, pages 139–145,
Vancouver, Canada, August 3, 2017. ©2017 Association for Computational Linguistics

embeddings using either sentence aligned or document aligned corpora (Bhattarai, 2012; Gouws et al., 2015; Kočiský et al., 2014). Our approach is significantly different as we obtain embeddings separately on monolingual corpora and then use supervision in the form of a small sparse bilingual dictionary, in some terms similar to Faruqui and Dyer (2014). We use a simple yet principled method to obtain a probabilistic conditional distribution of words directly and these probabilities allow us to expand the translation model for new words.

The rest of the paper is organised as follows. Section 2 presents the log-bilinear softmax model, and its integration into an SMT system. The experimental work is described in Section 3. Finally, we conclude and sketch some avenues for future work.

2 Mapping Continuous Word Representations using a Bilinear Model

Definitions. Let $\mathcal{E}$ and $\mathcal{F}$ be the vocabularies of the two languages, source and target, and let $e \in \mathcal{E}$ and $f \in \mathcal{F}$ be words in these languages respectively. Let us assume, we have a source word to target word $e \rightarrow f$ dictionary. We also assume that we have access to some kind of distributed word embeddings in both languages, ϕ_s for the source and ϕ_t for the target, where $\phi(.) \rightarrow \mathbb{R}^n$ denotes the n-dimensional distributed representation of the words. The task we are interested in is to learn a model for the conditional probability distribution $\Pr(f|e)$. That is, given a word in a source language, say English (e), we want to get a conditional probability distribution of all the words in a foreign language (f).

Log-Bilinear Softmax Model. We formulate the problem as a bilinear prediction task as proposed by Madhyastha et al. (2014a) and extend it for the bilingual setting. The proposed model makes use of word embeddings on both languages with no additional features. The basic function is formulated as log-bilinear softmax model and takes the following form:

$$\Pr(f|e; W) = \frac{\exp\{\phi_s(e)^\top W \phi_t(f)\}}{\sum_{f' \in \mathcal{F}} \exp\{\phi_s(e)^\top W \phi_t(f')\}} \quad (1)$$

Essentially, our problem reduces to: a) first obtaining the corresponding word embeddings of the vocabularies from both the languages using a sig-

nificantly large monolingual corpus and b) estimating W given a relatively small dictionary. That is, to learn W we use the source word to target word dictionary as training supervision. The dictionary can be a true bilingual dictionary or the word alignments generated by the SMT system, therefore, no additional resources to the training parallel corpus are needed.

We learn W by minimizing the negative log-likelihood of the dictionary using a regularized (relaxed low-rank regularization based) objective as: $L(W) = -\sum_{e,f} \log(\Pr(f|e; W)) + \lambda \|W\|_p$. λ is the constant that controls the capacity of W. To find the optimum, we follow previous (Madhyastha et al., 2014b) work and use an optimization scheme based on Forward-Backward Splitting (FOBOS) (Singer and Duchi, 2009).

We experiment with two regularization schemes, $p = 2$ or the ℓ_2 regularizer and $p = *$ or the ℓ_* (nuclear norm) regularizer. We find that both norms have approximately similar performance, however the trace norm regularized W has lower capacity and hence, smaller number of parameters. This is also observed by (Bach, 2008; Madhyastha et al., 2014a,b). In general, we can apply the ideas used by Mikolov et al. (2013b) to speed up the training as this model is equivalent to a softmax model. We can obtain models with similar properties if we change the loss from bilinear log softmax to a bilinear margin based loss. We leave this exploration for future work.

A by-product of regularizing with ℓ_* norm is a lower-dimensional, language aligned, and compressed embeddings for both languages. This is possible because of the induced low-dimensional properties of W. That is, assume W has rank k, where $k < n$, such that $W \approx U_k V_k^\top$, then the product:

$$\phi_s(e)^\top U_k V_k^\top \phi_t(f) \quad (2)$$

gives us $\phi_s(e)^\top U_k$ and $V_k^\top \phi_t(f)$ compressed embeddings with shared properties. These are similar to the CCA based projections obtained in Faruqui and Dyer (2014).

Integrating the Probabilistic List into the SMT System. We integrate the probabilistic list of translation options into the phrase-based decoder using the standard log-linear approach (Och and Ney, 2002). Consider a word pair (e, f), where the decoder searches for a foreign word $\hat{f}$ that maxi-

Table 1: Top-10 accuracy (in percentage) for bilingual dictionary induction for English–German and English–French.

		Strong supervision		Soft supervision			
l_1	l_2	BiSkip	BiCVM	BiCCA	BiVCD	Ours-300	Ours-100
en	de	79.7	74.5	72.4	62.5	73.8	71.1
en	fr	78.9	72.9	70.1	68.8	72.1	69.7

mizes a linear combination of feature functions:

$$\widehat{f} = \operatorname{argmax}_f \{ \sum \lambda_i \log \left(h_i(f, e) \right) + \lambda_{oov} \log \left(\Pr(f, e) \right) \}$$

here, λ_i is the weight associated with feature $h_i(f, e)$ and λ_{oov} is the weight associated with the unseen word.

3 Empirical Analysis

Quality of the Learned Embeddings. To understand the performance of the embedding projections in our model, we perform experiments to compute the top-10 accuracy of our models in the same setting provided in Upadhyay et al. (2016) for cross-lingual dictionary induction[1]. The evaluation task judges how good cross-lingual embeddings are at detecting word pairs that are semantically similar across languages. Similarly to Upadhyay et al. (2016), we compare against BiSkip embeddings (Luong et al., 2015a), BiCVM (Hermann and Blunsom, 2014), BiCCA (Faruqui and Dyer, 2014) and BiVCD (Vulic and Moens, 2015). We experiment with English–German and English–French language pairs, so that we can induce the dictionaries for the five systems. As seen in Table 1, our full 300-dimensional embeddings perform better than the BiCCA-based model, whereas 100-dimensional compressed embedding perform slightly worse, but still are competitive. Since our model and BiCCA use similar supervision, we obtain similar results and differ in a similar way to those that use stronger supervision like BiCVM and BiSkip based embeddings.

MT Data and System Settings. For estimating the monolingual WE, we use the CBOW algorithm as implemented in the `Word2Vec` package (Mikolov et al., 2013a) using a 5-token window. We obtain 300 dimension vectors for English and Spanish from a Wikipedia dump of 2015 and the Quest data[2]. The final corpus contains 2.27 bil-

lion tokens for English and 0.84 for Spanish. We remove any occurrence of sentences from the test set that are contained in our corpus. The coverage in our test sets is of 97% of the words.

To train the log-bilinear softmax based model, we use the dictionary from the `Apertium project`[3] (Forcada et al., 2011). The dictionary contains 37651 words, 70% of them are used for training and 30% as a development set for model selection. The average precision @1 is 86% for the best model over the development set.

A state-of-the-art phrase-based SMT system is trained on the Europarl corpus (Koehn, 2005) for the English-to-Spanish language pair. We use a 5-gram language model that is estimated on the target side of the corpus using interpolated Kneser-Ney discounting with `SRILM` (Stolcke, 2002). Additional monolingual data available within Quest corpora is used to build a larger language model with the same characteristics. Word alignment is done with `GIZA++` (Och and Ney, 2003) and both phrase extraction and decoding are done with the `Moses` package (Koehn et al., 2007). At decoding time, `Moses` allows to include additional translation pairs with their associated probabilities to selected words via xml markup. We take advantage of this feature to add our probabilistic estimations to each OOV. Since, by definition, OOV words do no appear in the parallel training corpus, they are not present in the translation model either and the new translation options only interact with the language model. The optimization of the weights of the model with the additional translation options is trained with MERT (Och, 2003) against the BLEU (Papineni et al., 2002) evaluation metric on the NewsCommentaries 2012[4] (NewsDev) set. We test our systems on the NewsCommentaries 2013 set (NewsTest) for an in-domain evaluation and on a test set

---

[1]We also used the script provided here: `https://github.com/shyamupa/biling-survey`

[2]`http://statmt.org/~buck/wmt13qe/wmt13qe_t13_t2_MT_corpus.tgz`

[3]The bilingual dictionary can be downloaded here: `http://goo.gl/TjH31q`.

[4]`http://www.statmt.org/wmt13/translation-task.html`

Table 2: OOVs on the dev and test sets.

	Sent.	Tokens	OOV_{all}	OOV_{CW}
NewsDev	3003	72988	1920 (2.6%)	378 (0.5%)
NewsTest	3000	64810	1590 (2.5%)	296 (0.5%)
WikiTest	500	11069	798 (7.2%)	201 (1.8%)

Table 3: Automatic evaluation of the translation systems defined in Section 3. The best system is bold-faced (see text for statistical significance).

| | NewsTest | | | WikiTest | | |
	TER	BLEU	MTR	TER	BLEU	MTR
noOOV	58.21	21.94	45.79	61.26	16.24	38.76
verbatimOOV	57.90	22.89	47.06	58.55	21.90	45.77
BWE	58.33	22.23	45.76	58.38	21.96	44.84
BWE_{CW50}	57.66	23.09	47.14	56.19	24.16	48.49
BWE_{CW10}	57.85	23.06	47.11	55.64	24.71	49.05
BLM	55.37	25.83	**49.19**	52.60	30.63	51.04
BLM+BWE	55.89	24.92	47.84	51.02	32.20	52.09
$BLM+BWE_{50}$	55.55	25.61	49.01	49.50	33.94	54.93
$BLM+BWE_{10}$	**55.31**	**25.86**	49.04	**49.12**	**34.58**	**55.52**

extracted from Wikipedia by Smith *et. al.* (2010) for an out-of-domain evaluation (WikiTest).

The *domainess* of the test set is established with respect to the number of OOVs. Table 2 shows the figures of these sets paying special attention to the OOVs in the basic SMT system. Less than a 3% of the tokens are OOVs for News data (OOV_{all}), whereas it is more than a 7% for Wikipedia's. In our experiments, we distinguish between OOVs that are named entities and the rest of content words (OOV_{CW}). Only about 0.5% (NewsTest) and 1.8% (WikiTest) of the tokens fall into this category, but we show that they are relevant for the final performance.

MT Experiments. We consider two baseline systems, the first one does not output any translation for OOVs (*noOOV*), it just ignores the token; the second one outputs a verbatim copy of the OOV as a translation (*verbatimOOV*). Table 3 shows the performance of these systems under three widely used evaluation metrics TER (Snover et al., 2006), BLEU and METEOR (MTR) (Banerjee and Lavie, 2005). Including the verbatim copy improves all the lexical evaluation metrics. Specially for NEs and acronyms (the 80% of OOVs in our sets), this is a hard baseline to be compared to as in most cases the same word is the correct translation.

We then enrich the systems with information gathered from the large monolingual corpora in two ways, using a bigger language model (*BLM*) and using our newly proposed log-bilinear model that uses word embeddings (*BWE*). BLMs are important to improve the fluency of the translations, however they may not be helpful for resolving OOVs as they can only promote translations available in the translation model. On the other hand, BWEs are important to make available to the decoder new vocabulary on the topic of the otherwise OOVs. Given the large percentage of NEs in the test sets (Table 2), our models add the source word as an additional option to the list of target words to mimic the *verbatimOOV* system.

Table 3 includes seven systems with the additional monolingual information. Three of them add, at decoding time, the top-n translation options given by the BWE for a OOV. *BWE* system uses the top-50 for all the OOVs, BWE_{CW50} also uses the top-50 but only for content words other than named entities[5], and BWE_{CW10} limits the list to 10 elements. *BLM* is the same as the baseline system *verbatimOOV* but with the large language model. *BLM+BWE*, $BLM+BWE_{50}$ and $BLM+BWE_{10}$ combine the three BWE systems with the large language model.

In the NewsTest, most of unseen words are named entities and using BWEs to translate them barely improves the translation. The reason is that embeddings of related NEs are usually equivalent. This affects the overall integration of the scores into the decoder and induces ambiguity in the system. However, we observe that the decoder benefits from the information on content words, specially for the out-of-domain WikiTest set. In this case, given the constrained list of alternative translations (BWE_{CW10}) one achieves 2.75 BLEU points of improvement.

The addition of the large language model improves the results significantly. When combined with the BWEs we observe that the BWEs clearly help in the translation of WikiTest but do not seem as relevant in the in-domain set. We achieve a statistically significant improvement of 3.9 points of BLEU with the BLM and BWE combo system – $BLM+BWE_{10}$ with respect to *BLM*– in WikiTest ($p<0.001$); the improvement in the NewsTest is not statistically significant (p-value=0.29). The number of translation options in the list is also

---

[5]We consider a named entity any word that begins with a capital letter and is not after a punctuation mark, and any fully capitalized word.

Table 4: Top-n list of translations obtained with the bilingual embeddings.

GALAXY	NYMPHS	STUART	FOLKSONG
galaxia	**ninfas**	William	música
planeta	ninfa	Henry	**folclore**
universo	crías	John	literatura
planetas	diosa	Charles	himno
galaxias	dioses	Thomas	folklore
...	...	Estuardo (#48)	**canción (#7)**

relevant, and for $BLM+BWE_{CW50}$ we have a significant but smaller improvement of 3.3 points on BLEU in WikiTest. All these results are consistent among different evaluation metrics.

In order to estimate the relevance of the bilingual embeddings into the final translation, we have manually evaluated the translation of WikiTest using the BWE_{CW50} model. For the translation of the OOVs, we obtain an accuracy of a 68%, that is, the BWE gives the correct translation option at least 68% of the times. We note that, even if the correct translation option is in the translation list obtained by the BWE, the decoder may choose not to consider it.

In general, we observe that when our model fails, in most of the cases, the words in the translated language happened to be either a multiword expression or a named entity. In Table 4 we present some of the these examples. The first two examples *galaxy* and *nymphs* are nouns where we obtain the first option as the correct translation. The problem is harder for named entities as we observe in the table, the name *Stuart* in English has *William* as most probable translation in Spanish, the correct translation *Estuardo* however appears as the 48th choice. Our model is also unable to generate multiword expressions, as shown in the table for the english word *folksong*, the correct translation being *canción folk*. This would need two words in Spanish in order to be translated correctly, however, our model does obtain words: *canción* and *folclore* as the most probable translation options.

4   Conclusions

We have presented a method for resolving OOVs in SMT that performs vocabulary expansion by using a simple log-bilinear softmax based model. The model estimates bilingual word embeddings and, as a by-product, generates low-dimensional compressed embeddings for both languages. The

addition of the new translation options to a mere 1.8% of the words has allowed the system to obtain a relative improvement of a 13% in BLEU (3.9 points) for out-of-domain data. For in-domain data, where the number of content words is small, improvements are more moderate.

The analysis of the results shows how the performance is damaged by not considering multiword expressions. The automatic detection of these elements in the monolingual corpus together with the addition of one-to-many dictionary entries for learning the W matrix can alleviate this problem and will be considered in future work.

We also note that this approach can be extended directly within neural machine translation systems, where its effects could be even larger due to the limited vocabulary. While one of the popular approaches to deal with OOVs is to use subword units (Sennrich et al., 2016) in order to resolve of unknown words, dictionary-based approaches, where an unknown word is translated by its corresponding translation in a dictionary or a (SMT) translation table, have also been used (Luong et al., 2015b). Our method can go further in the latter direction by learning correspondences of source and target vocabularies using large monolingual corpora and either a small dictionary or the word alignments.

References

Yaser Al-Onaizan and Kevin Knight. 2002. Machine transliteration of names in arabic text. In *Proceedings of the ACL-02 workshop on Computational approaches to semitic languages*. Association for Computational Linguistics, pages 1–13.

Francis R Bach. 2008. Consistency of the group lasso and multiple kernel learning. *The Journal of Machine Learning Research* 9:1179–1225.

Satanjeev Banerjee and Alon Lavie. 2005. METEOR: An Automatic Metric for MT Evaluation with Improved Correlation with Human Judgments. In *Proceedings of the ACL Workshop on Intrinsic and Extrinsic Evaluation Measures for Machine Translation and/or Summarization*. Association for Computational Linguistics, Ann Arbor, Michigan, pages 65–72.

Alexandre Klementiev Ivan Titov Binod Bhattarai. 2012. Inducing Crosslingual Distributed Representations of Words. In *Proceedings of COLING 2012*. The COLING 2012 Organizing Committee, Mumbai, India, pages 1459–1474.

Chris Callison-Burch, Philipp Koehn, and Miles Osborne. 2006. Improved Statistical Machine Translation Using Paraphrases. In *Proceedings of the Human Language Technology Conference of the North American Chapter of the Association of Computational Linguistics*. HLT-NAACL '06, pages 17–24.

Hal Daumé III and Jagadeesh Jagarlamudi. 2011. Domain adaptation for machine translation by mining unseen words. In *Association for Computational Linguistics*. Portland, OR, pages 407–412.

Qing Dou and Kevin Knight. 2012. Large scale decipherment for out-of-domain machine translation. In *Proceedings of the 2012 Joint Conference on Empirical Methods in Natural Language Processing and Computational Natural Language Learning*. Association for Computational Linguistics, pages 266–275.

Manaal Faruqui and Chris Dyer. 2014. Improving vector space word representations using multilingual correlation. In *Proceedings of the 14th Conference of the European Chapter of the Association for Computational Linguistics, EACL 2014, April 26-30, 2014, Gothenburg, Sweden*. pages 462–471.

Mikel L Forcada, Mireia Ginestí-Rosell, Jacob Nordfalk, Jim ORegan, Sergio Ortiz-Rojas, Juan Antonio Pérez-Ortiz, Felipe Sánchez-Martínez, Gema Ramírez-Sánchez, and Francis M Tyers. 2011. Apertium: a free/open-source platform for rule-based machine translation. *Machine translation* 25(2):127–144.

Stephan Gouws, Yoshua Bengio, and Greg Corrado. 2015. BilBOWA: Fast Bilingual Distributed Representations without Word Alignments. In *Proceedings of the 32nd International Conference on Machine Learning, ICML 2015, Lille, France, 6-11 July 2015*. pages 748–756.

Nizar Habash. 2008. Four Techniques for Online Handling of Out-of-Vocabulary Words in Arabic-English Statistical Machine Translation. In *ACL 2008, Proceedings of the 46th Annual Meeting of the Association for Computational Linguistics*. pages 57–60.

Karl Moritz Hermann and Phil Blunsom. 2014. Multilingual models for compositional distributed semantics. In *Proceedings of the 52nd Annual Meeting of the Association for Computational Linguistics*. Association for Computational Linguistics, Baltimore, Maryland, pages 58–68.

Ulf Hermjakob, Kevin Knight, and Hal Daumé III. 2008. Name translation in statistical machine translation: Learning when to transliterate. In *Proceedings of ACL-08: HLT*. pages 389–397.

Ann Irvine and Chris Callison-Burch. 2013. Combining bilingual and comparable corpora for low resource machine translation. In *Proceedings of the Eighth Workshop on Statistical Machine Translation*. pages 262–270.

Shonosuke Ishiwatari, Naoki Yoshinaga, Masashi Toyoda, and Masaru Kitsuregawa. 2016. Instant translation model adaptation by translating unseen words in continuous vector space. In *Proceedings of the 17th International Conference on Intelligent Text Processing and Computational Linguistics (CICLing 2016). Konya, Turkey*.

Philipp Koehn. 2005. Europarl: A Parallel Corpus for Statistical Machine Translation. In *Conference Proceedings: the Tenth Machine Translation Summit*. AAMT, AAMT, Phuket, Thailand, pages 79–86.

Philipp Koehn, Hieu Hoang, Alexandra Birch Mayne, Christopher Callison-Burch, Marcello Federico, Nicola Bertoldi, Brooke Cowan, Wade Shen, Christine Moran, Richard Zens, Chris Dyer, Ondrej Bojar, Alexandra Constantin, and Evan Herbst. 2007. Moses: Open source toolkit for statistical machine translation. In *Annual Meeting of the Association for Computation Linguistics (ACL), Demonstration Session*. pages 177–180.

Tomáš Kočiský, Karl Moritz Hermann, and Phil Blunsom. 2014. Learning bilingual word representations by marginalizing alignments. In *Proceedings of the 52nd Annual Meeting of the Association for Computational Linguistics*. Association for Computational Linguistics, Baltimore, Maryland, pages 224–229.

Thang Luong, Hieu Pham, and Christopher D Manning. 2015a. Bilingual word representations with monolingual quality in mind. In *Proceedings of the 1st Workshop on Vector Space Modeling for Natural Language Processing*. pages 151–159.

Thang Luong, Ilya Sutskever, Quoc Le, Oriol Vinyals, and Wojciech Zaremba. 2015b. Addressing the rare word problem in neural machine translation. In *Proceedings of the 53rd Annual Meeting of the Association for Computational Linguistics and the 7th International Joint Conference on Natural Language Processing (Volume 1: Long Papers)*. Association for Computational Linguistics, Beijing, China, pages 11–19.

Pranava Swaroop Madhyastha, Xavier Carreras, and Ariadna Quattoni. 2014a. Learning task-specific bilexical embeddings. In *Proceedings of COLING 2014, the 25th International Conference on Computational Linguistics: Technical Papers*. Dublin City University and Association for Computational Linguistics, pages 161–171.

Pranava Swaroop Madhyastha, Xavier Carreras, and Ariadna Quattoni. 2014b. Tailoring word embeddings for bilexical predictions: An experimental comparison. *International Conference on Learning Representations 2015, Workshop Track* .

Yuval Marton, Chris Callison-Burch, and Philip Resnik. 2009. Improved statistical machine translation using monolingually-derived paraphrases. In *Proceedings of the 2009 Conference on Empirical Methods in Natural Language Processing*. Association for Computational Linguistics, pages 381–390.

Tomas Mikolov, Kai Chen, Greg Corrado, and Jeffrey Dean. 2013a. Efficient Estimation of Word Representations in Vector Space. In *Proceedings of Workshop at ICLR*.

Tomas Mikolov, Quoc V. Le, and Ilya Sutskever. 2013b. Exploiting similarities among languages for machine translation. *CoRR* abs/1309.4168. http://arxiv.org/abs/1309.4168.

Franz Josef Och. 2003. Minimum Error Rate Training in Statistical Machine Translation. In *Proceedings of the Association for Computational Linguistics*. Sapporo, Japan, pages 160–167.

Franz Josef Och and Hermann Ney. 2002. Discriminative training and maximum entropy models for statistical machine translation. In *Proceedings of the 40th Annual Meeting on Association for Computational Linguistics*. Association for Computational Linguistics, Stroudsburg, PA, USA, ACL 2002, pages 295–302.

Franz Josef Och and Hermann Ney. 2003. A systematic comparison of various statistical alignment models. *Computational Linguistics* 29(1):19–51.

Kishore Papineni, Salim Roukos, Todd Ward, and Wei-Jing Zhu. 2002. BLEU: A Method for Automatic Evaluation of Machine Translation. In *Proceedings of the Association of Computational Linguistics*. pages 311–318.

Reinhard Rapp. 1999. Automatic identification of word translations from unrelated english and german corpora. In *Proceedings of the 37th annual meeting of the Association for Computational Linguistics on Computational Linguistics*. Association for Computational Linguistics, pages 519–526.

Rico Sennrich, Barry Haddow, and Alexandra Birch. 2016. Neural machine translation of rare words with subword units. In *Proceedings of the 54th Annual Meeting of the Association for Computational Linguistics, ACL 2016, August 7-12, 2016, Berlin, Germany, Volume 1: Long Papers*. pages 1715–1725.

Yoram Singer and John C Duchi. 2009. Efficient learning using forward-backward splitting. In *Advances in Neural Information Processing Systems*. pages 495–503.

Jason R. Smith, Chris Quirk, and Kristina Toutanova. 2010. Extracting Parallel Sentences from Comparable Corpora Using Document Level Alignment. In *In Proceedings of Human Language Technologies: The 11th Annual Conference of the North American Cha pter of the Association for Computational Linguistics (NAACL-HLT 2010)*. pages 403–411.

Matthew Snover, Bonnie Dorr, Richard Schwartz, Linnea Micciulla, and John Makhoul. 2006. A Study of Translation Edit Rate with Targeted Human Annotation. In *Proceedings of the Seventh Conference of the Association for Machine Translation in the Americas (AMTA 2006)*. Cambridge, Massachusetts, USA, pages 223–231.

Andreas Stolcke. 2002. SRILM - An Extensible Language Modeling Toolkit. In *Proceedings of the Seventh International Conference of Spoken Language Processing (ICSLP2002)*. Denver, Colorado, USA, pages 901–904.

Shyam Upadhyay, Manaal Faruqui, Chris Dyer, and Dan Roth. 2016. Cross-lingual models of word embeddings: An empirical comparison. In *Proceedings of the 54th Annual Meeting of the Association for Computational Linguistics, ACL 2016, August 7-12, 2016, Berlin, Germany*. pages 1661–1670.

Ivan Vulic and Marie-Francine Moens. 2015. Bilingual Word Embeddings from Non-Parallel Document-Aligned Data Applied to Bilingual Lexicon Induction. In *Proceedings of the 53rd Annual Meeting of the Association for Computational Linguistics and the 7th International Joint Conference on Natural Language Processing of the Asian Federation of Natural Language Processing, ACL 2015*. pages 719–725.

Haiyang Wu, Daxiang Dong, Xiaoguang Hu, Dianhai Yu, Wei He, Hua Wu, Haifeng Wang, and Ting Liu. 2014. Improve Statistical Machine Translation with Context-Sensitive Bilingual Semantic Embedding Model. In *Proceedings of the 2014 Conference on Empirical Methods in Natural Language Processing (EMNLP)*. Association for Computational Linguistics, Doha, Qatar, pages 142–146.

Jiajun Zhang, Shujie Liu, Mu Li, Ming Zhou, and Chengqing Zong. 2014. Bilingually-constrained phrase embeddings for machine translation. In *Proceedings of the 52nd Annual Meeting of the Association for Computational Linguistics*. Association for Computational Linguistics, Baltimore, Maryland, pages 111–121.

Jiajun Zhang, Feifei Zhai, and Chengqing Zong. 2012. Handling unknown words in statistical machine translation from a new perspective. In *Natural Language Processing and Chinese Computing*, Springer, pages 176–187.

Kai Zhao, Hany Hassan, and Michael Auli. 2015. Learning Translation Models from Monolingual Continuous Representations. In *The 2015 Conference of the North American Chapter of the Association for Computational Linguistics: Human Language Technologies, NAACL HLT 2015*. pages 1527–1536.

Will Y. Zou, Richard Socher, Daniel M. Cer, and Christopher D. Manning. 2013. Bilingual Word Embeddings for Phrase-Based Machine Translation. In *Proceedings of the 2013 Conference on Empirical Methods in Natural Language Processing, EMNLP 2013*. pages 1393–1398.

Prediction of Frame-to-Frame Relations in the FrameNet Hierarchy with Frame Embeddings

Teresa Botschen[§†], Hatem Mousselly-Sergieh[†], Iryna Gurevych[§†]
§Research Training Group AIPHES
†Ubiquitous Knowledge Processing (UKP) Lab
Department of Computer Science, Technische Universität Darmstadt
`www.aiphes.tu-darmstadt.de, www.ukp.tu-darmstadt.de`

Abstract

Automatic completion of frame-to-frame (F2F) relations in the FrameNet (FN) hierarchy has received little attention, although they incorporate meta-level commonsense knowledge and are used in downstream approaches. We address the problem of sparsely annotated F2F relations. First, we examine whether the manually defined F2F relations emerge from text by learning text-based frame embeddings. Our analysis reveals insights about the difficulty of reconstructing F2F relations purely from text. Second, we present different systems for predicting F2F relations; our best-performing one uses the FN hierarchy to train on and to ground embeddings in. A comparison of systems and embeddings exposes the crucial influence of knowledge-based embeddings to a system's performance in predicting F2F relations.

1 Introduction

FrameNet (FN) (Baker et al., 1998) is a lexical-semantic resource manually built by FN experts. It embodies the theory of frame semantics (Fillmore, 1976): the frames capture units of meaning corresponding to prototypical situations. Besides FN's definitions of frame-specific roles and frame-evoking elements that are used for the task of Semantic Role Labeling, it also contains manual annotations for relations that connect pairs of frames. There are thirteen *frame-to-frame (F2F) relations* of which five are antonym relations (e.g. `Precedes, Is_Preceded_by`). To give an example, the frame "Waking_up" is in relation `Precedes` to the frame "Being_awake". Figure 1 further elaborates this example by demon-

strating relationships to additional frames. Table 1 lists all F2F relation names with the number of frame pairs for each relation according to the FN hierarchy, and also restricted counts including only frame pairs that have lexical units (LU) in the FN hierarchy (e.g., the frame "Waking_up" can be evoked by the LU "awake.v" of the verb "awake"). The FN hierarchy, a report version of FN, does not provide lexical units for 125 frames (e.g., the frame "Sleep_wake_cycle" has no LU). In fact, such frames are used as meta-frames for abstraction purposes, thus, they exist only to participate in F2F relations with other frames (Ruppenhofer et al., 2006). In general, each frame pair is connected via only one F2F relation with occasional exceptions and the F2F relations situate the frames in semantic space (Ruppenhofer et al., 2006). F2F relations are used in the context of other tasks, such as text understanding (Fillmore and Baker, 2001), paraphrase rule generation for the system LexPar (Coyne and Rambow, 2009) and recognition of textual entailment (Aharon et al., 2010). Furthermore, F2F can be used as a form of commonsense knowledge (Rastogi and Van Durme, 2014).

The incompleteness of the FN hierarchy is a known issue not only at the frame level (Rastogi and Van Durme, 2014; Pavlick et al., 2015; Hartmann and Gurevych, 2013) but also at the

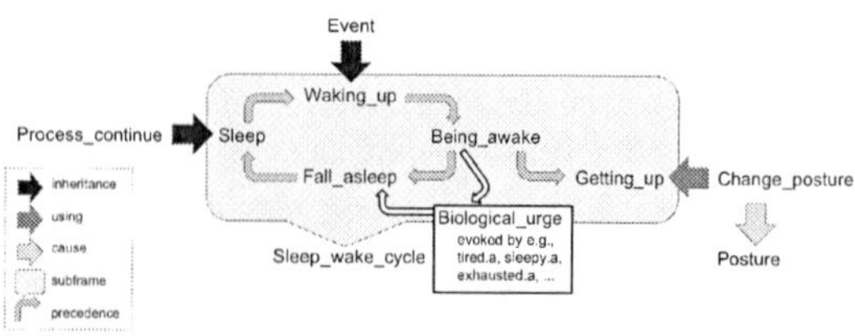

Figure 1: F2F relations example. Gray: FN hierarchy. White arrows: missing in FN hierarchy.

Proceedings of the 2nd Workshop on Representation Learning for NLP, pages 146–156,
Vancouver, Canada, August 3, 2017. ©2017 Association for Computational Linguistics

F2F Relation Name	Total	Restricted
Inherits_from	617	383
Is_inherited_by	617	383
Uses	491	430
Is_Used_by	490	430
Subframe_of	119	29
Has_Subframes	117	29
Perspective_on	99	15
Is_Perspectivized_in	99	15
Precedes	79	48
Is_Preceded_by	79	48
Is_Causative_of	48	47
See_also	41	40
Is_Inchoative_of	16	16
Sum	2,912	1,913

Table 1: F2F relation pair counts and restricted pair counts of frames with lexical units.

F2F relation level. Figure 1 exemplifies a missing precedence relation: "Fall_asleep" is preceded by "Being_awake" but inbetween yet another frame could be added, e.g. "Biological_urge" (evoked by the predicate "tired"). Rastogi (2014) note a lack of research on automatically enriching the F2F relations, which would be beneficial given the large number of possible frame pairs for a relation and their use in other tasks. The automatic annotation of F2F relations involves three difficulties accounted for by the nature of FN. First, F2F relation annotations occur sparsely and for the majority of pairs in each relation there are few instances (see Table 1). Second, the relations themselves have no direct lexical correspondences in text and hence inferring them from text is not trivial. Third, if a relation involves a frame that does not have any lexical unit (see restricted counts in Table 1), this frame does not occur in text and hence inferring this relation from text is even more difficult.

To the best of our knowledge there is no work (a) addressing the emergence of F2F relations from text data or (b) enriching F2F relations automatically. We aim to address these problems with the following contributions:

Contributions of the paper

1) We learn text-based frame embeddings and explore their limitations with respect to F2F relations to check whether the manually annotated F2F relations can naturally emerge from text. We find that, concerning the methods we explored, the embeddings have difficulties in showing structures directly corresponding to F2F relations.

2) We transfer the relation prediction task from research on Knowledge Graph Completion to the case of FN and present our best-performing system for predicting F2F relations. The system involves training on the FN hierarchy and uses embeddings also trained on the FN hierarchy.

3) We generically demonstrate the predictions of our best-performing system for unannotated frame pairs and suggest its application for automatic FN completion on the relation level.

Structure of the paper To start with, Section 2 reviews related research including algorithms and approaches that we will apply to our purposes. Next, Section 3 briefly presents the FN data that we will work with. Then, the paper is structured along our contributions: exploration of F2F relations in frame embedding space (Sec 4) and F2F Relation Prediction task (Sec 5), including a demonstration of predictions for unannotated frame pairs (Sec 5.3). Finally, Section 6 discusses our insights and traces options for future work.

2 Related Work

2.1 Frame Embeddings

Frame embeddings for frame identification To our knowledge, the only approach learning frame embeddings is a matrix factorization approach in the context of the task of Frame Identification (FrameId), which is the first step in FN Semantic Role Labeling. The state-of-the-art system (Hermann et al., 2014) for FrameId projects frames and predicates with their context words into the same latent space by using the *WSABIE* algorithm (Weston et al., 2011). Two projection matrices (one for frames and one for predicates) are learned using WARP loss and gradient-based updates such that the distance between the predicate's latent representation and that of the correct frame are minimized. Consequently, latent representations of frames will end up close to each other if they are evoked by similar predicates and context words. As the focus of such systems is on the FrameId task, the latent representations of the frames are rather a sub-step contributing to FrameId but not studied further or applied to other tasks. We will extract these frame embeddings and explore them with respect to F2F relations.

Word2Vec embeddings The Neural Network (NN) architecture of the *Word2Vec* algorithm (Mikolov et al., 2013a) learns word embeddings by either predicting a target word given its context words (*CBOW model*) or by predicting context words given their target word (*skip-gram model*).

There are different tasks specifically designed for the evaluation of word embeddings (Mikolov et al., 2013b). They are formulated as analogy questions about syntax or semantics of the form *"a is to b as c is to ___"*. Mikolov (2013b) suggest a **vector offset method** based on cosine distance to solve these analogy tasks. This assumes that relationships are expressed by vector offsets: given two word pairs (a, b) and (c, d), the question is to what extent the relations within the pairs are similar. We will apply this method to frame pairs that are connected via F2F relations in order to find out whether the frame embeddings incorporate F2F relations.

There is an interest in abstracting away from word embeddings towards embeddings for more coarse grained units: *Word2Vec* is used to learn embeddings for senses (Iacobacci et al., 2015) or for supersenses (Flekova and Gurevych, 2016). Iacobacci (2015) use the *CBOW model* on texts annotated with BabelNet senses (Navigli and Ponzetto, 2012). Flekova (2016) use the *skip-gram model* on texts with mapped WordNet supersenses (Miller, 1990; Fellbaum, 1990). For evaluation both works are oriented towards Mikolov's (2013b) analogy tasks and perform qualitative analyses for the top k most similar embeddings for (super)senses or visualize the embeddings in vector space. To have text-based frame embeddings in line with related work, we will also use the *Word2Vec* algorithm to learn an additional version for frame embeddings.

2.2 Relation Prediction

This task stems from automatic Knowledge Graph Completion (KGC) and is known as "Link Prediction" (Bordes et al., 2011, 2012, 2013). We will transfer this task to F2F Relation Prediction for frame pairs. For this task, knowledge-based embeddings are well suited, which are not learned on text but on triples of a KG.

TransE embeddings We leverage an embedding learning approach from KGC to obtain embeddings for frames and for F2F relations that are grounded in the FN hierarchy. In translation models, all entities and relations of the triples of head-entity, relation and tail-entity (h, r, t) are projected into one latent vector space such that the relation-vector connects from the head-vector to the tail-vector as a translating vector operation. *TransE* (Bordes et al., 2013) introduced the idea of mod-

eling relations as translations that operate on the embeddings of the entities. The model is formulated to minimize $| h + r - t |$ for a training set, with randomly initialized embeddings. The function to minimize resembles the idea of the vector offset by Mikolov (2013b).

Answer selection model Link Prediction is methodologically related to the key-task of Answer Selection from Question Answering (QA). The task is to rank a set of possible answer candidates with respect to a given question (Tan et al., 2015). State-of-the-art QA models are presented by (Feng et al., 2015) and by (Tan et al., 2015). They jointly learn vector representations for both the questions and the answers. Representations of the same dimensionality in the same space allow one to compute the cosine similarity between these vectors. We will orient ourselves by NN models for Answer Selection in order to adapt the ideas to F2F Relation Prediction. In our case, a question corresponds to a frame pair and an answer corresponds to a F2F relation. Optionally, pretrained frame embeddings can be used as initialization.

3 Data

Textual data In order to learn frame embeddings on textual data with *WSABIE* or *W2V*, we take the FrameNet 1.5 sentences provided by the Dependency-Parsed FrameNet Corpus (Bauer et al., 2012) which contains more than $170,000$ sentences annotated manually with frame labels for 700 frames. We denote a frame as f where $f \in F_t$ the set of frames in the textual data.

Hierarchy data The FN hierarchy lists for each frame of the overall $1,019$ frames the F2F relations to other frames. We denote with G the collection of triples (f_1, r, f_2) (standing for frame "f_1 is in relation r to frame f_2"), where f_1 and $f_2 \in F_h$ the set of frames in the FN hierarchy and $r \in R$ the set of F2F relations. As listed in Table 2, there are $2,912$ triples in the FN hierarchy with $1,913$ triples remaining if considering only those where both frames have lexical units and

Corpus	Frames	F2F Relations
FN Hierarchy	$1,019$	$2,912$
FN Hierarchy restricted to frames with LU	894	$1,913$
Textual data FN 1.5 sentences	700	$1,447$

Table 2: Counts for frames and F2F relations.

with $1,447$ triples remaining if considering only those where both frames occur in the textual data. We split the obtained triples whose frames have lexical units into a training and a test set such that the training set contains the first 70% of all the triples for each relation.

Table 2 summarizes frame counts per data source together with counts of F2F relations where both frames occur in the underlying source.

4 Exploration of Frame Embeddings

We aim at empirically analyzing whether F2F relations from the FN hierarchy are mirrored in frame embeddings learned on frame-labeled text in the context of other tasks. Thus, we want to identify whether a statistical analysis of text-based frame embeddings naturally yields the FN hierarchy. Indeed, the F2F relations are manually annotated by expert linguists but there is no guarantee that F2F relations can be observed in text. If these relations could emerge from raw text it would be reassuring for the definitions of the F2F relations that led to annotations of frame pairs and furthermore the annotations could be generated automatically. We hypothesize that distances and directions between frame embeddings learned on textual data can correspond to F2F relations. Figure 2 exemplifies this as known from word embeddings by Mikolov (Mikolov et al., 2013a): it highlights two frame pairs that are in the same relation: "Attempt" is in relation `precedes` with "Success_or_failure" and so is "Existence" in relation `precedes` with "Ceasing_to_be" and the connecting vectors are about the same direction and length.

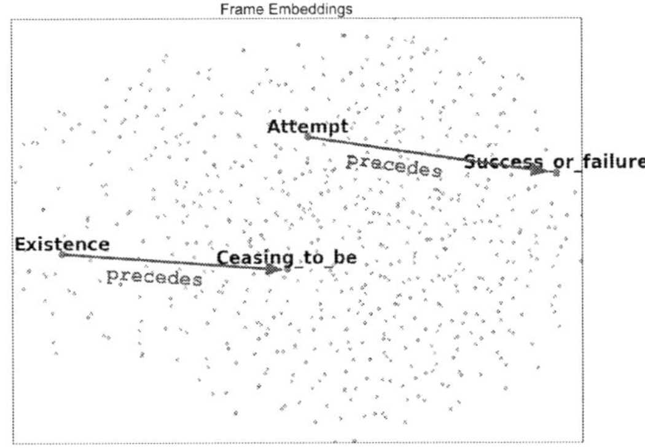

Figure 2: Intuition for frame embeddings incorporating F2F relations in vector space.

4.1 Methods

***WSABIE* frame embeddings** Concerning the matrix factorization approach for learning text-based frame embeddings, we use the code provided by (Hartmann et al., 2017) as it is publically available. It is leaned on Hermann's (2014) description of their state-of-the-art system and achieves comparable results on FrameId. Our hyperparameter choices are oriented towards (Hartmann et al., 2017): embedding dimension 100, maximum number of negative samples: 100, epochs: 1000 and initial representation of predicate and context: concatenation of pretrained dependency-based word embeddings (Levy and Goldberg, 2014).

***Word2Vec* frame embeddings** Concerning the NN approach for learning text-based frame embeddings, we use the *Word2Vec* implementation in the python library gensim (Řehůřek and Sojka, 2010). To obtain frame embeddings we follow the same steps as if we would learn word embeddings on FN sentences plus we replace all predicates with their frames. For instance, in the sequence *"Officials claim that Iran has produced bombs"* the predicates *"claim"* and *"bombs"* are replaced by *"STATEMENT"* and *"WEAPON"* respectively. This procedure corresponds to Flekova's (2016) setup for learning supersense embeddings and our hyperparameter choices are oriented towards their best performing ones: training algorithm: *skip-gram model*, embedding dimension: 300, minimal word frequency: 10, negative sampling of noise words: 5, window size 2, initial learning rate: 0.025 and iterations: 10.

Prototypical relation embeddings We denote learned embeddings with $\overrightarrow{e_1}$ (for frame f_1). We use the frame embeddings to infer prototypical F2F relation embeddings $\overrightarrow{e_r}$ with the vector offset method in the following way: we denote with I_r the relation-specific subset of G with all the instances (f_1, r, f_2) for this relation (see frame pair counts in Table 1). The vector offset $\overrightarrow{o_{e_1,e_2}}$ for two frames (f_1, f_2) is the difference of their embeddings, see Equation 1.

$$offset\{f_1, f_2\} = \overrightarrow{e_2} - \overrightarrow{e_1} \qquad (1)$$

We denote with O_r the relation-specific set of vector offsets of all $(f_1, f_2) \in I_r$. We define the prototypical embedding $\overrightarrow{e_r}$ for a relation r as the mean over all $\overrightarrow{o_{e_1,e_2}} \in O_r$. For visualizations in vector space we use t-SNE-plots (t-distributed Stochastic Neighbor Embedding (Maaten and Hinton, 2008) algorithm).

Difficulty of associating frame pairs with prototypical relations The association of the embedding of a frame pair $\overrightarrow{o_{e_1,e_2}} \in O_r$ with the correct prototypical relation embedding $\overrightarrow{e_r}$ is easier if the intra-relation variation (i.e. the deviation of frame pair embeddings from their prototypical embedding) is smaller than the inter-relation variation (i.e. the distances between prototypical embeddings). This means, the association is easier if two frame pairs which are members of the same F2F relation, on average, differ less from each other as they would differ from a member of another relation. As a way to capture this difficulty of association we compare the mean cosine distance between all prototypical relations embeddings $\overrightarrow{e_r}$ of all $r \in R$ to the relation-specific mean cosine distance between the frame pair embeddings in O_r and the prototypical embedding $\overrightarrow{e_r}$.

4.2 Experiments and Results

Frame embeddings Once the frame embeddings are learned, we perform a sanity check for frames and most similar frame embeddings by cosine similarity. Checking the top 10 most similar frame embeddings confirms that known properties from word or sense embeddings also apply to frame embeddings: their top 10 most similar frames are semantically related, both for frame embeddings learned with *WSABIE* and with *Word2Vec*. This is exemplified in Table 3 for the two most frequently occurring frames in the text data evoked by nouns ("Weapon") and by verbs ("Statement"). For both *WSABIE* and *Word2Vec*, in many cases the most similar frames are obviously semantically related (which we marked in bold), with some exceptions where it is hard to judge or related via an asso-

| frame | Top 10 most similar frames | |
	WSABIE	*Word2Vec*
Weapon	Substance, **Shoot_projectiles**, Manufacturing, **Bearing_arms**, **Toxic_substance**, **Hostile_encounter**, Ingredients, Information, **Smuggling**, Active_substance	**Military**, Substance, Operational_testing, Store, Electricity, Process_completed_state, Active_substance, Range, Estimated_value, Cause_to_make_progress
Statement	**Evidence**, Causation, **Topic**, **Chatting**, **Point_of_dispute**, **Request**, **Text_creation**, Cognitive_connection, **Make_agreement_on_action**, **Communication**	**Reveal_secret**, **Telling**, **Complaining**, **Reasoning**, **Communication_response**, Awareness, **Reassuring**, **Bragging**, **Questioning**, Cogitation

Table 3: Top 10 most similar frames to two exemplary most frequent frames.

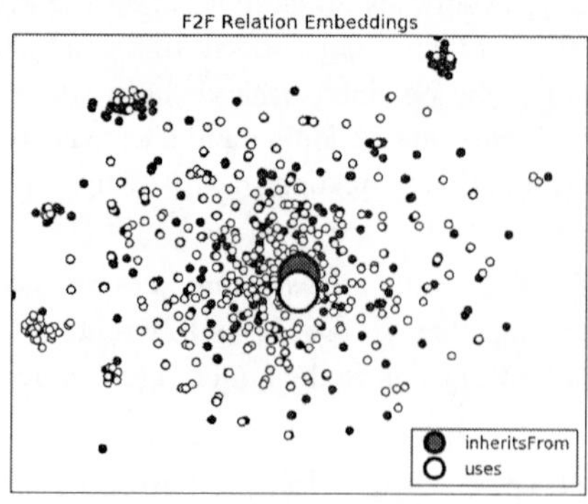

Figure 3: t-SNE plot of embeddings for two most frequent relations. Small: frame pair embeddings (offset). Large: prototypical embeddings (mean).

ciation chain. For the frame "Weapon", the most similar frames by *Word2Vec* are weaker compared to *WSABIE*, however this does not allow a general conclusion over all frames learned with *Word2Vec* or *WSABIE*.

F2F relations To check whether the frame embeddings directly mirror F2F relations, we measure the difficulty of associating frame pairs with the correct prototypical relation embedding.

First, we visualize the frame pair embeddings in the training set and the inferred prototypical relation embeddings in vector space with t-SNE-plots. Figure 3 depicts examples of *WSABIE* embeddings for the most frequently occurring F2F relations `inherits_from` and `uses`, and shows that the prototypical embeddings are very close to each other, whilst there are no separate relation-specific clusters for frame pairs. Vector space visualizations of embeddings stemming from both, *Word2Vec* and *WSABIE*, hint that the embeddings have difficulties in mirroring the F2F relations.

Second, we quantify the insights from the plots by comparing the distances between all prototypical embeddings to the mean over all mean distances between frame pair embeddings and their prototypical embeddings. Table 4 lists these vector space (cosine) distances. It shows that the distance between the prototypical embeddings (inter-relation) is smaller than that between frame pair embeddings and corresponding prototypical embeddings (intra-relation). In other words, two frame pairs which are members of the same relation, on average, differ as much from each other as

Mean distances between	WSABIE	Word2Vec
inter-relation variation (between prototypes)	0.73 ± 0.28	0.76 ± 0.28
intra-relation variation (between frame pairs and their prototypes)	0.75 ± 0.04	0.78 ± 0.05

Table 4: Cosine distances between the F2F relation embeddings.

they would differ from a member of another relation.

To sum up, we find that embeddings of frame pairs that are in the same relation do not have a similar vector offset which corresponds to the F2F relation. The FN hierarchy could not be reconstructed by the statistical analysis of text-based embeddings because there is as much intra-relation variation as inter-relation variation. We conclude that, concerning the methods we explored, the frame embeddings learned with *WSABIE* and *Word2Vec* have difficulties in showing structures in vector space corresponding to F2F relations and that F2F relations might not emerge purely from textual data. Hence, these text-based frame embeddings cannot be used as such to reliably infer the correct relation for a frame pair but might need some advanced learning. In the next section, we address the prediction of F2F relations with algorithms involving learning from the knowledge contained in the FN hierarchy.

5 Frame-to-Frame Relation Prediction

We aim at developing a system for finding the correct F2F relation given two frames, which can potentially be used for automatic completion of the F2F relation annotations in the FN hierarchy. This task transfers the principles of Link Prediction from KGC to the case of FN. As the previous experiment suggested that text-based frame embeddings do not mirror the F2F relations, we develop a system that learns from the knowledge contained in the FN hierarchy and that uses pretrained frame embeddings as input representations. Related work in KGC also demonstrates the strengths of representations trained directly on the KG for this task. For our systems involving learning, we experiment with different embeddings as input representations: in addition to the text-based frame embeddings, we also learn knowledge-based embeddings for frames and for F2F relations on the structure of the FN hierarchy with *TransE*, an approach well-known from KGC.

We want to quantify which combination of pretrained embeddings and system is most promising for the F2F Relation Prediction task.

5.1 Methods

TransE **embeddings** In addition to the text-based frame embeddings, we also learn embeddings for frames as well as for F2F relations by applying the well-known translation model *TransE*. *TransE* leverages the structure of the knowledge base, which is in our case the FN hierarchy with the collection of the $(frame, relation, frame)$ triples, and learns low dimensional vector representations for frames and for F2F relations in the same space. These embeddings will have the property of being learned explicitly for incorporating the annotations from the FN hierarchy. Concerning this knowledge-based approach for learning frame and F2F relation embeddings, we use an implementation of *TransE* provided by (Lin et al., 2015) yielding embeddings of dimension 50.

Neural network for relation selection We propose a nonlinear model based on NNs to identify the best F2F relation r between a frame pair (f_1, f_2). Figure 4 demonstrates the proposed NN architecture. Given a training instance, i.e. a triple (f_1, r, f_2), we feed a vector representation for each element into the NN. By default the input vector representations are initialized randomly but they can also stem from a pretraining step (more details in Sec 5.2). Within the NN, the initial vector representations of the two frames are combined into an internal dense layer c, followed by the calculation of the cosine similarity between this combina-

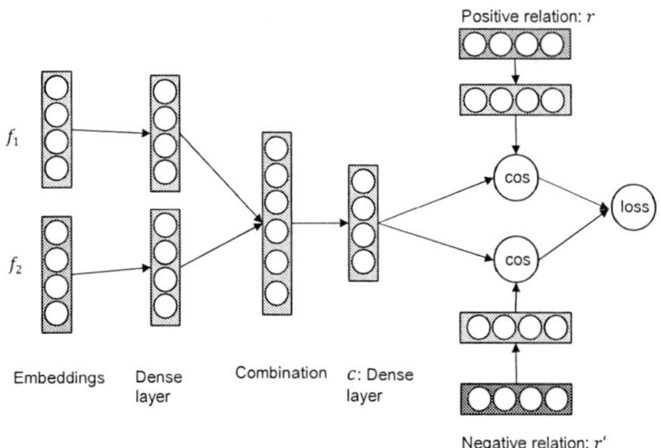

Figure 4: NN architecture for training on the F2F Relation Prediction task.

tion and the representation for the F2F relation r. Meanwhile, a negative relation r' is sampled randomly (by selecting a F2F relation which does not hold between the two frames) and its vector representation is also fed into the NN. The negative relation is processed as the correct one, yielding a second cosine similarity. Finally, the NN minimizes the following ranking loss:

$$loss = \max\{0, m - cos(c, r) + cos(c, r')\} \quad (2)$$

m is a margin and cos is the cosine similarity function. This means, the internal representations are trained to maximize the similarity between frame pair and correct relation and to minimize it for the negative relation. Our hyperparameter choices are: epochs: 550, size of dense layers: 128, dropout: 0.2, margin: 0.1, activation function: hyperbolic tangent, batch size: 2, learning rate 0.001.

5.2 Experiments and Results

Given a triple (f_3, r, f_4) from the test set, we want to predict the correct relation r for (f_3, f_4). As described in Sec 3, 70% of the triples in the FN hierarchy are used for training. Our systems are:

- **0a): rand.bsl** A random guessing baseline that chooses a relation randomly out of R.
- **0b): maj.bsl** Informed majority baseline that leverages the skewed distribution in the training set and predicts most frequent relation.
- **1: off** A test of the pretrained frame embeddings (*WSABIE* and *Word2Vec*) as introduced in Section 4. It computes the vector offset $\overrightarrow{o_{e_3,e_4}}$ (therefore "off") between the test frame embeddings, measures the similarity with the prototypical mean relation embeddings $\overrightarrow{e_r}$ of the training set and ranks the relations with respect to similarity (cosine) to output the closest one. No further training with respect to the FN hierarchy.
- **2: reg** A test of the pretrained frame embeddings (*WSABIE* and *Word2Vec*) as introduced in Section 4 involving training with respect to the FN hierarchy. It is a multinomial logistic regression model (therefore "reg") that trains the weights and biases on the training triples. It takes the test frame embeddings e_3, e_4 as input and ranks the prediction for a relation via the softmax function.
- **3: NN** NN architecture as described in Section 5.1 for training with respect to the FN hierarchy in the training triples. By de-

fault, it uses randomly initialized input representations, but it can also take pretrained representations as input: (a) the pretrained frame embeddings (*WSABIE* and *Word2Vec*) and inferred prototypical mean relation embeddings as introduced in Section 4 and (b) the *TransE* frame and relation embeddings trained on the training triples from the FN hierarchy as introduced in Section 5.1.

To evaluate the predictions of our systems for the F2F Relation Prediction task, we compare the measurements of accuracy, mean rank of the true relation and hits amongst the 5 first predictions, see Table 5.

Accuracy measures the proportion of correctly predicted relations amongst all predictions.

For the next two measures, not only the one predicted relation is of interest, but the ranked list of all relations with the predicted relation at rank 1.

Mean rank measures the mean of the rank of the true relation label over all predictions, aiming at low mean rank (best is $mr = 1$).

Hits@5 measures the proportion of true relation labels ranked in the top 5.

The random guessing baseline is a weak baseline that is outperformed by all approaches. The informed majority baseline, however, is a strong baseline given the skewed distribution of F2F relations in the FN hierarchy.

A comparison of this strong baseline with system 1 using the text-based frame embeddings (*WSABIE* and *Word2Vec*) and the similarity with prototypical relation embeddings, emphasizes the difficulties of these embeddings for reconstructing the F2F relations. Concerning accuracy scores, system 1 performs slightly better than the strong baseline but concerning the other two measures, mean rank and hits at 5, it is the other way round. An-

System	Embed.	acc ↑	mr ↓	hits@5 ↑
0: rand.bsl	-	7.69	6.5	38.46
0: maj.bsl	-	22.48	3.27	87.51
1: off	*WSABIE*	25.22	4.50	68.52
1: off	*Word2Vec*	30.61	4.53	66.96
1: off	*TransE*	51.13	2.99	83.30
2: reg	*WSABIE*	35.65	3.14	84.00
2: reg	*Word2Vec*	41.91	2.81	88.00
2: reg	*TransE*	**66.61**	**1.93**	**93.22**
3: NN	random	26.89	3.67	77.00
3: NN	*WSABIE*	27.46	3.59	79.98
3: NN	*Word2Vec*	30.55	3.27	82.61
3: NN	***TransE***	**67.73**	**1.83**	**94.39**

Table 5: Performances on relation prediction task.

other point made by system 1 is the fact that it does not involve training on the triples but is still competitive with the strong baseline that leverages the underlying distribution from the triples. This indicates that to some extent the textual frame embeddings still capture useful information for the F2F Prediction Task. In a further step, we also use the embeddings pretrained on the F2F relations of the FN hierarchy (*TransE*), even if in this setting we do not need to calculate prototypical relation embeddings as *TransE* provides embeddings for frames and relations. Thus, system 1 uses the *TransE* embeddings directly to calculate the similarity of the frame embeddings' vector offset and the relation embeddings. The large improvement in all performance measures shows the strength of knowledge-based embeddings over text-based embeddings and confirms the difficulty of text-based embeddings in reconstructing the F2F relations.

Performance increases with system 2, the softmax regression model involving learning. This shows the effect of training with respect to the F2F relations. It indicates that training should be involved for leveraging the text-based frame embeddings in the F2F Prediction Task. Using embeddings pretrained on the F2F relations of the FN hierarchy (*TransE*) instead, again leads to a large improvement in all performance measures. This confirms that embeddings designed to incorporate the knowledge from the FN hierarchy are better suited for the F2F relation prediction task and it emphasizes the large improvement over the textual embeddings.

Overall, we achieve best results in all performance measures with system 3, the NN approach, in combination with the knowledge-based *TransE* embeddings as input representations. Interestingly, the difference between NN and the regression model is only marginal when using the *TransE* embeddings, indicating the crucial influence of the knowledge-based embeddings and not necessarily the system. Moreover, when using the text-based *WSABIE* and *Word2Vec* the softmax regression model is stronger than the NN, which might be due to little training data. Furthermore, the randomly initialized embeddings for system 3 could be seen as another baseline which is not only beaten by the knowledge-based *TransE* embeddings but also by the text-based *WSABIE* and *Word2Vec* embeddings in systems 2 and 3. This again indicates the capability of the textual frame

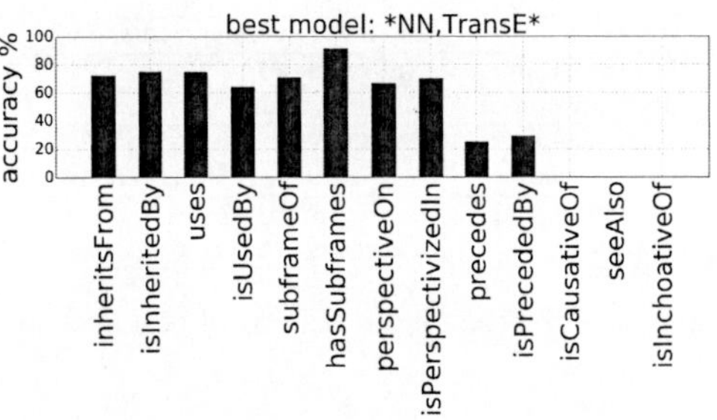

Figure 5: Relation-specific analysis of the best-performing model with respect to accuracy.

embeddings of capturing useful information for the F2F Prediction Task to at least some extent.

The systems could reach higher scores if the split of the data into training and test triples would be done random per relation such that the train and test set have some (random) relation-specific overlap in frames on the position f_1 in the triple. But in this case, it would not clear whether the systems would just perform "lexical memorization" as pointed out by (Levy et al., 2015) when the test set contains partial instances that were in the training set. We leave it for future work to contrast and explore different splits, e.g., random split, zero-overlap by relation or by all relations.

To sum up, on the one hand, the results confirm the conclusions from the exploration in Section 4: the frame embeddings learned on frame-labeled text in the context of other tasks are not able to reliably mirror the F2F relations, not even when used as input representations to a classifier. On the other hand, our results clearly emphasize the influence of the knowledge-based embeddings on the performance of our best-performing system. Thus, we propose this NN architecture in combination with the *TransE* embeddings as the first system for automatic F2F relation annotation for frame pairs in the FN hierarchy.

Figure 5 depicts a relation-specific analysis of the best-performing model showing good performances (above 60% accuracy) for frequent relations, a drop for the less frequent `precedence` relations and no capability at all in predicting infrequent relations, such as `is_Causative_of`, `see_Also` and `is_Inchoative_of`.

5.3 Demonstration of Predictions

We generically demonstrate the best-performing system's prediction for examples of frame pairs which are not annotated so far. Looking back at

(f_1, f_2)	top 3 F2F relation predictions
(Biological_urge, Sleep_wake_cycle)	**Subframe_of**, `Inherits_from`, `Uses`
(Biological_urge, Being_awake)	`Is_Inherited_by`, `Precedes`, **Is_Preceded_by**
(Biological_urge, Fall_asleep)	`Is_Inherited_by`, **Precedes**, `Is_Preceded_by`

Table 6: F2F relation predictions of best system.

the motivational example from the beginning, Figure 1 illustrated the incompleteness of the FN hierarchy at the F2F relation level with the example of a possibly missing `precedence` relation from "Being_awake" to "Biological_urge" (evoked by the predicate "tired"). Table 6 displays the top 3 F2F relation predictions for the frame pairs around "Biological_urge" in the figure. The expected F2F relation (printed bold) is indeed amongst the top 3 predictions of the best performing system for this example, even for the `precedence` relation which is rather underrepresented in the data. If this system was used to make suggestions to human expert annotators, they should be informed about the system being biased against the infrequent relations. However, it is hard to do a proper manual evaluation as judging the suggested relations requires expert knowledge of the definitions and annotation best-practices for the F2F relations. We propose using the best-performing system for semi-automatic FN completion on the relation level in cooperation with FN annotation experts. The system can be used to make reasonable suggestions of relations for frame pairs and the final decision could be made by experienced FN annotators. This would be a first step towards improving the incompleteness of F2F relation annotations in FN, which in turn could improve the performance in other tasks that take these F2F relations as input.

6 Discussion and Future Work

As the F2F relations of the FN hierarchy did not emerge from frame embeddings learned on frame-labeled text, the F2F relations should be seen as meta-structures not having direct evidence in text. On the one hand, more advanced approaches might be needed to distill F2F relations for frames occurring in raw text, by learning about common-sense knowledge involving frames, and then inferring the implicit relations. Here, it could also be helpful to exploit inter-sentential clues e.g., event chains, to enrich the frame embeddings which so far are built on sentence-level. On the other hand, the automatic completion of F2F relations can rely on knowledge-based embeddings trained on the hierarchy. To this end, an expert evaluation of the best-performing system's predictions for frame pairs could give clues for further system improvements. It could also yield an expert upper bound and may pave the way for developing advanced systems using frame embeddings for the prediction of F2F relations. Finally, we plan to investigate the case of FN for embeddings learned on both, frame-labeled texts and F2F relation annotations. By having such a combination, the limitation of the text-based embeddings on frames that have LUs (and hence occur in text) can be overcome as the knowledge-based embeddings also have access to frames without LUs. Last but not least, for different tasks, different representations of frames and relations might be better suited: embeddings purely learned on text, or embeddings purely learned on the FN hierarchy, or a combination of both.

7 Conclusion

We raised the question whether text-based frame embeddings naturally mirror F2F relations in the FN hierarchy. We set up the F2F Relation Prediction task as an adaptation of the link prediction task from KGC to the case of FN. Through this task, we quantify the ability of systems and embeddings to predict F2F relations. The F2F Relation Prediction task addresses the need for automatically completing F2F relations that are used in down-stream tasks. Our best-performing system for predicting F2F relations is a NN trained on the FN hierarchy and uses knowledge-based embeddings that by design incorporate the F2F relation. It can be used to suggest more F2F relation annotations in the FN hierarchy. The comparison of our different systems and embeddings reveals insights about the difficulty of reconstructing F2F relations purely from text. We encourage the development of advanced systems and embeddings for the F2F Relation Prediction task.

Acknowledgments

This work has been supported by the DFG-funded research training group "Adaptive Preparation of Information form Heterogeneous Sources" (AIPHES, GRK 1994/1). We also acknowledge the useful comments of the anonymous reviewers.

References

Roni Ben Aharon, Idan Szpektor, and Ido Dagan. 2010. Generating Entailment Rules from FrameNet. In *Proceedings of the ACL 2010 Conference Short Papers*. Association for Computational Linguistics, pages 241–246. http://www.aclweb.org/anthology/P10-2045.

Collin F Baker, Charles J Fillmore, and John B Lowe. 1998. The Berkeley FrameNet Project. In *Proceedings of the 36th Annual Meeting of the Association for Computational Linguistics and 17th International Conference on Computational Linguistics-Volume 1*. Association for Computational Linguistics, Montreal, Quebec, Canada, pages 86–90. https://doi.org/10.3115/980451.980860.

Daniel Bauer, Hagen Fürstenau, and Owen Rambow. 2012. The Dependency-Parsed FrameNet Corpus. In *Proceedings of the 8th Language Resources and Evaluation Conference (LREC 2012)*. Istanbul, Turkey, pages 3861–3867. http://hdl.handle.net/10022/AC:P:21192.

Antoine Bordes, Xavier Glorot, Jason Weston, and Yoshua Bengio. 2012. Joint Learning of Words and Meaning Representations for Open-Text Semantic Parsing. In Neil D. Lawrence and Mark Girolami, editors, *Proceedings of the Fifteenth International Conference on Artificial Intelligence and Statistics*. PMLR, La Palma, Canary Islands, volume 22 of *Proceedings of Machine Learning Research*, pages 127–135. http://proceedings.mlr.press/v22/bordes12.html.

Antoine Bordes, Nicolas Usunier, Alberto Garcia-Duran, Jason Weston, and Oksana Yakhnenko. 2013. Translating Embeddings for Modeling Multi-relational Data. In C. J. C. Burges, L. Bottou, M. Welling, Z. Ghahramani, and K. Q. Weinberger, editors, *Advances in Neural Information Processing Systems 26*. Curran Associates, Inc., pages 2787–2795. http://papers.nips.cc/paper/5071-translating-embeddings-for-modeling-multi-relational-data.pdf.

Antoine Bordes, Jason Weston, Ronan Collobert, and Yoshua Bengio. 2011. Learning Structured Embeddings of Knowledge Bases. In *Proceedings of the Twenty-Fifth AAAI Conference on Artificial Intelligence*. AAAI Press, AAAI'11, pages 301–306. http://dl.acm.org/citation.cfm?id=2900423.2900470.

Bob Coyne and Owen Rambow. 2009. LexPar: A Freely Available English Paraphrase Lexicon Automatically Extracted from FrameNet. In *Proceedings of the Third IEEE International Conference on Semantic Computing (ICSC 2009)*. pages 53–58. https://doi.org/10.1109/ICSC.2009.56.

Christiane Fellbaum. 1990. English Verbs as a Semantic Net. *International Journal of Lexicography* 3(4):278–301. https://doi.org/10.1093/ijl/3.4.278.

Minwei Feng, Bing Xiang, Michael R Glass, Lidan Wang, and Bowen Zhou. 2015. Applying Deep Learning to Answer Selection: A Study and An Open Task. In *2015 IEEE Workshop on Automatic Speech Recognition and Understanding (ASRU)*. IEEE, pages 813–820. https://doi.org/10.1109/ASRU.2015.7404872.

Charles J Fillmore. 1976. Frame Semantics and the Nature of Language. *Annals of the New York Academy of Sciences* 280(1):20–32. https://doi.org/10.1111/j.1749-6632.1976.tb25467.x.

Charles J Fillmore and Collin F Baker. 2001. Frame Semantics for Text Understanding. In *Proceedings of WordNet and Other Lexical Resources Workshop, NAACL*.

Lucie Flekova and Iryna Gurevych. 2016. Supersense Embeddings: A Unified Model for Supersense Interpretation, Prediction, and Utilization. In *Proceedings of the 54th Annual Meeting of the Association for Computational Linguistics (ACL 2016)*. Association for Computational Linguistics, Berlin, Germany, volume Volume 1: Long Papers, pages 2029–2041.

Silvana Hartmann and Iryna Gurevych. 2013. FrameNet on the Way to Babel: Creating a Bilingual FrameNet Using Wiktionary as Interlingual Connection. In *Proceedings of the 51st Annual Meeting of the Association for Computational Linguistics (ACL 2013)*. Association for Computational Linguistics, Stroudsburg, PA, USA, volume 1, pages 1363–1373.

Silvana Hartmann, Ilia Kuznetsov, Teresa Martin, and Iryna Gurevych. 2017. Out-of-domain FrameNet Semantic Role Labeling. In *Proceedings of the 15th Conference of the European Chapter of the Association for Computational Linguistics (EACL 2017)*. Association for Computational Linguistics, pages 471–482.

Karl Moritz Hermann, Dipanjan Das, Jason Weston, and Kuzman Ganchev. 2014. Semantic Frame Identification with Distributed Word Representations. In *Proceedings of the 52nd Annual Meeting of the Association for Computational Linguistics (Volume 1: Long Papers)*. Association for Computational Linguistics, Baltimore, Maryland, pages 1448–1458. http://www.aclweb.org/anthology/P14-1136.

Ignacio Iacobacci, Mohammad Taher Pilehvar, and Roberto Navigli. 2015. SensEmbed: Learning Sense Embeddings for Word and Relational Similarity. In *Proceedings of the 53rd Annual Meeting of the Association for Computational Linguistics and the 7th International Joint Conference on Natural Language Processing (Volume 1: Long Papers)*. Association for Computational Linguistics, Beijing, China, pages 95–105. http://www.aclweb.org/anthology/P15-1010.

Omer Levy and Yoav Goldberg. 2014. Dependency-Based Word Embeddings. In *Proceedings of the 52nd Annual Meeting of the Association for Computational Linguistics, ACL 2014, June 22-27, 2014, Baltimore, MD, USA, Volume 2: Short Papers*. The Association for Computer Linguistics, pages 302–308. https://doi.org/10.3115/v1/P14-2050.

Omer Levy, Steffen Remus, Chris Biemann, Ido Dagan, and Israel Ramat-Gan. 2015. Do Supervised Distributional Methods Really Learn Lexical Inference Relations? In *HLT-NAACL*. pages 970–976. https://doi.org/10.3115/v1/N15-1098.

Yankai Lin, Zhiyuan Liu, Maosong Sun, Yang Liu, and Xuan Zhu. 2015. Learning Entity and Relation Embeddings for Knowledge Graph Completion. In *AAAI*. pages 2181–2187.

Laurens van der Maaten and Geoffrey Hinton. 2008. Visualizing Data using t-SNE. *Journal of Machine Learning Research* 9(Nov):2579–2605.

Tomas Mikolov, Kai Chen, Greg Corrado, and Jeffrey Dean. 2013a. Efficient Estimation of Word Representations in Vector Space. *Proceedings of Workshop at ICLR* .

Tomas Mikolov, Wen-tau Yih, and Geoffrey Zweig. 2013b. Linguistic Regularities in Continuous Space Word Representations. In *Proceedings of the 2013 Conference of the North American Chapter of the Association for Computational Linguistics: Human Language Technologies (NAACL-HLT-2013)*. Association for Computational Linguistics, volume 13, pages 746–751. https://www.microsoft.com/en-us/research/publication/linguistic-regularities-in-continuous-space-word-representations/.

George A Miller. 1990. Nouns in WordNet: A Lexical Inheritance System. *International journal of Lexicography* 3(4):245–264. https://doi.org/10.1093/ijl/3.4.245.

Roberto Navigli and Simone Paolo Ponzetto. 2012. BabelNet: The automatic construction, evaluation and application of a wide-coverage multilingual semantic network. *Artificial Intelligence* 193:217–250. https://doi.org/10.1016/j.artint.2012.07.001.

Ellie Pavlick, Travis Wolfe, Pushpendre Rastogi, Chris Callison-Burch, Mark Dredze, and Benjamin Van Durme. 2015. FrameNet+: Fast Paraphrastic Tripling of FrameNet. In *Proceedings of the 53rd Annual Meeting of the Association for Computational Linguistics and the 7th International Joint Conference on Natural Language Processing (Short Papers)*. Beijing, China, pages 408–413.

Pushpendre Rastogi and Benjamin Van Durme. 2014. Augmenting FrameNet Via PPDB. In *Proceedings of the Second Workshop on EVENTS: Definition, Detection, Coreference, and Representation*. Association for Computational Linguistics, Baltimore, Maryland, USA, pages 1–5.

Radim Řehůřek and Petr Sojka. 2010. Software Framework for Topic Modelling with Large Corpora. In *Proceedings of the LREC 2010 Workshop on New Challenges for NLP Frameworks*. ELRA, Valletta, Malta, pages 45–50. http://is.muni.cz/publication/884893/en.

Josef Ruppenhofer, Michael Ellsworth, Miriam RL Petruck, Christopher R Johnson, and Jan Scheffczyk. 2006. FrameNet II: Extended Theory and Practice. Distributed with the FrameNet data.

Ming Tan, Bing Xiang, and Bowen Zhou. 2015. LSTM-based Deep Learning Models for Non-factoid Answer Selection. *arXiv preprint arXiv:1511.04108* .

Jason Weston, Samy Bengio, and Nicolas Usunier. 2011. WSABIE: Scaling Up to Large Vocabulary Image Annotation. In *Proceedings of the Twenty-Second International Joint Conference on Artificial Intelligence - Volume Volume Three*. AAAI Press, Barcelona, Catalonia, Spain, IJCAI'11, pages 2764–2770. https://doi.org/10.5591/978-1-57735-516-8/IJCAI11-460.

Learning Joint Multilingual Sentence Representations
with Neural Machine Translation

Holger Schwenk
Facebook
AI Research
schwenk@fb.com

Matthijs Douze
Facebook
AI Research
matthijs@fb.com

Abstract

In this paper, we use the framework of neural machine translation to learn joint sentence representations across six very different languages. Our aim is that a representation which is independent of the language, is likely to capture the underlying semantics. We define a new cross-lingual similarity measure, compare up to 1.4M sentence representations and study the characteristics of close sentences. We provide experimental evidence that sentences that are close in embedding space are indeed semantically highly related, but often have quite different structure and syntax. These relations also hold when comparing sentences in different languages.

1 Introduction

It is today common practice to use distributed representations of words, often called *word embeddings*, in almost all NLP applications. It has been shown that syntactic and semantic relations can be captured in this embedding space, see for instance (Mikolov et al., 2013). To process sequences of words, ie. sentences or small paragraphs, these word embeddings need to be *"combined"* into a representation of the whole sequence. Common approaches include: simple techniques like bag-of-words or some type of pooling, eg. (Arora et al., 2017), recursive neural networks, eg. (Socher et al., 2011), recurrent neural networks, in particular LSTMs, eg. (Cho et al., 2014), convolutional neural networks, eg. (Collobert and Weston, 2008; Zhang et al., 2015) or hierarchical approaches, eg. (Zhao et al., 2015).

In some NLP applications, both the input and output are sentences. A very popular approach to handle such tasks is the so-called *"encoder-decoder approach"*, also named *"sequence-to-sequence learning (seq2seq)"*. The main idea is to first encode the input sentence into an internal representation, and then to generate the output sentence from this representation. A very successful application of this paradigm is neural machine translation (NMT), see for instance (Kalchbrenner and Blunsom, 2013; Cho et al., 2014; Sutskever et al., 2014). Current best practice is to use recurrent neural networks for the encoder and decoder, but alternative architectures like convolutional networks have been also explored.

The performance of these vanilla seq2seq models substantially degrades with the sequence length since it is difficult to encode long sequences into a single, fixed-size representation. A plausible solution is the so-called attention mechanism (Bahdanau et al., 2015): where the generation of each target word is conditioned on a weighted subset of source words, instead of the full sentence. NMT has been also extended to handle several source and/or target languages at once, with the goal of achieving better translation quality than with separately trained NMT systems, in particular for under resourced languages, see for instance (Dong et al., 2015; Zoph and Knight, 2016; Luong et al., 2015a; Firat et al., 2016a).

In this work, we aim at learning *multilingual sentence representations*, i.e. which are independent of the language. Since we have to compare these representations among each other, for the same or between multiple languages, we only consider representations of fixed size.

There are many motivations to learn such a multilingual sentence representation, in particular:

- it is likely to capture the underlying semantics of the sentence (since the meaning is the only common characteristic of a sentence formulated in several languages);

- it has the potential to transfer many sentence

157

Proceedings of the 2nd Workshop on Representation Learning for NLP, pages 157–167,
Vancouver, Canada, August 3, 2017. ©2017 Association for Computational Linguistics

processing applications to other languages (classification, sentiment analysis, semantic similarity, etc), without the need for language specific training data;

- it enables multilingual search;

- such representation could be considered as sort of a *continuous space interlingua*.

To train these multilingual sentence embeddings we are using the framework of NMT with multiple encoders and decoders. We first describe our model in detail, relate it to existing research, and then present an experimental evaluation.

2 Architecture

We propose to use multiple encoders and decoders, one for each source and target language respectively. The notion of multiple input languages can be also extended to different modalities, e.g. speech and images. One can also envision to add classification tasks, in addition to sequence generation. Our ultimate goal is to jointly train this generic architecture on many tasks at once, to obtain a universal multilingual and -modal representation (see illustration in Figure 1). To ease the comparison and search, we are focusing on representations of fixed-size, independently of the length of the input (and output) sequence. This choice has certainly an impact on the performance for very long sequences, ie. in the order of more than fifty words, but we argue that such long sentences are probably not very frequent in every day communication. We would also like to emphasize that the goal of this work is not to improve NMT (for multiple languages), but to use the NMT framework to learn multilingual sentence embeddings. Once the system is trained, the decoders

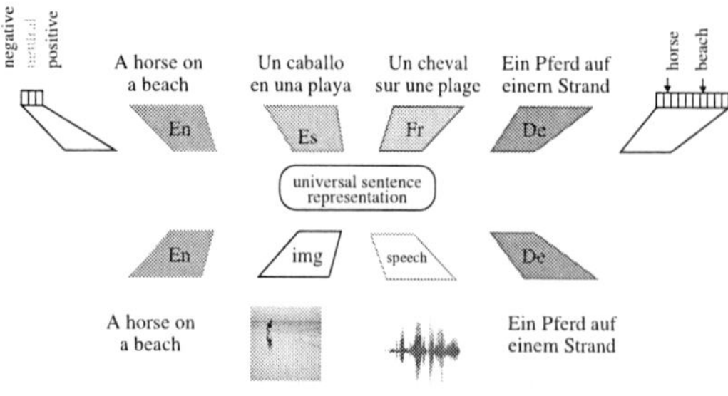

Figure 1: Generic multilingual and -modal encoder/decoder architecture.

are not used any more. This means in particular that the usual attention mechanism cannot be used since the attention weights are usually conditioned on the decoder outputs. A possible solution could be to condition the attention on the inputs only, for instance so-called *self-attention* (Liu et al., 2016) or *inner-attention* (Lin et al., 2017).

To fix ideas, let us consider that we have corpora in L different languages which can be pairwise or N-way parallel, $N \leq L$. This means that our architecture is composed of L encoders and L decoders respectively. However, this does not mean that we always provide input to all encoders, or targets for all decoders, but we change the used models at each mini-batch. One could for instance perform one mini-batch with two input languages and one output language (which requires an 3-way parallel corpus), and use one (different) input and output language in the next mini-batch (which require a bitext). We call this *partial training paths*. Note that we can also use monolingual data in this framework, ie. the input and output language is identical.

There are many possibilities to define partial training paths, with $1 < M, N \leq L$.

1:1 translating from one source into one target language respectively.

M:1 presenting simultaneously several source languages at the input.

1:N translating from one source language into multiple target languages.

M:N this is a combination of the preceding two strategies and the most general approach. Remember that not all inputs and outputs need to be present at each training step.

Our goal is to learn joint sentence representations, which are as close as possible when sentences are presented in different languages at the input. If we use 1:1 training, changing the language pair at each mini-batch (input and output), it is quite unlikely that the system would learn a common joint representation which is independent of the source language. A variant of 1:1 training is to always use the same decoder, but many different encoders. Since the decoder is shared for all the input languages, and the capacity of the model is limited, there's an incentive for the system to use the same representations for all the encoders.

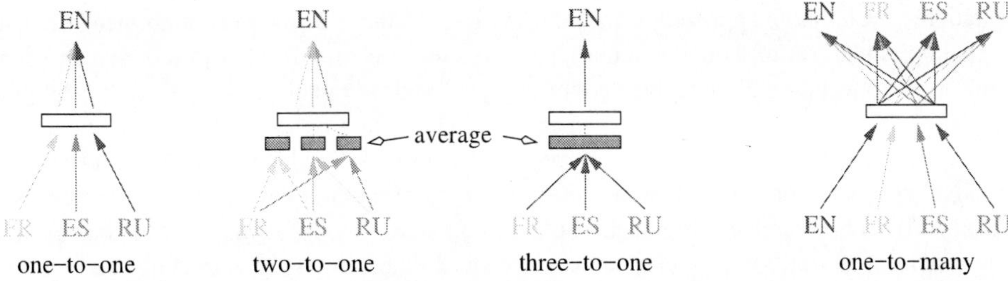

Figure 2: Possible partial training paths when four languages are available (En, Fr, Es and Ru). From left: 1:1, 2:1 and 3:1 strategy, using En as common target language. Right: 1:3 strategy, translating from one source to the three other target languages.

This training strategy only requires bitexts with one common language (usually English). An important drawback, however, is that we will not obtain an embedding of this common language since it is never used at the input.[1]

Using multiple languages at the input at the same time and combining the corresponding sentence embeddings, ie. the M:1 strategy, has in principle the potential to learn joint sentence embeddings, if an appropriate technique is used to combine the individual embeddings. The most straightforward approach is to average the embeddings. This was used for instance in (Firat et al., 2016b) in a multilingual NMT system with attention. The joint embedding could be also enforced by some type of regularizer. Again, having one dedicated output language makes it impossible to learn a representation for it.

The 1:N strategy is an interesting extension of 1:1. The idea is translate from one input language simultaneously to all L-1 other languages, excluding the one at the input (ie. no auto-encoder). The source and the set of target languages is changed at each mini-batch. By these means, every input language has at least one target language in common with all input languages, and each target language has at least one input language in common. On one hand hand, this strategy makes it possible to learn sentence embeddings for all languages, but one the other hand, it requires L-way parallel training data. Although bitexts are usually used in MT, there are also several corpora which can be aligned for more than two languages (eg. Eurpoarl, TED, UN). Finally, the N:M strat-

egy is the most generic one which combines all above techniques. These different training strategies are illustrated in Figure 2 for four languages.

2.1 Related work

The use of multiple encoders and decoders was first studied in the context of neural MT. Dong et al. (2015) used multiple decoders, i.e. 1:N training, to achieve improved NMT performance. Zoph and Knight (2016) and Firat et al. (2016b), on the other hand, used multiple encoders, i.e. M:1 training. It's not surprising that this complementarity improves MT quality, in comparison to one input language only. Many different configurations were explored by (Luong et al., 2015a) for seq2seq models. Firat et al. (2016a) were the first to use multiple encoders and decoders with a shared attention mechanism. This approach was further refined to enable zero-resource NMT (Firat et al., 2016b). Alternatively, it was proposed to handle multiple source and target languages with one encoder and decoder only, using a special token to indicate the target language (Johnson et al., 2016) to enable zero-shot NMT. To best of our knowledge, all these works focus on the improvement and extensions of seq2seq modeling, and fixed-sized vector representations have not analyzed in depth in a multilingual context.

Several publications consider joint representations in a multimodal context, usually text and images, for instance (Frome et al., 2013; Ngiam et al., 2011; Nakayama and Nishida, 2016). The usual approach is to optimize a distance or correlation between the two representations or *predictive auto-encoders* (Chandar et al., 2013). The same approach was applied to transliteration and captioning (Saha et al., 2016).

There is a large body of research on sentence

---

[1] One could also use the common output language at the input. This corresponds to training an auto-encoder which is easier than a translation model and may have an negative impact.

representations. Common approaches include: simple techniques like bag-of-words or some type of pooling, eg (Arora et al., 2017), recursive NNs, eg. (Socher et al., 2011), recurrent NNs, in particular LSTMs, eg. (Cho et al., 2014), convolutional NNs, eg. (Collobert and Weston, 2008; Zhang et al., 2015) or hierarchical approaches, eg. (Zhao et al., 2015). In all these works, the sentence representations are learned for one language only. It is important to note that our multiple encoder/decoder architecture and the different training paths make no assumption on the type of encoder and decoder used. In principle, all these sentence representations methods could be used. This is left for future research.

There are several works on learning multilingual representations at document level (Hermann and Blunsom, 2014; Zhou et al., 2016b; Pham et al., 2015). (Hermann and Blunsom, 2014) proposed a compositional vector model to learn document level representations. Their model is based on bag of words/bi-gram composition. (Pham et al., 2015) directly learn a vector representations for sentences in the absence of compositional property. (Zhou et al., 2016b) learn bilingual document representation by minimizing Euclidean distance between document representations and their translation.

Other multilingual sentence representation learning techniques include BAE (Chandar et al., 2013) which trains bilingual autoencoders with the objective of minimizing reconstruction error between two languages, and BRAVE (Bilingual paRAgraph VEctors) (Mogadala and Rettinger, 2016) which learns both bilingual word embeddings and sentence embeddings from either sentence-aligned parallel corpora (BRAVE-S), or label-aligned non-parallel corpora (BRAVE-D).

Finally, many papers address the problem of learning bi- or multilingual word representations which are used to perform cross-lingual document classification. They are trained either on word alignments or sentence-aligned parallel corpora, or both. I-Matrix (Klementiev et al., 2012) uses word alignments to do multi-task learning, where each word is a single task and the objective is to move frequently aligned words closer in the joint embeddings space. DWA (Distributed Word Alignment) (Kociský et al., 2014) learns word alignments and bilingual word embeddings simultaneously using translation probability as objec-

tive. Without using word alignments, BilBOWA (Gouews et al., 2014) optimizes both monolingual and bilingual objectives, uses Skip-gram as monolingual loss, while formulating the bilingual loss as Euclidean distance between bag-of-words representations of aligned sentences. UnsupAlign (Luong et al., 2015b) learns bilingual word embeddings by extending the monolingual Skip-gram model with bilingual contexts based on word alignments within the sentence. TransGram (Coulmance et al., 2015) is similar to (Pham et al., 2015) but treats all words in the parallel sentence as context words, thus eliminating the need for word alignments.

3 Evaluation protocol

An important question is how to evaluate multilingual joint sentence embeddings. Let us first define some desired properties of such embeddings:

- **multilingual closeness:** the representations of the same sentence for different languages should be as similar as possible;

- **semantic closeness:** similar sentences should be also close in the embeddings space, ie. sentences conveying the same meaning, but not necessarily the syntactic structure and word choice;

- **preservation of content:** sentence representations are usually used in the context of a task, eg. classification, multilingual NMT or semantic relatedness. This requires that enough information is preserved in the representations to perform the task;

- **scalability to many languages:** it is desirable that the metric can be extended to many languages without important computational cost or need for human labeling of data.

Two main approaches have been used in the literature to evaluate multilingual sentence embeddings: 1) cross-lingual document classification based on the Reuters corpus, first described in (Klementiev et al., 2012); and 2) cross-lingual evaluation of semantic textual similarity (in short STS). This task was first introduced in the 2016 edition of SemEval (Agirre et al., 2016). Both tasks focus on the evaluation of joint sentence representations of two languages only. In the Reuters task, a document classifier is trained on English sentence representations and then applied to texts in another language, and in the opposite direction respectively. STS seeks to measure the degree of semantic equivalence between two sentences (or small paragraphs). Semantic similarity is expressed by a score between 0 (the two sentences are completely dissimilar) and 5 (the two sentences are completely equivalent). In 2016, a cross lingual task was introduced (Es/En) and extended to two more language pairs in 2017 (Ar/En and Tr/En).

In this work, we propose an additional evaluation framework for multilingual joint representations, based on similarity search. Our metric can be automatically calculated without the need of new human-labeled data and scaled to many languages and large corpora. We only need collections of S sentences, and their translations in L different languages, ie. $s_i^p, i = 1 \ldots S, p = 1 \ldots L$. Such L-way parallel corpora are freely available, for instance Europarl[2] (20 languages), the UN corpus, 6 languages (Ziemski et al., 2016), or TED, 23 languages, (Cettolo et al., 2012).

Algorithm 1 Multilingual similarity search

1: L: number of languages
2: S: number of sentences
3: E_{pq}: error between languages p and q
4: $R(s_i^p)$: embedding of a sentence
5: $D()$: some distance metric
6: **for** $p = 1 \ldots L$ **do**
7:   **for** $q = 1 \ldots L, q \neq p$ **do**
8:     $E_{pq} = 0$
9:     **for** $i = 1 \ldots S$ **do**
10:       **if** $\arg \min_{j=1\ldots S} D(R(s_i^p), R(s_j^q)) \neq i$ **then**
11:         $E_{pq} + +$
12:       **end if**
13:     **end for**
14:   **end for**
15: **end for**

The details of our approach are given in algorithm 1. The basic idea is to search the closest sentence in all S sentences, and count an error if it is not the reference translation. This requires the calculation of S^2 distance metrics and makes only sense when there are no duplicate sentences in the corpus. With increasing S it may be also likely that the corpus contains several alternative valid translations which could be closer than the

---

reference one. This is difficult to handle automatically at large scale and counted as error by our algorithm.

Similarity search mainly evaluates the multilingual closeness property and can be easily scaled to many languages. We will report results how the similarity error rate is influenced by the number of language pairs and the size of the corpus. We have compared three distance metrics: L2, inner product and cosine. In general, cosine performed best. Note that all metrics are equivalent if the vectors are normalized.

4 Experimental evaluation

We have performed all our experiments with the freely available UN corpus. It contains about 12M sentences in six languages (En, Fr, Es, Ru, Ar and Zh). We have used the version which is 6-way parallel (about 8.3M sentences). This corpus comes with a predefined Dev and Test set (4000 sentences each). We lowercase all texts, limit the length of the training data to 50 words and use byte-pair encoding (BPE) with a 20k vocabulary. BPE allows to limit the size of the decoder output vocabulary, it has only a small impact on the sentence length ($\approx +20\%$) and it showed similar or even superior performance in NMT in comparison to many other techniques to limit the size of the output vocabulary (Sennrich et al., 2016). We have also found that BPE is very robust to spelling errors which is important when handling informal texts.

4.1 Different network architectures

In this work we only consider stacked LSTMs as encoders and decoders. In the vanilla seq2seq NMT model, the last state of the LSTM is used as sentence representation. There is also evidence that deeper architectures perform better in NMT than shallow ones, eg. (Zhou et al., 2016a; Wu et al., 2016). Following this tendency, we performed the first set of experiments with stacked LSTMs with three 512-dimensional hidden layers. Deeper architectures did not improve the performance.

We then switched to using BLSTMs followed by max-pooling (element-wise over the sequence length). We are not aware of works which use max-pooling in an NMT framework. One is indeed tempted to assume that max-pooling makes it more difficult to create a target sentence which preserves all information from the source sentence. On the other hand, max-pooling is success-

System	Average Similarity Error			
#pairs:	efs 6	efsr 10	efsra 15	efsraz 21
One-to-one systems:				
efs-r	1.97%	-	-	-
efs-a	2.09%	-	-	-
efsr-a	1.90%	2.40%	-	-
efsra-z	1.91%	2.26%	2.51%	-
One-to-many systems:				
efsraz-all	1.70%	1.97%	2.38%	2.59%
One-to-many systems, nhid=1024:				
efsraz-all	1.36%	1.64%	1.89%	1.95%

Three layer LSTM, nhid=512
Sentence representation: last LSTM state

System	Average Similarity Error			
#pairs:	efs 6	efsr 10	efsra 15	efsraz 21
One-to-one systems:				
efs-r	1.11%	-	-	-
efs-a	1.03%	-	-	-
efsr-a	1.11%	1.31%	-	-
efsra-z	1.01%	1.19%	1.25%	–
One-to-many systems:				
efsraz-all	0.92%	1.07%	1.15%	**1.20%**

One layer BLSTM, nhid=512
Sentence representation: max pooling

Table 1: Error rates of similarity search on the UN Dev corpus. Languages are abbreviated with the following letters: e=English, f=French, s=Spanish, r=Russian, a=Arabic, z=Chinese.

fully used in various sentence classification tasks, eg. (Conneau et al., 2017). It should be noted that the final sentence representation has twice the dimension of the BLSTM hidden layer.

The word embeddings are of size 384 for all models. We use vertical dropout with a value of 0.2 and gradients are clipped at 2. The initial learning rate is set to 0.01 and decreased each time performance on the Dev data does not improve. Performance is measured by perplexity for the decoders and similarity error at the embedding layer for the encoders. It is important to note that the similarity error rate can be only calculated once the whole development set is processed. Therefore it is not used to provide gradients to the encoders. Training is performed for up to five epochs with a batch size of 96. For the smallest models, one iteration through the training data takes about 11h. Most models converge after two to three epochs.

Table 1 summarizes our results on the UN Dev corpus for several systems using the one-to-one and one-to-many partial training paths. We compare training of joint representations for three to six languages using LSTM or BLSTM encoders. In each column, we give the average similarity error over all $n(n+1)/2$ language pairs. As an example, the system trained with En, Fr, Es and Ru at the input and Ar at the output (*"efsr-a"* in the third line), achieves an average similarity error of 1.90% over 6 language pairs[3], column *"efs"*, and 2.40% over 10 languages pairs[4], column *"efsr"*.

We can make the following observations. First, using an BLSTM with max-pooling (Table 1 right) performs much better than an LSTM and using the last hidden state as sentence representation (Table 1 left). This was also observed for many monolingual tasks, eg. (Conneau et al., 2017). This is particularly true when the number of languages is increased. This performance gain does not result from the increased dimension of the sentence representation ($2 \times$ nhid) since an 1024-dimensional LSTM only achieves 1.36% (see last line in Table 1 left). Second, increasing the number of languages for which we seek a joint sentence embedding does not seem to make the task harder: the system trained on all languages achieves the same results (1.01%) on three languages than when training only on these languages (1.03%). Third, the one-to-many training strategy (*efsraz-all*, 0.92%) performs better than 1:1 (*efsra-z*, 1.01%). In addition, it allows to obtain a sentence embedding for all languages, while the common output language is excluded in the 1:1 strategy.

Finally, we have explored whether deep architectures are needed when using an BLSTM encoder and a max-pooling sentence representation (see Table 2). We found no experimental evidence that stacking several BLSTM layers is useful.

4.2 Many-to-one training strategies

In this section, we study two M:1 training strategies, namely 2:1 and 3:1. Since the number of

---

[3]En-Es, En-Fr, Es-En, Es-Fr, Fr-En and Fr-Es.

[4]En-Es, En-Fr, En-Ru, Es-En, Es-Fr, Es-Ru, Fr-En, Fr-Es, Fr-Ru, Ru-En, Ru-Es and Ru-Fr.

Network	LSTM + last		BLSTM + max-pooling					
	3x512	3x1024	1x256	2x256	3x256	1x512	2x512	3x512
1:1, efsra-z	2.51	–	1.44	1.21	1,65	1.25	1.25	1.53
1:M, efsraz-all	2.38	1.89	1.27	1.30	1.53	**1.15**	1.17	1.30

Table 2: Error rates of similarity search on the UN Dev corpus for **five** language pairs (*efsra*). Comparision of LSTMs and BLSTMs of different size and depth.

combinations quickly increases with the number of input languages, we limit these experiences to three input languages (system *efs-a*). In that case, we have three 1:1 training paths (En→Ar, Fr→Ar and Es→Ar), three 2:1 training paths (En+Fr→Ar, En+Es→Ar and Fr+Es→Ar) and one 3:1 configuration (En+Fr+Es→Ar). This is illustrated in Figure 2. To obtain efficient training, we use homogeneous mini-batches, ie. the number of encoders and decoders is constant. Examples in a mini-batch are sampled according to a coefficient. In order to make a fair comparison, these resampling coefficient were chosen so that each encoders always sees the same number of sentences (roughly 8.3M). We refer to the different runs with an ID (first column in Table 3). As an example, for the experiment with ID 12_a, 90% of the mini-batches are 1:1 and 5% are 2:1. Note that that the 2:1 samples have a coefficient of 0.05 since two encoders are simultaneously used.

The first striking result is that presenting all input languages at once and averaging the three sentence representations (3:1, ID 3) does not allow to learn joint representations. We are however able to learn joint representations with the 2:1 strategy (ID 2), but the performance is worse than the 1:1 baseline (1.85% versus 1.03%). We are also tried to alternate between 1:1 and 2:1 mini-batches with increasing resampling coefficients (ID 12_a to 12_e). The idea is that each encoder learns to provide a sentence representation when used alone and when used with another one. However, we observe that adding 2:1 training paths is not useful: the similarity error increases. The same observation holds when adding 3:1 training paths (ID 13 and 123). Overall, we were not able to improve the baseline of 1.03% similarity error obtained with a simple 1:1 training strategy. Therefore, we did not try the even more complex M:N paths. This failure could be attributed to the fact that we simply average multiple sentence representations. In future research, we will investigate other possibilities, eg. based on correlation like proposed in (Saha et al., 2016; Chandar et al., 2016).

Detailed similarity search error rates for all **six** languages, including Zh, of our best system are given in Table 4. Overall, the error rates vary only slightly from the average of 1.2% although the six languages differ significantly with respect to morphology, inflection, word order, etc. In particular, Chinese is handled as well as the other languages. This is in nice contrast to many other NLP application, in particular NMT, for which the performances on Chinese are significantly below those of other languages. All error rates are below 1.7%.

4.3 Large scale out-of domain similarity search

In this section, we evaluate our sentence representation on out-of domain data. We are not aware of another huge corpus which is 6-way parallel for the same languages than the UN corpus. Therefore, we have selected the Europarl corpus and limit our study to three common languages (En,

ID	# input languages			Similarity Error
	1	2	3	
One M:1 strategy				
1	1	–	–	**1.03%**
2	–	0.5	–	1.85%
3	–	–	1	67.9%
Combining 1:1 and 2:1 strategies				
12_a	0.9	0.05	–	1.09%
12_b	0.8	0.10	–	1.16%
12_c	0.7	0.15	–	1.15%
12_d	0.6	0.20	–	1.13%
12_e	0.5	0.25	–	1.22%
Combining 1:1 and 3:1 strategies				
13	0.5	–	0.5	1.38%
Combining 1:1, 2:1 and 3:1 strategies				
123_a	0.33	0.16	0.33	1.39%
123_b	0.25	0.25	0.25	1.40%

Table 3: Different M:1 strategies for three input languages (system *efs-a*). The baseline with the 1:1 strategy is 1.03% (line with ID 1).

	Target language						
Src	En	Fr	Es	Ru	Ar	Zh	All
En	–	1.10	0.70	1.07	1.05	1.15	1.02
Fr	0.97	–	0.95	1.55	1.65	1.68	1.36
Es	0.68	1.10	–	1.20	1.35	1.27	1.12
Ru	0.78	1.52	1.23	–	1.32	1.32	1.23
Ar	0.78	1.52	1.07	1.48	–	1.23	1.22
Zh	0.97	1.55	1.12	1.35	1.30	–	1.26
All	0.83	1.36	1.02	1.33	1.33	1.33	**1.20**

Table 4: Pair-wise error rates of similarity search for 6 languages (UN Dev). Training was performed with a one layer BLSTM with 512 hiddens, max-pooling and the *"efsraz-all"* strategy.

Fr and Es). After excluding duplicates and limiting the sentence length to fifty tokens, we dispose of almost 1.5 million 3-way parallel sentences.

The two training strategies *"efsra-z"* and *"efsraz-all"* achieve the same similarity error rate of about 7.7%. We argue that this is an interesting result given the size of the corpus (1.46M sentences) and the fact that it contains several sentences which are very similar (e.g. *"The session resumes on DATE"*). Using the last state of an LSTM 3x512 achieves an error rate of 12.2%. Evaluating the similarity error requires the calculation of $1.46M^2$ distances for each language pair. This can be very efficiently performed with the FAISS open-source toolkit (Johnson et al., 2017) which offers many options to increase the speed of nearest neighbor search. Its implementation of brute-force L2 search was sufficient for our purposes.

4.4 Examples of multilingual search

On the next page, we give several examples of similarity search. For each example, we give the query and the five closest sentences. Remember that we use the cosine distance, i.e. the value of 1.0 is a perfect match and smaller values are worse.

The first example in Table 5 shows two simple query sentences for which four paraphrases were found in the Europarl corpus. A more complicated query sentence is used in the second example (see Table 6). For such longer sentences, it is unlikely to find several perfect paraphrases in the indexed corpus. However, the system was able to retrieve sentences which share a lot of the meaning of the query: all cover the topic *"punishment of (sexual) crimes, independently of the country the crime is*

committed in". Finally, examples of cross-lingual similarity search are given in Tables 7 and 8. In the first example, all five nearest French and Spanish sentences have very similar cosine distances, and all are indeed semantically related. Note that the closest French sentence is not the reference translation, but it nevertheless covers well the topic (its English translation is *"I should like to make one remark, however, in response to some of the opinions you have expressed"*).

Table 8 gives an example where not all retrieved sentences have similar cosine distances. The closest sentence is the correct translation, for French and for Spanish. Both second closest sentences are well related to the query and also have a cosine distance close to the best scoring sentence. The third and following sentences are less related with the query, which is clearly reflected in the substantially lower cosine distance. It's interesting to note that the three closest sentences are all identical, independently of the language. This can be seen as experimental evidence of the quality of the multilingual sentence embeddings.

5   Conclusion

We have shown that the framework of NMT with multiple encoders/decoders can be used to learn joint fixed-size sentence representations which exhibit interesting linguistic characteristics. We have explored several training paradigms which correspond to partial paths in the whole architecture. We have proposed a new evaluation protocol of multilingual similarity search which easily scales to many languages and large corpora. We were able to obtain an average cross-lingual similarity error rate of 1.2% for all 21 languages pairs between six languages[5] which differ significantly with respect to morphology, inflection, word order, etc. We have also studied the evolution of the similarity error rate when scaling up to 1.4 million sentences, drawn from an out-of-domain corpus.

Acknowledgments

We would like to thank Ke Tran (Informatics Institute University of Amsterdam, m.k.tran@uva.nl) and Orhan Firat (Middle East Technical University, orhan.firat@ceng.metu.edu.tr, now at Google) for their help with implementing some of the algorithms during their internship at Facebook AI Research in 2016.

[5]English, French, Spanish, Russian, Arabic and Chinese.

Query:	All kinds of obstacles must be eliminated.	Query:	I did not find out why.
D_2=0.970245	All kinds of barriers have to be removed.	D_2=0.913365	I have no idea why.
D_3=0.799097	All these things must be stopped.	D_3=0.913244	I fail to see the connection.
D_4=0.794444	All forms of provocation must be avoided.	D_4=0.906929	I do not understand why.
D_5=0.792740	All forms of violence must be prohibited.		

Table 5: Five closest sentences found by monolingual similarity search in English. All are some form of para-phrasing. The closest sentence (distance=1) is always identical to the query and therefore omitted.

Query	All citizens who commit sexual crimes against children must be punished, regardless of whether the crime is committed within or outside the EU.
D_2=0.650070	All kinds of sexual abuse of children are criminal and must be seen as the crimes that they are in all Member States.
D_3=0.580904	The perpetration of violence against women is a criminal act, whether in public or in private.
D_4=0.565544	The perpetrators of crimes cannot be allowed to believe that they will enjoy impunity, regardless of where they may reside, be it in Europe, in Africa or in any other part of the world.
D_5=0.560186	The impunity of those who commit terrible crimes against their own citizens and against other people regardless of their citizenship must be ended.

Table 6: A more complicated English sentence and the five closest sentences (excluding itself). All cover the punishment of (sexual) crimes.

EN_{59104}	Query	Allow me, however, to comment on certain issues raised by the honourable Members.
FR_{390378}	D_1=0.678347	Je voudrais toutefois apporter un commentaire à quelques-uns de vos avis.
FR_{59104}	D_2=0.676565	Permettez-moi toutefois de commenter certaines questions soulevées par les députés.
FR_{431699}	D_3=0.665086	Je voudrais toutefois formuler un certain nombre de commentaires concernant les remarques de M. Watson.
FR_{651418}	D_4=0.660149	Je voudrais toutefois faire part de quelques remarques qui cadrent très bien avec ce que vous avez évoqué.
FR_{269297}	D_5=0.647646	Je voudrais toutefois m'attarder sur certaines recommandations concrètes qui sont adressées à la Commission.
ES_{59104}	D_1=0.693376	No obstante, permítanme comentar ciertas cuestiones planteadas por sus Señorías.
ES_{390378}	D_2=0.663397	Sin embargo, quisiera añadir algunas observaciones en relación con algunas de las opiniones que han manifestado.
ES_{253861}	D_3=0.648316	Dicho esto, permítanme contestar algunos de los asuntos específicos que ustedes han planteado.
ES_{133167}	D_4=0.637314	Permítanme, no obstante, señalar algunas consideraciones que acaban de exponerse.
ES_{652101}	D_5=0.636661	No obstante, permítanme que conteste a algunos comentarios que se han realizado.

Table 7: **Cross-lingual similarity search**. English query and the five closest French and Spanish sentences. We also provide the index of the sentences (reference=59104). All the cosine distances are close and the sentences are indeed semantically related.

EN_{77777}	Query	And yet the report on the fight against racism does not demonstrate that the necessary conclusions have been drawn.
FR_{77777}	D=0.766306	Pourtant, le rapport sur la lutte contre le racisme n'indique pas que l'on en ait tiré les conclusions qui s'imposent.
$FR_{1081193}$	D=0.719267	Ainsi, le rapport sur la lutte contre le racisme n'indique pas que l'on en a tiré les conclusions qui s'imposent.
FR_{282752}	D=0.483043	Le rapport sur les femmes et le fondamentalisme n'offre toutefois aucune solution à cette problématique.
ES_{77777}	D=0.781921	Sin embargo, el informe sobre la lucha contra el racismo no muestra que se hayan extraído las conclusiones necesarias.
$ES_{1081193}$	D=0.735487	Así, el informe sobre la lucha contra el racismo no muestra que se hayan extraído las conclusiones necesarias.
ES_{282752}	D=0.474343	No obstante, el informe acerca de las mujeres y el fundamentalismo no ofrece ninguna solución para este problema.

Table 8: **Cross-lingual similarity search.** English query and the three closest French and Spanish sentences. In both cases, the correct translation was retrieved. The second closest sentences are also semantically well related to the query. However, the third (and following sentences) only cover some of the aspects of the query. This is indeed reflected in the lower similarity score.

References

Eneko Agirre, Carmen Banea, Daniel Cer, Mona Diab, Aitor Gonzalez-Agirre, Rada Mihalcea, German Rigau, and Janyce Wiebe. 2016. Semeval-2016 task 1: Semantic textual similarity, monolingual and cross-lingual evaluation. In *SemEval workshop*.

Sanjeev Arora, Yingyu Liang, and Tengyu Ma. 2017. A simple but tough-to-beat baseline for sentence embeddings. In *ICLR*.

Dzmitry Bahdanau, Kyunghyun Cho, and Yoshua Bengio. 2015. Neural machine translation by jointly learning to align and translate. In *ICLR*.

Mauro Cettolo, Christian Girardi, and Marcello Federico. 2012. Wit^3: Web inventory of transcribed and translated talks. In *EAMT*. pages 261–268.

Sarath Chandar, Mitesh M. Khapra, Hugo Larochelle, and Balaraman Ravindran. 2016. Correlation neural networks. *Neural Computation* 28:257–285.

Sarath Chandar, Mitesh M. Khapra, Balaraman Ravindran, Vikas Raykar, and Amrita Saha. 2013. Multilingual deep learning. In *NIPS DL wshop*.

Kyunghyun Cho, Bart van Merrienboer, Caglar Gulcehre, Fethi Bougares, Holger Schwenk, and Yoshua Bengio. 2014. Learning phrase representations using rnn encoder-decoder for statistical machine translation. In *EMNLP*.

Ronan Collobert and Jason Weston. 2008. A unified architecture for natural language processing: deep neural networks with multitask learning. In *ICML*. pages 160–167.

Alexis Conneau, Douwe Kiela, Holger Schwenk, Loic Barrault, and Antoine Bordes. 2017. Supervised learning of universal sentence representations from natural language inference data. In *https://arxiv.org/abs/1705.02364*.

J. Coulmance, J.M. Marty, G. Wenzek, and A. Benhaloum. 2015. Trans-gram, fast cross-lingual word embeddings. In *EMNLP*.

Daxiang Dong, Huan Wu, Wei He, Dianhai Yu, and Haifeng wang. 2015. Multi-task learning for multiple language translation. In *ACL*. pages 1723–1732.

Orhan Firat, Kyunghyun Choa, and Yoshua Bengio. 2016a. Multi-way, multilingual neural machine translation with shared attention mechanism. In *NAACL*.

Orhan Firat, Baskaran Sankaran, Yaser Al-Onaizan, Fatos T. Yarman Vural, and Kyunghyun Cho. 2016b. Zero-resource translation with multi-lingual neural machine translation. In *EMNLP*.

Andrea Frome, Grep S. Corrado, Jonathon Shlens, Samy Bengio, Jeffrey Dean, marc'Aurelio Ranzato, and Thomas Mikolov. 2013. DeViSa:E a deep visual-semantic embedding model. In *NIPS*.

S. Gouews, Y. Bengio, and G. Corrado. 2014. Bilbowa: Fast bilingual distributed representations without word alignments. In *ICML*.

Karl Moritz Hermann and Phil Blunsom. 2014. Multilingual models for compositional distributed semantics. In *ACL*. pages 58–68.

Jeff Johnson, Matthijs Douze, and Hervé Jégou. 2017. Billion-scale similarity search with gpus. *arXiv preprint arXiv:1702.08734* .

Melvin Johnson et al. 2016. Google's multilingual neural machine translation system: Enabling zero-shot translation. In *https://arxiv.org/abs/1611.04558*.

Nal Kalchbrenner and Phil Blunsom. 2013. Recurrent continuous translation models. In *EMNLP*. pages 1700–1709.

A. Klementiev, I. Titov, and B. Bhattarai. 2012. Inducing crosslingual distributed representations of words. In *Coling*.

T. Kociský, K.M. Hermann, and P. Blunsom. 2014. Learning bilingual word representations by marginalizing alignments. In *ACL*. pages 224–229.

Zhouhan Lin, Minwei Feng, Cicero Nogueira dos Santos, mo Yu, Bing Xiang, Bowen Zhou, and Yoshua Bengio. 2017. A structured self-attentive sentence embedding. In *ICLR*.

Yang Liu, Chenjie Sun, Lei Lin, and Xiaolong Wang. 2016. Learning natural language inference using bidirectional lstm model and inner-attention. In *https://arxiv.org/abs/1605.09090*.

Minh-Thang Luong, Quoc V. Le, Ilya Sutskever, Oriol Vinyals, and Lukasz Kaiser. 2015a. Multi-task sequence to sequence learning. In *ICLR*.

T. Luong, H. Pham, and C.D. Manning. 2015b. Bilingual word representations with monolingual quality in mind. In *ACL workshop on Vector Space Modeling for NLP*. pages 151–159.

Tomas Mikolov, Wen tau Yih, and Geoffrey Zweig. 2013. Linguistic regularities in continuous word space representations. In *NAACL*. pages 746–751.

Aditua Mogadala and Achim Rettinger. 2016. Bilingual word embeddings fomr parallel and non-parallel corpora for cross-language classification. In *NAACL*. pages 692–702.

Hideki Nakayama and Noriki Nishida. 2016. Zero-resource machine translation by multimodal encoder-decoder network with multimedia pivot. In *https://arxiv.org/abs/1611.04503*.

Jiquan Ngiam, Aditya Khosla, Mingyu Kim, Juhan Nam, Honglak Lee, and Andrew Y. Ng. 2011. Multimodal deep learning. In *ICML*.

Hieu Pham, Minh-Thang Luong, and Christopher D. Manning. 2015. Learning distributed representations for multilingual text sequences. In *Workshop on Vector Space Modeling for NLP*.

Amrita Saha, Mitesh M. Kharpa, Sarath Chandar, Janarthanan Rajendran, and Kyunghyun Cho. 2016. A correlational encoder decoder architecture for pivot based sequence generation. In *https://arxiv.org/abs/1606.04754*.

Rico Sennrich, Barry Haddow, and Alexandra Birch. 2016. Neural machine translation of rare words with subword units. In *ACL*. pages 1715–1725.

Richard Socher, Jeffrey Pennington, Eric H. Huang, Andrew Y. Ng, and Christopher D. Manning. 2011. Semi-supervised recursive autoencoders for predicting sentiment distributions. In *EMNLP*.

Ilya Sutskever, Oriol Vinyals, and Quoc V. Le. 2014. Sequence to sequence learning with neural networks. In *NIPS*. pages 3104–3112.

Yonghui Wu et al. 2016. Google's neural machine translation system: Bridging the gap between human and machine translation. In *https://arxiv.org/abs/1610.05011*.

Xiang Zhang, Junbo Zhao, and Yann LeCun. 2015. Character-level convolutional networks for text classification. In *NIPS*. pages 649–657.

Han Zhao, Zhengdong Lu, and Pascal Poupart. 2015. Self-adaptive hierarchical sentence model. In *https://arxiv.org/abs/1504.05070*.

Jie Zhou, Ying Cao, Xuguang Wang, Peng Li, and Wei Xu. 2016a. Deep recurrent models with fast-forward connections for neural machine translation. *TACL* 4:371–383.

Xinjie Zhou, Xiaojun Wan, and Jianguo Xiao. 2016b. Cross-lingual sentiment classification with bilingual document representation learning. In *ACL*.

M Ziemski, Marcin Juncys-Dowmunt, and B. Pouliquen. 2016. The united nations parallel corpus v1.0. In *LREC*.

Barret Zoph and Kevin Knight. 2016. Multi-source neural translation. In *NAACL*. pages 30–34.

Transfer Learning for Speech Recognition on a Budget

Julius Kunze[1], Louis Kirsch[1], Ilia Kurenkov[2], Andreas Krug[2],
Jens Johannsmeier[2], and Sebastian Stober[2]

[1]Hasso Plattner Institute, Potsdam, Germany
`juliuskunze@gmail.com, mail@louiskirsch.com`
[2]University of Potsdam, Potsdam, Germany
`{kurenkov,ankrug,johannsmeier,sstober}@uni-potsdam.de`

Abstract

End-to-end training of automated speech recognition (ASR) systems requires massive data and compute resources. We explore transfer learning based on model adaptation as an approach for training ASR models under constrained GPU memory, throughput and training data. We conduct several systematic experiments adapting a Wav2Letter convolutional neural network originally trained for English ASR to the German language. We show that this technique allows faster training on consumer-grade resources while requiring less training data in order to achieve the same accuracy, thereby lowering the cost of training ASR models in other languages. Model introspection revealed that small adaptations to the network's weights were sufficient for good performance, especially for inner layers.

1 Introduction

Automated speech recognition (ASR) is the task of translating spoken language to text in real-time. Recently, end-to-end deep learning approaches have surpassed previously predominant solutions based on Hidden Markov Models. In an influential paper, Amodei et al. (2015) used convolutional neural networks (CNNs) and recurrent neural networks (RNNs) to redefine the state of the art. However, Amodei et al. (2015) also highlighted the shortcomings of the deep learning approach. Performing forward and backward propagation on complex deep networks in a reasonable amount of time requires expensive specialized hardware. Additionally, in order to set the large number of parameters of a deep network properly, one needs to train on large amounts of audio recordings. Most of the time, the recordings need to be transcribed by hand. Such data in adequate quantities is currently available for few languages other than English.

We propose an approach combining two methodologies to address these shortcomings. Firstly, we use a simpler model with a lower resource footprint. Secondly, we apply a technique called *transfer learning* to significantly reduce the amount of non-English training data needed to achieve competitive accuracy in an ASR task. We investigate the efficacy of this approach on the specific example of adapting a CNN-based end-to-end model originally trained on English to recognize German speech. In particular, we freeze the parameters of its lower layers while retraining the upper layers on a German corpus which is smaller than its English counterpart.

We expect this approach to yield the following three improvements. Taking advantage of the representation learned by the English model will lead to shorter training times compared to training from scratch. Relatedly, the model trained using transfer learning requires less data for an equivalent score than a German-only model. Finally, the more layers we freeze the fewer layers we need to back-propagate through during training. Thus we expect to see a decrease in GPU memory usage since we do not have to maintain gradients for all layers.

This paper is structured as follows. Section 2 gives an overview of other transfer learning approaches to ASR tasks. Details about our implementation of the Wav2Letter model and how we trained it can be found in Section 3. The data we used and how we preprocessed it is described in Section 4. After a short introduction of the performed experiments in Section 5 we present and discuss the results in Section 6 followed by a conclusion in Section 7.

2 Related Work

Annotated speech data of sufficient quantity and quality to train end-to-end speech recognizers is scarce for most languages other than English. Nevertheless, there is demand for high-quality ASR

Proceedings of the 2nd Workshop on Representation Learning for NLP, pages 168–177,
Vancouver, Canada, August 3, 2017. ©2017 Association for Computational Linguistics

systems for these languages. Dealing with this issue requires specialized methods.

One such method, known as *transfer learning*, is a machine learning technique for enhancing a model's performance in a data-scarce domain by cross-training on data from other domains or tasks. There are several kinds of transfer learning. The predominant one being applied to ASR is *heterogeneous transfer learning* (Wang and Zheng, 2015) which involves training a base model on multiple languages (and tasks) simultaneously. While this achieves some competitive results (Chen and Mak, 2015; Knill et al., 2014), it still requires large amounts of data to yield robust improvements (Heigold et al., 2013).

In terms of how much data is needed for effective retraining, a much more promising type of transfer learning is called *model adaptation* (Wang and Zheng, 2015). With this technique, we first train a model on one (or more) languages, then retrain all or parts of it on another language which was unseen during the first training round. The parameters learned from the first language serve as a starting point, similar in effect to pre-training. Vu and Schultz (2013) applied this technique by first learning a multilayer perceptron (MLP) from multiple languages with relatively abundant data, such as English, and then getting competitive results on languages like Czech and Vietnamese, for which there is not as much data available.

The method presented in this paper differs from Vu and Schultz (2013) in that it does not force the representation to be compressed into *bottleneck features* (Grezl and Fousek, 2008) and use the result as the output of the pre-trained network. The idea of freezing only certain layers is another way in which our approach differs.

3 Model Architecture

One of the reasons Amodei et al. (2015) had to train their network using many GPUs was its complexity. It uses both convolutional and recurrent units stacked in many layers. Recently, a much simpler architecture called Wav2Letter has been proposed by Collobert et al. (2016). This model does not sacrifice accuracy for faster training. It relies entirely on its loss function to handle aligning the audio and the transcription sequences while the network itself consists only of convolutional units.

The resulting shorter training time and lower hardware requirements make Wav2Letter a solid basis for all of our transfer learning experiments. Since the general structure of the network is described in the original paper, we only mention what is notable in our adaptation of it in the following. An overview of their architecture is shown in Figure 1.

Collobert et al. (2016) do not specify the optimizer they used. We tried several conventional gradient descent optimizers and achieved best convergence with Adam (Kingma and Ba, 2014). Hyperparameters were slightly adapted from the defaults given by Kingma and Ba (2014), that is, we used the learning rate $\alpha = 10^{-4}$, $\beta_1 = 0.9$, $\beta_2 = 0.999$ and $\epsilon = 10^{-8}$. Collobert et al. (2016) note that the choice of activation function for the inner convolution layers does not seem to matter. We chose rectified linear units as our activation function because they have been shown to work well for acoustic models (Maas et al., 2013). Weights are initialized Xavier uniformly as introduced by Glorot and Bengio (2010).

At test time, decoding is performed using a beam search algorithm based on KenLM (Heafield et al., 2013). The decoding procedure follows the TensorFlow implementation based on (Graves, 2012). A beam is scored using two hyperparameters that were derived using a local search optimized to yield the best combined word error rate (WER) and letter error rate (LER) on the LibriSpeech (Panayotov et al., 2015) validation set. For the weight of the language model we chose $w_{lm} = 0.8$ and a weight multiplied with the number of vocabulary words in the transcription $w_{valid\_word} = 2.3$.

The CNN was implemented in Keras (Chollet, 2015). The language model and beam search were done in TensorFlow (Abadi et al., 2015) and the introspection in NumPy (van der Walt et al., 2011). The source code can be found at: https://github.com/transfer-learning-asr/transfer-learning-asr.

One of the innovations in Collobert et al. (2016) was the introduction of the AutoSegCriterion (ASG) loss function. The authors reported it mainly improving the model's throughput with negligible effect on WER and LER compared to the Connectionist Temporal Classification (CTC) loss introduced by Graves et al. (2006). Since there is currently no publicly available implementation of this loss function, we decided to stay with an existing TensorFlow implementation of the CTC loss instead.

The English model achieved a LER of 13.66% and WER of 43.58% on the LibriSpeech (Panayotov et al., 2015) test-clean corpus. This is worse than the results of Collobert et al. (2016). Since the authors of that paper did not publish their source code, we

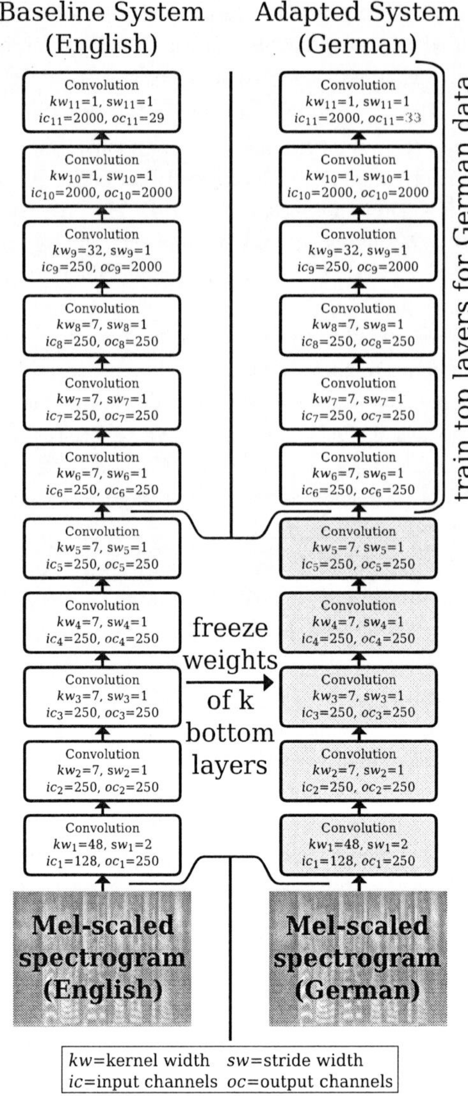

Figure 1: Network architecture adapted from Collobert et al. (2016).

were not able to reproduce their results reliably. All of our transfer learning experiments are based on this model and for our experiments it is assumed that such a model is already given for the transfer learning task that is to be performed.

4 Datasets

For training the English model, we used the LibriSpeech corpus (Panayotov et al., 2015). This dataset consists of about 1000 hours of read speech, sampled at 16 kHz, from the domain of audio books. This is the same dataset that was used to train the original Wav2Letter model.

The German models were trained on several corpora taken from the Bavarian Archive for Speech Signals (BAS) (Schiel, 1998; Reichel et al., 2016) as well as the dataset described in Radeck-Arneth et al. (2015), which will be referred to as "RADECK" from now on. Overall, we had a total of 383 hours of training data, which is only slightly more than one third of the English corpus. Additional quantitative information regarding each corpus, as well as any available references, is given in Table 1. Information about the kind of recording contained in each corpus is given in Table 2. It is also important to point out that some of the corpora pose additional challenges for speech recognition like partially intoxicated people, recordings over telephone, and different dialects.

Each German corpus was split into training and test sets. We grouped the audio by speakers and used 10% of the groups for testing. Therefore, no speaker appears in both training and test set ensuring that results are not due to overfitting to certain speakers. Exceptions to this procedure are: The VM corpora, which were used exclusively for training because obtaining a split based on speakers was not trivial here; SC10, which was used only for testing because it consists of recordings of speakers with German as a second language and strong foreign accents with only 5.8 hours in size; and RADECK, where we used the original splits.

We also rely on text corpora for the KenLM decoding step. For the English corpus (Panayotov et al., 2015), the provided 4-gram model based on all training transcriptions was used like in the original Wav2Letter implementation. For the German corpus, our n-gram model came from a preprocessed version of the German Wikipedia, the European Parliament Proceedings Parallel Corpus[1], and all the training transcriptions. Validation and test sets were carefully excluded.

4.1 Preprocessing

Since the English model was trained on data with a sampling rate of 16 kHz, the German speech data needed to be brought into the same format so that the convolutional filters could operate on the same timescale. To this end, all data was resampled to 16 kHz. Preprocessing was done using librosa (McFee et al., 2015) and consisted of applying a Short-time Fourier transform (STFT) to obtain power level spectrum features from the raw audio as described

---

[1] https://github.com/tudarmstadt-lt/kaldi-tuda-de/

Name	Size	Number of speakers	S LER	S WER	TL LER	TL WER
ALC (Schiel et al., 2012)	54.54h	162	13.48%	32.83%	8.23%	21.14%
HEMPEL (Draxler and Schiel, 2002)	14.21h	3909	34.05%	71.74%	19.13%	46.78%
PD1	19.36h	201	21.02%	34.37%	8.32%	11.85%
PD2	4.33h	16	7.60%	19.64%	1.97%	5.96%
RVG-J (Draxler and Schiel, 2002)	46.28h	182	17.43%	39.87%	10.85%	24.92%
SC10	5.80h	70	25.62%	78.82%	17.59%	57.84%
VM1 (Wahlster, 1993)	32.40h	654	-	-	-	-
VM2 (Wahlster, 1993)	43.90h	214	-	-	-	-
ZIPTEL (Draxler and Schiel, 2002)	12.96h	1957	22.87%	62.27%	15.07%	46.25%
RADECK (Radeck-Arneth et al., 2015)	181.96h	180	27.83%	65.13%	20.83%	56.17%
All corpora	415.7h	7545	22.78%	58.36%	15.05%	42.49%

Table 1: Quantitative information on the corpora used to train the German model. References to individual corpora are given where available. Size and number of speakers refer only to the subsets we used (including training and test sets). Test set LER and WER are reported for the best transfer learning (TL) model and the model from scratch (S) after 103h of training.

Name	Speech Type	Topic	Idiosyncrasies
ALC	read, spontaneous	car control commands, tongue twisters, answering questions	partially recorded in running car; speakers partially intoxicated
HEMPEL	spontaneous	answer: What did you do in the last hour?	recorded over telephone
PD1	read	phonetically balanced sentences, two stories: "Buttergeschichte" and "Nordwind und Sonne"	recordings were repeated until error-free
PD2	read	sentences from a train query task	recordings were repeated until error-free
RVG-J	read, spontaneous	numbers, phonetically balanced sentences, free-form responses to questions	speakers are adolescents mostly between the ages 13–15
SC10	read, spontaneous	phonetically balanced sentences, numbers, "Nordwind und Sonne", free dialogue, free retelling of "Der Enkel und der Grossvater"	multi-language corpus; only German data was used
VM1	spontaneous	dialogues for appointment scheduling	multi-language corpus; only German data was used
VM2	spontaneous	dialogues for appointment scheduling, travel planning and leisure time planning	multi-language corpus; only German data was used
ZIPTEL	read	street names, ZIP codes, telephone numbers, city names	recorded over telephone
RADECK	read, semi-spontaneous	Wikipedia, European Parliament transcriptions, commands for command-and-control settings	contains six microphone recordings of each speech signal

Table 2: Information on the kind of speech data contained in each corpus.

in Collobert et al. (2016). After that, spectrum features were mel-scaled and then directly fed into the CNN. Originally, the parameters were set to window length $w = 25$ms, stride $s = 10$ms and number of components $n = 257$. We adapted the window length to $w_{new} = 32$ms which equals a Fourier transform window of 512 samples, in order to follow the convention of using power-of-two window sizes. The stride was set to $s_{new} = 8$ms in order to achieve 75% overlap of successive frames. We observed that $n = 257$ results in many of the components being 0 due to the limited window length. We therefore decreased the parameter to $n_{new} = 128$. After the generation of the spectrograms, we normalized them to mean 0 and standard deviation 1 per input sequence.

Any individual recordings in the German corpora longer than 35 seconds were removed due to GPU memory limitations. This could have been solved instead by splitting audio files using their word alignments where provided (and their corresponding transcriptions), but we chose not to do so since the loss of data incurred by simply ignoring overly long files was negligible. Corpora sizes given in Table 1 are after removal of said sequences. We excluded 1046 invalid samples in the RADECK corpus due to truncated audio as well as 569 samples with empty transcriptions.

5 Experiments

Given the English model, we froze k of the lower layers and trained all $11 - k$ layers above with the

German corpora. This means the gradient was only calculated for the weights of those $11-k$ layers and gradient descent was then applied to update those as usual. The process of freezing k layers is visualized in Figure 1. The transfer training was performed based on both the original weights as well as a new random initialization for comparison. Except for changing the training data, the German corpora introduce four new class labels *äöüß* in addition to the original 28 labels. We set the initial weights and biases of the final softmax layer for these labels to zero. Additionally, as a baseline for the performance of a Wav2Letter based German ASR, we trained one model from scratch on all German training corpora. For all experiments we used a batch size of 64, both during training as well as evaluation.

6 Results and Discussion

As initially hypothesized, transfer learning could give us three benefits: Reduced computing time, lower GPU memory requirements and a smaller required amount of German speech data. In addition to that, we may find structural similarities between languages for the ASR task. In the subsequent sections, we will first report general observations, evaluate each hypothesis based on the performed experiments and then analyze the learned weights using introspection techniques. We report overall test scores and scores on each test set in the form of WERs and LERs. Finally, we discuss the language specific assumptions that were required for the experiments and how transfer learning may perform on other languages.

6.1 Retaining or reinitializing weights?

When the transfer learning training is performed, one could either continue training on the existing weights or reinitialize them. Reusing existing weights might lead to stochastic gradient descent (SGD) being stuck in a local minimum, reinitializing may take longer to converge. For $k=8$ we compared the speed of training for both methods. As it can be seen in Figure 2, using existing weights is much faster without a decrease in quality.

6.2 Reduced computing time

Given that languages share common features in their pronunciation, lower layers should contain common features that can be reused when transferring the model to a different language. Therefore, we subsequently froze k layers of the original English model, choosing a different k in each experiment. Our

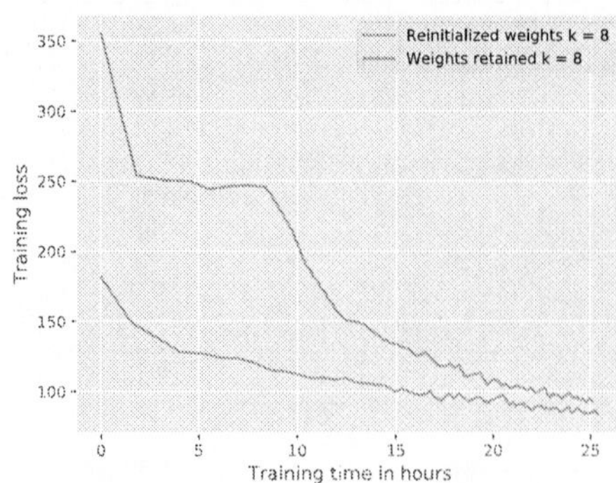

Figure 2: Comparison of learning curves for 25 hours of training with either reinitialized or retained weights. In both cases $k=8$ layers were frozen.

experiments showed that this assumption is indeed true, it is sufficient to adjust only at least two layers for achieving training losses below 100 after 25 hours. The loss curve for different k can be seen in Figure 3.

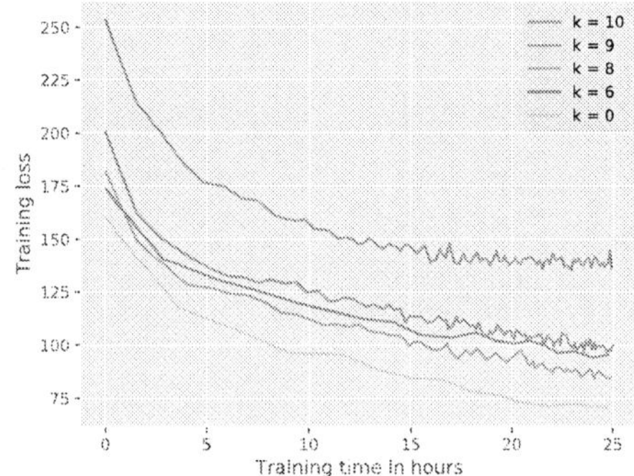

Figure 3: Learning curves for 25 hours of training with different numbers k of frozen layers. Note that due to the decreased time to process a batch (cf. Figure 4), training models with higher k (more frozen layers) allows to iterate over the training data more often in the same amount of time. But eventually, this does not help to beat the model with $k = 0$ which is trained with the fewest dataset iterations but still at any time achieves the lowest loss.

For bigger k we need to backpropagate through fewer layers, therefore training time per step (training one batch) decreases almost monotonically with k in Figure 4. Despite that boost in training time, experiments show that loss is almost always smaller at any given point in time for smaller k. In Figure 3 this manifests in $k = 0$ always having the smallest training loss. We conclude that in terms of achieving small loss, there is no reason to favor big values for k, freezing layers is not necessary.

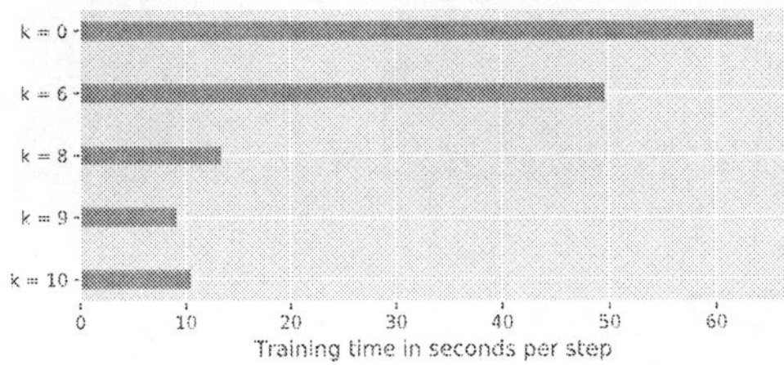

Figure 4: The more layers we freeze, the faster one batch of 64 is trained. Measured over 25h of training each.

When we compare the best transfer learning model with $k=0$ with a German model trained from scratch in Figure 5, we are able to see huge improvements in terms of computing time required for achieving the same loss. We conclude that a good weight starting configuration from another language's ASR is beneficial.

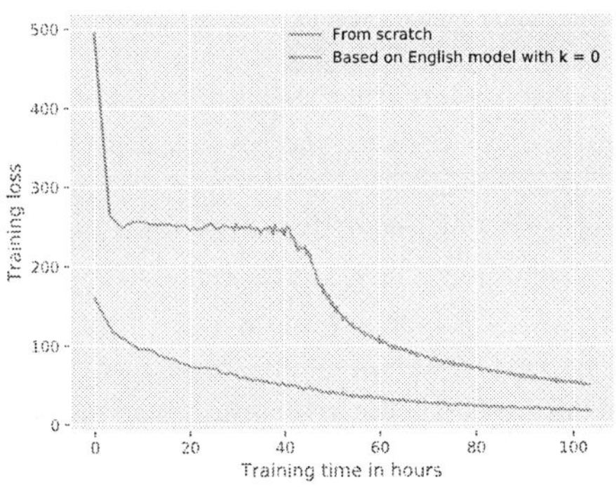

Figure 5: Applying transfer learning by using the weights from the English model leads to small losses more quickly than training from scratch.

6.3 Lower GPU memory requirements

Not only does it matter how long training takes with given resources, many researchers may also have only limited GPU memory at disposal. All of our experiments were performed on a single GeForce GTX Titan X graphics card, but the more layers k we freeze, the fewer layers we need to backpropagate through. Therefore, memory requirements for the GPU are lower. For a batch size of 64, forward propa-

gation takes less than 3 GB of memory, while training the whole network requires more than 10.4 GB. In contrast to that, freezing 8 layers already enables training with less than 5.5 GB of GPU memory.

6.4 Little German speech data required

We hypothesized that little training data may be required for the transfer learning task. Additionally to using the whole 383 hours of data we had available, we also tried an even more scarce variant. In order to prevent overfitting, we used a transfer learning model with $k = 8$ for our experiments. As it can be seen in Figure 6, for a model with $k=8$ that was trained for 25 hours, the LER using 100 hours of audio is almost equal to using the complete training data. Longer training causes overfitting. When using just 20 hours of training data this problem occurs even earlier. We can conclude that even though training for just 25 hours works well with only 100 hours of audio, beyond that overfitting appears nevertheless.

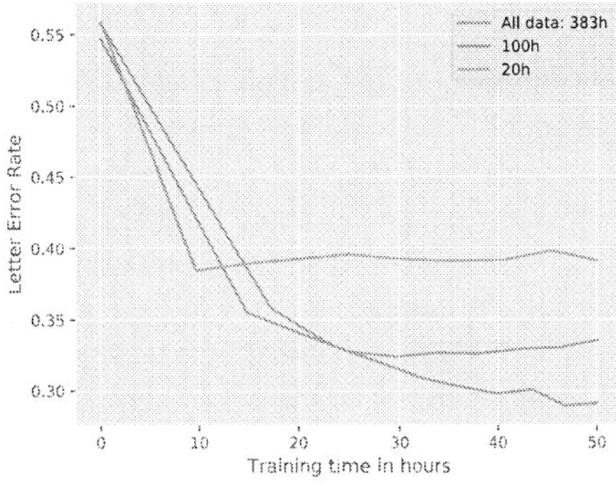

Figure 6: LER as a mean over all test samples for different training set sizes with k = 8 for all experiments

6.5 Model Introspection

When applying transfer learning, it is of interest how much the model needs to be adapted and which portions of the model are shared between different languages. To get insights into those differences, we compared the learned parameters both between the English model and adapted German model (for $k=0$) as well as between different points in time during training. Since the output layers of both models do not use the same number of output features, we excluded this layer from the comparison. First, we investigated the distribution of weights and corresponding changes between the English and adapted model, visualized on the left side of Figure 7. The plot shows the fraction

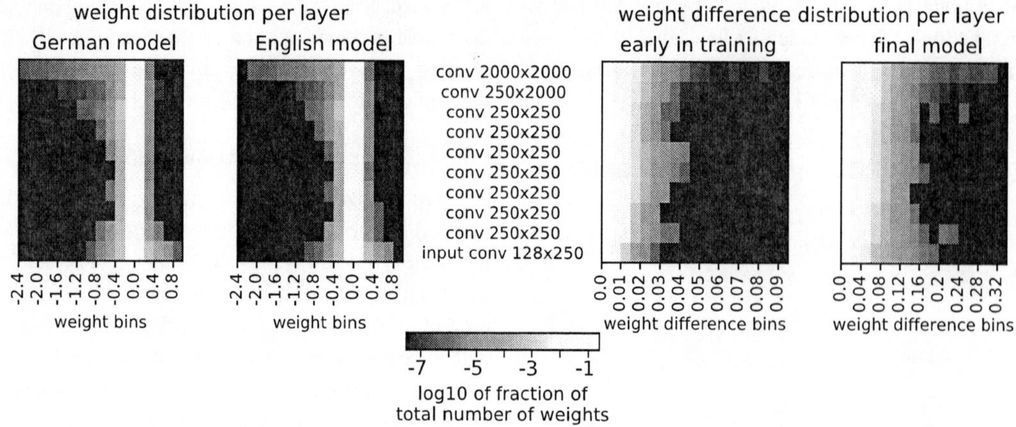

Figure 7: Weight distributions of the German and English model (left) and weight difference distributions both in an early stage and for the final model (right).

of weights in a layer lying in the respective range of values. Because most of the weights are between -0.2 and 0.2 (in just 2 bins), we used a $\log_{10}$-scale for the fraction of weights in each bin. We observed that the weights of highest absolute values are in the input and topmost layer. This indicates that the transformations in the middle layers are smaller than in the outer ones. Moreover, the weights of each layer are distributed with a mean value close to zero and very small variance. Due to the similar distributions, it is reasonable to compare the weights and their differences in the following. Between both models, there are only minor changes in the weight distributions, which supports the assumption that transfer learning is performing well because the English model is a suitable model for being adapted to German.

Since the adaptation to German is not explainable based on the distributions, we further investigated the differences between the individual weights. Therefore, we determined the absolute distance between weights as shown in Figure 7 on the right side. In the plot, we visualize the distribution of weight changes. We observed only small changes, therefore a $\log_{10}$-scale is used again. Figure 7 on the right side shows this analysis for the transfer learning model early in training as well as the final model after four days. In the early phase, weights had only been adapted little with a maximum difference of 0.1, while the final model weights changed up to 0.36. Additionally, we observed that the weights changed more in the middle and top layers earlier, but with progressing training the input layer experiences more changes. This higher variability in the outer layers can both be observed

in the weights of each individual model as well as in their differences. That is an indication that the model needs to alter the outer layers more than the inner ones in order to adapt to a particular language.

Finally, we looked into the changes of individual filters. Due to the large number of neurons, we provide the complete set of filters from all layers only in the supplement.[2] We present our findings for a selected set of neurons of the input layer that showed well-interpretable patterns. The weights of those filters and their differences between the English and German model are shown in Figure 8. The top row shows neurons that can be interpreted as detectors for short percussive sounds (e.g. t or k) and the end of high pitched noise (e.g. s). The bottom neurons might detect rising or falling pitch in vowels. Of these four filters, the upper left differs most between English and German with a maximum difference of 0.15. This supports that it is detecting percussive sounds as German language has considerably stronger pronunciation of corresponding letters than English. On the other hand, the bottom row filters experienced less change (both <0.1 maximum difference). This supports them being related to vocal detection since there are few differences in pronunciation between English and German speakers.

6.6 Overall test set accuracy

All test set LERs and WERs scores are consistent with the differences of loss in the performed experiments. After 103 hours of training, the best transfer learning model is therefore $k=0$ with a LER of 15.05% and WER of 42.49% as the mean over all test samples.

---

[2]supplements: https://doi.org/10.6084/m9.figshare.5048965

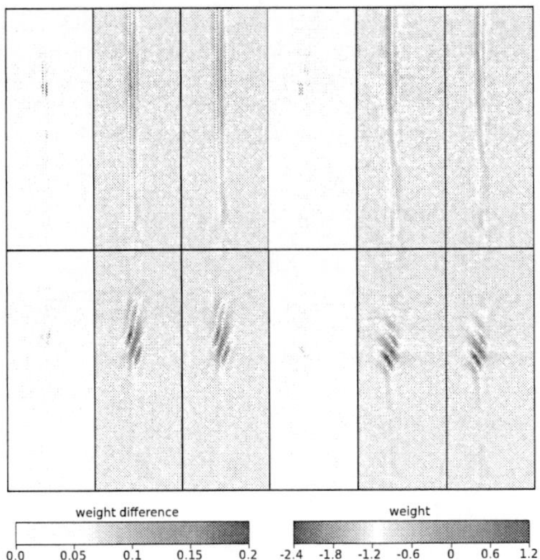

Figure 8: Differences in specific filters of the input layer. Neurons were chosen based on particular patterns. Each triplet of images shows the weight differences and the corresponding weights in the German and English model (from left to right).

The model that has been trained from scratch for the same amount of time achieves a LER of 22.78% and WER of 58.36%. Table 1 gives details about the accuracy on each test set.

Some very high WERs are due to heavy German dialect that is particularly problematic with numbers, e.g.

Expected: "sechsundneunzig"
Predicted: "sechs un nmeunsche"
LER 47%, WER 300%, loss: 43.15

This shows, that there is both room for improvement in terms of word compounds as well as ASR of different dialects where data is even more scarce.

6.7 Accuracy boost through language model decoding

The original Wav2Letter network did not report on improvements in LER and WER due to the KenLM integration. In Table 3 We compared decoding performed through KenLM scored beam search with a greedy decoding on the German corpora.

6.8 Transfer learning for other languages

In our speech recognizer, the lower layers of the network learn phonological features whereas the higher (deeper) ones map these features onto

	LER	WER
with LM	15.05%	42.49%
without LM	16.77%	56.14%

Table 3: Comparing LER and WER with and without KenLM based on model with $k=0$

graphemes. Thus for ASR these two types of features clearly matter the most. German and English have many phonemes and graphemes in common. The apparent success of our transfer learning approach was greatly facilitated by these similarities. Not all languages share as much in terms of these features. We anticipate that our approach will be less effective for such pairs. This means we expect the adaptation to a less similar language to require more data and training time. We further suspect that differences in grapheme inventories cause other effects than differences in phonemes. This is because only the mapping of phonological features to graphemes has to be adapted for a different orthography. In contrast, differences in phoneme inventories require more changes in features learned at lower layers of the network. Moreover, there could be differences in the importance of specific features. For instance, having vowels in common is potentially more important for transfer learning than sharing many consonants, because vowels experience higher variability in pronunciation. At the same time very drastic differences in orthography could probably trigger a stronger change of weights in lower network layers. We expect our transfer learning approach to encounter strong difficulties sharing knowledge between English and a logographic language like Mandarin Chinese. Despite those difficulties, using weights from a pre-trained ASR-network is a more reasonable initialization than random weights. This is because very basic audio features are shared between all languages. Therefore even for more different language pairs, we expect transfer learning to decrease the necessary amount of training data and time.

7 Conclusions

We were able to show that transfer learning using model adaptation can improve the speed of learning when only 383 hours of training data are available. Given an English model, we trained a German model that outperforms the German baseline model trained from scratch in the same amount of training time. Thus, with little time, our approach allows training better models. We showed that the English model's weights are a good starting configuration and allow the transfer learning model to reach smaller training losses in comparison to a weight reinitialization. When less GPU memory is available, freezing the lower 8 layers allows to train batches of 64 with less than 5.5 GB instead of more than 10.4 GB while still performing similar after 25 hours of training. Model introspection determined that lower and upper layers, in contrast to the layers in the center, need to change more thoroughly in order to adapt to the new language.

We identified several interesting directions for future work. Test accuracy showed that word compounds can be challenging and dialects pose difficulties when little training data is available. GPU memory consumption could be further reduced by caching the representation that needs only forward propagation. An open source version of the ASG loss would enable faster training. Finally, future research should investigate how well this transfer learning approach generalizes by applying it to more distinct languages.

Acknowledgments

This research was supported by the donation of a GeForce GTX Titan X graphics card from the NVIDIA Corporation.

References

Martín Abadi, Ashish Agarwal, Paul Barham, Eugene Brevdo, Zhifeng Chen, Craig Citro, Greg S. Corrado, Andy Davis, Jeffrey Dean, Matthieu Devin, Sanjay Ghemawat, Ian Goodfellow, Andrew Harp, Geoffrey Irving, Michael Isard, Yangqing Jia, Rafal Jozefowicz, Lukasz Kaiser, Manjunath Kudlur, Josh Levenberg, Dan Mané, Rajat Monga, Sherry Moore, Derek Murray, Chris Olah, Mike Schuster, Jonathon Shlens, Benoit Steiner, Ilya Sutskever, Kunal Talwar, Paul Tucker, Vincent Vanhoucke, Vijay Vasudevan, Fernanda Viégas, Oriol Vinyals, Pete Warden, Martin Wattenberg, Martin Wicke, Yuan Yu, and Xiaoqiang Zheng. 2015. TensorFlow: Large-scale machine learning on heterogeneous systems. http://tensorflow.org/.

Dario Amodei, Rishita Anubhai, Eric Battenberg, Carl Case, Jared Casper, Bryan Catanzaro, Jingdong Chen, Mike Chrzanowski, Adam Coates, Greg Diamos, Erich Elsen, Jesse Engel, Linxi Fan, Christopher Fougner, Tony Han, Awni Y. Hannun, Billy Jun, Patrick LeGresley, Libby Lin, Sharan Narang, Andrew Y. Ng, Sherjil Ozair, Ryan Prenger, Jonathan Raiman, Sanjeev Satheesh, David Seetapun, Shubho Sengupta, Yi Wang, Zhiqian Wang, Chong Wang, Bo Xiao, Dani Yogatama, Jun Zhan, and Zhenyao Zhu. 2015. Deep speech 2: End-to-end speech recognition in english and mandarin. *CoRR* abs/1512.02595. http://arxiv.org/abs/1512.02595.

Dongpeng Chen and Brian Kan-Wing Mak. 2015. Multitask learning of deep neural networks for low-resource speech recognition. *IEEE/ACM Trans. Audio, Speech & Language Processing* 23(7):1172–1183. http://dx.doi.org/10.1109/TASLP.2015.2422573.

François Chollet. 2015. Keras. https://github.com/fchollet/keras.

Ronan Collobert, Christian Puhrsch, and Gabriel Synnaeve. 2016. Wav2letter: an end-to-end convnet-based speech recognition system. *CoRR* abs/1609.03193. http://arxiv.org/abs/1609.03193.

Christoph Draxler and Florian Schiel. 2002. Three New Corpora at the Bavarian Archive for Speech Signals – and a First Step Towards Distributed Web-Based Recording. In *Third International Conference on Language Resources and Evaluation (LREC)*. Gonzles Rodriguez, Manual, pages 21–24.

Xavier Glorot and Yoshua Bengio. 2010. Understanding the difficulty of training deep feedforward neural networks. In *Aistats*. volume 9, pages 249–256.

Alex Graves. 2012. *Supervised Sequence Labelling with Recurrent Neural Networks*, volume 385 of *Studies in Computational Intelligence*. Springer. http://dx.doi.org/10.1007/978-3-642-24797-2.

Alex Graves, Santiago Fernández, Faustino Gomez, and Jürgen Schmidhuber. 2006. Connectionist temporal classification: labelling unsegmented sequence data with recurrent neural networks. In *Proceedings of the 23rd international conference on Machine learning*. ACM, pages 369–376.

Frantisek Grezl and Petr Fousek. 2008. Optimizing bottleneck features for lvcsr. In *International Conference on Acoustics, Speech and Signal Processing (ICASSP)*. IEEE, pages 4729–4732.

Kenneth Heafield, Ivan Pouzyrevsky, Jonathan H. Clark, and Philipp Koehn. 2013. Scalable modified Kneser-Ney language model estimation. In *Proceedings of the 51st Annual Meeting of the Association for Computational Linguistics*. Sofia, Bulgaria, pages 690–696.

Georg Heigold, Vincent Vanhoucke, Alan Senior, Patrick Nguyen, M. Ranzato, Matthieu Devin, and Jeffrey Dean. 2013. Multilingual acoustic models using distributed deep neural networks. In *International Conference on Acoustics, Speech and Signal Processing (ICASSP)*. IEEE, pages 8619–8623.

Diederik P. Kingma and Jimmy Ba. 2014. Adam: A method for stochastic optimization. *CoRR* abs/1412.6980. http://arxiv.org/abs/1412.6980.

Kate Knill, Mark J. F. Gales, Anton Ragni, and Shakti P. Rath. 2014. Language independent and unsupervised acoustic models for speech recognition and keyword spotting. In *15th Annual Conference of the International Speech (INTERSPEECH) Communication Association, Singapore, September 14-18, 2014*. pages 16–20. http://www.isca-speech.org/archive/interspeech_2014/i14_0016.html.

Andrew L Maas, Awni Y Hannun, and Andrew Y Ng. 2013. Rectifier nonlinearities improve neural network acoustic models. In *Proc. ICML*. volume 30.

Brian McFee, Colin Raffel, Dawen Liang, Daniel P.W. Ellis, Matt McVicar, Eric Battenberg, and Oriol Nieto. 2015. librosa: Audio and Music Signal Analysis in Python. In *Proceedings of the 14th python in science conference*. pages 18–25.

Vassil Panayotov, Guoguo Chen, Daniel Povey, and Sanjeev Khudanpur. 2015. LibriSpeech: an ASR corpus based on public domain audio books. In *International Conference on Acoustics, Speech and Signal Processing (ICASSP)*. IEEE, pages 5206–5210.

Stephan Radeck-Arneth, Benjamin Milde, Arvid Lange, Evandro Gouvêa, Stefan Radomski, Max Mühlhäuser, and Chris Biemann. 2015. Open source german distant speech recognition: Corpus and acoustic model. In *International Conference on Text, Speech, and Dialogue*. Springer International Publishing, pages 480–488.

Uwe D. Reichel, Florian Schiel, Thomas Kisler, Christoph Draxler, and Nina Pörner. 2016. The BAS Speech Data Repository .

Florian Schiel. 1998. Speech and speech-related resources at BAS. In *Proceedings of the First International Conference on Language Resources and Evaluation*. pages 343–349.

Florian Schiel, Christian Heinrich, and Sabine Barfüsser. 2012. Alcohol language corpus: the first public corpus of alcoholized German speech. *Language resources and evaluation* 46(3):503–521.

Stéfan van der Walt, S. Chris Colbert, and Gaël Varoquaux. 2011. The numpy array: a structure for efficient numerical computation. *CoRR* abs/1102.1523. http://arxiv.org/abs/1102.1523.

Ngoc Thang Vu and Tanja Schultz. 2013. Multilingual multilayer perceptron for rapid language adaptation between and across language families. In Frédéric Bimbot, Christophe Cerisara, Cécile Fougeron, Guillaume Gravier, Lori Lamel, François Pellegrino, and Pascal Perrier, editors, *INTERSPEECH*. ISCA, pages 515–519.

Wolfgang Wahlster. 1993. Verbmobil. In *Grundlagen und Anwendungen der Künstlichen Intelligenz*. Springer Berlin Heidelberg, pages 393–402.

Dong Wang and Thomas Fang Zheng. 2015. Transfer Learning for Speech and Language Processing. *arXiv:1511.06066 [cs]* http://arxiv.org/abs/1511.06066.

Gradual Learning of Matrix-Space Models of Language for Sentiment Analysis

Shima Asaadi[*] and **Sebastian Rudolph**
Faculty of Computer Science
TU Dresden, Germany
firstname.lastname@tu-dresden.de

Abstract

Learning word representations to capture the semantics and compositionality of language has received much research interest in natural language processing. Beyond the popular vector space models, matrix representations for words have been proposed, since then, matrix multiplication can serve as natural composition operation. In this work, we investigate the problem of learning matrix representations of words. We present a learning approach for compositional matrix-space models for the task of sentiment analysis. We show that our approach, which learns the matrices gradually in two steps, outperforms other approaches and a gradient-descent baseline in terms of quality and computational cost.

1 Introduction

Recently, a lot of NLP research has been devoted to word representations with the goal to capture language semantics, compositionality, and other linguistic aspects. A prominent class of approaches to produce word representations are Vector Space Models (VSMs) of language. In VSMs, a vector representation is created for each word in the text, mostly based on distributional information. One of the recent prominent methods to extract vector representations of words is Word2vec, introduced by Mikolov et al. (2013a; 2013b). These models measure both syntactic and semantic aspects of words and also seem to exhibit good compositionality properties. The principle of compositionality states that the meaning of a complex expression can be obtained from combining the meaning of its constituents (Frege, 1884). In the Word2vec case and many other VSM approaches, some vector space operations (such as vector addition) are used as composition operation.

One of the downsides of using vector addition (or other commutative operations like the component-wise product) as the compositionality operation is that word order information is inevitably lost. Alternative word-order-sensitive compositionality models for word representations have been introduced, such as Compositional Matrix-Space Models (CMSMs) (Rudolph and Giesbrecht, 2010). In such models, matrices instead of vectors are used as word representations and compositionality is realized via matrix multiplication. It has been proven that CMSMs are capable of simulating a wide range of VSM-based compositionality operations. The question, however, how to learn suitable word-to-matrix mappings has remained largely unexplored with few exceptions (Yessenalina and Cardie, 2011). The task is exacerbated by the fact that this amounts to a non-convex optimization problem, where a good initialization is crucial for the success of gradient descent techniques.

In this paper, we address the problem of learning CMSM in the domain of sentiment analysis. As has been observed before, the sentiment of a phrase is very much influenced by the presence and position of negators and modifiers, thus word order seems to be particularly relevant for establishing an accurate sentiment score.

We propose to apply a two-step learning method where the output of the first step serves as initialization for the second step. We evaluate the performance of our method on the task of fine-grained sentiment analysis and compare it to a previous work on learning CMSM for sentiment analysis (Yessenalina and Cardie, 2011). Moreover, the performance of our representation learning in sentiment composition is evaluated on sentiment composition in opposing polarity phrases

[*]Supported by DFG Graduiertenkolleg 1763 (QuantLA)

Proceedings of the 2nd Workshop on Representation Learning for NLP, pages 178–185,
Vancouver, Canada, August 3, 2017. ©2017 Association for Computational Linguistics

(Kiritchenko and Mohammad, 2016b).

The rest of the paper is organized as follows. Section 2 provides the related works. A detailed description of the approach is presented in Section 3, followed by experiments and discussion in Section 4, and the conclusion in the last section.

2 Related Work

Compositional Distributional Semantics: In compositional distributional semantics, different approaches for learning word and phrase representations and ways to compose the constituents are studied. As an early work in compositional distributional semantics, Mitchell and Lapata (2010) propose vector composition models with additive and multiplicative functions as the composition operations in semantic VSMs. These models outperform non-compositional approaches in semantic similarity of complex expressions. Mikolov et al. (2013a) propose Word2vec where continuous vector representations of words are trained through continuous bag-of-words and skip-gram models. These models are supposed to reflect syntactic and semantic similarities of words. An extension to these models is a vector representation of idiomatic phrases by considering a vector for each phrase and training Word2vec accordingly (Mikolov et al., 2013b). Moreover, compositionality is captured in these models by applying certain mathematical operations on word vectors.

Rudolph and Giesbrecht (2010) introduced compositional matrix-space models in which words are represented as matrices, and defined composition operation as a matrix multiplication function. Learning such matrix representations can be done by supervised machine learning algorithms (Yessenalina and Cardie, 2011). Other approaches using matrices for distributional representations of words have been introduced more recently. Socher et al. (2012) introduce a model in which a matrix and a vector is assigned to each word. The vector captures the meaning of the word by itself and the matrix shows how it modifies the meaning of neighboring words. The model is learned through recursive neural networks. In the model of Socher et al. (2013), a unique tensor-based composition function in a recursive neural tensor network is introduced which composes all word vectors. Maillard and Clark (2015) describe a compositional model for learning adjective-noun pairs where, first, a vector representation for each word is trained using a skip-gram model. Then, adjective matrices are trained in composition to their nouns, using back-propagation.

Sentiment Analysis: There is a lot of research interest in the sentiment analysis task in NLP. The task is to classify the polarity of a text (negative, positive, neutral) or assign a real-valued score, showing the polarity and intensity of the text. Some contributions focus on learning sentiment of a short text based on supervised machine learning techniques (Yessenalina and Cardie, 2011; Agrawal and An, 2014). Recent approaches have focused on learning different types of neural networks for sentiment analysis, such as the work of Socher et al. (2013) which apply recursive neural tensor networks for both fine-grained and binary classification of phrases and sentences. Timmaraju and Khanna (2015) use recursive-recurrent neural networks for sentiment classification of long text, and Hong and Fang (2015) apply long short-term memory and deep recursive-NNs. In a very recent work by Wang et al. (2016), convolutional neural networks and recurrent neural networks are combined leading to a significant improvement in sentiment analysis of short text.

Sentiment Composition: Compositionality in sentiment analysis is used to compute the sentiment of complex phrases and sentences. Recent works of Kiritchenko and Mohammad (2016a; 2016b) deal with sentiment composition of phrases. In (Kiritchenko and Mohammad, 2016a), they create a dataset of unigrams, bigrams and trigrams, which contains phrases with at least one negative and one positive word. They analyze the performance of different learning algorithms and word embeddings on the dataset with different linguistic patterns. In (Kiritchenko and Mohammad, 2016b), they create a sentiment composition lexicon for phrases containing negators, modals and adverbs with their associated sentiment scores, and study the effect of modifiers on the overall sentiment of phrases.

3 The Approach

Learning appropriate word representations to extract syntactic and semantic information of compositional phrases is a complex task in sentiment analysis. In order to learn a sentiment-aware representation model, we propose the following approach: We use a compositional matrix-space model, where, as opposed to vector-space models of language, words are represented by matrices. In the following, we describe the representation model itself and the training in detail.

3.1 Model Description: Compositional Matrix-Space Model

Compositional Matrix-Space Models (CMSMs) consider compositionality in language by the following general idea: the semantic space consists of quadratic matrices carrying real values. In other words, the semantics of each word is represented by a matrix. Then, considering the standard matrix multiplication as the composition operation, the semantics of phrases are obtained by multiplying the word-matrices in the appropriate order (Rudolph and Giesbrecht, 2010). Training CMSM using machine learning algorithms yields a type of word embedding for each word, which is a low-dimensional real-valued matrix. Like for word embeddings into vector spaces, each matrix representation is supposed to contain syntactic and semantic information about the word. Since we consider the task of sentiment analysis, word embeddings must be trained to contain sentiment-related information.

More formally, let $p = x_1 \cdots x_k$ be a phrase consisting of k words. The CMSM assigns to each word x_j a matrix $W_{x_i} \in \mathbb{R}^{m \times m}$. Then the representation of p which is the composition of words in the phrase, is shown as the matrix product of the words in the same order:

$$W_p = \prod_{i=1}^{k} W_{x_i} = W_{x_1} W_{x_2} \cdots W_{x_k}$$

To finally associate a real-valued score to a phrase p, we map the matrix representation of p to a real number using two mapping vectors $\alpha, \beta \in \mathbb{R}^m$ as follows:

$$\omega_p = \alpha^\top W_p \beta$$

In our case, the final score ω_p is supposed to indicate the sentiment polarity and strength of the phrase p.

The learning task is now, given a set of d training examples (p_j, ω_j) with $1 \leq j \leq d$, to find matrix representation for all words occurring in all p_j, such that $\omega_{p_j} \approx \omega_j$ for all j. Thereby, we fix

$$\alpha = e_1 = \begin{pmatrix} 1 \\ 0 \\ \vdots \\ 0 \end{pmatrix} \quad \text{and} \quad \beta = e_m = \begin{pmatrix} 0 \\ \vdots \\ 0 \\ 1 \end{pmatrix},$$

which only moderately restricts the expressivity of our model as made formally precise in the following theorem.

Theorem 1. *Given matrices $W_1, \ldots, W_\ell \in \mathbb{R}^{m \times m}$ and vectors $\alpha, \beta \in \mathbb{R}^m$, there are matrices $\hat{W}_1, \ldots, \hat{W}_\ell \in \mathbb{R}^{(m+1) \times (m+1)}$ such that for every sequence $i_1 \cdots i_k$ of numbers from $\{1, \ldots, \ell\}$ holds*

$$\alpha^\top W_{i_1} \cdots W_{i_k} \beta = e_1^\top \hat{W}_{i_1} \cdots \hat{W}_{i_k} e_{m+1}$$

Proof. If α is the zero vector, all scores will be zero, so we can let all $\hat{W}_h$ be the $(m+1) \times (m+1)$ zero matrix.

Otherwise let M be an arbitrary $m \times m$ matrix of full rank, whose first row is α, i.e., $e_1^\top M = \alpha^\top$. Now, let

$$\hat{W}_h := \begin{pmatrix} M W_h M^{-1} & M W_h \beta \\ 0 \cdots 0 & 0 \end{pmatrix}$$

for every $h \in \{1, \ldots, \ell\}$. Then, we obtain

$$\hat{W}_g \hat{W}_h = \begin{pmatrix} M W_g W_h M^{-1} & M W_g W_h \beta \\ 0 \cdots 0 & 0 \end{pmatrix}$$

for every $g, h \in \{1, \ldots, \ell\}$. This leads to

$$\begin{aligned} & e_1^\top \hat{W}_{i_1} \cdots \hat{W}_{i_k} e_{m+1} \\ = \; & e_1^\top M W_{i_1} \cdots W_{i_k} \beta \\ = \; & \alpha^\top W_{i_1} \cdots W_{i_k} \beta \end{aligned}$$

$\square$

In words, this theorem guarantees that for every CMSM-based scoring model with arbitrary vectors α and β there is another such model (with dimensionality increased by one) where α and β are distinct unit vectors. This justifies our above mentioned choice.

3.2 Model Training

Since the learning problem for CMSMs is not a convex problem, it must be trained carefully and specific attention has to be devoted to a good initialization (Yessenalina and Cardie, 2011). To this end, we (1) perform an "informed initialization" exploiting available scoring information for one-word phrases (unigrams), (2) apply a first learning step training only on parts of the matrices and using scored one- and two-word phrases from our training set, and (3) use the matrices obtained in this step as initialization for training the full matrices on the full training set.

Initialization: In this step, we first take all the words in the training data as our vocabulary, creating quadratic matrices of size $m \times m$ with entries from a normal distribution $\mathcal{N}(0, 0.1)$. Then, we consider the words which appear in unigram phrases $p_j = x$ with associated score ω_j in the training set. We exploit the fact that for any matrix W, computing $e_1^\top W e_m$ extracts exactly the entry of the first row, last column of W. Hence, we update this entry in every matrix corresponding to a scored unigram phrase by this value, i.e.:

$$W_{p_j} = \begin{pmatrix} \cdot & \cdots & \omega_j \\ \vdots & \ddots & \vdots \\ \cdot & \cdots & \cdot \end{pmatrix}$$

This way, we have initialized the word-to-matrix mapping such that it leads to perfect scores on the unigram phrases.

First Learning Step: After initialization, we consider bigram phrases. The sentiment value of a bigram phrase $p_j = xy$ is computed by the standard multiplication of word matrices of its constituents in the same order and mapping to the real value using the mapping vectors $\alpha = e_1$ and $\beta = e_m$:

$$\omega_j = e_1^\top W_x W_y e_m$$

$$= \begin{pmatrix} 1 \\ \vdots \\ 0 \end{pmatrix}^\top \begin{pmatrix} x_{1,1} \cdots x_{1,m} \\ \vdots \ddots \vdots \\ x_{m,1} \cdots x_{m,m} \end{pmatrix} \begin{pmatrix} y_{1,1} \cdots y_{1,m} \\ \vdots \ddots \vdots \\ y_{m,1} \cdots y_{m,m} \end{pmatrix} \begin{pmatrix} 0 \\ \vdots \\ 1 \end{pmatrix}$$

$$= \begin{pmatrix} x_{1,1} \\ \vdots \\ x_{1,m} \end{pmatrix}^\top \begin{pmatrix} y_{1,m} \\ \vdots \\ y_{m,m} \end{pmatrix} = \sum_{i=1}^m x_{1,i} y_{i,m}$$

We observe that for bigrams, multiplying the first row of the first matrix (row vector) with the last column of the second matrix (column vector) yields the sentiment score of the bigram phrase. Hence, as far as the scoring of unigrams and bigrams are concerned, only the matrix entries in the first row and the last column are relevant – thanks to our specific choice of the vectors α and β.

This observation justifies the next learning step: we use the unigrams and bigrams in the training set to learn optimal values for the relevant matrix entries only.

Second Learning Step: Using the entries obtained in the previous learning step for initialization, we finally repeat the optimization process, using the full training set and optimizing all the matrix values simultaneously.

For both learning steps, we apply the batch gradient descent optimization method on the training set to minimize the cost function defined as the summed squared error (SSE):

$$C(W) = \frac{1}{2} \sum_{j=1}^d (\hat{\omega}_j - \omega_j)^2$$

Then, update the word matrices as follows:

$$W_{x_i} = W_{x_i} - \eta \times \left(\frac{\partial C(W)}{\partial W_{x_i}} + \lambda W_{x_i} \right)$$

In order to avoid overfitting in optimization, a regularization term λW_{x_i} is used.

According to Petersen and Pedersen (2012) the derivative of a phrase with respect to the i-th word-matrix is computed as follows:

$$\frac{\partial \omega_j}{\partial W_{x_i}} = \frac{\partial (\alpha^\top W_{x_1} \cdots W_{x_i} \cdots W_{x_k} \beta)}{\partial W_{x_i}} =$$
$$(\alpha^\top W_{x_1} \cdots W_{x_{i-1}})^\top (W_{x_{i+1}} \cdots W_{x_k} \beta)$$

If a word x_i occurs several times in the phrase, then the partial derivative of the phrase with respect to W_{x_i} is the sum of partial derivatives with respect to each occurrence of W_{x_i}.

4 Experiments

We evaluate our approach on two different datasets which provide short phrases annotated with sentiment values. In both cases, we perform a ten-fold cross-validation.

4.1 Evaluation on Sentiment-Annotated Phrases from the MPQA Corpus

Experimental Setting: For the first evaluation of the proposed approach, we use the *MPQA corpus*[1]. This corpus contains newswire documents annotated with phrase-level polarity and intensity. We extracted the annotated phrases from the corpus documents, obtaining 9501 phrases. We removed phrases with low intensity similar to Yessenalina and Cardie (2011). The levels of polari-

---

[1] http://mpqa.cs.pitt.edu/corpora/mpqa_corpus/

ties and intensities and their translation into numerical values are as per Table 1. For the evaluation, we apply a ten-fold cross-validation process on the training data as follows: eight folds are used as training set, one fold as validation set and one fold as test set. The initial number of iterations in the first learning and second learning steps are set to $T = 200$ each, but we stop iterating when we obtain the minimum ranking loss, $e = \frac{1}{n}\sum_i |\hat{\omega}_i - \omega_i|$, on the validation set. Finally, we record the ranking loss of the obtained model for the test set. The learning rate η and regularization parameter λ in gradient descent are set to 0.01, by experiment. The dimension of matrices is set to $m = 3$ in order to be able to compare our results to the approach described by Yessenalina and Cardie (2011), called Matrix-space OLogReg+BowInit. We call our approach Gradual Gradient descent-based Matrix-Space Models (Grad-GMSM). All implementations have been done in Python 2.7.

Polarity	Intensity	Score
negative	high, extreme	-1
negative	medium	-0.5
neutral	medium, high, extreme	0
positive	medium	0.5
positive	high, extreme	1

Table 1: Phrase polarities and intensities in the MPQA corpus and their translation into sentiment scores.

Results and Discussion: In Yessenalina and Cardie's Matrix-space OLogReg+BowInit, matrices are initialized with a bag-of-words model. Then, ordered logistic regression is applied in order to minimize the negative log-likelihood of the training data, as the objective function. L-BFGS-B is used as their optimizer. To avoid ill-conditioned matrices, a projection step is added to matrices during training, by shrinking the singular value of matrices to one.

The ranking losses obtained by Yessenalina and Cardie's and by our method are shown in Table 2. As we observe, Grad-GMSM obtained a significantly lower ranking loss than Matrix-space OLogReg+BowInit.

Table 3 shows the sentiment scores of some example phrases trained using these two methods. As shown in the table, the two approaches' results coincide regarding the order of basic phrases: the score of *"very good"* is greater than *"good"* (and both are positive) and the score of *"very bad"* is

Method	Ranking loss
Grad-GMSM	0.3126
Matrix-space OLogReg+BowInit	0.6375

Table 2: Ranking loss of compared methods.

Phrase	Grad-GMSM	Matrix-space OLogReg+BowInit
good	0.73	2.81
very good	0.95	3.53
not good	-0.43	-0.16
not very good	-0.29	0.66
bad	-0.80	-1.67
very bad	-1.04	-2.01
not bad	0.38	-0.54
not very bad	0.32	-1.36

Table 3: Frequent phrases with average sentiment scores

less than *"bad"* (and both are negative). Also, *"not good"* is characterized as negative by both approaches.

On the other hand, there are significant differences between the two approaches: for example, our approach characterizes the phrase *"not bad"* as mildly positive while their's associates a negative score to it, the same discrepancy occurs for *"not very bad"*. Intuitively, we tend to agree more with our method's verdict on these phrases.

In general, our findings confirm those of Yessenalina and Cardie: *"very"* seems to intensify the value of the subsequent word, while the *"not"* operator does not just flip the sentiment of the word after it, but also dampens the sentiment of the words gradually. On the other hand, the scores of phrases starting with *"not very"* defy the assumption that the described effects of these operators can be combined in a straightforward way.

Figure 1 provides a more comprehensive selection of phrases and their associated scores by our approach. We obtained an average of $\omega(very\ very\ good) = 1.23$, which is greater than *"very good"*, and $\omega(very\ very\ bad) = -1.34$ less than *"very bad"*. Therefore, we can also consider *"very very"* as an intensifier operator. Moreover, we observe that the average score of $\omega(not\ really\ good) = -0.463$ is not equal to the average score of $\omega(really\ not\ good) = -0.572$, which demonstrates that the matrix-based compositionality operation shows sensitivity to word orders, arguably reflecting the meaning of phrases

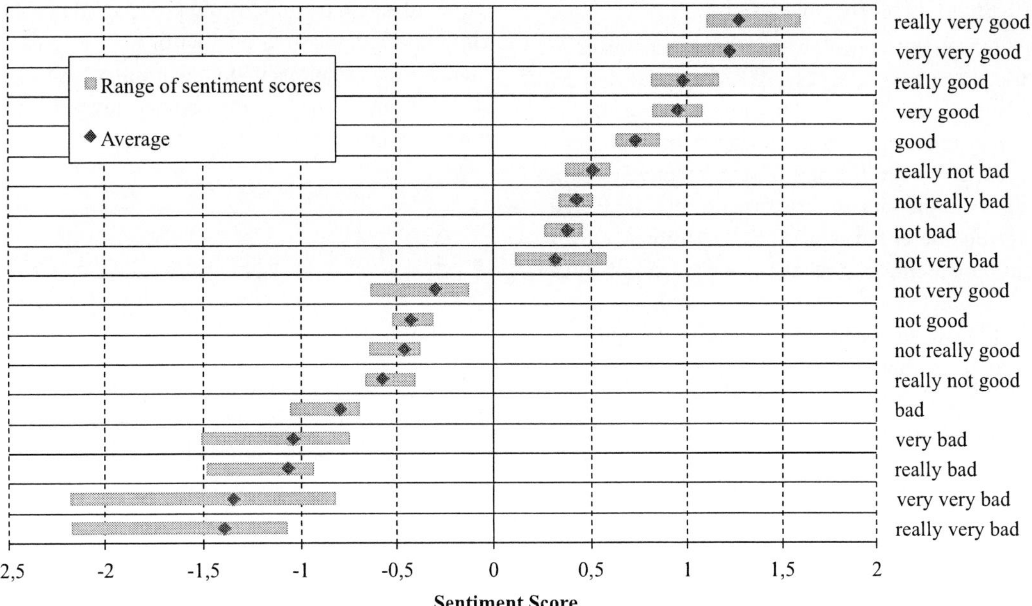

Figure 1: The order of sentiment scores for sample phrases (trained on MPQA corpus).

better than any commutative operation could.

Although the training data consists of only the values of Table 1, the training of the model is done in a way that sentiment scores for phrases with more extreme intensity might yield real values greater than $+1$ or lower than -1, since we do not constrain the sentiment scores to $[-1, +1]$. Moreover, in our experiments we observed that no extra precautions were needed to avoid ill-conditioned matrices or abrupt changes in the scores while training.

To assess the effect of our gradual two-step training method, we compared the results of Grad-GMSM against those obtained by random initialization followed by a single training phase where the full matrices were optimized (randIni-GMSM). The results, averaged over 10 runs each, are reported in Table 4. On top of a significantly better result in terms of ranking loss, we also observe faster convergence in Grad-GMSM, since the lowest ranking loss is obtained on average after 78 iterations, including both training steps. In randIni-GMSM, the lowest ranking lost happens on average after 162 iterations.

To observe the effect of a higher number of dimensions on our approach, we repeated the experiments with $m = 50$, and observed a ranking loss of $c = 0.3125$ (i.e., virtually the same as for

Method	Ranking loss	Total number of iterations
Grad-GMSM	0.3126	21.1 (Step 1) + 56.5 (Step 2) = 77.6
randIni-GMSM	0.3480	161.5

Table 4: Performance comparison for different initializations in MPQA

$m = 3$) and similar values for the number of iterations confirming the observation of Yessenalina and Cardie, that increasing the number of dimensions does not significantly improve the prediction quality of the obtained model.

4.2 Evaluation on Sentiment Composition Lexicon with Opposing Polarity Phrases

Experimental Setting: For the second evaluation of the proposed approach we use the *Sentiment Composition Lexicon for Opposing Polarity Phrases (SCL-OPP)*[2]. SCL-OPP consists of 602 unigrams, 311 bigrams, and 265 trigrams, which are taken from a corpus of tweets, and annotated with real-valued sentiment scores in the interval $[-1, +1]$ by Kiritchenko and Mohammad (2016b). The multi-word phrases contain at least one negative word and one positive word. Therefore, we find this lexicon as an interesting and suitable dataset to evaluate our approach in sentiment pre-

---

[2]http://www.saifmohammad.com/WebPages/SCL.html

diction of opposing polarity phrases.

In this experiment, we set the dimension of matrices to $m = 200$ as in (Kiritchenko and Mohammad, 2016b) and $T = 50$. The learning rate η and regularization parameter λ in gradient descent are set to 0.1 and 0.01, respectively. In addition to the ranking loss, we also use the Pearson correlation coefficient (r) for performance evaluation, which measures the linear relation between the predicted and the annotated sentiment polarity of phrases in training data. Again, we apply tenfold cross-validation in the same way as described before and average over ten repeated runs.

Results and Discussion: Kiritchenko and Mohammad (2016b) study different patterns of sentiment composition in phrases. They analyze the efficacy of several supervised and unsupervised methods on these phrases, and the effect of POS tags, word vector representations, etc. as their features in learning sentiment classification and regression. The word embeddings are obtained by the Word2vec model. For the task of regression, RBF kernel-based Support-Vector Regression (SVR) is applied as a supervised method, which we call *RBF-SVR*. RBF-SVR uses all unigrams, their sentiment scores, POS tags, and word embeddings as features during the training. For composition, they use maximal, average or concatenation of the embeddings. They perform learning for trigrams and bigrams separately. The best results reported by RBF-SVR on bigrams and trigrams are $r = 0.802$ and $r = 0.753$, respectively.

As opposed to the experimental scheme of RBF-SVR, we apply our regular training procedure on SCL-OPP lexicon. We consider it important that the learned model generalizes well to phrases of variable length, hence we consider the training of one model per phrase length not conducive. Rather, we argue that training CMSM can and should be done independent of the length of phrases, by ultimately using the combination of different length phrases for training and testing. Also, our approach does not use information extracted from other resources (such as Word2vec) nor POS tagging, i.e., we perform a light-weight training with fewer features. Still, we were able to obtain Pearson $r = 0.759$ in the task of regression.

Table 5 presents the results obtained by random initialization in CMSM and Grad-GMSM on the SCL-OPP dataset. In both methods we apply early

stopping and perform ten-fold cross-validation. In Grad-GMSM, the total number of iterations again includes the iterations in both learning phases, and still it shows a faster convergence toward minimum ranking loss.

Method	Ranking loss	Pearson r	Total number of iterations
Grad-GMSM	0.249	0.759	2.5 (Step 1) + 7.7 (Step 2) = 10.2
randIni-GMSM	0.376	0.441	77

Table 5: Performance comparison for different initializations in SCL-OPP

Finally, we repeated the experiments on the Grad-GMSM model with values of m, i.e., different numbers of dimensions. For each dimension number, we took the average of 5 runs. As shown in Table 6, the results do improve only marginally when increasing m over several orders of magnitude. Also the number of required iterations remains essentially the same, except for $m = 1$, which does not exploit the matrix properties. We see that – as opposed to vector space models – good performance can be achieved already with a very low number of dimensions.

Number of dimensions	Ranking loss	Pearson r	Total number of iterations
1	0.441	0.487	20.3
2	0.270	0.728	12.8
3	0.269	0.731	10.6
10	0.266	0.736	12.3
20	0.263	0.741	11.1
50	0.258	0.748	10.6
100	0.253	0.754	9.6
300	0.245	0.763	9.6

Table 6: Performance comparison for different dimensions in SCL-OPP

5 Conclusion

In this paper, we addressed the problem of learning compositional matrix-space models for the task of sentiment analysis. As opposed to the standard gradient descent approach, the novelty of our approach consists in a two-step learning procedure, where the result of the first step is used as initialization for the second step. We showed that with this alternative initialization step added to the learning process, we get lower ranking loss than (1) a previously described learning method on CMSM and (2) the standard gradient descent method starting from a random initializations. Moreover, we evaluated the performance of training CMSMs in sentiment prediction of phrases with opposing polarities and observed that the model captures compositionality well in such phrases. Since CMSMs turn out to be very robust against the choice of dimensionality, we conclude that choosing low-dimensional matrices as word representations lead to a reduced training time and still very good performance. In the future, we plan to extensively compare the learning of word matrix representations with vector space models in the task of sentiment analysis on several datasets.

References

Ameeta Agrawal and Aijun An. 2014. Kea: Sentiment analysis of phrases within short texts. In Preslav Nakov and Torsten Zesch, editors, *Proceedings of the 8th International Workshop on Semantic Evaluation (SemEval 2014)*. pages 380–384.

Gottlob Frege. 1884. *Die Grundlagen der Arithmetik: eine logisch-mathematische Untersuchung über den Begriff der Zahl*. Breslau, Germany: W. Koebner.

James Hong and Michael Fang. 2015. Sentiment analysis with deeply learned distributed representations of variable length texts. Technical report, Stanford University.

Svetlana Kiritchenko and Saif M Mohammad. 2016a. The effect of negators, modals, and degree adverbs on sentiment composition. In Alexandra Balahur, Erik van der Goot, Piek Vossen, and Andrés Montoyo, editors, *Proceedings of the 7th Workshop on Computational Approaches to Subjectivity, Sentiment and Social Media Analysis (WASSA)*. pages 43–52.

Svetlana Kiritchenko and Saif M Mohammad. 2016b. Sentiment composition of words with opposing polarities. In Kevin Knight, Ani Nenkova, and Owen Rambow, editors, *Proceedings of North American Chapter of the Association for Computational Linguistics: Human Language Technologies (NAACL-HLT 2016)*. pages 1102–1108.

Jean Maillard and Stephen Clark. 2015. Learning adjective meanings with a tensor-based skip-gram model. In Afra Alishahi and Alessandro Moschitti, editors, *Proceedings of the Nineteenth Conference on Computational Natural Language Learning (CoNLL 2015)*. pages 327–331.

Tomas Mikolov, Kai Chen, Greg Corrado, and Jeffrey Dean. 2013a. Efficient estimation of word representations in vector space. *arXiv preprint arXiv:1301.3781* .

Tomas Mikolov, Ilya Sutskever, Kai Chen, Greg S Corrado, and Jeff Dean. 2013b. Distributed representations of words and phrases and their compositionality. In Chris J.C. Burges, Léon Bottou, Max Welling, Zoubin Ghahramani, and Kilian Q. Weinberger, editors, *Advances in neural information processing systems (NIPS 2013)*. pages 3111–3119.

Jeff Mitchell and Mirella Lapata. 2010. Composition in distributional models of semantics. *Cognitive science* 34(8):1388–1429.

Kaare B. Petersen and Michael S. Pedersen. 2012. *The Matrix Cookbook*. Technical University of Denmark. Version 20121115.

Sebastian Rudolph and Eugenie Giesbrecht. 2010. Compositional matrix-space models of language. In Jan Hajic, Sandra Carberry, and Stephen Clark, editors, *Proceedings of the 48th Annual Meeting of the Association for Computational Linguistics (ACL 2010)*. pages 907–916.

Richard Socher, Brody Huval, Christopher D Manning, and Andrew Y Ng. 2012. Semantic compositionality through recursive matrix-vector spaces. In Jun'ichi Tsujii, James Henderson, and Marius Pasca, editors, *Proceedings of the 2012 Joint Conference on Empirical Methods in Natural Language Processing and Computational Natural Language Learning (EMNLP-CoNLL 2012)*. pages 1201–1211.

Richard Socher, Alex Perelygin, Jean Y Wu, Jason Chuang, Christopher D Manning, Andrew Y Ng, and Christopher Potts. 2013. Recursive deep models for semantic compositionality over a sentiment treebank. In *Proceedings of the conference on empirical methods in natural language processing (EMNLP 2013)*. pages 1631–1642.

Aditya Timmaraju and Vikesh Khanna. 2015. Sentiment analysis on movie reviews using recursive and recurrent neural network architectures. *Semantic Scholar*.

Xingyou Wang, Weijie Jiang, and Zhiyong Luo. 2016. Combination of convolutional and recurrent neural network for sentiment analysis of short texts. In Yuji Matsumoto and Rashmi Prasad, editors, *Proceedings of the 26th International Conference on Computational Linguistics (COLING 2016)*. pages 2428–2437.

Ainur Yessenalina and Claire Cardie. 2011. Compositional matrix-space models for sentiment analysis. In *Proceedings of the Conference on Empirical Methods in Natural Language Processing (EMNLP 2011)*. pages 172–182.

Improving Language Modeling using
Densely Connected Recurrent Neural Networks

Fréderic Godin, Joni Dambre and Wesley De Neve

IDLab - ELIS, Ghent University - imec, Ghent, Belgium
`firstname.lastname@ugent.be`

Abstract

In this paper, we introduce the novel concept of densely connected layers into recurrent neural networks. We evaluate our proposed architecture on the Penn Treebank language modeling task. We show that we can obtain similar perplexity scores with six times fewer parameters compared to a standard stacked 2-layer LSTM model trained with dropout (Zaremba et al., 2014). In contrast with the current usage of skip connections, we show that densely connecting only a few stacked layers with skip connections already yields significant perplexity reductions.

1 Introduction

Language modeling is a key task in Natural Language Processing (NLP), lying at the root of many NLP applications such as syntactic parsing (Ling et al., 2015), machine translation (Sutskever et al., 2014) and speech processing (Irie et al., 2016).

In Mikolov et al. (2010), recurrent neural networks were first introduced for language modeling. Since then, a number of improvements have been proposed. Zaremba et al. (2014) used a stack of Long Short-Term Memory (LSTM) layers trained with dropout applied on the outputs of every layer, while Gal and Ghahramani (2016) and Inan et al. (2017) further improved the perplexity score using variational dropout. Other improvements are more specific to language modeling, such as adding an extra memory component (Merity et al., 2017) or tying the input and output embeddings (Inan et al., 2017; Press and Wolf, 2016).

To be able to train larger stacks of LSTM layers, typically four layers or more (Wu et al., 2016),

skip or residual connections are needed. Wu et al. (2016) used residual connections to train a machine translation model with eight LSTM layers, while Van Den Oord et al. (2016) used both residual and skip connections to train a pixel recurrent neural network with twelve LSTM layers. In both cases, a limited amount of skip/residual connections was introduced to improve gradient flow.

In contrast, Huang et al. (2017) showed that densely connecting more than 50 convolutional layers substantially improves the image classification accuracy over regular convolutional and residual neural networks. More specifically, they introduced skip connections between *every* input and *every* output of *every* layer.

Hence, this motivates us to densely connect all layers within a stacked LSTM model using skip connections between every pair of layers.

In this paper, we investigate the usage of skip connections when stacking multiple LSTM layers in the context of language modeling. When every input of every layer is connected with every output of every other layer, we get a densely connected recurrent neural network. In contrast with the current usage of skip connections, we demonstrate that skip connections significantly improve performance when stacking only a *few* layers. Moreover, we show that densely connected LSTMs need fewer parameters than stacked LSTMs to achieve similar perplexity scores in language modeling.

2 Background: Language Modeling

A language model is a function, or an algorithm for learning such a function, that captures the salient statistical characteristics of sequences of words in a natural language. It typically allows one to make probabilistic predictions of the next word, given preceding words (Bengio, 2008). Hence, given a sequence of words $[w_1, ... w_T]$, the

Proceedings of the 2nd Workshop on Representation Learning for NLP, pages 186–190,
Vancouver, Canada, August 3, 2017. ©2017 Association for Computational Linguistics

goal is to estimate the following joint probability:

$$Pr(w_1, ..., w_T) = \prod_{t=1}^{T} Pr(w_t | w_{t-1}, ..w_1) \quad (1)$$

In practice, we try to minimize the negative log-likelihood of a sequence of words:

$$L_{neg}(\theta) = -\sum_{t=1}^{T} log(Pr(w_t | w_{t-1}, ..w_1)). \quad (2)$$

Finally, perplexity is used to evaluate the performance of the model:

$$Perplexity = \exp\left(\frac{L_{neg}(\theta)}{T}\right) \quad (3)$$

3 Methodology

Language Models (LM) in which a Recurrent Neural Network (RNN) is used are called Recurrent Neural Network Language Models (RNNLMs) (Mikolov et al., 2010). Although there are many types of RNNs, the recurrent step can formally be written as:

$$h_t = f_\theta(x_t, h_{t-1}) \quad (4)$$

in which x_t and h_t are the input and the hidden state at time step t, respectively. The function f_θ can be a basic recurrent cell, a Gated Recurrent Unit (GRU), a Long Short Term Memory (LSTM) cell, or a variant thereof.

The final prediction $Pr(w_t | w_{t-1}, ..w_1)$ is done using a simple fully connected layer with a soft-max activation function:

$$y_t = softmax(W h_t + b). \quad (5)$$

Stacking multiple RNN layers To improve performance, it is common to stack multiple recurrent layers. To that end, the hidden state of a a layer l is used as an input for the next layer $l + 1$. Hence, the hidden state $h_{l,t}$ at time step t of layer l is calculated as:

$$x_{l,t} = h_{l-1,t}, \quad (6)$$

$$h_{l,t} = f_{\theta_l}(x_{l,t}, h_{l,t-1}). \quad (7)$$

An example of a two-layer stacked recurrent neural network is illustrated in Figure 1a.

However, stacking too many layers obstructs fluent backpropagation. Therefore, skip connections or residual connections are often added. The latter is in most cases a way to avoid increasing the

size of the input of a certain layer (i.e., the inputs are summed instead of concatenated).

A skip connection can be defined as:

$$x_{l,t} = [h_{l-1,t}; h_{l-2,t}] \quad (8)$$

while a residual connection is defined as:

$$x_{l,t} = h_{l-1,t} + h_{l-2,t}. \quad (9)$$

Here, $x_{l,t}$ is the input to the current layer as defined in Equation 7.

Densely connecting multiple RNN layers In analogy with DenseNets (Huang et al., 2017), a densely connected set of layers has skip connections from every layer to every other layer. Hence, the input to RNN layer l contains the hidden states of all lower layers at the same time step t, including the output of the embedding layer e_t:

$$x_{l,t} = [h_{l-1,t}; ...; h_{1,t}; e_t]. \quad (10)$$

Due to the limited number of RNN layers, there is no need for compression layers, as introduced for convolutional neural networks (Huang et al., 2017). Moreover, allowing the final classification layer to have direct access to the embedding layer showed to be an important advantage. Hence, the final classification layer is defined as:

$$y_t = softmax(W[h_{L,t}; ...; h_{1,t}; e_t] + b). \quad (11)$$

An example of a two-layer densely connected recurrent neural network is illustrated in Figure 1b.

4 Experimental Setup

We evaluate our proposed architecture on the Penn Treebank (PTB) corpus. We adopt the standard train, validation and test splits as described in Mikolov and Zweig (2012), containing 930k training, 74k validation, and 82k test words. The vocabulary is limited to 10,000 words. Out-of-vocabulary words are replaced with an UNK token.

Our baseline is a stacked Long Short-Term Memory (LSTM) network, trained with regular dropout as introduced by Zaremba et al. (2014). Both the stacked and densely connected LSTM models consist of an embedding layer followed by a variable number of LSTM layers and a single fully connected output layer. While Zaremba et al. (2014) only report results for two stacked

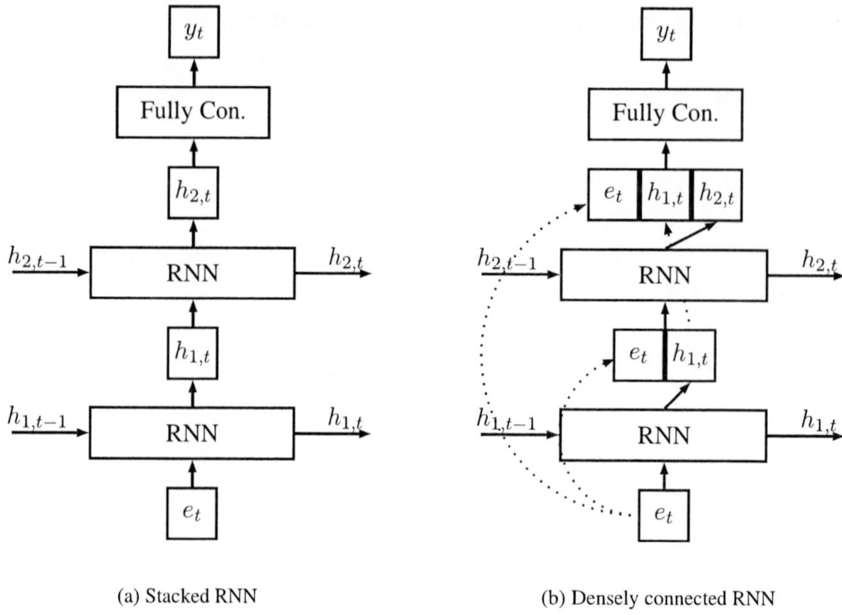

(a) Stacked RNN   (b) Densely connected RNN

Figure 1: Example architecture for a model with two recurrent layers.

LSTM layers, we also evaluate a model with three stacked LSTM layers, and experiment with two, three, four and five densely connected LSTM layers. The hidden state size of the densely connected LSTM layers is either 200 or 650. The size of the embedding layer is always 200.

We applied standard dropout on the output of every layer. We used a dropout probability of 0.6 for models with size 200 and 0.75 for models with hidden state size 650 to avoid overfitting. Additionally, we also experimented with Variational Dropout (VD) as implemented in Inan et al. (2017). We initialized all our weights uniformly in the interval [-0.05;0.05]. In addition, we used a batch size of 20 and a sequence length of 35 during training. We trained the weights using standard Stochastic Gradient Descent (SGD) with the following learning rate scheme: training for six epochs with a learning rate of one and then applying a decay factor of 0.95 every epoch. We constrained the norm of the gradient to three. We trained for 100 epochs and used early stopping. The evaluation metric reported is perplexity as defined in Equation 3. The number of parameters reported is calculated as the sum of the total amount of weights that reside in every layer.

Note that apart from the exact values of some hyperparameters, the experimental setup is identical to Zaremba et al. (2014).

5   Discussion

The results of our experiments are depicted in Table 1. The first three results, marked with *stacked LSTM (Zaremba et al., 2014)*, follow the setup of Zaremba et al. (2014) while the other results are obtained following the setup described in the previous section.

The smallest densely connected model which only uses two LSTM layers and a hidden state size of 200, already reduces the perplexity with 20% compared to a two-layer stacked LSTM model with a hidden state size of 200. Moreover, increasing the hidden state size to 350 to match the amount of parameters the two-layer densely connected LSTM model contains, does not result in a similar perplexity. The small densely connected model still realizes a 9% perplexity reduction with an equal amount of parameters.

When comparing with Zaremba et al. (2014), the smallest densely connected model outperforms the stacked LSTM model with a hidden state size of 650. Moreover, adding one additional layer is enough to obtain the same perplexity as the best model used in Zaremba et al. (2014) with a hidden state size of 1500. However, our densely connected LSTM model only uses 11M parameters while the stacked LSTM model needs six times more parameters, namely 66M. Adding a fourth layer further reduces the perplexity to 76.8.

188

Table 1: Evaluation of densely connected recurrent neural networks for the PTB language modeling task.

Name	Hidden state size	# Layers	# Parameters	Valid	Test
Stacked LSTM (Zaremba et al., 2014)[1]	200	2	5M	104.5	100.4
	650	2	20M	86.2	82.7
	1500	2	66M	82.2	78.4
Stacked LSTM	200	2	5M	105	100.9
	200	3	5M	113	108.8
	350	2	9M	91.5	87.9
Densely Connected LSTM	200	2	9M	83.4	80.4
	200	3	11M	81.5	78.5
	200	4	14M	79.2	76.8
	200	5	17M	79.7	76.9
Densely Connected LSTM	650	2	23M	81.5	78.9
Dens. Con. LSTM + Var. Dropout	650	2	23M	81.3	78.3

Increasing the hidden state size is less beneficial compared to adding an additional layer, in terms of parameters used. Moreover, a dropout probability of 0.75 was needed to reach similar perplexity scores. Using variational dropout with a probability of 0.5 allowed us to slightly improve the perplexity score, but did not yield significantly better perplexity scores, as it does in the case of stacked LSTMs (Inan et al., 2017).

In general, adding more parameters by increasing the hidden state and performing subsequent regularization, did not improve the perplexity score. While regularization techniques such as variational dropout help improving the information flow through the layers, densely connected models solve this by adding skip connections. Indeed, the higher LSTM layers and the final classification layer all have direct access to the current input word and corresponding embedding. When simply stacking layers, this embedding information needs to flow through all stacked layers. This poses the risk that embedding information will get lost. Increasing the hidden state size of every layer improves information flow. By densely connecting all layers, this issue is mitigated. Outputs of lower layers are directly connected with higher layers, effectuating efficient information flow.

Comparison to other models In Table 2, we list a number of closely related models. A densely connected LSTM model with an equal number of parameters outperforms a combination of RNN, LDA and Kneser Ney (Mikolov and Zweig, 2012). Applying Variational Dropout (VD) (Inan et al., 2017) instead of regular dropout (Zaremba et al., 2014) can further reduce the perplexity score of stacked LSTMs, but does not yield satisfactory results for our densely connected LSTMs. However, a densely connected LSTM with four layers still outperforms a medium-sized VD-LSTM while using fewer parameters. Inan et al. (2017) also tie the input and output embedding together (cf. model VD-LSTM+REAL). This is, however, not possible in densely connected recurrent neural networks, given that the input and output embedding layer have different sizes.

6 Conclusions

In this paper, we demonstrated that, by simply adding skip connections between *all* layer pairs of a neural network, we are able to achieve similar perplexity scores as a large stacked LSTM model (Zaremba et al., 2014), with six times fewer parameters for the task of language modeling. The simplicity of the skip connections allows them to act as an easy add-on for many stacked recurrent neural network architectures, significantly reducing the number of parameters. Increasing the size of the hidden states and variational dropout did not yield better results over small hidden states and regular dropout. In future research, we would like to investigate how to properly regularize larger models to achieve similar perplexity reductions.

---

[1]There are no results reported in Zaremba et al. (2014) for a small network with dropout. These are our own results, following the exact same setup as for the medium-sized architecture.

Table 2: Comparison to other language models evaluated on the PTB corpus.

Model	# Parameters	Perplexity Test
RNN (Mikolov and Zweig, 2012)	6M	124.7
RNN+LDA+KN-5+Cache (Mikolov and Zweig, 2012)	9M	92.0
Medium stacked LSTM (Zaremba et al., 2014)	20M	82.7
Densely Connected LSTM (small - 2 layers)	**9M**	**80.4**
Char-CNN (Kim et al., 2016)	19M	78.9
Densely Connected LSTM (small - 3 layers)	**11M**	**78.5**
Large stacked LSTM (Zaremba et al., 2014)	66M	78.4
Medium stacked VD-LSTM (Inan et al., 2017)	20M	77.7
Densely Connected LSTM (small - 4 layers)	**14M**	**76.8**
Large stacked VD-LSTM (Inan et al., 2017)	66M	72.5
Large stacked VD-LSTM + REAL (Inan et al., 2017)	51M	68.5

Acknowledgments

The research activities as described in this paper were funded by Ghent University, imec, Flanders Innovation & Entrepreneurship (VLAIO), the Fund for Scientific Research-Flanders (FWO-Flanders), and the EU.

References

Yoshua Bengio. 2008. Neural net language models. *Scholarpedia* 3(1):3881. revision #91566.

Yarin Gal and Zoubin Ghahramani. 2016. A theoretically grounded application of dropout in recurrent neural networks. In *Advances in Neural Information Processing Systems*.

Gao Huang, Zhuang Liu, Kilian Q Weinberger, and Laurens van der Maaten. 2017. Densely connected convolutional networks. In *Proceedings of the IEEE Conference on Computer Vision and Pattern Recognition*.

Hakan Inan, Khashayar Khosravi, and Richard Socher. 2017. Tying word vectors and word classifiers: A loss framework for language modeling. In *Proceedings of the International Conference on Learning Representations*.

Kazuki Irie, Zoltán Tüske, Tamer Alkhouli, Ralf Schlüter, and Hermann Ney. 2016. Lstm, gru, highway and a bit of attention: an empirical overview for language modeling in speech recognition. In *Proceedings of Interspeech*.

Yoon Kim, Yacine Jernite, David Sontag, and Alexander M. Rush. 2016. Character-aware neural language models. In *Proceedings of the Thirtieth AAAI Conference on Artificial Intelligence*.

Wang Ling, Chris Dyer, Alan W. Black, Isabel Trancoso, Ramon Fermandez, Silvio Amir, Lus Marujo, and Tiago Lus. 2015. Finding function in form: Compositional character models for open vocabulary word representation. In *Proceedings of the International Conference on Empirical Methods in Natural Language Processing*.

Stephen Merity, Caiming Xiong, James Bradbury, and Richard Socher. 2017. Pointer sentinel mixture models. In *Proceedings of the International Conference on Learning Representations*.

Tomas Mikolov, Martin Karafit, Luks Burget, Jan Cernock, and Sanjeev Khudanpur. 2010. Recurrent neural network based language model. In *Proceedings of Interspeech*.

Tomas Mikolov and Geoffrey Zweig. 2012. Context dependent recurrent neural network language model. In *Proceedings of the IEEE Workshop on Spoken Language Technology*.

Ofir Press and Lior Wolf. 2016. Using the output embedding to improve language models. *CoRR* abs/1608.05859. http://arxiv.org/abs/1608.05859.

Ilya Sutskever, Oriol Vinyals, and Quoc V. Le. 2014. Sequence to sequence learning with neural networks. In *Proceedings of the International Conference on Neural Information Processing Systems*.

Aäron Van Den Oord, Nal Kalchbrenner, and Koray Kavukcuoglu. 2016. Pixel recurrent neural networks. In *Proceedings of the 33rd International Conference on International Conference on Machine Learning*.

Yonghui Wu, Mike Schuster, and Zhifeng Chen et al. 2016. Google's neural machine translation system: Bridging the gap between human and machine translation. *CoRR* abs/1609.08144. http://arxiv.org/abs/1609.08144.

Wojciech Zaremba, Ilya Sutskever, and Oriol Vinyals. 2014. Recurrent neural network regularization. *CoRR* abs/1409.2329. http://arxiv.org/abs/1409.2329.

NewsQA: A Machine Comprehension Dataset

Adam Trischler[*]   **Tong Wang**[*]   **Xingdi Yuan**[*]   **Justin Harris**

Alessandro Sordoni   **Philip Bachman**   **Kaheer Suleman**

{adam.trischler, tong.wang, eric.yuan, justin.harris,
alsordon, phbachma, kasulema}@microsoft.com
Microsoft Maluuba
Montréal, Québec, Canada

Abstract

We present *NewsQA*, a challenging machine comprehension dataset of over 100,000 human-generated question-answer pairs. Crowdworkers supply questions and answers based on a set of over 10,000 news articles from CNN, with answers consisting of spans of text in the articles. We collect this dataset through a four-stage process designed to solicit exploratory questions that require reasoning. Analysis confirms that *NewsQA* demands abilities beyond simple word matching and recognizing textual entailment. We measure human performance on the dataset and compare it to several strong neural models. The performance gap between humans and machines (13.3% F1) indicates that significant progress can be made on *NewsQA* through future research. The dataset is freely available online.

1   Introduction

Almost all human knowledge is recorded in the medium of text. As such, comprehension of written language by machines, at a near-human level, would enable a broad class of artificial intelligence applications. In human students we evaluate reading comprehension by posing questions based on a text passage and then assessing a student's answers. Such comprehension tests are objectively gradable and may measure a range of important abilities, from basic understanding to causal reasoning to inference (Richardson et al., 2013). To teach literacy to machines, the research community has taken a similar approach with machine comprehension (MC).

Recent years have seen the release of a host of MC datasets. Generally, these consist of (document, question, answer) triples to be used in a supervised learning framework. Existing datasets vary in size, difficulty, and collection methodology; however, as pointed out by Rajpurkar et al. (2016), most suffer from one of two shortcomings: those that are designed explicitly to test comprehension (Richardson et al., 2013) are too small for training data-intensive deep learning models, while those that are sufficiently large for deep learning (Hermann et al., 2015; Hill et al., 2016; Bajgar et al., 2016) are generated synthetically, yielding questions that are not posed in natural language and that may not test comprehension directly (Chen et al., 2016). More recently, Rajpurkar et al. (2016) proposed *SQuAD*, a dataset that overcomes these deficiencies as it contains crowdsourced natural language questions.

In this paper, we present a challenging new largescale dataset for machine comprehension: *NewsQA*. It contains 119,633 natural language questions posed by crowdworkers on 12,744 news articles from CNN. In *SQuAD*, crowdworkers are tasked with both asking and answering questions given a paragraph. In contrast, *NewsQA* was built using a collection process designed to encourage exploratory, curiosity-based questions that may better reflect realistic information-seeking behaviors. Particularly, a set of crowdworkers were tasked to answer questions given a summary of the article, i.e. the CNN article highlights. A separate set of crowdworkers selects answers given the full article, which consist of word spans in the corresponding articles. This gives rise to interesting patterns such as questions that may not be answerable by the original article.

As Trischler et al. (2016a), Chen et al. (2016), and others have argued, it is important for datasets to be sufficiently challenging to teach models

---

[*]Equal contribution.

Proceedings of the 2nd Workshop on Representation Learning for NLP, pages 191–200,
Vancouver, Canada, August 3, 2017. ©2017 Association for Computational Linguistics

the abilities we wish them to learn. Thus, in line with Richardson et al. (2013), our goal with *NewsQA* was to construct a corpus of challenging questions that necessitate reasoning-like behaviors—for example, synthesis of information across different parts of an article. We designed our collection methodology explicitly to capture such questions.

NewsQA is closely related to the *SQuAD* dataset: it is crowdsourced, with answers given by spans of text within an article rather than single words or entities, and there are no candidate answers from which to choose. The challenging characteristics of *NewsQA* that distinguish it from *SQuAD* are as follows:

1. Articles in *NewsQA* are significantly longer (6x on average) and come from a distinct domain.

2. Our collection process encourages lexical and syntactic divergence between questions and answers.

3. A greater proportion of questions requires reasoning beyond simple word- and context-matching.

4. A significant proportion of questions have no answer in the corresponding article.

We demonstrate through several metrics that, consequently, *NewsQA* offers a greater challenge to existing comprehension models. Given their similarities, we believe that *SQuAD* and *NewsQA* can be used to complement each other, for instance to explore models' ability to transfer across domains.

In this paper we describe the collection methodology for *NewsQA*, provide a variety of statistics to characterize it and contrast it with previous datasets, and assess its difficulty. In particular, we measure human performance and compare it to that of two strong neural-network baselines. Humans significantly outperform powerful question-answering models, suggesting *NewsQA* could drive further advances in machine comprehension research.

2   Related Datasets

NewsQA follows in the tradition of several recent comprehension datasets. These vary in size, difficulty, and collection methodology, and each has its own distinguishing characteristics.

2.1   MCTest

MCTest (Richardson et al., 2013) is a crowdsourced collection of 660 elementary-level children's stories with associated questions and answers. The stories are fictional, to ensure that the answer must be found in the text itself, and carefully limited in language and depth. Each question comes with a set of 4 candidate answers that range from single words to full sentences. Questions are designed to require rudimentary reasoning and synthesis of information across sentences, making the dataset quite challenging. This is compounded by the dataset's size, which limits the training of expressive statistical models. Nevertheless, recent comprehension models have performed well on *MCTest* (Sachan et al., 2015; Wang et al., 2015), including a highly structured neural model (Trischler et al., 2016a). These models all rely on access to the small set of candidate answers, a crutch that *NewsQA* does not provide.

2.2   CNN/Daily Mail

The *CNN/Daily Mail* corpus (Hermann et al., 2015) consists of news articles scraped from those outlets with corresponding cloze-style questions. Cloze questions are constructed synthetically by deleting a single entity from abstractive summary points that accompany each article (written presumably by human authors). As such, determining the correct answer relies mostly on recognizing textual entailment between the article and the question. The named entities within an article are identified and anonymized in a preprocessing step and constitute the set of candidate answers; contrast this with *NewsQA* in which answers often include longer phrases and no candidates are given. Performance of the strongest models (Kadlec et al., 2016; Trischler et al., 2016b; Sordoni et al., 2016) on this dataset now nearly matches that of humans.

2.3   Children's Book Test

The *Children's Book Test* (*CBT*) (Hill et al., 2016) was collected using a process similar to that of *CNN/Daily Mail*. Text passages are 20-sentence excerpts from children's books available through Project Gutenberg; questions are generated by deleting a single word in the next (*i.e.*, 21st) sentence. Consequently, *CBT* evaluates word prediction based on context.

2.4 BookTest

Bajgar et al. (2016) convincingly argue that, because existing datasets are not large enough, we have yet to reach the full capacity of existing comprehension models. As a remedy they present *Book-Test*. This is an extension to the named-entity and common-noun strata of *CBT* that increases their size by over 60 times.

2.5 SQuAD

The comprehension dataset most closely related to *NewsQA* is *SQuAD* (Rajpurkar et al., 2016). It consists of natural language questions posed by crowdworkers on paragraphs from Wikipedia articles with high PageRank score. As in *NewsQA*, each answer consists of a span of text from the related paragraph and no candidates are provided. *SQuAD* provides 107,785 question-answer pairs based on 536 articles. In contrast, our questions are based on a larger number of articles, i.e. 12,744.

Although *SQuAD* is a more realistic and more challenging comprehension task than the other largescale MC datasets, machine performance has rapidly improved towards that of humans in recent months. This suggests that new, more difficult alternatives like *NewsQA* could further push the development of advanced MC systems.

3 Collection methodology

We collected *NewsQA* through a four-stage process: article curation, question sourcing, answer sourcing, and validation. We also applied a post-processing step to consolidate near-duplicate answers and to merge multiple spans in order to enhance the dataset's usability. These steps are detailed below.

3.1 Article curation

We retrieve articles from CNN using the script created by Hermann et al. (2015) for *CNN/Daily Mail*. From the returned set of 90,266 articles, we select 12,744 uniformly at random. These cover a wide range of topics that includes politics, economics, and current events. Articles are partitioned at random into a training set (90%), a development set (5%), and a test set (5%).

3.2 Question sourcing

It was important to us to collect challenging questions that could not be answered using straightforward word- or context-matching. Like Richardson et al. (2013) we want to encourage reasoning in comprehension models. We are also interested in questions that, in some sense, model human curiosity and reflect actual human use-cases of information seeking. Along a similar line, we consider it an important (though as yet overlooked) capacity of a comprehension model to recognize when given information is inadequate, so we are also interested in questions that may not have sufficient evidence in the text. Our question sourcing stage was designed to solicit questions of this nature, and deliberately separated from the answer sourcing stage for the same reason.

Questioners (a distinct set of crowdworkers) see *only* a news article's headline and its summary points (also available from CNN); they do not see the full article itself. They are asked to formulate a question from this incomplete information. This encourages curiosity about the contents of the article and prevents questions that are simple reformulations of sentences in the text. It also increases the likelihood of questions whose answers do not exist in the text. We reject questions that have significant word overlap with the summary points to ensure that crowdworkers do not treat the summaries as mini-articles, and further discourage this in the instructions. During collection each Questioner is solicited for up to three questions about an article. They are provided with positive and negative examples to prompt and guide them (detailed instructions are available at `datasets.maluuba.com`).

3.3 Answer sourcing

A second set of crowdworkers (*Answerers*) provide answers. Although this separation of question and answer increases the overall cognitive load, we hypothesized that unburdening Questioners in this way would encourage more complex questions. Answerers receive a full article along with a crowdsourced question and are tasked with determining the answer. They may also reject the question as nonsensical, or select the *null* answer if the article contains insufficient information. Answers are submitted by clicking on and highlighting words in the article, while instructions encourage the set of answer words to consist of a single continuous span (an example prompt is given at `datasets.maluuba.com`). For each question we solicit answers from multiple crowdworkers (avg. 2.73) with the aim of achieving agreement between at least two Answerers.

3.4 Validation

Crowdsourcing is a powerful tool but it is not without peril (collection glitches; uninterested or malicious workers). To obtain a dataset of the highest possible quality we use a validation process that mitigates some of these issues. In validation, a third set of crowdworkers sees the full article, a question, and the set of unique answers to that question. We task these workers with choosing the best answer from the candidate set or rejecting all answers. Each article-question pair is validated by an average of 2.48 crowdworkers. Validation was used on those questions *without* answer-agreement after the previous stage, amounting to 43.2% of all questions.

3.5 Answer marking and cleanup

After validation, 86.0% of all questions in *NewsQA* have answers agreed upon by at least two separate crowdworkers—either at the initial answer sourcing stage or after validation. This improves the dataset's quality. We choose to include the questions without agreed answers in the corpus also, but they are specially marked. Such questions could be treated as having the *null* answer and used to train models that are aware of poorly posed questions.

As a final cleanup step, if two answer spans are less than 3 words apart (punctuation is discounted), we take the start of the first span and the end of the second span as the new boundary of the answer span. We find that 5.68% of answers consist of multiple spans, while 71.3% of multi-spans are within the 3-word threshold. Looking more closely at the data reveals that the multi-span answers often represent lists. These may present an interesting challenge for comprehension models moving forward.

4 Data analysis

We analyze questions and answers in *NewsQA* to demonstrate its challenge and usefulness as a machine comprehension benchmark. Our analysis focuses on the types of answers that appear in the dataset and the various forms of reasoning required to solve it.[1]

---

[1]Additional statistics are available at `datasets.maluuba.com`.

Table 1: The variety of answer types appearing in *NewsQA*, with proportion statistics and examples.

Answer type	Example	Proportion (%)
Date/Time	March 12, 2008	2.9
Numeric	24.3 million	9.8
Person	Ludwig van Beethoven	14.8
Location	Torrance, California	7.8
Other Entity	Pew Hispanic Center	5.8
Common Noun Phr.	federal prosecutors	22.2
Adjective Phr.	5-hour	1.9
Verb Phr.	suffered minor damage	1.4
Clause Phr.	trampling on human rights	18.3
Prepositional Phr.	in the attack	3.8
Other	nearly half	11.2

4.1 Answer types

Following Rajpurkar et al. (2016), we categorize answers based on their linguistic type in Table 1. This categorization relies on Stanford CoreNLP to generate constituency parses, POS tags, and NER tags for answer spans (see Rajpurkar et al. (2016) for more details). From the table we see that the majority of answers (22.2%) are common noun phrases. Thereafter, answers are fairly evenly spread among the clause phrase (18.3%), person (14.8%), numeric (9.8%), and other (11.2%) types.

The proportions in Table 1 only account for cases when an answer span exists. The complement of this set comprises questions with an agreed *null* answer (9.5% of the full corpus) and answers without agreement after validation (4.5% of the full corpus).

4.2 Reasoning types

The forms of reasoning required to solve *NewsQA* directly influence the abilities that models will learn from the dataset. We stratified reasoning types using a variation on the taxonomy presented by Chen et al. (2016) in their analysis of the *CNN/Daily Mail* dataset. Types are as follows, in ascending order of difficulty:

1. **Word Matching:** Important words in the question exactly match words in the immediate context of an answer span, such that a keyword search algorithm could perform well on this subset.

2. **Paraphrasing:** A single sentence in the article entails or paraphrases the question. Paraphrase recognition may require synonymy and world knowledge.

3. **Inference:** The answer must be inferred from incomplete information in the article or by rec-

ognizing conceptual overlap. This typically draws on world knowledge.

4. **Synthesis:** The answer can only be inferred by synthesizing information distributed across multiple sentences.

5. **Ambiguous/Insufficient:** The question has no answer or no unique answer in the article.

For both *NewsQA* and *SQuAD*, we manually labelled 1,000 examples (drawn randomly from the respective development sets) according to these types and compiled the results in Table 2. Some examples fall into more than one category, in which case we defaulted to the more challenging type. We can see from the table that word matching, the easiest type, makes up the largest subset in both datasets (32.7% for *NewsQA* and 39.8% for *SQuAD*). Paraphrasing constitutes a larger proportion in *SQuAD* than in *NewsQA* (34.3% vs 27.0%), possibly a result of the explicit encouragement of lexical variety in *SQuAD* question sourcing. However, *NewsQA* significantly outnumbers *SQuAD* on the distribution of the more difficult forms of reasoning: synthesis and inference make up a combined 33.9% of the data in contrast to 20.5% in *SQuAD*.

5 Baseline models

To benchmark *NewsQA* for the MC task, we compare the performance of four comprehension systems: a heuristic sentence-level baseline, two neural models, and human data analysts. The first neural model is the match-LSTM (mLSTM) of Wang and Jiang (2016b). The second is the FastQA model of Weissenborn et al. (2017). We describe these models below but omit the personal details of our analysts.

5.1 Sentence-level baseline

First we investigate a simple baseline that we found to perform surprisingly well on *SQuAD*. Given a document and question, the baseline aims to indicate which sentence contains the answer (rather indicating the specific answer span). Although this task is easier, we hypothesized that naive techniques like word-matching would yet be inadequate if *NewsQA* required more involved reasoning as intended.

The baseline uses a variation on inverse document frequency (*idf*), which we call inverse sentence frequency (*isf*).[2] Given a sentence S_i from an article and its corresponding question Q, the *isf* score is given by the sum of the *idf* scores of the words common to S_i and Q (each sentence is treated as a document for the *idf* computation). The sentence with the highest *isf* is taken as the answer sentence S_*, that is,

$$S_* = \arg\max_i \sum_{w \in S_i \cap Q} idf(w).$$

5.2 Match-LSTM

The mLSTM model (Wang and Jiang, 2016b) is straightforward to implement and offers strong, though not state-of-the-art, performance on the similar *SQuAD* dataset. There are three stages involved. First, LSTM networks encode the document and question (represented by GloVe word embeddings (Pennington et al., 2014)) as sequences of hidden states. Second, an mLSTM network (Wang and Jiang, 2016a) compares the document encodings with the question encodings. This network processes the document sequentially and at each token uses an attention mechanism to obtain a weighted vector representation of the question; the weighted combination is concatenated with the encoding of the current token and fed into a standard LSTM. Finally, a Pointer Network uses the hidden states of the mLSTM to select the boundaries of the answer span. We refer the reader to Wang and Jiang (2016a,b) for full details.

5.3 FastQA

We additionally report the results obtained by Weissenborn et al. (2017) using their FastQA model, which was near state-of-the-art on *SQuAD* at the time of writing. FastQA first augments the standard word embeddings with character-based embeddings computed using a convolutional network. These are projected and augmented with word-in-question features, then fed to a bidirectional LSTM to encode both the question and document. In the answer layer, a weighted representation of the question is combined with the document encodings and fed through a 2-layer feedforward network followed by a softmax layer, which induces a probability distribution over the document words. Separate networks point to the answer span's start and end. A unique aspect of this model is that

---

[2]We also experimented with normalizing the *isf* score by sentence length and the performance difference is negligible (<0.02%).

Table 2: Reasoning mechanisms needed to answer questions. For each we show an example question with the sentence that contains the answer span. Words relevant to the reasoning type are in **bold**. The corresponding proportion in the human-evaluated subset of both *NewsQA* and *SQuAD* (1,000 samples each) is also given.

Reasoning	Example	Proportion (%) *NewsQA*	*SQuAD*
Word Matching	Q: **When were** the **findings published**? S: Both sets of research **findings were published Thursday**...	32.7	39.8
Paraphrasing	Q: **Who** is the **struggle between** in Rwanda? S: The **struggle pits ethnic Tutsis**, supported by Rwanda, **against ethnic Hutu**, backed by Congo.	27.0	34.3
Inference	Q: **Who** drew **inspiration** from **presidents**? S: **Rudy Ruiz** says the lives of US **presidents** can make them **positive role models** for students.	13.2	8.6
Synthesis	Q: **Where** is **Brittanee Drexel** from? S: The mother of a 17-year-old **Rochester, New York** high school student ... says she did not give her daughter permission to go on the trip. **Brittanee** Marie **Drexel**'s mom says...	20.7	11.9
Ambiguous/Insufficient	Q: **Whose mother** is **moving** to the White House? S: ... **Barack Obama's mother-in-law**, Marian Robinson, will **join** the Obamas at the **family's private quarters** at 1600 Pennsylvania Avenue. [Michelle is never mentioned]	6.4	5.4

it uses beam search to maximize (approximately) the answer span probability. We refer the reader to Weissenborn et al. (2017) for full details. Note that we report results of the "extended" FastQA model from that work.

6 Experiments

All of our present experiments use the subset of *NewsQA* with agreed or validated answers (92,549 samples for training, 5,166 for validation, and 5,126 for testing). We leave the challenge of identifying the unanswerable questions for future work.

6.1 Human performance

We tested four English speakers on a total of 1,000 questions from the *NewsQA* development set. We used four performance measures: F1 and exact match (EM) scores (the same measures used by *SQuAD*), as well as BLEU and CIDEr.[3] BLEU is a precision-based metric popular in machine translation that uses a weighted average of variable length phrase matches (n-grams) against the reference sentence (Papineni et al., 2002). CIDEr was designed to correlate better with human judgements of sentence similarity, and uses *tf-idf* scores over n-grams (Vedantam et al., 2015).

As given in Table 3, humans averaged 69.4% F1

on *NewsQA*. The human EM scores are relatively low at 46.5%. These lower scores are a reflection of the fact that, particularly in a dataset as complex as *NewsQA*, there are multiple ways to select semantically equivalent answers, *e.g.*, "1996" versus "in 1996". Although these answers are equally correct they would be measured at 50% F1 and 0% EM relative to each other. This suggests that simpler automatic metrics are not equal to the task of complex MC evaluation, a problem that has been noted in other domains, *e.g.*, dialogue (Liu et al., 2016). It is for this reason that we consider BLEU and CIDEr scores, also: humans score 56.0 and 3.596 on these metrics, respectively.

The original evaluation of human performance on *SQuAD* compares distinct answers given by crowdworkers according to EM and F1; for a closer comparison with *NewsQA*, we replicated our human test on the same number of development questions (1,000) with the same humans. We measured human answers against the second group of crowdsourced responses in *SQuAD*'s development set, giving 80.7% F1, 62.5 BLEU, and 3.998 CIDEr. Note that the F1 score is close to the performance of 78.9% achieved by the FastQA model and reported in Table 5.

We finally compared human performance on the answers with crowdworker agreement with and without validation, finding a difference of only

---

[3] We calculate these two scores using `https://github.com/tylin/coco-caption`.

Table 3: Human performance on *SQuAD* and *NewsQA* datasets. The first row is taken from Rajpurkar et al. (2016).

Dataset	Exact Match	F1	BLEU	CIDEr
SQuAD	80.3	90.5	-	-
SQuAD (ours)	65.0	80.7	62.5	3.998
NewsQA	46.5	69.4	56.0	3.596

Table 4: Sentence-level accuracy on standard and artificially-lengthened *SQuAD* documents.

	SQuAD				*NewsQA*
# documents	1	5	7	9	1
Avg # sentences	4.9	23.2	31.8	40.3	30.7
isf score	79.6	73.0	72.3	71.0	35.4

1.4% F1. This suggests our validation stage yields good-quality answers.

6.2 Model performance

6.2.1 ISF sentence selection

As reported in Table 4, the heuristic *isf* baseline achieves an impressive 79.6% accuracy in determining the correct answer sentence for *SQuAD*'s development set; however, it reaches only 35.4% sentence-selection accuracy on *NewsQA*'s development set. Selecting the answer sentence in *NewsQA* should be inherently more difficult, since *SQuAD* documents are on average 4.9 sentences long, while *NewsQA* articles are on average 30.7 sentences. To eliminate this difference in article length as a possible cause of the observed performance gap, we concatenated adjacent *SQuAD* paragraphs that come from the same Wikipedia article and ran the baseline on these lengthened documents. Accuracy decreases as expected with increased *SQuAD* document length, yet remains significantly higher than on *NewsQA* even when the lengthened documents are longer than the news articles (see Table 4).

6.2.2 Neural models

Performance of the neural baselines is measured by EM and F1 using the official evaluation script from *SQuAD*. Results are listed in Table 5. We see that on both datasets, FastQA outperforms our implementation of the mLSTM according to all measures. Moreover, comparing with Table 3, the gap between human and FastQA performance on *SQuAD* is 1.8% F1 under our evaluation scheme compared with 13.3% F1 on *NewsQA*. This suggests a large

margin for improvement remains for machine comprehension methods to master *NewsQA*.

For a finer-grained analysis, we measured our implementation of mLSTM's performance on questions from the human-evaluated portion of the development set. We stratified performance according to answer type and reasoning type as defined in Sections 4.1 and 4.2, respectively. Results are presented in Figure 1.

Answer-type stratification suggests that the model is better at pointing to named entities compared to other answer types. The reasoning-type stratification, on the other hand, shows that questions requiring *inference* and *synthesis* are, not surprisingly, most difficult for the model. Consistent with observations in Table 5, stratified performance on *NewsQA* is significantly lower than on *SQuAD*. The difference is smallest on word matching and largest on synthesis. We postulate that the longer stories in *NewsQA* make synthesizing information from separate sentences more difficult, since the relevant sentences may be farther apart. This requires the model to track longer-term dependencies. The details of our mLSTM implementation are given in the Appendix.

7 Conclusion

We have introduced a challenging new comprehension dataset: *NewsQA*. We collected the 100,000+ examples of *NewsQA* using teams of crowdworkers, who variously read CNN articles or highlights, posed questions about them, and determined answers. Our methodology yields diverse answer types and a significant proportion of questions that require some reasoning ability to solve. This makes the corpus challenging, as confirmed by the large performance gap between humans and deep neural models. By its size and complexity, we believe *NewsQA* makes a significant extension to the existing body of comprehension datasets, in particular complementing *SQuAD*. We hope that our corpus will spur further advances in machine comprehension and foster the development of more literate machines.

References

Ondrej Bajgar, Rudolf Kadlec, and Jan Kleindienst. 2016. Embracing data abundance: Booktest dataset for reading comprehension. *arXiv preprint arXiv:1610.00956* .

Table 5: Neural model performance on *SQuAD* and *NewsQA*. mLSTM results on *SQuAD* are derived from our implementation of Wang and Jiang (2016b), and all FastQA results are taken from Weissenborn et al. (2017).

SQuAD	Dev		Test		*NewsQA*	Dev		Test	
Model	F1	EM	F1	EM	**Model**	F1	EM	F1	EM
mLSTM	73.9	63.1	-	-	mLSTM	51.0	35.7	50.5	35.4
FastQA	78.5	70.3	78.9	70.8	FastQA	56.1	43.7	56.1	42.8

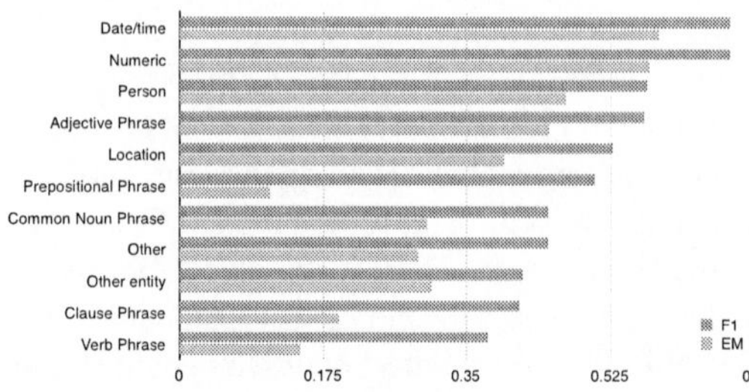
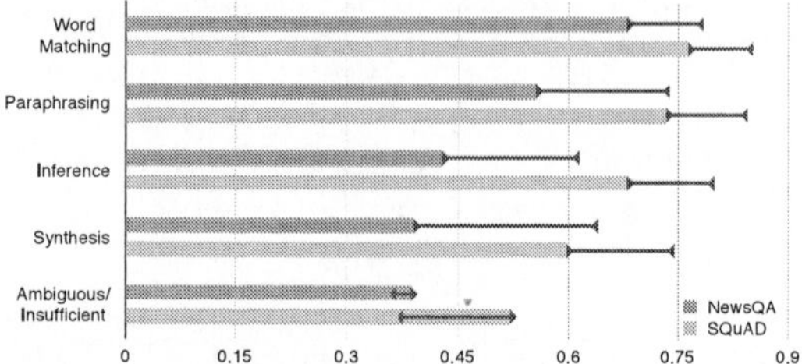

Figure 1: *Left*: mLSTM performance (F1 and EM) stratified by answer type on the full development set of *NewsQA*. *Right*: mLSTM performance (F1) stratified by reasoning type on the human-assessed subset on both *NewsQA* and *SQuAD*. Error bars indicate performance differences between mLSTM and human annotators.

J. Bergstra, O. Breuleux, F. Bastien, P. Lamblin, R. Pascanu, G. Desjardins, J. Turian, D. Warde-Farley, and Y. Bengio. 2010. Theano: a CPU and GPU math expression compiler. In *In Proc. of SciPy*.

Danqi Chen, Jason Bolton, and Christopher D. Manning. 2016. A thorough examination of the cnn / daily mail reading comprehension task. In *Association for Computational Linguistics (ACL)*.

François Chollet. 2015. keras. `https://github.com/fchollet/keras`.

Karl Moritz Hermann, Tomas Kocisky, Edward Grefenstette, Lasse Espeholt, Will Kay, Mustafa Suleyman, and Phil Blunsom. 2015. Teaching machines to read and comprehend. In *Advances in Neural Information Processing Systems*. pages 1684–1692.

Felix Hill, Antoine Bordes, Sumit Chopra, and Jason Weston. 2016. The goldilocks principle: Reading children's books with explicit memory representations. *ICLR* .

Rudolf Kadlec, Martin Schmid, Ondrej Bajgar, and Jan Kleindienst. 2016. Text understanding with the attention sum reader network. *arXiv preprint arXiv:1603.01547* .

Diederik Kingma and Jimmy Ba. 2015. Adam: A method for stochastic optimization. *ICLR* .

Chia-Wei Liu, Ryan Lowe, Iulian V Serban, Michael Noseworthy, Laurent Charlin, and Joelle Pineau. 2016. How not to evaluate your dialogue system: An empirical study of unsupervised evaluation metrics for dialogue response generation. *arXiv preprint arXiv:1603.08023* .

Kishore Papineni, Salim Roukos, Todd Ward, and Wei-Jing Zhu. 2002. Bleu: a method for automatic evaluation of machine translation. In *Proceedings of the 40th annual meeting on association for computational linguistics*. Association for Computational Linguistics, pages 311–318.

Razvan Pascanu, Tomas Mikolov, and Yoshua Bengio. 2013. On the difficulty of training recurrent neural networks. *ICML (3)* 28:1310–1318.

Jeffrey Pennington, Richard Socher, and Christopher D Manning. 2014. Glove: Global vectors for word representation. In *EMNLP*. volume 14, pages 1532–43.

Pranav Rajpurkar, Jian Zhang, Konstantin Lopyrev, and Percy Liang. 2016. Squad: 100,000+ questions for machine comprehension of text. *arXiv preprint arXiv:1606.05250* .

Matthew Richardson, Christopher JC Burges, and Erin Renshaw. 2013. Mctest: A challenge dataset for the open-domain machine comprehension of text. In *EMNLP*. volume 1, page 2.

Mrinmaya Sachan, Avinava Dubey, Eric P Xing, and Matthew Richardson. 2015. Learning answer entailing structures for machine comprehension. In *Proceedings of ACL*.

Andrew M Saxe, James L McClelland, and Surya Ganguli. 2013. Exact solutions to the nonlinear dynamics of learning in deep linear neural networks. *arXiv preprint arXiv:1312.6120* .

Alessandro Sordoni, Philip Bachman, Adam Trischler, and Yoshua Bengio. 2016. Iterative alternating neural attention for machine reading. *arXiv preprint arXiv:1606.02245* .

Adam Trischler, Zheng Ye, Xingdi Yuan, Jing He, Philip Bachman, and Kaheer Suleman. 2016a. A parallel-hierarchical model for machine comprehension on sparse data. In *Proceedings of the 54th Annual Meeting of the Association for Computational Linguistics*.

Adam Trischler, Zheng Ye, Xingdi Yuan, and Kaheer Suleman. 2016b. Natural language comprehension with the epireader. In *EMNLP*.

Ramakrishna Vedantam, C Lawrence Zitnick, and Devi Parikh. 2015. Cider: Consensus-based image description evaluation. In *Proceedings of the IEEE Conference on Computer Vision and Pattern Recognition*. pages 4566–4575.

Hai Wang, Mohit Bansal, Kevin Gimpel, and David McAllester. 2015. Machine comprehension with syntax, frames, and semantics. In *Proceedings of ACL, Volume 2: Short Papers*. page 700.

Shuohang Wang and Jing Jiang. 2016a. Learning natural language inference with lstm. *NAACL* .

Shuohang Wang and Jing Jiang. 2016b. Machine comprehension using match-lstm and answer pointer. *arXiv preprint arXiv:1608.07905* .

Dirk Weissenborn, Georg Wiese, and Laura Seiffe. 2017. Fastqa: A simple and efficient neural architecture for question answering. *arXiv preprint arXiv:1703.04816* .

Appendices

A   Implementation details

mLSTM was implemented with the Keras framework (Chollet, 2015) using the Theano (Bergstra et al., 2010) backend. Word embeddings are initialized using GloVe vectors (Pennington et al., 2014) pre-trained on the 840-billion *Common Crawl* corpus. The word embeddings are not updated during training. Embeddings for out-of-vocabulary words are initialized with zero.

The training objective is to maximize the log likelihood of the boundary pointers. Optimization is performed using stochastic gradient descent (with a batch-size of 32) with the ADAM optimizer (Kingma and Ba, 2015). The initial learning rate is 0.003. The learning rate is decayed by a factor of 0.7 if validation loss does not decrease at the end of each epoch. Gradient clipping (Pascanu et al., 2013) is applied with a threshold of 5. Parameter tuning is performed on both models using `hyperopt`[4]. Configuration for the best observed performance was as follows:

In *SQuAD* experiments, both the pre-processing layer and the answer-pointing layer use RNNs with a hidden size of 150. These settings are consistent with those used by Wang and Jiang (2016b). In *NewsQA* experiments, both the pre-processing layer and the answer-pointing layer use RNNs with a hidden size of 192.

Model parameters are initialized with either the normal distribution ($\mathcal{N}(0, 0.05)$) or the orthogonal initialization ($\mathcal{O}$, Saxe et al. 2013) in Keras. All weight matrices in the LSTMs are initialized with $\mathcal{O}$. In the Match-LSTM layer, W^q, W^p, and W^r are initialized with $\mathcal{O}$, b^p and w are initialized with $\mathcal{N}$, and b is initialized as 1.

In the answer-pointing layer, V and W^a are initialized with $\mathcal{O}$, b^a and v are initialized with $\mathcal{N}$, and c is initialized as 1.

---

[4] `https://github.com/hyperopt/hyperopt`

Intrinsic and Extrinsic Evaluation of Spatiotemporal Text Representations in Twitter Streams

Lawrence Phillips and **Kyle Shaffer** and **Dustin Arendt** and **Nathan Hodas** and **Svitlana Volkova**
Pacific Northwest National Laboratory
Richland, Washington 99354

Abstract

Language in social media is a dynamic system, constantly evolving and adapting, with words and concepts rapidly emerging, disappearing, and changing their meaning. These changes can be estimated using word representations in context, over time and across locations. A number of methods have been proposed to track these spatiotemporal changes but no general method exists to evaluate the quality of these representations. Previous work largely focused on qualitative evaluation, which we improve by proposing a set of visualizations that highlight changes in text representation over both space and time. We demonstrate usefulness of novel spatiotemporal representations to explore and characterize specific aspects of the corpus of tweets collected from European countries over a two-week period centered around the terrorist attacks in Brussels in March 2016. In addition, we quantitatively evaluate spatiotemporal representations by feeding them into a downstream classification task – event type prediction. Thus, our work is the first to provide both intrinsic (qualitative) and extrinsic (quantitative) evaluation of text representations for spatiotemporal trends.

1 Introduction

Language in social media presents additional challenges for textual representations. Being able to represent texts in social media streams requires a methodology with the following properties:

1. Capable of handling *large amounts* of data.
2. In a *streaming* rather than static fashion.
3. Across *many geographic regions*.

While there has been some recent work for representing change over time in embedding spaces, these methods largely did not take into account geographic variation (Costa et al., 2014; Kim et al., 2014; Kulkarni et al., 2015; Hamilton et al., 2016b,a). Likewise, papers examining geographic variations of language tend not to examine data temporally (Bamman et al., 2014; Kulkarni et al., 2016; Pavalanathan and Eisenstein, 2015; Hovy et al., 2015). Although Kulkarni et al. (2016) incorporate temporal information, they treat each timestep as a separate corpus, learning unique representations. We propose two algorithms to learn spatiotemporal text representations from large amounts of social media data and investigate their utility both from a qualitative and quantitative standpoint.

Indeed, the broader question of how to evaluate the quality of an embedding is one which has received a great deal of attention (Schnabel et al., 2015; Gladkova et al., 2016). Previous spatial and temporal embedding algorithms have been evaluated primarily with qualitative evidence, investigating the ability of the embedding to capture a small number of known meaning shifts and providing some form of visualization (Costa et al., 2014; Kim et al., 2014; Kulkarni et al., 2015, 2016; Hamilton et al., 2016b,a). While it is important to capture known changes of interest, without some form of quantitative evaluation it cannot be known whether these embedding methods actually produce good vector spaces. Because of these issues we not only provide the first spatiotemporal algorithms for learning text embeddings from social media data, but we also evaluate our embedding algorithms through a variety of means.

For **qualitative evaluation**, we develop a set of novel visualizations[1] which allow us to investigate

---

[1] Live Demo: https://esteem.labworks.org/

Proceedings of the 2nd Workshop on Representation Learning for NLP, pages 201–210,
Vancouver, Canada, August 3, 2017. ©2017 Association for Computational Linguistics

word representation shifts across space and time. In particular, we demonstrate that the model captures temporal shifts related to events in our corpus and these shifts vary across distinct countries. For **quantitative evaluation**, we estimate the effectiveness of spatiotemporal embeddings through a downstream event-classification task, demonstrating that temporal and spatial algorithms vary in their usefulness. We choose an extrinsic evaluation task rather than the more standard intrinsic embedding evaluation because of recent work demonstrating weak relationships between intrinsic measures and extrinsic performance (Schnabel et al., 2015; Gladkova et al., 2016).

2 Background

Text Representations Most existing algorithms for learning text representations model the context of words using a continuous bag-of-words approach (Mikolov et al., 2013a), skip-grams with negative sampling (Mikolov et al., 2013b), modified skip-grams with respect to the dependency tree of the sentence (Levy and Goldberg, 2014), or optimized ratio of word co-occurrence probabilities (Pennington et al., 2014).

Text representations have been learned mainly from well-written texts (Al-Rfou et al., 2013). Only recent work has focused on learning embeddings from social media data e.g., Twitter (Pennington et al., 2014). Moreover, most of the existing approaches learn text embeddings in a static (batch) setting. Learning embeddings from streaming social media data is challenging because of problems such as noise, sparsity, and data drift (Kim et al., 2014; Kulkarni et al., 2015).

Embedding Evaluation There are two principle ways one can evaluate embeddings: (a) intrinsic and (b) extrinsic.

(a) **Intrinsic evaluations** directly test syntactic or semantic relationships between the words, and rely on existing NLP resources e.g., WordNet (Miller, 1995) and subjective human judgements e.g., crowdsourcing or expert judgment.

(b) **Extrinsic methods** evaluate word vectors by measuring their performance when used for downstream NLP tasks e.g., dependency parsing, named entity recognition etc. (Passos et al., 2014; Godin et al., 2015)

Recent work suggests that intrinsic and extrinsic measures correlate poorly with one another (Schn-

abel et al., 2015; Gladkova et al., 2016). In many cases we want an embedding not just to capture relationships within the data, but also to do so in a way which can be usefully applied. In these cases, both intrinsic and extrinsic evaluation must be taken into account.

Temporal Embeddings Preliminary work on studying changes in text representations over time has focused primarily on changes over large timescales (e.g. decades or centuries) and in well-structured text such as books. For instance, Kim et al. (2014) present a method to measure change in word semantics across the 20th century by comparing each word's initial meaning with its meanings in later years. Other work explores a wider range of corpora (all based on text from books) and embedding methods and report similar qualitative findings (Hamilton et al., 2016b). What quantitative evidence they do provide is limited to intrinsic evaluations of word similarities as well as the model's ability to recognize a small set of hand-selected known shifts. One attempt at learning over time from social media comes from Costa et al. (2014) that explore a number of online learning methods for updating embeddings across timesteps. They measure the ability of their temporal embeddings to predict Twitter hashtags, but do not compare their results against a non-temporal baseline which makes it difficult to assess the usefulness of learning temporal embeddings. Finally, more recent work learns from Twitter, among other data sources, but presents only qualitative evaluations (Kulkarni et al., 2015).

Spatial Embeddings Work on incorporating space into low-dimensional text representations has been less well researched. Only recent work presents an approach to train embedding models independently across a variety of English-speaking countries as well as US states (Kulkarni et al., 2016). Their model creates a general embedding space which is shared across all regions, as well as a region-specific embedding space which captures local meaning. Although they are able to report a number of meaning differences captured by the model, no general quantitative evaluation is given. The lack of extrinsic evaluation both for temporal and spatial representations highlights a major difficulty for future research. Although it is clear that temporal and spatial patterns can be captured by distributed text representations, unlike other approaches, our work is the first to quali-

Event Types (A)	Clusters	Tweets	Tweet / Cluster	Event Types (B)	Clusters	Tweets	Tweet / Cluster
Arts	321	18,926	144	Politics	329	36,908	270
Business	157	8,961	276	Entertainment	315	18,977	147
Politics	190	18,729	105	Business	208	9,092	97
Justice	138	1,296	27	Crime	175	16,194	233
Conflict	101	1,623	46	Terrorism	97	1,369	41
Life	93	602	20	Transportation	46	196	15
Personnel	53	8,457	412	Celebrity	43	401	22
Contact	28	226	19	Death	35	9,021	646
Transaction	20	175	872	Health	33	178	20
Nature	20	6,960	746	Natural disaster	20	6,953	873

Table 1: Distributions of event types in two annotation schemes: A from Doddington et al. (2004) and B from Metzler et al. (2012).

tatively and quantitatively evaluate whether these patterns can be useful in applied tasks.

Event Type Classification To do this, we focus on event detection, a popular NLP task to detect mentions of relevant real-world events within text documents. Some earlier efforts include TABARI (Schrodt, 2001), GDELT (Leetaru and Schrodt, 2013), TDT (Allan, 2012) challenges, and the Automatic Content Extraction (ACE) program (Doddington et al., 2004). This task can take the form of summarizing events from text (Kedzie et al., 2016), querying information on specific events (Metzler et al., 2012), or clustering together event mentions (Ritter et al., 2012) that all describe the same event.

In this work, we focus on building predictive models to classify event types from raw tweets. Only limited work in event classification has also tried to codify events into specific event types, such as "political" vs. "economic" (Bies et al., 2016). Because the desired granularity of an event type can vary depending on the end-task, we analyze our tweets using modified versions of event types from the ACE program (Doddington et al., 2004) and more topical event types defined by Metzler et al. (2012).

3 Datasets

We make use of three datasets in our experiments. First, we use a large corpus of European Twitter data captured over two weeks in order to learn text representations across time and space. For our event classification task, we chose a subset of tweets in the larger corpus which were made by news accounts. These "news-worthy" tweets were then manually annotated for event type. To leverage the additional available data annotated with real-world events, we train our models on a larger event dataset from Wikipedia and then use transfer learning to apply it to our smaller event data.

Brussels Bombing Twitter Dataset We collected a large sample of tweets (with geo-locations and language IDs assigned to each tweet) from 240 countries in 66 languages from Twitter. Data collection lasted two weeks, beginning on March 15th, 2016 and ending March 29th, 2016. Tweets were filtered based on geo-location and language tags to include only English-language tweets from a set of 34 European countries that had at least 10,000 English tweets per day in the corpus. This resulted in a set of 140M tweets we use to learn different types of embeddings.

Twitter Event Dataset We selected "news-worthy" tweets that discuss real-world events from 400M English tweets generated in 240 countries. Our criterion for selecting "news-worthy" tweets was to only select tweets that contain an action word from the connotation frame lexicon (Rashkin et al., 2016) and either come from a verified account, from a news account e.g., @bbc, @wsj, or contain the hashtag "#breaking" or "#news". We identified 600,000 English *subject-predicate-object* tuples using SyntaxNet (Andor et al., 2016).

Three annotators labeled event types for all tuples based on two previously defined lists of event categories: the ACE event categories (Doddington et al., 2004) and those from a related paper on querying event types (Metzler et al., 2012). Because of missing values for the third annotator, we used Krippendorff's alpha to judge inter-annotator agreement (like Fleiss' kappa, Krippendorff's alpha is ≤ 1 with 1 indicating complete agreement and 0 indicating random chance). This subset of labeled clusters without ties have high inter-annotator agreement: 0.71 and 0.78, respectively. Finally, we subsampled our "news-worthy" tweets to match the 34 European countries in the Brussels dataset. We show the final number of clusters and tweets per event category in Table 1.

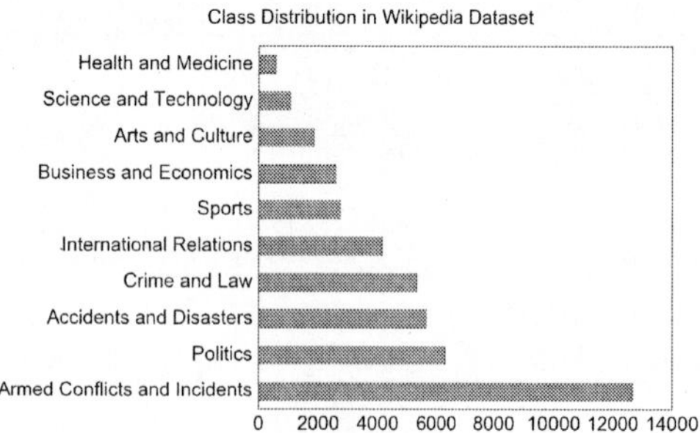

Figure 1: Top 10 classes in the Wikipedia event dataset.

Wikipedia Event Dataset   Given the small size of our Twitter event dataset, we explore additional resources for training an effective event detection model. We construct a larger event dataset by scraping the English language Wikipedia Current Events Portal from the time period of January 2010 to October 2016. Each event in this portal is described in a short summary and is labeled by date along with a subject heading such as *Armed Conflicts and Attacks*. We use these summaries and headings as training data for a neural network to be used for transfer learning.

Overall, the Wikipedia event dataset contains 43,098 total event samples and 31 event type classes. For training, we use the 42,906 samples that correspond to the ten most frequent classes within the dataset, approximately 99.5% of the original data. The distribution of these ten most frequent classes is shown in Figure 1.

4   Methodology

All embeddings were trained using gensim's continuous bag-of-words word2vec algorithm (Řehůřek and Sojka, 2010). All of our embeddings were 100 dimensional with embeddings learned over the full vocabulary. For evaluation, we limit ourselves to vocabulary occurring at least 1,000 times in the Brussels dataset, resulting in a vocabulary size of 36,200.

Temporal Embeddings   We build upon the state-of-the-art algorithm to learn embeddings (Mikolov et al., 2013a). In order to learn embeddings over time we separate our corpus into 8-hour windows, resulting in 45 timesteps. For each timestep, we train a model using the previous timestep's embeddings to initialize the model at time $t + 1$ as shown in Algorithm 1.

This results in an embedding space specific to each timestep capturing any change in meaning which has just occurred. Because timesteps are connected through initialization, we can examine how word representations shift over time.

Spatial Embeddings   The simplest method for learning embeddings across countries is to train a separate set of embeddings for each country independently as shown in Algorithm 2. We use these spatial embeddings without time to investigate the ability of this simple method to capture task-relevant information.

Spatiotemporal Embeddings   We train each spatial region separately, but rather than training over the entire corpus, we train in 8 hour time chunks using the previous timestep for initialization as shown in Algorithm 3.

Global2Specific Embeddings   The disadvantage of training each country's embeddings independently is that countries with more tweets will necessarily possess better learned embeddings. We explore an alternative method where for each timestep, we train a joint embedding using tweets from all countries and use it to initialize the country-specific embeddings on the *following* timestep as shown in Algorithm 4.

By initializing with joint embeddings, high quality vectors for infrequent words can be retained across countries. In cases where a country's usage for a word does not differ from overall

---

Algorithm 1 Temporal Text Representations

1: Initialize $\mathbf{W}^{(0)}$ randomly
2: $\mathbf{W}^{(0)} = $ LearnEmbeddings(C, t_0)
3: **for** timestep t in T **do**
4:     Initialize $\mathbf{W}^{(t)}$ with $\mathbf{W}^{(t-1)}$
5:     $\mathbf{W}^{(t)} = $ LearnEmbeddings(C, t)

Algorithm 2 Spatial Text Representations

1: **for** country c in C **do**
2:     Initialize $\mathbf{W}_{(c)}$ randomly
3:     $\mathbf{W}_{(c)} = $ LearnEmbeddings(c, T)

Algorithm 3 Spatiotemporal Embeddings

1: **for** country c in C **do**
2:     Initialize $\mathbf{W}^{(0)}_{(c)}$ randomly
3:     $\mathbf{W}^{(0)}_{(c)} = $ LearnEmbeddings(c, t_0)
4:     **for** timestep t in T **do**
5:         Initialize $\mathbf{W}^{(t)}_{(c)}$ with $\mathbf{W}^{(t-1)}_{(c)}$
6:         $\mathbf{W}^{(t)}_{(c)} = $ LearnEmbeddings(c, t)

Algorithm 4 Global2Specific Embeddings

1: Initialize $\mathbf{G}^{(0)}$ randomly
2: $\mathbf{G}^{(0)} = \text{LearnEmbeddings}(C, t_0)$
3: **for** timestep t in T **do**
4:     **for** country c in C **do**
5:        Initialize $\mathbf{W}_{(c)}^{(t)}$ with $\mathbf{G}^{(t-1)}$
6:        $\mathbf{W}_{(c)}^{(t)} = \text{LearnEmbeddings}(c, t)$
7:     Initialize $\mathbf{G}^{(t)}$ with $\mathbf{G}^{(t-1)}$
8:     $\mathbf{G}^{(t)} = \text{LearnEmbeddings}(C, t)$

usage, it can still rely on the embeddings learned from a larger data. If the meaning of a word does change in a particular country, this will still be captured as the model learns from that timestep.

Aligning Embeddings Following Hamilton et al. (2016b), we use Procrustes analysis to align embeddings across space and time for more accurate comparison. Procrustes analysis provides an optimal rotation of one matrix with respect to a "target" matrix (in this case a word embedding matrix in the joint space) by minimizing the sum of squared (Euclidean) distances between elements in each of the matrices.

Predictive Models for Wikipedia Events We use subject headings from the Wikipedia event dataset as noisy labels to train a model to predict the ten most frequent classes within the dataset. Weights of the LSTM layer of this model are used to initialize the LSTM layer in the Twitter event classification models.

We divide the Wikipedia event dataset using 10-fold cross-validation, optimizing the network for F_1 score on the validation sets. We searched over hyper-parameters for dropout on all layers, number of units in the fully-connected layer, activation function (rectified linear unit, hyperbolic tangent, or sigmoid), and batch size using the Hyperas library.[2]. The model was trained for 10 epochs, implemented using Keras.[3] Hyperoptimized parameters were then used to train the model on the full dataset to be transferred to the event detection model. We compare the LSTM performance against three simpler models trained on TFIDF features using scikit-learn.[4]

Predictive Models for Twitter Events For each word in each tweet, we first look up the appropriate embedding vector. If a word does not have a corresponding embedding vector, we create an "average vector" from all the word vectors for the appropriate embedding type, and use this as the representation of the word. Preliminary results indicated that averaging produced better results than using a zero-vector. These embedding representations of tweets are fed to a fully-connected dense layer of 100 units. This layer is regularized with 30% dropout, and its outputs are then fed to 100 LSTM units whose weights have been initialized with the LSTM weights learned from our Wikipedia neural network. We tried both freezing these weights in the LSTM layer as well as allowing them to be tuned in the training process, and found that further tuning helped model performance. The output of this LSTM layer is then fed to another densely connected layer of 128 units regularized with 50% dropout, before passing these outputs to a final softmax layer to compute class probabilities and final predictions. We use rectified linear units as the activation function for both densely connected layers, and use the Adam optimization algorithm with a learning rate set to 0.001. We experimented with various other architectures, including adding 1-dimensional convolutional and max-pooling layers between the first dense layer and the LSTM layer, but did not find these to be advantageous.

Baselines and Evaluation Metrics As a baseline, we compare our spatiotemporal embeddings against openly available, pre-trained embeddings – 300-dimensional Word2Vec embeddings trained on Google News, and 100-dimensional GloVe embeddings trained on 2 billion tweets. In addition, we evaluate three simpler classifiers on the the 5- and 10-way event classification problems. We train logistic regression (LR), linear SVM, and a random forest classifier (RF) with 100 decision trees on TFIDF features from our labeled Twitter dataset, and report micro and macro F1 scores over 10-fold c.v. in Table 4 below.

5 Results

Qualitative Evaluation We analyze the results of temporal embeddings when trained over all countries of the Brussels dataset in Figure 2. Time is plotted on the x-axis with every tick indicating a single 8-hour timestep. The distance between ticks is proportional to the change in the keyword's vector representation (Euclidean distance) during that time. Vertical gray bars indicate a change greater than one standard deviation above the mean. For

----

[2]Hyperas: https://github.com/maxpumperla/hyperas
[3]Keras: https://keras.io/
[4]Scikit-learn: http://scikit-learn.org/

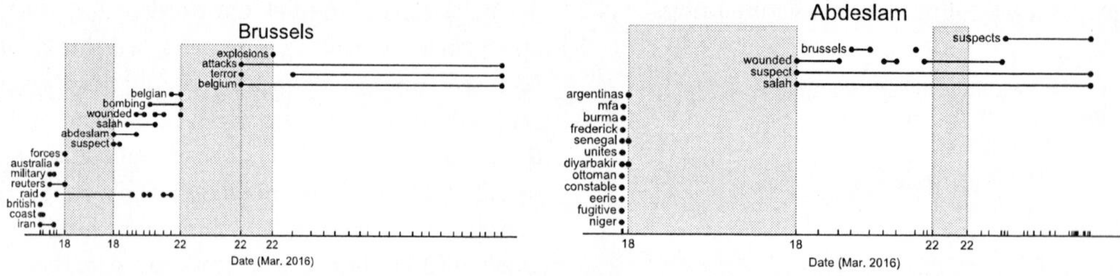

Figure 2: Visualizing temporal embeddings: Top-3 similar keywords to the concepts *Brussels* and *Abdeslam* for each timestamp (similarity is measured using Euclidean distance).

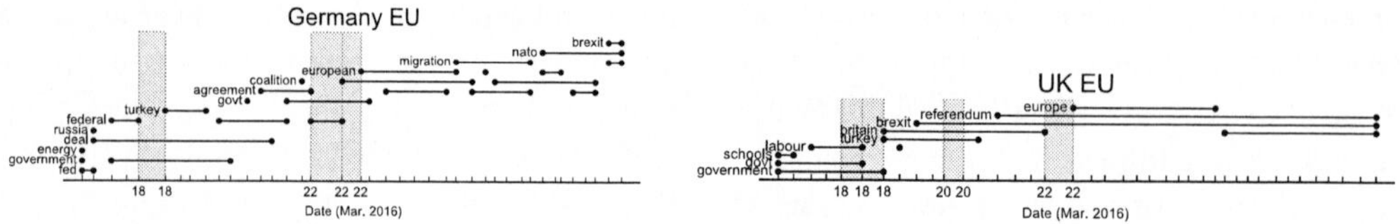

Figure 3: Visualizing spatial (country-specific) embeddings: Top-3 similar keywords to the concept *EU (European Union)* for each timestamp (similarity is measured using Euclidean distance).

each timestep, the three most similar keywords are plotted on the y-axis, with horizontal lines indicating that the keyword was in the top three over that period. We plot the keywords *Brussels* as well as *Abdeslam*, which is the last name of a suspect in the 2015 Paris bombing. For both words we see large shifts in meaning both on March 18th and 22nd. On March 18th, Salah Abdeslam was captured in Brussels during a police raid.[5] Before that date, Abdeslam was not widely mentioned on Twitter and the meaning of his name was not well learned. After his capture, Twitter users picked up the story and the embedding quickly relates Abdeslam to *Salah* (his first name), *suspect*, and *wounded*. Mention of Salah Abdeslam is also visible in the most similar keywords to *Brussels*. On March 22nd the Brussels bombing occurred.[6] and one can see that the embedding of *Brussels* quickly shifts, with *belgium*, *terror*, and *attacks* remaining as the top three similar keywords for all following timesteps.

To understand how different countries discuss a global event, we examined keywords of interest and identified for each country the top k most similar words. Table 2 presents the top-4 similar words to the keyword *Belgium* across five countries in our dataset from the spatial embeddings learned over all timesteps. Each country refer-

Belgium	France	Russia	UK
killed	terrorism	bombers	pakistan
attack	suspect	belgian	bombing
isis	bombings	condolences	iraq
pakistan	turkey	bomber	lahore

Table 2: Most similar words to a query word *Belgium* for country-specific text representations.

ences the bombing which took place on March 22nd, but each country is referring to Belgium in different ways. Belgium and the UK, for instance, draw parallels to the suicide bombing in Lahore, Pakistan on March 27th,[7] while *Brussels* in France and Russia is more linked to the suspect and bomber of the Brussels attack.

Countries discuss topics in ways that grow more similar or distant over time. Looking at the keywords *Brussels* and *Radovan*, we calculate the cosine distance between the word vectors of any two countries and plot the three most extreme country pairs becoming more or less similar over time. For Brussels, we see that before the terror attack on the 22nd, there is a great amount of divergence between countries. After the 22nd, many of these differences disappear as can be seen in the blue lines which indicate the three most-converging country pairs. Belgium itself, however, continues to diverge from other countries even after the 22nd as can be seen in the red lines. Another event during our corpus was the conviction and sentencing

---

[5]https://www.theguardian.com/world/2016/mar/18/paris-attacks-suspect-salah-abdeslam-wounded-in-brussels-terror-raid-reports

[6]http://www.bbc.com/news/world-europe-35869254

[7]http://www.nytimes.com/2016/03/28/world/asia/explosion-lahore-pakistan-park.html

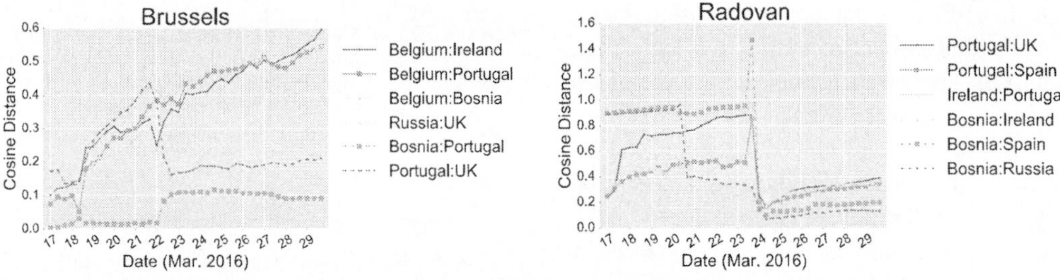

Figure 4: Converging and diverging country pairs for the keywords *Brussels* and *Radovan*. Converging country pairs (in blue) became more similar over time than other pairs. Diverging country pairs (in red) became more dissimilar over time.

Embedding	A5 (4,325)		A10 (5,480)		B5 (5,017)		B10 (5,940)	
	Macro	Micro	Macro	Micro	Macro	Micro	Macro	Micro
Baseline 1: Word2Vec[6]	0.64	0.68	0.49	0.62	0.67	0.68	0.45	0.61
Baseline 2: Glove[7] (2B tweets)	0.66	0.69	0.46	0.59	0.65	0.66	0.43	0.59
Static (140M tweets; upperbound)	0.81	0.82	0.53	0.69	0.78	0.79	0.53	0.72
Temporal (1.4–4.6M tweets)	0.74	0.76	**0.51**	**0.66**	0.75	**0.77**	**0.52**	**0.67**
Spatial (0.2M–81.7M tweets)	0.62	0.66	0.36	0.55	0.65	0.67	0.39	0.57
Spatiotemporal (2K–2.8M tweets)	0.67	0.70	0.41	0.59	0.69	0.71	0.43	0.63
Global2Specific (2K–2.8M tweets)	**0.76**	**0.77**	0.46	0.65	**0.75**	0.77	0.49	0.67

Table 3: Embedding evaluation results (F1) for event detection task (best performance is marked in bold). Tweets from specific timesteps and countries make use of relevant temporal and spatial embeddings where applicable.

of Radovan Karadžić who was found guilty on the 24th for, among many other crimes, the Srebrenica massacre in 1995.[8]

While the cases listed above represent a number of real-world events that can be visualized and captured by the embedding models, we note that not all events will necessarily be captured in this same way. For instance, an event discussed many months in advance, and with many related tweets, may not see the same shifts that characterize the examples provided here. Still, our visualization techniques are able to extract meaningful relations demonstrating possible utility for social scientists hoping to better understand their data.

Quantitative Evaluation We investigate which of our embedding types are most useful for a downstream event classification task. We present a performance comparison between using our embeddings and using pre-trained Word2Vec and GloVe embeddings, as well as performance comparison between a recurrent neural network and three other models. The neural network uses the same batch size, number of epochs, and 10-fold cross-validation scheme as before. Results from our experiments are presented in Tables 3, 4 and 5. We present results of 5- and 10-way classification for each of the annotation schemes (A or B), and denote these as abbreviations of the annotation letter and number of classes e.g., A5.

Table 4 demonstrates the clear effectiveness of our LSTM model, which outperforms all other models in all classification tasks. At minimum, we see a 4.2% increase in $F1$ score over the next best model and in some cases we see an 8.5% increase in $F1$ score. While we see the largest gains in the 5-way classification task, we also see an 8.2% $F1_{macro}$ increase in the 10-way classification task for annotation B. This suggests that at least some of our embeddings are more effective at capturing information relevant to a downstream classification task than other more straightforward linguistic features such as TFIDIF weights. However, this analysis does not determine whether the increased predictive power of the LSTM or the increased information from our embeddings contributes most to this performance boost.

For a more rigorous analysis of our embedding types, we compare their effectiveness as inputs for our LSTM for this event classification task. This is the first attempt to quantitatively measure the performance of spatiotemporal embeddings on a sizable evaluation task made of non-simulated

[8]http://www.nytimes.com/2016/03/25/world/europe/radovan-karadzic-verdict.html

data. In addition to comparing the different types of embeddings, we also compare our embeddings against pre-trained static embeddings. Results for these experiments are given in Table 3. We experimented with increased embedding dimensionality but find only a modest gain and therefore report only for our 100-dimension embeddings.

We find that *static* embeddings trained on the two-week corpus of Twitter data outperform pre-trained embeddings (both Word2Vec and GloVe), even when trained on a much larger quantity of tweets e.g., 140M vs. the 2B used by GLoVe. *Static* embeddings also outperform all spatiotemporal embeddings, likely due to the amount of training data used by each embedding. The spatial algorithm has the worst performance, which also coincides with the fact that the spatial model is unable to share information between different locations. This differs from the temporal, spatiotemporal, and Global2Specific models which are able to share information across timesteps, reducing data sparsity somewhat. Although we find generally lower performance, increased data may improve the spatiotemporal models and these models have the additional advantage that they can be trained online, allowing researchers to study changes as they occur.

The difficulty for naive spatial embeddings is countered by our *Global2Specific* strategy. Recall that in the training process for these embeddings, at each timestep a joint embedding is trained using tweets from all countries. These joint embeddings are then used to initialize the embedding learned for a given country. Intuitively, this initialization should result in better learned embeddings since it leverages all of the data in the joint space (140M tweets) as well as spatiotemporal aspects of the data. While these embeddings do not outperform those learned completely in the joint space, they demonstrate that this training process transfers useful information, outperforming the *spatial* and *spatiotemporal* embeddings.

6   Summary and Discussion

Discourse on social media varies widely over space and time, thus, any static embedding method will have difficulty resolving how events influence discourse. It can be difficult to *a priori* define an effective embedding scheme to capture this without explicitly encoding space and time. In demonstrating the value of spatiotemporal embeddings,

Annotation	F1	LR	SVM	RF	LSTM
A5	Macro	0.68	0.72	0.62	**0.80**
	Micro	0.71	0.74	0.66	**0.82**
A10	Macro	0.42	0.48	0.41	**0.53**
	Micro	0.61	0.64	0.58	**0.69**
B5	Macro	0.70	0.72	0.64	**0.78**
	Micro	0.72	0.72	0.65	**0.79**
B10	Macro	0.37	0.45	0.37	**0.53**
	Micro	0.64	0.65	0.59	**0.72**

Table 4: Results of baseline models and LSTM trained on static embeddings. Best performance is marked in bold.

A10	F1	B10	F1
Arts	0.74	Entertainment	0.79
Business	0.73	Politics	0.71
Conflict	0.73	Business	0.73
Justice	0.64	Crime	0.54
Politics	0.53	Terrorism	0.64
Life	0.56	Celebrity	0.39
Personnel	0.49	Death	0.39
Contact	0.36	Transportation	0.44
Nature	0.24	Natural disaster	0.52
Transaction	0.01	Health	0.42

Table 5: Error analysis: classification results (F1 per class) using Global2Specific embeddings.

we can clearly observe the variation in discourse caused by significant events. We can pinpoint the event, such as the Brussels bombing, down to the resolution of our temporal embedding technique – 8 hours, in this case. We also observe general differences in how discourse varies over geography.

What previous work has not made clear is whether spatiotemporal embeddings also have value in a quantitative sense. Our event classification results show that simple spatiotemporal strategies are not necessarily useful. The value of spatiotemporal learning must be weighed against loss of data when multiple embeddings must be separately trained. The success of our *Global2Specific* embeddings compared to other strategies demonstrates that explicitly accounting for this loss of data is a useful strategy. Future work will need to investigate whether spatiotemporal embeddings have value only when trained on very large data or if better strategies can be incorporated to explicitly model space and time.

7   Acknowledgments

The authors would like to thank Hannah Rashkin (University of Washington), Ian Stewart (Georgia Institute of Technology), Jacob Hunter, Josh Harrison, Eric Bell (PNNL) for their support and assistance with this project.

References

Rami Al-Rfou, Bryan Perozzi, and Steven Skiena. 2013. Polyglot: Distributed word representations for multilingual NLP. *Proceedings of CoNNL* .

James Allan. 2012. *Topic detection and tracking: event-based information organization*, volume 12. Springer Science & Business Media.

Daniel Andor, Chris Alberti, David Weiss, Aliaksei Severyn, Alessandro Presta, Kuzman Ganchev, Slav Petrov, and Michael Collins. 2016. Globally normalized transition-based neural networks. *arXiv preprint arXiv:1603.06042* .

David Bamman, Chris Dyer, and Noah A Smith. 2014. Distributed representations of geographically situated language. In *Proceedings of ACL.*

Ann Bies, Zhiyi Song, Jeremy Getman, Joe Ellis, Justin Mott, Stephanie Strassel, Martha Palmer, Teruko Mitamura, Marjorie Freedman, Heng Ji, and Tim O'Gorman. 2016. A comparison of event representations in deft. In *Workshop on Events: Definition, Detection, Coreference, and Representation.*

Joana Costa, Catarina Silva, Mário Antunes, and Bernardete Ribeiro. 2014. Concept drift awareness in twitter streams. In *Proceedings of ICMLA.* pages 294–299.

George R Doddington, Alexis Mitchell, Mark A Przybocki, Lance A Ramshaw, Stephanie Strassel, and Ralph M Weischedel. 2004. The automatic content extraction (ace) program-tasks, data, and evaluation. In *Proceedings of LREC.*

Anna Gladkova, Aleksandr Drozd, and Computing Center. 2016. Intrinsic evaluations of word embeddings: What can we do better? *Proceedings of ACL* .

Fréderic Godin, Baptist Vandersmissen, Wesley De Neve, and Rik Van de Walle. 2015. Named entity recognition for twitter microposts using distributed word representations. In *Proceedings of ACL-IJCNLP.*

William L Hamilton, Jure Leskovec, and Dan Jurafsky. 2016a. Cultural shift or linguistic drift? comparing two computational measures of semantic change. *Proceedings of EMNLP* .

William L Hamilton, Jure Leskovec, and Dan Jurafsky. 2016b. Diachronic word embeddings reveal statistical laws of semantic change. *Proceedings of ACL* .

Dirk Hovy, Anders Johannsen, and Anders Søgaard. 2015. User review sites as a resource for large-scale sociolinguistic studies. In *Proceedings of WWW.* ACM, pages 452–461.

Chris Kedzie, Fernando Diaz, and Kathleen Mckeown. 2016. Real-Time Web Scale Event Summarization Using Sequential Decision Making. *Proceedings of IJCAI* .

Yoon Kim, Yi-I Chiu, Kentaro Hanaki, Darshan Hegde, and Slav Petrov. 2014. Temporal analysis of language through neural language models. *Proceedings of ACL* .

Vivek Kulkarni, Rami Al-Rfou, Bryan Perozzi, and Steven Skiena. 2015. Statistically significant detection of linguistic change. In *Proceedings of WWW.* pages 625–635.

Vivek Kulkarni, Bryan Perozzi, and Steven Skiena. 2016. Freshman or fresher? quantifying the geographic variation of language in online social media. In *Proceedings of AAAI-WSM.*

Kalev Leetaru and Philip A Schrodt. 2013. Gdelt: Global data on events, location, and tone, 1979–2012. In *ISA.* 4.

Omer Levy and Yoav Goldberg. 2014. Dependency-based word embeddings. In *Proceedings of ACL.* pages 302–308.

Donald Metzler, Congxing Cai, and Eduard Hovy. 2012. Structured event retrieval over microblog archives. *Proceedings of NAACL* pages 646–655.

Tomas Mikolov, Kai Chen, Greg Corrado, and Jeffrey Dean. 2013a. Efficient estimation of word representations in vector space .

Tomas Mikolov, Ilya Sutskever, Kai Chen, Greg S Corrado, and Jeff Dean. 2013b. Distributed representations of words and phrases and their compositionally. In *Proceedings of NIPS.* pages 3111–3119.

George A Miller. 1995. Wordnet: a lexical database for english. *Communications of the ACM* 38(11):39–41.

Alexandre Passos, Vineet Kumar, and Andrew McCallum. 2014. Lexicon infused phrase embeddings for named entity resolution. In *Proceedings of CoNLL.*

Umashanthi Pavalanathan and Jacob Eisenstein. 2015. Confounds and consequences in geotagged twitter data. In *Proceedings of EMNLP.*

Jeffrey Pennington, Richard Socher, and Christopher D Manning. 2014. Glove: Global vectors for word representation. In *Proceedings of EMNLP.* volume 14, pages 1532–43.

Hannah Rashkin, Sameer Singh, and Yejin Choi. 2016. Connotation frames: A data-driven investigation. In *Proceedings of ACL.*

Radim Řehůřek and Petr Sojka. 2010. Software Framework for Topic Modelling with Large Corpora. In *Workshop on New Challenges for NLP Frameworks.*

Alan Ritter, Oren Etzioni, and Sam Clark. 2012. Open domain event extraction from twitter. In *Proceedings of SIGKDD.*

Tobias Schnabel, Igor Labutov, David Mimno, and Thorsten Joachims. 2015. Evaluation methods for unsupervised word embeddings. In *Proceedings of EMNLP*.

Philip A Schrodt. 2001. Automated coding of international event data using sparse parsing techniques. In *ISA*.

Rethinking Skip-thought: A Neighborhood based Approach

Shuai Tang[1], Hailin Jin[2], Chen Fang[2], Zhaowen Wang[2], Virginia R. de Sa[1]
[1]Department of Cognitive Science, UC San Diego, La Jolla CA 92093, USA
[2]Adobe Research, 345 Park Ave., San Jose CA 95110, USA
{shuaitang93,desa}@ucsd.edu, {hljin,cfang,zhawang}@adobe.com

Abstract

We study the skip-thought model proposed by Kiros et al. (2015) with neighborhood information as weak supervision. More specifically, we propose a skip-thought neighbor model to consider the adjacent sentences as a neighborhood. We train our skip-thought neighbor model on a large corpus with continuous sentences, and then evaluate the trained model on 7 tasks, which include semantic relatedness, paraphrase detection, and classification benchmarks. Both quantitative comparison and qualitative investigation are conducted. We empirically show that, our skip-thought neighbor model performs as well as the skip-thought model on evaluation tasks. In addition, we found that, incorporating an autoencoder path in our model didn't aid our model to perform better, while it hurts the performance of the skip-thought model.

1 Introduction

We are interested in learning distributed sentence representation in an unsupervised fashion. Previously, the skip-thought model was introduced by Kiros et al. (2015), which learns to explore the semantic continuity within adjacent sentences (Harris, 1954) as supervision for learning a generic sentence encoder. The skip-thought model encodes the current sentence and then decodes the previous sentence and the next one, instead of itself. Two independent decoders were applied, since intuitively, the previous sentence and the next sentence should be drawn from 2 different conditional distributions, respectively.

By posing a hypothesis that the adjacent sentences provide the same neighborhood informa-

tion for learning sentence representation, we first drop one of the 2 decoders, and use only one decoder to reconstruct the surrounding 2 sentences at the same time. The empirical results show that our skip-thought neighbor model performs as well as the skip-thought model on 7 evaluation tasks. Then, inspired by Hill et al. (2016), as they tested the effect of incorporating an autoencoder branch in their proposed FastSent model, we also conduct experiments to explore reconstructing the input sentence itself as well in both our skip-thought neighbor model and the skip-thought model. From the results, we can tell that our model didn't benefit from the autoencoder path, while reconstructing the input sentence hurts the performance of the skip-thought model. Furthermore, we conduct an interesting experiment on only decoding the next sentence without the previous sentence, and it gave us the best results among all the models. Model details will be discussed in Section 3.

2 Related Work

Distributional sentence representation learning involves learning word representations and the compositionality of the words within the given sentence. Previously, Mikolov et al. (2013b) proposed a method for distributed representation learning for words by predicting surrounding words, and empirically showed that the additive composition of the learned word representations successfully captures contextual information of phrases and sentences. Similarly, Le and Mikolov (2014) proposed a method that learns a fixed-dimension vector for each sentence, by predicting the words within the given sentence. However, after training, the representation for a new sentence is hard to derive, since it requires optimizing the sentence representation towards an objective.

Using an RNN-based autoencoder for language

Proceedings of the 2nd Workshop on Representation Learning for NLP, pages 211–218,
Vancouver, Canada, August 3, 2017. ©2017 Association for Computational Linguistics

representation learning was proposed by Dai and Le (2015). The model combines an LSTM encoder, and an LSTM decoder to learn language representation in an unsupervised fashion on the supervised evaluation datasets, and then finetunes the LSTM encoder for supervised tasks on the same datasets. They successfully show that learning the word representation and the compositionality of words could be done at the same time in an end-to-end machine learning system.

Since the RNN-based encoder processes an input sentence in the word order, it is obvious that the dependency of the representation on the starting words will decrease as the encoder processes more and more words. Tai et al. (2015) modified the plain LSTM network to a tree-structured LSTM network, which helps the model to address the long-term dependency problem. Other than modifying the network structure, additional supervision could also help. Bowman et al. (2016) proposed a model that learns to parse the sentence at the same time as the RNN is processing the input sentence. In the proposed model, the supervision comes from the objective function for the supervised tasks, and the parsed sentences, which means all training sentences need to be parsed prior to training. These two methods require additional preprocessing on the training data, which could be slow if we need to deal with a large corpus.

Instead of learning to compose a sentence representation from the word representations, the skip-thought model Kiros et al. (2015) utilizes the structure and relationship of the adjacent sentences in the large unlabelled corpus. Inspired by the skip-gram model (Mikolov et al., 2013a), and the sentence-level distributional hypothesis (Harris, 1954), the skip-thought model encodes the current sentence as a fixed-dimension vector, and instead of predicting the input sentence itself, the decoders predict the previous sentence and the next sentence independently. The skip-thought model provides an alternative way for unsupervised sentence representation learning, and has shown great success. The learned sentence representation encoder outperforms previous unsupervised pretrained models on 8 evaluation tasks with no finetuning, and the results are comparable to supervised trained models. In Triantafillou et al. (2016), they finetuned the skip-thought models on the Stanford Natural Language Inference (SNLI)

corpus (Bowman et al., 2015), which shows that the skip-thought pretraining scheme is generalizable to other specific NLP tasks.

In Hill et al. (2016), the proposed FastSent model takes summation of the word representations to compose a sentence representation, and predicts the words in both the previous sentence and the next sentence. The results on this semantic related task is comparable with the RNN-based skip-thought model, while the skip-thought model still outperforms the FastSent model on the other six classification tasks. Later, Siamese CBOW (Kenter et al., 2016) aimed to learn the word representations to make the cosine similarity of adjacent sentences in the representation space larger than that of sentences which are not adjacent.

Following the skip-thought model, we designed our skip-thought neighbor model by a simple modification. Section 3 presents the details.

3 Approach

In this section, we present the skip-thought neighbor model. We first briefly introduce the skip-thought model (Kiros et al., 2015), and then discuss how to explicitly modify the decoders in the skip-thought model to get the skip-thought neighbor model.

3.1 Skip-thought Model

In the skip-thought model, given a sentence tuple (s_{i-1}, s_i, s_{i+1}), the encoder computes a fixed-dimension vector as the representation $\mathbf{z}_i$ for the sentence s_i, which learns a distribution $p(\mathbf{z}_i|s_i; \theta_e)$, where θ_e stands for the set of parameters in the encoder. Then, conditioned on the representation $\mathbf{z}_i$, two separate decoders are applied to reconstruct the previous sentence s_{i-1}, and the next sentence s_{i+1}, respectively. We call them previous decoder $p(s_{i-1}|\mathbf{z}_i; \theta_p)$ and next decoder $p(s_{i+1}|\mathbf{z}_i; \theta_n)$, where $\theta.$ denotes the set of parameters in each decoder.

Since the two conditional distributions learned from the decoders are parameterized independently, they implicitly utilize the sentence order information within the sentence tuple. Intuitively, given the current sentence s_i, inferring the previous sentence s_{i-1} is considered to be different from inferring the next sentence s_{i+1}.

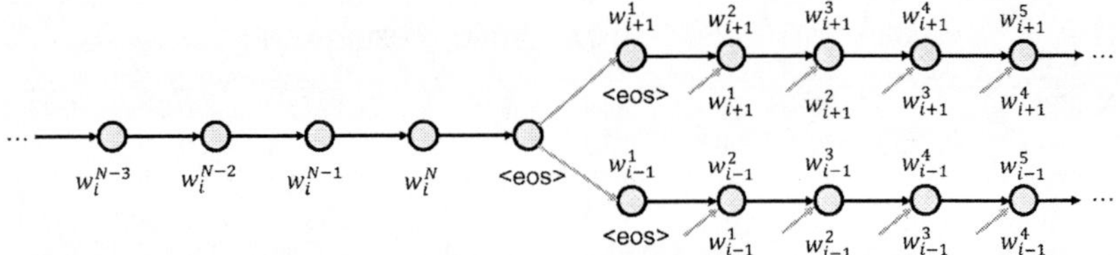

Figure 1: The skip-thought neighbor model. The shared parameters are indicated in colors. The blue arrow represents the dependency on the representation produced from the encoder. For a given sentence s_i, the model tries to reconstruct its two neighbors, s_{i-1} and s_{i+1}.

3.2 Encoder: GRU

In order to make the comparison fair, we choose to use a recurrent neural network with the gated recurrent unit (GRU) (Cho et al., 2014), which is the same recurrent unit used in Kiros et al. (2015). Since the comparison among different recurrent units is not our main focus, we decided to use GRU, which is a fast and stable recurrent unit. In addition, Chung et al. (2014) shows that, on language modeling tasks, GRU performs as well as the long short-term memory (LSTM) (Hochreiter and Schmidhuber, 1997).

Suppose sentence s_i contains N words, which are $w_i^1, w_i^2, ..., w_i^N$. At an arbitrary time step t, the encoder produces a hidden state $\mathbf{h}_i^t$, and we regard it as the representation for the previous subsequence through time t. At time N, the hidden state $\mathbf{h}_i^N$ represents the given sentence s_i, which is $\mathbf{z}_i$. The computation flow of the GRU in our experiments is shown below (omitting the subscript i) :

$$\begin{bmatrix} \mathbf{m}^t \\ \mathbf{r}^t \end{bmatrix} = \sigma \left(\mathbf{W}_h \mathbf{h}^{t-1} + \mathbf{W}_x \mathbf{x}^t \right) \tag{1}$$

$$\hat{\mathbf{h}}^t = \tanh \left(\mathbf{W} \mathbf{x}^t + \mathbf{U} \left(\mathbf{r}^t \odot \mathbf{h}^{t-1} \right) \right) \tag{2}$$

$$\mathbf{h}^t = (1 - \mathbf{m}^t) \odot \mathbf{h}^{t-1} + \mathbf{m}^t \odot \hat{\mathbf{h}}^t \tag{3}$$

where $\mathbf{x}^t$ is the embedding for the word w_i^t, $\mathbf{W}$. and $\mathbf{U}$ are the parameter matrices, and $\odot$ is the element-wise product.

3.3 Decoder: Conditional GRU

The decoder needs to reconstruct the previous sentence s_{i-1} and the next sentence s_{i+1} given the representation $\mathbf{z}_i$. Specifically, the decoder is a recurrent neural network with conditional GRU, and it takes the representation $\mathbf{z}_i$ as an additional input at each time step.

3.4 Skip-thought Neighbor Model

Our hypothesis is that, even without the order information within a given sentence tuple, the skip-thought model should behave similarly in terms of the reconstruction error, and perform similarly on the evaluation tasks. To modify the skip-thought model, given s_i, we assume that inferring s_{i-1} is the same as inferring s_{i+1}. If we define $\{s_{i-1}, s_{i+1}\}$ as the two neighbors of s_i, then the inferring process can be denoted as $s_j \sim p(s|\mathbf{z}_i; \theta_d)$, for any j in the neighborhood of s_i. The conditional distribution learned from the decoder is parameterized by θ_d.

In experiments, we directly drop one of the two decoders, and use only one decoder to reconstruct the previous sentence s_{i-1} and next sentence s_{i+1} at the same time, given the representation $\mathbf{z}_i$ of s_i. Our skip-thought neighbor model can be considered as sharing the parameters between the previous decoder and the next decoder in the original skip-thought model. An illustration is shown in Figure 1.

The objective at each time step is defined as the log-likelihood of the predicted word given the previous words, which is

$$\ell_{i,j}^t(\theta_e, \theta_d) = \log p(w_j^t | w_j^{<t}, \mathbf{z}_i; \theta_e, \theta_d) \tag{4}$$

$$\max_{\theta_e, \theta_d} \sum_i \sum_{j \in \{i-1, i+1\}} \sum_t \ell_{i,j}^t(\theta_e, \theta_d) \tag{5}$$

where θ_e is the set of parameters in the encoder, and θ_d is the set of parameters in the decoder. The loss function is summed across the whole training corpus.

3.5 Skip-thought Neighbor with Autoencoder

Previously, we defined $\{s_{i-1}, s_{i+1}\}$ as the two neighbors of s_i. In addition, we assume that s_i could also be a neighbor of itself. Therefore, the neighborhood of s_i becomes $\{s_{i-1}, s_i, s_{i+1}\}$. In-

Model	MR	CR	SUBJ	MPQA	TREC	MSRP (Acc/F1)	SICK		
							r	ρ	MSE
uni-N-1200	71.5	78.4	90.1	83.4	85.2	72.1 / 81.7	0.8108	0.7382	0.3498
bi-N-1200	71.9	79.3	90.8	85.2	88.8	72.8 / 81.5	0.8294	0.7594	0.3192
combine-N-1200	73.6	80.2	91.4	85.7	89.0	73.5 / 82.1	0.8381	0.7721	0.3039
uni-skip-1200	72.1	77.8	90.5	84.2	86.0	71.5 / 80.8	0.8196	0.7510	0.3350
bi-skip-1200	72.9	79.3	90.6	85.2	87.6	72.9 / 81.6	0.8264	0.7535	0.3237
combine-skip-1200	74.0	80.4	91.5	86.1	87.8	73.7 / 81.7	0.8312	0.7610	0.3164
uni-N-1200+AE	70.8	75.9	90.4	82.7	87.2	73.3 / 81.7	0.8128	0.7450	0.3493
bi-N-1200+AE	71.1	78.4	90.8	83.7	**89.6**	73.2 / 81.7	0.8198	0.7572	0.3389
combine-N-1200+AE	72.4	78.6	91.5	84.3	88.7	**75.4 / 83.0**	0.8347	0.7680	0.3135
uni-skip-1200+AE	68.4	76.5	89.4	81.4	81.6	72.2 / 81.4	0.7888	0.7224	0.3874
bi-skip-1200+AE	70.0	76.4	89.6	81.4	86.0	72.8 / 81.4	0.7908	0.7249	0.3824
combine-skip-1200+AE	71.6	78.0	90.7	83.2	83.2	73.2 / 81.4	0.8086	0.7410	0.3562
uni-N-next-1200	73.3	80.0	90.7	84.9	84.8	73.8 / 81.9	0.8207	0.7512	0.3330
bi-N-next-1200	75.0	80.5	91.1	86.5	87.4	72.3 / 81.3	0.8271	0.7630	0.3223
combine-N-next-1200	**75.8**	**81.8**	**91.9**	**86.8**	88.6	75.0 / 82.5	**0.8396**	**0.7739**	**0.3013**

Table 1: The model name is given by *encoder type - model type - model size* with or without autoencoder branch *+AE*. Bold numbers indicate the best results among all models. Without the autoencoder branch, our skip-thought neighbor models perform as well as the skip-thought models, and our "next" models slightly outperform the skip-thought models. However, with the autoencoder branch, our skip-thought neighbor models outperform the skip-thought models.

ferring $s_j \sim p(s|\mathbf{z}_i; \theta_d)$ for any j in the neighborhood of s_i then involves adding an autoencoder path into to our skip-thought neighbor model. In experiments, the decoder in the model is required to reconstruct all three sentences $\{s_{i-1}, s_i, s_{i+1}\}$ in the neighborhood of s_i at the same time. The objective function becomes

$$\max_{\theta_e, \theta_d} \sum_i \sum_{j \in \{i-1, i, i+1\}} \sum_t \ell_{i,j}^t(\theta_e, \theta_d) \quad (6)$$

Previously Hill et al. (2016) tested adding an autoencoder path into their FastSent model. Their results show that, with the additional autoencoder path, the performance on the classification tasks slightly improved, while there was no significant performance gain or loss on the semantic relatedness task.

We tested both our skip-thought neighbor model and the original skip-thought model with the autoencoder path, respectively. The results are presented in Sections 4, 5 and 6.

3.6 Skip-thought Neighbor with One Target

In our skip-thought neighbor model, for a given sentence s_i, the decoder needs to reconstruct the sentences in its neighborhood $\{s_{i-1}, s_{i+1}\}$, which are two targets. We denote the inference process as $s_i \rightarrow \{s_{i-1}, s_{i+1}\}$. For the next sentence s_{i+1},

the inference process is $s_{i+1} \rightarrow \{s_i, s_{i+2}\}$. In other words, for a given sentence pair $\{s_i, s_{i+1}\}$, the inference process includes $s_i \rightarrow s_{i+1}$ and $s_{i+1} \rightarrow s_i$.

In our hypothesis, the model doesn't distinguish between the sentences in a neighborhood. In this case, an inference process that includes $s_i \rightarrow s_{i+1}$ and $s_{i+1} \rightarrow s_i$ is equivalent to an inference process with only one of them. Thus, we define a skip-thought neighbor model with only one target, and the target is always the next sentence. The objective becomes

$$\max_{\theta_e, \theta_d} \sum_i \sum_t \ell_{i,i+1}^t(\theta_e, \theta_d) \quad (7)$$

4 Experiment Settings

The large corpus that we used for unsupervised training is the BookCorpus dataset (Zhu et al., 2015), which contains 74 million sentences from 7000 books in total.

All of our experiments were conducted in Torch7 (Collobert et al., 2011). To make the comparison fair, we reimplemented the skip-thought model under the same settings, according to Kiros et al. (2015), and the publicly available theano code[1]. We adopted the multi-GPU train-

---

[1] https://github.com/ryankiros/skip-thoughts

ing scheme from the Facebook implementation of ResNet[2].

We use the ADAM (Kingma and Ba, 2014) algorithm for optimization. Instead of applying the gradient clipping according to the norm of the gradient, which was used in Kiros et al. (2015), we directly cut off the gradient to make it within $[-1, 1]$ for stable training.

The dimension of the word embedding and the sentence representation are 620 and 1200. respectively. For the purpose of fast training, all the sentences were zero-padded or clipped to have the same length.

5 Quantitative Evaluation

We compared our proposed skip-thought neighbor model with the skip-thought model on 7 evaluation tasks, which include semantic relatedness, paraphrase detection, question-type classification and 4 benchmark sentiment and subjective datasets. After unsupervised training on the BookCorpus dataset, we fix the parameters in the encoder, and apply it as a sentence representation extractor on the 7 tasks.

For semantic relatedness, we use the SICK dataset (Marelli et al., 2014), and we adopt the feature engineering idea proposed by Tai et al. (2015). For a given sentence pair, the encoder computes a pair of representations, denoted as u and v, and the concatenation of the component-wise product $u \cdot v$ and the absolute difference $|u - v|$ is regarded as the feature for the given sentence pair. Then we train a logistic regression on top of the feature to predict the semantic relatedness score. The evaluation metrics are Pearsons r, Spearmans ρ, and mean squared error MSE.

The dataset we use for the paraphrase detection is the Microsoft Paraphrase Detection Corpus (Dolan et al., 2004). We follow the same feature engineering idea from Tai et al. (2015) to compute a single feature for each sentence pair. Then we train a logistic regression, and 10-fold cross validation is applied to find the optimal hyperparameter settings.

The 5 classification tasks are question-type classification (TREC) (Li and Roth, 2002), movie review sentiment (MR) (Pang and Lee, 2005), customer product reviews (CR) (Hu and Liu, 2004), subjectivity/objectivity classification (SUBJ) (Pang and Lee, 2004), and opinion polarity (MPQA) (Wiebe et al., 2005).

In order to deal with more words besides the words used for training, the same word expansion method, which was introduced by Kiros et al. (2015), is applied after training on the BookCorpus dataset.

The results are shown in Table 1, where the model name is given by *encoder type - model type - model size*. We tried with three different types of the encoder, denoted as *uni-*, *bi-*, and *combine-* in Table 1. The first one is a uni-directional GRU, which computes a 1200-dimension vector as the sentence representation. The second one is a bi-directional GRU, which computes a 600-dimension vector for each direction, and then the two vectors are concatenated to serve as the sentence representation. Third, after training the uni-directional model and the bi-directional model, the representation from both models are concatenated together to represent the sentence, denoted as *combine-*.

In Table 1, *-N-* refers to our skip-thought neighbor model, *-N-next-* refers to our skip-thought neighbor with only predicting the next sentence, and *-skip-* refers to the original skip-thought model.

5.1 Skip-thought Neighbor vs. Skip-thought

From the results we show in Table 1, we can tell that our skip-thought neighbor models perform as well as skip-thought models but with fewer parameters, which means that the neighborhood information is effective in terms of helping the model capture sentential contextual information.

5.2 Skip-thought Neighbor+AE vs. Skip-thought+AE

For our skip-thought neighbor model, incorporating an antoencoder (+AE) means that, besides reconstructing the two neighbors s_{i-1} and s_{i+1}, the decoder also needs to reconstruct s_i. For the skip-thought model, since the implicit hypothesis in the model is that different decoders learn different conditional distributions, we add another decoder in the skip-thought model to reconstruct the sentence s_i. The results are also shown in Table 1.

As we can see, our skip-thought neighbor+AE models outperform skip-thought+AE models significantly. Specifically, in skip-thought model, adding an autoencoder branch hurts the performance on SICK, MR, CR, SUBJ and MPQA

---

[2]https://github.com/facebook/fb.resnet.torch

dataset. We find that the reconstruction error on the autoencoder branch decreases drastically during training, while the sum of the reconstruction errors on the previous decoder and next decoder fluctuates widely, and is larger than that in the model without the autoencoder branch. It seems that, the autoencoder branch hurt the skip-thought model to capture sentential contextual information from the surrounding sentences. One could vary the weights on the three independent branches to get better results, but it is not our main focus in this paper.

In our skip-thought neighbor model, the inclusion of the autoencoder constraint did not have the same problem. With the autoencoder branch, the model gets lower errors on reconstructing all three sentences. However, it doesn't help the model to perform better on the evaluation tasks.

5.3 Increasing the Number of Neighbors

We also explored adding more neighbors into our skip-thought neighbor model. Besides using one decoder to predict the previous 1 sentence, and the next 1 sentence, we expand the neighborhood to contain 4 sentences, which are the previous 2 sentences, and the next 2 sentences. In this case, the decoder is required to reconstruct 4 sentences at the same time. We ran experiments with our model, and we evaluated the trained encoder on 7 tasks.

There is no significant performance gain or loss on our model trained with 4 neighbors; it seems that, increasing the number of neighbors doesn't improve the performance, but it also doesn't hurt the performance. Our hypothesis is that, reconstructing four different sentences in a neighborhood with only one set of parameters is a hard task, which might distract the model from capturing the sentential contextual information.

5.4 Skip-thought Neighbor with One Target

Compared to the skip-thought model, our skip-thought neighbor model with one target contains fewer parameters, and runs faster during training, since for a given sentence, our model only needs to reconstruct its next sentence while the skip-thought model needs to reconstruct its surrounding two sentences. The third section in Table 1 presents the results of our model with only one target. Surprisingly, it overall performs as well as the skip-thought models as all previous models.

5.5 A Note on Normalizing the Representation

An interesting observation was found when we were investigating the publicly available code for Kiros et al. (2015), which is, during training, the representation produced from the encoder will be directly sent to the two decoders, however, after training, the output from the encoder will be normalized to keep the l2-norm as 1, so the sentence representation is a normalized vector.

Model	SICK		
	r	ρ	MSE
uni-N-1200	0.8174	0.7409	0.3404
bi-N-1200	0.8339	0.7603	0.3102
combine-N-1200	0.8360	0.7645	0.3054
uni-skip-1200	0.8232	0.7493	0.3292
bi-skip-1200	0.8280	0.7526	0.3203
combine-skip-1200	0.8340	0.7600	0.3100
uni-N-1200+AE	0.8210	0.7450	0.3493
bi-N-1200+AE	0.8302	0.7610	0.3169
combine-N-1200+AE	0.8326	0.7621	0.3285
uni-skip-1200+AE	0.7959	0.7255	0.3760
bi-skip-1200+AE	0.7986	0.7282	0.3693
combine-skip-1200+AE	0.8129	0.7400	0.3508
uni-N-next-1200	0.8253	0.7508	0.3245
bi-N-next-1200	0.8296	0.7621	0.3175
combine-N-next-1200	**0.8402**	**0.7706**	**0.2999**

Table 2: Evaluation on SICK dataset without normalizing the representation. Bold numbers indicate the best values among all models.

We conducted experiments on the effect of normalization during the evaluation, and we evaluated both on our skip-thought neighbor model, and our implemented skip-thought model. Generally, the normalization step slightly hurts the performance on the semantic relatedness SICK task, while it improves the performance across all the other classification tasks. The Table 1 presents the results with the normalization step, and Table 2 presents the results without normalization on SICK dataset.

6 Qualitative Investigation

We conducted investigation on the decoder in our trained skip-thought neighbor model.

6.1 Sentence Retrieval

We first pick up 1000 sentences as the query set, and then randomly pick up 1 million sentences as the database. In the previous section, we

i wish i had a better answer to that question .
i wish i knew the answer .
i only wish i had an answer .
i kept my eyes on the shadowed road , watching my every step .
i kept my eyes at my feet and up ahead on the trail .
i kept on walking , examining what i could out of the corner of my eye .
the world prepared to go into its hours of unreal silence that made it seem magical , and it really was .
the world changed , and a single moment of time was filled with an hour of thought .
everything that was magical was just a way of describing the world in words it could n't ignore .
my phone buzzed and i awoke from my trance .
i flipped my phone shut and drifted off to sleep .
i grabbed my phone and with groggy eyes , shut off the alarm .
i threw my bag on my bed and took off my shoes .
i sat down on my own bed and kicked off my shoes .
i fell in bed without bothering to remove my shoes .

Table 3: In each section, the first sentence is the query, the second one is the nearest neighbor retrieved from the database, and the third one is the 2nd nearest neighbor. The similarity between every sentence pair is measure by the cosine similarity in the representation space.

mentioned that normalization improves the performance of the model, so the distance measure we applied in the sentence retrieval experiment is the cosine distance. Most of retrieved sentences look semantically related and can be viewed as the sentential contextual extension to the query sentences. Several samples can be found in Table 3.

6.2 Conditional Sentence Generation

" i do n't want to talk about it . "
" i 'm not going to let you drive me home . "
" hey , what 's wrong ? "
i 'm not sure how i feel about him .
i was n't going to be able to get to the beach .
he was n't even looking at her .
" i guess you 're right . "

Table 4: Samples of the generated sentences.

Since the models are trained to minimizing the reconstruction error across the whole training corpus, it is reasonable to analyze the behavior of the decoder on the conditional sentence generation. We first randomly pick up sentences from the training corpus, and compute a representation for each of them. Then, we greedily decode the representations to sentences. Table 4 presents the generated sentences. Several interesting observations worth mentioning here.

The decoder in our skip-thought neighbor model aims to minimize the distance of the generated sentence to two targets, which lead us to doubt if the decoder is able to generate at least grammatically-correct English sentences. But, the results shows that the generated sentences are both grammatically-correct and generally meaningful.

We also observe that, the generated sentences tend to have similar starting words, and usually have negative expression, such as *i was n't, i 'm not, i do n't*, etc. After investigating the training corpus, we noticed that this observation is caused by the dataset bias. A majority of training sentences start with *i* and *i 'm* and *i was* , and there is a high chance that the negation comes after *was* and *'m*. In addition, the generated sentences rarely are the sentential contextual extension of their associated input sentences, which is same for the skip-thought models. More investigations are needed for the conditional sentence generation.

7 Conclusion

We proposed a hypothesis that the neighborhood information is effective in learning sentence representation, and empirically tested our hypothesis. Our skip-thought neighbor models were trained in an unsupervised fashion, and evaluated on 7 tasks. The results showed that our models perform as well as the skip-thought models. Furthermore, our model with only one target performs better than the skip-thought model. Future work could explore more on the our skip-thought neighbor model with only one target, and see if the proposed model is able to generalize to even larger corpora, or another corpus that is not derived from books.

Acknowledgments

We gratefully thank Jeffrey L. Elman, Benjamin K. Bergen, Seana Coulson, and Marta Kutas for insightful discussion, and thank Thomas Andy Keller, Thomas Donoghue, Larry Muhlstein, and Reina Mizrahi for suggestive chatting. We also thank Adobe Research Lab for GPUs support, and thank NVIDIA for DGX-1 trial as well as support from NSF IIS 1528214 and NSF SMA 1041755.

References

Samuel R. Bowman, Gabor Angeli, Christopher Potts, and Christopher D. Manning. 2015. A large annotated corpus for learning natural language inference. In *EMNLP*.

Samuel R. Bowman, Jon Gauthier, Abhinav Rastogi, Raghav Gupta, Christopher D. Manning, and Christopher Potts. 2016. A fast unified model for parsing and sentence understanding. *CoRR* abs/1603.06021.

Kyunghyun Cho, Bart van Merrienboer, Caglar Gulcehre, Dzmitry Bahdanau, Fethi Bougares, Holger Schwenk, and Yoshua Bengio. 2014. Learning phrase representations using rnn encoder-decoder for statistical machine translation. In *EMNLP*.

Junyoung Chung, Caglar Gulcehre, Kyunghyun Cho, and Yoshua Bengio. 2014. Empirical evaluation of gated recurrent neural networks on sequence modeling. *CoRR* abs/1412.3555.

R. Collobert, K. Kavukcuoglu, and C. Farabet. 2011. Torch7: A matlab-like environment for machine learning. In *BigLearn, NIPS Workshop*.

Andrew M. Dai and Quoc V. Le. 2015. Semi-supervised sequence learning. *CoRR* abs/1511.01432.

William B. Dolan, Chris Quirk, and Chris Brockett. 2004. Unsupervised construction of large paraphrase corpora: Exploiting massively parallel news sources. In *COLING*.

Zellig S Harris. 1954. Distributional structure. *Word* 10(2-3):146–162.

Felix Hill, Kyunghyun Cho, and Anna Korhonen. 2016. Learning distributed representations of sentences from unlabelled data. In *HLT-NAACL*.

Sepp Hochreiter and Juergen Schmidhuber. 1997. Long short-term memory. *Neural Computation* 9:1735–1780.

Minqing Hu and Bing Liu. 2004. Mining and summarizing customer reviews. In *KDD*.

Tom Kenter, Alexey Borisov, and Maarten de Rijke. 2016. Siamese cbow: Optimizing word embeddings for sentence representations. *CoRR* abs/1606.04640.

Diederik P. Kingma and Jimmy Ba. 2014. Adam: A method for stochastic optimization. *CoRR* abs/1412.6980.

Jamie Ryan Kiros, Yukun Zhu, Ruslan Salakhutdinov, Richard S. Zemel, Raquel Urtasun, Antonio Torralba, and Sanja Fidler. 2015. Skip-thought vectors. In *NIPS*.

Quoc V. Le and Tomas Mikolov. 2014. Distributed representations of sentences and documents. In *ICML*.

Xin Li and Dan Roth. 2002. Learning question classifiers. In *COLING*.

Marco Marelli, Stefano Menini, Marco Baroni, Luisa Bentivogli, Raffaella Bernardi, and Roberto Zamparelli. 2014. A sick cure for the evaluation of compositional distributional semantic models. In *LREC*.

Tomas Mikolov, Kai Chen, Gregory S. Corrado, and Jeffrey Dean. 2013a. Efficient estimation of word representations in vector space. *CoRR* abs/1301.3781.

Tomas Mikolov, Ilya Sutskever, Kai Chen, Gregory S. Corrado, and Jeffrey Dean. 2013b. Distributed representations of words and phrases and their compositionality. *CoRR* abs/1310.4546.

Bo Pang and Lillian Lee. 2004. A sentimental education: Sentiment analysis using subjectivity summarization based on minimum cuts. In *ACL*.

Bo Pang and Lillian Lee. 2005. Seeing stars: Exploiting class relationships for sentiment categorization with respect to rating scales. In *ACL*.

Kai Sheng Tai, Richard Socher, and Christopher D. Manning. 2015. Improved semantic representations from tree-structured long short-term memory networks. In *ACL*.

Eleni Triantafillou, Jamie Ryan Kiros, Raquel Urtasun, and Richard Zemel. 2016. Towards generalizable sentence embeddings.

Janyce Wiebe, Theresa Wilson, and Claire Cardie. 2005. Annotating expressions of opinions and emotions in language. *Language Resources and Evaluation* 39:165–210.

Yukun Zhu, Jamie Ryan Kiros, Richard S. Zemel, Ruslan Salakhutdinov, Raquel Urtasun, Antonio Torralba, and Sanja Fidler. 2015. Aligning books and movies: Towards story-like visual explanations by watching movies and reading books. *CoRR* abs/1506.06724.

A Frame Tracking Model
for Memory-Enhanced Dialogue Systems

Hannes Schulz[*] and **Jeremie Zumer**[*] and **Layla El Asri** and **Shikhar Sharma**
Microsoft Maluuba
`first.last@microsoft.com`

Abstract

Recently, resources and tasks were proposed to go beyond state tracking in dialogue systems. An example is the frame tracking task, which requires recording multiple frames, one for each user goal set during the dialogue. This allows a user, for instance, to compare items corresponding to different goals. This paper proposes a model which takes as input the list of frames created so far during the dialogue, the current user utterance as well as the dialogue acts, slot types, and slot values associated with this utterance. The model then outputs the frame being referenced by each triple of dialogue act, slot type, and slot value. We show that on the recently published Frames dataset, this model significantly outperforms a previously proposed rule-based baseline. In addition, we propose an extensive analysis of the frame tracking task by dividing it into sub-tasks and assessing their difficulty with respect to our model.

1 Introduction

Conversational agents can seamlessly integrate into our lives by offering a natural language interface for complex tasks. However, the complexity of conversations with current slot-filling dialogue systems is limited. One limitation is that the user usually cannot refer back to an earlier state in the dialogue, which is essential *e.g.*, when comparing alternatives or researching a complex subject.

The recently published Frames dataset (El Asri et al., 2017) provides 1369 goal-oriented human-human dialogues where the participants had to decide on a vacation package to purchase. The authors observed that in order to make up their minds, participants often compared different packages and referred to items that had been previously discussed during the dialogue. Current dialogue systems do not model the dialogue history in a way that a user can go back-and-forth between the different things that have been discussed. To address this shortcoming, El Asri et al. (2017) introduced a new task called *frame tracking*. Frame tracking is an extension of the state tracking (Henderson, 2015; Williams et al., 2016) task.

In a task-oriented dialogue system, the state tracker keeps track of the user goal. The user goal is often represented as the set of constraints that the user has (*e.g.*, a budget) as well as the questions that the user has about the items presented to her by the dialogue system (*e.g.*, the price of the vacation package). It is assumed that the dialogue system only needs to keep track of the last set of constraints given by the user. As a consequence, the user can change her goal during the dialogue but never come back to a previous goal. Frame tracking consists of recording all the different goals set by the user during the dialogue. This requires creating a new frame for each new user goal, which is the annotation provided with the Frames corpus.

A frame tracker needs to be able to assign each new user utterance to the frames it references. This requires understanding which frame the user is talking about and recognizing when the user changes her goal, which implies that a new frame is created. For *e.g.* comparisons, multiple referenced frames need to be identified. This paper proposes a neural model that attempts to solve these tasks.

Proceedings of the 2nd Workshop on Representation Learning for NLP, pages 219–227,
Vancouver, Canada, August 3, 2017. ©2017 Association for Computational Linguistics

[*] Both authors contributed equally.

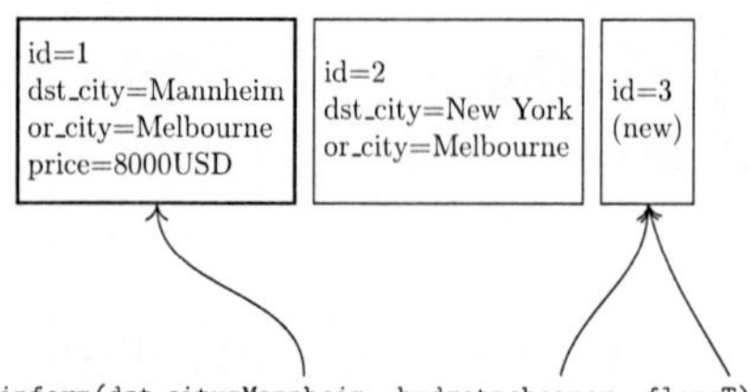

Figure 1: Illustration of the frame tracking task. The model must choose, for each slot, which frame it is referring to, given the set of available frames, the previous active frame (bold), and the potential new frame (marked "(new)").

We show that the model significantly outperforms the baseline proposed by El Asri et al. on all the tasks required to perform frame tracking except for when the user switches frames without specifying slots. We also provide an analysis of frame tracking. In particular, we show that our model knows what frame anaphora refer to almost 90% of the time, and which hotel is being talked about 84.6% of the time. On the other hand, it does not perform well on slots which tend to be repeated in many frames, such as `dst_city` (destination city). It also has difficulties selecting the right frame among similar `offers` introduced in the same dialogue turn.

2 Frame Tracking: An Extension of State Tracking

In a goal-oriented dialogue system, the state tracker records the user goal in a semantic frame (Singh et al., 2002; Raux et al., 2003; El Asri et al., 2014; Laroche et al., 2011). The Dialogue State Tracking Challenge (DSTC) (Williams et al., 2016) defines this semantic frame with the following components:

- User constraints: slots which have been set to a particular value by the user.
- User requests: slots whose values the user wants to know.
- User's search method: the user's way of searching the database (*e.g.*, by constraints or alternatives).

In state tracking, when a new user constraint is set, it overwrites the previous one in the frame. In frame tracking, a new user constraint creates a new frame and thus, there are as many frames as user goals explored during the dialogue.

To deal with user goals, two components specific to this setting were added to a frame, namely:

- User's comparison requests: user requests for this frame and one or more other frames.
- User's binary questions: user questions with slot types and slot values for this frame and possibly one or more other frames.

The user's search method is not part of the semantic frame defined for frame tracking. In addition, a frame is also created when the wizard proposes a vacation package to the user. This type of frame contains the same components as the ones defining a user goal except that the constraints are set by the wizard and not the user. A new frame is created so that if the user wants to consider the package, it is possible to switch to this frame and consider it to be the current user goal.

An example of comparison request is *"Could you tell me which of these resorts offers free wifi?"* and an example of binary question is *"Is this hotel in the downtown area of the city?"* or *"Is the this trip cheaper than the previous one?"*. A user request only has a slot type, *e.g.*, *"Where is this hotel?"* whereas a binary question has a slot type and a slot value. In other words, a binary question amounts to a confirmation and a request, to an open question.

Frames was collected using a Wizard-of-Oz method (WOz, Kelley, 1984; Rieser et al., 2005; Wen et al., 2016): for each dialogue a user and a wizard were paired. The user had a set of constraints and was tasked with finding a good vacation package that fits these constraints. The wizard had access to a database of vacation packages and helped the user find a suitable package. The wizards were thus playing the role of the dialogue system.

Each dialogue turn in the dataset is annotated with the currently active frame, *i.e.*, the frame that is being currently discussed. The corpus was annotated in such a way that both users and wizards could create new frames. On the wizard side, a new frame is created whenever the wizard proposes a new package to the user. However, only the user can switch the currently active frame, for instance, by asking questions about a package proposed by the wizard. The motivation is that the user should have control of the frame being discussed throughout the dialogue, the dialogue system being an assistant to the user.

El Asri et al. (2017) define the frame tracking task as follows:

> For each user turn τ, the full dialogue history $H = \{F_1, ..., F_{n_{\tau-1}}\}$ is available, where F_i is a frame and $n_{\tau-1}$ is the number of frames created up to that turn. The following labels are known for the user utterance u_τ at time τ: dialogue acts, slot types, and slot values. The task is to predict if a new frame is created and to predict the frame or frames that are referenced in each dialogue act. A referenced frame can be the currently active frame or a previous one.

This task is illustrated in Figure 1. We propose a model that tries to solve this task and analyze this model's behavior on several sub-tasks.

3   Related Work

As discussed in the previous section, frame tracking extends state tracking from only tracking the current user goal to tracking all the user goals that occur during the dialogue.

Recently, several approaches to state tracking have attempted to model more complex behaviors than sequential slot-filling. The closest approach to ours is the Task Lineage-based Dialog State Tracking (TL-DST) setting proposed by Lee and Stent (2016). TL-DST is a framework that allows keeping track of multiple tasks across different domains. Similarly to frame tracking, Lee and Stent propose to learn a dynamic structure of the dialogue composed of several frames corresponding to different tasks. TL-DST encompasses several sub-tasks among which *task frame parsing* which consists of assigning a set of new dialogue acts to frames. This relates to frame tracking except that they impose constraints on how a dialogue act can be assigned to a frame and a

dialogue act can only reference one frame. Lee and Stent (2016) trained their tracking model on datasets released for DSTC (DSTC2 and DSTC3, Henderson et al., 2014b,a) because no appropriate data for the task was available at the time. With this data, they could artificially mix different tasks within one dialogue, *e.g.*, looking for a restaurant and looking for a pub, but they could not study human behavior and how humans switch between tasks and frames. Besides, TL-DST allows switching between different tasks but does not allow comparisons which is an important aspect of frame tracking.

Another related approach was proposed by Perez and Liu (2016), who re-interpreted the state tracking task as a question-answering task. Their state tracker is based on a memory network (Weston et al., 2014) and can answer questions about the user goal at the end of the dialogue. They also propose adding other skills such as keeping a list of the constraints expressed by the user during the dialogue. This work did not attempt to formalize the different constraints as separate states to record.

Before describing our frame tracking model, we analyze the frame-switching and frame-creation behavior in Frames.

4   Analysis of Frame References

4.1   Reasons for Referencing Other Frames

The Frames dataset contains 19986 turns, among which 10407 are user turns. In 3785 (36%) of these user turns, the active frame is changed. When the active frame is not changed, the user refers to one or more other frames in 7.5% of the turns.

If we consider only `inform` acts[1], a dialogue system with a traditional state tracker which tracks only a single semantic frame would be able to deal with the subset of frame changes which correspond to overriding an already established value (1684 turns or 44% of the turns where frame changes occur). The remaining 2102 (56%) turns contain `switch_frame` acts from the user. The `switch_frame` act indicates when a user switches from the currently active frame to a previously-defined frame. A `switch_frame` act directly follows one or sev-

---

[1]Utterances where the user informs the wizard of constraints.

eral vacation-package offers from the wizard in 1315 (38%) of the frame-changing turns. In 428 turns, the user selects between multiple offers made by the wizard and in 887 turns, she accepts a single offer made by the wizard. A total of 787 (20%) frame switches are made to a point in the dialogue which is anterior to the directly preceding turn. Note that in this work, we assume that we know the list of all previous frames at each turn of the dialogue but a practical dialogue system should generate this list dynamically during the dialogue. For this reason, it is crucial to also correctly interpret the user's `inform` acts so that if a user appeals to an old frame, this frame exists and is correctly identified.

Most of the turns where the user does not change the active frame but refers to other frames contain `request_compare` (asking to compare different frames, 191), `negate` (98), `request` (28), and `request_alts` (asking for another package, 17) acts.

4.2 Examples

In this section, we categorize instances of interesting frame-related user behavior and discuss the resulting requirements for a frame tracker.

- **Switching to a frame by mentioning a slot value.** "Oh, the Rome deal sounds much better!", "Can you tell me more about the Frankfurt package?", "I'll take the 13 day trip then!".
  For this case, we need to find which frames match the identified slot values, for instance, the destination city in the first example. Since there might be multiple matching frames, we have to incorporate recency information as well. In addition, equivalences have to be taken into account (13 – thirteen, September – sept, NY – Big Apple, etc.). Furthermore, in some cases, we need to learn equivalences between slots. *E.g.*, the user has a budget, but the wizard typically only mentions prices.
- **Switching to a frame without referencing it directly, usually by accepting an offer explicitly or implicitly.** "yeah tell me more!", "yes please", "Reasonable. any free wifi for the kids?".
  The difficult part here is to identify whether the user actually accepted an offer at all, which also modifies the frame if the user asks follow-up questions in the same turn like in the third example. Some users ignore irrelevant wizard offers completely.
- **Switching to a frame using anaphora.** "Yeah, how much does the second trip cost?", "When is this trip and what is the price?", "Give me the first option, thank you".
  This is a slightly more explicit version of the previous case, and requires additional logic to determine the referenced frame based on recency and other mentioned slot values.
- **Implicit reference for comparisons.** "Do these packages have different departure dates?".
- **Explicit reference for comparisons.** "Can you compare the price of this and the one to the package in St. Luis?" (sic)
- **Creating a new frame by specifying a conflicting slot value.** "okaaay, how about to Tijuana then?", "what's the cheapest you got?", "Can I get a longer package if I opt for economy first?"
  Here, the mentioned slot values need to be explicitly compared with the ones in the current frame to identify contradicting values. The same similarities discussed in frame switching above must be considered. The context in which the slot values occur may be crucial to decide whether this is a switch to an old frame or the creation of a new one.
- **Creating a new frame with an explicit reference to a previous one.** "Are there flights from Vancouver leaving around the same time from another departure city?", "I'd like to also compare the prices for a trip to Kobe between the same dates.", "Is there a shorter trip to NY?".
  In these examples, the slots time, date, and duration depend on references to frames (the current frame and the NY frame, respectively).

5 Frame Tracking Model

In the previous section, we identified various ways employed by the users to reference past frames or create new ones. In the following sections, we describe a model for frame tracking, *i.e.*, a model which takes as input the history of past frames as well as the current user utterance and the associated dialogue acts, and which outputs the frames references for each dialogue act.

5.1 Input Encoding

Our model receives three kinds of inputs: the frames that were created before the current turn, the current turn's user dialogue acts without frame references, and the user's utterance. We encode these three inputs before passing them to the network. The frames and the dialogue acts in particular are complex data structures whose encodings are crucial for the model's performance.

5.1.1 Text Encoding

We encode the user text as well as all the slot values by tokenizing the strings[2] and converting each token to letter trigrams[3]. Each trigram $t \in \mathcal{T}$ is represented as its index in a trainable trigram dictionary $D_\mathcal{T}$.

5.1.2 Frame Encoding

We encode only the constraints stored in the set $\mathcal{F}$ containing the frames created before the current turn. In the Frames dataset, each frame $F \in \mathcal{F}$ contains constraints composed of slot-value pairs, where for one slot $s \in \mathcal{S}$ multiple equivalent values (*e.g.*, NY and New York) and additional negated values (for instance if the user says that she does not want to go to a city proposed by the wizard) may be present. We encode a string representation of the most recent non-negated value v as described in Section 5.1.1. The slot type is encoded as an index in a slot type dictionary $D_\mathcal{S}$. The final frame encoding is the concatenation of all slot-value pairs in the frame.

In addition to the encoded frames, we also provide two vectors to the model: a one-hot code f_c marking the frame that was active in the last turn (the bold frame in Figure 1) and a one-hot code f_n marking the frame that will be added if a new frame is created by the user in this turn (the frame marked "(new)" in Figure 1).

---

[2]using nltk's `TweetTokenizer`, www.nltk.org

[3]*E.g.*, "hello" is converted to #he, hel, ell, llo, lo#

5.1.3 Similarity Encoding

To simplify learning of plain value matching, we precompute a matrix $S_L \in \mathbb{R}^{N \times \mathcal{F}}$, which contains the normalized string edit distance of the slot values in the user act to the value of the same slot in each frame, if present.

5.1.4 Recency Encoding

We also provide the model with information about the history of the dialogue by marking recently added as well as recently active frames, coded as h_d^τ and h_c^τ, respectively, at turn τ. For a frame f introduced or last active at turn τ_f, we set

$$
h_\cdot^\tau(f) = \begin{cases} 0 & \text{if } \tau < \tau_f \\ 1 & \text{if } \tau = \tau_f \\ \gamma h_\cdot^{\tau-1} & \text{otherwise.} \end{cases}
$$

5.1.5 Act Encoding

A dialogue act in the current turn has an act name $a \in \mathcal{A}$ and a number of arguments. Each argument has a slot type $s \in \mathcal{S}$ and an optional slot value v. We use a dictionary $D_\mathcal{A}$ to assign a unique index to each act a, and use the same method as described in Section 5.1.2 to encode slot-value pairs. In addition to the N triples (a, s, v), we encode every act a separately, since an act may not have any arguments but still refer to a frame (cf. frame switching examples in Section 4.2).

5.2 Output Encoding

For each triple (a, s, v), our model outputs a multinomial distribution $p_{asv,F}$ over the frames $F \in \mathcal{F}$. Additionally, for each act $a \in \mathcal{A}$ and frame $F \in \mathcal{F}$, we determine the probability $p_{a,F}$ that F is referenced by a.

It can be difficult for the model to correctly predict the cases when the referenced frame is the currently active frame, especially in situations where (a) the slot values do not match and (b) the active frame was changed by an earlier act within the same turn. To address this challenge, in the target, we replace all occurrences of the active frame with a special frame with index 0. In the example of Figure 1, the value `flex=T` would point to this frame 0 since the active frame is changed by a previous value, in this case, the `budget`.

In the loss function, we do not penalize the model for confusing the active frame and the

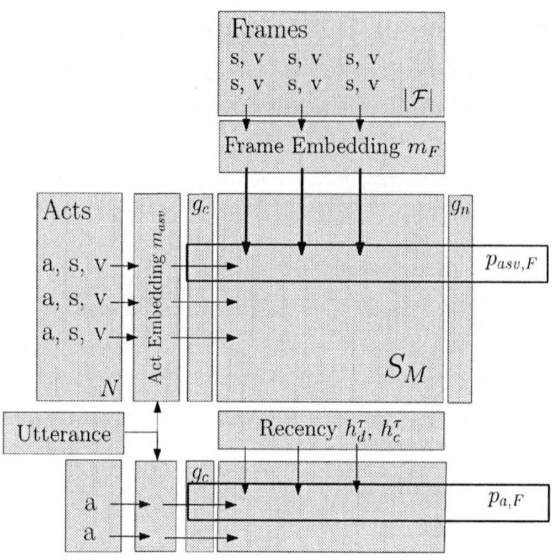

Figure 2: Simplified overview of our model. N triples of acts a with slot-value arguments s, v are matched to frames F by computing a model similarity metric S_M. Frames are described by their constraints (slot-value pairs s, v). Together with the current and new frame indicators (g_c, g_n), S_M represents a multinomial distribution $p_{asv,F}$ over the frames $F \in \mathcal{F}$. The same acts a can refer to additional frames regardless of slot-value arguments, predicted in $p_{a,F}$ with the help of recency information h^τ.

special frame except for `switch_frame` and frame-creating `inform` acts, for which we want the model to predict the referenced frame.

During prediction, we distribute $p_{asv,0}$ over $\mathcal{F}$ according to the predicted active frame:

$$g_s = \begin{cases} 1 & \text{if a } \texttt{switch\_frame} \text{ act is present} \\ 0 & \text{otherwise} \end{cases}$$

$$p_{\text{new}} = p_{asv,|\mathcal{F}|+1}$$

$$p_{asv,F} := p_{asv,F} + p_{asv,0}\big((1 - g_s) \times p_{\text{new}} + g_s \times p_{\text{switch},F}\big),$$

where $p_{\text{switch},\cdot}$ is the distribution assigned by the model to the `switch_frame` act. If no new frame was predicted and no `switch_frame` act is present, the remaining probability mass is assigned to the previously active frame.

5.3 Model Structure

For each user turn, we first embed all dialogue acts a, slot types s, and letter trigrams t using

the dictionaries $D_\mathcal{A}$, $D_\mathcal{S}$, and $D_\mathcal{T}$, respectively. We sum the letter trigram embeddings for every token to generate trigram hashes (Huang et al., 2013). A bidirectional GRU (Cho et al., 2014) r_t over the hashes of values and the utterance generates summary vectors for both. The summary vector is the concatenation of the final hidden state of the forward and backward computation.

A second bi-directional GRU r_{asv} computes a hidden activation for each of the (act, slot, value) triples in the current turn. We compute a value summary vector m_{asv} by appending each hidden state of r_{asv} with the utterance embedding and projecting to a 256-dimensional space.

For the frames, we proceed in a similar manner, except that the frames do not contain dialogue acts nor an utterance, so we use a GRU r_F to compute hidden states for all slot-value pairs

$$\begin{pmatrix} D_\mathcal{S}[s_1], r_t(D_\mathcal{T}[v_1]) \\ D_\mathcal{S}[s_2], r_t(D_\mathcal{T}[v_2]) \\ \dots \end{pmatrix}. \tag{1}$$

During training, the constraint order within frames is shuffled. The final hidden of the state r_F is projected to a 256-dimensional space, resulting in a frame summary vector m_F.

By comparing slot values m_{asv} mentioned by the user to the frames m_F, and taking into account the recently-active and recently-added information, we can determine which frame the user is referencing. To this end, we compute the dot-product between m_{asv} and m_F, resulting in a model similarity matrix $S_M \in \mathbb{R}^{N \times |\mathcal{F}|}$. It is important to have the user utterance in the value summary vector because without it, the comparison with the frames would only work if slot values were explicitly mentioned, which is not true in general. Boolean values, for example, are usually only present implicitly (*cf.* Section 4.2). We learn the weights of a linear combination of the model similarity matrix with the input S_L, yielding the final similarity matrix S.

Two special cases remain: (1) no match could be found and (2) a new frame should be created. To handle these cases, we extend S with two columns corresponding to the active frame g_c and the new frame g_n. Intuitively, g_n

Lesion	Accuracy (%)								
	Full Acts	Only Acts	Frames	Text	h_c^τ	h_d^τ	f_n	S_L	f_c
Slot-based	58.3	66	63.7	74.5	65.4	78.8	79.5	64.4	82.7
Act-based	98	98.3	93.9	94.2	89.8	85.8	90.2	97.1	92.8

Table 1: Accuracy when removing model inputs.

is high if no frame matches the user turn and if there is a strong discrepancy with the active frame. On the other hand, g_c is high only if no frame matches the user turn. Since again, the actual user utterance sometimes contains crucial information, we condition g_n and g_c on the maximum match with any frame, the match with the previously active frame, and the user utterance embedding.

For a user input triple (a, s, v), the slot-based frame prediction is then computed as

$$p_{asv} = \mathrm{softmax}(g_c, S_{asv,1}, S_{asv,2}, \dots, \quad (2)$$
$$S_{asv,|\mathcal{F}|}, g_n).$$

Finally, we determine the act-based probability of frame references $p_{a,F}$. For every pair (a, F), this probability is computed by a 2 layer densely connected network conditioned on the dialogue act, the recency information, and the user utterance embedding. We also set $p_{a,0}$ to $1 - \max_F p_{a,F}$ to produce an implicit reference to the active frame by default.

6   Experiments

6.1   Learning Protocol and Metrics

We train the model by splitting the dataset into 10 folds as described by El Asri et al. (2017). For each fold, we further split the training corpus into training and validation sets by withholding a random selection of 20% of the dialogues from training. We use the Adam (Kingma and Ba, 2014) algorithm to minimize the sum of the loss for p_{asv} and $p_{a,F}$, with a learning rate of 10^{-3}. Learning is stopped when the minimum validation error has not changed for ten epochs. We compare our model to the simple rule-based baseline described by El Asri et al. (2017).

For slot-based predictions $(p_{asv,F})$, we report mean accuracy over the ten folds of the Frames dataset. For act-based predictions $(p_{a,F})$, *i.e.*, we determine for every act a whether the

	Accuracy (%)	
	Ours	**Baseline**
Slot-based	**76.43**±4.49	61.32±2.19
Act-based	**95.66**±2.34	66.81±2.58

Table 2: Performance comparison between the baseline of El Asri et al. (2017) and our model.

	Accuracy (%)	
	Ours	**Baseline**
Frame change (new val)	52.5	4.2
No frame change (new val)	93.8	74.3
Frame change (no offer)	36.4	22.7
Frame change (offer)	67	62.2
request_compare	70.5	40.9

Table 3: Partial comparison table of performance for different dialogue settings (cf Section 4), including frame changes/lack of frame changes upon the introduction of new values, as well as when preceded by an offer or not, demonstrating our model's improvements over the baseline.

ground truth set of referenced frames is equal to the predicted set of referenced frames (with a cutoff at $p_{a,F} = \frac{1}{2}$), and again average accuracy scores over the ten folds.

Results are summarized in Table 2. Our model strongly outperforms the baseline both on references with and without slots. In particular, we observe that our model excels at predicting frame references based on acts alone, while the baseline struggles to solve this task.

6.2   Comparison with the Baseline

We further analyze the difference in performance between our frame tracking model and the rule-based baseline on classes of predictions on a single fold of the data. We organize turns in the test set into 11 classes and measure performance by computing accuracy only on

	Accuracy (%)	
	Ours	**Baseline**
`switch_frame(dst_city)`	66.1	21.4
`switch_frame(duration)`	52.6	26.3
`inform(seat)`	60.0	36.0
`request(end_date)`	66.7	0.0

Table 4: Partial comparison table of act-slot combinations between our model and the baseline of (El Asri et al., 2017).

turns that fall into the respective class.

We first observe that the baseline model almost completely fails to identify frame changes when a new value is introduced by a user (4% accuracy over 303 turns), frame changes associated with `switch_frame` acts that do not have slot values, or when a `switch_frame` act is present in a turn following one that does not contain an `offer` act. On the other hand, the baseline model predicts lacks of frame changes (74.3% over 1111 instances) and frame changes after an `offer` (62.2% over 312 instances) quite well.

Our model dominates the rule-based baseline on all classes except for the prediction of frame changes with `switch_frame` acts that do not have slot values (4.2% over 24 occurrences). Partial comparison results are presented in Table 3.

Perhaps surprisingly, our model correctly predicts 70.5% of frames associated with `request_compare` acts whereas the baseline only correctly identifies 40.9% of them.

We then computed the accuracy on the set of unique act and slot combinations in the dataset. Here, our model outperforms the baseline on all act-slot pairs with more than 10 occurrences in the test set. We observe that the baseline performs quite poorly on `switch_frames` with `dst_city` (destination city) slots, whereas our model does not have such a drawback. The same is true for a `switch_frame` with a `duration` or for an `inform` with a `seat` (economy or business flight seat) or even a `request` with an `end_date`. Results are presented in Table 4. We note that our model performs worse on combinations that should express a match with a frame whose slot values use very different spellings (such as rich abbreviations

and synonyms) whereas the baseline model is the weakest when slot values can be easily confused for values of other slots (*e.g.* a rating of 5 (stars) vs. a duration of 5 (days)). Our model is also currently unable to distinguish between similar offers introduced in the same turn.

Code to generate the full set of metrics will be made available.

6.3 Lesion Studies

To assess which of the features are useful for the model, we remove the model's inputs one at a time and measure the model's performance. Results are shown in Table 1. We observe that the model stops learning (*i.e.* its performance does not exceed the baseline's) on the act-slot-value triples when any of the input is removed except for the new frame history, new frame candidate, and previous frame inputs. Similarly, the model performance suffers when the new frame candidate, any historical data, or the frames are removed. We observe that all the inputs are used by the model in its predictions either for $p_{asv,F}$ or p_{a},F.

7 Discussion

Our model makes use of the text to correctly predict the frames associated with acts. Dependence on input text means our method is domain-dependent. The annotation process for the Frames dataset is costly, so it would be beneficial if we could transfer learned frame switching behavior to other domains, possibly with already existing NLU components. A possible solution might be to standardize the text after NLU, and use anonymous placeholders instead of domain-specific words.

Additionally, our current model assumes a perfect NLU to provide acts, slots, and values as inputs. While this is helpful for researching the frame referencing issues in isolation, both components should work together. For example, currently, we assume that a `switch_frame` act is correctly identified, but we do not know the frame the user wants to switch to. In a more realistic pipeline, these decisions are closely related and also need to take more of the dialogue history into account.

7.1 Conclusion

In this paper, we provided a thorough analysis of user behavior concerning switching between different user goals in the Frames dataset. Based on this analysis, we have designed a frame tracking model that outperforms the baseline of El Asri et al. (2017) by almost 20% relative performance. This model assigns the dialogue acts of a new user utterance to the semantic frames created during the dialogue, each frame corresponding to a goal. We analyzed the strengths and weaknesses of the rule-based baseline and of our model on different subtasks of frame tracking. Our model outperforms the baseline on all but one subtasks. We showed that further improvement is necessary for matching slot values when they are present in many distinct frames. We have demonstrated that the frame tracking task can be performed effectively by learning from data (our model correctly identifies frame changes in about 3 out of 4 cases). This represents a first step toward memory-enhanced dialogue systems which understand when a user refers to an older topic in a conversation and which provide more accurate advice by understanding the full context of a request.

References

Kyunghyun Cho, Bart van Merrienboer, Dzmitry Bahdanau, and Yoshua Bengio. 2014. On the Properties of Neural Machine Translation: Encoder-Decoder Approaches. *arXiv:1409.1259 [cs, stat]* .

L. El Asri, H. Schulz, S. Sharma, J. Zumer, J. Harris, E. Fine, R. Mehrotra, and K. Suleman. 2017. Frames: A Corpus for Adding Memory to Goal-Oriented Dialogue Systems. *arXiv:1704.00057 [cs.CL]* https://datasets.maluuba.com/Frames.

Layla El Asri, Remi Lemonnier, Romain Laroche, Olivier Pietquin, and Hatim Khouzaimi. 2014. NASTIA: Negotiating Appointment Setting Interface. In *LREC.* pages 266–271.

M. Henderson, B. Thomson, and J. Williams. 2014a. The Third Dialog State Tracking Challenge. In *Proc. of IEEE Spoken Language Technology.*

Matthew Henderson. 2015. Machine learning for dialog state tracking: A review. In *Proc. of The First International Workshop on Machine Learning in Spoken Language Processing.*

Matthew Henderson, Blaise Thomson, and Jason D. Williams. 2014b. The second dialog state tracking challenge. In *Proc. of SIGDIAL.*

Po-Sen Huang, Xiaodong He, Jianfeng Gao, Li Deng, Alex Acero, and Larry Heck. 2013. Learning deep structured semantic models for web search using clickthrough data. In *Proc. of ACM.* pages 2333–2338.

John F. Kelley. 1984. An iterative design methodology for user-friendly natural language office information applications. *ACM Transactions on Information Systems (TOIS)* 2(1):26–41.

Diederik Kingma and Jimmy Ba. 2014. Adam: A method for stochastic optimization. *arXiv:1412.6980 [cs.LG]* .

Romain Laroche, Ghislain Putois, Philippe Bretier, Martin Aranguren, Julia Velkovska, Helen Hastie, Simon Keizer, Kai Yu, Filip Jurcicek, Oliver Lemon, and others. 2011. Final evaluation of classic towninfo and appointment scheduling systems. Technical report.

Sungjin Lee and Amanda Stent. 2016. Task lineages: Dialog state tracking for flexible interaction. In *Proc. of SIGDIAL.*

Julien Perez and Fei Liu. 2016. Dialog state tracking, a machine reading approach using memory network. In *Proc. of EACL.*

Antoine Raux, Brian Langner, Black Alan, and Maxine Eskenazi. 2003. LET's GO: Improving Spoken Dialog Systems for the Elderly and Non-natives. In *Proc. of Eurospeech.*

Verena Rieser, Ivana Kruijff-Korbayov, and Oliver Lemon. 2005. A corpus collection and annotation framework for learning multimodal clarification strategies. In *SIGdial Workshop on Discourse and Dialogue.*

Satinder Singh, Diane Litman, Michael Kearns, and Marilyn Walker. 2002. Optimizing dialogue management with reinforcement learning: Experiments with the NJFun system. *Journal of Artificial Intelligence Research* 16:105–133.

Tsung-Hsien Wen, David Vandyke, Nikola Mrksic, Milica Gasic, Lina M. Rojas-Barahona, Pei-Hao Su, Stefan Ultes, and Steve Young. 2016. A Network-based End-to-End Trainable Task-oriented Dialogue System. *arXiv:1604.04562 [cs, stat]* .

Jason Weston, Sumit Chopra, and Antoine Bordes. 2014. Memory networks. *arXiv:1410.3916 [cs.AI]* .

Jason D. Williams, Antoine Raux, and Matthew Henderson. 2016. The dialog state tracking challenge series: A review. *Dialogue and Discourse* .

Plan, Attend, Generate: Character-Level Neural Machine Translation with Planning

Caglar Gulcehre[*]
University of Montreal

Francis Dutil[*]
University of Montreal

Adam Trischler
Microsoft Research

Yoshua Bengio
University of Montreal

Abstract

We investigate the integration of a planning mechanism into an encoder-decoder architecture with attention. We develop a model that can plan ahead when it computes alignments between the source and target sequences not only for a single time-step, but for the next k timesteps as well by constructing a matrix of proposed future alignments and a commitment vector that governs whether to follow or recompute the plan. This mechanism is inspired by strategic attentive reader and writer (STRAW) model, a recent neural architecture for planning with hierarchical reinforcement learning that can also learn higher level temporal abstractions. Our proposed model is end-to-end trainable with differentiable operations. We show that our model outperforms strong baselines on character-level translation task from WMT'15 with less parameters and computes alignments that are qualitatively intuitive.

1 Introduction

Character-level neural machine translation (NMT) is an attractive research problem (Lee et al., 2016; Chung et al., 2016; Luong and Manning, 2016) because it addresses important issues encountered in word-level NMT. Word-level NMT systems can suffer from problems with rare words(Gulcehre et al., 2016) or data sparsity, and the existence of compound words without explicit segmentation in certain language pairs can make learning alignments and translations more difficult. Character-level neural machine translation mitigates these issues.

In this work we propose integrating a planning algorithm with the standard encoder-decoder architecture for character-level NMT, using planning

specifically to improve the alignment between source and target sequences. We cast alignment (also called *attention*) as a planning problem, whereas it has traditionally been treated as a search problem.

The model we propose creates an explicit plan of source-target alignments to use at future time-steps, based on its current observation and a summary of its past actions; it may modify this plan as needed. The planning mechanism itself is inspired by the *strategic attentive reader and writer* (STRAW) of Vezhnevets et al. (2016).

Our work is motivated by the intuition that, although natural language (speech and writing) is *generated* sequentially because of human physiological constraints, it is almost certainly not *conceived* word-by-word.

Planning, i.e., choosing some goal along with candidate macro-actions to arrive at it, is one way to induce *coherence* in natural language. Learning to generate long coherent sequences or how to form alignments over long source contexts is difficult for existing models. In the case of machine translation, performance of encoder-decoder models with attention deteriorates as sequence length increases (Cho et al., 2014; Sutskever et al., 2014). This effect can be more pronounced in character-level NMT, because the length of sequences in character-level translation can be much longer than word-level translation. A planning mechanism could make the decoder's search for alignments more tractable and scalable.

Our model is based on the well-known encoder-decoder framework for NMT. Its encoder is a recurrent neural network (RNN) that reads the source (a sequence of byte pairs representing text in some language) and encodes it as a sequence of vector representations; the decoder is a second RNN that generates the target translation character-by-character in the target language. The decoder uses an attention mechanism to align its internal state to vectors in the source encoding that are relevant to the current generation step

---

[*] Equal Contribution

Proceedings of the 2nd Workshop on Representation Learning for NLP, pages 228–234,
Vancouver, Canada, August 3, 2017. ©2017 Association for Computational Linguistics

(see Bahdanau et al. (2015) for the original description). To plan ahead explicitly rather than focusing primarily on what is relevant at the present time, our model's internal state is augmented with (i) an *action plan* matrix and (ii) a *commitment plan* vector. The action plan matrix is a template of alignments that the model intends to follow at future time-steps, specifically a sequence of probability distributions over source tokens. The commitment plan vector governs whether to recompute the action plan or to continue following it, and as such models discrete decisions.

Because of computational constraints we here apply planning only on the input sequence, via searching for alignments. We find this alignment-based planning to be helpful in the translation task. For other NLP tasks, however, planning could be applied explicitly for generation as well. Recent work by Bahdanau et al. (2016) on actor-critic methods for sequence prediction, for example, can be seen as this kind of generative planning.

We evaluate our model and report results on character-level translation tasks from WMT'15 for English to German, English to Finnish, and English to Czech language pairs. On almost all pairs we observe improvements over a baseline that represents the state-of-the-art in neural character-level translation. In our NMT experiments, our model outperforms the baseline despite using significantly fewer parameters and converges faster in training.

2 Planning for Character-level Neural Machine Translation

We now describe how to integrate a planning mechanism into a sequence-to-sequence architecture with attention (Bahdanau et al., 2015). Our model first creates a *plan*, then computes a soft *alignment* based on the plan, and *generates* at each time-step in the decoder. We refer to our model as PAG (Plan-Attend-Generate).

2.1 Notation and Encoder

As input our model receives a sequence of tokens, $X = (x_0, \cdots, x_{|X|})$, where $|X|$ denotes the length of X. It processes these with the encoder, a bidirectional RNN. At each input position i we obtain annotation vector $\mathbf{h}_i$ by concatenating the forward and backward encoder states, $\mathbf{h}_i = [\mathbf{h}_i^{\rightarrow}; \mathbf{h}_i^{\leftarrow}]$, where $\mathbf{h}_i^{\rightarrow}$ denotes the hidden state of the encoder's forward RNN and $\mathbf{h}_i^{\leftarrow}$ denotes the hidden state of the encoder's backward RNN.

Through the decoder the model predicts a sequence of output tokens, $Y = (y_1, \cdots, y_{|Y|})$. We denote by $\mathbf{s}_t$ the hidden state of the decoder RNN generating the target output token at time-step t.

2.2 Alignment and Decoder

Our goal is a mechanism that plans which parts of the input sequence to focus on for the next k time-steps of decoding. For this purpose, our model computes an alignment plan matrix $\mathbf{A}_t \in \mathbb{R}^{k \times |X|}$ and commitment plan vector $\mathbf{c}_t \in \mathbb{R}^k$ at each time-step. Matrix $\mathbf{A}_t$ stores the alignments for the current and the next $k-1$ timesteps; it is conditioned on the current input, i.e. the token predicted at the previous time-step $\mathbf{y}_t$, and the current context ψ_t, which is computed from the input annotations $\mathbf{h}_i$. The recurrent decoder function, $f_{\text{dec-rnn}}(\cdot)$, receives $\mathbf{s}_{t-1}$, $\mathbf{y}_t$, ψ_t as inputs and computes the hidden state vector

$$\mathbf{s}_t = f_{\text{dec-rnn}}(\mathbf{s}_{t-1}, \mathbf{y}_t, \psi_t). \tag{1}$$

Context ψ_t is obtained by a weighted sum of the encoder annotations,

$$\psi_t = \sum_i^{|X|} \alpha_{ti} \mathbf{h}_i, \tag{2}$$

where the soft-alignment vector $\alpha_t = \mathtt{softmax}(\mathbf{A}_t[0]) \in \mathbb{R}^{|X|}$ is a function of the first row of the alignment matrix. At each time-step, we compute a candidate alignment-plan matrix $\bar{\mathbf{A}}_t$ whose entry at the ith row is

$$\bar{\mathbf{A}}_t[i] = f_{\text{align}}(\mathbf{s}_{t-1}, \mathbf{h}_j, \beta_t^i, \mathbf{y}_t), \tag{3}$$

where $f_{\text{align}}(\cdot)$ is an MLP and β_t^i denotes a summary of the alignment matrix's i^{th} row at time $t-1$. The summary is computed using an MLP, $f_r(\cdot)$, operating row-wise on $\mathbf{A}_{t-1}$: $\beta_t^i = f_r(\mathbf{A}_{t-1}[i])$.

The commitment plan vector $\mathbf{c}_t$ governs whether to follow the existing alignment plan, by shifting it forward from $t-1$, or to recompute it. Thus, $\mathbf{c}_t$ represents a discrete decision. For the model to operate discretely, we use the recently proposed Gumbel-Softmax trick (Jang et al., 2016; Maddison et al., 2016) in conjunction with the straight-through estimator (Bengio et al., 2013) to backpropagate through $\mathbf{c}_t$.[1] The model further learns the temperature for the Gumbel-Softmax as proposed in (Gulcehre et al., 2017). Both the commitment vector and the action plan matrix are initialized with ones; this initialization is not modified through training.

---

[1] We also experimented with training $\mathbf{c}_t$ using REINFORCE (Williams, 1992) but found that Gumbel-Softmax led to better performance.

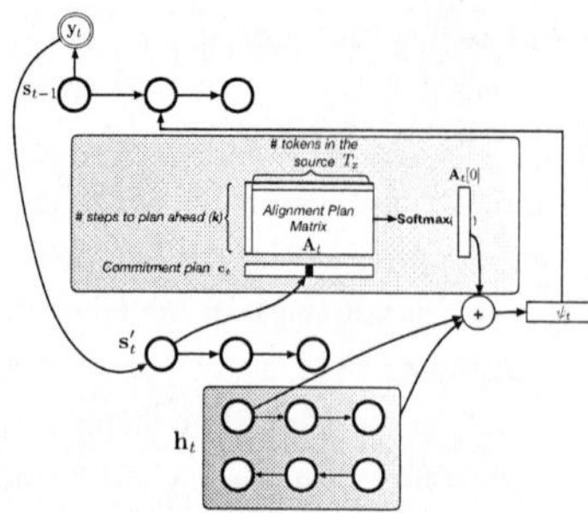

Figure 1: Our planning mechanism in a sequence-to-sequence model that learns to plan and execute alignments. Distinct from a standard sequence-to-sequence model with attention, rather than using a simple MLP to predict alignments our model makes a plan of future alignments using its alignment-plan matrix and decides when to follow the plan by learning a separate commitment vector. We illustrate the model for a decoder with two layers $\mathbf{s}'_t$ for the first layer and the $\mathbf{s}_t$ for the second layer of the decoder. The planning mechanism is conditioned on the first layer of the decoder ($\mathbf{s}'_t$).

Alignment-plan update Our decoder updates its alignment plan as governed by the commitment plan. Denoted by g_t the first element of the discretized commitment plan $\bar{\mathbf{c}}_t$. In more detail, $g_t = \bar{\mathbf{c}}_t[0]$, where the discretized commitment plan is obtained by setting $\mathbf{c}_t$'s largest element to 1 and all other elements to 0. Thus, g_t is a binary indicator variable; we refer to it as the commitment switch. When $g_t = 0$, the decoder simply advances the time index by shifting the action plan matrix $\mathbf{A}_{t-1}$ forward via the shift function $\rho(\cdot)$. When $g_t = 1$, the controller reads the action-plan matrix to produce the summary of the plan, β^i_t. We then compute the updated alignment plan by interpolating the previous alignment plan matrix $\mathbf{A}_{t-1}$ with the candidate alignment plan matrix $\bar{\mathbf{A}}_t$. The mixing ratio is determined by a learned update gate $\mathbf{u}_t \in \mathbb{R}^{k \times |X|}$, whose elements $\mathbf{u}_{ti}$ correspond to tokens in the input sequence and are computed by an MLP with sigmoid activation, $f_{\mathrm{up}}(\cdot)$:

$$\mathbf{u}_{ti} = f_{\mathrm{up}}(\mathbf{h}_i, \mathbf{s}_{t-1}),$$
$$\mathbf{A}_t[:,i] = (1 - \mathbf{u}_{ti}) \odot \mathbf{A}_{t-1}[:,i] + \mathbf{u}_{ti} \odot \bar{\mathbf{A}}_t[:,i].$$

To reiterate, the model only updates its alignment plan when the current commitment switch g_t is active. Otherwise it uses the alignments planned and committed at previous time-steps.

Algorithm 1: Pseudocode for updating the alignment plan and commitment vector.

```
for j ∈ {1,···|X|} do
    for t ∈ {1,···|Y|} do
        if g_t = 1 then
            c_t = softmax(f_c(s_{t-1}))
            β_t^j = f_r(A_{t-1}[j])  {Read alignment plan}
            Ā_t[i] = f_align(s_{t-1}, h_j, β_t^i, y_t)
            {Compute candidate alignment plan}
            u_{ti} = f_up(h_i, s_{t-1}, ψ_{t-1})  {Compute update gate}
            A_t = (1 − u_{ti}) ⊙ A_{t-1} + u_{ti} ⊙ Ā_t
            {Update alignment plan}
        else
            A_t = ρ(A_{t-1})  {Shift alignment plan}
            c_t = ρ(c_{t-1})  {Shift commitment plan}
        end if
        Compute the alignment as α_t = softmax(A_t[0])
    end for
end for
```

Commitment-plan update The commitment plan also updates when g_t becomes 1. If g_t is 0, the shift function $\rho(\cdot)$ shifts the commitment vector forward and appends a 0-element. If g_t is 1, the model recomputes $\mathbf{c}_t$ using a single layer MLP ($f_c(\cdot)$) followed by a Gumbel-Softmax, and $\bar{\mathbf{c}}_t$ is recomputed by discretizing $\mathbf{c}_t$ as a one-hot vector:

$$\mathbf{c}_t = \texttt{gumbel\_softmax}(f_c(\mathbf{s}_{t-1})), \qquad (4)$$
$$\bar{\mathbf{c}}_t = \texttt{one\_hot}(\mathbf{c}_t). \qquad (5)$$

We provide pseudocode for the algorithm to compute the commitment plan vector and the action plan matrix in Algorithm 2. An overview of the model is depicted in Figure 1.

2.2.1 Alignment Repeat

In order to reduce the model's computational cost, we also propose an alternative approach to computing the candidate alignment-plan matrix at every step. Specifically, we propose a model variant that reuses the alignment from the previous time-step until the commitment switch activates, at which time the model computes a new alignment. We call this variant *repeat, plan, attend, and generate* (rPAG). rPAG can be viewed as learning an explicit segmentation with an implicit planning mechanism in an unsupervised fashion. Repetition can reduce the computational complexity of the alignment mechanism drastically; it also eliminates the need for an explicit alignment-plan matrix, which reduces the model's memory consumption as well. We provide pseudocode for rPAG in Algorithm 2.

Algorithm 2: Pseudocode for updating the repeat alignment and commitment vector.

> **for** $j \in \{1, \cdots |X|\}$ **do**
>   **for** $t \in \{1, \cdots |Y|\}$ **do**
>   **if** $g_t = 1$ **then**
> $\mathbf{c}_t = \texttt{softmax}(f_c(\mathbf{s}_{t-1}, \psi_{t-1}))$
> $\alpha_t = \texttt{softmax}(f_{\text{align}}(\mathbf{s}_{t-1}, \mathbf{h}_j, \mathbf{y}_t))$
>   **else**
> $\mathbf{c}_t = \rho(\mathbf{c}_{t-1})$ {Shift the commitment vector $\mathbf{c}_{t-1}$}
> $\alpha_t = \alpha_{t-1}$ {Reuse the old the alignment}
>   **end if**
>   **end for**
> **end for**

2.3 Training

We use a deep output layer (Pascanu et al., 2013) to compute the conditional distribution over output tokens,

$$p(\mathbf{y}_t | \mathbf{y}_{<t}, \mathbf{x}) \propto \mathbf{y}_t^{\top} \exp(\mathbf{W}_o f_o(\mathbf{s}_t, \mathbf{y}_{t-1}, \psi_t)), \quad (6)$$

where $\mathbf{W}_o$ is a matrix of learned parameters and we have omitted the bias for brevity. Function f_o is an MLP with $\tanh$ activation.

The full model, including both the encoder and decoder, is jointly trained to minimize the (conditional) negative log-likelihood

$$\mathcal{L} = -\frac{1}{N} \sum_{n=1}^{N} \log p_\theta(\mathbf{y}^{(n)} | \mathbf{x}^{(n)}),$$

where the training corpus is a set of $(\mathbf{x}^{(n)}, \mathbf{y}^{(n)})$ pairs and θ denotes the set of all tunable parameters. As noted in (Vezhnevets et al., 2016), the proposed model can learn to recompute very often which decreases the utility of planning. In order to avoid this behavior, we introduce a loss that penalizes the model for committing too often,

$$\mathcal{L}_{\text{com}} = \lambda_{\text{com}} \sum_{t=1}^{|X|} \sum_{i=0}^{k} || \frac{1}{k} - \mathbf{c}_{ti} ||_2^2, \quad (7)$$

where λ_{com} is the commitment hyperparameter and k is the timescale over which plans operate.

3 Experiments

Character-level neural machine translation (NMT) is an attractive research problem (Lee et al., 2016; Chung et al., 2016; Luong and Manning, 2016) because it addresses important issues encountered in word-level NMT. Word-level NMT systems can suffer from problems with rare words (Gulcehre et al., 2016) or data sparsity, and the existence of compound words without explicit segmentation in some language pairs can make learning alignments between different languages and translations to be more difficult. Character-level neural machine translation mitigates these issues.

In our NMT experiments we use byte pair encoding (BPE) (Sennrich et al., 2015) for the source sequence and characters at the target, the same setup described in Chung et al. (2016). We also use the same preprocessing as in that work.[2] We present our experimental results in Table 2. Models were tested on the WMT'15 tasks for English to German (En→De), English to Czech (En→Cs), and English to Finnish (En→Fi) language pairs. The table shows that our planning mechanism improves translation performance over our baseline (which reproduces the results reported in (Chung et al., 2016) to within a small margin). It does this with fewer updates and fewer parameters. We trained (r)PAG for 350K updates on the training set, while the baseline was trained for 680K updates. We used 600 units in (r)PAG's encoder and decoder, while the baseline used 512 in the encoder and 1024 units in the decoder. In total our model has about 4M fewer parameters than the baseline. We tested all models with a beam size of 15.

As can be seen from Table 2, layer normalization (Ba et al., 2016) improves the performance of PAG model significantly. However, according to our results on En→De, layer norm affects the performance of our rPAG only marginally. Thus, we decided not to train rPAG with layer norm on other language pairs.

In Table 1, we present the results for PAG using the biscale decoder.

Table 1: WMT'15 En→De Results

	Beam Size	Development	Test Set
Baseline	8	20.39	20.11
Baseline	24	20.52	20.39
PAG	8	21.19	20.84
PAG	24	**21.26**	**20.98**

In Figure 2, we show qualitatively that our model constructs smoother alignments. At each word that the baseline decoder generates, it aligns the first few characters to a word in the source sequence, but for the remaining characters places the largest alignment weight on the last, empty token of the source sequence. This is because the baseline becomes confident of which word to generate after the first few

---

[2] Our implementation is based on the code available at `https://github.com/nyu-dl/dl4mt-cdec`

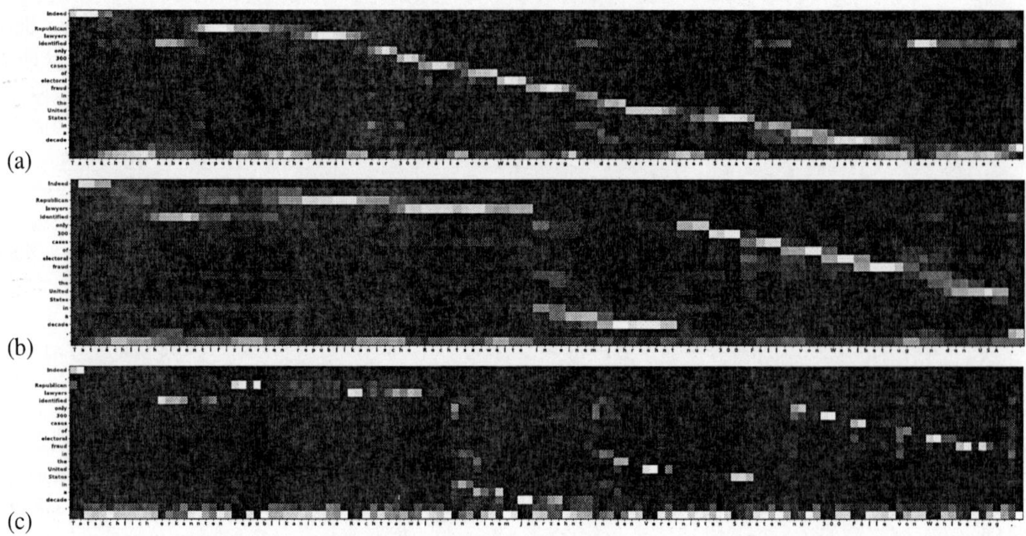

Figure 2: We visualize the alignments learned by PAG in (a) and the biscale baseline model in (b). As depicted, the alignments learned by PAG look more accurate intuitively and appear smoother than those of the baseline. The baseline tends to focus too much attention on the last word of the sequence, which is sensible to do on average because of German's structure, whereas our model places higher weight on the last word mainly when it generates a space token.

	Model	Layer Norm	Dev	Test 2014	Test 2015
	Baseline	✗	21.57	21.33	**23.45**
	Baseline[†]	✗	21.4	21.16	22.1
En→De	PAG	✗	21.52	21.35	22.21
		✓	**22.12**	**21.93**	22.83
	rPAG	✗	21.81	21.71	22.45
		✓	21.67	21.81	22.73
	Baseline	✗	17.68	19.27	16.98
En→Cs	PAG	✗	17.44	18.72	16.99
		✓	**18.78**	**20.9**	**18.59**
	rPAG	✗	17.83	19.54	17.79
	Baseline	✗	11.19	-	10.93
En→Fi	PAG	✗	11.51	-	11.13
		✓	**12.67**	-	**11.84**
	rPAG	✗	11.50	-	10.59

Table 2: The results of different models on WMT'15 task on English to German, English to Czech and English to Finnish language pairs. We report BLEU scores of each model computed via the *multi-blue.perl* script. The best-score of each model for each language pair appears in bold-face. We use *newstest2013* as our development set, *newstest2014* as our "Test 2014" and *newstest2015* as our "Test 2015" set. ([†]) denotes the results of the baseline that we trained using the hyperparameters reported in (Chung et al., 2016) and the code provided with that paper. For our baseline, we only report the median result, and do not have multiple runs of our models.

characters, and it generates the remainder of the word mainly by relying on language-model predictions. We observe that (r)PAG converges faster with the help of the improved alignments, as illustrated by the learning curves in Figure 3.

4 Conclusions and Future Work

In this work we addressed a fundamental issue in neural generation of long sequences by integrating *planning* into the alignment mechanism of sequence-to-sequence architectures. We proposed two different planning mechanisms: PAG, which constructs explicit plans in the form of stored matrices, and rPAG, which plans implicitly and is computationally cheaper. The

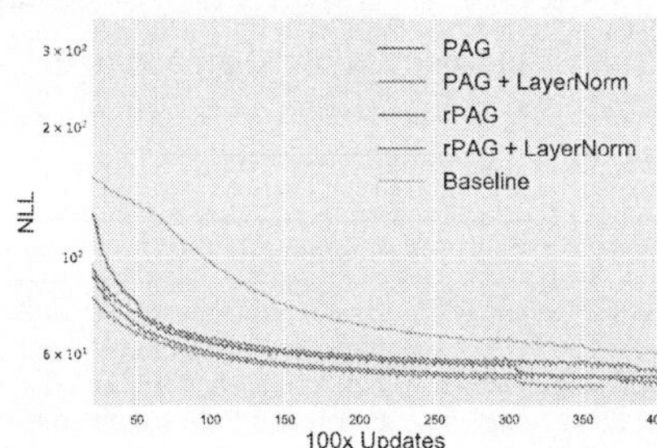

Figure 3: Learning curves for different models on WMT'15 for En→De. Models with the planning mechanism converge faster than our baseline (which has larger capacity).

(r)PAG approach empirically improves alignments over long input sequences. We demonstrated our models' capabilities through results on character-level machine translation, an algorithmic task, and question generation. In machine translation, models with planning outperform a state-of-the-art baseline on almost all language pairs using fewer parameters. As a future work, we plan to test our planning mechanism at the outputs of the model and other sequence to sequence tasks as well.

References

Jimmy Lei Ba, Jamie Ryan Kiros, and Geoffrey E Hinton. 2016. Layer normalization. *arXiv preprint arXiv:1607.06450* .

Dzmitry Bahdanau, Philemon Brakel, Kelvin Xu, Anirudh Goyal, Ryan Lowe, Joelle Pineau, Aaron Courville, and Yoshua Bengio. 2016. An actor-critic algorithm for sequence prediction. *arXiv preprint arXiv:1607.07086* .

Dzmitry Bahdanau, Kyunghyun Cho, and Yoshua Bengio. 2015. Neural machine translation by jointly learning to align and translate. *International Conference on Learning Representations (ICLR)* .

Yoshua Bengio, Nicholas Léonard, and Aaron Courville. 2013. Estimating or propagating gradients through stochastic neurons for conditional computation. *arXiv preprint arXiv:1308.3432* .

Kyunghyun Cho, Bart Van Merriënboer, Dzmitry Bahdanau, and Yoshua Bengio. 2014. On the properties of neural machine translation: Encoder-decoder approaches. *arXiv preprint arXiv:1409.1259* .

Junyoung Chung, Kyunghyun Cho, and Yoshua Bengio. 2016. A character-level decoder without explicit segmentation for neural machine translation. *arXiv preprint arXiv:1603.06147* .

Caglar Gulcehre, Sungjin Ahn, Ramesh Nallapati, Bowen Zhou, and Yoshua Bengio. 2016. Pointing the unknown words. *arXiv preprint arXiv:1603.08148* .

Caglar Gulcehre, Sarath Chandar, and Yoshua Bengio. 2017. Memory augmented neural networks with wormhole connections. *arXiv preprint arXiv:1701.08718* .

Eric Jang, Shixiang Gu, and Ben Poole. 2016. Categorical reparameterization with gumbel-softmax. *arXiv preprint arXiv:1611.01144* .

Jason Lee, Kyunghyun Cho, and Thomas Hofmann. 2016. Fully character-level neural machine translation without explicit segmentation. *arXiv preprint arXiv:1610.03017* .

Minh-Thang Luong and Christopher D Manning. 2016. Achieving open vocabulary neural machine translation with hybrid word-character models. *arXiv preprint arXiv:1604.00788* .

Chris J Maddison, Andriy Mnih, and Yee Whye Teh. 2016. The concrete distribution: A continuous relaxation of discrete random variables. *arXiv preprint arXiv:1611.00712* .

Razvan Pascanu, Caglar Gulcehre, Kyunghyun Cho, and Yoshua Bengio. 2013. How to construct deep recurrent neural networks. *arXiv preprint arXiv:1312.6026* .

Rico Sennrich, Barry Haddow, and Alexandra Birch. 2015. Neural machine translation of rare words with subword units. *arXiv preprint arXiv:1508.07909* .

Ilya Sutskever, Oriol Vinyals, and Quoc V Le. 2014. Sequence to sequence learning with neural networks. In *Advances in neural information processing systems*. pages 3104–3112.

Alexander Vezhnevets, Volodymyr Mnih, John Agapiou, Simon Osindero, Alex Graves, Oriol Vinyals, and Koray Kavukcuoglu. 2016. Strategic attentive writer for learning macro-actions. In *Advances in Neural Information Processing Systems*. pages 3486–3494.

Ronald J Williams. 1992. Simple statistical gradient-following algorithms for connectionist reinforcement learning. *Machine learning* 8(3-4):229–256.

A   Qualitative Translations from both Models

In Table 3, we present example translations from our model and the baseline along with the ground-truth. [3]

Table 3: Randomly chosen example translations from the development-set.

	Groundtruth	Our Model (PAG + Biscale)	Baseline (Biscale)
1	Eine republikanische Strategie , um der Wiederwahl von Obama entgegenzutreten	Eine republikanische Strategie gegen die Wiederwahl von Obama	Eine republikanische Strategie zur Bekämpfung der Wahlen von Obama
2	Die Führungskräfte der Republikaner rechtfertigen ihre Politik mit der Notwendigkeit , den Wahlbetrug zu bekämpfen .	Republikanische Führungspersönlichkeiten haben ihre Politik durch die Notwendigkeit gerechtfertigt , Wahlbetrug zu bekämpfen .	Die politischen Führer der Republikaner haben ihre Politik durch die Notwendigkeit der Bekämpfung des Wahlbetrugs gerechtfertigt .
3	Der Generalanwalt der USA hat eingegriffen , um die umstrittensten Gesetze auszusetzen .	Die Generalstaatsanwälte der Vereinigten Staaten intervenieren , um die umstrittensten Gesetze auszusetzen .	Der Generalstaatsanwalt der Vereinigten Staaten hat dazu gebracht , die umstrittensten Gesetze auszusetzen .
4	Sie konnten die Schäden teilweise begrenzen	Sie konnten die Schaden teilweise begrenzen	Sie konnten den Schaden teilweise begrenzen
5	Darüber hinaus haben Sie das Recht von Einzelpersonen und Gruppen beschränkt , jenen Wählern Hilfestellung zu leisten , die sich registrieren möchten .	Darüber hinaus begrenzten sie das Recht des Einzelnen und der Gruppen , den Wählern Unterstützung zu leisten , die sich registrieren möchten .	Darüber hinaus unterstreicht Herr Beaulieu die Bedeutung der Diskussion Ihrer Bedenken und Ihrer Familiengeschichte mit Ihrem Arzt .

---

[3]These examples are randomly chosen from the first 100 examples of the development set. None of the authors of this paper can speak or understand German.

Does the Geometry of Word Embeddings Help Document Classification?
A Case Study on Persistent Homology Based Representations

Paul Michel[*]
Carnegie Mellon University
pmichel1@cs.cmu.edu

Abhilasha Ravichander[*]
Carnegie Mellon University
aravicha@cs.cmu.edu

Shruti Rijhwani[*]
Carnegie Mellon University
srijhwan@cs.cmu.edu

Abstract

We investigate the pertinence of methods from algebraic topology for text data analysis. These methods enable the development of mathematically-principled isometric-invariant mappings from a set of vectors to a document embedding, which is stable with respect to the geometry of the document in the selected metric space. In this work, we evaluate the utility of these topology-based document representations in traditional NLP tasks, specifically document clustering and sentiment classification. We find that the embeddings do not benefit text analysis. In fact, performance is worse than simple techniques like *tf-idf*, indicating that the geometry of the document does not provide enough variability for classification on the basis of topic or sentiment in the chosen datasets.

1 Introduction

Given a embedding model mapping words to n dimensional vectors, every document can be represented as a finite subset of $\mathbb{R}^n$. Comparing documents then amounts to comparing such subsets. While previous work shows that the Earth Mover's Distance (Kusner et al., 2015) or distance between the weighted average of word vectors (Arora et al., 2017) provides information that is useful for classification tasks, we wish to go a step further and investigate whether useful information can also be found in the 'shape' of a document in word embedding space.

Persistent homology is a tool from algebraic topology used to compute topological signatures (called *persistence diagrams*) on compact metric spaces. These have the property of being stable with respect to the Gromov-Haussdorff distance (Gromov et al., 1981). In other words, compact metric spaces that are close, up to an isometry, will have similar embeddings. In this work, we examine the utility of such embeddings in text classification tasks. To the best of our knowledge, no previous work has been performed on using topological representations for traditional NLP tasks, nor has any comparison been made with state-of-the-art approaches.

We begin by considering a document as the set of its word vectors, generated with a pretrained word embedding model. These form the metric space on which we build persistence diagrams, using Euclidean distance as the distance measure. The diagrams are a representation of the document's geometry in the metric space. We then perform clustering on the Twenty Newsgroups dataset with the features extracted from the persistence diagram. We also evaluate the method on sentiment classification tasks, using the Cornell Sentence Polarity (CSP) (Pang and Lee, 2005) and IMDb movie review datasets (Maas et al., 2011).

As suggested by Zhu (2013), we posit that the information about the intrinsic geometry of documents, found in the persistence diagrams, might yield information that our classifier can leverage, either on its own or in combination with other representations. The primary objective of our work is to empirically evaluate these representations in the case of sentiment and topic classification, and assess their usefulness for real-world tasks.

2 Method

2.1 Word embeddings

As a first step we compute word vectors for each document in our corpus using a word2vec (Mikolov et al., 2013) model trained on the Google

---

*The indicated authors contributed equally to this work.

Proceedings of the 2nd Workshop on Representation Learning for NLP, pages 235–240,
Vancouver, Canada, August 3, 2017. ©2017 Association for Computational Linguistics

News dataset[1]. In addition to being a widely used word embedding technique, word2vec has been known to exhibit interesting linear properties with respect to analogies (Mikolov et al., 2013), which hints at rich semantic structure.

2.2 Gromov-Haussdorff Distance

Given a dictionary of word vectors of dimension n, we can represent any document as a finite subset of $\mathbb{R}^n$. The *Haussdorff distance* gives us a way to evaluate the distance between two such sets. More precisely, the Haussdorff distance d_H between two finite subsets A, B of $\mathbb{R}^n$ is defined as:

$$d_H(A, B) = \max(\sup_{a \in A} d(a, B), \sup_{b \in B} d(b, A))$$

where $d(x, Y) = \inf_{y \in Y} \|x - y\|_2$ is the distance of point x from set Y.

However, this distance is sensitive to translations and other isometric[2] transformations. Hence, a more natural metric is the **Gromov-Haussdorff distance** (Gromov et al., 1981), simply defined as

$$d_{GH}(A, B) = \inf_{f \in E_n} d_H(A, f(B))$$

where E_n is the set of all isometries of $\mathbb{R}^n$.

Figure 1 provides an example of practical Gromov-Haussdorff (GH) distance computation between two sets of three points each. Both sets are embedded in $\mathbb{R}^2$ (middle panel) using isometries i.e the distance between points in each set is conserved. The Haussdorff distance between the two embedded sets corresponds to the length of the black segment. The GH distance is the minimum Haussdorff distance under all possible isometric embeddings.

We want to compare documents based on their intrinsic geometric properties. Intuitively, the GH distance measures how far two sets are from being isometric. This allows us to define the geometry of a document more precisely:

Definition 1 (Document Geometry) *We say that two documents A, B have the same* geometry *if $d_{GH}(A, B) = 0$, ie if they are the same up to an isometry.*

Mathematically speaking, this amounts to defining the geometry of a document as its equivalence class under the equivalence relation induced by the GH distance on the set of all documents.

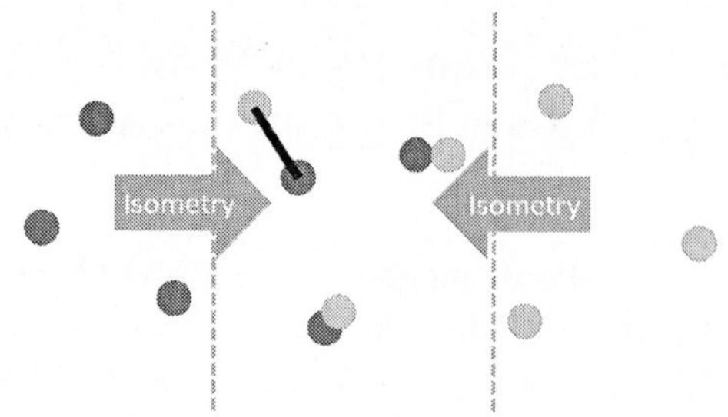

Figure 1: Gromov-Haussdorff distance between two sets (red, green). The black bar represents the actual distance (given that the isometric embedding is optimal).

Comparison to the Earth Mover Distance : Kusner et al. (2015) proposed a new method for computing a distance between documents based on an instance of the Earth Mover Distance (Rubner et al., 1998) called Word Mover Distance (WMD). While WMD quantifies the total cost of matching all words of one document to another, the GH distance is the cost, up to an isometry, of the worst-case matching.

2.3 Persistence diagrams

Efficiently computing the GH distance is still an open problem despite a lot of recent work in this area (Mémoli and Sapiro, 2005; Bronstein et al., 2006; Mémoli, 2007; Agarwal et al., 2015).

Fortunately, Carrière et al. (2015) provides us with a way to derive a signature which is stable with respect to the GH distance. More specifically, given a finite point cloud $A \subset \mathbb{R}^n$, the persistence diagram of the Vietori-Rips filtration on A, $Dg(A)$, can be computed. This approach is inspired by persistent homology, a subfield of algebraic topology.

The rigorous definition of these notions is not the crux of this paper and we will only present them informally. The curious reader is invited to refer to Zhu (2013) for a short introduction. More details are in Delfinado and Edelsbrunner (1995); Edelsbrunner et al. (2002); Robins (1999).

A persistence diagram is a scatter plot of 2-D points representing the appearance and disappearance of geometric features[3] under varying resolutions. This can be imagined as replacing each point by a sphere of increasing radius.

We use the procedure described in Carrière et al.

---

[1] https://code.google.com/archive/p/word2vec/

[2] $f : \mathbb{R}^n \longrightarrow \mathbb{R}^n$ is *isometric* if it is distance preserving, ie $\forall x, y \in \mathbb{R}^n, \|f(x) - f(y)\|_2 = \|x - y\|_2$. Rotations, translations and reflections are examples of (linear) isometries.

[3] such as connected components, holes or empty hulls

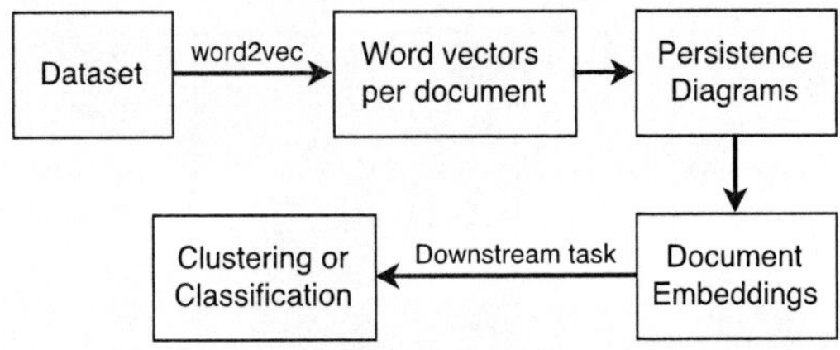

Figure 2: Method Pipeline

(2015) to derive fixed-sized vectors from persistence diagrams. These vectors have the following property: if A and B are two finite subsets of $\mathbb{R}^n$, $Dg(A)$ and $Dg(B)$ are their persistence diagrams, $N = \max(|Dg(A)|, |Dg(B)|)$ and $V_A, V_B \in \mathbb{R}^{\frac{N(N-1)}{2}}$, then

$$\|V_A - V_B\|_2 \leqslant \sqrt{2N(N-1)}d_{GH}(A, B)$$

In other words, the resulting signatures V_A and V_B are stable with respect to the GH distance. The size of the vectors are dependent on the underlying sets A and B. However, as is argued in Carrière et al. (2015), we can truncate the vectors to a dimension fixed across our dataset while preserving the stability property (albeit losing some of the representative ability of the signatures).

3 Experiments

3.1 Experiments

The pipeline for our experiments is shown in Figure 2. In order to build a persistence diagram, we convert each document to the set of its word vectors. We then use Dionysus (Morozov, 2008–2016), a C++ library for computing persistence diagrams, and form the signatures described in 2.3. We will subsequently refer to these diagrams as Persistent Homology (PH) embeddings. Once we have the embeddings for each document, they can be used as input to standard clustering or classification algorithms.

As a baseline document representation, we use the average of the word vectors for that document (subsequently called Aw2v embeddings).

For clustering, we experiment with K-means and Gaussian Mixture Models (GMM) on a subset[4] of the Twenty Newsgroups dataset. The subset was selected to ensure that most documents are from related topics, making clustering non-trivial, and the documents are of reasonable length to compute the representation.

For classification, we perform both sentence-level and document-level binary sentiment classification using logistic regression on the CSP and IMDb corpora respectively.

4 Results

4.1 Hyper-parameters

Our method depends on very few hyper-parameters. Our main choices are listed below.

Choice of distance We experimented with both euclidean distance and cosine similarity (angular distance). After preliminary experiments, we determined that both performed equally and hence, we only report results with the euclidean distance.

Persistence diagram computation The hyper-parameters of the diagram computation are monotonic and mostly control the degree of approximation. We set them to the highest values that allowed our experiment to run in reasonable time[5].

4.2 Document Clustering

We perform clustering experiments with the baseline document features (Aw2v), *tf-idf* and our PH signatures. Figure 3 shows the B-Cubed precision, recall and F1-Score of each method (metrics as defined in Amigó et al. (2009)). To further assess the utility of PH embeddings, we concatenate them with Aw2v to obtain a third representation, Aw2v+PH.

With GMM and Aw2v+PH, the F1-Score of clustering is 0.499. In terms of F1 and precision, we see that *tf-idf* representations perform better than PH, for reasons that we will discuss in later sections. In terms of recall, PH as well as Aw2v perform fairly well. Importantly, we see that all the metrics for PH are significantly above the random baseline, indicating that some valuable information is contained in them.

4.3 Sentiment Classification

4.3.1 Sentence-Level Sentiment Analysis

We evaluate our method on the CSP dataset[6]. The results are presented in Table 1. For comparison, we provide results for one of the state of the art models, a CNN-based sentence classifier (Kim,

---

[4]alt.atheism, sci.space and talk.religion.misc categories

[5]Selected such that the computation of the diagram of the longest file in the training data took less than 10 minutes.

[6]For lack of a canonical split, we use a random 10% of the dataset as a test set

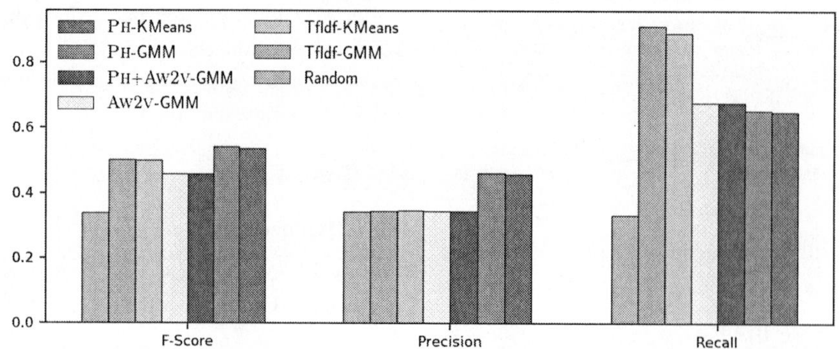

Figure 3: Results for clustering on 3 subclasses of the Twenty Newsgroups dataset

Model	Accuracy
CNN Non-Static	81.5%
PH + LogReg	53.19%
Aw2v + LogReg	77.13%
Aw2v + PH + LogReg	77.13%

Table 1: Performance on the CSP dataset

Model	Accuracy
Paragraph Vector	92.58%
PH + LogReg	53.16%
Aw2v + LogReg	82.94%
Aw2v + PH + LogReg	83.08%

Table 2: Performance on the IMDb dataset

2014). We observe that by themselves, PH embeddings are not useful at predicting the sentiment of each sentence. Aw2v gives reasonable performance in this task, but combining the two representations does not impact the accuracy at all.

4.3.2 Document-Level Sentiment Analysis

We perform document-level binary sentiment classification on the IMDb Movie Reviews Dataset (Maas et al., 2011). We use sentence vectors in this experiment, each of which is the average of the word vectors in that sentence. The results are presented in Table 2. We compare our results with the paragraph-vector approach (Le and Mikolov, 2014). We observe that PH embeddings perform poorly on this dataset. Similar to the CSP dataset, Aw2v embeddings give acceptable results. The combined representation performs slightly better, but not by a margin of significance.

5 Discussion and Analysis

As seen in Figure 3, the PH representation does not outperform *tf-idf* or Aw2v, and in fact often doesn't perform much better than chance.

One possible reason is linked to the nature of our datasets: the computation of the persistence diagram is very sensitive to the size of the documents. The geometry of small documents, where the number of words is negligible with respect to the dimensionality of the word vectors, is not very rich. The resulting topological signatures are very sparse, which is a problem for CSP as well as documents in IMDb and Twenty Newsgroups that contain only one line. On the opposite side of the spectrum, persistence diagrams are intractable to compute without down-sampling for very long documents (which in turn negatively impacts the representation of smaller documents).

We performed an additional experiment on a subset of the IMDb corpus that only contained documents of reasonable length, but obtained similar results. This indicates that the poor performance of PH representations, even when combined with other features (Aw2v), cannot be explained only by limitations of the data.

These observations lead to the conclusion that, for these datasets, the intrinsic geometry of documents in the word2vec semantic space does not help text classification tasks.

6 Related Work

Learning distributed representations of sentences or documents for downstream classification and information retrieval tasks has received recent attention owing to their utility in several applications, be it representations trained on the sentence/paragraph level Le and Mikolov (2014); Kiros et al. (2015) or purely word vector based methods Arora et al. (2017).

Document classification and clustering (Willett, 1988; Hotho et al., 2005; Steinbach et al., 2000; Huang, 2008; Xu and Gong, 2004; Kuang et al., 2015; Miller et al., 2016) and sentiment classification (Nakagawa et al., 2010; Kim, 2014; Wang and Manning, 2012) are relatively well studied.

Topological data analysis has been used for various tasks such as 3D shapes classification (Chazal et al., 2009) or protein structure analysis (Xia and Wei, 2014). However, such techniques have not been used in NLP, primarily because the theory is inaccessible and suitable applications are scarce. Zhu (2013) offers an introduction to using persistent homology in NLP, by creating representations of nursery-rhymes and novels, as well as highlights structural differences between child and adolescent writing. However, these techniques have not been applied to core NLP tasks.

7 Conclusion

Based on our experiments, using persistence diagrams for text representation does not seem to positively contribute to document clustering and sentiment classification tasks. There are certainly merits to the method, specifically its strong mathematical foundation and its domain-independent, unsupervised nature. Theoretically, algebraic topology has the ability to capture structural context, and this could potentially benefit syntax-based NLP tasks such as parsing. We plan to investigate this connection in the future.

Acknowledgments

This work was supported in part by the Defense Advanced Research Projects Agency (DARPA) Information Innovation Office (I2O) under the Low Resource Languages for Emergent Incidents (LORELEI) program issued by DARPA/I2O under Contract No. HR0011-15-C-0114. The views expressed are those of the authors and do not reflect the official policy or position of the Department of Defense or the U.S. Government.

We are grateful to Matt Gormley, Hyun Ah Song, Shivani Poddar and Hai Pham for their suggestions on the writing of this paper as well as to Steve Oudot for pointing us to helpful references. We would also like to thank the anonymous ACL reviewers for their valuable suggestions.

References

Pankaj K Agarwal, Kyle Fox, Abhinandan Nath, Anastasios Sidiropoulos, and Yusu Wang. 2015. Computing the gromov-hausdorff distance for metric trees. In *International Symposium on Algorithms and Computation*. Springer, pages 529–540.

Enrique Amigó, Julio Gonzalo, Javier Artiles, and Felisa Verdejo. 2009. A comparison of extrinsic clustering evaluation metrics based on formal constraints. *Information retrieval* 12(4):461–486.

Sanjeev Arora, Yingyu Liang, and Tengyu Ma. 2017. A simple but tough-to-beat baseline for sentence embeddings. In *International Conference on Learning Representations. To Appear*.

Alexander M Bronstein, Michael M Bronstein, and Ron Kimmel. 2006. Efficient computation of isometry-invariant distances between surfaces. *SIAM Journal on Scientific Computing* 28(5):1812–1836.

Mathieu Carrière, Steve Y Oudot, and Maks Ovsjanikov. 2015. Stable topological signatures for points on 3d shapes. In *Computer Graphics Forum*. Wiley Online Library, volume 34, pages 1–12.

Frédéric Chazal, David Cohen-Steiner, Leonidas J Guibas, Facundo Mémoli, and Steve Y Oudot. 2009. Gromov-hausdorff stable signatures for shapes using persistence. In *Computer Graphics Forum*. Wiley Online Library, volume 28, pages 1393–1403.

Cecil Jose A Delfinado and Herbert Edelsbrunner. 1995. An incremental algorithm for betti numbers of simplicial complexes on the 3-sphere. *Computer Aided Geometric Design* 12(7):771–784.

Herbert Edelsbrunner, David Letscher, and Afra Zomorodian. 2002. Topological persistence and simplification. *Discrete and Computational Geometry* 28(4):511–533.

Mikhael Gromov, Jacques Lafontaine, and Pierre Pansu. 1981. Structures métriques pour les variétés riemanniennes .

Andreas Hotho, Andreas Nürnberger, and Gerhard Paaß. 2005. A brief survey of text mining. In *Ldv Forum*.

Anna Huang. 2008. Similarity measures for text document clustering. In *Proceedings of the sixth new zealand computer science research student conference (NZCSRSC2008), Christchurch, New Zealand*. pages 49–56.

Yoon Kim. 2014. Convolutional neural networks for sentence classification. In *In EMNLP*.

Ryan Kiros, Yukun Zhu, Ruslan R Salakhutdinov, Richard Zemel, Raquel Urtasun, Antonio Torralba, and Sanja Fidler. 2015. Skip-thought vectors. In *Advances in neural information processing systems*. pages 3294–3302.

Da Kuang, Jaegul Choo, and Haesun Park. 2015. Nonnegative matrix factorization for interactive topic modeling and document clustering. In *Partitional Clustering Algorithms*, Springer, pages 215–243.

Matt J Kusner, Yu Sun, Nicholas I Kolkin, Kilian Q Weinberger, et al. 2015. From word embeddings to document distances. In *ICML*. volume 15, pages 957–966.

Quoc V. Le and Tomas Mikolov. 2014. Distributed representations of sentences and documents. In *Proceedings of the 31th International Conference on Machine Learning, ICML 2014, Beijing, China, 21-26 June 2014*. pages 1188–1196.

Andrew L. Maas, Raymond E. Daly, Peter T. Pham, Dan Huang, Andrew Y. Ng, and Christopher Potts. 2011. Learning word vectors for sentiment analysis. In *Proceedings of the 49th Annual Meeting of the Association for Computational Linguistics: Human Language Technologies*. Association for Computational Linguistics, Portland, Oregon, USA, pages 142–150. http://www.aclweb.org/anthology/P11-1015.

Facundo Mémoli. 2007. On the use of gromov-hausdorff distances for shape comparison .

Facundo Mémoli and Guillermo Sapiro. 2005. A theoretical and computational framework for isometry invariant recognition of point cloud data. *Foundations of Computational Mathematics* 5(3):313–347.

Tomas Mikolov, Ilya Sutskever, Kai Chen, Greg S Corrado, and Jeff Dean. 2013. Distributed representations of words and phrases and their compositionality. In *Advances in neural information processing systems*. pages 3111–3119.

Timothy A Miller, Dmitriy Dligach, and Guergana K Savova. 2016. Unsupervised document classification with informed topic models. *ACL* .

Dmitriy Morozov. 2008–2016. Dyonisus : a c++ library for computing persistent homology. `http://mrzv.org/software/dionysus/`.

Tetsuji Nakagawa, Kentaro Inui, and Sadao Kurohashi. 2010. Dependency tree-based sentiment classification using crfs with hidden variables. In *Human Language Technologies: The 2010 Annual Conference of the North American Chapter of the Association for Computational Linguistics*. Association for Computational Linguistics, Stroudsburg, PA, USA, HLT '10, pages 786–794. http://dl.acm.org/citation.cfm?id=1857999.1858119.

Bo Pang and Lillian Lee. 2005. Seeing stars: Exploiting class relationships for sentiment categorization with respect to rating scales. In *Proceedings of the ACL*.

Vanessa Robins. 1999. Towards computing homology from finite approximations. In *Topology proceedings*. volume 24, pages 503–532.

Yossi Rubner, Carlo Tomasi, and Leonidas J Guibas. 1998. A metric for distributions with applications to image databases. In *Computer Vision, 1998. Sixth International Conference on*. IEEE, pages 59–66.

Michael Steinbach, George Karypis, Vipin Kumar, et al. 2000. A comparison of document clustering techniques. In *KDD workshop on text mining*.

Sida Wang and Christopher D. Manning. 2012. Baselines and bigrams: Simple, good sentiment and topic classification. In *Proceedings of the 50th Annual Meeting of the Association for Computational Linguistics: Short Papers - Volume 2*. Association for Computational Linguistics, Stroudsburg, PA, USA, ACL '12, pages 90–94. http://dl.acm.org/citation.cfm?id=2390665.2390688.

Peter Willett. 1988. Recent trends in hierarchic document clustering: a critical review. *Information Processing & Management* 24(5):577–597.

Kelin Xia and Guo-Wei Wei. 2014. Persistent homology analysis of protein structure, flexibility, and folding. *International journal for numerical methods in biomedical engineering* 30(8):814–844.

Wei Xu and Yihong Gong. 2004. Document clustering by concept factorization. In *Proceedings of the 27th Annual International ACM SIGIR Conference on Research and Development in Information Retrieval*. ACM, New York, NY, USA, SIGIR '04, pages 202–209. https://doi.org/10.1145/1008992.1009029.

Xiaojin Zhu. 2013. Persistent homology: An introduction and a new text representation for natural language processing. In *Proceedings of the 23rd International Joint Conference on Artificial Intelligence*.

Adversarial Generation of Natural Language

Sandeep Subramanian♠* **Sai Rajeswar**♠* **Francis Dutil**♠
Christopher Pal ♣♠ **Aaron Courville**♠†

♠MILA, Université de Montréal   ♣École Polytechnique de Montréal   †CIFAR Fellow

{sandeep.subramanian.1,sai.rajeswar.mudumba,aaron.courville}@umontreal.ca,
frdutil@gmail.com, christopher.pal@polymtl.ca

Abstract

Generative Adversarial Networks (GANs) have gathered a lot of attention from the computer vision community, yielding impressive results for image generation. Advances in the adversarial generation of natural language from noise however are not commensurate with the progress made in generating images, and still lag far behind likelihood based methods. In this paper, we take a step towards generating natural language with a GAN objective alone. We introduce a simple baseline that addresses the discrete output space problem without relying on gradient estimators and show that it is able to achieve state-of-the-art results on a Chinese poem generation dataset. We present quantitative results on generating sentences from context-free and probabilistic context-free grammars, and qualitative language modeling results. A conditional version is also described that can generate sequences conditioned on sentence characteristics.

1 Introduction

Deep neural networks have recently enjoyed some success at modeling natural language (Mikolov et al., 2010; Zaremba et al., 2014; Kim et al., 2015). Typically, recurrent and convolutional language models are trained to maximize the likelihood of observing a word or character given the previous observations in the sequence $P(w_1 \ldots w_n) = p(w_1) \prod_{i=2}^{n} P(w_i | w_1 \ldots w_{i-1})$. These models are commonly trained using a technique called *teacher forcing* (Williams and Zipser, 1989) where the inputs to the network are fixed and the model is trained to predict only the next

item in the sequence given all previous observations. This corresponds to maximum-likelihood training of these models. However this one-step ahead prediction during training makes the model prone to *exposure bias* (Ranzato et al., 2015; Bengio et al., 2015). Exposure bias occurs when a model is only trained conditioned on ground-truth contexts and is not exposed to its own errors (Wiseman and Rush, 2016). An important consequence to exposure bias is that generated sequences can degenerate as small errors accumulate. Many important problems in NLP such as machine translation and abstractive summarization are trained via a maximum-likelihood training objective (Bahdanau et al., 2014; Rush et al., 2015), but require the generation of extended sequences and are evaluated based on sequence-level metrics such as BLEU (Papineni et al., 2002) and ROUGE (Lin, 2004).

One possible direction towards incorporating a sequence-level training objective is to use Generative Adversarial Networks (GANs) (Goodfellow et al., 2014). While GANs have yielded impressive results for modeling images (Radford et al., 2015; Dumoulin et al., 2016), advances in their use for natural language generation has lagged behind. Some progress has been made recently in incorporating a GAN objective in sequence modeling problems including natural language generation. Lamb et al. (2016) use an adversarial criterion to match the hidden state dynamics of a teacher forced recurrent neural network (RNN) and one that samples from its own output distribution across multiple time steps. Unlike the approach in Lamb et al. (2016), sequence GANs (Yu et al., 2016) and maximum-likelihood augmented GANs (Che et al., 2017) use an adversarial loss at outputs of an RNN. Using a GAN at the outputs of an RNN however isn't trivial since sampling from these outputs to feed to the discrimi-

---

Proceedings of the 2nd Workshop on Representation Learning for NLP, pages 241–251,
Vancouver, Canada, August 3, 2017. ©2017 Association for Computational Linguistics

nator is a non-differentiable operation. As a result gradients cannot propagate to the generator from the discriminator. Yu et al. (2016) use policy gradient to estimate the generator's gradient and (Che et al., 2017) present an importance sampling based technique. Other alternatives include REINFORCE (Williams, 1992), the use of a Gumbel softmax (Jang et al., 2016) and the straightthrough estimator (Bengio et al., 2013) among others.

In this work, we address the discrete output space problem by simply forcing the discriminator to operate on continuous valued output distributions. The discriminator sees a sequence of probabilities over every token in the vocabulary from the generator and a sequence of 1-hot vectors from the true data distribution as in Fig. 1. This technique is identical to that proposed by Gulrajani et al. (2017), which is parallel work to this. In this paper we provide a more complete empirical investigation of this approach to applying GANs to discrete output spaces. We present results using recurrent as well as convolutional architectures on three language modeling datasets of different sizes at the word and character-level. We also present quantitative results on generating sentences that adhere to a simple context-free grammar (CFG), and a richer probabilistic context-free grammar (PCFG). We compare our method to previous works that use a GAN objective to generate natural language, on a Chinese poetry generation dataset. In addition, we present a conditional GAN (Mirza and Osindero, 2014) that generates sentences conditioned on sentiment and questions.

2 Generative Adversarial Networks

GANs (Goodfellow et al., 2014) are a general framework used in training generative models by formulating the learning process as a two player minimax game as formulated in the equation below. A generator network G tries to generate samples that are as close as possible to the true data distribution $P(x)$ of interest from a fixed noise distribution $P(z)$. We will refer to the samples produced by the generator as $G(z)$. A discriminator network is then trained to distinguish between $G(z)$ and samples from the true data distribution $P(x)$ while the generator network is trained using gradient signals sent by the discriminator by minimizing $\log(1 - D(G(z)))$. Goodfellow et al. (2014) have shown that, with respect to an optimal discriminator, the minimax formulation can be shown to minimize the Jensen Shannon Divergence (JSD) between the generator's output distribution and the true data distribution.

$$\min_G \max_D V(D, G) = \mathbb{E}_{x \sim P(x)} [\log D(x)]$$
$$+ \mathbb{E}_{z \sim P(z)} [\log(1 - D(G(z)))]$$

However, in practice, the generator is trained to maximize $\log(D(G(z)))$ instead, since it provides stronger gradients in the early stages of learning (Goodfellow et al., 2014).

GANs have been reported to be notoriously hard to train in practice (Arjovsky and Bottou, 2017) and several techniques have been proposed to alleviate some of the complexities involved in getting them to work including modified objective functions and regularization (Salimans et al., 2016; Arjovsky et al., 2017; Mao et al., 2016; Gulrajani et al., 2017). We discuss some of these problems in the following subsection.

Nowozin et al. (2016) show that it is possible to train GANs with a variety of f-divergence measures besides JSD. Wasserstein GANs (WGANs) (Arjovsky et al., 2017) minimize the earth mover's distance or Wasserstein distance, while Least Squared GANs (LSGANs) (Mao et al., 2016) modifies replaces the log loss with an L2 loss. WGAN-GP (Gulrajani et al., 2017) incorporate a gradient penalty term on the discriminator's loss in the WGAN objective which acts as a regularizer. In this work, we will compare some of these objectives in the context of natural language generation.

2.1 Importance of Wasserstein GANs

Arjovsky and Bottou (2017) argue that part of the problem in training regular GANs is that it seeks to minimize the JSD between the $G(z)$ and $P(x)$. When the generator is trying to optimized $log(1 - D(G(z)))$, the gradients that it receives vanish as the discriminator is trained to optimality. The authors also show that when trying to optimize the more practical alternative, $-log(D(G(z)))$, the generator might not suffer from vanishing gradients but receives unstable training signals. It is also important to consider the fact that highly structured data like images and language lie in low-dimensional manifolds (as is evident by studying their principal components). Wassterstein GANs (Arjovsky et al., 2017) overcome some of the problems in regular GAN training by providing a softer metric to compare the distributions lying in low dimensional manifolds. A key contribution of this work was identifying the importance of a lipschitz constraint which is achieved by clamping the weights of the discriminator to lie in a fixed interval. The lipschitz constraint and training the discriminator multiple times for every generator gradient update creates a strong learning signal for the generator.

Gulrajani et al. (2017) present an alternative to weight clamping that they call a gradient penalty to enforce lipschitzness since model performance was reported to be highly sensitive to the clamping hyperparameters. They add the following penalty to the discriminator training objective - $(\|\nabla_{G(z)} D(G(z))\|_2 - 1)^2$. A potential concern regarding our strategy to train our discriminator to distinguish between sequence of 1-hot vectors from the true data distribution and a sequence of probabilities from the generator is that the discriminator can easily exploit the sparsity in the 1-hot vectors to reach optimality. However, Wasserstein distance with a lipschitz constraint / gradient penalty provides good gradients even under an optimal discriminator and so isn't a problem for us in practice. Even though it is possible to extract some performance from a regular GAN objective with the gradient penalty (as we show in one of our experiments), WGANs still provide better gradients to the generator since the discriminator doesn't saturate often.

3 Model architecture

Let $\mathbf{z} \sim \mathcal{N}(\mathbf{0}, \mathbf{I})$ be the input to our generator network G from which we will attempt to generate natural language. For implementation convenience, the sample $\mathbf{z}$ is of shape $n \times d$ where n is the length of sequence and d is a fixed length dimension of the noise vector at each time step. The generator then transforms $\mathbf{z}$ into a sequence of probability distributions over the vocabulary $G(z)$ of size $n \times k$ where k is the size of our true data distribution's vocabulary. The discriminator network D is provided with fake samples $G(z)$ and samples from the true data distribution $P(x)$. Samples from the true distribution are provided as a sequence of 1-hot vectors with each vector serving as an indicator of the observed word in the sample. As described in section 2, the discriminator is trained to discriminate between real and fake samples and the generator is trained to fool

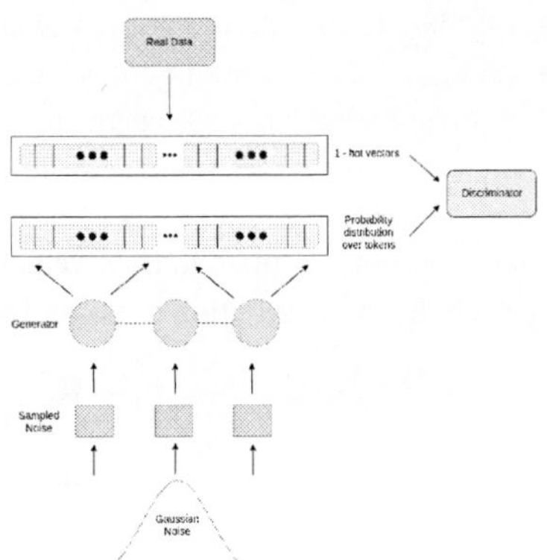

Figure 1: Model architecture

the discriminator as in Fig. 1.

We investigate recurrent architectures as in (Lamb et al., 2016; Yu et al., 2016; Che et al., 2017) and convolutional architectures in both the generator as well as the discriminator. The following subsections detail our architectures.

3.1 Recurrent Models

Recurrent Neural Networks (RNNs), particularly Long short-term memory networks (LSTMs) (Hochreiter and Schmidhuber, 1997) and Gated Recurrent Networks (Cho et al., 2014) are powerful models that have been successful at modeling sequential data (Graves and Schmidhuber, 2009; Mikolov et al., 2010). They transform a sequence of input vectors $\mathbf{x} = x_1 \dots x_n$ into a sequence of hidden states $\mathbf{h} = h_1 \dots h_n$ where each hidden state maintains a summary of the input up until then. RNN language models are autoregressive in nature since the input to the network at time t depends on the output at time $t - 1$. However, in the context of generating sequences from noise, the inputs are pre-determined and there is no direct correspondence between the output at time $t - 1$ and the input at time t this fundamentally changes the auto-regressiveness of the RNN. The RNN does however carry forward information about its output at time t through subsequent time steps via its hidden states $\mathbf{h}$ as evident from its recurrent transition function. In order to incorporate an explicit dependence between subsequent RNN outputs, we add a peephole connection between the *output* probability distribution $\mathbf{y_{t-1}}$ at time $t - 1$ and the hidden state $\mathbf{h_t}$ at time t as show in the LSTM equations below. Typical RNN language models have a shared affine transformation matrix $\mathbf{W_{out}}$ that is shared across time all steps that projects the hidden state vector to a vector of the same size as the target vocabulary to generate a sequence of outputs $\mathbf{y} = y_1 \ldots y_t$. Subsequently a softmax function is applied to each vector to turn it into a probability distribution over the vocabulary.

$$\mathbf{y}_t = \mathrm{softmax}(\mathbf{W}_{out}\mathbf{h}_t + \mathbf{b}_{out}),$$

During inference, an output is sampled from the softmax distribution and becomes the input at the subsequent time step. While training the inputs are pre-determined. In all of our models, we perform greedy decoding where we always pick argmax y_t. When using the LSTM as a discriminator we use a simple binary logistic regression layer on the last hidden state h_n to determine the probability of the sample being from the generator's data distribution or from the real data distribution. $P(real) = \sigma(\mathbf{W}_{pred}\mathbf{h}_n + \mathbf{b}_{pred})$.

The LSTM update equations with an output peephole are :

$$\mathbf{i}_t = \sigma(\mathbf{W}_{xi}\mathbf{x}_t + \mathbf{W}_{hi}\mathbf{h}_{t-1} + \mathbf{W}_{pi}\mathbf{y}_{t-1} + \mathbf{b}_i)$$
$$\mathbf{f}_t = \sigma(\mathbf{W}_{xf}\mathbf{x}_t + \mathbf{W}_{hf}\mathbf{h}_{t-1} + \mathbf{W}_{pf}\mathbf{y}_{t-1} + \mathbf{b}_f)$$
$$\mathbf{o}_t = \sigma(\mathbf{W}_{xo}\mathbf{x}_t + \mathbf{W}_{ho}\mathbf{h}_{t-1} + \mathbf{W}_{po}\mathbf{y}_{t-1} + \mathbf{b}_o)$$
$$\mathbf{c}_t = \tanh(\mathbf{W}_{xc}\mathbf{x}_t + \mathbf{W}_{hc}\mathbf{h}_{t-1} + \mathbf{W}_{pc}\mathbf{y}_{t-1} + \mathbf{b}_c)$$
$$\mathbf{c}_t = \mathbf{f}_t \odot \mathbf{c}_{t-1} + \mathbf{i}_t \odot \mathbf{c}_t$$
$$\mathbf{h}_t = \mathbf{o}_t \odot \tanh(\mathbf{c}_t),$$

where σ is the element-wise sigmoid function, $\odot$ is the hadamard product, tanh is the element-wise tanh function. $\mathbf{W}$. and $\mathbf{b}$. are learn-able parameters of the model and $\mathbf{i_t}, \mathbf{f_t}, \mathbf{o_t}$ and $\mathbf{c_t}$ constitute the input, forget, output and cell states of the LSTM respectively.

3.2 Convolutional Models

Convolutional neural networks (CNNs) have also shown promise at modeling sequential data using 1-dimensional convolutions (Dauphin et al., 2016; Zhang et al., 2015). Convolution filters are convolved across time and the input dimensions are treated as channels. In this work, we explore convolutional generators and discriminators with residual connections (He et al., 2016).

Gulrajani et al. (2017) use a convolutional model for both the generator and discriminator. The generator consists of 5 residual blocks with 2 1-D convolutional layers each. A final 1-D convolution layer transforms the output of the resid-

ual blocks into a sequence of un-normalized vectors for each element in the input sequence (noise). These vectors are then normalized using the softmax function. All convolutions are 'same' convolutions with a stride of 1 followed by batch-normalization (Ioffe and Szegedy, 2015) and the ReLU (Nair and Hinton, 2010; Glorot et al., 2011) activation function without any pooling so as to preserve the shape of the input. The discriminator architecture is identical to that of the generator with the final output having a single output channel.

3.3 Curriculum Learning

In likelihood based training of generative language models, models are only trained to make one-step ahead predictions and as a result it is possible to train these models on relatively long sequences even in the initial stages of training. However, in our adversarial formulation, our generator is encouraged to generate entire sequences that match the true data distribution without explicit supervision at each step of the generation process. As a way to provide training signals of incremental difficulty, we use curriculum learning (Bengio et al., 2009) and train our generator to produce sequences of gradually increasing lengths as training progresses.

4   Experiments & Data

GAN based methods have often been critiqued for lacking a concrete evaluation strategy (Salimans et al., 2016), however recent work (Wu et al., 2016) uses an annealed importance based technique to overcome this problem.

In the context of generating natural language, it is possible to come up with a simpler approach to evaluate compute the likelihoods of generated samples. We synthesize a data generating distribution under which we can compute likelihoods in a tractable manner. We propose a simple evaluation strategy for evaluating adversarial methods of generating natural language by constructing a data generating distribution from a CFG or P−CFG. It is possible to determine if a sample belongs to the CFG or the probability of a sample under a P−CFG by using a constituency parser that is provided with all of the productions in a grammar. Yu et al. (2016) also present a simple idea to estimate the likelihood of generated samples by using a randomly initialized LSTM as their data generating distribution. While this is a viable strategy to evaluate generative models of language, a randomly initialized LSTM provides little visibility into the complexity of the data distribution itself and presents no obvious way to increase its complexity. CFGs and PCFGs however, provide explicit control of the complexity via their productions. They can also be learned via grammar induction (Brill, 1993) on large treebanks of natural language and so the data generating distribution is not synthetic as in (Yu et al., 2016).

Typical language models are evaluated by measuring the likelihood of samples from the true data distribution under the model. However, with GANs it is impossible to measure likelihoods under the model itself and so we measure the likelihood of the model's samples under the true data distribution instead.

We divide our experiments into four categories:

- Generating language that belongs to a toy CFG and an induced PCFG from the Penn Treebank (Marcus et al., 1993).

- Chinese poetry generation with comparisons to (Yu et al., 2016) and (Che et al., 2017).

- Generated samples from a dataset consisting of simple English sentences, the 1-billion-word and Penn Treebank datasets.

- Conditional GANs that generate sentences conditioned on certain sentence attributes such as sentiment and questions.

4.1 Simple CFG

We use a simple and publicly available CFG[1] that contains 248 productions. We then generate two sets of data from this CFG - one consisting of samples of length 5 and another of length 11. Each set contains 100,000 samples selected at random from the CFG. The first set has a vocabulary of 36 tokens while the second 45 tokens. We evaluate our models on this task by measuring the fraction of generated samples that satisfy the rules of the grammar and also measure the diversity in our generated samples. We do this by generating 1,280 samples from noise and computing the fraction of those that are valid under our grammar using the Earley parsing algorithm (Earley, 1970). In order to measure sample diversity, we simply

count the number of unique samples; while this assumes that all samples are orthogonal it still serves as a proxy measure of the entropy. We compare various generator, discriminator and GAN objectives on this problem.

4.2 Penn Treebank PCFG

To construct a more challenging problem than a simple CFG, we use sections 0-21 of the WSJ subsection of the Penn Treebank to induce a PCFG using simple count statistics of all productions.

$$P(A \rightarrow BC) = \frac{count(A \rightarrow BC)}{count(A \rightarrow *)}$$

We train our model on all sentences in the treebank and restrict the output vocabulary to the top 2,000 most frequently occurring words. We evaluate our models on this task by measuring the likelihood of a sample using a Viterbi chart parser (Klein and Manning, 2003). While such a measure mostly captures the grammaticality of a sentence, it is still a reasonable proxy of sample quality.

4.3 Chinese Poetry

Zhang and Lapata (2014) present a dataset of Chinese poems that were used to evaluate adversarial training methods for natural language in (Yu et al., 2016) and (Che et al., 2017). The dataset consists of 4-line poems with a variable number of characters in each line. We treat each line in a poem as a training example and use lines of length 5 (poem-5) and 7 (poem-7) with the train/validation/test split[2] specified in (Che et al., 2017). We use BLEU-2 and BLEU-3 to measure model performance on this task. Since there is no obvious "target" for each generated sentence, both works report corpus-level BLEU measures using the entire test set as the reference.

4.4 Language Generation

We generate language from three different datasets of varying sizes and complexity. A dataset comprising simple English sentences[3] which we will henceforth refer to as CMU−SE, the version of the Penn Treebank commonly used in language modeling experiments (Zaremba et al., 2014) and the Google 1-billion word dataset (Chelba et al.,

---

[1] `http://www.cs.jhu.edu/~jason/465/ hw-grammar/extra-grammars/holygrail`

[2] `http://homepages.inf.ed.ac.uk/mlap/ Data/EMNLP14/`

[3] `https://github.com/clab/sp2016. 11-731/tree/master/hw4/data`

2013). We perform experiments at generating language at the word as well as character-level. The CMU−SE dataset consists of 44,016 sentences with a vocabulary of 3,122 words, while the Penn Treebank consists of 42,068 sentences with a vocabulary of 10,000 words. We use a random subset of 3 million sentences from the 1-billion word dataset and constrain our vocabulary to the top 30,000 most frequently occurring words. We use a curriculum learning strategy in all of our LSTM models (with and without the output peephole connection) that starts training on sentences of length 5 at the word level and 13 for characters and increases the sequence length by 1 after a fixed number of epochs based on the size of the data. Convolutional methods in (Gulrajani et al., 2017) are able to generate long sequences even without a curriculum, however we found it was critical in generating long sequences with an LSTM.

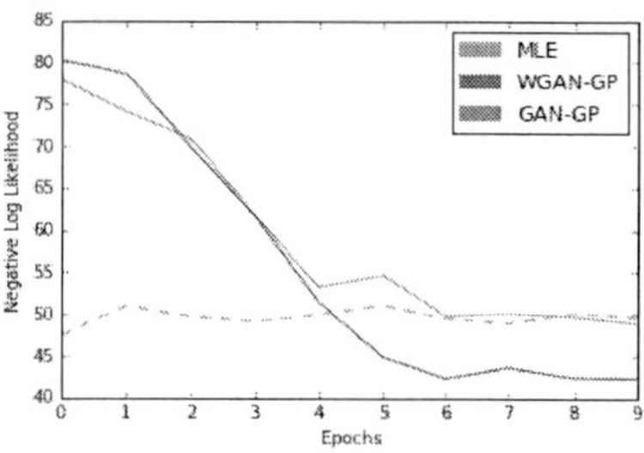

Figure 2: Negative log-likelihood of generated samples under the PCFG using an LSTM trained with the WGAN-GP, GAN-GP and a standard MLE objective on the PTB dataset

4.5 Conditional Generation of Sequences

GANs are able to leverage explicit conditioning on high-level attributes of data (Mirza and Osindero, 2014; Gauthier, 2014; Radford et al., 2015) to generate samples which contain these attributes. Recent work (Hu et al., 2017) generates sentences conditioned on certain attributes of language such as sentiment using a variational autoencoders (VAEs) (Kingma and Welling, 2013) and holistic attribute discriminators. In this paper, we use two features inherent in language - sentiment and questions. To generate sentences that are questions, we use the CMU−SE dataset and label sentences that contain a "?" as being questions and the rest as been statements. To generate sentences of positive and negative sentiment we use the Amazon review polarity dataset collected

in (Zhang et al., 2015) and use the first 3 million *short* reviews with a vocabulary of the top 4,000 most frequently occurring words. Conditioning on sentence attributes is achieved by concatenating a single feature map containing either entirely ones or zeros to indicate the presence or absence of the attribute as in (Radford et al., 2015) at the output of each convolutional layer. The conditioning is done on both the generator and the discriminator. We experiment with conditional GANs using only convolutional methods since methods adding conditioning information has been well studied in these architectures.

4.6 Training

All models are trained using the back-propagation algorithm updating our parameters using the Adam optimization method (Kingma and Ba, 2014) and stochastic gradient descent (SGD) with batch sizes of 64. A learning rate of 2×10^{-3}, $\beta_1 = 0.5$ and $\beta_2 = 0.999$ is used in our LSTM generator and discriminators while convolutional architectures use a learning rate of 1×10^{-4}. The noise prior and all LSTM hidden dimensions are set to 128 except for the Chinese poetry generation task where we set it to 64.

5 Results and Discussion

Table. 1 presents quantitative results on generating sentences that adhere to the simple CFG described in Section 4.1. The Acc column computes the accuracy with which our model generates samples from the CFG using a sample of 1,280 generations. We observe that all models are able to fit sequences of length 5 but only the WGAN, WGAN-GP objectives are able to generalize to longer sequences of length 11. This motivated us to use only the WGAN and WGAN-GP objectives in our subsequent experiments. The GAN-GP criterion appears to perform reasonably as well but we restrict our experiments to use the WGAN and WGAN-GP criteria only. GANs have been shown to exhibit the phenomenon of "mode dropping" where the generator fails to capture a large fraction of the modes present in the data generating distribution (Che et al., 2016). It is therefore important to study the diversity in our generated samples. The Uniq column computes the number of unique samples in a sample 1,280 generations serves as a rough indicator of sample diversity. The WGAN-GP objective appears to encourage the generation

Gen	Disc	Objective	Length 5		Length 11	
			Acc (%)	Uniq	Acc (%)	Uniq
LSTM	LSTM	GAN	99.06	0.913	0	0.855
LSTM	LSTM	LSGAN	99.45	0.520	0	0.855
LSTM	LSTM	WGAN	93.98	0.972	98.04	0.924
LSTM-P	LSTM	WGAN	97.96	0.861	99.29	0.653
LSTM	LSTM	WGAN-GP	99.21	0.996	96.25	0.992
CNN	CNN	WGAN-GP	98.59	0.990	97.01	0.771
LSTM-P	LSTM	GAN-GP	98.68	0.993	96.32	0.995

Table 1: Accuracy and uniqueness measure of samples generated by different models. LSTM, LSTM-P refers to the LSTM model with the output peephole and the WGAN-GP and GAN-GP refer to models that use a gradient penalty in the discriminator's training objective

Models	Poem 5				Poem 7			
	BLEU-2		BLEU-3		BLEU-2		BLEU-3	
	Val	Test	Val	Test	Val	Test	Val	Test
MLE (Che et al., 2017)	-	0.693	-	-	-	0.318	-	-
Sequence GAN (Yu et al., 2016)	-	0.738	-	-	-	-	-	-
MaliGAN-basic (Che et al., 2017)	-	0.740	-	-	-	0.489	-	-
MaliGAN-full (Che et al., 2017)	-	0.762	-	-	-	0.552	-	-
LSTM (ours)	0.840	0.837	0.427	**0.372**	0.660	0.655	0.386	**0.405**
LSTM Peephole (ours)	0.845	**0.878**	0.439	0.363	0.670	**0.670**	0.327	0.355

Table 2: BLEU scores on the poem-5 and poem-7 datasets

of diverse samples while also fitting the data distribution well.

Fig. 2 shows the negative-log-likelihood of generated samples using a LSTM architecture using the WGAN-GP, GAN-GP and MLE criteria. All models used an LSTM generator. The sequence length is set to 7 and the likelihoods are evaluated at the end of every epoch on a set of 64 samples.

Table. 2 contains quantitative results on the Chinese poetry generation dataset. The results indicate that our straightforward strategy to overcome back-propagating through discrete states is competitive and outperforms more complicated methods.

Table. 5 contains sequences generated by our model conditioned on sentiment (positive/negative) and questions/statements. The model is able to pick up on certain consistent patterns in questions as well as when expressing sentiment and use them while generating sentences.

Tables 3 and 4 contain sequences generated at the word and character-level by our LSTM and CNN models. Both models are able to produce realistic sentences. The CNN model with a WGAN-GP objective appears to be able to maintain context over longer time spans.

6 Conclusion and Future work

In conclusion, this work presents a straightforward but effective method to train GANs for natural language. The simplicity lies in *forcing the discriminator to operate on continuous values* by presenting it with a sequence of probability distributions from the generator and a sequence of 1-hot vectors corresponding to data from the true distribution. We propose an evaluation strategy that involves learning the data distribution defined by a CFG or PCFG. This lets us evaluate the likelihood of a sample belonging to the data generating distribution. The use of WGAN and WGAN-GP objectives produce realistic sentences on datasets of varying complexity (CMU-SE, Penn Treebank and the 1-billion dataset). We also show that it is possible to perform conditional generation of text on high-level sentence features such as sentiment and questions. In future work, we would like to explore GANs in other domains of NLP such as non goal-oriented dialog systems where a clear train-

Level	Method	1-billion-word
Word	LSTM	An opposition was growing in China . This is undergoing operation a year . It has his everyone on a blame . Everyone shares that Miller seems converted President as Democrat . Which is actually the best of his children . Who has The eventual policy and weak ?
	CNN	Companies I upheld , respectively patented saga and Ambac. Independence Unit have any will MRI in these Lights It is a wrap for the annually of Morocco The town has Registration matched with unk and the citizens
Character	CNN	To holl is now my Hubby , The gry timers was faller After they work is jith a But in a linter a revent

Table 3: Word and character-level generations on the 1-billion word dataset

Level	Model	PTB	CMU-SE
Word	LSTM	what everything they take everything away from . may tea bill is the best chocolate from emergency . can you show show if any fish left inside . room service , have my dinner please .	<s>will you have two moment ? </s> <s>i need to understand deposit length . </s> <s>how is the another headache ? </s> <s>how there , is the restaurant popular this cheese ? </s>
	CNN	meanwhile henderson said that it has to bounce for. I'm at the missouri burning the indexing manufacturing and through .	<s>i 'd like to fax a newspaper . </s> <s>cruise pay the next in my replacement . </s> <s>what 's in the friday food ? ? </s>

Table 4: Word level generations on the Penn Treebank and CMU-SE datasets

POSITIVE	NEGATIVE
best and top notch newtonmom . good buy homeostasis money well spent kickass cosamin of time and fun . great britani ! I lovethis.	usuall the review omnium nothing non-functionable extreme crap-not working and eeeeew a horrible poor imposing se400
QUESTION	**STATEMENT**
<s>when 's the friday convention on ? </s> <s>how many snatched crew you have ? </s> <s>how can you open this hall ? </s>	<s>i report my run on one mineral . </s> <s>we have to record this now . </s> <s>i think i deeply take your passenger .</s>

Table 5: Coditional generation of text. Top row shows generated samples conditionally trained on amazon review polarity dataset with two attributes 'positive' and 'negative'. Bottom row has samples conditioned on the 'question' attribute

ing and evaluation criterion does not exist.

Acknowledgements

The Authors would like to thank Ishaan Gulrajani, Martin Arjovsky, Guillaume Lample, Rosemary Ke, Juneki Hong and Varsha Embar for their advice and insightful comments. We are grateful to the Fonds de Recherche du Québec – Nature et Technologie for their financial support. We would also like to acknowledge NVIDIA for donating a DGX-1 computer used in this work.

Appendix

We demonstrate that our approach to solve the problem of discrete outputs produces reasonable outputs even when applied to images. Figure 3 shows samples generated on the binarized MNIST dataset (Salakhutdinov and Murray, 2008). We used a generator and discriminator architecture identical to (Radford et al., 2015) with the WGAN-GP criterion. The generator's outputs are continuous while samples from the true data distribution are binarized.

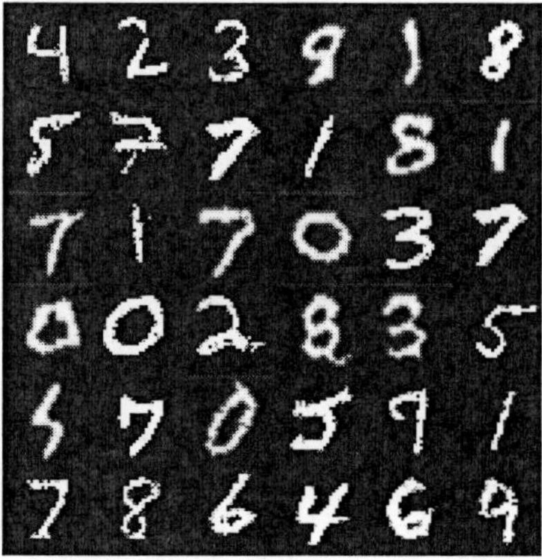

Figure 3: Binarized MNIST samples using a DCWGAN with gradient penalty

References

Martin Arjovsky and Léon Bottou. 2017. Towards principled methods for training generative adversarial networks. In *NIPS 2016 Workshop on Adversarial Training. In review for ICLR*. volume 2016.

Martin Arjovsky, Soumith Chintala, and Léon Bottou. 2017. Wasserstein gan. *arXiv preprint arXiv:1701.07875*.

Dzmitry Bahdanau, Kyunghyun Cho, and Yoshua Bengio. 2014. Neural machine translation by jointly learning to align and translate. *arXiv preprint arXiv:1409.0473*.

Samy Bengio, Oriol Vinyals, Navdeep Jaitly, and Noam Shazeer. 2015. Scheduled sampling for sequence prediction with recurrent neural networks. In *Advances in Neural Information Processing Systems*. pages 1171–1179.

Yoshua Bengio, Nicholas Léonard, and Aaron Courville. 2013. Estimating or propagating gradients through stochastic neurons for conditional computation. *arXiv preprint arXiv:1308.3432*.

Yoshua Bengio, Jérôme Louradour, Ronan Collobert, and Jason Weston. 2009. Curriculum learning. In *Proceedings of the 26th annual international conference on machine learning*. ACM, pages 41–48.

Eric Brill. 1993. Automatic grammar induction and parsing free text: A transformation-based approach. In *Proceedings of the workshop on Human Language Technology*. Association for Computational Linguistics, pages 237–242.

Tong Che, Yanran Li, Athul Paul Jacob, Yoshua Bengio, and Wenjie Li. 2016. Mode regularized generative adversarial networks. *arXiv preprint arXiv:1612.02136*.

Tong Che, Yanran Li, Ruixiang Zhang, R Devon Hjelm, Wenjie Li, Yangqiu Song, and Yoshua Bengio. 2017. Maximum-likelihood augmented discrete generative adversarial networks. *arXiv preprint arXiv:1702.07983*.

Ciprian Chelba, Tomas Mikolov, Mike Schuster, Qi Ge, Thorsten Brants, Phillipp Koehn, and Tony Robinson. 2013. One billion word benchmark for measuring progress in statistical language modeling. *arXiv preprint arXiv:1312.3005*.

Kyunghyun Cho, Bart Van Merriënboer, Caglar Gulcehre, Dzmitry Bahdanau, Fethi Bougares, Holger Schwenk, and Yoshua Bengio. 2014. Learning phrase representations using rnn encoder-decoder for statistical machine translation. *arXiv preprint arXiv:1406.1078*.

Yann N Dauphin, Angela Fan, Michael Auli, and David Grangier. 2016. Language modeling with gated convolutional networks. *arXiv preprint arXiv:1612.08083*.

Vincent Dumoulin, Ishmael Belghazi, Ben Poole, Alex Lamb, Martin Arjovsky, Olivier Mastropietro, and Aaron Courville. 2016. Adversarially learned inference. *arXiv preprint arXiv:1606.00704*.

Jay Earley. 1970. An efficient context-free parsing algorithm. *Communications of the ACM* 13(2):94–102.

Jon Gauthier. 2014. Conditional generative adversarial nets for convolutional face generation. *Class Project for Stanford CS231N: Convolutional Neural Networks for Visual Recognition, Winter semester* 2014(5):2.

Xavier Glorot, Antoine Bordes, and Yoshua Bengio. 2011. Deep sparse rectifier neural networks. In *Aistats*. volume 15, page 275.

Ian Goodfellow, Jean Pouget-Abadie, Mehdi Mirza, Bing Xu, David Warde-Farley, Sherjil Ozair, Aaron Courville, and Yoshua Bengio. 2014. Generative adversarial nets. In *Advances in neural information processing systems*. pages 2672–2680.

Alex Graves and Jürgen Schmidhuber. 2009. Offline handwriting recognition with multidimensional recurrent neural networks. In *Advances in neural information processing systems*. pages 545–552.

Ishaan Gulrajani, Faruk Ahmed, Martin Arjovsky, Vincent Dumoulin, and Aaron Courville. 2017. Improved training of wasserstein gans. *arXiv preprint arXiv:1704.00028*.

Kaiming He, Xiangyu Zhang, Shaoqing Ren, and Jian Sun. 2016. Deep residual learning for image recognition. In *Proceedings of the IEEE Conference on Computer Vision and Pattern Recognition*. pages 770–778.

Sepp Hochreiter and Jürgen Schmidhuber. 1997. Long short-term memory. *Neural computation* 9(8):1735–1780.

Zhiting Hu, Zichao Yang, Xiaodan Liang, Ruslan Salakhutdinov, and Eric P Xing. 2017. Controllable text generation. *arXiv preprint arXiv:1703.00955*.

Sergey Ioffe and Christian Szegedy. 2015. Batch normalization: Accelerating deep network training by reducing internal covariate shift. *arXiv preprint arXiv:1502.03167*.

Eric Jang, Shixiang Gu, and Ben Poole. 2016. Categorical reparameterization with gumbel-softmax. *arXiv preprint arXiv:1611.01144*.

Yoon Kim, Yacine Jernite, David Sontag, and Alexander M Rush. 2015. Character-aware neural language models. *arXiv preprint arXiv:1508.06615*.

Diederik Kingma and Jimmy Ba. 2014. Adam: A method for stochastic optimization. *arXiv preprint arXiv:1412.6980*.

Diederik P Kingma and Max Welling. 2013. Auto-encoding variational bayes. *arXiv preprint arXiv:1312.6114* .

Dan Klein and Christopher D Manning. 2003. A parsing: fast exact viterbi parse selection. In *Proceedings of the 2003 Conference of the North American Chapter of the Association for Computational Linguistics on Human Language Technology-Volume 1*. Association for Computational Linguistics, pages 40–47.

Alex M Lamb, Anirudh Goyal ALIAS PARTH GOYAL, Ying Zhang, Saizheng Zhang, Aaron C Courville, and Yoshua Bengio. 2016. Professor forcing: A new algorithm for training recurrent networks. In *Advances In Neural Information Processing Systems*. pages 4601–4609.

Chin-Yew Lin. 2004. Rouge: A package for automatic evaluation of summaries. In *Text summarization branches out: Proceedings of the ACL-04 workshop*. Barcelona, Spain, volume 8.

Xudong Mao, Qing Li, Haoran Xie, Raymond YK Lau, and Zhen Wang. 2016. Least squares generative adversarial networks. *arXiv preprint ArXiv:1611.04076* .

Mitchell P Marcus, Mary Ann Marcinkiewicz, and Beatrice Santorini. 1993. Building a large annotated corpus of english: The penn treebank. *Computational linguistics* 19(2):313–330.

Tomas Mikolov, Martin Karafiát, Lukas Burget, Jan Cernockỳ, and Sanjeev Khudanpur. 2010. Recurrent neural network based language model. In *Interspeech*. volume 2, page 3.

Mehdi Mirza and Simon Osindero. 2014. Conditional generative adversarial nets. *arXiv preprint arXiv:1411.1784* .

Vinod Nair and Geoffrey E Hinton. 2010. Rectified linear units improve restricted boltzmann machines. In *Proceedings of the 27th international conference on machine learning (ICML-10)*. pages 807–814.

Sebastian Nowozin, Botond Cseke, and Ryota Tomioka. 2016. f-gan: Training generative neural samplers using variational divergence minimization. In *Advances in Neural Information Processing Systems*. pages 271–279.

Kishore Papineni, Salim Roukos, Todd Ward, and Wei-Jing Zhu. 2002. Bleu: a method for automatic evaluation of machine translation. In *Proceedings of the 40th annual meeting on association for computational linguistics*. Association for Computational Linguistics, pages 311–318.

Alec Radford, Luke Metz, and Soumith Chintala. 2015. Unsupervised representation learning with deep convolutional generative adversarial networks. *arXiv preprint arXiv:1511.06434* .

Marc'Aurelio Ranzato, Sumit Chopra, Michael Auli, and Wojciech Zaremba. 2015. Sequence level training with recurrent neural networks. *arXiv preprint arXiv:1511.06732* .

Alexander M Rush, Sumit Chopra, and Jason Weston. 2015. A neural attention model for abstractive sentence summarization. *arXiv preprint arXiv:1509.00685* .

Ruslan Salakhutdinov and Iain Murray. 2008. On the quantitative analysis of deep belief networks. In *Proceedings of the 25th international conference on Machine learning*. ACM, pages 872–879.

Tim Salimans, Ian Goodfellow, Wojciech Zaremba, Vicki Cheung, Alec Radford, and Xi Chen. 2016. Improved techniques for training gans. In *Advances in Neural Information Processing Systems*. pages 2226–2234.

Ronald J Williams. 1992. Simple statistical gradient-following algorithms for connectionist reinforcement learning. *Machine learning* 8(3-4):229–256.

Ronald J Williams and David Zipser. 1989. A learning algorithm for continually running fully recurrent neural networks. *Neural computation* 1(2):270–280.

Sam Wiseman and Alexander M. Rush. 2016. Sequence-to-sequence learning as beam-search optimization. *CoRR* abs/1606.02960. http://arxiv.org/abs/1606.02960.

Yuhuai Wu, Yuri Burda, Ruslan Salakhutdinov, and Roger Grosse. 2016. On the quantitative analysis of decoder-based generative models. *arXiv preprint arXiv:1611.04273* .

Lantao Yu, Weinan Zhang, Jun Wang, and Yong Yu. 2016. Seqgan: sequence generative adversarial nets with policy gradient. *arXiv preprint arXiv:1609.05473* .

Wojciech Zaremba, Ilya Sutskever, and Oriol Vinyals. 2014. Recurrent neural network regularization. *arXiv preprint arXiv:1409.2329* .

Xiang Zhang, Junbo Zhao, and Yann LeCun. 2015. Character-level convolutional networks for text classification. In *Advances in neural information processing systems*. pages 649–657.

Xingxing Zhang and Mirella Lapata. 2014. Chinese poetry generation with recurrent neural networks. In *EMNLP*. pages 670–680.

Deep Active Learning for Named Entity Recognition

Yanyao Shen
UT Austin
Austin, TX 78712
shenyanyao@utexas.edu

Hyokun Yun
Amazon Web Services
Seattle, WA 98101
yunhyoku@amazon.com

Zachary C. Lipton
Amazon Web Services
Seattle, WA 98101
liptoz@amazon.com

Yakov Kronrod
Amazon Web Services
Seattle, WA 98101
kronrod@amazon.com

Animashree Anandkumar
Amazon Web Services
Seattle, WA 98101
anima@amazon.com

Abstract

Deep neural networks have advanced the state of the art in named entity recognition. However, under typical training procedures, advantages over classical methods emerge only with large datasets. As a result, deep learning is employed only when large public datasets or a large budget for manually labeling data is available. In this work, we show that by combining deep learning with active learning, we can outperform classical methods even with a significantly smaller amount of training data.

1 Introduction

Over the past several years, a series of papers have used deep neural networks (DNNs) to advance the state of the art in named entity recognition (NER) (Collobert et al., 2011; Huang et al., 2015; Lample et al., 2016; Chiu and Nichols, 2015; Yang et al., 2016). Historically, the advantages of deep learning have been less pronounced when working with small datasets. For instance, on the popular CoNLL-2003 English dataset, the best DNN model outperforms the best shallow model by only 0.4%, as measured by F1 score, and this is a small dataset containing only 203,621 words. On the other hand, on the OntoNotes-5.0 English dataset, which contains 1,088,503 words, a DNN model outperforms the best shallow model by 2.24% (Chiu and Nichols, 2015).

In this work, we investigate whether we can train DNNs using fewer samples under the active learning framework. Active learning is the paradigm where we actively select samples to be used during training. Intuitively, if we are able to select the most informative samples for training,

we can vastly reduce the number of samples required. In practice, we can employ Mechanical Turk or other crowdsourcing platforms to label the samples actively selected by the algorithm. Reducing sample requirements for training can lower the labeling costs on these platforms.

We present positive preliminary results demonstrating the effectiveness of deep active learning. We perform incremental training of DNNs while actively selecting samples. On the standard OntoNotes-5.0 English dataset, our approach matches 99% of the F1 score achieved by the best deep models trained in a standard, supervised fashion despite using only a quarter

2 NER Model Description

We use CNN-CNN-LSTM model from Yun (2017) as a representative DNN model for NER. The model uses two convolutional neural networks (CNNs) (LeCun et al., 1995) to encode characters and words respectively, and a long short-term memory (LSTM) recurrent neural network (Hochreiter and Schmidhuber, 1997) as a decoder. This model achieves the best F1 scores on the OntoNotes-5.0 English and Chinese dataset, and its use of CNNs in encoders enables faster training as compared to previous work relying on LSTM encoders (Lample et al., 2016; Chiu and Nichols, 2015). We briefly describe the model:

Data Representation We represent each input sentence as follows. First, special [BOS] and [EOS] tokens are added at the beginning and the end of the sentence, respectively. In order to batch the computation of multiple sentences, sentences with similar length are grouped together into buckets, and [PAD] tokens are added at the end of sentences to make their lengths uniform inside of the

Proceedings of the 2nd Workshop on Representation Learning for NLP, pages 252–256,
Vancouver, Canada, August 3, 2017. ©2017 Association for Computational Linguistics

Formatted Sentence	[BOS]	Kate	lives	on	Mars	[EOS]	[PAD]
Tag	O	S-PER	O	O	S-LOC	O	O

Table 1: Example formatted sentence. To avoid clutter, [BOW] and [EOW] symbols are not shown.

bucket. We follow an analogous procedure to represent the characters in each word. For example, the sentence 'Kate lives on Mars' is formatted as shown in Table 1. The formatted sentence is denoted as $\{\mathbf{x}_{ij}\}$, where $\mathbf{x}_{ij}$ is the one-hot encoding of the j-th character in the i-th word.

Character-Level Encoder For each word i, we use CNNs to extract character-level features $\mathbf{w}_i^{\text{char}}$ (Figure 1). We apply ReLU nonlinearities (Nair and Hinton, 2010) and dropout (Srivastava et al., 2014) between CNN layers, and include a residual connection between input and output of each layer (He et al., 2016). So that our representation of the word is of fixed length, we apply max-pooling on the outputs of the topmost layer of the character-level encoder (Kim, 2014).

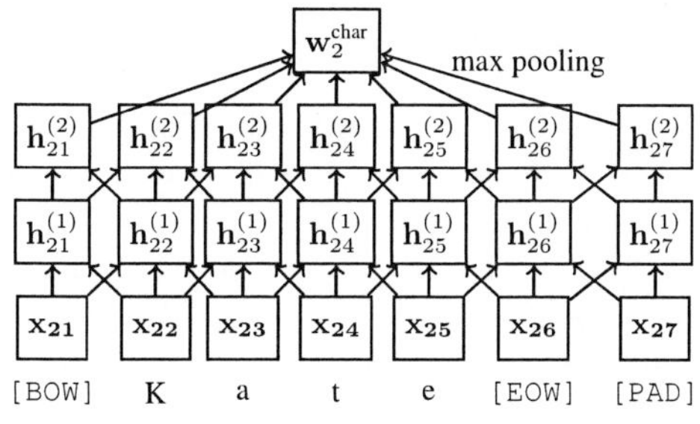

Figure 1: Example CNN architecture for Character-level Encoder with two layers.

Word-Level Encoder To complete our representation of each word, we concatenate its character-level features with $\mathbf{w}_i^{\text{emb}}$, a latent word embedding corresponding to that word:

$$\mathbf{w}_i^{\text{full}} := \left(\mathbf{w}_i^{\text{char}}, \mathbf{w}_i^{\text{emb}}\right).$$

In order to generalize to words unseen in the training data, we replace each word with a special [UNK] (unknown) token with 50% probability during training, an approach that resembles the word-drop method due to Lample et al. (2016).

Given the sequence of word-level input features $\mathbf{w}_1^{\text{full}}, \mathbf{w}_2^{\text{full}}, \ldots, \mathbf{w}_n^{\text{full}}$, we extract word-level representations $\mathbf{h}_1^{\text{Enc}}, \mathbf{h}_2^{\text{Enc}}, \ldots, \mathbf{h}_n^{\text{Enc}}$ for each word position in the sentence using a CNN. In Figure 2,

we depict an instance of our architecture with two convolutional layers and kernels of width 3. We concatenate the representation at the l-th convolutional layer $\mathbf{h}_i^{(l)}$, with the input features $\mathbf{w}_i^{\text{full}}$:

$$\mathbf{h}_i^{\text{Enc}} = \left(\mathbf{h}_i^{(l)}, \mathbf{w}_i^{\text{full}}\right)$$

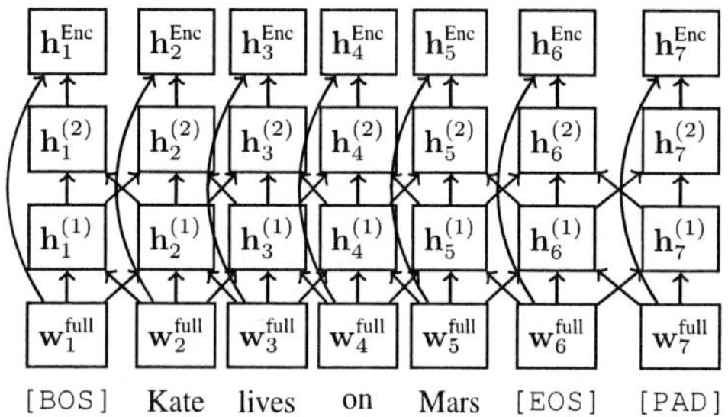

Figure 2: Example CNN architecture for Word-level Encoder with two layers.

Tag Decoder The tag decoder induces a probability distribution over sequences of tags, conditioned on the word-level encoder features: $\mathbb{P}\left[y_2, y_3, \ldots, y_{n-1} \mid \left\{\mathbf{h}_i^{\text{Enc}}\right\}\right]^1$. We use an LSTM RNN for the tag decoder, as depicted in Figure 3. At the first time step, the [GO]-symbol is provided as y_1 to the decoder LSTM. At each time step i, the LSTM decoder computes $\mathbf{h}_{i+1}^{\text{Dec}}$, the hidden state for decoding word $i + 1$, using the last tag y_i, the current decoder hidden state $\mathbf{h}_i^{\text{Dec}}$, and the learned representation of next word $\mathbf{h}_{i+1}^{\text{Enc}}$. Using a softmax loss function, y_{i+1} is decoded; this is further fed as an input to the next time step.

While it is computationally intractable to find the best sequence of tags with an LSTM decoder, Yun (2017) reports that greedily decoding tags from left to right often yields performance superior to chain CRF decoder (Lafferty et al., 2001), for which exact inference is tractable.

---

[1] y_1 and y_n are ignored because they correspond to auxiliary words [BOS] and [EOS]. If [PAD] words are introduced, they are ignored as well.

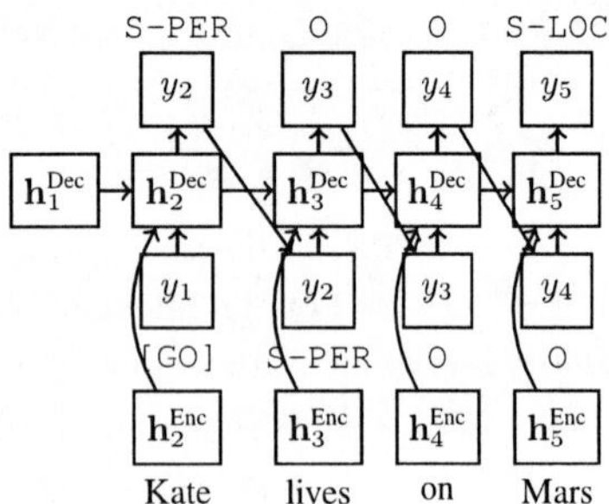

Figure 3: LSTM architecture for Tag Decoder.

3 Active Learning

As with most tasks, labeling data for NER usually requires manual annotations by human experts, which are costly to acquire at scale. Active learning seeks to ameliorate this problem by strategically choosing which examples to annotate, in the hope of getting greater performance with fewer annotations. To this end, we consider the following setup for interactively acquiring annotations. The learning process consists of multiple rounds: At the beginning of each round, the active learning algorithm chooses sentences to be annotated up to the predefined budget. After receiving annotations, we update the model parameters by training on the augmented dataset, and proceeds to the next round. We assume that the cost of annotating a sentence is proportional to the number of words in the sentence, and that every word in the selected sentence needs to be annotated; the algorithm cannot ask workers to partially annotate the sentence.

While various existing active learning strategies suit this setup (Settles, 2010), we explore the uncertainty sampling strategy, which ranks unlabeled examples in terms of current model's uncertainty on them, due to its simplicity and popularity. We consider three ranking methods, each of which can be easily implemented in the CNN-CNN-LSTM model as well as most common models for NER.

Least Confidence (LC): This method sorts examples in descending order by the probability of *not* predicting the most confident sequence from the current model (Lewis and Gale, 1994; Culotta and McCallum, 2005):

$$1 - \max_{y_1,\ldots,y_n} \mathbb{P}\left[y_1,\ldots,y_n \mid \{\mathbf{x}_{ij}\}\right]. \quad (1)$$

Since exactly computing (1) is not feasible with the LSTM decoder, we approximate it with the probability of a greedily decoded sequence.

Maximum Normalized Log-Probability (MNLP): Our preliminary analysis revealed that the LC method disproportionately selects longer sentences. Note that sorting unlabeled examples in descending order by (1) is equivalent to sorting in ascending order by the following scores:

$$\max_{y_1,\ldots,y_n} \mathbb{P}\left[y_1,\ldots,y_n \mid \{\mathbf{x}_{ij}\}\right]$$

$$\Leftrightarrow \max_{y_1,\ldots,y_n} \prod_{i=1}^{n} \mathbb{P}\left[y_i \mid y_1,\ldots,y_{n-1},\{\mathbf{x}_{ij}\}\right]$$

$$\Leftrightarrow \max_{y_1,\ldots,y_n} \sum_{i=1}^{n} \log \mathbb{P}\left[y_i \mid y_1,\ldots,y_{n-1},\{\mathbf{x}_{ij}\}\right]. \quad (2)$$

Since (2) contains summation over words, LC method naturally favors longer sentences. Because longer sentences require more labor for annotation, however, we find this undesirable, and propose to normalize (2) as follows, which we call Maximum Normalized Log-Probability method:

$$\max_{y_1,\ldots,y_n} \frac{1}{n} \sum_{i=1}^{n} \log \mathbb{P}\left[y_i \mid y_1,\ldots,y_{n-1},\{\mathbf{x}_{ij}\}\right].$$

Bayesian Active Learning by Disagreement (BALD): We also consider the Bayesian metric proposed by Gal et al. (2017). Denote $\mathbb{P}^1, \mathbb{P}^2, \ldots \mathbb{P}^M$ as models sampled from the posterior. Then, one measure of our uncertainty on the ith word is f_i, the fraction of models which disagreed with the most popular choice:

$$f_i = 1 - \frac{\max_y \left| \{m : \mathrm{argmax}_{y'} \mathbb{P}^m\left[y_i = y'\right] = y\} \right|}{M},$$

where $|\cdot|$ denotes cardinality of a set. We normalize this by the number of words as $\frac{1}{n}\sum_{j=1}^{n} f_j$, and sort sentences in decreasing order by this score. Following Gal et al. (2017), we used Monte Carlo dropout (Gal and Ghahramani, 2016) to sample from the posterior, and set M as 100.

4 Experiments

We use OntoNotes-5.0 English and Chinese data (Pradhan et al., 2013) for our experiments. The training datasets contain 1,088,503 words and 756,063 words respectively. State-of-the-art models trained the full training sets achieve F1 scores of 86.86 and 75.63 on the test sets (Yun, 2017).

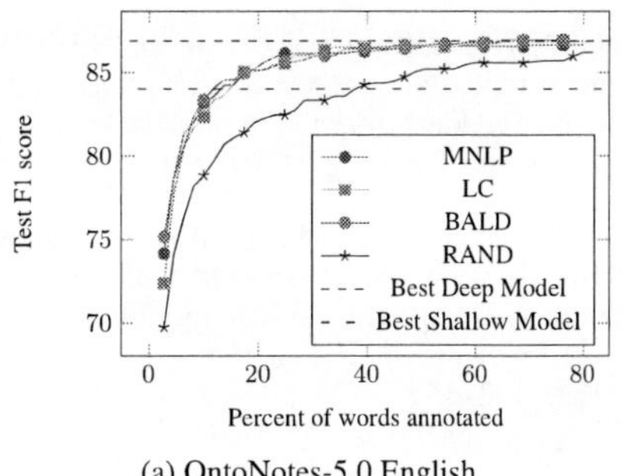 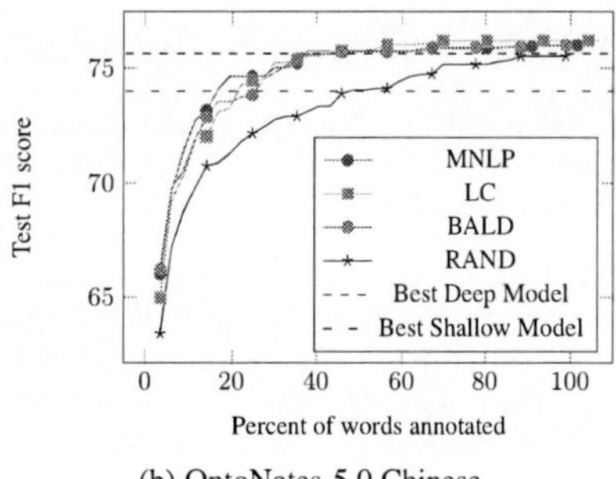

(a) OntoNotes-5.0 English   (b) OntoNotes-5.0 Chinese

Figure 4: F1 score on the test dataset, in terms of the number of words labeled.

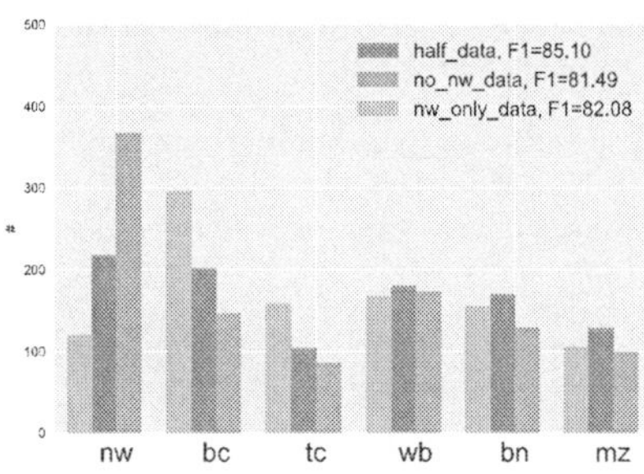

Figure 5: Genre distribution of top 1,000 sentences chosen by an active learning algorithm

Comparisons of selection algorithms We empirically compare selection algorithms proposed in Section 3, as well as uniformly random baseline (**RAND**). All algorithms start with an identical 1% of original training data and a randomly initialized model. In each round, every algorithm chooses sentences from the rest of the training data until 20,000 words have been selected, adding this data to its training set. Then, the algorithm updates its model parameters by stochastic gradient descent on its augmented training dataset for 50 passes. We evaluate the performance of each algorithm by its F1 score on the test dataset.

Figure 4 shows results. All active learning algorithms perform significantly better than the random baseline. Among active learners, **MNLP** slightly outperformed others in early rounds. Impressively, active learning algorithms achieve 99% performance of the best deep model trained on full data using only 24.9% of the training data on the English dataset and 30.1% on Chinese. Also, 12.0% and 16.9% of training data were enough for deep active learning algorithms to surpass the performance of the shallow models from Pradhan et al. (2013) trained on the full training data.

Detection of under-explored genres To better understand how active learning algorithms choose informative examples, we designed the following experiment. The OntoNotes datasets consist of six genres: broadcast conversation (bc), broadcast news (bn), magazine genre (mz), newswire (nw), telephone conversation (tc), weblogs (wb). We created three training datasets: **half-data**, which contains random 50% of the original training data, **nw-data**, which contains sentences only from newswire (51.5% of words in the original data), and **no-nw-data**, which is the complement of **nw-data**. Then, we trained CNN-CNN-LSTM model on each dataset. The model trained on **half-data** achieved 85.10 F1, significantly outperforming others trained on biased datasets (**no-nw-data**: 81.49, **nw-only-data**: 82.08). This showed the importance of good genre coverage in training data. Then, we analyzed the genre distribution of 1,000 sentences **MNLP** chose for each model (see Figure 5). For **no-nw-data**, the algorithm chose many more newswire (nw) sentences than it did for unbiased **half-data** (367 vs. 217). On the other hand, it undersampled newswire sentences for **nw-only-data** and increased the proportion of broadcast news and telephone conversation, which are genres distant from newswire. Impressively, although we did not provide the genre of sentences to the algorithm, it was able to automatically detect underexplored genres.

5 Conclusion

We proposed deep active learning algorithms for NER and empirically demonstrated that they achieve state-of-the-art performance with much less data than models trained in the standard supervised fashion.

255

References

Jason PC Chiu and Eric Nichols. 2015. Named entity recognition with bidirectional lstm-cnns. *arXiv preprint arXiv:1511.08308* .

Ronan Collobert, Jason Weston, Léon Bottou, Michael Karlen, Koray Kavukcuoglu, and Pavel Kuksa. 2011. Natural language processing (almost) from scratch. *Journal of Machine Learning Research* 12(Aug):2493–2537.

Aron Culotta and Andrew McCallum. 2005. Reducing labeling effort for structured prediction tasks. In *AAAI*. volume 5, pages 746–51.

Yarin Gal and Zoubin Ghahramani. 2016. A theoretically grounded application of dropout in recurrent neural networks. In *Advances in Neural Information Processing Systems*. pages 1019–1027.

Yarin Gal, Riashat Islam, and Zoubin Ghahramani. 2017. Deep bayesian active learning with image data. *arXiv preprint arXiv:1703.02910* .

Kaiming He, Xiangyu Zhang, Shaoqing Ren, and Jian Sun. 2016. Deep residual learning for image recognition. In *Proceedings of the IEEE Conference on Computer Vision and Pattern Recognition*. pages 770–778.

Sepp Hochreiter and Jürgen Schmidhuber. 1997. Long short-term memory. *Neural computation* 9(8):1735–1780.

Zhiheng Huang, Wei Xu, and Kai Yu. 2015. Bidirectional lstm-crf models for sequence tagging. *arXiv preprint arXiv:1508.01991* .

Yoon Kim. 2014. Convolutional neural networks for sentence classification. *arXiv preprint arXiv:1408.5882* .

John Lafferty, Andrew McCallum, Fernando Pereira, et al. 2001. Conditional random fields: Probabilistic models for segmenting and labeling sequence data. In *Proceedings of the eighteenth international conference on machine learning, ICML*. volume 1, pages 282–289.

Guillaume Lample, Miguel Ballesteros, Sandeep Subramanian, Kazuya Kawakami, and Chris Dyer. 2016. Neural architectures for named entity recognition. *arXiv preprint arXiv:1603.01360* .

Yann LeCun, Yoshua Bengio, et al. 1995. Convolutional networks for images, speech, and time series. *The handbook of brain theory and neural networks* 3361(10):1995.

David D Lewis and William A Gale. 1994. A sequential algorithm for training text classifiers. In *Proceedings of the 17th annual international ACM SIGIR conference on Research and development in information retrieval*. Springer-Verlag New York, Inc., pages 3–12.

Vinod Nair and Geoffrey E Hinton. 2010. Rectified linear units improve restricted boltzmann machines. In *Proceedings of the 27th international conference on machine learning (ICML-10)*. pages 807–814.

Sameer Pradhan, Alessandro Moschitti, Nianwen Xue, Hwee Tou Ng, Anders Björkelund, Olga Uryupina, Yuchen Zhang, and Zhi Zhong. 2013. Towards robust linguistic analysis using ontonotes. In *CoNLL*. pages 143–152.

Burr Settles. 2010. Active learning literature survey. *University of Wisconsin, Madison* 52(55-66):11.

Nitish Srivastava, Geoffrey E Hinton, Alex Krizhevsky, Ilya Sutskever, and Ruslan Salakhutdinov. 2014. Dropout: a simple way to prevent neural networks from overfitting. *Journal of Machine Learning Research* 15(1):1929–1958.

Zhilin Yang, Ruslan Salakhutdinov, and William Cohen. 2016. Multi-task cross-lingual sequence tagging from scratch. *arXiv preprint arXiv:1603.06270* .

Hyokun Yun. 2017. Design choices for named entity recognition. Manuscript in preparation.

Learning when to skim and when to read

Alexander R. Johansen and **Richard Socher**
Salesforce Research, Palo Alto, CA, USA
{ajohansen, rsocher}@salesforce.com

Abstract

Many recent advances in deep learning for natural language processing have come at increasing computational cost, but the power of these state-of-the-art models is not needed for every example in a dataset. We demonstrate two approaches to reducing unnecessary computation in cases where a fast but weak baseline classier and a stronger, slower model are both available. Applying an AUC-based metric to the task of sentiment classification, we find significant efficiency gains with both a probability-threshold method for reducing computational cost and one that uses a secondary decision network. [1]

1 Introduction

Deep learning models are getting bigger, better and more computationally expensive in the quest to match or exceed human performance (Wu et al., 2016; He et al., 2015; Amodei et al., 2015; Silver et al., 2016). With advances like the sparsely-gated mixture of experts (Shazeer et al., 2017), pointer sentinel (Merity et al., 2016), or attention mechanisms (Bahdanau et al., 2015), models for natural language processing are growing more complex in order to solve harder linguistic problems. Many of the problems these new models are designed to solve appear infrequently in real-world datasets, yet the complex model architectures motivated by such problems are employed for every example. For example, fig. 1 illustrates how a computationally cheap model (continuous bag-of-words) represents and clusters sentences.

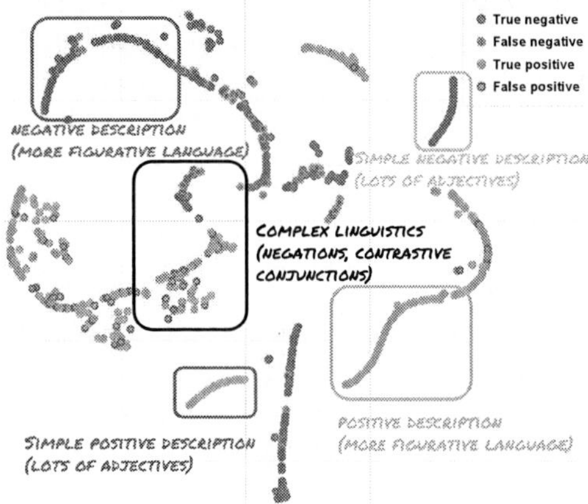

Figure 1: Illustration with t-SNE (van der Maaten and Hinton, 2008) of the activations of the last hidden layer in a computationally cheap bag-of-words (BoW) model on the binary Stanford Sentiment Treebank (SST) dataset (Socher et al., 2013). Each data point is one sentence, while the plot has been annotated with qualitative descriptions.

Clusters with simple syntax and semantics ("simple linguistic content") tend to be classified correctly more often than clusters with difficult linguistic content. In particular, the BoW model is agnostic to word order and fails to accurately classify sentences with contrastive conjunctions.

This paper starts with the intuition that exclusively using a complex model leads to inefficient use of resources when dealing with more straightforward input examples. To remedy this, we propose two strategies for reducing inefficiency based on learning to classify the difficulty of a sentence. In both strategies, if we can determine that a sentence is easy, we use a computationally cheap bag-of-words ("skimming"). If we cannot, we default

---

[1]Blog post with interactive plots is available at https://metamind.io/research/learning-when-to-skim-and-when-to-read

Proceedings of the 2nd Workshop on Representation Learning for NLP, pages 257–264,
Vancouver, Canada, August 3, 2017. ©2017 Association for Computational Linguistics

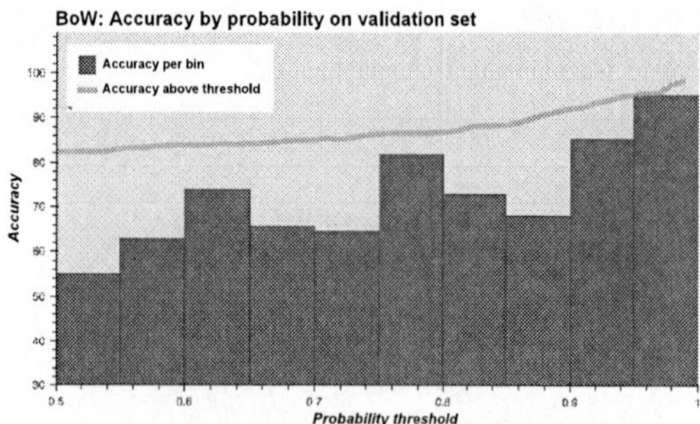

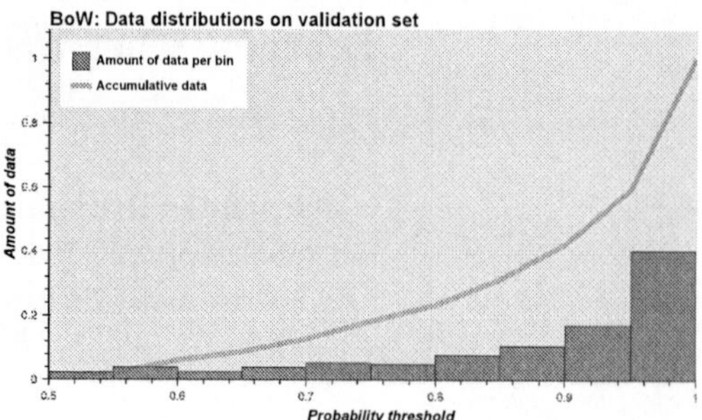

Figure 2: Accuracy for thresholding on binary SST. Probability thresholds are the maximum of the probability for the two classes. The green bars corresponds to accuracy for each probability bucket (examples within a given probability span, e.g. $0.5 < \Pr(Y|X, \theta_{\mathrm{BoW}}) < 0.55$), while the orange curve corresponds the accuracy of all examples with a probability above a given threshold (e.g. $\Pr(Y|X, \theta_{\mathrm{BoW}}) < 0.7$).

Figure 3: Histogram showing frequency of each BoW probability bin on the SST validation set. The line represents the cumulative frequency, or the fraction of data for which the expensive LSTM is triggered given a probability threshold.

SST Valid		BoW 82%	
		True	**False**
LSTM	**True**	76%	12%
88%	**False**	6%	6%

Table 1: Confusion matrix for the BoW and the LSTM, where **True** means that the given model classifies correctly.

to an LSTM (reading). The first strategy uses the probability output of the BoW system as a confidence measure. The second strategy employs a decision network to learn the relationship between the BoW and the LSTM. Both strategies increase efficiency as measured by an area-under-the-curve (AUC) metric.

2 When to skim: strategies

To keep total computation time down, we investigate cheap strategies based on the BoW encoder. Where the probability thresholding strategy is a cost-free byproduct of BoW classification and the decision network strategy adding a small additional network.

2.1 Probability strategy

Since we use a softmax cross entropy loss function, our BoW model is penalized more for confident but wrong predictions. We should thus expect that confident answers are more likely correct. Figure 2 investigates the accuracy by thresholding probabilities empirically on the SST based on the BoW outputs, strengthening such hypothesis. The probability strategy uses a threshold τ to determine which model to use, such that:

$$\hat{Y}_{\Pr(Y|X,\theta_{\mathrm{BoW}})>\tau} = \arg\max_{Y} \Pr(Y|X, \theta_{\mathrm{BoW}})$$

$$\hat{Y}_{\Pr(Y|X,\theta_{\mathrm{BoW}})<\tau} = \arg\max_{Y} \Pr(Y|X, \theta_{\mathrm{LSTM}})$$

where Y is the prediction, X the input, θ_{BoW} the BoW model and θ_{LSTM} the LSTM model. The LSTM is used only when the probability of the BoW is below the threshold. Figure 3 illustrates how much data is funneled to the LSTM when increasing the probability threshold, τ.

2.2 Decision network

In the probability strategy we make our decision based on the expectation that the more powerful LSTM will do a better job when the bag-of-words system is in doubt, which is not necessarily the case. Section 2.1 illustrates the confusion matrix between the BoW and the LSTM. It turns out that the LSTM is only strictly better 12% of the time, whereas 6% of the sentences neither the BoW or the LSTM is correct. In such case, there is no reason to run the LSTM and we might as well save time by only using the BoW.

2.2.1 Learning to skim, the setup

We propose a trainable decision network that is based on a secondary supervised classification task. We use the confusion matrix between the BoW and the LSTM from Section 2.1 as labels. We consider the case where the LSTM is correct and the BoW is wrong as the LSTM class and all

Model	Cost per sample
Bag-of-words (BoW)	0.16 ms
LSTM	1.36 ms

Table 2: Computation time per sample for each model, with batch size 64.

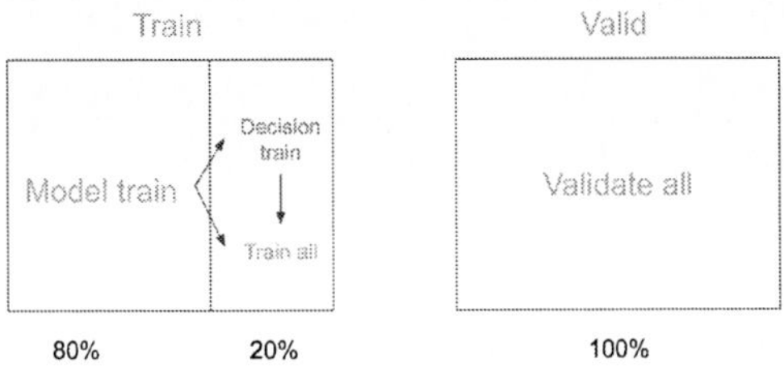

Figure 4: We train both models (BoW and LSTM) on "model train", then generate labels and train the decision network on "decision train" and lastly fine tune the models on the full train set. The full validation set is used for validation.

other combinations as the BoW class.

However, the confusion matrix on the train set is biased due to the models overfitting—which is why cannot co-train the decision network and our models (BoW, LSTM) on the same data. Instead we create a new held-out split for training the decision network in a way that will generalize to the test set. We split the training set into a model training set (80% of training data) and a decision training set (remaining 20% of training data). We first train the BoW and the LSTM models on the model training set, generate labels for the decision training set and train the decision network on the decision training set, and lastly fine-tune the BoW and the LSTM on the original full training set while holding the decision network fixed. We find that the decision network will still generalize to models that are fine-tuned on the full training set. The entire pipeline is illustrated in 4.

3   Related Work

The idea of penalizing computational cost is not new. Adaptive computation time (ACT) (Graves, 2016) employs a cost function to penalize additional computation and thereby complexity. Concurrently with our work, two similar methods have been developed to choose between computationally cheap and expensive models. Odena et al. (2017) propose the composer model, which chooses between computationally inexpensive and

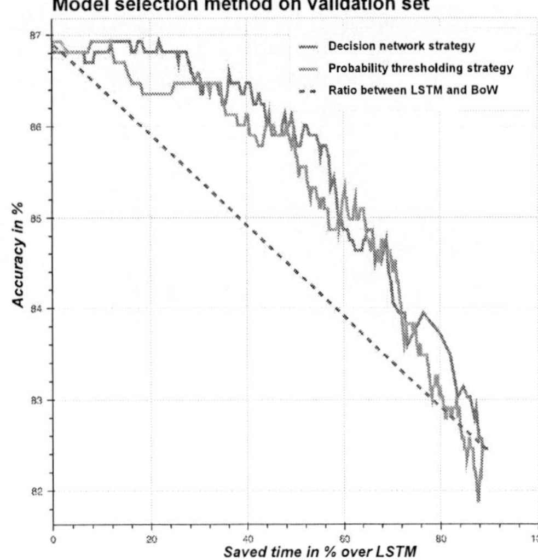

Figure 5: Model usage strategies plotted with thresholds for the probability and decision network strategies chosen to save a given fraction of computation time. The curve stops at around 90% savings as this represents using only the BoW model. The dashed red line represents the naïve approach of using the BoW and LSTM models at random with a fixed ratio.

expensive layers. To model the compute versus accuracy tradeoff they use a test-time modifiable loss function that resembles our probability strategy. The composer model, similar to our decision network, is not restrained to the binary choice of two models. Further, their model, similar to our decision network, does not have the drawbacks of probability thresholding, which requires every model of interest to be sequentially evaluated. Instead, it can in theory support a multi-class setting; choosing from several networks Bolukbasi et al. (2017) similarly use probability output to choose between increasingly expensive models. They show results on ImageNet (Deng et al., 2009) and provides encouraging time-savings with minimal drop in performance. This further suggest that the probability thresholding strategy is a viable alternative to exclusively using SoTA models.

4   Results

4.1   Model setup

The architecture and training details of all models are all available in section 5. In table 2 is an overview of the computational cost of our models. Our dataset is the binary version of the Stan-

Strategy	Validation AUC	Test AUC
Naïve ratio	84.84	83.77
Probability thresholding	$\mu = 86.03, \sigma = 0.3$	$\mu = 85.49, \sigma = 0.3$
Decision network	$\mu = \mathbf{86.13}, \sigma = 0.3$	$\mu = \mathbf{85.49}, \sigma = 0.3$

Table 3: Results for each decision strategy. The AUC is the mean value of the curve from 5. Each model is trained ten times with different initialization, and results are reported as mean and standard deviation over the ten runs.

ford Sentiment Treebank (SST), where "very positive" is combined with "positive", "very negative" is combined with "negative" and all "neutral" examples are removed.

4.2 Benchmark model

To compare the two decision strategies we evaluate the trade-off between speed and accuracy, shown in fig. 5. Speedup is gained by using the BoW more frequently. We vary the probability threshold in both strategies and compute the fraction of samples dispatched to each model to calculate average computation time. We measure the average value of the speed-accuracy curve, a form of the area-under-the-curve (AUC) metric.

To construct a baseline we consider a naïve ratio between the two models, i.e. let Y_{ratio} be the random variable to represent the average accuracy on an unseen sample. Then Y_{ratio} has the following properties:

$$\begin{cases} \Pr(Y_{\text{ratio}} = A_{\text{BoW}}) = \alpha \\ \Pr(Y_{\text{ratio}} = A_{\text{LSTM}}) = 1 - \alpha \end{cases} \quad (1)$$

Where A is the accuracy and $\alpha \in [0, 1]$ is the proportion of data used for BoW. According to the definition of the expectation of the random variable, we have the expected accuracy be:

$$\mathrm{E}(Y_{\text{ratio}}) = \sum \Pr(Y_{\text{ratio}} = y) \times y \quad (2)$$

$$= \alpha \times A_{\text{BoW}} + (1 - \alpha) \times A_{\text{LSTM}} \quad (3)$$

We calculate the cost of our strategy and benchmark ratio in the following manner.

$$C_{\text{strategy}} = C_{\text{BoW}} + (1 - \alpha) \times C_{\text{LSTM}} \quad (4)$$

$$C_{\text{ratio}} = \alpha \times C_{\text{BoW}} + (1 - \alpha) \times C_{\text{LSTM}} \quad (5)$$

Where C is the cost. Notice that the decision network is not a byproduct of BoW classification and requires running a second MLP model, but for simplicity we consider the cost equivalent to the probability strategy.

4.3 Quantitative results

In fig. 5 and Table 3 we find that using either guided strategy outperforms the naïve ratio benchmark by **1.72 AUC**.

4.4 Qualitative results

One might ask why the decision network is performing equivalently to the computationally simple probability thresholding technique. In 5 we have provided illustrations for qualitative analysis of why that might be the case. For example, A1 provides a t-SNE visualization of the last hidden layer in the BoW (used by both policies), from which we can assess that the probability strategy and the decision network follow similar predictive patterns. There are a few samples where the probabilities assigned by both strategies differ significantly; it would be interesting to inspect whether or not these have been clustered differently in the extra neural layers of the decision network. Towards that end, A2 is a t-SNE plot of the last hidden layer of the decision network. What we hope to see is that it learns to cluster when the LSTM is correct and the BoW is incorrect. However, from the visualization it does not seem to learn the tendencies of the LSTM. As we base our decision network on the last hidden state of the BoW, which is needed to reach a good solution, the decision network might not be able to discriminate where the BoW could not or it might have found the local minimum of imitating BoW probabilities too compelling. Furthermore, learning the reasoning of the LSTM solely by observing its correctness on a slim dataset could be too weak of a signal. Co-training the models in similar fashion to (Odena et al., 2017) might have yielded better results.

5 Conclusion

We have investigated if a cheap bag-of-words model can decide when samples, in binary sentiment classification, are easy or difficult. We found that a guided strategy, based on a bag-of-words neural network, can make informed decisions on the difficulty of samples and when to run an expensive classifier. This allow us to save computational time by only running complex classifiers on difficult sentences. In our attempts to build a more general decision network, we found that it is difficult to use a weaker network to learn the behavior of a stronger one by just observing its correctness.

References

D. Amodei, R. Anubhai, E. Battenberg, C. Case, J. Casper, B. Catanzaro, J. Chen, M. Chrzanowski, A. Coates, G. Diamos, E. Elsen, J. Engel, L. Fan, C. Fougner, T. Han, A. Hannun, B. Jun, P. LeGresley, L. Lin, S. Narang, A. Ng, S. Ozair, R. Prenger, J. Raiman, S. Satheesh, D. Seetapun, S. Sengupta, Y. Wang, Z. Wang, C. Wang, B. Xiao, D. Yogatama, J. Zhan, and Z. Zhu. 2015. Deep speech 2: End-to-end speech recognition in english and mandarin. *CoRR* abs/1512.02595. http://arxiv.org/abs/1512.02595.

D. Bahdanau, K. Cho, and Y. Bengio. 2015. Neural Machine Translation by Jointly Learning to Align and Translate. In *ICLR*.

T. Bolukbasi, J. Wang, O. Dekel, and V. Saligrama. 2017. Adaptive neural networks for fast test-time prediction. *CoRR* abs/1702.07811. http://arxiv.org/abs/1702.07811.

J. Deng, W. Dong, R. Socher, L.-J. Li, K. Li, and L. Fei-Fei. 2009. ImageNet: A Large-Scale Hierarchical Image Database. In *CVPR*.

F. Gers, J. Schmidhuber, and F. Cummins. 2000. Learning to forget: Continual prediction with lstm. *Neural Comput.* 12(10):2451–2471.

A. Graves. 2012. Neural networks. In *Supervised Sequence Labelling with Recurrent Neural Networks*, Springer Berlin Heidelberg, pages 15–35.

A. Graves. 2016. Adaptive computation time for recurrent neural networks. *CoRR* abs/1603.08983. http://arxiv.org/abs/1603.08983.

K. He, X. Zhang, S. Ren, and J. Sun. 2015. Deep residual learning for image recognition. *CoRR* abs/1512.03385. http://arxiv.org/abs/1512.03385.

S. Hochreiter and J. Schmidhuber. 1997. Long Short-Term Memory. *Neural Computation* 9(8):1735–1780.

D. Kingma and J. Ba. 2014. Adam: A method for stochastic optimization. *arXiv preprint arXiv:1412.6980* .

S. Merity, C. Xiong, J. Bradbury, and R. Socher. 2016. Pointer sentinel mixture models. *CoRR* abs/1609.07843. http://arxiv.org/abs/1609.07843.

T. Mikolov, K. Chen, G. Corrado, and J. Dean. 2013. Efficient Estimation of Word Representations in Vector Space. In *ICLR (workshop)*.

A. Odena, D. Lawson, and C. Olah. 2017. Changing model behavior at test-time using reinforcement learning. *arXiv preprint arXiv:1702.07780* .

J. Pennington, R. Socher, and C. D. Manning. 2014. Glove: Global vectors for word representation. In *EMNLP*.

D. Ruck, S. Rogers, M. Kabrisky, M. Oxley, and B. Suter. 1990. The multilayer perceptron as an approximation to a bayes optimal discriminant function. *Neural Networks, IEEE Transactions on* 1(4):296–298.

M. Schuster and K. Paliwal. 1997. Bidirectional recurrent neural networks. *Signal Processing, IEEE Transactions* .

N. Shazeer, A. Mirhoseini, K. Maziarz, A. Davis, Q. Le, G. Hinton, and J. Dean. 2017. Outrageously large neural networks: The sparsely-gated mixture-of-experts layer. *CoRR* abs/1701.06538.

D. Silver, A. Huang, C. Maddison, A. Guez, L. Sifre, G. van den Driessche, J. Schrittwieser, I. Antonoglou, V. Panneershelvam, M. Lanctot, S. Dieleman, D. Grewe, J. Nham, N. Kalchbrenner, I. Sutskever, T. Lillicrap, M. Leach, K. Kavukcuoglu, T. Graepel, and D. Hassabis. 2016. Mastering the game of Go with deep neural networks and tree search. *Nature* 529(7587):484–489. https://doi.org/10.1038/nature16961.

R. Socher, A. Perelygin, J. Wu, J. Chuang, C. Manning, A. Ng, and C. Potts. 2013. Recursive deep models for semantic compositionality over a sentiment treebank. In *EMNLP*.

N. Srivastava, G. Hinton, A. Krizhevsky, I. Sutskever, and R. Salakhutdinov. 2014. Dropout: a simple way to prevent neural networks from overfitting. *Journal of Machine Learning Research* 15(1):1929–1958.

L. van der Maaten and G. Hinton. 2008. Visualizing data using t-sne. *Journal of Machine Learning Research* 9(Nov):2579–2605.

Y. Wu, M. Schuster, Z. Chen, Q. Le, M. Norouzi, W. Macherey, M. Krikun, Y. Cao, Q. Gao, K. Macherey, J. Klingner, A. Shah, M. Johnson, X. Liu, L. Kaiser, S. Gouws, Y. Kato, T. Kudo, H. Kazawa, K. Stevens, G. Kurian, N. Patil, W. Wang, C. Young, J. Smith, J. Riesa, A. Rudnick, O. Vinyals, G. Corrado, M. Hughes, and J. Dean. 2016. Google's neural machine translation system: Bridging the gap between human and machine translation. *CoRR* abs/1609.08144. http://arxiv.org/abs/1609.08144.

Supplementary material

Visualizations

t-SNE plots for the qualitative analysis section.

t-SNE BoW with probability outputs   **t-SNE BoW with decision network labels**

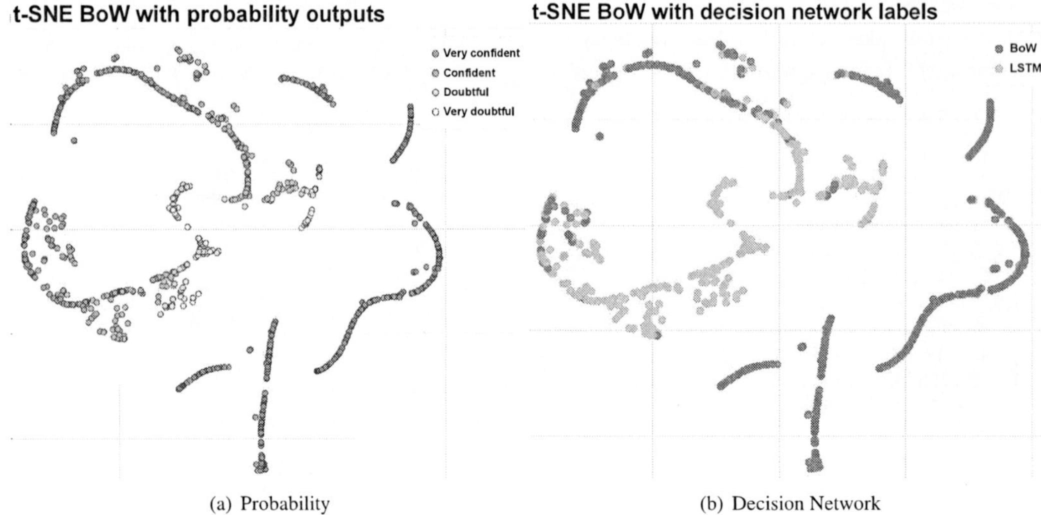

(a) Probability   (b) Decision Network

Figure A1: t-SNE plot of the last hidden layer of the BoW model. The probabilities are colored by the confidence of the probability strategy. The colors in the decision network plot are the predictions of which model should be used at a given threshold of the decision network.

Model training

All models are optimized with Adam (Kingma and Ba, 2014) with a learning rate of 5×10^{-4}. We train our models with early stopping based on maximizing accuracy of all models, except the decision network where we maximize the AUC as described in section 4.2. We use SST subtrees in both the model and decision train splits and for training both models.

Model illustration: The bag of words (BoW)

As shown in fig. A3, the BoW model's embeddings are initialized with pretrained GloVe (Pennington et al., 2014) vectors, then updated during training. The embeddings are followed by an average-pooling layer (Mikolov et al., 2013) and a two layer MLP (Ruck et al., 1990) with dropout of $p = 0.5$ (Srivastava et al., 2014). The network is first trained on the model train dataset (80% of training data, as shown in fig. 4) until convergence (early stopping, at max 50 epochs) and afterwards on the full train dataset (100% of training data) until convergence (early stopping, at max 50 epochs).

Model illustration: The LSTM

The LSTM is visualized in fig. A3. The LSTM's word embeddings are initialized with GloVe (Pennington et al., 2014). Instead of updating the embeddings, as is done in the BoW, we apply a trainable projection layer. We find that this reduces overfitting. After the projection layer a bi-directional (Schuster and Paliwal, 1997) recurrent neural network (Graves, 2012) with long short-term memory cells (Hochreiter and Schmidhuber, 1997; Gers et al., 2000) is applied, followed by concatenated mean- and max-pooling of the hidden states across time. We then employ a two layer MLP (Ruck et al., 1990) with dropout of $p = 0.5$ (Srivastava et al., 2014). The network is first trained on the model train dataset (80% of training data) until convergence (early stopping, max 50 epochs) and afterwards on the full train dataset (100% of training data) until convergence (early stopping, max 50 epochs).

t-SNE decision network with BoW vs LSTM comparison

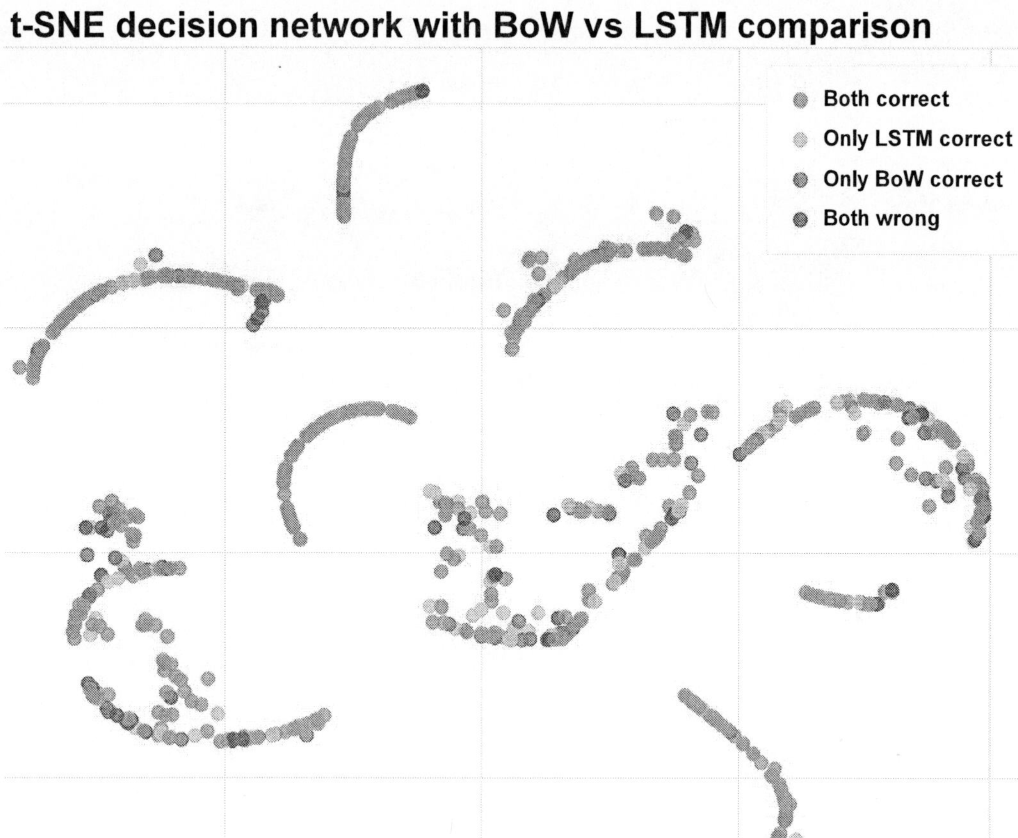

Figure A2: We compare the predictions of the BoW and the LSTM to assess when one might be more correct than the other. We train the decision network to separate the yellows (only LSTM correct) from the rest. This plot enables us to evaluate if the model is able to learn the relationship between the correctness of the two models, even though it only has access to the BoW model.

Model illustration: The Decision Network

The decision network is pictured in fig. A4, it inherits all but the output layer of the BoW model trained on the model train dataset, without dropouts. The layers originating from the BoW are not updated during training. We find that it overfits if we allow such. From the last hidden layer of the BoW model, a two layer MLP (Ruck et al., 1990) with dropout of $p = 0.5$ (Srivastava et al., 2014) is applied on top.

The network is trained on the decision train portion of the dataset (20% of training data) until convergence. We use early stopping by measuring the AUC metric between the BoW and LSTM trained only on the model train dataset.

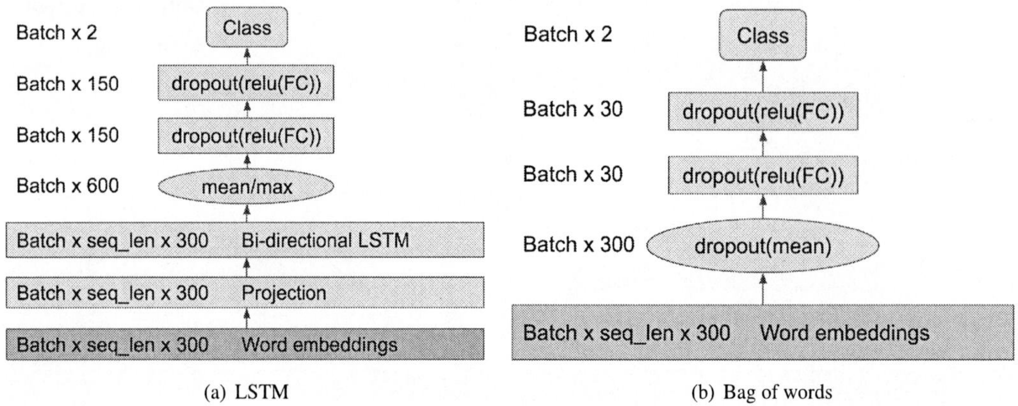

Figure A3: Visualization of the BoW and LSTM model. Green refers to initialization by GloVe and updating during training. Grey is randomly initialized and updated during training. Turquoise means fixed GloVe vectors.

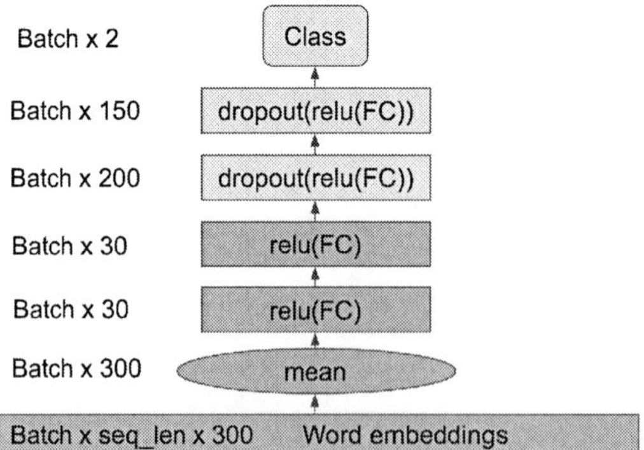

Figure A4: Architecture of the decision network. Turquoise boxes represent layers shared with the BoW model trained on the model train dataset and not updated during decision model training.

Learning to Embed Words in Context for Syntactic Tasks

Lifu Tu   **Kevin Gimpel**   **Karen Livescu**

Toyota Technological Institute at Chicago, Chicago, IL, 60637, USA

{lifu,kgimpel,klivescu}@ttic.edu

Abstract

We present models for embedding words in the context of surrounding words. Such models, which we refer to as **token embeddings**, represent the characteristics of a word that are specific to a given context, such as word sense, syntactic category, and semantic role. We explore simple, efficient token embedding models based on standard neural network architectures. We learn token embeddings on a large amount of unannotated text and evaluate them as features for part-of-speech taggers and dependency parsers trained on much smaller amounts of annotated data. We find that predictors endowed with token embeddings consistently outperform baseline predictors across a range of context window and training set sizes.

1   Introduction

Word embeddings have enjoyed a surge of popularity in natural language processing (NLP) due to the effectiveness of deep learning and the availability of pretrained, downloadable models for embedding words. Many embedding models have been developed (Collobert et al., 2011; Mikolov et al., 2013; Pennington et al., 2014) and have been shown to improve performance on NLP tasks, including part-of-speech (POS) tagging, named entity recognition, semantic role labeling, dependency parsing, and machine translation (Turian et al., 2010; Collobert et al., 2011; Bansal et al., 2014; Zou et al., 2013).

The majority of this work has focused on a single embedding for each word type in a vocabulary.[1]   We will refer to these as **type embed-**

---

[1]A word type is an entry in a vocabulary, while a word token is an instance of a word type in a corpus.

dings. However, the same word type can exhibit a range of linguistic behaviors in different contexts. To address this, some researchers learn *multiple* embeddings for certain word types, where each embedding corresponds to a distinct sense of the type (Reisinger and Mooney, 2010; Huang et al., 2012; Tian et al., 2014). But token-level linguistic phenomena go beyond word sense, and these approaches are only reliable for frequent words.

Several kinds of token-level phenomena relate directly to NLP tasks. Word sense disambiguation relies on context to determine which sense is intended. POS tagging, dependency parsing, and semantic role labeling identify syntactic categories and semantic roles for each token. Sentiment analysis and related tasks like opinion mining seek to understand word connotations in context.

In this paper, we develop and evaluate models for embedding word tokens. Our **token embeddings** capture linguistic characteristics expressed in the context of a token. Unlike type embeddings, it is infeasible to precompute and store all possible (or even a significant fraction of) token embeddings. Instead, our token embedding models are parametric, so they can be applied on the fly to embed any word in its context.

We focus on simple and efficient token embedding models based on local context and standard neural network architectures. We evaluate our models by using them to provide features for downstream low-resource syntactic tasks: Twitter POS tagging and dependency parsing. We show that token embeddings can improve the performance of a non-structured POS tagger to match the state of the art Twitter POS tagger of Owoputi et al. (2013). We add our token embeddings to Tweeboparser (Kong et al., 2014), improving its performance and establishing a new state of the art for Twitter dependency parsing.

Proceedings of the 2nd Workshop on Representation Learning for NLP, pages 265–275,
Vancouver, Canada, August 3, 2017. ©2017 Association for Computational Linguistics

2 Related Work

The most common way to obtain context-sensitive embeddings is to learn separate embeddings for distinct senses of each type. Most of these methods cluster tokens into senses and learn vectors for each cluster (Vu and Parker, 2016; Reisinger and Mooney, 2010; Huang et al., 2012; Tian et al., 2014; Chen et al., 2014; Piña and Johansson, 2015; Wu and Giles, 2015). Some use bilingual information (Guo et al., 2014; Šuster et al., 2016; Gonen and Goldberg, 2016), nonparametric methods to avoid specifying the number of clusters (Neelakantan et al., 2014; Li and Jurafsky, 2015), topic models (Liu et al., 2015), grounding to Word-Net (Jauhar et al., 2015), or senses defined as sets of POS tags for each type (Qiu et al., 2014).

These "multi-type" embeddings are restricted to modeling phenomena expressed by a single clustering of tokens for each type. In contrast, token embeddings are capable of modeling information that cuts across phenomena categories. Further, as the number of clusters grows, learning multi-type embeddings becomes more difficult due to data fragmentation. Instead, we learn *parametric* models that transform a type embedding and those of its context words into a representation for the token. While multi-type embeddings require more data for training, parametric models require less.

There is prior work in developing representations for tokens in the context of unsupervised or supervised training, whether with long short-term memory (LSTM) networks (Kågebäck et al., 2015; Ling et al., 2015; Choi et al., 2016; Melamud et al., 2016), convolutional networks (Collobert et al., 2011), or other architectures. However, learning to represent tokens in supervised training can suffer from limited data. We instead focus on learning token embedding models on unlabeled data, then use them to produce features for downstream tasks. So we focus on efficient architectures and unsupervised learning criteria.

The most closely related work consists of efforts to train LSTMs to represent tokens in context using unsupervised training objectives. Kawakami and Dyer (2015) use multilingual data to learn token embeddings that are predictive of their translation targets, while Melamud et al. (2016) and Peters et al. (2017) use unsupervised learning with monolingual sentences. We experiment with LSTM token embedding models as well, though we focus on different tasks: POS tagging and de-pendency parsing. We generally found that very small contexts worked best for these syntactic tasks, thereby limiting the usefulness of LSTMs as token embedding models.

3 Token Embedding Models

We assume access to pretrained type embeddings. Let $\mathcal{W}$ denote a vocabulary of word types. For each word type $x \in \mathcal{W}$, we denote its type embedding by $\boldsymbol{v}_x \in \mathbb{R}^d$.

We define a word sequence $\boldsymbol{x} = \langle x_1, x_2, ..., x_{|\boldsymbol{x}|} \rangle$ in which each entry x_j is a word type, i.e., $x_j \in \mathcal{W}$. We define a word token as an element in a word sequence. We consider the class of functions f that take a word sequence $\boldsymbol{x}$ and index j of a particular token in $\boldsymbol{x}$ and output a vector of dimensionality d'. We will refer to choices for $f(\boldsymbol{x}, j)$ as **encoders**.

3.1 Feedforward Encoders

Our first encoder is a basic feedforward neural network that embeds the sequence of words contained in a window of text surrounding word j. We use a fixed-size window containing word j, the w' words to its left, and the w' words to its right. We concatenate the vectors for each word type in this window and apply an affine transformation followed by a nonlinearity:

$$f_{\mathrm{FF}}(\boldsymbol{x}, j) =$$
$$g\left(W^{(D)}[\boldsymbol{v}_{x_{j-w'}}; \boldsymbol{v}_{x_{(j-w')+1}}; ...; \boldsymbol{v}_{x_{j+w'}}] + \boldsymbol{b}^{(D)}\right)$$

where g is an elementwise nonlinear function (e.g., tanh), $W^{(D)}$ is a d' by $d(2w'+1)$ parameter matrix, semicolon (;) denotes vertical concatenation, and $\boldsymbol{b}^{(D)} \in \mathbb{R}^{d'}$ is a bias vector. We assume that $\boldsymbol{x}$ is padded with start-of-sequence and end-of-sequence symbols as needed. The resulting d'-dimensional token embedding can be transformed by additional nonlinear layers.

This encoder does not distinguish word j other than by centering the window at its position. It is left to the training objectives to place emphasis on word j as needed (see Section 3.3). Varying w' will influence the phenomena captured by this encoder, with smaller windows capturing similarity in terms of local syntactic category (e.g., noun vs. verb) and larger windows helping to distinguish word senses or to identify properties of the discourse (e.g., topic or style).

3.2 Recurrent Neural Network Encoders

The above feedforward DNN encoder will be brittle with large window sizes. We therefore also consider encoders based on recurrent neural networks (RNNs). RNNs have recently enjoyed a great deal of interest in the deep learning, speech recognition, and NLP communities (Sundermeyer et al., 2012; Graves et al., 2013; Sutskever et al., 2014), most frequently used with "gated" connections like long short-term memory (LSTM) (Hochreiter and Schmidhuber, 1997; Gers et al., 2000).

We use an LSTM to encode the sequence of words containing the token and take the final hidden vector as the d'-dimensional encoding. While we can use longer sequences, such as the sentence containing the token (Kawakami and Dyer, 2015), we restrict the input sequence to a fixed-size context window around word j, so the input is identical to that of the feedforward encoder above. For the syntactic tasks we consider, we did not find large context windows to be helpful.

3.3 Training

We consider unsupervised ways to train the encoders described above. Throughout training for both models, the type embeddings are kept fixed. We assume that we are given a corpus $X = \{x^{(i)}\}_{i=1}^{|X|}$ of unannotated word sequences.

One widely-used family of unsupervised criteria is that of reconstruction error and its variants. These are used when training autoencoders, which use an encoder f to convert the input x to a vector followed by a decoder g that attempts to reconstruct the input from the vector. The typical loss function is the squared difference between the input and reconstructed input. We use a generalization that is sensitive to the position of elements. Since our primary interest is in learning useful representations for a *particular* token in its context, we use a weighted reconstruction error:

$$\text{loss}_{\text{WRE}}(f, g, x, j) = \sum_{i=1}^{|x|} \omega_i \, \|g(f(x, j))_i - v_{x_i}\|_2^2$$

$$(1)$$

where $g(f(x, j))_i$ is the subvector of $g(f(x, j))$ corresponding to reconstructing v_{x_i}, and where ω_i is the weight for reconstructing the ith entry.

For our feedforward encoder f, we use analogous fully-connected layers in the decoder g, forming a standard autoencoder architecture. To train the LSTM encoder, we add an LSTM decoder to form a sequence-to-sequence ("seq2seq") autoencoder (Sutskever et al., 2014; Li et al., 2015; Dai and Le, 2015). That is, we use one LSTM as the encoder f and another LSTM for the decoder g, initializing g's hidden state to the output of f. Since we use the same weighted reconstruction error described above, the decoder must output a single vector at each step rather than a distribution over word types. So we use an affine transformation on the LSTM decoder hidden vector at each step in order to generate the output vector for each step. Reconstruction error has efficiency advantages over log loss here in that it avoids the costly summation over the vocabulary.

4 Qualitative Analysis

Before discussing downstream tasks, we perform a qualitative analysis to show what our token embedding models learn.

4.1 Experimental Setup

We train a feedforward DNN token embedding model on a corpus of 300,000 unlabeled English tweets. We use a window size $w' = 3$ for the qualitative results reported here; for downstream tasks below, we will vary w'. For training, we use our weighted reconstruction error (Eq. 1). The encoder uses one hidden layer of size 512 followed by the token embedding layer of size $d' = 256$. The decoder also uses a single hidden layer of size 512. We use ReLU activations except the final encoder/decoder layers which use linear activations.

In preliminary experiments we compared 3 weighting schemes for ω in the objective: for token index j, "uniform" weighting sets $\omega_i = 1$ for all i; "focused" sets $\omega_j = 2$ and $\omega_i = 1$ for $i \neq j$; and "tapered" sets $\omega_j = 4$, $\omega_{j\pm1} = 3$, $\omega_{j\pm2} = 2$, and 1 otherwise. The non-uniform schemes place more emphasis on reconstructing the target token, and we found them to slightly outperform uniform weighting. Unless reported otherwise, we use focused weighting for all experiments below.

We train using stochastic gradient descent with momentum for 1 epoch, saving the model that reaches the best objective value on a held-out validation set of 3,000 unlabeled tweets. For the type embeddings used as input to our token embedding model, we train 100-dimensional skip-gram embeddings on 56 million English tweets using the `word2vec` toolkit (Mikolov et al., 2013).

Q	my first **one was like** $\underline{2}$ **minutes long and** has	Q	**jus listenin** $\underline{2}$ **mr hudson and** drake crazyness
1	my fav **place- was there** $\underline{2}$ **years ago and** am	1	@mention **deaddddd u go** $\underline{2}$ **mlk high up** n
2	thought it **was more like** $\underline{2}$ **..... either way** , i	2	only a **cups tho tryin** $\underline{2}$ **feed the whole** family
3	to **backup everything from** $\underline{2}$ **years before i**	3	bored on mars **i kum down** $\underline{2}$ **earth ... yupp** !!
4	i **slept for like** $\underline{2}$ **sec lol** . freakin chessy	4	i miss **you i trying** $\underline{2}$ **looking oud my** mind girl
Q	the lines : **i am** $\underline{so}$ **thrilled about this** . may	Q	fighting **off a headache** $\underline{so}$ **i can work** on my
1	and work . **i am** $\underline{so}$ **glad you asked** . let	1	im **on my phone** $\underline{so}$ **i cant see** who @mention
2	i was $\underline{so}$ **excited to sleep** in tomorrow	2	did some **things that hurt** $\underline{so}$ **i guess i** was doing
3	@mention **that is** $\underline{so}$ **funny** ! **i know** which	3	my **phone keeps beeping** $\underline{so}$ **i know ralph** must
4	little girl ! **i was** $\underline{so}$ **touched when she** called	4	randomly obsessed **with this song** $\underline{so}$ **i bought it**

Table 1: Query tokens of two polysemous words and their four nearest neighboring tokens. The target token is underlined and the encoder context (3 words to either side) is shown in bold. See text for details.

4.2 Nearest Neighbor Analysis

We inspect the ability of the encoder to distinguish different senses of ambiguous types. Table 1 shows query tokens (Q) followed by their four nearest neighbor tokens (with the same type), all from our held-out set of 3,000 tweets. We choose two polysemous words that are common in tweets: "2" and "so". As queries, we select tokens that express different senses. The word "2" can be both a number (left) and a synonym of "to" (right). The word "so" is both an intensifier (left) and a connective (right). We find that the nearest neighbors, though generally differing in context words, have the same sense and same POS tag.

In Table 2 we consider nearest neighbors that may have different word types from the query type. For each query word, we permit the nearest neighbor search to consider tokens from the following set: {"4", "for", "2", "to", "too", "1", "one"}. In the first two queries, we find that tokens of "4" have nearest neighbors with different word types but the same syntactic category. That is, tokens of *different* word types are more similar to the query than tokens of the *same* type. We see this again with neighbors of "2" used as a synonym for "to". The encoder appears to be doing a kind of canonicalization of nonstandard word uses, which suggests applications for token embeddings in normalization of social media text (Clark and Araki, 2011). See neighbor 8, in which "too" is understood as having the intended meaning despite its misleading surface form.

4.3 Visualization

In order to gain a better qualitative understanding of the token embeddings, we visualize the learned token embeddings using t-SNE (Maaten and Hinton, 2008). We learn token embeddings as above except with $w' = 1$. Figure 1 shows a two-dimensional visualization of token embed-

Q	masters **swimmers annual swim** $\underline{4}$ **your heart** !
1	so **many miles loking** $\underline{for}$ **her and handing**
2	off to **the rehearsal space** $\underline{for}$ **a weekend long**
3	on **the inauguration** $\underline{for}$ **your enjoyment**
Q	#canucks **now have a** $\underline{4}$ **point lead on** the
1	way lol . **it's the** $\underline{1}$ **mile trail and** then you
2	my first **one was like** $\underline{2}$ **minutes long and**
3	my fav **place- was there** $\underline{2}$ **years ago and**
Q	**jus listenin** $\underline{2}$ **mr hudson and** drake crazyness
1	@mention **deaddddd u go** $\underline{2}$ **mlk high up** n bk
2	only a **cups tho tryin** $\underline{2}$ **feed the whole** family
3	**are ya'll listening** $\underline{to}$ **the annointed one** ? he's on
4	@mention well **could u come** $\underline{to}$ **mrs wilsons for**
5	i'm bored on mars **i kum down** $\underline{2}$ **earth ... yupp** !!
6	**i am listening** $\underline{to}$ **amar prtihibi** - black
7	about **neopets and listening** $\underline{to}$ **yelle** (URL
8	high ritee **now -______-** $\underline{too}$ **troop to the** crib

Table 2: Nearest neighbors for token embeddings, where we consider neighbors that may have different word types from that in the query token. See text for details.

dings for the word type "4". For this visualization, we embed tokens in the POS-annotated tweet datasets from Gimpel et al. (2011) and Owoputi et al. (2013), so we have their gold standard POS tags. We show the left and right context words (using $w' = 1$) along with the token and its gold standard POS tag. We find that tokens of "4" with the same gold POS tag are close in the embedded space, with prepositions appearing in the upper part of the plot and numbers appearing in the lower part.

5 Downstream Tasks

We evaluate our token embedding models on two downstream tasks: POS tagging and dependency parsing. Given an input sequence $x = \langle x_1, x_2, ..., x_n \rangle$, we want to predict its tag sequence and dependency parse. We focus on Twitter since there is limited annotated data but abundant unlabeled data for training token embeddings.

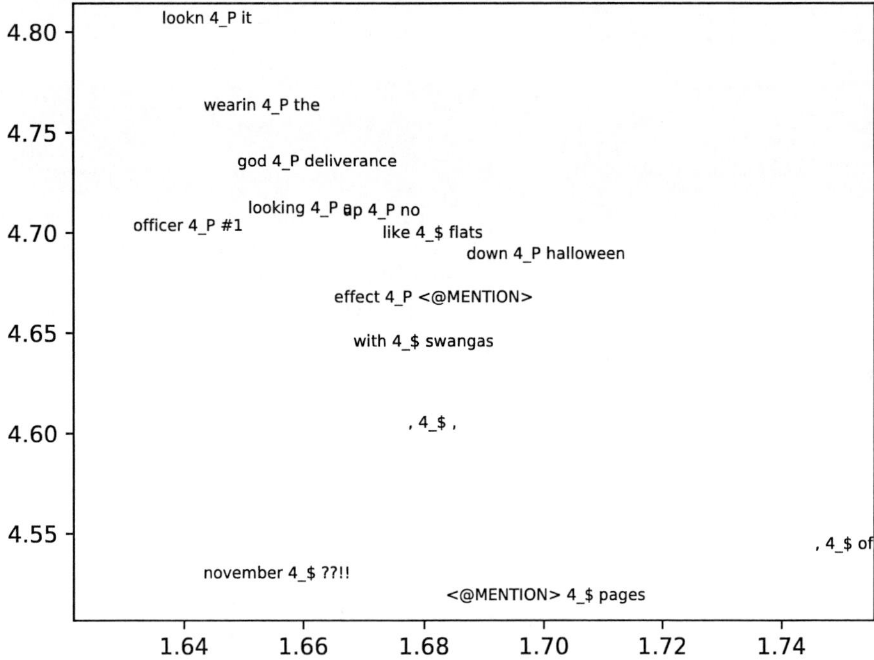

Figure 1: t-SNE visualization of token embeddings for word type "4". Each point shows the left and right context words ($w' = 1$) for the token along with the gold standard POS tag following an underscore ("_"). The tag "P" is preposition and "$" is number. Following the t-SNE projection, points were subsampled for this visualization for clarity.

5.1 Part-of-Speech Tagging

Baseline We use a simple feedforward DNN as our baseline tagger. It is a local classifier that predicts the tag for a token independently of all other predictions for the tweet. That is, it does not use structured prediction. The input to the network is the type embedding of the word to be tagged concatenated with the type embeddings of w words on either side. The DNN contains two hidden layers followed by one softmax layer. Figure 2(a) shows this architecture for $w = 1$ when predicting the tag of *4* in the tweet *thanks 4 follow*. We concatenate a 10-dimensional binary feature vector computed for the word being tagged (Table 3).[2]

We train the tagger by minimizing the log loss (cross entropy) on the training set, performing early stopping on the validation set, and reporting accuracy on the test set. We consider both learning the type embeddings ("updating") and keeping

---

[2]The definition of punctuation is taken from Python's `string.punctuation`.

x begins with @ and $|x| > 1$
x begins with # and $|x| > 1$
lowercase(x) is rt (retweet indicator)
x matches URL regular expression
x only contains digits
x contains \$
x is : (colon)
x is … (ellipsis)
x is punctuation and $|x| = 1$ and x is not : or \$
x is punctuation and $|x| > 1$ and x is not …

Table 3: Rules for binary feature vector for word x. If multiple rules apply, the first has priority. The tagger uses this feature vector only for the word to be tagged; the parser uses one for the child and another for the parent in the dependency arc under consideration.

them fixed. When we update the embeddings we include an ℓ_2 regularization term penalizing the divergence from the initial type embeddings.

Token Embedding Tagger When using token embeddings, we concatenate the d'-dimensional token embedding to the tagger input. The rest of

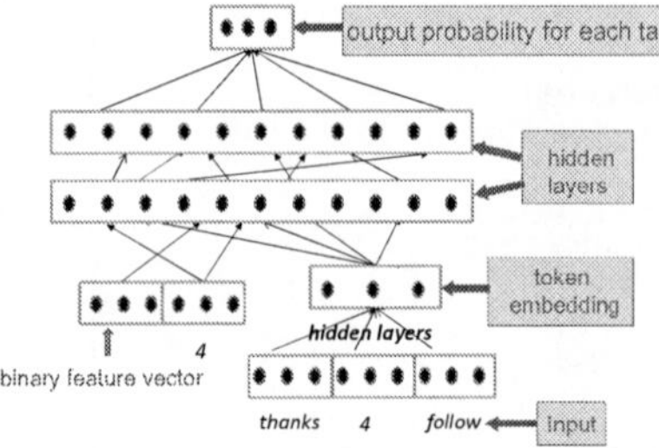

Figure 2: (a) Baseline DNN tagger, (b) tagger augmented with token embeddings.

the architecture is the same as the baseline tagger. Figure 2(b) shows the model when using type embedding window size $w = 0$ and token embedding window size $w' = 1$.

While training the DNN tagger with the token embeddings, we do not fine-tune the token embedding encoder parameters, leaving them fixed.

5.2 Dependency Parser

Baseline   As our baseline, we use a simple DNN to do parent prediction independently for each word. That is, we use a local classifier that scores parents for a word. To infer a parse at test time, we independently choose the highest-scoring parent for each word. We also use our classifier's scores as additional features in Twee-boParser (Kong et al., 2014).

Our parent prediction DNN has two hidden layers and an output layer with 1 unit. This unit corresponds to a value $S(x_i, x_j)$ that serves as the score for a dependency arc with child word x_i and parent word x_j. The input to the DNN is the concatenation of the type embeddings for x_i and x_j, the type embeddings of w words on either side of x_i and x_j, the features for x_i and x_j from Table 3, and features for the pair, including relative positions, direction, and distance (shown in Table 4).[3]

---

[3]When considering the root attachment (i.e., x_j is the wall symbol $), the type embeddings for x_j and its neighbors are all zeroes, the feature vector for x_j is all zeroes, and the dependency pair features are all zeroes except the first and last.

For a sentence of length n, the loss function we use for a single arc (x_i, x_j) follows:

$$\text{loss}_{\text{arc}}(x_i, x_j) =$$

$$- S(x_i, x_j) + \log \left(\sum_{k=0, k \neq i}^{n} \exp\{S(x_i, x_k)\} \right) \tag{2}$$

where $k = 0$ indicates the root attachment for x_i. We sum over all possible parents even though the model only computes a score for a binary decision.[4] Where $\text{head}(x_i)$ returns the annotated parent for x_i, the loss for a sequence x is:

$$\sum_{i=1}^{n} \text{loss}_{\text{arc}}(x_i, \text{head}(x_i)) \tag{3}$$

After training, we predict the parent for a word x_i as follows:

$$\overline{\text{head}}(x_i) = \underset{k \neq i}{\arg\max} \, S(x_i, x_k) \tag{4}$$

Token Embedding Parser   For the token embedding parser, we use the d'-dimensional token embeddings for x_i and x_j. We simply concatenate the two token embeddings to the input of the DNN parser. When $x_j = \$$, the token embedding for x_j is all zeroes. The other parts of the input are the same as the baseline parser. While training this parser, we do not optimize the token embedding encoder parameters. As with the tagger, we tune over the decision to keep type embeddings fixed or update them during learning, again using ℓ_2 regularization when doing so. We tune this decision for both the baseline parser and the parser that uses token embeddings.

6   Experimental Setup

For training the token embedding models, we mostly use the same settings as in Section 4.1 for the qualitative analysis. The only difference is that we train the token embedding models for 5 epochs, again saving the model that reaches the best objective value on a held-out set of 3,000 unlabeled tweets. We also experiment with several values for the context window size w' and the hidden layer size, reported below.

---

[4]We found this to work better than only summing over the exponentiated scores of an arc or no arc for the pair $\langle x_i, x_j \rangle$.

$\frac{i}{n}$	$\frac{j}{n}$	$\Delta = 1$	$\Delta = 2$	$3 \leq \Delta \leq 5$	$6 \leq \Delta \leq 10$	$\Delta \geq 11$	$i < j$	$i > j$	x_j is wall symbol

Table 4: Dependency pair features for arc with child x_i and parent x_j in an n-word sentence and where $\Delta = |i - j|$. The final feature is 1 if x_j is the wall symbol (\$), indicating a root attachment for x_i. In that case, all features are zero except for the first and last.

6.1 Part-of-Speech Tagging

We use the annotated tweet datasets from Gimpel et al. (2011) and Owoputi et al. (2013). For training, we combine the 1000-tweet OCT27TRAIN set and the 327-tweet OCT27DEV development set. For validation, we use the 500-tweet OCT27TEST test set and for final testing we use the 547-tweet DAILY547 test set. The DNN tagger uses two hidden layers of size 512 with ReLU nonlinearities and a final softmax layer of size 25 (one for each tag). The input type embeddings are the same as in the token embedding model. We train using stochastic gradient descent with momentum and early stopping on the validation set.

6.2 Dependency Parsing

We use data from Kong et al. (2014), dividing their 717 training tweets randomly into a 573-tweet train set and a 144-tweet validation set. We use their 201-tweet TEST-NEW as our test set. Kong et al. annotated whether particular tokens are contained in the syntactic structure of each tweet ("token selection"). We use the same automatic token selection (TS) predictions as they did, which are 97.4% accurate. We use a pipeline architecture in which unselected tokens are not considered as possible parents when performing the summation in Eq. 2 or the argmax in Eq. 4.

Like Kong et al., we use gold standard POS tags and gold standard TS during training and tuning. For final testing on TEST-NEW, we use automatically-predicted POS tags and automatic TS (using their same automatic predictions for both). Like them, we use attachment F_1 score (%) for evaluation. Our DNN parsers use two hidden layers of size 1024 with ReLU nonlinearities. The final layer has size 1 (the score $S(x_i, x_j)$). We train using SGD with momentum.

7 Results

7.1 Part-of-Speech Tagging

We first train our baseline tagger without the binary feature vector using different amounts of training data and window sizes $w \in \{0, 1, 2, 3\}$. Figure 3 shows accuracies on the validation set.

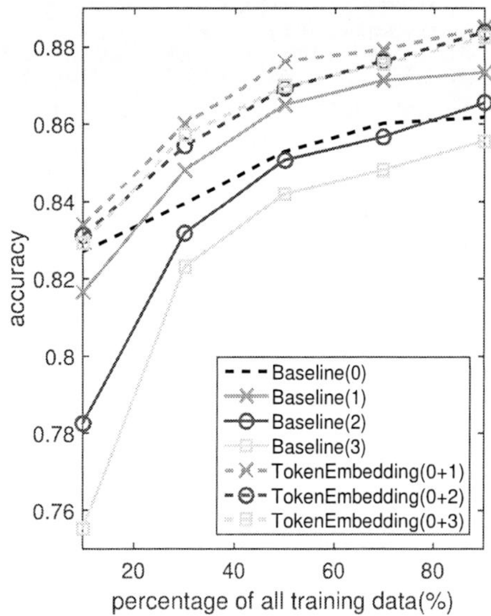

Figure 3: Tagging results. "Baseline(w)" refers to the baseline tagger with context of $\pm w$ words; "TokenEmbedding(w+w')" refers to the token embedding tagger with tagger context of $\pm w$ words and token embedding context of $\pm w'$ words.

When using only 10% of the training data, the baseline tagger with $w = 0$ performs best. As the amount of training data increases, the larger window sizes begin to outperform $w = 0$, and with the full training set, $w = 1$ performs best.

Figure 3 also shows the results of our token embedding tagger for $w = 0$ and $w' \in \{1, 2, 3\}$.[5] We see consistent gains when using token embeddings, higher than the best baseline window for all values of w', though the best performance is obtained with $w' = 1$. When using small amounts of data, the baseline accuracy drops when increasing w, but the token embedding tagger is much more robust, always outperforming the $w = 0$ baseline.

We then perform experiments using the full training set, showing results in Table 5. For all experiments with the baseline DNN tagger, we fix

---

[5]We used focused weighting for the results in Figure 3 using $\omega_j = 2$, but found slightly more stable results by increasing ω_j to 3, still keeping the other weights to 1. Our final tagging results use $\omega_j = 3$.

	val.	test
(1) Baseline	88.4	88.9
(1) + DNN TE	+1.6	+0.9
(2) Baseline + updating	89.4	89.4
(2) + DNN TE	+0.6	+0.5
(3) Baseline + features	89.2	89.3
(3) + DNN TE*	+0.6	+0.3
(3) + DNN TE	+1.2	+1.2
(3) Baseline + features	89.2	89.3
(3) + seq2seq TE*	-0.6	-1.0
(3) + seq2seq TE	+1.3	+1.0

Table 5: Tagging accuracies (%) on validation (OCT27TEST) and test (DAILY547) sets. Accuracy deltas are always relative to the respective baseline in each section of the table. "updating" = updates type embeddings during training, "features" = uses binary feature vector for center word, * = omits center word type embedding.

	val.	test
(4) Baseline + all features	92.1	92.2
(4) + updating	92.2	92.4
(4) + DNN TE + without updating	92.4	92.8
Owoputi et al.	91.6	92.8

Table 6: Tagging accuracies (%) on validation (OCT27TEST) and test (DAILY547) sets using all features: Brown clusters, tag dictionaries, name lists, and character n-grams. Last row is best result from Owoputi et al. (2013).

$w = 1$; when using token embeddings, we fix $w = 0$ and $w' = 1$. We also consider updating the initial word type embeddings during tagger training ("updating") and using the binary feature vector for the center word ("features").

Using token embeddings consistently outperforms using type embeddings alone. On the test set, we see gains from token embeddings across all settings, ranging from 0.5 to 1.2. The gains from DNN and seq2seq token embeddings are similar (possibly because we again use $w = 0$ and $w' = 1$ for the latter). The baseline taggers improve substantially by updating type embeddings or adding features (settings (2) or (3)), but adding token embeddings still yields additional improvements. When we use token embeddings but remove the type embedding for the word being tagged (denoted "*"), DNN TEs can still improve over the baseline, though seq2seq TEs yield lower accuracy. This suggests that the seq2seq TE model is focusing on other information in the window that is not necessarily related to the center word.

Comparison to State of the Art. Owoputi et al. (2013) achieve 92.8% on this train/test setup, us-

ing structured prediction and additional features from annotated and curated resources. We add several additional features inspired by theirs. We use features based on their generated Brown clusters, namely, binary vectors representing indicators for cluster string prefixes of length 2, 4, 6, and 8. We add tag dictionary features constructed from the Wall Street Journal portion of the Penn Treebank (Marcus et al., 1993). We use the concatenation of the binary tag vectors for the three most common tags in the tag dictionary for the word being tagged. We use the 10-dimensional binary feature vector and a binary feature indicating whether the word begins with a capital letter. All features above are used for the center word as well as one word to the left and one word to the right.

We add several more features only for the word being tagged. We use name list features, adding a binary feature for each name list used by Owoputi et al. (2013), where the feature indicates membership on the corresponding name list of the word being tagged. We also include character n-gram count features for $n \in \{2, 3\}$, adding features for the 3,133 bi/trigrams that appear 3 or more times in the tagging training data.

After adding these features, we increase the hidden layer size to 2048. We use dropout, using a dropout rate of 0.2 for the input layer and 0.4 for the hidden layers. The other settings remain the same. The results are shown in Table 6. Our new baseline tagger improves from 89.2% to 92.1% on validation, and improves further with updating.

We then add DNN token embeddings to this new baseline. When doing so, we set $w = 0$, as in all earlier experiments. We add two sets of DNN token embedding features to the tagger, one with $w' = 1$ and another with $w' = 3$. The results improve by 0.4 over the strongest baseline on the test set, matching the accuracy of Owoputi et al. (2013). This is notable since they used structured prediction while we use a simple local classifier, enabling fast and maximally-parallelizable test-time inference.

7.2 Dependency Parsing

We show results with our head predictors in Table 7. The baseline head predictor actually does best with $w = 0$. The predictors with token embeddings are able to leverage larger context: with DNN token embeddings, performance is best with $w' = 1$ while with seq2seq token embeddings,

w or w'	Baseline	DNN TE	seq2seq TE
0	**75.8**	-	-
1	75.4	**77.8**	77.8
2	73.2	77.3	**77.9**
3	72.3	77.2	76.9

Table 7: Attachment F_1 (%) on validation set using different models and window sizes. For TE columns, the input does not include any type embeddings at all, only token embeddings. Best result in each column is in boldface.

performance is strong with $w' = 1$ and 2. When using token embeddings, we actually found it beneficial to drop the center word type embedding from the input, only using it indirectly through the token embedding functions. We use $w = -1$ to indicate this setting.

The upper part of Table 8 shows the results when we simply use our parsers to output the highest-scoring parents for each word in the test set. Token embeddings are more helpful for this task than type embeddings, improving performance from 73.0 to 75.8 for DNN token embeddings and improving to 75.0 for the seq2seq token embeddings.

We also use our head predictors to add a new feature to TweeboParser (Kong et al., 2014). TweeboParser uses a feature on every candidate arc corresponding to the score under a first-order dependency model trained on the Penn Treebank. We add a similar feature corresponding to the arc score under our model from our head predictors. Because TweeboParser results are nondeterministic, presumably due to floating point precision, we train TweeboParser 10 times for both its baseline configuration and all settings using our additional features, using TweeboParser's default hyperparameters each time. We report means and standard deviations.

The final results are shown in the lower part of Table 8. While adding the feature from the baseline parser hurts performance slightly (80.6→ 80.5), adding token embeddings improves performance. Using the feature from our DNN TE head predictor improves performance to 81.5, establishing a new state of the art for Twitter dependency parsing.

8 Conclusion

We have presented a simple and efficient way of learning representations of words in their contexts using unlabeled data, and have shown how

(1) Baseline parser ($w = 0$)	73.0
(1) + DNN TE ($w = -1, w' = 1$)	75.8
(1) + seq2seq TE ($w = -1, w' = 1$)	75.0
(1) + seq2seq TE ($w = -1, w' = 2$)	74.2
(2) Kong et al.	80.6 ± 0.25
(2) + Baseline parser ($w = 0$)	80.5 ± 0.30
(2) + DNN TE ($w = -1, w' = 1$)	81.5 ± 0.25
(2) + seq2seq TE ($w = -1, w' = 1$)	81.0 ± 0.17
(2) + seq2seq TE ($w = -1, w' = 2$)	80.9 ± 0.33

Table 8: Dependency parsing unlabeled attachment F_1 (%) on test (TEST-NEW) sets for baseline parser and results when augmented with token embedding features. Following Kong et al., we report three significant digits.

they can be used to improve syntactic analysis of Twitter. Qualitatively, our token embeddings are shown to encode sense and POS information, grouping together tokens of different types with similar in-context meanings. Quantitatively, using token embeddings in simple predictors consistently improves performance, even rivaling the performance of strong structured prediction baselines. Our code and trained token embedding models are publicly available at the authors' websites. Future work includes further exploration of token embedding models, unsupervised objectives, and their integration with supervised predictors.

Acknowledgments

We thank the anonymous reviewers, Chris Dyer, and Lingpeng Kong. We also thank the developers of Theano (Theano Development Team, 2016) and Lasagne (Dieleman et al., 2015) as well as NVIDIA Corporation for donating GPUs used in this research.

References

Mohit Bansal, Kevin Gimpel, and Karen Livescu. 2014. Tailoring continuous word representations for dependency parsing. In *Proc. of ACL*.

Xinxiong Chen, Zhiyuan Liu, and Maosong Sun. 2014. A unified model for word sense representation and disambiguation. In *Proc. of EMNLP*.

Heeyoul Choi, Kyunghyun Cho, and Yoshua Bengio. 2016. Context-dependent word representation for neural machine translation. *arXiv preprint arXiv:1607.00578*.

Eleanor Clark and Kenji Araki. 2011. Text normalization in social media: progress, problems and applications for a pre-processing system of casual English. *Procedia-Social and Behavioral Sciences* 27.

Ronan Collobert, Jason Weston, Léon Bottou, Michael Karlen, Koray Kavukcuoglu, and Pavel Kuksa. 2011. Natural language processing (almost) from scratch. *Journal of Machine Learning Research* 12.

Andrew M. Dai and Quoc V. Le. 2015. Semi-supervised sequence learning. In *Advances in NIPS*.

Sander Dieleman, Jan Schlüter, Colin Raffel, Eben Olson, Søren Kaae Sønderby, Daniel Nouri, Daniel Maturana, Martin Thoma, Eric Battenberg, Jack Kelly, et al. 2015. Lasagne: First release. http://dx.doi.org/10.5281/zenodo.27878.

Felix A. Gers, Jürgen Schmidhuber, and Fred Cummins. 2000. Learning to forget: Continual prediction with LSTM. *Neural Computation* 12(10).

Kevin Gimpel, Nathan Schneider, Brendan O'Connor, Dipanjan Das, Daniel Mills, Jacob Eisenstein, Michael Heilman, Dani Yogatama, Jeffrey Flanigan, and Noah A. Smith. 2011. Part-of-speech tagging for Twitter: annotation, features, and experiments. In *Proc. of ACL*.

Hila Gonen and Yoav Goldberg. 2016. Semi supervised preposition-sense disambiguation using multilingual data. In *Proc. of COLING*.

Alan Graves, Abdel-rahman Mohamed, and Geoffrey Hinton. 2013. Speech recognition with deep recurrent neural networks. In *Proc. of ICASSP*.

Jiang Guo, Wanxiang Che, Haifeng Wang, and Ting Liu. 2014. Learning sense-specific word embeddings by exploiting bilingual resources. In *Proc. of COLING*.

Sepp Hochreiter and Jürgen Schmidhuber. 1997. Long short-term memory. *Neural Computation* 9(8).

Eric Huang, Richard Socher, Christopher D. Manning, and Andrew Ng. 2012. Improving word representations via global context and multiple word prototypes. In *Proc. of ACL*.

Sujay Kumar Jauhar, Chris Dyer, and Eduard Hovy. 2015. Ontologically grounded multi-sense representation learning for semantic vector space models. In *Proc. of NAACL-HLT*.

Mikael Kågebäck, Fredrik Johansson, Richard Johansson, and Devdatt Dubhashi. 2015. Neural context embeddings for automatic discovery of word senses. In *Proc. of NAACL-HLT*.

Kazuya Kawakami and Chris Dyer. 2015. Learning to represent words in context with multilingual supervision. In *Proc. of ICLR Workshop*.

Lingpeng Kong, Nathan Schneider, Swabha Swayamdipta, Archna Bhatia, Chris Dyer, and Noah A. Smith. 2014. A dependency parser for tweets. In *Proc. of EMNLP*.

Jiwei Li and Dan Jurafsky. 2015. Do multi-sense embeddings improve natural language understanding? In *Proc. of EMNLP*.

Jiwei Li, Thang Luong, and Dan Jurafsky. 2015. A hierarchical neural autoencoder for paragraphs and documents. In *Proc. of ACL*.

Wang Ling, Chris Dyer, Alan W. Black, Isabel Trancoso, Ramon Fermandez, Silvio Amir, Luis Marujo, and Tiago Luis. 2015. Finding function in form: Compositional character models for open vocabulary word representation. In *Proc. of EMNLP*.

Yang Liu, Zhiyuan Liu, Tat-Seng Chua, and Maosong Sun. 2015. Topical word embeddings. In *Proc. of AAAI*.

Laurens van der Maaten and Geoffrey Hinton. 2008. Visualizing data using t-SNE. *Journal of Machine Learning Research* 9.

Mitchell P. Marcus, Mary Ann Marcinkiewicz, and Beatrice Santorini. 1993. Building a large annotated corpus of English: The Penn Treebank. *Computational Linguistics* 19(2).

Oren Melamud, Jacob Goldberger, and Ido Dagan. 2016. context2vec: Learning generic context embedding with bidirectional LSTM. In *Proc. of CoNLL*.

Tomas Mikolov, Ilya Sutskever, Kai Chen, Greg S. Corrado, and Jeff Dean. 2013. Distributed representations of words and phrases and their compositionality. In *Advances in NIPS*.

Arvind Neelakantan, Jeevan Shankar, Alexandre Passos, and Andrew McCallum. 2014. Efficient nonparametric estimation of multiple embeddings per word in vector space. In *Proc. of EMNLP*.

Olutobi Owoputi, Brendan O'Connor, Chris Dyer, Kevin Gimpel, Nathan Schneider, and Noah A. Smith. 2013. Improved part-of-speech tagging for online conversational text with word clusters. In *Proc. of NAACL*.

Jeffrey Pennington, Richard Socher, and Christopher D. Manning. 2014. GloVe: Global vectors for word representation. In *Proc. of EMNLP*.

Matthew E. Peters, Waleed Ammar, Chandra Bhagavatula, and Russell Power. 2017. Semi-supervised sequence tagging with bidirectional language models. In *Proc. of ACL*.

Luis Nieto Piña and Richard Johansson. 2015. A simple and efficient method to generate word sense representations. In *Proc. of RANLP*.

Lin Qiu, Yong Cao, Zaiqing Nie, and Yong Rui. 2014. Learning word representation considering proximity and ambiguity. In *Proc. of AAAI*.

Joseph Reisinger and Raymond J. Mooney. 2010. Multi-prototype vector-space models of word meaning. In *Proc. of NAACL*.

Martin Sundermeyer, Ralf Schlüter, and Hermann Ney. 2012. LSTM neural networks for language modeling. In *Proc. of Interspeech*.

Simon Šuster, Ivan Titov, and Gertjan van Noord. 2016. Bilingual learning of multi-sense embeddings with discrete autoencoders. In *Proc. of NAACL*.

Ilya Sutskever, Oriol Vinyals, and Quoc V. Le. 2014. Sequence to sequence learning with neural networks. In *Advances in NIPS*.

Theano Development Team. 2016. Theano: A Python framework for fast computation of mathematical expressions. *arXiv e-prints* abs/1605.02688.

Fei Tian, Hanjun Dai, Jiang Bian, Bin Gao, Rui Zhang, Enhong Chen, and Tie-Yan Liu. 2014. A probabilistic model for learning multi-prototype word embeddings. In *Proc. of COLING*.

Joseph Turian, Lev Ratinov, and Yoshua Bengio. 2010. Word representations: a simple and general method for semisupervised learning. In *Proc. of ACL*.

Thuy Vu and D. Stott Parker. 2016. k-embeddings: Learning conceptual embeddings for words using context. In *Proc. of NAACL-HLT*.

Zhaohui Wu and C. Lee Giles. 2015. Sense-aware semantic analysis: A multi-prototype word representation model using Wikipedia. In *Proc. of AAAI*.

Will Y. Zou, Richard Socher, Daniel Cer, and Christopher D. Manning. 2013. Bilingual word embeddings for phrase-based machine translation. In *Proc. of EMNLP*.

Author Index